Crime Victims

An Introduction to Victimology

SEVENTH EDITION

ANDREW KARMEN
John Jay College of Criminal Justice

WADSWORTH
CENGAGE Learning

Australia • Brazil • Japan • Korea • Mexico • Singapore • Spain • United Kingdom • United States

Crime Victims: An Introduction to Victimology, Seventh Edition
Andrew Karmen

Senior Acquisitions Editor, Criminal Justice: Carolyn Henderson Meier

Development Editor: Meaghan Banks

Assistant Editor: Meaghan Banks

Editorial Assistant: John Chell

Associate Media Editor: Andy Yap

Marketing Manager: Michelle Williams

Marketing Associate: Jillian Myers

Marketing Communications Manager: Tami Strang

Content Project Management: Pre-PressPMG

Creative Director: Rob Hugel

Art Director: Maria Epes

Print Buyer: Karen Hunt

Rights Acquisition Account Manager, Text: Roberta Broyer

Production Service: Pre-PressPMG

Copy Editor: Ellen M. Cosgrove

Illustrator: Pre-PressPMG

Cover Designer: Dustin York, Riezebos Hozbaur Design Group

Cover Image: Corbis

Compositor: Pre-PressPMG

Text and Cover Printer: West Group

For product information and technology assistance, contact us at
Cengage Learning Academic Resource Center, 1-800-423-0563
For permission to use material from this text or product, submit all requests online at **www.cengage.com/permissions**.
Further permissions questions can be e-mailed to
permissionrequest@cengage.com.

Library of Congress Control Number: 2008942263

ISBN-13: 978-0-495-59929-6

ISBN-10: 0-495-59929-8

Wadsworth Cengage Learning
10 Davis Drive
Belmont, CA 94002-3098
USA

Cengage Learning products are represented in Canada by Nelson Education, Ltd.

For your course and learning solutions, visit **academic.cengage.com**.

Purchase any of our products at your local college store or at our preferred online store **www.ichapters.com**.

Printed in the United States of America
1 2 3 4 5 6 7 13 12 11 10 09

*To those whose suffering is intensified or prolonged needlessly because of
ignorance about the plight of crime victims or a lack of commitment to assist their recovery.*

About the Author

Andrew Karmen earned a Ph.D. in sociology from Columbia University in 1977. Since 1978, he has been a professor in the Sociology Department at John Jay College of Criminal Justice of the City University of New York. He has taught courses on victimology, criminology, drug abuse, delinquency, social problems, race relations, criminal justice, policy analysis, research methods, statistics, introductory sociology, and an overview of crime and justice in New York City. At John Jay College, he has served as a co-director of the master's program in criminal justice, an advisor for undergraduates majoring in criminal justice and in criminology, and a member of the doctoral faculty.

Dr. Karmen has co-edited (with Donal MacNamara) a reader called *Deviants: Victims or Victimizers?* (Sage, 1983). He has authored journal articles and chapters in books on a number of subjects, including drug abuse, auto theft, police use of deadly force, the zero-tolerance crackdown on quality-of-life infractions in New York City, vigilantism, research taboos, the Rosenberg atomic spy case, news media ethics, providing lawyers for indigents, providing advocates for victims, victims' rights, the victimization of women, and the likely situation of crime victims in the future. In *New York Murder Mystery: The True Story Behind the Crime Crash of the 1990s* (NYU Press, 2006, paperback), all the leading explanations about why crime rates rise and fall are tested, but none turn out to be unequivocally supported by the available statistical evidence.

Brief Contents

Contents

Boxes, Tables, and Figures

TABLES

FIGURES

Foreword

"What about the victim?"

This may seem like a mundane question, but most of the time, when we hear it, we are hearing a rhetorical way to advocate for a philosophy of justice, one that takes account of the problems and costs suffered by victims of crime. While the plight of victims of crime is an old one, the philosophy that embraces the plight as a justice priority is not. For most of the history of our nation, victims of crime were largely invisible in the criminal justice process. The very way we referred to criminal cases, *Wilson v. State*, made clear an overriding idea that criminal justice was concerned with a controversy between a defendant and the state. Victims, if they were considered at all, were only important as potential witnesses in that controversy.

Beginning in the last third of the twentieth century, however, this isolation of victims from the justice process began to change. With concern about the rising crime rate in the 1960s and 1970s came an increasing interest in the impact of crime and the criminal justice process on victims. Perhaps this concern was inevitable, as rising rates of crime meant there were increasing numbers of crime victims, families with victims, and friends of victims, many of whom could recount all-too-frequent negative experiences with the way their cases were handled. The concern about victims was also a bit of a backlash against that same era when the rights of criminal suspects were such a prominent issue in Supreme Court holdings and public policy debates. And it is also likely that as the U.S. citizenry came to demand more services in general, it would only be natural that one of the constituencies calling for help would be crime victims.

Whatever the causes—and there are probably several—victims of crime became an important constituency. They also became a significant political force, and their effects could be seen in the new cornerstone of almost every politician's campaign promises: to get "tough on crime." Even people who had never been victims of serious crime and knew no one in that category came to believe that a tough stance on crime was a victim-friendly stance on crime. For more than

30 years, penalties for crime have become ever more severe—often with the justification that a concern for victims required tougher measures against offenders. But
this was not the only expression of pro-victim sentiment in the political arena.

Numerous local victims' advocacy organizations were formed, the most notable
of which might be Mothers Against Drunk Driving. The federal government established a national office on victims of crime in the U.S. Department of Justice, while
many states passed new legislation that enumerated the rights of victims of crime. In
many ways, the latest generation of criminal justice has been one dominated by the
voice of the victim, at least as a symbol of alarm and a call for change. No set of
ideas has had a more profound impact on the criminal justice system in the past
30 years than has the institutionalized, public concern about the victims of crime.

As public sentiment about the predicament of the victim grew, social scientists developed an interest in the victim as well. A new field, called victimology,
was established to investigate all aspects of victims of crime, from prevalence and
demographics to needs and perspectives. Lessons about the social significance of
crime gleaned through an active social science of the victim have reshaped our
understanding of crime and justice. From the time when it became popular to
ask "What about the victim?" to the contemporary ease with which we embrace
concern about the victim in the justice system, much has changed and much has
been learned. Today, anyone who wishes to be informed in crime and justice
must understand what we know about victims of crime.

That is why I am delighted to announce the Seventh Edition of Andrew
Karmen's superb, seminal text on the topic: *Crime Victims: An Introduction to
Victimology*. Professor Karmen was one of the first scholars to write about the
problems faced by victims, and his book remains one of the most authoritative
and accessible studies of victims available today. This new edition retains the reliable data, even-handed analysis, and thought-provoking presentation of the
previous editions. It adds completely updated statistics, new discussions of recent
developments in victimology, and fresh perspectives on the future of the field.

No book currently available provides a more balanced, comprehensive, or
reliable discussion of the important controversies and dilemmas in the criminal
justice policy and practice regarding victims. This book supports its positions
with data, provides statistics that question some of the typical myths about victims, and provokes the reader to think carefully about the importance of the
victims' movement for criminal justice policy.

Professor Karmen's earlier editions of this book were received with praise.
This new edition continues and strengthens its contribution to our knowledge.
I commend the book to you. To read it is to have your thoughts and opinions
about crime victims become more informed and more effective. You will be
changed by this book.

Todd R. Clear
President of the American Society of Criminology
Distinguished Professor of Criminal Justice
John Jay College of Criminal Justice
City University of New York

Preface

In the early 1980s, I became interested in the victims' rights movement that was campaigning to reform criminal justice policies. I wanted to develop a course about victimology, but I found that no comprehensive and up-to-date textbook existed. Accepting the challenge, I decided to write one.

When I began the first edition, it was difficult to locate reliable social science data or even well-informed speculation about a number of crucial aspects of criminal victimization. When I prepared the second edition in the late 1980s, I encountered the opposite problem. Instead of a scarcity of material, there was too much: massive amounts of data and lengthy analyses, especially about rape, spouse abuse, child abuse, and elder abuse. By the mid-1990s, when I prepared the third edition, this "knowledge explosion" had become even more difficult to manage. Entire issues of scholarly journals had been devoted to, and whole books had been written about, the plight of these victims. When I wrote the fourth edition, the most striking change that I encountered was how the Internet could provide readily available and continuously updated information about a wide variety of victims. As a result, I added an appendix of websites that faculty and students could check out periodically to find out the latest statistics and the most recent developments concerning new laws, programs, and services. (The appendix for this new edition can be found at www.cengage.com/criminaljustice). The fifth edition introduced readers to the problems faced by victims of identity theft, cyberstalking, sexual abuse by clergy, drug-facilitated date rape, bias-driven hate crimes, and unfortunately, terrorist attacks. It also contained many more research findings and statistics as a large number of studies about victimization found their way onto the information highway. So many new topics and controversial issues accumulated over 20 years that I had to break up seven long chapters into thirteen more manageable chapters in the sixth edition. This re-packaging of themes and issues should work out very well for courses that run fourteen or fifteen weeks.

WHAT'S NEW?

In revising this book once again, I have retained all the coverage of the previous six editions. I have changed the sequence of subjects in a few chapters, and I have given greater attention to several topics. In response to reviewer feedback, this edition was revised with the aim of not only providing students with fresh statistics and more discussions of theories, but also of humanizing the victims themselves. This new, emotionally compelling material will promote students' engagement with the text.

The most noteworthy changes for each of the thirteen chapters are described below:

- Chapter 1, "What Is Victimology?" has been substantially rewritten. Up-to-date references and the most recent statistics available appear throughout the chapter. It also contains new cases that dramatize the suffering of victims, real-life incidents with college students as the targets. Another set of actual cases illustrates how the reactions of victims under attack can often be inspirational and uplifting. This chapter also includes a new table that assembles "victimology-bashing" quotes. This table shows how victimology is often confused with victimism, giving the discipline an undeserved "bad reputation." All of these additions will help your students connect with the material.

- Chapter 2, "The Rediscovery of Crime Victims," provides many new references that can be useful to students who want to take part in the rediscovery process by investigating the plights of particular groups that had been overlooked. Also, a new box assembles the latest material about differing estimates of the seriousness of these problems: road rage, violence among prisoners, and human trafficking.

- Chapter 3, "Sources of Information about Crime Victims: The *UCR* and the *NCVS*," has been reorganized for clarity, as well as revised with a new discussion of the changes in data gathering, up-to-date references, and the most recent statistics available.

- Chapter 4, "Violent Crimes: Murders and Robberies," includes an in-depth analysis of these two crimes, additional references and the most recent statistics available concerning patterns, trends, differential risks, comparative risks, murder rates for U.S. cities, and international comparisons. The pedagogical tools, "Murder Rates Across the Globe: Selected Countries" and "Murder Rates Across the Globe: Selected Cities," have been expanded to reflect several new sources of data. More information about gang-related murders was added.

- Chapter 5, "Victims' Contribution to the Crime Problem," presents all sides of this controversial topic. There is considerably more material on automobile theft, including which cars are stolen most often, and what cities are the most dangerous for parked cars, which will be of great interest to many students. I have also extensively updated the section on identity theft, discussing both the statistics, methods, and careless behaviors associated with this crime. The expanded coverage of these timely topics provides a bridge to an analysis of risk reduction and crime prevention strategies.

- Chapter 6, "Victims and the Criminal Justice System: Cooperation and Conflict; Part 1: The Police," contains updated material, including several new cases, and the latest statistics about reporting, stolen property recovery, and clearance rates (this table includes additional cities and covers more years). A section on the code of the streets as it relates to "snitching" should provoke a lively classroom discussion.

- Chapter 7, "Victims and the Criminal Justice System: Cooperation and Conflict; Part 2: Prosecutors, Defense Attorneys, Judges, and Corrections Officials," contains updated statistics and some new, real-life cases. The section on "recognizing 'second-class' treatment" in victims' interactions with law enforcement now includes a real-life case that compares how two kidnappings were handled by the police.

- Chapter 8, "Children as Victims," contains expanded discussions and updated statistics, especially about missing children and sexually abused youngsters. Several cases have been added along with new material about sexual abuse in religious communities. The clash between maximalist and minimalist perspectives has been expanded.

- Chapter 9, "Victims of Violence by Lovers and Family Members" features a new discussion of the differences between criminal and non-criminal forms of abuse. "Recognizing Warning Signs" is now a distinct section; this information has been expanded. A section on "The Legislative Response" to abuse has been added, encouraging students to think about how pro-victim movements can lead to policy change. The chapter also benefits from new cases and updated statistics.

- Chapter 10, "Victims of Rapes and Other Sexual Assaults," contains the latest statistics and some new, real-life cases. Early in the chapter, students are encouraged to think about the very language used to describe rapes and sexual assaults, and its implications for victims. The sections on acquaintance rape, on rape underreporting, and on sexual violence among inmates have been expanded. Finally, a box identifying "rape myths" has been added.

- Chapter 11, "Additional Groups of Victims with Special Problems," has been reorganized for flow and clarity. The chapter now includes more information about students harmed on campus, including a section on shootings on college grounds (a new box presents a timeline of the worst campus shootings, and the aftermath of the 2007 and 2008 rampages is discussed). The maximalist-minimalist debates surrounding date rapes and drug-facilitated sexual assaults have been sharpened. Updated statistics and expanded discussions are provided about terrorism, hate crimes, stalking, and line-of-duty deaths of police officers.

- Chapter 12, "Repaying Victims," contains new material about the costs of crime. Students are encouraged to think about both the physical and psychological effects of crime on a victim and his or her community. The information on restitution programs has been expanded, and the benefits and current limitations of compensation programs are discussed at greater length.

- Chapter 13, "Victims in the Twenty-First Century: Alternative Directions," features new examples about arming for self-defense as well as vigilantism. A new box, "Dramatic Examples of Victim Activism," provides students with inspirational accounts of survivors who channeled their grief into constructive efforts to expand victims' rights.

As in the previous six editions, I have highlighted the many controversies that surround victims and their strained relations with offenders, criminal justice officials and agencies, policy makers, the news media, social movements, and profit-oriented enterprises selling security products and services. I continue to strive for objectivity as I summarize both sides of issues that are emotionally gripping, hotly debated, and politically divisive. I do not necessarily endorse the points of view that I present or their implications for social policy. But I firmly believe that a textbook ought to call attention whenever possible to sharp clashes between well-meaning people with differing evidence-based views and divergent interpretations of the same data.

It appears that the passions inflamed by the burning issues of the 1980s and early 1990s have abated, especially concerning the whereabouts of missing children, allegations about human sacrifices by satanic cults, claims about repressed memories of childhood sexual abuse, and estimates about the frequency of husband beating and marital rape. However, new controversies have emerged, especially between the advocates of restorative justice (which seeks to bring about reconciliation between victims and their offenders) and the adherents of retributive justice (which emphasizes punishment), including staunch proponents of armed self-defense against criminal attacks.

This edition accentuates the positive: the unanticipated but much-welcomed trend that became evident by the late 1990s, namely, the impressive nationwide drop in victimization rates. Across the country, fewer people are being murdered, robbed, raped, or assaulted, or are suffering losses from burglaries and car thefts. This improvement in public safety is well documented in the many tables and graphs throughout the text. This "crime crash," which was particularly dramatic in New York City, was an unforeseen development that has not yet been satisfactorily explained.

Of course, no one knows how much longer the ebbing of the crack-fueled crime wave of the late 1980s and early 1990s will last because no consensus exists among criminologists and victimologists about why crime rates rise and fall. The latest statistics from the Bureau of Justice Statistics' *National Crime Victimization Survey* and the FBI's *Uniform Crime Report* can be found on the Internet. Those who are interested in monitoring these trends can compare the data as it becomes available on the FBI and BJS websites to the 2006 statistics (and in a few instances, for 2007) that appear throughout this seventh edition.

USING THIS TEXTBOOK

This seventh edition is intended to meet several distinct needs. The optimal situation is to use this text as the foundation for an undergraduate elective course on victimology that runs for an entire term. In fact, more than enough material is provided to sustain even a graduate-level course. If other topics must be covered in either an advanced criminology or criminal justice course, certain victim issues can be selected to address the major concerns of these two disciplines and of the general public.

Many discussions are important in criminology, criminal justice, policy analysis and research methods. For courses that require a term paper or class project, this edition provides up-to-date references, suggestions for short research projects at the end of each chapter, plenty of statistics, and numerous observations about problems of measurement and interpretation. The extensive compilation of the types of victimization that recently have been recognized or are just waiting to be "rediscovered" (see the listing at the end of Chapter 2) can serve as a launching pad for exploratory research and term projects. For courses that incorporate writing requirements via essay exams, several questions for discussion and debate plus a few that stimulate critical thinking appear at the end of each chapter. An instructor's manual with short answer questions is also available, as are Microsoft PowerPoint® visual aids.

MY GROWING "CREDENTIALS"
AS A CRIME VICTIM

Each time I revise this textbook, my credentials (unfortunately) broaden and deepen. Direct experience often is the best teacher and a source of sensitivity and insight about life's problems and personal challenges. In all the prefaces of the previous editions, I listed my credentials not only as a criminologist and victimologist but also as a crime victim.

I know from personal encounters what it is like to be a victim of a range of street and white-collar crimes (thankfully, none of them were really serious). In fact, my very first experience was something to laugh at, in retrospect. After I graduated from college, I got my first car: a brand new 1966 Mustang. I drove it around upstate New York, where I was attending graduate school, for about a week before a thief stole its gleaming wire wheel covers—all four of them in a single night! Amazingly enough, crime was not yet a widespread problem, so my minor misfortune actually appeared in the police blotter of the local newspaper. This incident contributed to my lifelong interest in lawbreaking, victimization, and the search for justice.

Before the first edition was written:

- I was held up twice (in one month!) by pairs of knife-wielding robbers.
- I lost a car to thieves. The police discovered it completely stripped, burned, and abandoned.

- I experienced a series of thefts of car radios and batteries.
- I suffered a break-in that left my apartment in shambles.

By the time the second edition of this textbook came out, my already impressive résumé as a street crime victim had grown considerably:

- A thief stole the bicycle that I used to ride to the train station by cutting the fence to which it was chained.
- Someone ran off with a fishing rod I had left unattended for a few minutes on a pier while I was buying more bait.
- A teenager singled out my car in a crowded parking lot for some reason and smashed the rear window with a rock. An eyewitness pointed out the young man to the police, and his foster parents volunteered to pay my bills for the damage. (I minimized their expenses by going to a salvage yard to find a low-cost replacement window.)
- A thief broke into the trunk of my car and stole my wallet and my wife's pocketbook while we spent an afternoon at the beach. Our wallets were later recovered from a nearby mailbox, emptied of our cash and credit cards.
- One hot summer night, an intruder entered our kitchen through an unlocked screen door. He ran off with a purse while we talked to guests in the living room.
- A car I was riding in was sideswiped by a vehicle driven by a fugitive who was being hotly pursued by a patrol car. No one was hurt, and the offender escaped.
- A thief smashed the side window of my car, which was parked at a meter a block away from the college where I teach. Sitting in the passenger seat, he began to pry out the radio. When the alarm went off, he fled, leaving his screwdriver behind (it is now my favorite tool).

By the third edition, I had a few more misfortunes to add to the list:

- My car was broken into two more times, on busy streets, during the day.
- In each incident, the alarm sounded and apparently scared off the thief, cutting short his depredations and minimizing my losses to a handful of quarters kept for tolls in an ashtray and some items in the glove compartment.

Shortly before the fourth edition was completed, my family was the victim of a con game that turned out to be a rather common scam:

- We picked a moving company out of the Yellow Pages because it advertised low rates and accepted credit cards. I should have been suspicious when they arrived in a rented truck, but I foolishly signed some papers authorizing them to charge me for packing materials. While we loaded computer components, valuables, and pets into our cars and shuttled them to our new house, they quickly used an enormous amount of shrink-wrap and cardboard boxes on our old furniture, cheap picture frames, and clothing. When their rented van arrived at our new home ten miles away, they presented me with a bill that was inflated by about $1,000 worth of unnecessary packaging. Then they demanded immediate payment in cash before they would unload our stuff that Saturday night, or else they would drive away with all our possessions and charge us for unloading and storage. I called the police but they insisted it was a business dispute and said that they could not intervene. I had no choice but to visit several ATMs and use all our credit cards and then to hand over the cash. On Monday, I contacted some colleagues at John Jay College of Criminal Justice who have close connections with law enforcement agencies. They made inquiries and warned me that this company was known to have mob ties. Because these gangsters literally knew where we lived, a fear of reprisals intimidated me from pursuing my claims about fraud in civil court or through state regulatory agencies or consumer affairs bureaus. Years later, I read in the newspaper that some victims received protection as witnesses for the prosecution and that these moving scam operators eventually were put out of business and incarcerated.

By the time I completed the fifth edition, my credentials had grown some more.

- Just like many other New Yorkers, I knew some victims of terrorism who barely escaped death by evacuating the World Trade Center before the Twin Towers collapsed.

- My daughter's backpack was stolen by a thief who pried open the trunk of our automobile after watching her park the car and walk away.

- More importantly, I received just a taste of what it is like to be a victim of identity theft. The fraud detection unit of a credit card company called one morning and asked if anyone in my family had recently charged exactly $400 at a department store and $200 at a computer software store about 40 miles away. When I answered no, and wondered aloud how such round number amounts could be charged for merchandise that is taxed, they simply said, "Don't worry, just fill out an affidavit." When the paperwork finally arrived weeks later, I did what they asked and never heard anything about these peculiar financial transactions again.

By the time the sixth edition came out, I had received plenty of fraudulent e-mails (called "phishing"—see the discussion of identity theft in Chapter 11) warning me that I must immediately update my account at some bank or credit card company or eBay before it is frozen. Besides these pathetic attempts to con me, very little else happened, which probably reflected the nationwide drop in crime that has lowered virtually everyone's risks of being victimized (see Chapter 4).

However, while preparing this seventh edition, my family was victimized twice—in other countries! My daughter's car was broken into near a museum in Montreal, Canada, and her husband's digital camera was stolen (and I paid a hefty bill for a new door lock and rear window for the damaged vehicle). In London's theater district, a pickpocket deftly removed my wife's wallet from her backpack (see Chapter 1). Fortunately, although she lost some cash and her driver's license, whoever ended up with her credit cards was not able to purchase anything or steal her identity. Meanwhile, back home, I suspected that someone entered our car one night while it was parked unlocked in our driveway because the glove compartment was open the next morning. As far as I could tell, nothing was taken. Sure enough, the next night the thief returned and stole the remote for our garage door opener from the car's sun visor while we were eating dinner. Fortunately, just an hour later I discovered that the remote was missing due to my habitual carelessness about locking my car door (see Chapter 5), so I disconnected the garage door opener. I did not report these two minor matters to the police. The incidents in Montreal and London were reported to the authorities, but they have not contacted us, so presumably the car thief and the pickpocket were never caught and our stolen property was not recovered (see Chapter 6).

One other recent incident is worth recounting because it is humorous:

- I keep my canoe chained to a rack at the town beach during warm weather. I came down one hot summer day to do some paddling and discovered that someone had stolen the chain and the padlock—but the canoe was undamaged. Go figure!

Obviously, victimization is rarely a laughing matter. Others have suffered far more severely than I have; some survive life-shattering events and endure devastating losses. But these many brushes with an odd assortment of offenders over recent decades have sensitized me to the kinds of expenses, emotional stresses, and physical injuries that taken together constitute the "victim's plight." I suspect that many victimologists and victim advocates have been drawn to this humanistic discipline because their own painful experiences inspired them to try to alleviate the suffering of others.

ANCILLARIES

To further enhance the teaching of victimology courses, the following supplements are available to qualified adopters. Please consult your local sales representative for details.

Instructor's Resource Manual with Test Bank

By Debra Heath-Thornton of Messiah College. Prepare for class more quickly and effectively with such resources as detailed chapter outlines, learning objectives, key terms, lecture suggestions, and handouts. A Test Bank with more than 800 questions in multiple choice, true/false, fill-in-the-blank, and essay formats saves you time creating tests.

Microsoft® PowerPoint® Presentation Slides

By Michael Chabries of Weber State University. Microsoft PowerPoint® slides let you incorporate art from the book right into your lectures. These handy slides outline the key points of the text to help you give visually engaging lectures.

ACKNOWLEDGMENTS

I would like to thank the following people who helped me prepare this seventh edition of my textbook:

Carolyn Henderson Meier, Senior Acquisitions Editor for Criminal Justice; Meaghan Banks, Development Editor; Michelle Williams, Marketing Manager; Jennie Redwitz, Senior Production Manager, all at Cengage; Ellen M. Cosgrove, copy editor; Mary Stone, Project Manager at Pre-PressPMG; Ramya Jayaraman, Proofreader at Pre-PressPMG; and Sonya Dintaman, indexer.

I also want to continue to thank those who assisted me on the revision of the sixth edition, which was a major undertaking: Jana Davis, Rebecca Johnson, Carol Henderson Meier, Jennie Redwitz, and Terra Schultz at Thomson Wadsworth; copy editor Janet Tilden; and Merrill Peterson at Matrix Productions.

I would like to express my appreciation to the reviewers of this and all previous editions:

Kelly Asmussen, Peru State College.
Frankie Bailey, State University of New York, Albany.
Susan Beecher, Aims Community College.
Bonnie Black, Mesa Community College.
Faith Coburn, University of Wisconsin–Milwaukee.
Ellen G. Cohn, Florida International University.
Andria L. Cooper, Fort Hays State University.
Susan Craig, University of Central Florida.
Elizabeth DeValve, Fayetteville State University.
Rhonda Dobbs, The University of Texas at Arlington.
William Doerner, Florida State University, Tallahassee.
John Dussich, California State University, Fresno.
Gerald P. Fisher, Georgia College and State University.
Linda Fleischer, The Community College of Baltimore County.
Gilbert Geis, University of California at Irvine.
Alan Harland, Temple University.
Sidney Harring, John Jay College of Criminal Justice.
Matasha Harris, John Jay College of Criminal Justice.
Carrie Harter, Sam Houston State University.
Debra Heath-Thornton, Messiah College.
Scott Hedlund, Pierce College.
Elizabeth Hegeman, John Jay College of Criminal Justice.

Michael Herbert, Bemidji State University.

Eric W. Hickey, California State University, Fresno.

Lin Huff-Corzine, Kansas State University.

David Johnson, University of Baltimore.

Janice Joseph, Richard Stockton College of New Jersey.

Betsy Kreisel, University of Central Missouri.

Fred Kramer, John Jay College of Criminal Justice.

Janet Lauritsen, University of Missouri–St. Louis.

Daniel P. LeClair, Boston University.

Joseph Linskey, Centenary College.

Donal MacNamara, John Jay College of Criminal Justice.

Liz Marciniak, University of Pittsburgh at Greensburg.

Michael G. Maxfield, Rutgers University.

Thomas McDonald, North Dakota State University.

Jackye McClure, San Jose State University.

Christine Mouton, University of Central Florida.

Ann Weaver Nichols, Arizona State University.

Sharon Ostrow, Temple University.

Leanne Owen, Holy Family University.

Elicka S. L. Peterson, Florida State University.

Roy Roberg, San Jose State University.

Kevin Roberts, Grace College.

Edward Sagarin, John Jay College of Criminal Justice.

Stanley Saxton, University of Dayton.

Brent Smith, University of Alabama, Birmingham.

David Sternberg, John Jay College of Criminal Justice.

Mark Stevens, North Carolina Wesleyan College.

Thomas Underwood, Washburn University.

Joseph Victor, Mercy College.

Tamara Tucker Wilkins, Minnesota State University, Mankato.

Janet Wilson, University of Central Arkansas.

1

What Is Victimology?

THE PLIGHT OF CRIME VICTIMS

The concept of a "**victim**" can be traced back to ancient societies. It was connected to the notion of sacrifice. In the original meaning of the term, a victim was a person or an animal put to death during a religious ceremony in order to appease some supernatural power or deity. Over the centuries, the word has picked up additional meanings. Now it commonly refers to individuals who suffer injuries, losses, or hardships for any reason. People can become victims of accidents, natural disasters, diseases, or social problems such as warfare, discrimination, political witch hunts, and other injustices. Crime victims are harmed by illegal acts.

1

Victimization is an asymmetrical interpersonal relationship that is abusive, painful, destructive, parasitical, and unfair. While a crime is in progress, offenders temporarily force their victims to play roles (almost as if following a script) that mimic the dynamics between predator and prey, winner and loser, victor and vanquished, and even master and slave. Many types of victimization have been outlawed over the centuries—specific oppressive and exploitative acts, like raping, robbing and swindling. But not all types of hurtful relationships and deceitful practices are forbidden by law. It is permissible to overcharge a customer for an item that can be purchased for less elsewhere; or to underpay a worker who could receive higher wages for the same tasks at another place of employment; or impose exorbitant interest rates and hidden fees on borrowers who take out mortgages and use credit cards; and to deny food and shelter to the hungry and the homeless who cannot pay the required amount.

Victimology is the scientific study of the physical, emotional, and financial harm people suffer because of illegal activities. Victimologists first and foremost investigate the victims' plight: the impact of the injuries and losses inflicted by offenders on the people they target. In addition, victimologists carry out research into the public's political, social, and economic reactions to the plight of victims. Victimologists also study how victims are handled by officials and agencies within the criminal justice system, especially interactions with police officers, detectives, prosecutors, defense attorneys, judges, probation officers, and members of parole boards.

Victimologists want to know whether and to what degree crime victims experience physical wounds, economic hardships, or emotional turmoil. One aim, of course, is to devise ways to help them recover. In the aftermath of the incident, are they frightened, terrorized, depressed, traumatized, infuriated, or embittered? Also, victimologists want to find out how effectively the injured parties are being assisted, served, accommodated, rehabilitated, and educated to avoid further trouble. Victimologists are equally curious to determine the extent to which their plight is being ignored, neglected, belittled, manipulated, and commercially or politically exploited. Some individuals who sustain terrible injuries and devastating losses might be memorialized, honored, and even idolized, while others might be mocked, discredited, defamed, demeaned, socially stigmatized, and even condemned for bringing about their own misfortunes. Why is this so?

Victimologists also want to examine why some injured parties find their ordeals life-transforming. Some become deeply alienated and withdraw from social relationships. They may become burdened by bouts of depression, sleep disorders, panic attacks, and stress-related illnesses. Their healing process may require overcoming feelings of helplessness, frustration, and self-blame. Others might react to their fear and fury by seeking out fellow sufferers, building alliances, and discovering ways to exercise their "agency"—to assess their options and make wise decisions, take advantage of opportunities, regain control of their lives, rebuild their self-confidence, and restore a sense of trust and security. Why do people experience such a wide range of responses and what personality and social factors determine how a person reacts?

Direct or **primary victims** experience the criminal act and its consequences firsthand. Perhaps the term "survivors" is preferable to "victims" because it is more upbeat and empowering, emphasizing the prospect of overcoming adversity. However, the established usage of the term "**survivors**" is to refer to the close relatives of people killed by murderers. Survivors or **indirect** or **secondary victims** (such as family members and lovers) are not immediately involved or physically injured in confrontations. But they might be burdened, even devastated, as the following example illustrates.

> A teenager who shot and killed a high school athlete is about to be sentenced to prison. The distraught father of the murdered boy tells the judge "We always hope our little guy will come through the door, and it will never be. We don't have lives. We stay in every day. We can't function." (MacGowan, 2007)

First responders and rescue workers who race to crime scenes (such as police officers, forensic evidence technicians, paramedics, and firefighters) are exposed to emergencies and trauma on such a routine basis that they also can be considered secondary or indirect victims who periodically might need emotional support themselves (see Regehr and Bober, 2005).

Note that victimologists are social scientists and researchers, as opposed to practitioners who directly assist injured parties to recover from their ordeals or who advocate on their behalf. Doctors, nurses, psychiatrists, psychologists, therapists, counselors, social workers, caseworkers, lawyers, clergy, and dedicated volunteers provide hands on services, emotional support, and practical advice to their clients (see Williams, 2002). Victimologists step back and evaluate the effectiveness of these well-intentioned efforts by members of the healing and helping professions. Conversely, people who minister to those in distress can gain valuable insights and useful suggestions from the findings of studies carried out by victimologists.

STUDYING VICTIMIZATION SCIENTIFICALLY

The suffering of victims and survivors always has been a popular theme for artists and writers to interpret and for political and religious leaders to address. But this long and rich tradition embodies what might be categorized as the **subjective approach** to the plight of victims, since issues are approached from the standpoint of morality, ethics, philosophy, personalized reactions, and intense emotions. Victimologists examine these same topics and incidents from a fresh, new angle: a social science perspective. **Objectivity** is the hallmark of any social scientific endeavor. Scientific objectivity requires that the observer try to be fair, open-minded, evenhanded, dispassionate, neutral, and unbiased. Objectivity means not taking sides, not showing favoritism, not allowing personal prejudices to sidetrack analyses, not permitting emotion to cloud reasoning, and not letting the dominant views of the times dictate conclusions and recommendations.

Prescriptions to remain disinterested and uninvolved are easier to abide by when the incidents under scrutiny happened long ago and far away. It is much harder to maintain social distance when investigating the plight of real people right here and right now. These scientific tenets are extremely difficult to live up to when the subject matter—the depredations inflicted by lawbreakers—draws upon widely held beliefs about good and evil, right and wrong, justice and unfairness. Most offenders show such callous disregard and depraved indifference toward the human beings they have cold-bloodedly targeted as depersonalized objects that it is difficult to avoid being caught up and swept away by strong emotional currents. Consider how natural it is to identify with those on the receiving end of violent attacks, feel empathy and sympathy toward them, and to bristle with hostility toward the aggressors, as in the following real-life cases (all involving college students):

> Two freshmen returning to their Jeep in a shopping center parking lot are confronted by a junior pre-med student from another college who is home for Christmas break.
>
> He draws a gun and forces his two hostages to drive to a deserted area. There he orders his captives out, reassuring them, "Don't be nervous. I'm not going to hurt you." As they lie face-down in the snow, he shoots each of them in the back of the head, killing one young man and injuring the other. Then he drives off with his prize—the Jeep. (Hanley, 1994b)

***

A 24-year-old woman disappears while hiking with her dog on the Appalachian Trail on New Years Day. Assuming that she is lost, a search-and-rescue crew combs the area. Her parents arrive at the scene and at first are optimistic, describing her as a feisty and gregarious person who could handle herself outdoors in chilly weather. A week later the authorities stumble upon some bloody clothing and her dog wandering around a parking lot. When the police arrest a 61-year-old drifter who has her wallet and college identification card, he quickly confesses to avoid the death penalty, leads detectives to her decapitated corpse, and admits he held her captive for several days before slaying her. (Goodman, 2008)

***

A classroom door swings open, and a mentally deranged undergraduate barges in and shoots the professor who is lecturing by the blackboard. Then, starting with those in the front rows, the silent and expressionless gunman methodically starts firing away at the horrified students, who hit the floor and turn over desks to shield themselves. "There were a couple of screams, but for the most part it was eerily silent, other than the gunfire," a student reports. As the mass murderer wanders off, another student recalls, "I told people that were still up and conscious, 'Just be quiet because we don't want him to think there are people in here because he'll come back in.'" Indeed, he tries to return to resume the slaughter, but a wounded student keeps the door wedged shut. Still determined to re-enter into the classroom, the deranged undergrad fires repeatedly at the door. When he eventually stalks off, the survivors call 911 on their cell phones and holler for help out the window. The attacker is later found dead from a self-inflicted gunshot wound to the head, in another classroom, alongside the bodies of some of his other victims. (Hernandez, 2007)

Doesn't basic human decency demand that observers identify with the wounded, downtrodden, and underdogs and condemn predatory behavior? Why would victimologists even consider maintaining objectivity to be an indispensable prerequisite of each and every scientific analysis?

WHY OBJECTIVITY IS DESIRABLE

At first glance, the importance of reserving judgments, refraining from jumping to conclusions, and resisting the urge to side with those who are in pain might not be self-evident. An angry, gut

reaction might be to ask, "What kind of person would try to remain dispassionate in the midst of intense suffering? What is wrong with championing the interests of people who have been harmed by unjust and illegal actions? Why is neutrality a worthwhile starting point in any analysis?"

The simple and direct answer to the question "Why shouldn't victimologists be openly and squarely pro-victim?" is that, unlike the situations described in the examples above, on many occasions this formula provides no real guidance. So when is a person worthy of sympathy and support? Most people would consider an individual who sustained injuries and losses to be an innocent victim only when the following conditions apply (what sociologists would call the **ideal type** or positive stereotype): the person who suffered harm was weaker in comparison to the apparent aggressor and was acting virtuously (or at least was engaged in conventional activities and was not looking for trouble or breaking any laws); and the wrongdoer was a complete stranger whose behavior obviously was illegal and unprovoked, and was not a member of a powerful group protected by vested interests (such as police officers or prison guards). In other words, the status of being a legitimate or bona fide victim is socially constructed and conferred (see Christie, 1986; and Dignan, 2005).

Victims or Offenders?

But real-life confrontations do not consistently generate simple clear-cut cases that neatly fall into the dichotomies of good and evil, and innocence and guilt. Not all victims were weak, defenseless, unsuspecting "lambs" who, through tragic or ironic circumstances or just plain bad luck, were pounced upon by cunning, vicious "wolves." In some instances, observers may have reasonable doubts and honest disagreements over which party in a conflict should be labeled the victim and which should be stigmatized as the villain. These complicated situations dramatize the need for impartiality when untangling convoluted relationships in order to make a rational argument and a sound legal determination that one person should be arrested, prosecuted, and punished, and the other defended, supported, and assisted. Unlike the black-and-white examples presented above, many messy incidents reported in the news and processed by the courts embody "shades of gray." Clashes frequently take place between two people who, to varying degrees, are both victims, or both wrongdoers. Consider the following accounts of high-profile cases that illustrate just how difficult it can be to try to establish exactly who seriously misbehaved and who acted appropriately:

***

A man riding a subway train is approached by a pair of teenagers who ask him for $5 while two of their friends look on. Fearing that he is about to be robbed and injured, as in a previous incident, the man rises from his seat, draws an unlicensed revolver, and empties it of the bullets he has hollowed out for greater impact. He shoots two of the teens in the chest, one in the side, and the fourth twice, once in the back at close range. Dubbed the "Subway Vigilante" by reporters, he is widely hailed as a hero who stood up and fought back, striking a symbolic blow on behalf of all victims against all street criminals. Others, however (including some high officials), depict him as a trigger-happy gunman who overreacted to stereotypes and mowed down four unarmed teenagers—two of them fleeing—before they made their intentions clear. Amidst a growing controversy, a grand jury does not indict him, but the case is brought before a second grand jury which agrees to put him on trial for attempted murder, assault, and reckless endangerment. His lawyer pursues a prosecutorial defense, arguing that the four wounded youths are really injured robbers and that the accused is actually their intended prey who justifiably resorted to deadly force to protect himself. The jury convicts him only of possessing an unlicensed handgun. But the judge sentences him not only to a jail term followed by probation, but also to community service, psychiatric observation, and a fine (Fletcher, 1990). The young man who was shot

twice ends up in a wheelchair, paralyzed from the waist down. More than ten years later he wins a multimillion-dollar lawsuit against the subway rider who crippled him when a civil jury decides that the fifth shot in the back was not fired in self-defense. (Nossiter, 1996)

***

Two brothers, 18 and 21, barge in upon their wealthy parents who are watching television and eating ice cream in their mansion. The sons slay their father and mother with a salvo of fifteen shotgun blasts. For six months the police search for the killers; then these two college students concede that they did it. On trial for first-degree murder and facing possible execution, the sons give emotionally compelling (but uncorroborated) testimony describing how their father sexually molested and emotionally abused them when they were little boys. The brothers contend they acted in self-defense, believing that their parents were about to murder them to keep the alleged incestuous acts a family secret. The prosecution argues that the boys killed their parents in order to get their hands on their $14 million inheritance (they quickly spent $700,000 on luxury cars, condos, and fashionable clothing before they were arrested). The jurors become deadlocked over whether to find them guilty of murder or only of the lesser charge of voluntary manslaughter, and the judge declares a mistrial. In the second trial the prosecution ridicules their abuse defense. They are convicted of premeditated murder and are sentenced to life in prison without parole. (Berns, 1994; Mydans, 1994; Associated Press, 1996a)

***

An ex-Marine who works as a bouncer in a bar wakes up in his bed and discovers to his horror that his wife has sliced off his penis with a kitchen knife. Arrested for "malicious wounding," she tells the police that she mutilated him because earlier that evening in a drunken stupor he forced himself upon her. He is put on trial for marital sexual abuse but is acquitted by a jury that does not believe her testimony about a history of beatings, involuntary rough sex, and other humiliations. When she is indicted on felony charges (ironically, by the same prosecutor) for the bloody bedroom assault, many people rally to her side. To her supporters, she has undercut the debilitating stereotype of female passivity; she literally disarmed him with a single stroke and threw the symbol of male sexual dominance out the window. To her detractors, she is a master at manipulation, publicly playing the role of sobbing, sympathetic victim to divert attention from her act of rage against a sleeping husband who had lost his sexual interest in her. Facing up to twenty years in prison, she declines to plead guilty to a lesser charge and demands her day in court. The jury accepts her defense—that she was a traumatized battered wife, deeply depressed, beset by flashbacks, and susceptible to "irresistible impulses" because of years of cruelty and abuse—and finds her not guilty by reason of temporary insanity. After forty-five days under observation in a mental hospital, she is released. Soon afterwards, the couple divorces, and then they each take financial advantage of all the international media coverage, sensationalism, titillation, voyeurism, and sexual politics surrounding their deeply troubled relationship. (Margolick, 1994; Sachs, 1994)

In each of these cases, the people officially designated as the victims by the police and prosecutors—the wounded teenagers, the dead parents, the slashed husband—arguably could be considered by certain standards as wrongdoers who "got what was coming to them," and, indeed, they were viewed just that way by substantial segments of the public and by some jurors. The defendants who got in trouble with the law—the pistol-packing subway passenger, the shotgun-toting brothers, and the knife-wielding wife—insisted that they should not be portrayed as criminals. On the contrary, they contended that they actually were the genuine victims: an innocent commuter about to be robbed, sons sexually molested by

their father, a battered woman who was subjected to marital rape.

When different interpretations of the facts lead to sharply divergent conclusions about who is actually the guilty party and who is the injured party, any knee-jerk anti-offender, pro-victim impulses provide no guidance for action. The confusion inherent in the unrealistically simplistic labels of 100% criminal and 100% victim underscores the need for objectivity when trying to figure out who is primarily responsible for what happened. Clearly, the dynamics between victims and victimizers need to be sorted out in an even-handed and open-minded manner, not only by victimologists but also by police officers, prosecutors, judges, and juries.

Criminals as Victims

To further complicate matters, impartiality is called for when the injured party turns out to be an undeniable lawbreaker. To put it bluntly, predators prey upon each other as well as upon innocent members of the general public. Some assaults and slayings surely can be characterized as "criminal-on-criminal." Researchers (see Singer, 1981; Fattah, 1990) have noted that people who routinely engage in illegal activities are more likely to get hurt than their law-abiding counterparts. When an organized crime syndicate "takes out a contract" on a rival faction's chieftain, the gangster who was "whacked" in a "mob rubout" was not an upstanding citizen struck down by an act of randomly directed violence. Similarly, when a turf battle erupts between drug dealers and one vanquishes the other, it must be remembered that the loser aspired to be the victor. When youth gangs feud with each other by carrying out "drive-by" shootings, the young members who get gunned down are casualties of their own brand of retaliatory "street justice." Hustlers, con men, high-stakes gamblers, pimps, prostitutes, fences, swindlers, smugglers, traffickers, and others living life in the fast lane of the underworld often get hurt because they enter into conflicts with volatile persons known to be armed and dangerous. What could it possibly mean to be pro-victim in these rather common cases in which lawbreakers harm other wrongdoers? The designations "victim" and "offender" are not always at opposite poles but sometimes can be pictured as overlapping categories somewhere near the middle of a continuum bounded by complete innocence and full legal responsibility.

Of course, it is possible for people engaged in illicit activities to be genuine victims deserving of protection and redress through the courts. For example, prostitutes who trade sexual favors for money are frequently beaten by sadistic johns, robbed of their earnings by exploitative pimps (see Boyer and James, 1983; Brents and Hausbeck, 2005), and occasionally targeted by serial killers. The harms they suffer are more serious than the offenses they commit (see Coston, 2004). In bar-room brawls, individuals who pick fights might wind up badly beaten or even killed by their intended targets who turn the tables, gain the upper hand, and respond to their attackers' belligerent initiatives with unreasonable, excessive force, be-yond what the law permits in self-defense. In penal institutions, convicts become victims entitled to press charges when they are assaulted, gang raped, or robbed by other, more vicious inmates.

Next, consider the possibility of a cycle of violence over time that transforms a victim into a victimizer (see Fagan, Piper, and Cheng, 1987). For example, a group of picked-upon students might band together to ambush their bullying tormentors; a battered wife might launch a vengeful surprise attack against her brutal husband; or a child sub-jected to periodic beatings might grow up to parent his sons in the same excessively punitive way he was raised. A study that tracked the fortunes of boys and girls known to have been physically and sexually abused over a follow-up period of several decades concluded that being harmed at an early age sub-stantially increased the odds of future delinquency and criminality (Widom and Maxfield, 2001). Another longitudinal study of molested males estimated that although most did not become ped-ophiles, more than 10 percent grew up to become sexual aggressors and exploiters (Skuse et al., 2003). Similarly, the results of a survey of convicts revealed that they were much more likely to have been abused physically or sexually as children than their

law-abiding counterparts (Harlow, 1999). About half of all inmates in state prisons told interviewers that they had been shot at in the past, and more than a fifth had been wounded by gunfire (Harlow, 2001). Violence begets violence, to the extent that those who suffer today may be inclined to inflict pain on others tomorrow.

Even more confusing are the situations of cer-tain groups of people who continuously switch roles as they lead their twisted daily lives. For instance, desperate heroin addicts are repeatedly subjected to consumer fraud (dealers constantly cheat them by selling heavily adulterated packets of this forbidden powder). Nevertheless, after being swindled over and over again by their suppliers, they routinely go out and steal other people's property to raise the cash that pays for their habits (see Kelly, 1983). Similarly, teenage girls who engage in prostitution are arrested by the police and sent to juvenile court as delinquents, in accordance with the law. But reformers see them more as victims of sexual abuse by pimps and johns who actually commit statutory rape upon these underage sex workers, who are in need of help rather than punishment (Herbert, 2008). To further complicate matters, offenders can morph into victims right under the noses of the authorities. For example, when delinquents are thrown in with older and tougher inmates in adult jails, these teenagers face grave risks of being physically and sexually assaulted ("New study," 2008).

Victims Versus "Good Guys"

Striving for objectivity is important for another reason. Victimologists do not limit their studies to the clashes between victims and offenders. They are very interested in the social reaction to victimization—how others respond to these crimes. Crime victims can and do become embroiled in conflicts with persons and groups besides the perpe-trators who have directly inflicted physical wounds and economic losses. Injured parties might nurse grievances against journalists reporting about their cases; police officers and detectives investigating their complaints; prosecutors ostensibly representing them in court; defense attorneys working on behalf of the accused; juries and judges deciding how to resolve their cases; probation, parole, and corrections officers supervising convicts who harmed them; lawyers handling their lawsuits in civil court; governmental agencies and legislative bodies shaping their legal rights; social movements either speaking on their behalf or opposing their wishes; and businesses viewing them as eager customers for security products and services. Impartiality helps social scientists to understand why friction can develop in these situations, and how to find solutions if these relationships become antagonistic.

Consider the dilemmas many people face because of their competing loyalties: to side with crime victims but also to remain true to their other commitments (for instance, to support a free press, local police forces, the U.S. military, and the pro-life movement), as the following examples will illustrate.

Often, victims of highly publicized crimes are outraged by the way the news media portrays them. For example, the families of homicide victims often complain about **sensationalism**, a kind of coverage that can be branded as "scandal-mongering," "pandering," "yellow journalism," and "tabloidism." Newspapers, magazines, radio stations, and television networks may engage in sensationalism because they are profit-oriented businesses. Shocking stories attract readers, listeners, and viewers. Blaring headlines, gripping accounts, colorful phrases, memorable quotes, and other forms of media "hype" build the huge audiences that enable media enterprises to charge advertisers high rates. Producers, editors, and reporters who seek to play up the human-interest angle may exploit the victims' plight, having found that crime stories attract a lot of notice if they are spiced up with a heavy dose of sex, gore, and raw emotions. Rather than side with the injured parties or with the journalists covering their cases, shouldn't a victimologist adopt the stance of a detached and disinterested observer who investigates these charges of sensationalism by carrying out a content analysis of press coverage in high-profile cases?

Consider how important it is for researchers to remain neutral whenever angry victims or their next of kin raise explosive charges against law enforcement agencies whose duty it is to "protect and serve," while highly respected police officials issue denials and rebuttals. For example, a child held captive by her intoxicated father was killed by a hail of bullets from a SWAT team during an attempted rescue. The mother blamed the police more so than her hostage-taking husband for the tragic outcome, triggering an investigation by outside agencies (see Winton, 2005; and Rubin, 2008). In another incident, after a hearing a defendant overpowered a court officer and used the service revolver to kill innocent bystanders. The families of the dead faulted the department's lax security practices and inadequate training for the slaughter of their loved ones (Dewan, 2005). In instances like these, would a person who is both ardently pro-victim and pro-police agree with the distraught relatives that law enforcement agencies were too reluctant to take responsibility for procedural mistakes that cost innocent lives? After two unarmed auxiliary police officers were gunned down by a deranged killer, their parents applied to a compensation fund for line-of-duty-deaths administered by the U.S. Department of Justice, which is widely viewed as the pro-victim branch of government. When their request was rejected because the two murdered auxiliaries technically were not peace officers with the power to arrest, the federal agency's decision was denounced by the parents, the police commissioner, and newspaper editorial boards (Lueck, 2008). Where would people who are both pro-victim and pro-Department of Justice stand in this controversy?

One more ambiguous and divisive situation involving the criminal justice system needs to be confronted. Isn't objectivity indispensable when two competing approaches both claim to be pro-victim? Consider two alternative ways of handling wife-beating. One policy insists that a battered woman should be permitted to remain in control of "her" case and ultimately decide if she wants to continue to press charges against her husband/boyfriend who was arrested for assaulting her. The other policy mandates that the prosecution of the arrestee should go forward on the basis of the available evidence (police officer testimony, photos of bruises, eyewitness accounts, hospital records), even if the injured party wants to drop the charges (either because she fears reprisals or seeks rapprochement). Only an objective analysis can determine which of these two ostensibly "pro-victim" approaches best serves the long-term interests of different types of domestic violence victims (see O'Sullivan et al., 2007).

In the midst of a global war on terrorism, strong unquestioning support for the armed forces of the United States abounds in Congress as well as among the citizenry. But what happens when people who are zealously pro-military learn of charges that the leadership of the Department of Defense has not done enough to assist victims and prosecute offenders in cases of wife-beating on military bases, and of sexual assaults by servicemen against women in uniform from the battlefields of Iraq and Afghanistan to the U.S. Air Force Academy? These accusations from female soldiers, plus concerns voiced by elected officials, have caused the Pentagon to investigate domestic violence and sexual misconduct in the military and to issue sweeping policy reforms eighteen times over sixteen years (see Moss, 2003; Office of the Inspector General, 2003; CBS News, 2005; and Houppert, 2005; and Corbett, 2007).

Most people would agree that a girl or woman who has been compelled to submit to a sexual assault that results in a pregnancy should not have to bear the rapist's child. But those who are both staunchly pro-victim and passionately anti-abortion might find themselves torn between competing loyalties when it comes to policies surrounding the "morning-after pill." Lawmakers and political interest groups are divided over whether or not hospitals (especially those closely affiliated with religious orders) should be required to offer this form of emergency contraception to rape victims who have reported the crime to the police. Even more controversial is the question whether pharmacists could be allowed to dispense the pill without a prescription (for example, to a woman who does not want to inform the authorities and file a formal complaint against some man in her family who forced himself upon her) (Greenberger, 2005).

SOURCES OF BIAS

To sum up the arguments presented in earlier sections, when choosing projects to research and when gathering and interpreting data, victimologists must put aside their personal political orientations towards criminal justice policies (such as conservatism or liberalism); their allegiances to causes (such as preserving civil liberties or advancing women's rights); and any positive or negative feelings toward entire groups (such as being pro-police or anti-gun owners). Advocacy, whether for or against some policy or practice, should be kept separate from assessing the facts or drawing conclusions based on evidence. Scientific skepticism—not self-interest or preconceived notions—must prevail when evaluating whether victims' rights legislation, prevention strategies, antitheft hardware, and recovery programs genuinely work or are ineffective or even counterproductive in reaching their stated goals. Expert opinion, in reports, in court testimony, or in the classroom must be based on facts, not faith. Like all social scientists, victimologists must declare: "Prove it! Show me! Where is the evidence?" when presented with claims (for example, that restraining orders issued by judges consistently fail to protect battered women, or that installing burglar alarms limit losses by panicking thieves). Victimological research must tell the whole truth, no matter who is disappointed or insulted.

Three types of biases undermine the ability of any social scientists (not just victimologists) to achieve objectivity (see Myrdal, 1944). The first may arise from personal experiences, taking the form of individual preferences and prejudices. For example, victimologists who have been personally harmed in some way (by a burglary, robbery, or rape, for example) might become so sensitized to the plight of their fellow victims that they can see issues only from the victim's point of view. Conversely, those who have never been through such an ordeal might be unable to truly grasp what the victim must endure. In either case, the victimologist may develop a bias, whether it be oversensitivity and over-identification or insensitivity and lack of identification with injured persons.

A second type of bias derives from the legacy of the discipline itself. The language, concepts, theories, and research priorities can reflect the collective preferences and priorities of its founders and their followers. For instance, it is widely acknowledged that the pioneers in this field of study introduced a victim-blaming orientation into the new discipline, but over the decades the tide has decisively turned. Today, the vast majority of victimologists make no secret of their pro-victim commitments to devise effective means of aid, support, and recovery.

Although subtle, a third type of bias can be traced back to the mood of the times. Victimologists, like all other members of a society, are influenced by their social environment. The events that shape public opinion during different periods of time can also affect scientific thought. During the 1960s and early 1970s, for example, many people demanded that the government devise ways to help victims get back on their feet financially, medically, and emotionally. This insistence about expanding the social safety net to cushion the blows inflicted by offenders reflected the spirit of egalitarianism of this stage in American history, and inspired a great deal of research and policy advocacy by victimologists. But these ambitious goals have been voiced less often ever since the 1980s, when the themes of "self-reliance," "reduce social spending by government," and "cut taxes" gained popularity. Consequently, research projects about government-funded victim assistance programs have shifted their focus to matters such as cost effectiveness and the feasibility of privately financed or faith-based charitable alternatives.

Clearly, inquiries into how victims suffer at the hands of criminals and other groups such as criminal justice officials is unavoidably a value-laden pursuit that arouses intense passions and sharply opposing views. As a result, some people believe that objectivity is an impossible and unrealistic goal that should be abandoned in favor of a forthright affirmation of values and allegiances. They say that victimologists (and other social scientists) should acknowledge their biases at the outset to alert their audiences to the slant that their analyses and policy recommendations will take. Others argue that objectivity is worth striving for because subjectivity thwarts attempts to accurately describe, understand, and explain what is happening, why it came about, and how conditions can be improved.

For the purposes of a textbook, the best course of action is to present all sides of controversial issues. Nevertheless, space limitations impose hard choices. This book focuses almost entirely on victims of street crimes (murder, rape, robbery, assault, kidnapping, burglary, larceny, and motor vehicle theft). There are many other categories of lawbreaking: crimes in the "suites" involving a betrayal of trust and an abuse of power by high government officials against their rivals or to the detriment of the general public; and by corporate executives who can illegally inflict massive losses and injuries upon their company's workers, customers, stock owners, or competitors. White collar crimes such as embezzlement by employees against their employers or fraud by citizens against government programs also impose much greater financial costs than street crimes. Organized rackets run by mobsters (drug smuggling, gun trafficking, counterfeiting of documents and currency, gambling, extortion) generate millions of dollars, undermine everyday life, and stimulate official corruption (bribes to look the other way). Crimes without complainants—victimless activities to some, vice to others—are controversial because the social reaction and criminal justice response might be worse than the original deviant behavior involving transactions between consenting adults (such as prostitution, illegal wagering, and street level drug selling and buying). Clearly these other categories of crimes are as serious and merit attention from scholars, law enforcement agencies, and concerned citizens. But they are not the types of lawless deeds that come to mind when people talk about "the crime problem" or express fears about being harmed. Street crime scares the public, preoccupies the media, keeps police departments busy, and captures the notice of politicians. These conventional, ordinary, depressingly familiar, and all-too-common predatory acts have tangible, visible, readily identifiable victims who are directly affected and immediately aware of their injuries and losses.

In contrast, in the other categories of crime, especially white-collar crime and crime in the

---

B O X 1.1 What the Police Mean by the Term Victimology

When homicide squad detectives say they are engaged in victimology, they mean piecing together the dead person's life in order to help discover the killer's identity. Police investigators want to find out as much as possible about the deceased from interviews with the next of kin and eyewitnesses, email messages, diaries, banking deposits and withdrawals, and records of telephone calls. Detectives look into the victim's associates (by compiling lists of contacts, including friends, family members, acquaintances, rivals, and enemies); social background (lifestyle, occupation, education, marital status, secret lovers); criminal background (any prior record of arrests, convictions, and any cases in which the departed served as a complainant, plaintiff, or witness against others); financial situation (sources of income, debts owed, investments, and who is next-in line to inherit the victim's property); and health issues (drinking habits, drug-taking, and other problems). Autopsy findings shed light on the final meal, drinking and drug-taking, the cause of death, and the approximate time interval when the fatal confrontation took place.

For example, if a drug dealer is found shot to death in an alley, detectives would construct a timeline of his last known whereabouts and activities. What were his known hangouts (bars, clubs, pool halls, etc.)? Investigators would seek clues to determine whether he was killed by someone above him in the hierarchy of drug trafficking or someone below who worked for him or bought controlled substances from him. Was he recently embroiled in any disputes or court cases and did he secretly serve as a confidential informant? Who had a motive and an opportunity to slay him?

Clearly, whereas victimologists want to uncover trends, patterns, and regularities that hold true for many victims in general, police investigators seek to reconstruct in great detail everything that can be uncovered about the life and death of just one particular person. The contribution of this effort at "forensic victimology" in this very pragmatic and immediate sense is to increase the odds of solving the case, apprehending a suspect, and advocating in court on behalf of a person who is no longer able to pursue justice (NYPD homicide detectives, 2008; also see Petherick and Turvey, 2008).

---

suites, the deleterious consequences are experienced by abstractions (such as "a competitive economy" or "national security"), impersonal entities (such as the U.S. Treasury or multi-national corporations), or vaguely defined collectivities (such as taxpayers, voters, shareholders, or consumers). It is difficult to grasp precisely "who" has suffered in these cases, and it is nearly impossible to describe or measure the background characteristics or reactions of the injured parties. It is extremely tough to establish in court specifically who the flesh-and-blood victims are in cases of drug smuggling, money laundering, insurance scams, false advertising, bribe-taking, software piracy, counterfeiting of trademarked goods, dumping of toxic wastes, insider trading, electoral fraud, illegal campaign contributions, and income tax evasion. But people hurt by street crimes can be easily identified, observed, contacted, interviewed, studied, counseled, assisted legally, and treated medically. As a result, a wealth of statistical data has accumulated about their

wounds, losses, and emotional reactions. For these reasons, victims of interpersonal violence and theft will be the primary focus of attention and concern throughout this text, even though many of the illegal activities cited above inflict much more severe social and economic damage (see Naim, 2005). But note that this decision immediately introduces a bias into this introduction to the field of victimology, one that reflects the experiences of authors of articles and textbooks, the collective priorities of the discipline's founders and most prolific researchers, and the mood of the times!

Clearly the term victimology can have different meanings to different people, and the scope of the field can vary depending upon a group's purposes. To detectives, victimology has a very restricted meaning: learning as much as possible about a person who was murdered in order to help figure out who the killer is. In police work, the term victimology is applied to a type of background investigation (see Box 1.1).

B O X 1.2   Some Striking Examples of "Victimology-Bashing"

The context and then the statement denouncing "victimology"

Concerning male / female relations:

■ During a nationally televised interview, a critic of contemporary feminism (Paglia, 1993) declared, *"I hate victimology. I despise a victim-centered view of the universe. Do not teach young women that their heritage is nothing but victimization."*

■ A collection of letters written to the editors of *The New York Times* (1996, p. E8) was published under the headline *"What women want is a lot less victimology."*

■ A reviewer (Harrop, 2003) of a book about the difficulties facing boys wrote, *"The art of victimology requires three easy steps: (1) Identify a group suffering real or perceived injustices. (2) Exaggerate the problem. (3) Blame the problem on a group you don't like. Conservatives have long condemned the "victimology industry" as a racket, especially when practiced by women and minorities. As it happens, conservatives also play the game, and very well indeed.... The latest victimized group seems to be American boys."*

■ A political analyst subtitled her provocative article about an alleged "Campus Rape Myth" as *"The reality: bogus statistics, feminist victimology, and university-approved sex toys"* (MacDonald, 2008a).

Concerning heterosexual / homosexual relations:

■ In a newspaper opinion piece about the controversy surrounding homosexuals serving in the military, the author (Sullivan, 1993, p. A21) observed, *"The effect that ending the ban could have on the gay community is to embolden the forces of responsibility and integration and weaken the impulses of victimology and despair.... A defeat would send a signal to a gay community at a crossroads between hopeful integration and a new relapse into the victimology of the ghetto."*

Concerning race and ethnic relations:

■ An author of a book about race relations called a well-known reverend and civil rights activist a *"professional Victimologist"* (see Dreher, 2001).

■ A former governor of Colorado (Lamm, 2004) warned that a plot to "destroy America" through immigration and multiculturalism would include the following strategy: *"establish the cult of victimology ... start a grievance industry blaming all minority failure on the majority population."*

■ A political commentator (Goldberg, 2008) observed during the 2008 presidential campaign: *"Democratic politicians have carried the baggage of black victimology and white guilt for generations."*

Concerning international relations:

■ A former Soviet intelligence officer (Pacepa, 2005) denounced the United Nations as a breeding ground for *"a virulent strain of hatred for America, grown from the bacteria of Communism, anti-Semitism, nationalism, jingoism, and victimology."*

■ A prominent commentator (Brooks, 2006) wrote about the public's perception of the

---

Victimology's Undeserved "Bad Reputation"

As the previous sections demonstrated, objectivity is desirable within victimology. Ironically, many outsiders do not approach the field of victimology in an objective way. They seem hostile to it on a gut level because they believe it is hopelessly biased. Some prominent and insightful people who ought to know better use the word "victimology" as an epithet spit out through clenched teeth. Not very long after the term entered mainstream culture, victimology (undeservedly!) became a "dirty word." This disturbing trend emerged during the 1990s and unfortunately is becoming even more entrenched and pronounced during the twenty-first century. Some dramatic illustrations of how victimology has been bad-mouthed in the media as muddled thinking or even denounced as a contemptible point of view appear in Box 1.2.

Middle East: *"What these Americans see is fanatical violence, a rampant culture of victimology and grievance, a tendency by many Arabs to blame anyone but themselves for the problems they create."*

- A reviewer (Anderson, 2008) of a book about the war on terrorism wrote: *"The Left's victimology now sickens [the author]."*

Concerning "Culture Wars":

- In his syndicated column, a leading conservative partisan (Buckley, 1994, p. 30a) condemned the thinking of the 1960s Woodstock generation: *"The countercultural music is the perfect accompaniment for the culture of sexual self-indulgence, of exhibitionism, of crime and illegitimacy and ethnic rancor and victimology."*

Concerning courtroom strategies:

- A news magazine columnist (Leo, 2002) took a swipe at certain lawsuits: *"Yes, everybody is a victim now, but some breakthroughs in victimology are more noteworthy than others. The year's best example was the trio of supersize teens who sued McDonald's, claiming the burger chain made them fat by enticing them to eat its meals nearly every day for five years."*
- In a critique of several jury verdicts that found defendants "not guilty," a news magazine commentator (Leo, 1994) complained, *"We are deep into the era of the abuse excuse. The doctrine of victimology—claiming victim status means you are not responsible for your actions—is beginning to*

warp the legal system.... The irony of this seems to escape victimologists. A movement that began with the slogan, 'Don't blame the victim' now strives to blame murder victims for their own deaths."

Concerning academia and life on college campuses:

- A columnist (Seebach, 1999, p. 2B) berated liberal professors for producing college grads whom employers would reject because the students were *"experts only in victimology or oppression studies."*
- A political analyst (MacDonald, 2007) interpreted the selection of a new university president as evidence that *"Harvard will now be the leader in politically correct victimology."*
- Arguing that resentment against highly educated candidates might be going too far during the 2008 presidential campaign, a political analyst (MacDonald, 2008c) agreed with her allies: *"I am as depressed as anyone by the university's descent into ignorant narcissism and victimology over the last 30 years."*

Concerning everyday life:

- A Pulitzer-Prize–winning conservative commentator (Will, 1998, p. 42) titled his syndicated column opposing the Clinton administration's antismoking campaign as *"President feeds the culture of victimology."*
- One journalist (Parker, 1999, p. B10) even insisted that *"Americans are fed up with twentieth-century victimology."*

What were these commentators thinking when they issued these sweeping denunciations of what they labeled "victimology"? Why is this relatively new academic discipline being singled out for such harsh criticisms?

Evidently, those who condemn victimology are railing at something other than scientific research focused on people harmed by criminals. The mistake these commentators are making is parallel to the improper usage of the phrase "sociological forces" rather than "social forces," and "psychological

problems" instead of "mental problems." Victimology is just one of many "-ologies" (including such narrowly focused fields of study as penology or suicidology, or such broad disciplines as sociology and psychology). The suffix "-ology" merely means "the study of." If the phrase "the objective study of crime victims" is substituted for "victimology" in the excerpts quoted above, the sentences make no sense. Victimology, sociology, and psychology are disciplines that adopt a certain approach to their subject matter or a method of analysis that maintains a particular focus, but they do not impose a partisan point of view or yield a set of predictably biased conclusions.

It appears that what these strident denunciations are deriding is a victimization-centered orientation which can be categorized as the ideology of **victimism** (see Sykes, 1992). An **ideology** is a coherent, integrated set of beliefs that shapes interpretations and leads to political action. Victimism is the outlook of people who share a sense of common victimhood. Individuals who accept this outlook believe that they gain insight from an understanding of history: of how their fellow group members (such as women, homosexuals, or racial and religious minorities) have been seriously "wronged" by another group (to put it mildly; viciously slaughtered would be a better way to phrase it in many historical cases!) or held back and kept down by unfair social, economic, or political institutions built upon oppressive and exploitative roles and relationships.

For example, in a well-known speech in 1964 (right before Congress passed civil rights legislation officially dismantling segregation), Malcolm X, the fiery spokesman for the black nationalist movement, proclaimed (see Breitman, 1966) "I'm one of the 22 million black people who are the victims of Americanism ... victims of democracy, nothing but disguised hypocrisy ... I'm speaking as a victim of this American dream system. And I see America through the eyes of the victim. I don't see any American dream; I see an American nightmare." Today, African-American activists combating the lingering embodiments of the old racist double standards within criminal justice might stress the legacy of centuries of government-sanctioned slavery followed by decades of crippling "Jim Crow" segregation (based on a U.S. Supreme Court decision that promulgated the dishonest doctrine of "separate but equal") that was enforced by lynch mobs and Klan terrorism.

Similarly, a leading figure in the women's liberation movement of the late 1960s analyzed "sexual politics" in this way (Millet, 1970): "Oppressed groups have been denied education, economic independence, the power of office, representation, an image of dignity and self-respect, equality of status and recognition as human beings. Throughout history women have been consistently denied all of these,

and their denial today, while attenuated and partial, is nevertheless consistent." Feminists struggling against stubborn vestiges of sexism within criminal justice might point out how in the past rape victims felt as if they were on trial; how battered women's pleas for help were ignored by the men at the helm of the criminal justice system; and how women were unable to serve on juries, and were strongly discouraged from seeking various careers such as becoming a police officer, lawyer, or judge. Staunch critics of current conditions often connect the dots by tracing the roots of today's social problems back through centuries of systematic injustices. But the commentators cited in Box 1.2 above claim that adopting this kind of victimist orientation leads to an unhealthy preoccupation with the past that impedes progress.

This debate over who or what is to blame for persisting injustices is part of an ongoing political battle for the hearts and minds of the American people—a continuing ideological struggle that is often categorized as "identity politics" which is part of the "culture wars." Unfortunately, victimology has become confused with victimism and as a result has been caught up in the crossfire between partisans on both sides. But victimology, as an "-ology" and not an "-ism," is an objective, neutral, open-minded and evenhanded scientific endeavor that does not take sides, play favorites, or speak with just one voice in these political debates. So there is no reason to condemn the whole scholarly enterprise of victimology and dismiss it as flawed, distorted, or slanted, as the commentators quoted above did. To put it bluntly, victimology has received a bum rap by those who mistakenly mock it and equate it with victimism. Read on and this confusion will be dispelled. Victimology will take shape as a challenging, meaningful, balanced, enlightening, constructive, and relevant field of study that focuses on a very old problem from a fresh, new angle.

THE ORIGINS OF VICTIMOLOGY

The beginnings of the academic discipline of victimology can be traced back to several articles, books, and research projects initiated by criminologists during the 1940s and 1950s. Until that time, criminology's attention was focused entirely on those who violated the law: who they were, why they engaged in illegal activities, how they were handled by the criminal justice system, whether they should be incarcerated, and how they might be rehabilitated. Eventually, perhaps through the process of elimination, several criminologists searching for solutions to the crime problem were drawn to—or stumbled upon—the important role played by victims.

These criminologists considered victims to be worthy of serious study primarily because they were the completely overlooked half of the dyad (pair). The first scholars to consider themselves victimologists examined the resistance put up by rape victims (Mendelsohn, 1940); the presumed vulnerabilities of certain kinds of people, such as the very young, the very old, recent immigrants, and the mentally disturbed (Von Hentig, 1948); and the kinds of people, in terms of factors such as age and sex, whose actions contributed to their own violent deaths (Wolfgang, 1958). The first use in English of the term victimology to refer to the study of people harmed by criminals appeared in a book about murderers written by a psychiatrist (Wertham, 1949).

During the 1960s, as the problem of street crime intensified, the President's Commission on Law Enforcement and the Administration of Justice argued that criminologists ought to pay more attention to victims (thereby inspiring some to become victimologists). The Commission's Task Force on Assessment (1967, p. 80) concluded:

> One of the most neglected subjects in the study of crime is its victims: the persons, households, and businesses that bear the brunt of crime in the United States. Both the part the victim can play in the criminal act and the part he could have played in preventing it are often overlooked. If it could be determined with sufficient specificity that people or businesses with certain characteristics are more likely than others to be crime victims, and that crime is more likely to occur in some places

rather than in others, efforts to control and prevent crime would be more productive. Then the public could be told where and when the risks of crime are greatest. Measures such as preventive police patrol and installation of burglar alarms and special locks could then be pursued more efficiently and effectively. Individuals could then substitute objective estimation of risk for the general apprehensiveness that today restricts—perhaps unnecessarily and at best haphazardly—their enjoyment of parks and their freedom of movement on the streets after dark.

In this call for a shift in focus, the Commission's Task Force stressed the potential practical benefits: More crimes could be prevented and more criminals caught, unrealistic fears could be calmed and unwarranted complacency dispelled, and needless expenditures could be eliminated or reduced. These ambitious goals have not yet been attained. Other goals not cited by the commission that have been added over the years include reducing suffering, making the criminal justice system more responsive, and restoring victims to the financial condition they were in before the crime occurred.

During the 1960s and 1970s, criminologists, reformers, and political activists argued persuasively that offenders themselves were in some sense "victims" too—of grinding poverty, dysfunctional families, failing school systems, rundown housing, job shortages, discrimination, police brutality, and other social problems (for example, see Ryan, 1971). In reaction to this sympathetic characterization of lawbreakers, many people asked, "But what about the real flesh-and-blood individuals that they preyed upon who were innocent, law-abiding, and vulnerable? What can be done to ease their suffering?" While grappling with that question, reformers came to recognize that persons targeted by criminals were being systematically abandoned to their fates, and that institutionalized neglect had prevailed for too long. A consensus began to emerge that people harmed by illegal acts deserved better treatment. Plans for financial assistance were the focus of early discussions; campaigns for enhanced rights within the legal system soon followed.

By the 1970s, victimology had become a recognized field of study with its own national and international professional organizations, conferences, and journals. By the end of the 1990s, students were taking courses in victimology at more than 240 colleges and universities. Box 1.3 lists a compilation of the major events in victimology's short history.

VICTIMOLOGY COMPARED TO CRIMINOLOGY

Victimology is an interdisciplinary field that benefits from the contributions of sociologists, psychologists, social workers, political scientists, doctors, nurses, criminal justice officials, lawyers, spiritual leaders, and other professionals, volunteers, advocates, and activists. But academically and organizationally, victimology is best conceived of as an area of specialization within **criminology**, on par with other fields of intensive study, such as delinquency, drug abuse, and penology. All these subdisciplines merit elective courses and textbooks of their own in colleges and graduate programs. In other words, criminology is the older parent discipline and victimology is the recent offshoot.

Criminology can be defined as encompassing the scientific study of illegal activities, offenders, their victims, criminal law and the justice system, and societal reactions to the crime problem.

Parallels Between Criminology and Victimology

Even though it is a rapidly evolving subdiscipline, victimology parallels its parent, criminology, in many ways. Criminologists ask why certain individuals become involved in lawbreaking while others do not. Their studies concentrate on the offenders' backgrounds and motives in order to uncover the root causes of their misbehavior. Victimologists ask why some individuals, households, and entities (such as banks) are targeted while others are not. Research projects aim to discover the sources of vulnerability to criminal attack and the reasons why some victims might act carelessly, behave recklessly, or even instigate others to assault them. Criminologists recognize that most people occasionally break certain laws (especially during adolescence) but are otherwise law-abiding; only some who engage in delinquent acts graduate to become hardcore offenders and career criminals. Victimologists realize that anyone can suffer the misfortune of being at the wrong place at the wrong time but wonder why certain individuals are targeted over and over again.

Although the law holds offenders personally accountable for their illegal conduct, criminologists explore how social, economic, and political conditions generate criminal activity. Similarly, although certain victims might be accused of sharing some degree of responsibility with their offenders for the outbreak of specific incidents, victimologists examine personality traits, agents of socialization, and cultural imperatives that compel some people to take chances and put their lives in danger, while others seem to accept their fate. Just as aggressive criminal behavior can be learned, victims may have been taught to lead high-risk lifestyles or even to play their subordinate roles.

Both criminologists and victimologists place a great emphasis on following the proper ways of gathering and interpreting data. Criminologists and victimologists rely upon the same methods used by all social scientists: case studies, surveys and polls based on questionnaires and interviews, carefully designed social experiments, content analyses of various forms of communication (like movies and song lyrics), secondary analyses of documents and files, and up-close and personal ethnographic approaches relying upon systematic observations. Criminologists and victimologists calculate statistics, compute rates, compile profiles, draw graphs, and search for patterns and trends. Criminologists collect and analyze information about individuals engaging in illegal behaviors, such as their typical ages and social backgrounds. Victimologists look over statistics about the ages and social backgrounds of the people who are harmed by unlawful activities.

B O X 1.3   Highlights in the Brief History of Victimology and Victim Assistance

Year	Event
1941	Hans Von Hentig publishes an article focusing on the interaction between victims and criminals.
1947	Benjamin Mendelsohn coins the term victimology in an article written in French.
1957	In Great Britain, Margery Fry proposes legislation that would authorize the government to reimburse victims for their losses.
1958	Marvin Wolfgang studies the circumstances surrounding the deaths of murder victims, and discovers that some contributed to their own demise.
1964	The U.S. Congress holds hearings on the plight of crime victims but rejects legislative proposals to cover their losses.
1965	California becomes the first U.S. state to set up a special fund to repay victims for crime inflicted expenses.
1966	A research team carries out a nationwide survey to find out about crimes that were not reported to the police.
1967	A presidential commission recommends that criminologists study victims.
1968	Stephen Schafer writes the first textbook about victims.
Early 1970s	The first sex crime squads and rape crisis centers are organized.
Mid-1970s	Prosecutors initiate victim-witness assistance programs.
1972	The federal government initiates a yearly National Crime Victimization Survey of the general public to uncover firsthand information about street crimes.
1973	The first international conference of victimologists is convened in Jerusalem.
1974	The first shelter for battered women is set up in Minnesota.
1976	The first scholarly journal devoted to victimology begins publication.
1977	New York State enacts the first "Son of Sam" law to prevent offenders from profiting from telling about their exploits.
1979	The World Society of Victimology is founded.

Year	Event
1981	President Reagan proclaims Victims' Rights Week every April.
1982	Congress passes a Victim and Witness Protection Act that suggests standards for fair treatment of victims within the federal court system.
1983	The President's Task Force on Victims of Crime recommends changes in the Constitution and in federal and state laws to guarantee victims' rights.
1984	Congress passes the Victims of Crime Act, which provides federal subsidies to state victim compensation and assistance programs.
1985	The United Nations General Assembly unanimously adopts a resolution that urges all members to respect and extend the rights of victims of crimes and of abuses of power.
1986	Victims' rights activists seek the passage of constitutional amendments on the federal and state levels guaranteeing victims' rights.
1987	The U.S. Department of Justice opens a National Victims Resource Center in Rockville, Maryland, to serve as a clearinghouse for information.
1990	Congress passes the Victims' Rights and Restitution Act.
1994	Congress passes the Violence Against Women Act.
2003	The American Society of Victimology holds its first annual national symposium.
2004	Congress enacts the Crime Victims' Rights Act, which pledges fair treatment and opportunities for input in federal court proceedings.
2005	A bipartisan group of 18 members of Congress forms a Victim's Rights Caucus.
2007	VictimLaw, a user-friendly website, provides a searchable database about state legislation concerning restitution and compensation for financial losses.
2008	A National Museum of Crime & Punishment opens in Washington, D.C., with exhibits that dramatize the plights of victims.

SOURCE: Galaway and Hudson, 1981; Schneider, 1982; Lamborn, 1985; National Organization for Victim Assistance (NOVA), 1989, 1995; Garlock, 2007; and Rothstein, 2008.

Criminologists apply their findings to devise local, regional, and national crime-prevention strategies. Victimologists scrutinize the patterns and trends they detect to develop personalized victimization-prevention strategies and risk reduction tactics.

Both criminologists and victimologists study how the criminal justice system actually works, in contrast to the way the system is supposed to work according to agency regulations, official roles, federal and state legislation, court decisions, and politicians' promises. Criminological research reveals how suspects, defendants, and convicts are really handled, while victimological studies examine the way injured parties are actually treated by police officers, prosecutors, defense attorneys, and judges. Criminologists assess the needs of offenders for counseling, psychotherapy, additional education, job training, and drug treatment. In addition, criminologists evaluate the effectiveness of various rehabilitation programs offered behind bars or available to probationers or parolees that are intended to reduce recidivism rates. Similarly, victimologists want to diagnose the emotional problems that beset people after they have been harmed by offenders, and to test out the usefulness of programs designed to facilitate their recovery (see Roberts, 1990; and Lurigio, 1990). Criminologists try to calculate the social and economic costs that criminal activity imposes on a community or on society as a whole. Victimologists estimate the losses and expenses that individuals and businesses incur due to acts of violence, theft, or fraud.

Differences and Boundaries

Criminology and victimology differ in several important ways. Criminology is several hundred years old, whereas victimology did not emerge until the second half of the 20th century. Criminologists agree among themselves that they should limit their studies to illegal activities (and not those expressions of social deviance that do not violate any laws). Victimologists cannot reach a consensus about the appropriate boundaries of their field. Some victimologists argue that their scientific studies should not be restricted to criminal victimization. They

believe that additional sources of suffering are worthy of systematic analysis: harm caused by oppressive political regimes, man-made disasters (such as wars and genocide), natural disasters (such as floods and earthquakes), and sheer accidents. The common goals would be to develop effective strategies for short-run relief, as well as government programs and long-term solutions to alleviate suffering from all kinds of calamities. However, the majority of victimologists believe that their studies should remain focused on criminal victimization so that there are precise, readily identifiable limits and clear directions for further research and theorizing. Criminal victimization may not be more serious (financially), more injurious (medically), or more traumatic and longer lasting (emotionally) than other types of harm and sources of suffering. But it is necessary to rein in the boundaries of the field in order to make it manageable for the practical purposes of holding conferences, publishing journals, writing textbooks, and teaching college courses. (For the pros and cons of these alternative visions of what the scope of victimology ought to be, see Schafer, 1968; Viano, 1976, 1983, and 1990a; Galaway and Hudson, 1981; Flynn, 1982; Scherer, 1982; Schneider, 1982; Friedrichs, 1983; Elias, 1986; and Fattah, 1991).

The boundary between victimology and mainstream criminology is not always clear-cut; sometimes the two overlap. Historically, much of criminology can be characterized as "offenderology" because of its preoccupation with the question of etiology: the wrongdoers' motives and the underlying causes of criminal behavior. Lawbreakers always have been under a spotlight while the people they harmed remained shadowy figures on the fringes. But now victimology enriches criminology by yielding a more balanced and comprehensive approach that sheds light on both parties and their interactions.

To illustrate the central concerns of each field and their areas of common interest, consider the problem of sexual predators preying on youngsters. Uncovering the kinds of emotional disorders and cultural themes about domination and exploitation that drive adults to molest and rape children are obviously subjects for criminological research, as is the controversy surrounding the alleged ineffectiveness of various "cures" for pedophilia. Whether threats of harsher punishments actually deter future attacks and whether satellite tracking of formerly incarcerated offenders is a worthwhile investment of government funds also falls squarely within the realm of criminology. Criminologists might launch their inquiries by examining the files maintained by police departments to draw a profile of the typical offender. Victimologists would use the same records to derive a statistical portrait of the children most at risk (in terms of age ranges, gender, class, race, and ethnicity, for example). Victimologists would focus their inquiries on which treatments best speed the recovery of molested children, and whether reforms in the way their cases are handled in court are minimizing the stress endured by these young witnesses who testify for the prosecution. Whether the relatively recent and rapidly spreading community notification policies (such as "Megan's Law") about the arrival of a new resident with a past history of sexual predation eases or intensifies parental fears for their children's safety is a subject for criminological research (because it explores the reactions of the general public to the threat of crime). Whether this kind of advanced warning about potentially dangerous strangers in the neighborhood who should be avoided makes previously molested children feel more or less anxious is a topic for victimologists to investigate. Whether these community notification requirements actually lead to fewer incidents is a research topic that straddles the line between criminology and victimology (because it leads to the calculation of crime rates which are simultaneously victimization rates).

The Interface with Other Disciplines

A number of academic orientations enrich victimology. Victimologists who pursue a mental health/forensic psychology orientation might explore how victims react to their misfortunes. They ask why some people experience **post-traumatic stress disorder** (PTSD) while others who suffer through comparable calamities do not. Members of the helping professions also want to know what personality traits, coping skills, inner resources, and belief systems (perhaps based on spirituality and religiosity) enable individuals who have endured shattering experiences to get through their period of bereavement, recover from depression, reconsider their priorities, and reorient their lives (see Ai and Park, 2005). Professionals engaged in therapeutic relationships with survivors of vicious violence need to discover which crisis intervention techniques work best (see Roberts, 2005). Victimologists who take an historical perspective trace developments from the past to better understand the present, while those who adopt an economic perspective try to measure individual and collective costs, losses, and expenses that result from criminal activities. The anthropological orientation compares victimization in other societies far away and long ago in order to transcend the limitations of analyses mired in the here and now. Victimologists who adopt a sociological perspective develop victim profiles (statistical portraits), analyze the interactions within the victim-offender relationship, examine the way other people and social institutions (such as the public welfare and health care systems) deal with injured parties, and seek to evaluate the effectiveness of new policies and programs. Victimologists who apply a legalistic/criminal justice orientation explore how victims are supposed to be handled by the police, prosecutors, defense attorneys, judges, probation officers, and parole boards, and they scrutinize the provisions of recently enacted laws designed to empower victims as the adversary system resolves "their" cases.

Divisions within the Discipline

Victimology does not have the distinct schools of thought that divide criminologists into opposing camps, probably because this new subdiscipline lacks its own well-developed theories of human behavior. However, in both criminology and victimology, political ideologies—conservative, liberal, and radical left/critical/conflict—can play a significant role in influencing the choice of research topics and in shaping policy recommendations.

The conservative tendency within victimology focuses primarily upon street crimes. A basic tenet of conservative thought is that everyone—both victims and offenders—must be held strictly accountable for their decisions and actions. This translates into an emphasis on self-reliance rather than governmental assistance. Individuals should strive to take personal responsibility for preventing, avoiding, resisting, and recovering from criminal acts and for defending themselves, their families, and their homes from outside attack. In accordance with the **crime control** model of criminal justice, lawbreakers must be strictly punished on behalf of their victims (retribution, or **just deserts**). Inflicting suffering on lawbreakers should further general deterrence (to make a negative example of them, to serve as a warning to other would-be offenders that they should think twice and decide not to break the law), and specific deterrence (to teach them a lesson not to commit any harmful acts in the future). Incapacitating predators behind bars keeps them away from the targets they would like to prey upon.

The liberal tendency sees the scope of the field as stretching beyond street crime to include criminal harm inflicted on persons by reckless corporate executives and corrupt officials. A basic theme within liberal thought is to endorse governmental intervention to try to ensure fair treatment and to alleviate needless suffering. This position leads to efforts to extend the "safety net" mechanisms of the welfare state to cushion shocks and losses due to all kinds of misfortunes, including crime. To "make the victim whole again," aid must be available from such programs as state compensation funds, subsidized crime insurance plans, rape crisis centers, and shelters for battered women. Some liberals are enthusiastic about restorative justice experiments that, instead of punishing offenders by imprisoning them, attempt to make wrongdoers pay restitution to their victims so that reconciliation between the two estranged parties might become possible.

The radical left/critical/conflict tendency seeks to demonstrate that the problem of victimization arises from the exploitative and oppressive relations that are pervasive throughout the social system. Therefore, the scope of the field should not be limited simply to the casualties of criminal activity in the streets. Inquiries must be extended to cover the harm inflicted by industrial polluters, owners and managers of hazardous workplaces, fraudulent advertisers, predatory lenders (for example, of mortgages with deceptive provisions for repayment of the loan), brutally violent law enforcement agencies, and discriminatory institutions. Victims might not be particular individuals but whole groups of people, such as factory workers, minority groups, customers, or neighborhood residents. From the radical/critical/conflict perspective, victimology can be faulted for preferring to study the more obvious, less controversial kinds of harmful behaviors, mostly acts of personal violence and crude theft by desperate individuals, instead of the more fundamental injustices that mar everyday life: the inequitable distribution of wealth and power that results in poverty, malnutrition, homelessness, family dysfunction, chronic structural unemployment, substance abuse, and other social problems. The legal system and the criminal justice apparatus are considered part of the problem by criminologists as well as victimologists working within this tradition because these institutions primarily safeguard the interests of influential groups and privileged classes (see Birkbeck, 1983; Friedrichs, 1983; Viano, 1983; Elias, 1986, 1993; Fattah, 1986, 1990, 1992a, 1992b; Miers, 1989; Reiman, 1990; Walklate, 1991; and Mawby and Walklate, 1993).

Why Study Victimology?

One last parallel between criminology and victimology merits highlighting. Criminology and victimology are not well-paying fields ripe with opportunities for employment and advancement. Becoming a criminologist or a victimologist rarely leads to fame and fortune, and certainly doesn't make a person invincible to physical attacks, thefts, or swindles. Yet for several reasons a growing number of people are investing time, energy, and money to study victimology.

First of all, victimologists benefit intellectually, as do all social scientists, by gaining insights into everyday life, solving puzzling and troubling issues, better appreciating life's subtleties, seeing phenomena more clearly, and understanding complex situations more profoundly. Second, individuals profit from pursuits that expand their horizons, transcend the limits of their own experiences, free them from irrational fears and unfounded concerns, and enable them to overcome gut reactions of fatalism, cynicism, emotionalism, and deep-seated prejudices. Third, the findings generated from theorizing and applied research have practical applications that simultaneously ease the suffering of others and give the victimologist a sense of purpose, worth, accomplishment, and satisfaction.

It is true that criminologists and victimologists may appear to be guilty of impersonal detachment when, for example, they study murder victims by counting corpses and noting the circumstances of death. But the dilemma of treating real flesh-and-blood casualties as mere "cases" or "abstract statistics" is largely unavoidable and arises just as sharply in other fields, such as medicine, military history, police science, and suicidology. The redeeming value of victimology lies in its potential for human betterment. Victimology's allegiance to the principle of striving for objectivity when conducting research doesn't detract from the discipline's overall commitment to alleviate needless suffering.

Victimology is not the cold or dismal discipline it might appear to be at first glance. Victimologists are not morbidly curious about or preoccupied with misfortune, loss, tragedy, pain, grief, death, and mourning. Of course, because of its negative subject matter, the discipline is problem-oriented by nature. However, victimologists also take part in furthering positive developments and constructive activities when they seek to discover effective ways of coping with hardships, transcending the vicissitudes of life, reimbursing financial damages, speeding up recovery, promoting reconciliation between parties enmeshed in conflicts, and restoring harmony to a strife-torn community.

On occasion, victimologists—and the general public—can find the attitudes and actions of individuals who have suffered terrible ordeals to be uplifting, exemplary, even inspiring. Consider what can be learned from these cases:

A young man returns home to discover that a burglar has spirited off his television, an old laptop, and his Xbox 360. He contacts a local pawn shop and sure enough, someone tried to sell his computer and the store's camera contains an image of the thief. He alerts the police, but they never contact him. However, the burglar leaves him a message, demanding money for the return of the stolen property. The young man calls the police again, but they take no action. So he traces the message back to its sender and identifies the thief, his address, even the high school he attends. The victim circulates this information about the thief via internet websites, and when the bombardment through instant messaging becomes unbearable, the burglar returns all the stolen property. (Crecente, 2008)

***

A 4 foot, 5 inch, 90 pound 27-year-old woman is behind the counter of her family's suburban convenience store when a 6-foot-tall man wearing a mask pulls a gun and brandishes it in her face. The angry gunman screams "Hurry up! Give me the money!" but she stalls and makes believe she can't open the cash register. When the robber turns to see if anyone is looking, she grabs a 3 foot ax hidden behind the counter and starts swinging it wildly, yelling "Get out of here!" He flees, and then she confides to detectives and a reporter that "I was scared, I was shaking. I didn't want to hit him, I just wanted him to get out." (Crowley, 2007)

***

A "gentleman" holds a lobby door open for a 101-year-old woman who is on her way to church. But then he hits her so hard that blood spurts out her mouth and nose. A surveillance camera in the hallway shows the robber striking her over and over until she finally relinquishes her grip on her handbag containing $23. Her face bleeds for two weeks and her right arm never heals properly. But nearly a year later, she hobbles into a courtroom to identify the 45-year-old defendant as the man who mugged her. Her testimony at this special evidentiary hearing is preserved on videotape just in case she is unable to appear as a witness for the prosecution at the trial, which is anticipated to begin a year later. (Farmer, 2008)

***

A 35-year-old woman … is beaten, robbed, and repeatedly raped for two hours in a dingy garage. In court, the courageous single mother testifies that while the gunman kept sexually assaulting her, "I had to keep myself from going crazy. I just hummed to myself." Realizing that the humming also calmed the rapist, she begins to give him a massage and to talk soothingly to him. As they converse, the 45-year-old assailant apologizes, and then discloses his name and even his date of birth, which later leads to his arrest. (Shifrel, 2007a)

***

A 45-year-old teacher is kidnapped in a shopping mall parking lot by a gun-toting teenage carjacker. She secretly turns on a micro-cassette recorder to gather evidence just in case she can't convince the youth to let her go. During her final 46 minutes, she persuades the carjacker to discuss his childhood and his experiences in the military, descriptions which later provide investigators with valuable clues. She also reads passages to him from a psychology textbook; urges him to live a meaningful life and to find God; promises to help him land a job; and sobs as she describes how she treasures being a mother to her young son. But it is all to no avail. He doesn't shoot her but smothers her with her own coat, which contains the cassette in a pocket. (Jones, 2007)

***

A 31-year-old social worker is about to go to dinner after a long day on a cold night when he is suddenly confronted by a teenager wielding a knife. He hands over his wallet to the young robber and then offers him his coat too, surmising "If you are willing to risk your freedom for a few dollars, then I guess you must really need the money." Then he takes the emotionally confused adolescent to a restaurant. When it is time to pay for the meal, the teenager gives back his wallet, and even hands over his knife. The social worker sums up their encounter to an interviewer: "If you treat people right, you can only hope that they treat you right. That's as simple as it gets in this complicated world." (NPR, 2008)

***

A mentally deranged 60-year-old woman shoots a member of a sheriff's department SWAT team in the neck. Formerly known as "the most in shape" deputy by his fellow officers, he wakes up paralyzed as a quadriplegic confined to a wheel chair. But with great determination he remains focused on his goal of returning to work at a desk job in the narcotics squad, observing "Your future is kind of bleak when you've got tubes coming out of you and everyone is saying you'll never walk again… But if you stay mad about it all the time, you're not doing anything good for yourself." Supported by his family and colleagues, he optimistically reports signs of progress. "There have been a lot of little instances, like being able to pick up a … potato chip and eat it with my hands." (Young, 2008)

Evidently, studying how injured parties respond to their plight can yield some unanticipated benefits. Victimologists can gain a more complete understanding and appreciation of the full range of possible reactions to attacks. Some victims respond to their misfortunes in ways that are clever, bold, even courageous, and demonstrate a determination to behave with dignity and to pursue a commitment to justice. These individuals can serve as positive role models for overcoming adversity. Victimology is not hopelessly mired in suffering and negativity.

WHAT VICTIMOLOGISTS DO

The current parameters of the field are evident in the kinds of questions victimologists try to answer. In general, these questions transcend the basics about "who, how, where, and when," and tackle the questions of "why" and "what can be done." Victimologists explore the interactions between victims and offenders, victims and the criminal justice system, and victims and the larger society. In the process, victimologists, like all social scientists, gather data to test hypotheses and refine theories. In the face of bold claims for credit (for example, about a financial records monitoring service that prevents customers' identities from being stolen) or accusations about blame (about why identity theft strikes certain individuals), victimologists must adopt a critical spirit and a skeptical stance to see where the trail of evidence leads. In the search for truth, myths must be exposed, unfounded charges dismissed, and commonsense notions put to the test. The following guidelines outline the step-by-step reasoning process that victimologists follow when carrying out their research (see Parsonage, 1979; Birkbeck, 1983; and Burt, 1983).

Step 1: Identify, Define, and Describe the Problem

The most basic task for victimologists is to determine all the different ways that a violation of the law can inflict immediate and long-term harm: the extent of any physical injuries, emotional damage, and economic costs, plus any social consequences (such as loss of status). For example, severely abused children might suffer from posttraumatic stress disorder, dysfunctional interpersonal relationships, personality problems, and self-destructive impulses (see Briere, 1992).

Sometimes a group is difficult to study because there isn't an adequate expression to describe their common misfortune or to capture the nature of their plight. Now that terms like date rape, stalking, cyberstalking, carjacking, battering, elder abuse, road rage, identity theft, and bias crime have entered everyday speech, government agencies and researchers are exploring in what manner and how frequently people are harmed by these offenses. Sometimes a familiar problem, such as bullying among juveniles, receives renewed attention (see Unnever and Cornell, 2003), especially in the aftermath of a massacre on the grounds of a high school by a teenager deeply resentful of the cruel teasing of other students (see De Gette, Jenson, and Colomy, 2000). On occasion, victimologists help to break the silence about situations that long have been considered taboo topics, by studying activities such as sibling abuse, incestuous sexual impositions in stepfamilies, and marital rape (see Hines and Malley-Morrison, 2005).

Victimologists analyze how the status of being a "legitimate victim" is socially defined. They explore why only some people who suffer physical, emotional, or economic harm are designated and treated as full-fledged, bona fide, and officially recognized victims and as such, are eligible for aid and encouraged to exercise rights within the criminal justice process. But why are other injured parties left to fend for themselves? One key question is, "Is the social standing of each of the two parties taken into account when government officials and members of the general public evaluate whether one person should get into legal trouble for what happened and the other should be granted assistance?" Another important query is, "Who decides what is unacceptable and illegal?" For example, what official action should be taken when workers are killed in on-the-job incidents? Are they victims of criminal negligence? When customers claim they were deceived by exaggerated claims in advertisements, are they victims of fraud, and therefore entitled to certain legal remedies? In what situations should elementary school students who are subjected to corporal punishment by headmasters, deans, and teachers (even with parental permission) be considered victims of a physical assault?

Clearly, the status of being an officially recognized victim of a crime is "socially constructed." The determination of who is included and who is excluded from this privileged category is carried out by actors within the criminal justice process (police officers and detectives, prosecutors, judges, even juries) and is heavily influenced by legislators (who formulate criminal laws) and the media that shapes public opinion about specific incidents.

Step 2: Measure the True Dimensions of the Problem

Because policy makers and the general public want to know how serious various kinds of illegal activities are, victimologists must devise ways to keep track of the frequency and consequences of prohibited acts. The accuracy of statistics kept by government bureaus and private agencies must be critically examined to ferret out any biases that might inflate or deflate these estimates to the advantage of those who, for some self-serving reason, wish to either exaggerate or downplay the real extent of the problem.

In order to make measurements, victimologists have to **operationalize** their concepts by developing working definitions that specify essential characteristics and also mark boundaries, clarifying which cases should be included and which should be excluded. For example, when trying to determine how many students have been victims of school violence, should youngsters who were threatened with a beating be counted, even if they were not actually physically attacked? Once victimologists measure the frequency of some unwanted event per year, they can begin to search for changes over time to see if a particular type of criminal activity is marring the lives of a greater number or fewer people as time passes. To grasp the importance of making accurate measurements, consider the problem of child abuse. Statistics gathered by child protection agencies may indicate a huge increase in the number of reported instances of suspected abuse. How can this upsurge be explained? One possibility is that parents are neglecting, beating, and molesting their children these days like never before. But another explanation

could be that new compulsory reporting requirements recently imposed on physicians, school nurses, and teachers are bringing many more cases to the attention of the authorities. Thus, a sharp rise in reports might not reflect a genuine crime wave directed at children by their caretakers but merely a surge in official reports because of improvements in detecting and keeping records of maltreatment. Victimologists can make a real contribution toward resolving this controversy by devising ways to estimate with greater precision the actual dimensions of the child abuse problem. Other pressing questions that can be answered by careful measurements and accurate statistics include the following: Are huge numbers of children being snatched up by kidnappers demanding ransoms? Or are abductions by strangers rare? Are husbands assaulted by their wives about as often as wives are battered by their husbands? Or is female aggression of minor concern when compared to male violence? Is forced sex a common outcome at the end of an evening, or is date rape less of a danger than some people believe (see Loseke, Gelles, and Cavanaugh, 2005)?

After determining **incidence rates** (how often a type of victimization takes place during a given time period, usually one year), **prevalence rates** (the fraction of the population that has ever experienced this type of misfortune) can also be estimated. Using various assumptions it then becomes possible to project **lifetime likelihoods** (the proportion of the population that will someday suffer in this way, if current rates prevail). Additionally, researchers can discern which categories of people are preyed upon the most and the least. That information can be used to draw a **profile** (statistical portrait) of the characteristics of typical victims (people who fall into high-risk groupings).

Once injured parties have been identified and located, researchers can carry out a **needs assessment** through interviews or via a survey to discover what kinds of assistance and support they require to resolve their problems and return to the lives they were leading before the crime occurred. Such studies of help-seeking behaviors might reveal unmet material and emotional needs, weaknesses in existing programs and policies, and the significant contributions of informal support systems (primarily family and friends).

Step 3: Investigate How Victims Are Handled

Victimologists scrutinize how victims actually are treated by the criminal justice and social service systems that are ostensibly designed to help them. Researchers carry out needs assessments to identify just what the injured parties want, require, and get. Studies pinpoint the sources of tension, conflict mistreatment, and dissatisfaction that alienate victims from the agencies that are supposed to serve them. Program evaluations determine whether stated goals are being met. For instance, victimologists want to know how well or how poorly the police, prosecutors, judges, and family therapists are responding to the plight of abused children and battered women (see Hilton, 1993; Roberts, 2002; Hines and Malley-Morrison, 2005; and Barnett, Miller-Perrin, and Perrin, 2005). Similarly, victimologists explore whether promises are being kept, and if reforms granting new rights are having any impact on business as usual within the legal system. Are most victims wasting their time if they appear before parole boards to argue that the prisoners who harmed them should not receive early release, or are victims' arguments taken seriously? Additionally, victimologists monitor the way the public, the news media, elected officials, nonprofit organizations, and profit-oriented enterprises react to the plight of people who are robbed, raped, beaten, or murdered.

Step 4: Gather Evidence to Test Hypotheses

Victimologists investigate claims, suspicions, hunches, and predictions. They collect data to see if there is any basis for widely held hypotheses, such as that

wives beaten mercilessly by their husbands often don't flee their unhappy homes because they are too frightened of being hunted down and killed. Similarly, researchers want to determine the "red flags" or warning signs that indicate trouble ahead in a stormy relationship. Should women who have suffered beatings during courtship or cohabitation quickly break-up with their abusive boyfriends, or can these turbulent relationships be salvaged? (See Roberts and Roberts, 2005.) Are most women who were raped angry or relieved if their cases are resolved through **plea negotiations** (in which the assailants admit their guilt in return for some concession) rather than by highly publicized trials in which they would be a key prosecution witness? Are a significant proportion of survivors of homicides opposed to the execution of the murderers of their loved ones? Are the practical suggestions offered on Web sites for women who are being stalked by ex-lovers likely to reduce the risks of violent outbursts, or does following this advice actually heighten dangers? Testing hypotheses yields interesting findings, especially discoveries that cast doubt on common-sense notions (challenging what everyone "knows" to be true). Victimologists try to sort out myths from realities.

All research findings serve to build victimology's knowledge base, and some have obvious practical applications. For example, how often do people who were robbed fail to recognize the suspect and pick out an innocent person at a station house lineup (how accurate are eyewitness identifications)? After elderly persons are robbed and injured, are they more likely than victims of other ages to adopt extreme precautions, such as staying home at night? If police departments become more user-friendly, will many more victims be willing to come forward and lodge charges against assailants, robbers, and rapists? Ironically, does the public get the impression that a crime wave is taking place and that their local law enforcement officials are incompetent?

A selection of some intriguing and imaginative studies that illustrate the kinds of issues addressed by victimologists over the years appears in Box 1.4.

B O X 1.4   A Sampling of the Wide Range Of Studies Victimologists Undertake

Identifying the Cues That Trigger a Mugger into Action

Pedestrians, through their body language, may signal to prowling robbers that they are "easy marks." Men and women walking down a city street were secretly video-taped for several seconds, about the time it takes a criminally inclined person to size up a potential victim. The tapes were then shown to a panel of "experts"— prisoners convicted of assaulting strangers—who sorted out those who looked as if they would be easy to corner from those who might give them a hard time. Individuals who received high **muggability ratings** tended to move along awkwardly, unaware that their nonverbal communication might cause them trouble (Grayson and Stein, 1981).

Explaining Public Indifference toward Victims of Fraud and Con Games

People who have lost money to swindlers and con artists often are portrayed as undeserving of sympathy in the media, and they may encounter callousness, suspicion, or contempt when they turn to the police or consumer fraud bureaus for help. This second-class treatment seems to be due to negative stereotypes and ambivalent attitudes that are widely held by the public as well as criminal justice officials. A number of aphorisms place blame on the "suckers" themselves—fraud only befalls those of questionable character, an honest man can't be cheated, and people must have larceny in their hearts to fall for a con game.

The stereotype of defrauded parties is that they disregarded the basic rules of sensible conduct regarding financial matters. They don't read contracts before signing and don't demand that guarantees be put in

writing before making purchases. Their apparent naivety, carelessness, or complicity undermines their credibility and makes others reluctant to activate the machinery of the criminal justice system and regulatory agencies on their behalf and to validate their claims to be treated as authentic victims worthy of support rather than to be ignored as mere dupes who were outsmarted (Walsh and Schram, 1980; Moore and Mills, 1990; and Shichor, Sechrest, and Doocy, 2001). And yet a nationwide survey using a broad definition of fraudulent schemes (including dishonest home, auto, and appliance repairs and inspections; useless warranties; fake subscription, insurance, credit, and investment scams; phony charities, contests, and prizes; and expensive 900-number telephone ploys, among other rip-offs) found the problem to be widespread. More than half the respondents had been caught up in some deception or an attempt at least once in their lives, costing an average loss of more than $200. Contrary to the prevailing negative stereotype, the elderly were not any more trusting and compliant; in fact, they were deceived less often than younger people (Titus, Heinzelmann, and Boyle, 1995).

Examining How Victims Are Viewed by Pickpockets

According to a sample of twenty "class cannons" (professional pickpockets) working the streets of Miami, Florida, their preferred marks (victims) are tourists who are relaxed, off guard, loaded with money, and lacking in clout with criminal justice officials. Some pickpockets choose "paps" (elderly men) because their reaction time is slower, but others favor bates (middle-aged men) because they tend to carry fatter wallets. A "moll buzzer" or "hanger binger" (sneak thief who preys on women) is looked down on

SUMMARY

Victimization is an asymmetrical relationship that is abusive, parasitical, destructive, unfair, and illegal. Offenders harm their victims physically, financially, and emotionally. Laws that recognized that injured parties deserved governmental support and economic

aid were passed centuries ago, but until the middle of the twentieth century the plight of crime victims was largely overlooked, even by most criminologists. When some researchers began to study victims, their initial interest betrayed an anti-victim in the underworld fraternity as a bottom feeder who acts without skill or courage. Interaction with victims is kept to a minimum. Although pickpockets may "trace a mark" (follow a potential target) for some time, they need just a few seconds to "beat him of his poke" (steal his wallet). This is done quietly and deftly, without a commotion or any jostling. They rarely "make a score" (steal a lot in a single incident). The class cannon "passes" (hands over) "the loot" (wallet, wad of bills) to a member of his "mob" (an accomplice) and swiftly leaves the scene of the crime. Only about one time in a hundred do they get caught by the mark. And on those rare occasions when the theft is detected, they can usually persuade their victims not to call the police. They give back what they took (maybe more than they stole) and point out that pressing charges can ruin a vacation because of the need to surrender the wallet as evidence, plus waste precious time in court appearances. Cannons show no hatred or contempt for their marks. In general, they rationalize their crimes as impersonal acts directed at targets who can easily afford the losses or who would otherwise be fleeced by businesses or allow their money to be taken from them in other legally permissible ways (Inciardi, 1976).

Exploring the Bonds between Captives and Their Captors

Hostages (of terrorists, skyjackers, kidnappers, bank robbers, rebelling prisoners, and gunmen who go berserk) are used by their captors to exert leverage on a third party—perhaps a family, the police, or a government agency. These captives frequently react in an unanticipated way to being trapped and held against their will. Instead of showing anger and seeking revenge, these pawns in a larger drama may emerge from a lengthy siege with positive feelings for, and attachments to, their keepers. Their outrage is likely to be directed at the authorities who rescued them for acting with apparent indifference to their well-being during the protracted negotiations. This surprising emotional realignment has been termed the **Stockholm Syndrome** because it was first noted after a 1973 bank holdup in Sweden. Several psychological explanations for this "pathological transference" are plausible. The hostages could be identifying with the aggressor and they might have become sympathetic to acts of defiance aimed at the power structure. As survivors, they might harbor intense feelings of gratitude toward their keepers for sparing their lives; or as helpless dependents, they might cling to the powerful figures who controlled their every action because of a primitive emotional response called "traumatical infantilism." After the ordeal, terrorized hostages need to be welcomed back and reassured that they did nothing wrong during—and right after—their captivity. People in occupations that place them at high risk of being taken prisoner—ranging from convenience-store clerks and bank tellers to airline personnel and diplomats—need to be trained about how to act, what to say, and what not to do if they are held and used as a bargaining chip during a stand-off. Law enforcement agencies need to set up and train hostage negotiation units as an alternative to solely relying on heavily armed SWAT teams whose military style assaults endanger the lives of the captives they are trying to save (see Fattah, 1979; Ochberg, 1978; Symonds, 1980a; Turner, 1990; Wolff, 1993; and Louden, 1998).

bias: They sought evidence that the victims' behavior before and during the incidents contributed to their own downfall. Since the 1960s, the majority of the social scientists attracted to this new discipline have labored to find ways to ease the suffering of victims and to prevent future incidents. But a commitment to strive for objectivity rather than to be reflexively "pro-victim" is the best stance to adopt when carrying out research or evaluating the effectiveness of policies.

Victimology is best viewed as an area of specialization within criminology. Both criminologists and victimologists seek to be impartial in their roles as social scientists when investigating lawbreaking, its social consequences, and the official responses by the justice system. But much of criminology in the past can be characterized as "offenderology," so the new focus on those who suffer provides some balance and rounds out any analysis of problems arising from lawbreaking behavior.

Victimologists carry out studies that seek to identify, define, and describe all the ways that illegal activities harm targeted individuals; to measure the seriousness of the problem; to discover how victims' cases are actually handled by the legal system; and to test research hypotheses to see if they are supported by the available evidence.

KEY TERMS

victim, 1

victimization, 2

victimology, 2

direct or primary victims, 2

survivors, 2

indirect or secondary victims, 2

subjective approach, 3

objectivity, 3

ideal type, 4

sensationalism, 8

victimism, 14

ideology, 14

criminology, 16

post-traumatic stress disorder, 19

crime control, 20

just deserts, 20

operationalization, 24

incidence rates, 24

prevalence rates, 24

lifetime likelihoods, 24

profile, 24

needs assessment, 24

muggability ratings, 26

plea negotiations, 25

Stockholm Syndrome, 27

QUESTIONS FOR DISCUSSION AND DEBATE

1. Why should victimologists strive for objectivity rather than automatically adopt a pro-victim bias?

2. Give several examples of the kinds of research questions that victimologists find interesting and the kinds of studies they carry out.

3. In what ways are victimology and criminology similar, and in what ways do they differ?

4. What are some of the important milestones in the history of victimology and victim assistance?

CRITICAL THINKING QUESTIONS

1. How should the police and the public react when hard-core criminals, such as mobsters, drug dealers, and street gang members become victims of violence?

2. Generate a list of questions about forcible rapes that would be of great interest to a victimologist working within (a) an anthropological framework; (b) an historical approach; and (c) an economic perspective.

SUGGESTED RESEARCH PROJECTS

1. Perform a keyword search of a comprehensive database of magazines and newspaper articles to discover whether the term victimology is still being misused and confused with the ideology of victimism.

2. Use a comprehensive database of magazines and newspaper articles to determine whether any cases currently in the news illustrate the difficulty of identifying which party clearly is the criminal and which is the victim.

2

The Rediscovery of
Crime Victims

THE DISCOVERY OF CRIME VICTIMS

Each law that prohibits a certain act as being harmful defines the wrongdoer as a criminal subject to punishment, and at the same time specifies that the injured party is a victim deserving some sort of redress. The laws forbidding what are now called **street crimes**—murder, rape, robbery, assault, burglary, and theft—can be traced back to biblical times. When the thirteen American colonies were settled by immigrants from Great Britain, the earliest penal codes were based on religious values as well as **English common law**. Hence, victims of interpersonal violence and theft were "discovered" ages ago, in the sense that they were formally identified and officially recognized.

THE DECLINE OF CRIME VICTIMS

Scholars of the history of the legal system report that in past centuries victims played a leading role in the resolution of criminal matters. To discourage retaliation by victims and their families—acts that could lead to endless feuding if offenders and their kin counterattacked—societies in simpler times established direct repayment schemes. Legal codes around the world enabled injured parties to receive money or valuables from wrongdoers to compensate for the pain, suffering, and losses they endured.

This process of victim-oriented justice prevailed mostly in small villages engaged in farming, where social relations were based on personal obligations, clear-cut family ties, strong religious beliefs, and sacred traditions. But the injured party's role diminished as industrialization and urbanization brought about business relations that were voluntary, secular, impersonal, rationalized, and contractual.

Over the centuries, victims lost control over the process of determining the fate of the offenders who harmed them. Instead, the local governmental structure dominated judicial proceedings and extracted fines from convicts, physically punished them, or even executed them. The seriousness of the wounds and losses inflicted upon victims were of importance only for determining the charges and penalties wrongdoers faced upon conviction. Restoring injured parties to the condition they were in before the crimes occurred was no longer the main concern. In fact, the recovery of damages became a separate matter that was handled in another arena (**civil court**) according to a different set of rules (**tort law**) after criminal proceedings were concluded (Schafer, 1968).

Historically, in the United States and in other parts of the world, the situations of victims followed the same evolutionary path from being at the center of the legal process to being relegated to the sidelines. During the colonial era, police forces and public prosecutors had not yet been established. Victims were the key decision makers within the rudimentary criminal justice system and were its direct beneficiaries. They conducted their own investigations, paid for warrants to have sheriffs make arrests, and hired private attorneys to indict and prosecute their alleged attackers. Convicts were forced to repay those they harmed up to three times the value of the goods they had damaged or stolen (Schafer, 1968).

But after the American Revolution and the adoption of the Constitution and the Bill of Rights, crimes were reconceptualized as hostile acts directed against the authority of the government, which was defined as the representative of the people. Addressing the suffering imposed upon individuals was deemed to be less important than dealing with the symbolic threat to the social order posed by lawbreakers. **Public prosecutors**, acting on behalf of the state and in the name of the entire society, took over the powers and responsibilities formerly exercised by victims. Federal, state, and county (district) attorneys were granted the discretion to decide whether to press charges against defendants and what sanctions to ask judges to impose upon convicts.

The goals of deterring crime through punishment, protecting society by incapacitating dangerous people in prisons or through executions, and rehabilitating transgressors through treatment came to overshadow victims' demands to be restored to financial, emotional, and physical health.

Over the last two centuries, the government increasingly has assumed the obligation of providing jail detainees and prison inmates with food, clothing, housing, supervision, medical care, recreational opportunities, schooling, job training, psychological counseling, and legal representation—while leaving victims to fend for themselves. As they lost control over "their" cases, their role dwindled to just two contributions: filing a complaint with the police that initiated an investigation and, if necessary, testifying for the prosecution as another piece of evidence in the state's presentation of damning facts against the accused.

When **plea negotiations** replaced trials as the means of resolving most cases, victims lost their last opportunity to actively participate in the process by presenting their firsthand experiences on the witness stand to a jury. Victims rarely were included and consulted when the police and prosecution team decided upon their strategies and goals. To add insult to injury, often they were not even informed of the outcomes of "their" cases. Thoroughly marginalized, victims often sensed that they had been taken advantage of twice: first by the offender and then by a system that ostensibly was set up to help them but in reality seemed more intent on satisfying the needs of its core agencies and key officials (see Schafer, 1968; McDonald, 1977; and Davis, Kunreuther, and Connick, 1984).

THE REDISCOVERY OF CRIME VICTIMS

After centuries of neglect, those on the receiving end of violence and theft were given renewed attention and, in effect, were rediscovered during the late 1950s and early 1960s. A small number of self-help advocates, social scientists, crusading journalists, enlightened criminal justice officials, and responsive lawmakers helped to direct public concern to a serious problem: the total disregard of the needs and wants of victims. Through publications, meetings, rallies, and petition drives, these activists promoted their message: that victims were forgotten figures in the criminal justice process whose best interests had been systematically overlooked but merited attention. Discussion and debate emerged during the late 1960s and has intensified throughout the following decades over why this injustice existed, and what could be done about it. Various groups with their own distinct agendas formed coalitions and mobilized to campaign for reforms. As a result, new laws favorable to victims are being passed and criminal justice policies are being overhauled.

Social Movements: Taking Up the Victims' Cause

Aside from suffering harm at the hands of criminals, victims as a group may have very little else in common. They differ in terms of age, sex, race/ethnicity, religion, social class, political orientation, and many other important characteristics. Therefore, it has been difficult to organize them into self-help groups and to harness their energies into a political force for change. Despite these obstacles, a crime victims' movement emerged during the 1970s. It has developed into a broad alliance of activists, support groups, and advocacy organizations that lobbies for increased rights and expanded services, demonstrates at trials, maintains a variety of Web sites, educates the public, trains criminal justice professionals and caregivers, sets up research institutes and information clearinghouses, designs and evaluates experimental policies, and holds conferences to share experiences and develop innovative programs.

The guiding principle holding this diverse coalition together is the belief that victims who otherwise would feel powerless and enraged can attain a sense of empowerment and regain control over their lives through practical assistance, mutual support, and involvement in the criminal justice process (see Friedman, 1985; Smith, 1985; Smith, Sloan, and Ward, 1990; and Weed, 1995).

Major Sources of Inspiration, Guidance and Support   Several older and broader social movements have greatly influenced the growth and orientation of the victims' movement. The most important contributions have been made by the law-and-order movement, the **women's movement**, and the **civil rights movement**.

The **law-and-order movement** of the 1960s raised concerns about the plight of victims of street crimes of violence and theft. Alarmed by surging crime rates, conservative advocates of the "crime control" perspective adopted a hard-line, get-tough stance. They insisted that the criminal justice system was society's first line of defense against internal enemies who threatened chaos and destruction. The "thin blue line" of law enforcement needed to be strengthened. A willingness to tolerate too much misbehavior was the problem and a crackdown on social and political deviants who disobeyed society's rules and disrupted the lives of conventional people was the solution. To win over people who might have been reluctant to grant more power to government agencies—police, prosecutors, and prison authorities—they argued that the average American should be more worried about becoming a victim than about being falsely accused, mistakenly convicted, and unjustly punished (Hook, 1972). Crime control advocates pictured the scales of justice as being unfairly tilted in favor of the "bad guys" at the expense of the "good guys"—the innocent, law-abiding citizens and their allies on the police force and in the prosecutor's office. In the smooth-running justice system that these crime control advocates envisioned, punishment would be swift and sure. Attorneys for defendants would no longer be able to take advantage of practices that were dismissed as "loopholes" and "technicalities" that undermined the government's efforts to arrest, detain, convict, deter, incapacitate, and impose retribution on wrongdoers.

"Permissiveness" (unwarranted leniency) and any "coddling of criminals" would end: more offenders would be locked up for longer periods of time, and fewer would be granted bail, probation, or parole. Liberals and civil libertarians who opposed these policies as politically repressive and overly punitive were branded as "pro-criminal" and "anti-victim" (see Miller, 1973; and Carrington, 1975).

Since the late 1960s, some liberal activists in the **women's movement** have focused their energies on aiding one group of victims in particular: females who were harmed by males and then failed to receive the support they deserved from the male-dominated criminal justice system. Feminists launched both an anti-rape and an anti-battering movement. The anti-rape movement set up the first rape crisis centers in Berkeley, California, and Washington, D.C., in 1972. These centers were not just places of aid and comfort in a time of pain and confusion. They also were rallying sites for outreach efforts to those who were suffering in isolation, meeting places for consciousness-raising groups exploring the patriarchal cultural traditions that encouraged males to subjugate females, and hubs for political organizing to change laws and policies (see Rose, 1977; Largen, 1981; and Schechter, 1982).

Some anti-rape activists went on to protest street harassment, uniting behind the slogan "Take back the night" (see Lederer, 1980). Other activists helped to organize battered women's shelters. They established the first "safe house" in St. Paul, Minnesota, in 1974. Campaigns to end battering paralleled activities to combat rape in a number of ways. Both projects were initiated for the most part by former victims who viewed their plight as an outgrowth of larger societal problems and institutional arrangements rather than personal troubles and individual shortcomings. Both sought to empower women by confronting established male authority, challenging existing procedures, providing peer support and advocacy, and devising alternative places to turn to for help in a time of need. The overall analysis that originally guided these pro-victim efforts was that male versus female offenses (such as rape, wife beating, sexual harassment in the streets and at work, and incest at home) pose a threat to all women, and that this kind of illegal sexual oppression slows progress toward equality between the sexes. The gravest dangers are faced by women who are socially disadvantaged because of racial discrimination and economic insecurity. According to this philosophy, girls and women victimized by boys and men cannot count on the men at the helm of the criminal justice system to lead the struggle to effectively protect or assist them—instead, women must empower each other (see Brownmiller, 1975).

Similarly, some liberal activists in the **civil rights movement** of the 1960s focused their energies on opposing entrenched racist beliefs and discriminatory practices that encouraged members of the white majority to intimidate, harass, and attack people of color. Over the decades, this movement has brought together organizations representing the interests of a wide range of minority groups in order to direct attention to the special threats posed by racist violence, from lynch mobs to Ku Klux Klan bombings and assassinations.

In recent years, one of the movement's major concerns has been convincing the government to provide enhanced protection to individuals who are the targets of bias-motivated **hate crimes**, which can range from harassment and vandalism to arson, beatings, and slayings. Civil rights groups have been instrumental in lobbying state legislatures to impose stiffer penalties on attackers whose behavior is fueled by bigotry and in establishing specialized police squads to deter or solve these divisive and inflammatory violations of the law that would otherwise polarize communities along racial and ethnic lines (see Levin and McDevitt, 2003).

Civil rights organizations try to mobilize public support to demand evenhandedness in the administration of justice. A double standard, although more subtle today than in the past, may still infect the operations of the criminal justice system. Crimes by black perpetrators against white victims always have been taken very seriously—thoroughly investigated, quickly solved, vigorously prosecuted, and severely punished. However, crimes by white offenders against black victims, as well as by blacks against other blacks (see Ebony, 1979) have rarely evoked the same governmental response and public outrage. The more frequent imposition of the death penalty on those who kill whites, especially blacks who kill whites, is the clearest example of a discriminatory double standard (see Baldus, 2003). Civil rights activists also point out that members of minority groups still face graver risks of becoming victims of official misconduct in the form of police brutality—or even worse, the unjustified use of deadly force—as well as false accusations, frame-ups, wrongful convictions, and other miscarriages of justice.

Additional Contributions by Other Social Movements Social movements that champion the causes of civil liberties, children's rights, senior citizens' rights, homosexual rights, and self-help also have made significant contributions to bettering the situation of victims.

The **civil liberties movement**'s primary focus is to preserve constitutional safeguards and due-process guarantees that protect suspects, defendants, and prisoners from abuses of governmental power by overzealous criminal justice officials. However, civil liberties organizations have won court victories that have benefited victims of street crime in two ways: by furthering police professionalism and by extending the doctrine of "equal protection under the law."

In professionalized police departments, officers must meet higher educational and training requirements and must abide by more demanding standards. As a result, victims are more likely to receive prompt responses, effective service, and sensitive treatment. If they don't, channels exist through which they can redress their grievances. Guarantees of equal protection enable minority communities to gain access to the police and prosecutorial assistance to which they are entitled, and to insist upon their right to improved, more professional law enforcement in contrast to the under-policing they endured until recently. This improves the prospects for sensitive and responsive handling for complainants whose calls for help were given short shrift in the past when officials discriminated against them due to their race, ethnicity, sex, age, social class, disability, or some other disadvantage (Walker, 1982; Stark and Goldstein, 1985).

Children's rights groups campaign against sexual abuse, physical abuse, severe corporal punishment, gross neglect, and other forms of maltreatment of youngsters. Their successes include stricter reporting requirements of cases of suspected abuse; improved procedures for arrest, prosecution, and conviction of offenders; greater sensitivity to the needs of victimized children as complaining witnesses; enhanced protection and prevention services; and more effective parenting instruction programs. Activists in senior citizens' groups have pressured some police departments to establish special squads to protect older people from younger robbers and swindlers, and have brought about greater awareness of the problem of **elder abuse**—financial, emotional, and physical mistreatment by family members or caretakers (see Smith and Freinkel, 1988).

The **gay rights movement** originally called attention to the vulnerability of male homosexuals and lesbians to blackmail, exploitation by organized crime syndicates that ran bars and clubs, and police harassment of those who needed protection (see Maghan and Sagarin, 1983). The movement now focuses on preventing street assaults ("gay-bashing") against suspected homosexuals and lesbians—bias crimes that are motivated by the offenders' hatred for the victims' presumed sexual orientation.

Groups that are part of the **self-help movement** have set up dependable support systems for injured parties by combining the participatory spirit of the grass-roots protest movements of the 1960s with the self-improvement ideals of the human potential movement of the 1970s. The ideology of self-help is based upon a fundamental organizing principle that people who have directly experienced the pain and suffering of being harmed and are still struggling to overcome these hardships themselves can foster a sense of solidarity and mutual support that is more comforting and effective than the services offered by impersonal bureaucracies and emotionally detached professional caregivers (Gartner and Riessman, 1980).

Even the prisoners' rights movement of the late 1960s and early 1970s may have inspired victim activism. Inmates rebelled at a number of correctional institutions, often in vicious and counterproductive ways. They protested overcrowded conditions; demanded decent living standards; insisted on greater ways of communicating with the outside world (via uncensored mail, access to the mass media, more family visits and meetings with lawyers); asked for freedom of religion; called for more opportunities for rehabilitation, education, and job training; and complained about mistreatment and brutality by guards (see ACLU, 2008). Many people harmed by these incarcerated offenders surely asked, if convicts deserve better treatment, don't we, too?

The task for victimologists is to assess the impact these social movements have had on shaping the course of the victims' movement over the decades, as well as on easing the plight of today's crime victims. How effective and influential have they really been?

Elected Officials: Enacting Legislation Named After Victims

During the 1980s, elected officials engaged in the political process of enacting new laws helped to rediscover and publicize the plight of victims. They realized that proposing a new law to be named after someone who suffered terribly in an incident that received a great deal of media coverage helps to build support for its passage; few officeholders would dare to argue against the bill, lest they be branded "anti-victim."

Probably the best-known example of a law bearing the name of a crime victim is the **Brady Bill**, named after James Brady, President Reagan's press secretary, who was shot in 1981 by an assassin trying to kill the president. This federal legislation passed by Congress imposes restrictions on gun purchases (background checks and "cooling-off" periods) that are intended to head-off shootings by unstable individuals eager to get their hands on a firearm.

The nationwide **Amber Alert** system was named after an abducted girl who was killed by a sexual predator; it provides federal funding that enables the authorities to use the media to quickly disseminate descriptions of the kidnapper, the child, and any vehicle they are traveling in. These announcements mobilize the public so that thousands of people can immediately help the police to watch out for the missing youngster.

Many state legislatures have passed statutes named after victims. For example, most states have passed some variation of New Jersey's **Megan's Law**, named after a little girl slain by her new neighbor, a habitual child molester. It mandates that community residents be notified of the arrival of formerly incarcerated sex offenders, so that parents—in theory, at least—can take measures to better shield their children from potentially dangerous strangers.

In New York State, a number of recent statutes have been named after victims:

- Lawmakers enacted a measure requiring convicts to serve lengthier sentences before becoming eligible for parole, referring to it as Jenna's Law, in honor of a 22-year-old college student murdered by a man out on parole.

- A law mandating background checks of employees was dubbed Kathy's Law, in memory of a comatose woman in a nursing home who was raped and impregnated by a health care worker and then died after childbirth.

- A regulation that prohibited imprisoned fathers who killed their spouses from demanding visitation rights to see their children is called Lee-Anne's Law after the deceased wife and mother of three whose husband petitioned the court to require their children to visit him while he was serving his prison sentence for killing her (Henican, 1998).

- Kendra's Law, named in memory of a young woman who was pushed in front of a speeding subway train by a man who had not taken his prescribed medication for schizophrenia, empowered courts to impose compulsory treatment on mentally ill patients (Cox, 1998).

- Stephanie's Law, named after a woman whose peeping-tom landlord placed a hidden camera in her apartment, made it a felony to secretly videotape a person in a place where there is a reasonable expectation of privacy (Lovett, 2003).

- VaSean's Law was named in honor of an 11-year-old who was run over by a drunk driver. It stiffened the penalties for serious injuries and deaths caused by intoxicated motorists (Silverman, 2005).

Two very different reactions are possible to the rediscovery of the victim's plight by lawmakers. One response is to suspect that vote-seeking politicians are exploiting the media attention surrounding highly emotional but very complicated situations for their own personal advantage (to advance their careers). They grab headlines by proposing a change in the law that will allegedly prevent such incidents from happening again. The strong feelings evoked by a recent tragedy make it difficult for opponents to question the wisdom and potential flaws of the measures proposed in the name of the victim. (During the last 20 years, legislatures nationwide reportedly have enacted thousands of new laws named after victims) (see Lovett, 2006; and Editors, New York Post, 2006). The other response is to view certain highly publicized tragedies as a final straw that finally focused much-needed attention on a festering problem, mobilized public opinion, and triggered long overdue legislative action by elected officials.

The task for victimologists is to start out as impartial observers and to gather data to see whether the legislation bearing the name of a victim actually offers any tangible assistance to ease the plight of people harmed in this particular manner. Also, are these measures really effective in preventing innocent people from being harmed by these kinds of offenses in the future, or do they just punish offenders more severely in behalf of those they already injured? Some of these recent legal reforms allegedly enacted in the name of honoring victims might turn out to be ill-conceived, ineffective, or even counterproductive (for example, see Cooper, 2005).

The News Media: Portraying the Victims' Plight

The news media deserve a great deal of credit for rediscovering victims. In the past, offenders received the lion's share of coverage in newspapers, magazines, and on radio and television stations. Stories delved into their backgrounds, their motives, and what should be done with them—usually how severely they should be punished. Scant attention was paid to the flesh-and-blood individuals who suffered because of illegal activities.

But now those who are on the receiving end of criminal behavior are no longer invisible or forgotten people. Details about the injured parties are routinely included to inject some human interest into crime stories. Balanced accounts can vividly describe the victims' plight: how they were harmed, what losses they incurred, what intense emotions distressed them, what helped or even hindered their recovery, how they were treated by caregivers, and how their cases were handled by the legal system. By remaining faithful to the facts, journalists can enable their audiences to transcend their own limited experiences with lawbreakers and to see emergencies, tragedies, and triumphs through the eyes of victims. Skillful reporting and insightful observations allow the public to better understand and empathize with the actions and reactions of those who suffered harm.

In highly publicized cases, interviews by journalists have given victims a voice in how their cases are resolved in court, and even how the problem (such as kidnappings, easy access to firearms, or collisions caused by drunk drivers) should be handled by the criminal justice system. Media coverage has given these activists with firsthand experiences a public platform to campaign for wider societal reforms (Dignan, 2005). It appears that incidents receive intensive and sustained coverage only when some aspect of the victim-offender relationship stands out as an attention-grabber: The act, the perpetrator, or the target must be unusual, unexpected, strange, or perverse. Causing harm in ways that is typical, commonplace, or predictable is just not newsworthy. Editors and journalists sift through an overwhelming number of real-life tragedies that come to their attention (largely through contacts within the local police department) and select the cases that are most likely to shock people out of their complacency or arouse the public's social conscience.

The stories that are featured strike a responsive chord in audiences because the incidents symbolize some significant theme—for example, that anyone can be chosen at random and be attacked brutally (simply for being at the wrong place at the wrong time); that bystanders might not come to a person's aid, especially in anonymous, big-city settings; or that complete strangers cannot be trusted (Roberts, 1989).

Historically, heinous crimes that have received the most press attention have had one or more of these elements in common: Either the injured party or the defendant is a child, woman, or a prominent or wealthy person; intimations of "promiscuous" behavior by the victim or defendant help to explain

the event; and some doubts linger about the guilt of the convict (Stephens, 1988).

However, a study of homicides in Houston, Texas, determined that the amount of coverage depended more upon the particular circumstances and situations surrounding the slaying than the characteristics of the killer or victim (Buckler and Travis, 2005). For example, it is predictable that the unsolved Christmas Eve murder of a six-year-old beauty contest winner in her own upscale home with her parents upstairs would be the subject of incessant tabloid sensationalism, as was the murder of a young woman jogging in a park who was having an affair with a married Congressman.

Furthermore, media coverage may reflect the unconscious biases of talk show hosts, correspondents, and editors who work in the newsroom. For example, members of minority communities have charged that national news outlets, especially on cable TV, focus relentless attention on the disappearance of attractive white people, especially young women and children, but overlook equally compelling cases involving individuals who do not share these characteristics (see Lyman, 2005; Memmott, 2005; and Gardiner, 2008).

If these charges are true, the problem may go deeper and may reflect the shortcomings of market-driven journalism. The gatekeepers, under organizational pressures to sell their product, sift through a huge pool of items and select stories they perceive will resonate with the general public, at the expense of presenting an accurate sampling of the full range of tragedies taking place locally, nationally, and around the world (see Buckler and Travis, 2005).

A related problem is that in the quest for higher ratings, coverage can sink to an "If it bleeds, it leads" orientation characterizing commercially driven "infotainment." If reporters turn a personal tragedy into a media circus and a public spectacle, their intrusive behavior might be considered an invasion of privacy. Overzealous journalists are frequently criticized for showing corpses lying in a pool of blood, maintaining vigils outside a grieving family's home, or shoving microphones into the faces of bereaved, dazed, or hysterical relatives at funerals. The injured party receives unwanted publicity and experiences a loss of control as others comment upon, draw lessons from, and impose judgments on what he or she allegedly did or did not do.

And yet, it can be argued that media coverage of crime stories is an absolute necessity in an open society. Reporters and news editors have a constitutional right, derived from the First Amendment's guarantee of a free press, to present information about lawbreaking to the public without interference from the government. Illegal activities not only harm particular individuals but also pose a threat to those who may be next. People have a right as well as a need to know about the emergence of dangerous conditions and ominous developments, and the media has an obligation to communicate this information accurately.

The problem is that the public's right to know about crime and the media's right to report these incidents clash with the victim's right to privacy. Journalists, editors, and victims' advocates are addressing questions of fairness and ethics in a wide variety of forums, ranging from blogs and posted comments on the Web and letters to the editor in newspapers, to professional conferences and lawsuits in civil court.

Several remedies have been proposed to curb abusive coverage of a victim's plight. One approach would be to enact new laws to shield those who suffer from needless public exposure such as unnecessary disclosure of names and addresses in news coverage or on Web sites. An alternative approach would be to rely on the self-restraint of reporters and their editors. The fact that most news accounts of sexual molestations of children and of rapes no longer reveal the names of those who were harmed is an example of this self-policing approach in action. A third remedy would be for the media to adopt a code of professional ethics. Journalists who abide by the code would "read victims their rights" at the outset of interviews, just as police officers read suspects their Miranda rights when taking them into custody (see Thomason and Babbilli, 1987; and Karmen, 1989).

Victimologists could play an important role in monitoring progress by studying how frequently and how seriously news reporters insult and defame the subjects of their stories and how successfully the different reform strategies prevent this kind of exploitation, or at least minimize abusive invasions of privacy.

Then there is the question of accuracy in media imagery. For example, the most publicized stories about mass killings center on a lone gunman who randomly shoots complete strangers in a public setting. However, a careful analysis of multiple homicides reveals that the most frequent category of mass killings is the head of a household slaying all the members of his family, so the widely disseminated image misidentifies the greatest source of danger (Duwe, 2000). Journalists often put forward intriguing possibilities without sufficient documentation in their coverage of victims' issues. A story in the news might hypothesize that there are a great many battered women living in insular, devoutly religious communities who are extremely reluctant to turn to outside authorities for help. It is up to victimologists to treat these plausible assertions as research hypotheses to be tested, to see if the available data support or undermine these impressions circulating in the media.

Commercial Interests: Selling Security Products and Services to Victims

Just as the rediscovery of victims by elected officials and the news media has benefits as well as drawbacks, so too does the new attention paid to injured parties by businesses. The development of this new market of people seeking out protective services and antitheft devices simultaneously raises the possibility of commercial exploitation. Profiteers can engage in fear mongering and false advertising in order to cash in on the legitimate concerns and desires of customers who feel particularly vulnerable and even panicky. In situations where entrepreneurs issue bold claims about their products' effectiveness, objectivity takes the form of scientific skepticism. Victimologists must represent the public interest and demand, "Prove those assertions! Where is the evidence?"

Consider the question of whether expensive automobile security systems actually work as well as their manufacturers' advertisements say they do. For instance, do car alarms really provide the layer of protection against break-ins that their purchasers want and that sales pitches claim? In New York, the City Council passed regulations restricting the installation of new car alarms because the devices were deemed to be largely ineffective as well as a serious source of noise pollution. Rather than agreeing with frustrated motorists that the wailing sirens do no good, or trying to defend the alarm industry's reputation and profits, nonpartisan victimologists can independently evaluate the effectiveness of these antitheft devices. Are car alarms really useful in deterring break-ins; in minimizing losses of accessories such as car stereos, navigation systems or air bags; in preventing vehicles from being driven away; and in aiding the police to catch thieves red-handed?

VICTIMOLOGY CONTRIBUTES TO THE REDISCOVERY PROCESS

The emergence and acceptance of victimology has furthered the rediscovery of new groups of victims. This process—in which people whose plight was recognized long ago, neglected for many years, and now again gains the attention it deserves—goes on and on with no end in sight. Such rediscovered groups include battered women; females who have suffered date rapes; kidnapped children; people targeted by bigots; drivers attacked by enraged fellow motorists; pedestrians, passengers, and drivers killed in collisions caused by drunkards; prisoners sexually assaulted by fellow inmates; and detainees killed while in government custody.

The rediscovery process is more than just a well-intentioned humanitarian undertaking, media campaign, or example of special pleading. It has far-reaching consequences for everyday life, and the stakes are high. Injured people who gain legitimacy

as innocent victims and win public backing are in a position to make compelling claims on government resources (asking for compensation payments to cover the expenses they incurred from their physical wounds, for example). People who know from firsthand experience about the suffering caused by illegal acts also can advance persuasive arguments about reforming criminal justice policies concerning arrest, prosecution, trial procedures, appropriate sentences, and custodial control over prisoners. Finally, rediscovered victims can assert that preventing others from suffering the same fate requires a change in prevailing cultural values about tolerating social conditions that generate criminal behavior. Victims even can make recommendations that are taken seriously about the ways people should and should not behave (for instance, how husbands should treat their wives, and how closely parents should supervise their children); the proper role of government (such as how readily the state should intervene in "private" matters such as violence between intimates); and how convicts should be handled (whether certain offenders should be imprisoned or sent to treatment programs for their underlying disorders).

The process of rediscovery usually unfolds through a series of steps and stages. The sequential model that is proposed below incorporates observations drawn from several sources. The notion of developmental stages arises from the **self-definition of the victimization process** (Viano, 1989). The natural history, career, or life-cycle perspective comes from examining models of ongoing social problems (see Fuller and Myers, 1941; Ross and Staines, 1972; and Spector and Kitsuse, 1987). The focus on how concerns about being harmed are first raised, framed, and then publicized arises from the **constructionist approach** (see Best, 1989b). The idea of inevitable clashes of opposing interest groups battling over governmental resources and influence over legislation comes from sociology's **conflict approach**. The realization that there is an ongoing struggle by victimized groups for respect and support in the court of public opinion is an application of the concept of **stigma contests** (Schur, 1984).

Stage 1: Calling Attention to an Overlooked Problem

The rediscovery process is set in motion whenever activists begin to raise the public's consciousness about some type of illegal situation that "everybody knows" happens but few have cared enough to investigate or try to correct. These **moral entrepreneurs**, who lead campaigns to change laws and win people over to their point of view, usually have firsthand experience with a specific problem as well as direct, personal knowledge of the pain and suffering that accompany it. Particularly effective self-help and advocacy groups have been set up by mothers whose children were killed in collisions caused by drunk drivers, survivors of officers slain in the line of duty, and parents who endured the agony of searching for their missing children, among others. Additional individuals who deserve credit for arousing an indifferent public include the targets of hate-filled bias crimes; adults haunted by the way they were molested when they were young; women brutally raped by acquaintances they trusted; and wives viciously beaten by their husbands. These victims called attention to a state of affairs that people took for granted as harmful but shrugged off with a "What can anyone do?" attitude.

These activists responded, "Things don't have to be this way!" Exploitative and hurtful relationships don't have to be tolerated—they can be prevented, avoided, and outlawed; governmental policies can be altered; and the criminal justice system can be made more accountable and responsive to its "clients." As Stage 1 moves along, activists function as the inspiration and nucleus for the formation of self-help groups that provide mutual aid and solace and also undertake campaigns for reform. Members of support networks believe that only people who have suffered through the same ordeal can really understand and appreciate what others just like them are going through (a basic tenet borrowed from therapeutic communities that assist substance abusers to recover from drug addiction).

Activists also state that victims' troubles stem from larger social problems that are beyond any individual's ability to control; consequently those who suffer should not be blamed for causing their own misfortunes. Finally, activists argue that recovery requires empowerment within the criminal justice process so that victims can pursue what they define as their own best interests, whether to see to it that the offender receives the maximum punishment permitted by law, is compelled to undergo treatment, and/or is ordered to pay their bills for crime-related expenses.

To build wider support for their causes, moral entrepreneurs and self-help groups organize themselves into loosely structured coalitions such as the anti-rape and anti-battering movements. Usually, one or two well-publicized cases are pointed to as symbolic of the problem. Soon many other victims come forward to tell about similar personal experiences. Then experts such as social workers, detectives, and lawyers testify about the suffering that these kinds of victims routinely endure and plead that legal remedies are urgently needed. Extensive media coverage is a prerequisite for success. The group's plight becomes known because of investigative reports on television, talk radio discussions, magazine cover stories, newspaper editorials, and the circulation of these accounts on blogs. Meanwhile, press conferences, demonstrations, marches, candlelight vigils, petition drives, ballot initiatives, lawsuits, and lobbying campaigns keep the pressure on and the issue alive.

Sociologically, what happens during the first stage can be termed the **social construction** of a social problem, along with **claims-making** and **typification** (see Spector and Kitsuse, 1987; Best, 1989b), when a consensus about a pattern of behavior that is harmful and should be subjected to criminal penalties is *constructed*. This crystallization of public opinion is a product of the activities of moral entrepreneurs, support groups, and their allies. Spokespersons engage in a claims-making process to air grievances, estimate how many people are hurt in this manner, suggest appropriate remedies to facilitate recovery, and recommend measures that could prevent this kind of physical, emotional, and financial suffering from burdening others. Through the process of typification, advocates point out classic cases and textbook examples that illustrate the menace to society against which they are campaigning.

Stage 2: Winning Victories, Implementing Reforms

The rediscovery process enters its second stage whenever activists and advocacy groups begin to make headway toward their goals.

At first, it might be necessary to set up independent demonstration projects or pilot programs to prove the need for special services. Then government grants can be secured, or federal, state, and local agencies can copy successful models or take over some responsibility for providing information, assistance, and protection. For instance, the battered women's movement set up shelters, and the anti-rape movement established crisis centers. Eventually local governments funded safe houses where women and their young children could seek refuge, and hospitals (and even some universities) organized their own 24-hour rape hotlines and crisis-intervention services.

Individuals subjected to bias crimes were rediscovered during the 1990s. During the 1980s, only private organizations monitored incidents of hate-motivated violence and vandalism directed against racial and religious minorities, as well as homosexuals. But in 1990, the government got involved when Congress passed the Hate Crime Statistics Act, which authorized the FBI to undertake the task of collecting reports about bias crimes from local police departments. Achievements that mark this second stage in the rediscovery process include legislative hearings at which victims' testimonies can lead to new laws—for instance, more severe punishment for hate-motivated bias crimes because they polarize communities and undermine the mutual respect and good will needed to enable multiculturalism to succeed. Specially trained law enforcement units have been set up in many jurisdictions to more effectively recognize, investigate, solve, and prosecute bias crimes. Self-help groups offer injured parties tangible forms of support.

The best example of a rediscovery campaign that has raised consciousness, won victories, and secured reforms is the struggle waged since the early 1980s by Mothers Against Drunk Driving (MADD). It is an organization of parents, mostly mothers, whose sons or daughters were injured or killed by drunk drivers. These anguished survivors argued that for too long the "killer drunk" was able to get away with a socially acceptable and judicially excusable form of homicide because more people identified with the intoxicated driver than with the innocent person who died from injuries sustained in the collision.

Viewing themselves as the relatives of bona fide crime victims, not merely accident victims, these crusaders were able to move the issue from the obituary page to the front page by using a wide range of tactics to mobilize public support, including candlelight vigils, pledges of responsible behavior by children and family cooperation by their parents, and demonstrations outside courthouses. Local chapters of their national self-help organizations offered concrete services: pamphlets were distributed through hospital emergency rooms and funeral parlors, bereavement support groups assisted grieving relatives, and volunteers accompanied victims and their families to police stations, prosecutors' offices, trials, and sentencing hearings.

Buoyed by very favorable media coverage, their lobbying campaigns brought about a crackdown on DUI (driving under the influence) and DWI (driving while intoxicated) offenders. Enforcement measures include roadblocks, license suspensions and revocations, more severe criminal charges, and on-the-spot confiscations of vehicles. Their efforts also led to reforms of drinking laws, such as raising the legal drinking age to 21 and lowering the blood-alcohol concentration levels that officially define impairment and intoxication (Thompson, 1984). Along with the 55-mph speed limit, mandatory seat belt laws, improved vehicle safety engineering, better roads, and breakthroughs in emergency medical services, the achievements of MADD and its allies have saved countless lives (Ayres, 1994).

Stage 3: Emergence of an Opposition and Development of Resistance to Further Changes

The third stage in the rediscovery process is marked by the emergence of groups that oppose the goals sought by victims of rediscovered crimes. The victims had to overcome public apathy during Stage 1 and bureaucratic inertia during Stage 2, and they encounter resistance from other quarters during Stage 3. A backlash arises against perceived excesses in their demands. The general argument of opponents is that the pendulum is swinging too far in the other direction, that people are uncritically embracing a point of view that is too extreme, unbalanced, and one-sided, and that special interests are trying to advance an agenda that does not really benefit the law-abiding majority.

Spokespersons for a group of recently rediscovered victims might come under fire for a number of reasons. They might be criticized for overestimating the numbers of people harmed when the actual threat to the public, according to the opposition, is much smaller. Advocates might be condemned for portraying those who were harmed as totally innocent of blame—and therefore deserving of unqualified support—when in reality some are partly at fault and shouldn't get all the assistance that they demand. Activists might be castigated for making unreasonable demands that will cost the government (and taxpayers) too much money. They also might be denounced for insisting upon new policies that would undermine cherished constitutional rights, such as the presumption of innocence of people accused of breaking the law (for example, allegations about child abuse or elder abuse can lead to investigations that permanently stigmatize the accused even if the charges later turn out to be unfounded) (see Crystal, 1988).

When the anti-rape movement claimed to have discovered an outbreak of date rapes against college students, skeptics asked why federally mandated statistics about incidents reported to campus security forces showed no such upsurge. They contended that hard-to-classify liaisons were being redefined as full-fledged sexual assaults, thereby maligning some admittedly sexually aggressive and exploitative college men as hard-core criminals (see Gilbert, 1991; Hellman, 1993; and MacDonald, 2008). When the battered women's movement organized a clemency drive to free certain imprisoned wives who had slain (allegedly in self-defense) their abusive husbands, critics charged that these women would be getting away with revenge killings. When incest survivors insisted that new memory retrieval techniques had helped them recall repressed recollections of sexual molestations by parents, stepparents, and other guardians, some accused family members banded together and insisted they were being unfairly slandered because of a therapist-induced **false memory syndrome**. Claims by some child-search organizations that each year tens of thousands of children were being kidnapped by complete strangers created near hysteria among parents until some journalists challenged their estimates as gross exaggerations (see Chapters 8, 9, and 10 for an in-depth analysis of these controversies).

Even the many accomplishments of the entire victims' movement can be questioned (see Weed, 1995). Under the banner of advancing victims' rights, pressure groups might advocate policies that undermine whatever progress has been made toward securing humane treatment for offenders and ex-prisoners and inadvertently "widen the net" of formal social control exercised by the police and prosecutors over deviants and rebels. Victim activism can unnecessarily heighten fear and anxiety levels about the dangers of violence and theft and divert funds away from social programs designed to tackle the root causes of street crime.

Groups that focus their energies on the plight of individuals harmed by street crimes also can distract attention from other socially harmful activities such as polluting the environment or marketing unsafe products, and their reforms can raise expectations about full recovery that just cannot be reasonably met (Fattah, 1986). It is even possible that what was formerly a grassroots movement run by volunteers who solicited donations has metamorphosed into a virtual "victim industry." It engages in a type of mass production, churning out newly identified groups of victims by dwelling on kinds of suffering that can arise from non-criminal sources such as bullying, emotional abuse, sexual harassment, sexual addiction, eating disorders, and credit card dependency (Best, 1997).

Stage 4: Research and Temporary Resolution of Disputes

It is during the fourth and last stage of the rediscovery process that victimologists can make their most valuable contributions. By getting to the bottom of unsolved mysteries and by intervening in bitter conflicts, victimologists can become a source of accurate assessments, helping to evaluate competing claims issued by those who, assuming the worst, generate high estimates, and by those at the opposite end of the spectrum who downplay threats and come up with very low estimates.

During Stage 4, a standoff, deadlock, or truce might develop between victims' advocates who want more changes, and their opponents who resist any further reforms. But the fourth phase is not necessarily the final phase. The findings and policy recommendations of neutral parties such as victimologists and criminologists do not settle questions once and for all. Concern about some type of victimization can recede from public consciousness for years to reappear only when social conditions are ripe for a new rediscovery cycle of claims-making, reform, opposition, and temporary resolution.

By maintaining objectivity, victimologists can serve as arbiters in these heated disputes. For instance, since the early 1980s, parents have been petrified about the specter of kidnappers spiriting off their children. Highly publicized cases of vicious pedophiles abducting, molesting, and then slaying youngsters periodically rekindle this smoldering panic. But skeptics voice concerns that fears about "stranger danger" are causing over-reactions and are being exploited for commercial gain. A blue-ribbon panel of experts convened by the U.S. Department of Justice in the 1980s and again in the late 1990s sought to make sense out of competing claims about just how often such infuriating tragedies take place each year. The researchers concluded that killings and long-term abductions by complete strangers were, thankfully, very rare and did not pose a dire threat to the well-being of the next generation (see Chapter 8).

During the 1980s, a series of shocking shootings by disgruntled gun-toting employees led to the rediscovery of victims of "workplace violence." In the aftermath of these slaughters, worried workers insisted that employers call in occupational safety specialists to devise prevention and protection programs. Anxious managers feared expensive lawsuits and lowered morale. But researchers have determined that these highly publicized multiple murders accounted for just a tiny fraction of a multifaceted but far less newsworthy set of dangers. Most of the cases of workplace violence across the country involve robberies, unarmed assaults, and complaints about stalkers acting in a menacing way. Many incidents that disrupt the smooth functioning of factories and offices are not even criminal matters, such as incidents of verbal abuse, bullying, and sexual harassment (Rugala, 2004) (see Chapter 11).

A number of aspects of the crime problem have reached Stage 4; data is now becoming available that can be used to try to put the public's fears into perspective, to attempt to resolve controversies, and to evaluate the effectiveness of countermeasures and prevention strategies (see Box 2.1).

REDISCOVERING ADDITIONAL GROUPS OF VICTIMS

Academics, practitioners, social movements, elected officials, the news media, and commercial interests continue to drive the process of rediscovery forward. A steady stream of fresh revelations serves as a reminder that neglected groups still are "out there" and that they have compelling stories to tell, unmet needs, and legitimate demands for assistance and

---

B O X   2.1   Research on Controversies About Certain Types of Victimization

---

Road Rage

Research is needed to address widespread fears about the chances of becoming a victim of **road rage**. Flare-ups between drivers with short fuses must have been taking place since the dawn of the automobile age. But the rediscovery of the suffering caused by these spontaneous confrontations between people encountering one another for the first time did not take place until the phrase "road rage" was coined in the late 1980s. During the 1990s, news media outlets carried many accounts about "ugly acts of freeway fury" in which cursing, seething, and stressed-out motorists were "driven to destruction," because it was "high noon on the country's streets and highways." Drivers lost their tempers and took their frustrations out on each other in numerous ways, ranging from running their antagonists off the road to intentional collisions to gunfire (see Fumento, 1998).

Road rage is generally defined to include all vehicular incidents in which one driver intentionally injures or kills another motorist, passenger, or pedestrian. The term also includes an infuriated driver using his vehicle as a weapon to attack someone. Those who are injured or killed often share responsibility to some degree with the complete strangers who attack them because the violations of traffic laws would not have escalated into criminal matters were it not for the victim's furious overreaction to the offender's bad driving. The eruption of repressed anger by both parties initially takes the form of shouting out some curse or slur or the making of an obscene gesture. Angry words over minor slights can escalate into assaults. A driver who is threatened can be considered a victim of harassment, and if a gun is pointed, the crime becomes "menacing." Assaults with a deadly weapon can result in tragically pointless deaths, as this incident illustrates:

> Late at night a car, with three young men who had been drinking heavily, is cut off and swerves out of its lane. The infuriated driver speeds up, pulls even with the other vehicle, and uses his fingers to make a gesture that resembles pointing a gun and pulling the trigger. The other driver lowers his window and fatally shoots him. He later turns himself in, claims he acted in self-defense, and reveals that he is an off-duty police officer. (Baker, 2007).

As the process of rediscovery gathered momentum during the 1990s, polls revealed that many motorists have been targets of or witnesses to acts of road rage. Some, fearful that aggressive driving was getting out of hand, kept weapons in their cars for self-protection. Researchers sifting through police and insurance company files and news accounts attributed thousands of injuries and several hundred deaths to outbursts by "road warriors."

After the House Subcommittee on Surface Transportation held hearings about a reported epidemic of "auto anarchy" that was "transforming the nation's roadways into crime scenes," state legislatures passed tough new laws against recklessly aggressive driving. Police departments and state highway patrol agencies devised new ways of monitoring and videotaping incidents and accidents and enforcing traffic laws. Awareness and education campaigns were developed by the National Safety Council, the AAA Foundation for Traffic Safety, insurance companies, and government agencies such as the National Highway Traffic Safety Administration. In the midst of all this publicity, however, skeptics argued that statistics showed that the numbers of accidents, highway deaths, and crash-related injuries actually were trending downward, especially when the increases in the number of drivers, registered vehicles, and the total miles traveled were taken into account. Perhaps the problem had been blown way out of proportion by journalists engaging in media sensationalism, vote-seeking politicians, therapists looking to profit from heightened fears of a newly recognized emotional "disorder," and lobbyists representing publicity-hungry agencies and associations (see Drivers.com staff, 1997; Fumento, 1998; Rathbone and Huckabee, 1999; Hennessy and Wiesenthal, 2002; and "Rising rage," 2005).

The problem for victimologists is that the definition of road rage has expanded far beyond the original narrow notion of violence on wheels. Now several Web sites welcome postings by people infuriated by encounters (and sometimes accidents) triggered by aggressive, inconsiderate, rude, careless, or just plain inept drivers who cut them off, honked incessantly, braked hard without warning, or tailgated. These might be annoying violations of traffic ordinances, but they don't rise to the level of criminal matters, and the aggrieved parties are not victims of violence or intentional property destruction. The task for victimologists is to sort through this collection of accounts about bad driving and sift out the incidents of intentional collisions, assaults, shootings, and even murders in order to estimate the true dimensions of the problem and the effectiveness of the recently devised solutions. Attempts to measure the actual extent of attacks that can be attributed to expressions of road rage will be facilitated by improvements in police record-keeping and media coverage. Now, with the term firmly entrenched in the vocabulary of criminal justice and journalism, news media accounts periodically highlight outrageous and tragic incidents, and on occasion raise the specter that isolated outbursts of road rage are somehow contagious or reflect surges in hostility levels in the general public (for example, see AP, 2008).

Violence Among Prisoners

In 2008, the number of people in U.S. jails and prisons set a record, exceeding 2.3 million, or more than 1 in every 100 adults (Pew Charitable Trust, 2008).

It is well known that when large numbers of criminally inclined men are held against their will in conditions of intense confinement and utter subjugation, they vent their anger and frustration on each other. Inmates target one another in a number of ways, including thefts of their meager possessions, extortion, assaults with homemade weapons, and gang fights (see Silberman, 1995; Schneider, 1996; and O'Connell and Straub, 1999). But the worst expressions of violence born of frustration—sexual assaults and murders resulting from fatal beatings and stabbings—are receiving renewed attention from corrections administrations intent on running orderly institutions.

The rape of weaker inmates by stronger prisoners, once a taboo topic, has been written about and depicted in movies for decades (see Lockwood, 1980; and MacNamara, 1983). But it was not until 2003 that those who endured sexual assaults while incarcerated were rediscovered officially when Congress passed the Prison Rape Reduction Act. Public Law 108-79 promulgated a zero tolerance policy and mandated that preventing, detecting, and prosecuting sexual attacks become a top priority in each federal, state, and local correctional institution in order to protect the Eighth Amendment rights of individuals subjected to the government's care and custody.

Acknowledging that there was insufficient solid research and data about the extent and seriousness of sexual aggression behind bars, the legislation assigned the task of administering a survey to the Bureau of Justice Statistics (BJS) to determine the frequency and consequences of inmate-on-inmate sexual contacts,

both non-consensual and consensual. Experts provided an initial estimate that about 13 percent of the more than 2 million detainees and convicts in the nation's jails and prisons (more than 270,000 people) have been sexually abused during their period of incarceration. The Commission's first national survey in 2007, based on a representative sample of state and federal prison inmates, yielded an estimate that 4.5 percent (about 70,000 individuals) had endured sexual violence during a single year (NPREC, 2007). During 2004, more than 8,000 allegations of sexual assaults were lodged by inmates, and more than 2,000 of these complaints were substantiated after investigations by the authorities.

About 90 percent of the non-consensual acts could be summarized as inmate-on-inmate as well as male-on-male. The remainder were perpetrated by corrections officers, and female inmates were often the targets. The highest levels of reported sexual assaults took place in juvenile facilities, where about five youths out of every 1,000 were forced to submit to the demands of other inmates—or sometimes even members of the custodial staff—according to the officials who ran these institutions (Beck and Hughes, 2005). The most vulnerable of all inmates are teenagers confined in adult institutions ("New Study," 2008).

But determining the true scope of the problem is difficult. Many inmates conceal their ordeals from the authorities because they fear retaliation or don't want to be labeled as a "snitch." Other prisoners may lodge false accusations in order to get an enemy into serious trouble, or to justify a transfer to a more favorable setting.

A National Prison Rape Elimination Commission holds annual hearings to identify the common characteristics of both perpetrators and victims, and to examine why some facilities have had more success in reducing sexual violence than others. The Commission believes it is in the enlightened self-interest of law-abiding citizens to be concerned about sexual violence behind bars: young men who have been gang-raped when corrections officers weren't present to intervene are likely to suffer from deep-seated rage, intense shame, low self-esteem, self-loathing, and an inability to trust others. They are prone to substance abuse and a return to criminal behavior upon release ("What sheriffs need to know ...," 2004; Parsell, 2005). Yet in most correctional institutions, inmates who have suffered sexual assaults still cannot find safe, reliable, and responsive ways to report these attacks; nor are they are able to access adequate and

(Continued)

B O X 2.1   Continued

timely medical and mental health services behind bars (National Sheriffs Association, 2008).

Even worse than being forcibly raped is to be murdered while ostensibly under the government's care and control. Controversies often break out when suspects, defendants, and convicts die while in the custody of law enforcement agencies (police station lockups), the courts (holding pens), or the correctional system (jails, prisons, and juvenile facilities). Some deaths might be attributed to medical conditions (heart attacks and strokes), drug abuse (overdoses or adverse reactions), suicides, or the use of necessary force by officers during an escape attempt. But on oc-casion the relatives of the deceased insist he is a victim and that either fellow inmates or the authorities (po-lice or correctional officers) committed a serious crime. Researchers were unable to seek the truth about these allegations until Congress officially rediscovered the existence of homicides behind bars, and passed the "Deaths in Custody Reporting Act of 2000."

The Bureau of Justice Statistics now maintains a database about all fatalities while in custody, whether under suspicious circumstances or not. The information includes the gender, race/ethnicity, and age of the de-ceased; the date, time, and location of the incident; and a brief narrative about the circumstances. The first analysis of this new database indicated that nearly 70 homicides of inmates in jails and prisons took place during 2002 (BJS, 2005; Mumola, 2005). Focusing only on state prisons, the BJS reported that fewer than 200 convicts were murdered by other prisoners during the years 2001 through 2004, for a homicide rate of about four per 100,000 (mostly male) inmates per year, which was lower than the murder rate for the general public (of men, women, and children) (Mumola, 2007). The murder rate for jail inmates over the six-year period from 2000 to 2005 was an even lower average rate of three slayings for every 100,000 confined people per year. As for long-term trends, over the decades from 1980 to 2002, the annual murder rate of prison inmates plunged an astonishing 93 percent. As for the backgrounds of these men slain in jails and

prisons, most were serving time for violent offenses (Mumola, 2005).

The next step is for victimologists to develop more detailed statistical profiles of the deceased inmates and their killers; to figure out where, when, and why these slayings happen; to determine circumstances that would heighten the risks that a prisoner will be beaten or stabbed to death; and to examine what can be done to prevent such needless losses of life of people under governmental control in the future.

Victims of Human Trafficking

People-smuggling by unscrupulous syndicates presum-ably began decades ago when immigration restrictions between nations were first established. Organized-crime families (who also smuggle guns and drugs) provide a service, helping border-crossers to get to their destinations. Some individuals who paid exorbi-tant fees (considering their limited ability to raise such large sums of money) to "coyotes" and other smug-glers surely knew they would have to work off their debts before they left their country of origin. They can't really be considered victims. But others must have been deceived and did not realize how traffickers could force them into virtual servitude. Many of the women and certainly all the children who wind up mired in prostitution were unknowing victims. **Trafficking in human beings** has emerged as a lucrative racket and major problem in a great many source, transit, and destination countries across the globe.

The rediscovery of people trapped in a modern equivalent of the slave trade officially took place in 1994 when the U.S. Department of State began to collect reports about trafficking across borders as a severe violation of human rights. Its Office to Monitor and Combat Trafficking in Persons originally focused on the sexual exploitation of women and girls smug-gled by international prostitution rings. But over the years, its concerns—and the United Nation's definition of trafficking—have broadened to cover anyone recruited, transported, transferred, harbored, and compelled to work in prostitution, domestic service,

support. Usually, they continue to escape public notice until some highly unusual or horrific inci-dent reveals how they are being harmed and attracts the interest of the news media and criminal justice

agencies. The types of victims whose plight is now being rediscovered—but who require much more scrutiny and analysis, and creative remedies—are listed in Box 2.2.

agriculture, construction work, or factory sweatshops by means of threat, coercion, force, abduction, fraud, or deception. Physical transport across borders is no longer an essential part of the definition (U.S. State Department, 2007; www.humantrafficking.org, 2008).

From the standpoint of victimological research and policy evaluation, the first hurdle is to distinguish between those who are genuinely tricked, abused, enticed, terrorized, and caught up in debt bondage (peonage) from those economically desperate immigrants who knowingly and willingly pay smugglers huge fees. That entails identifying actual trafficking victims from the ranks of "illegal immigrants," asylum seekers, and political refugees. Victimologists want to discover exactly how the traffickers lure or deceive their targets (probably through false promises of a better life and ploys about legitimate jobs); how they recruit children (by capitalizing on their innocence and naivete, sometimes with parental complicity); and how they dominate and intimidate into submission those who find themselves trapped into involuntary servitude, even if chances to escape their predicament arise—presumably this occurs by confiscating all their documents, exploiting language barriers, threatening reprisals against loved ones at home, and scaring them about deportation if they turn to the authorities for help (see George, 2003; Landesman, 2004; Bureau of Public Affairs, 2005; Glaberson, 2005; and Saunders, 2005).

The United Nations, federal agencies, and nonprofit and nongovernmental organizations work to rescue individuals caught in the clutches of transnational organized crime syndicates. As for legislation, the Trafficking Victims Protection Act, passed by Congress in 2000 and reauthorized and strengthened in 2003 and 2005, established a federal interagency task force, imposed stiff penalties on profiteers, and promised victims certain legal benefits and services if they cooperated with prosecutors and testified against their exploiters.

The United States is principally a transit and destination country as opposed to a source country. Concerned individuals in diplomatic circles, law enforcement, and social services are developing and then recommending "best practices" of a victim-centered approach to prevent the smuggling and sale of human beings, safeguarding these individuals from further harm, and repatriating these displaced people to their country of origin or reintegrating them into the destination society with citizenship rights. In the United States, hotlines invite tipsters to report suspicious relationships, and trained professionals as well as volunteers stand ready to provide comfort and support to escapees or to those "confirmed victims" who are rescued after a raid of a brothel or sweatshop.

By the start of 2007, 27 states had passed antitrafficking legislation and 42 regional task forces had been set up and funded by the Department of Justice. But between 2000 and early 2007, federal agencies had certified only 1,175 people from 77 countries as victims of human trafficking (U.S. State Department, 2007). Yet the official estimate in Congress's 2005 reauthorization legislation was that the human cargo smuggled into the United States each year numbered between 18,000 to 20,000 people, primarily women and children (www.humantrafficking.org, 2008). And on New York's Long Island, an area reputed to be a hotbed of trafficking, not one arrest was made during 2005, and only one woman was rescued from prostitution (Mead, 2006).

The murder of several border-crossers in Arizona by smugglers holding them hostage in frustrated attempts to extort more money from their families back home indicates the depth of the perils victims face (Fulginiti, 2008). Furthermore, a study based on a survey completed by more than 160 municipal and county police departments concluded that most of these law enforcement agencies lacked sufficient policies and training to adequately identify trafficking victims and investigate their cases (Wilson, Walsh, and Kleuber, 2006). Clearly, the true level of seriousness of the problem, and the effectiveness of well-intentioned efforts to reach out to trafficking victims in the United States, requires additional research, which is why the situation can be considered to be at Stage 4 of the rediscovery process.

SUMMARY

Victimologists are social scientists who strive for objectivity when studying the characteristics of victims, the suffering they endure, their reactions to their plight, their interactions with offenders, and the way others (such as journalists, elected officials, and people allied with social movements

B O X 2.2   The Process of Rediscovery Goes On and On

These recently recognized groups of victims face special problems that require imaginative solutions:

- Disabled individuals (deaf, blind, mentally retarded, mentally ill, or afflicted in other ways) who were assaulted or molested (Office for Victims of Crime, 2003)

- People whose attackers cannot be arrested and prosecuted because they are members of foreign delegations granted diplomatic immunity (Ashman and Trescott, 1987; Sieh, 1990; and Lynch, 2003)

- Immigrants who feel they cannot come forward and ask the police for help without revealing that they are "illegal aliens" who lack the proper documents and are subject to deportation (Davis and Murray, 1995; Davis, Erez, and Avitabile, 2001; Chan, 2007)

- Homeless adults robbed, assaulted, and murdered on the streets and in shelters (Fitzpatrick, LaGory, and Ritchey, 1993; and Green, 2008)

- Homeless runaway teens who are vulnerable to sexual exploitation and rape (Tyler et al., 2005)

- Hotel guests who suffer thefts and assaults because of lax security measures (Prestia, 1993; Owsley, 2005)

- Tourists who blunder into dangerous situations avoided by streetwise locals (Rohter, 1993a; 1993b; and Murphy, 2006) and are easy prey because they let their guard down (Boyle, 1994; and Lee, 2005)

- Delivery-truck drivers who are preyed upon by robbers, hijackers, and highway snipers (Sexton, 1994; and Duret and Patrick, 2004)

- Motorists and pedestrians slammed into during high speed chases by fugitives seeking to avoid arrest or by squad cars in hot pursuit (Gray, 1993; Crew, Fridell, and Pursell, 1995; and San Mateo Section, 2006)

- Good Samaritans who try to break up crimes in progress and rescue the intended victims but wind up injured or killed themselves (McFadden, 1993; and Eligon, 2008)

- Innocent bystanders wounded or killed by bullets intended for others, often when caught in cross-fire between rival street gangs or drug dealers fighting over turf (Sherman, Steele, Laufersweiler, Hoffer, and Julian, 1989; Onishi, 1994; and Williams, 2009)

- People deceived by robbers and rapists impersonating plainclothes detectives (Lenkowitz, 2003; Topping, 2005; and Wilson, 2008)

- Unrelated individuals whose lives are snuffed out by vicious and demented serial killers (Holmes and DeBurger, 1988; Hickey, 1991; Egger and Egger, 2002)

- Prostitutes soliciting customers on the streets who face risks of being beaten, raped, and murdered that are many times higher than for other women in their age bracket (Boyer and James, 1983; and Salfati, James, and Ferguson, 2008)

- Newborns abandoned or killed by their distraught mothers (Yardley, 1999; and Buckley, 2007)

- Frantic relatives of "missing persons" who have vanished and are presumed dead but, since they were adults with the right to privacy, cannot be

and commercial interests) respond to them. Victimology's findings contribute to an ongoing re-discovery process, which constantly brings the plight of additional overlooked groups to the public's attention. The rediscovery process goes through several stages. After a group's plight becomes known and

reforms are implemented, an opposition frequently arises that resists further changes that might be to the group's advantage. Victimologists can help resolve disputes by studying how newly rediscovered groups suffer and whether efforts to assist them are really working as intended.

the objects of intense police manhunts unless there is evidence of foul play (McPhee, 1999; Gardiner, 2008; and NCMA, 2008)

- Suspects brutally beaten by police officers (Amnesty International USA, 1999; Davey and Einhorn, 2007)
- Teachers attacked, injured, and even killed by their students (Fine, 2001)
- Students sexually molested or physically abused through prohibited forms of corporal punishment by teachers (Goodnough, 2003)
- High school and college students subjected to abusive hazing and bullying by older students that results in injury or death (Salmivalli and Nieminen, 2002; Meadows, Johnson, and Downey, 2003)
- Students assaulted, robbed, even fatally shot by fellow students or by intruders in school buildings and schoolyards (Bastian and Taylor, 1991; Toby, 1983; NCES, 1998; and DeGette, Jenson, and Colomy, 2000)
- Terrified residents whose homes were invaded by armed robbers (Lambert, 2005; and Henican, 2007)
- "Mail-order brides," lured to the United States by unregulated international matchmaking services on the Internet, who fear deportation if they complain to the authorities about their husbands' violence (Briscoe, 2005)
- Teenage girls and young women kidnapped and held captive as "sex slaves" by vicious rapists (Hoffman, 2003; and Jacobs, 2003)
- Unsuspecting people, usually women, who feel symbolically raped after being secretly videotaped during private moments by voyeurs using hidden spy cameras (Lovett, 2003; Williams, 2005)
- Female motorists sexually abused by highway patrol officers (Tyre, 2001)
- Female inmates sexually abused by corrections officers (Struckman-Johnson and Struckman-Johnson, 2002)
- Youngsters physically and sexually abused by child-care workers and babysitters (Finkelhor and Ormrod, 2001)
- People being blackmailed who are reluctant to turn to the authorities for help because that would lead to exposure of their embarrassing secrets (see Katz, Fletcher, and Altman, 1993; Patrick, 2006; and Niesse, 2008)
- Recipients of crank phone calls, laced with threats or obscenities, made by individuals that range from "heavy breathers" and bored teenagers to dangerous assailants (Savitz, 1986; Associated Press, 2005a)
- Residents injured by fires or burned out of their homes, unaware that they were harmed by a criminal act until fire marshals determine that the suspicious blazes were intentionally set (Sclafani, 2005)
- Consumers who lose money in Internet cyber-swindles and "dotcons" such as online pyramid investment (Ponzi) schemes, bogus auctions, fake escrow accounts, and other computer-based frauds (Lee, 2003b)
- Homeowners who become victims of mortgage fraud and foreclosure-rescue fraud and lose their homes because they are swindled (FBI, 2008).

KEY TERMS

street crimes, 30

English common law, 30

civil court, 31

tort law, 31

public prosecutors, 31

plea negotiations, 32

law-and-order movement, 32

women's movement, 33

civil rights movement, 33

civil liberties movement, 34

children's rights groups, 34

elder abuse, 34

gay rights movement, 34

hate crimes, 34

self-help movement, 35

Brady Bill, 35

Amber Alert, 35

Megan's Law, 35

self-definition of the victimization process, 39

QUESTIONS FOR DISCUSSION AND DEBATE

1. Describe what happens at each stage of the rediscovery process.

2. Argue that the rediscovery of victims by the news media, elected officials, and commercial enterprises is a "mixed blessing" by stressing the downside: the potential for exploitation.

CRITICAL THINKING QUESTIONS

1. Identify a group of victims of illegal activities who still has not been rediscovered and was not mentioned in this chapter. Describe the kinds of harm this group might be experiencing.

2. Argue that victimology would be enriched by expanding its boundaries to include studies about people around the world who suffer because of war crimes, government repression of political dissidents, and torture by the authorities.

SUGGESTED RESEARCH PROJECTS

1. Find out proposed or recently passed laws in your state that have been named in honor of crime victims. In each case, ask whether this legislation offers anything specific—other than stepped-up punishment of the offender—to ease the victim's plight.

2. Choose a group from the list in Box 2.2 whose plight is currently being rediscovered. Pose questions that researchers ought to examine. Find out what you can about this group.

Sources of Information
about Crime Victims
The *UCR* and the *NCVS*

CRIME IN THE STREETS: THE BIG PICTURE

Victimologists gather and interpret data to answer questions such as: How many people are harmed by criminals each year? How rapidly are the ranks of people who have suffered misfortunes growing? And, a matter of particular concern, which groups are targeted the most and the least often? Researchers want to find out where and when the majority of crimes occur, whether predators on the prowl intimidate and subjugate their prey with weapons and if so, what kinds of weapons. Victimologists also want to determine whether individuals are attacked by complete strangers or people they know, and how these intended targets act when confronted by assailants. What proportion try to escape or fight back, how many are injured, what percentage need to be hospitalized, and how much money do they typically lose in an incident?

The answers to basic questions like these, when taken together, constitute what can be termed the **big picture**—an overview of what is really happening across the United States during the first decade of this new century. The big picture serves as an antidote to impressions based on direct but limited personal experiences, as well as self-serving reports circulated by organizations with vested interests, misleading media images, crude stereotypes, and widely held myths. But putting together the big picture is not easy. Compiling an accurate portrayal requires careful planning, formulation of the right questions, proper data-collection techniques, and insightful analyses.

Until the 1970s, few efforts were made to routinely monitor and systematically measure various indicators of a victim's plight. In the 1980s, a great many social scientists and agencies were conducting the research needed to bring the big picture into focus. By the 1990s, all sorts of special-interest groups began keeping count and disseminating their own estimates about the suffering of a wide variety of victims, including youngsters wounded at school, college students hurt or killed on campus, children reported missing by their parents, and people singled out by assailants who hate their "kind."

Most of the statistics and analyses presented in this chapter concern the dreaded crimes of murder and robbery. Statistics about murders are more complete, consistent (over time and from place to place), accurate, and detailed than those for any other crime. Robbery statistics are far less precise and reliable but are still extremely important because hold-ups fuel the public's fears about strangers committing "crime in the streets." Other street crimes, involving violence (assaults) or stealing (burglaries, vehicle thefts) will also share the focus of attention in this chapter.

The Use and Abuse of Statistics

Statistics are meaningful numbers that reveal important information. Statistics are of crucial importance to social scientists, policy analysts, and decision makers because they replace vague adjectives such as "many," "most," and "few" with precise numbers. Criminologists and victimologists both gather their own data to make their own calculations, or they scrutinize **official statistics** compiled and published by government agencies. By collecting, computing, and analyzing statistics, victimologists can derive answers to the intriguing research questions they must tackle. Accurate statistics about crimes and victims are vital because they can shed light on a number of important matters:

- Statistics can be calculated to estimate **victimization rates**, which are realistic assessments of threat levels that criminal activities pose to particular individuals and groups. What are the chances or odds various categories of people face of getting harmed during a certain time period, such as a year, or even over an entire lifetime? Counts (such as death tolls), or better yet, rates (per 100,000 people per year) can provide answers to these disturbing questions.

- Statistics can expose **patterns** of criminal activity. Patterns reflect predictable relationships or regular occurrences that show up during an analysis of the data. For instance, a search for patterns in the data could answer these questions: Do murders generally occur at a higher rate in urban neighborhoods than in suburban and rural areas? Also, is homicide a bigger problem year after year in the South than in other regions of the country? Are robberies committed more often at certain locations than others, and more often against men than women?

- Statistical **trends** can demonstrate how situations have changed as time goes by. Is the burden of crime intensifying or subsiding as years pass? Are the dangers of getting killed by robbers increasing or decreasing with each successive year?

- Statistics can provide estimates of the costs and losses imposed by illegal behavior. For example, insurance companies can determine what premiums to charge their customers based on calculations of the average financial expenses suffered by motorists whose cars are stolen.

- Statistics can be used for planning purposes to project a rough or "ballpark figure" of how many people are likely to need assistance in the immediate future. Law enforcement agencies, service providers, and insurance companies can anticipate the approximate size of their case-loads for the following year if they know how many people were harmed the previous year.

- Statistics also can be computed to evaluate the effectiveness of criminal justice operations, and to assess the usefulness of recovery efforts and prevention strategies. Are battered women likely to lead safer lives after their violent mates are arrested? How well are police departments doing in returning stolen property to burglarized households? Does installing a car alarm with a flashing red warning light really deter thieves?

- Finally, statistical **profiles** can be assembled to yield an impression of what is usual or typical about a victim in terms of characteristics such as sex, age, and race/ethnicity. For example, is there any truth in the stereotype that most of the people who die violently are young men from troubled families living in poverty-stricken big-city neighborhoods? Also, statistical portraits can provide a reality check to help ground theories that purport to explain why some groups experience higher rates of preda-tion than others. For example, if it turns out that the frail elderly are robbed less often than teenagers, then a theory that emphasizes the physical vulnerability of robbers' targets will be off-base or incomplete as an explanation of which groups suffer the most and why.

Interpreting Statistics

Cynics joke that statistics can be used by special interest groups just like a lamppost is used by a drunkard—for support rather than for illumination.

Officials, agencies, and organizations with their own particular agendas may release statistics to influence decision makers or the public. Alarming figures can be circulated by law enforcement agencies to support their arguments at budget hear-ings that more personnel, equipment, and money are needed to better protect and serve the public. Other numbers can be used to reduce fears and to demonstrate that those in charge are doing their jobs well, such as tracking down murderers or pre-venting robberies. Their opponents will try to make the contrary point by releasing numbers that seem to indicate that the crime problem is getting worse and that the incumbents are incompetent at com-bating crime and need to be replaced. Statistics might also be cited to prove that existing laws and policies are having the intended effects (such as in-stalling surveillance cameras reduces the number of robberies) or, conversely, to persuade people that the old methods are not working and new ap-proaches are necessary.

Interpretations of mathematical findings can be given a **spin** that may be debatable—for example, emphasizing that a shelter for battered women is "half empty" rather than "half full," or stressing how much public safety has improved, as opposed to how much more progress is needed before street crime can be considered under control. As useful and necessary as statistics are, they should always be viewed with a healthy dose of scientific skepticism.

Although some mistakes are honest and un-avoidable, it is easy to "lie" with statistics by using impressive and scientific-sounding numbers to ma-nipulate or mislead. Whenever statistics are pre-sented to underscore or clinch some point in an argument, their origin and interpretation must be questioned, and certain methodological issues must be raised. What was the source of the data, and does this organization have a vested interest in shaping public opinion? Are different estimates available from other sources? What kinds of biases and inaccuracies could have crept into the collec-tion and analysis of the data? How valid and precise were the measurements? How were key concepts defined and measured ("operationalized")? What was included and what was excluded, and why?

For example, officials in New York like to at-tract tourists by pointing out that it is the safest big city in America. That claim has been true since the late 1990s (see Karmen, 2000) and even was accurate for 2001 because the terrible death toll from the September 11 terrorist attacks on the World Trade Center, in which more than 2,700 people perished, was not counted by the FBI in its official calculation of New York City's murder rate (evidently, its rate of "ordinary" murders). However, the body count of 168 deaths resulting from the bombing of the Oklahoma City federal building by home-grown terrorists in 1995 was added to the number of "ordinary" homicides that year, making it look like that urban area was an exceptionally dangerous place. To make definitional matters even more complicated, the six people who were killed from a blast in the underground garage in the first terrorist attack on the World Trade Center in 1993 were counted as murder victims by the FBI.

Victimologists committed to objectivity try to gather and interpret statistics without injecting any particular "spin" into their conclusions because (it is hoped) they have no "ax to grind" other than enlightening people about myths and realities surrounding the crime problem.

THE TWO OFFICIAL SOURCES OF VICTIMIZATION DATA

As early as the 1800s, public officials began keeping records about crimes to gauge the "moral health" of society. Then, as now, high rates of interpersonal violence and theft were taken as signs of social pathology—indications that something was desperately wrong with the way many people interacted. Sets of yearly data were compiled to determine whether illegal activities were being brought under control as time passed. This monitoring of trends is even more important today than it was then; over the centuries many innovative but intrusive and expensive criminal justice policies intended to curb crime have been implemented.

Two government reports published annually contain statistical data that enable victimologists to monitor trends. The Federal Bureau of Investigation's *Uniform Crime Report: Crime in the United States*, is a massive compilation of incidents known to police departments across the country. This virtual "bible" of crime statistics is older and better known than the other official source, the Bureau of Justice Statistics' *National Crime Victimization Survey: Criminal Victimization in the United States*, which is a compilation of incidents voluntarily disclosed by victims to interviewers. Both of these official sources of facts and figures about crime and its victims are disseminated each year by the U.S. Department of Justice in Washington, D.C. Each of these government data-collection systems has its own strengths and weaknesses in terms of providing the information victimologists are seeking to answer their key questions.

The establishment of a second, independent reporting system to measure the amount of street crime in contemporary American society initially appeared to be a major breakthrough in terms of bringing the big picture into sharper focus. In theory, the federal government's two monitoring systems should support and confirm each other's findings, lending greater credence to all official statistics published for the public's benefit. But in practice, estimates from the **Uniform Crime Report (UCR)** and the **National Crime Victimization Survey (NCVS)** have diverged substantially for particular categories of offenses and certain brief stretches of time.

On occasion during the 1970s and 1980s, victimization rates appeared to go up according to the *UCR* but down according to the *NCVS*, or vice versa, as a number of graphs presented later in this book will show (see Chapter 4 in particular). This lack of close correspondence (technically speaking, this absence of a very strong positive **correlation**) caused confusion and touched off debates about inaccuracies among victimologists, criminologists, and criminal justice professionals (see Lynch and Addington, 2007). The divergence enabled some interest groups to contend that America's street crime problem was getting worse, while their opponents could marshal evidence from the other reporting system to argue that the situation was improving. During the second half of the 1990s, trend lines drawn from the data from both government agencies were in synch, confirming that an across-the-board decline in criminal activity was taking place throughout the country. However, the two reporting systems again gave out conflicting signals concerning short term trends in certain offenses during the early years of the twenty-first century, yielding different impressions about whether the "big picture" was relatively stable or slowing changing.

A First Glance at the Big Picture: Looking at the FBI's Crime Clock   Statistics never speak for themselves. Numbers must always be scrutinized carefully and placed within context, or put into

perspective. Sometimes the same numbers can be interpreted quite differently, depending on what spin commentators give them—what is stressed and what is downplayed. For example, consider a set of statistics issued yearly to summarize the big picture by the FBI in its authoritative *Uniform Crime Report* (*UCR*). The picture it presents is called the **"Crime Clock."** The Crime Clock dramatizes the fact that with the passing of each and every second, minute, hour, and day, the toll keeps mounting as more and more people join the ranks of crime victims (see Figure 3.1).

The Crime Clock's statistics are calculated in a straightforward manner. The number of incidents of each kind reported to police departments is divided

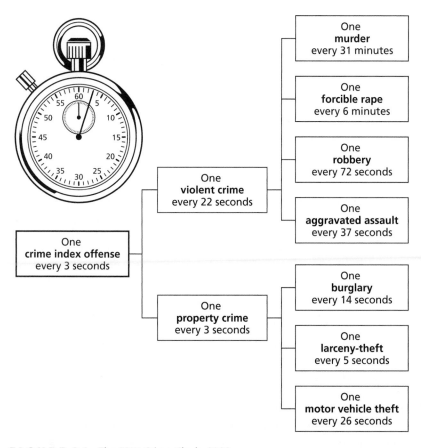

FIGURE 3.1   The FBI's Crime Clock, 2006

into the number of seconds ($60 \times 60 \times 24 \times 365 = 31,536,000$) or minutes ($60 \times 24 \times 365 = 525,600$) in an entire year. For instance, during 2006, about 17,000 people were slain in the United States. The calculation $(525,600)/(17,000) = 31$ indicates that approximately every 31 minutes one American was murdered that year (FBI, 2007).

Just a glance at this chart alerts even the casual reader to its chilling message. The big picture it portrays is that crimes of violence (one every 22 seconds) and theft (one every three seconds) are all too common. As the Crime Clock ticks away, a stream of casualties flows into morgues, hospital emergency rooms, and police stations throughout the land. Practically every moment somewhere in the United States another person is experiencing what it feels like to be harmed by a criminal. These grim reminders give the impression that being victimized is virtually inevitable. It seems to be just a matter of time before one's "number is called" and disaster strikes. Sooner or later, it will be every American's "turn"—or so it appears.

The FBI (2005: 44) offers a disclaimer that points out that crimes do not take place with such rigid predictability. "The Crime Clock should be viewed with care. The most aggregate representation of *UCR* data, it conveys the annual reported crime experience by showing a relative frequency of occurrence of the Part I index offenses [referred to as "street crimes" in this textbook; see below]. It should not be taken to imply a regularity in the commission of crime. The Crime Clock represents the annual ratio of crime to fixed time intervals." In other words, the FBI's Uniform Crime Reporting Division is reminding the reader that in reality the number of offenses carried out by lawbreakers ebbs and flows, varying with the time of day, day of the week, and season. These frequencies represent projections over the course of an entire year and not the actual timing of the attacks.

Because the future seems so ominous, this Crime Clock mode of presentation has inherent shock value. It lends itself to media sensationalism, fear-mongering political campaigns, and marketing ploys. Heightened anxieties can be exploited to garner votes and to boost the sales of burglar alarms, automobile antitheft devices, or crime insurance. Customers can be frightened into thinking they may be next or that their time is nearly up—if they haven't already suffered in some manner at least once.

Furthermore, it can be argued on methodological grounds that the alarming figures revealed on the Crime Clock are actually underestimates of how dangerous the streets of the United States really are. The big picture is much worse. The FBI's calculations are based solely upon crimes known to the police across the country. But not all illegal acts are reported. The police find out about only a small fraction of all the incidents of violence and even a smaller proportion of the thefts that actually take place.

Many victims do not bring their troubles to the attention of their local police departments. The reporting rate varies from crime to crime, place to place, year to year, and group to group (see Chapter 6 about victim reporting rates). Hence, one way to look at these Crime Clock statistics is to assume that they represent the tip of the iceberg: The actual number of people harmed by offenders in these various ways must be considerably higher.

However, these impressions about the risks to life and limb in the United States today can legitimately be given an opposite spin. It can be argued on justifiable methodological grounds that conditions inferred from these numbers are overly dramatic and unduly pessimistic, and consequently misleading. The numbers lack "context"—the recognition that there are millions of potential targets throughout the nation. The ticking away of the Crime Clock is an unnecessarily frightening way of depicting the big picture because it uses a formula that ignores population size. Instead of seconds and minutes, another figure could be used in the calculation that takes into account the actual (huge) number of people or possessions at risk. Because there are so many hundreds of millions of residents, homes, and automobiles that could be selected by predators on the prowl, the actual chances of any given individual getting targeted during the course of a year may not be so high or so worrisome.

Although the FBI's Crime Clock infers that being singled out by an offender is a shockingly common occurrence, a different set of authoritative numbers circulated by another branch of the U.S. Department of Justice yields a very different impression. Estimates about the chances of being victimized from a different source—a nationwide survey (*NCVS*)—are presented as rates per 1,000 persons for violent crimes and per 1,000 households for property crimes per year. Adding a "denominator" ("for every 1,000 each year") seems to make a world of difference in terms of "context." The implicit message when rates are calculated is almost the opposite: Don't worry so much about being targeted. These misfortunes will probably strike other people, not you. Indeed, the survey's yearly findings seem relatively reassuring, suggesting that the odds of being harmed are not at all as ominous as the Crime Clock implies.

For example, the Crime Clock warned that a robbery took place nearly every minute during 2006. That understandably sounds frightening because robbery is *the* street crime most people worry about. However, when the *UCR* findings are presented with a denominator as a rate, the figure seems less worrisome. For every 100,000 Americans, "only" 160 were robbed during 2006; therefore, 99,840 made it through the year without being accosted. Put another way, only about 0.16 percent of the public complained to the police that they had been robbed that year.

Similarly, the *NCVS*'s findings indicated that 290 out of every 100,000 residents age 12 and over (or just about three of every 1,000 people in the United States, or 0.3 percent) were robbed during that year (this statistic is about double the *UCR* figure because it includes those incidents not reported to the police but that were disclosed on the survey). Furthermore, the victim was not physically injured in roughly two-thirds of the confrontations. An additional bit of good news was that victims did not lose anything of value to robbers in about one-third of the hostile encounters (no possessions were stolen or damaged, according to a detailed BJS statistical breakdown). In sum, despite widespread public concern, and accentuating

the positive, for every 1,000 residents of the United States, 997 were never confronted; 999 were not wounded; and 998 did not suffer any financial losses due to robberies during 2006 (see Rand and Catalano, 2007).

In sum, both sets of data published by agencies in the federal government are reasonably accurate and trustworthy. What differs is the way the statistics are presented. Each format lends itself to a particular interpretation or spin. The *UCR*'s Crime Clock calculations accentuate the negative by highlighting the number of people harmed per hour, minute, or even second. But stripped of perspective, this "numerator" without a denominator is unduly alarming. It ignores the fact that the overwhelming majority of Americans went about their daily lives throughout the year without interference from criminals. The rates per 100,000 published in the *UCR* and per 1,000 in the *NCVS* juxtapose the small numbers who were preyed upon against the huge numbers who got away unscathed in any given year. This mode of presenting the same statistics yields a very different impression: a rather reassuring message that being targeted is a relatively unusual event.

The FBI's *Uniform Crime Report* (*UCR*)

The *UCR* was established in 1927 by a committee set up by the International Association of Chiefs of Police. The goal was to develop a uniform set of definitions and reporting formats for gathering crime statistics. Since 1930, the FBI has published crime data in the *UCR* that was forwarded voluntarily by police departments across the United States. In recent years, more than 17,000 village, town, municipal, county, and state police departments and sheriff's departments in all 50 states, the District of Columbia, and several territories that serve about 94 percent of the roughly 300 million inhabitants of the United States participate in the data collection process, usually via state criminal justice clearinghouses. Unfortunately, both Parts I and Part II of the *UCR* have been of limited value to those interested in studying victims rather than incidents or arrestees.

Part I of the *UCR* focuses on eight **index crimes**, illegal acts most people think about when they hear the term "street crime." Four index crimes count violent attacks directed "against persons": murder, forcible rape, robbery, and aggravated assault. The other four constitute crimes "against property": burglary, larceny (thefts of all kinds), motor vehicle theft, and arson. The category of arson was added in 1979 at the request of Congress when poor neighborhoods in big cities experienced many blazes of suspicious origin. However, incidents of arson are still unreliably measured because intentionally set fires might remain classified by fire marshals as being "of unknown origin."

The ranking of these eight offenses, from murder to arson, is considered by the FBI for record-keeping purposes to correspond to their relative degree of seriousness (see below). The number of acts of violence and theft known to the authorities is presented for cities, counties, states, regions of the country, and even many college campuses (since the mid-1990s; see Chapter 11). For each crime, the FBI compiles information about the number of incidents reported to the police, the total estimated losses in billions of dollars due to property crimes, the proportion of cases that were solved, and some characteristics of the suspects arrested—but, unfortunately for victimologists, nothing about the people who filed the complaints.

In Part II, the *UCR* furnishes data about the number of people arrested (without estimates of the number of illegal acts committed) for 21 assorted offenses. Some of these crimes that led to arrests do not have clearly identifiable victims—examples include counterfeiting, prostitution, gambling, drunkenness, disorderly conduct, weapons possession, and drug offenses. Other Part II crimes do have flesh-and-blood victims, such as "offenses against women and children," as well as sex offenses other than forcible rape and prostitution. Still other Part II arrests could have arisen from incidents that directly harmed identifiable individuals, including embezzlement, fraud, vandalism, and buying/receiving/possessing stolen property.

Another part of the report furnishes data about how many hate crimes were reported to police

departments (see Chapter 11). The Uniform Crime Reporting Division also issues a yearly analysis of how many law enforcement officers were feloniously assaulted and killed in the line of duty, the weapons used against them, and the assignments they were carrying out when they were slain (see Chapter 11).

From a victimologist's point of view, the *UCR*'s method of data collection suffers from several shortcomings that undermine its accuracy and usefulness (see Savitz, 1982; and O'Brien, 1985). First of all, under-reporting remains a major intractable problem. Because many victims do not inform their local law enforcement agencies about illegal acts committed against them and their possessions (see Chapter 6), the FBI's compilation of "crimes known to the police" is unavoidably incomplete. The statistics about the number of crimes committed inevitably are lower than the actual (but unknown) number of crimes that occurred. Second, the *UCR* focuses on accused offenders (keeping track of the age, sex, and race) but does not provide any information about the complainants who reported the incidents. (However, characteristics of murder victims are collected routinely—see Chapter 4.) Third, the *UCR* mixes reports of attempted crimes (usually not as serious for victims) with completed crimes (in which offenders achieved their goals). Fourth, when computing crime rates for cities, counties, and states, the FBI counts incidents directed against all kinds of targets, adding together crimes against impersonal entities (such as corporations and government offices) and commercial establishments (stores and restaurants) on the one hand, and individuals and households on the other. For example, figures for robberies include bank holdups as well as muggings; statistics about burglaries combine attempted warehouse break-ins with ransackings of homes; figures for larcenies include shoplifting in addition to thefts from pocket-pickings and car break-ins.

Finally, the FBI instructs local police departments to observe the **hierarchy rule** when reporting incidents: List the event under the heading of the most serious crime. For instance, if an armed intruder breaks into a home and finds a woman alone, rapes her, steals her jewelry, and drives off in her car, the entire incident will be counted only as a forcible rape (the worst crime she suffered). If the rapist is caught, he could also be charged with armed robbery, burglary, motor vehicle theft, possession of a deadly weapon, and possession of stolen property, but the lesser offenses are not noted in that year's *UCR*'s totals.

Phasing-In a National Incident-Based Reporting System Fortunately, the *UCR* is being overhauled and is becoming a much more useful source of information for researchers. The FBI is converting its data collection format to a National Incident-Based Reporting System (NIBRS).

One major change is the abandonment of the hierarchy rule of reporting only the worst offense that happened during a sequence of events. Preserving a great many details will make it possible to determine how often one crime evolves into another, such as a carjacking escalating into a kidnapping, or a robbery intensifying into a life-threatening shooting. For the incident cited above that was categorized as a forcible rape under the hierarchy rule, this new record-keeping system also would preserve information about the initial burglary; the resulting robbery; the vehicle theft; other property stolen from the victim, its value, and whether it was recovered; other injuries sustained; the woman's age, sex, and race; whether there was a previous relationship between the victim and the assailant; and the date, time, and location of the incident (IBR Resource Center, 2002). Until the advent of the NIBRS computer database, only in cases of homicide were some of these facts extracted from police files and collected.

Instead of just eight closely watched *UCR* index offenses, FBI computers are now prepared to keep track of 46 Group A offenses derived from 22 categories of crimes. In addition to the four "crimes against persons" and the four "against property" of Part I, the new Group A embraces offenses against individual victims that had been listed in Part II or not collected at all. These crimes, for which victim-oriented data are becoming available, include justifiable homicide and negligent manslaughter (classified as types of homicides); simple assault (including

intimidation); vandalism (property damage and destruction); blackmail (extortion); fraud (swindles and con games); forcible sex crimes (sodomy, sexual assault with an object, and fondling); nonforcible sex offenses (statutory rape and incest); and kidnapping (including parental abductions) (IBR Resource Center, 2002).

Although these changes will yield useful information for researchers, keeping track of these details about victims and arrestees (in addition to simply counting offenses and incidents) leads to many complications. Entering all the data from police files into the proper computer fields is very time consuming, costly, and complex, especially when a single incident involves several different offenses, more than one victim, many offenders, and multiple arrests. Eventually routine analyses of in-depth statistics from the NIBRS database will appear in an annual supplement called *Victims and Offenders: Incident-Based Uniform Crime Reports* (Reaves, 1993; Office of Justice Programs, 1997; Chilton, Major, and Propheter, 1998; FBI, 1999).

Already, some data-mining studies exclusively from the NIBRS archives answer some troubling questions. For example, an analysis of roughly 1,200 cases of abductions in the 12 states that had switched over to NIBRS by 1997 shed light on a previously overlooked subcategory of "holding of a person against his or her will": acquaintance kidnapping. This newly recognized offense includes situations such as when a teenage boy isolates his former girlfriend to punish her for spurning him, or to pressure her to return to him, or to force her to submit sexually, or to evade her parents' efforts to break them up. Also included are incidents in which gang members spirit off rivals to intimidate them, retaliate against them, or even to recruit them. In these types of hostage-takings, the perpetrators tend to be juveniles just like their teenage targets (as opposed to adult strangers who snatch little children); the abductions take place in homes as opposed to public places; and the victims are more likely to be assaulted (Finkelhor and Ormrod, 2000).

Several studies using NIBRS data have revealed important findings about murders. Elderly people are more likely to be fatally assaulted by attackers they know than by complete strangers such as robbers (Chu and Kraus, 2004). Murders of intimate partners tend to be committed late at night, during weekends, and in the midst of certain holidays more often than at other times (Vazquez, Stohr, and Purkiss, 2005). Also, the higher homicide rate in Southern cities may not be due to a presumed subculture of violence or "code of honor" that compels individuals likely to lose fights and suffer beatings to stand up to the aggressors to save face (Chilton, 2004).

The police force in Austin, Texas, was the first to switch to this comprehensive data collection and reporting system, but other big-city police departments that deal with a huge volume of crime reports have had trouble meeting NIBRS goals and timetables so complete implementation has been postponed repeatedly. North Dakota and South Carolina were the first two states to adopt NIBRS formatting in 1991. By 2006, 29 states and the District of Columbia had converted their data-gathering and record-keeping systems (Barnett-Ryan, 2007). As greater numbers of local law enforcement agencies and state data-collection clearinghouses phase in the NIBRS format, the wealth of details in the FBI's Uniform Crime Report will increasingly resemble the information derived from the *National Crime Victimization Survey*. But one major difference will persist: *UCR* and NIBRS figures will continue to be based solely on crimes known to local police forces and sheriff's departments.

The BJS's *National Crime Victimization Survey (NCVS)*

Criminologists and victimologists have reservations about the accuracy of official records kept by police that form the basis of the FBI's *UCR*. Tallies maintained by local law enforcement agencies surely are incomplete due to victim non-reporting. Occasionally these closely watched statistics may be distorted as a result of political pressures to either downplay or inflate the total number of incidents in order to manipulate public opinion (for example, see Blau, 2006).

Dissatisfaction with official record-keeping practices has led criminologists to collect their own data. The first method used was the **self-report survey**. Small samples of people were promised anonymity and confidentiality if they would "confess" on questionnaires about the crimes they had committed. This line of inquiry consistently revealed greater volumes of illegal acts than were indicated by official statistics in government reports. Self-report surveys confirmed the hypothesis that large numbers of people broke the law (especially during their teens and twenties), but most were never investigated, arrested, or convicted, especially if they were members of middle- or upper-class families.

After establishing the usefulness of self-report surveys about offenses, the next logical step for researchers was to query people from all walks of life about any street crimes that may have been committed against them rather than by them. These self-report studies originally were called "victim surveys." But that label was somewhat misleading because most respondents answered that they were not victims—they had not been harmed by street crimes during the time period in question.

The first national survey about victimization (based on a random sample of 10,000 households) was carried out in 1966 for the President's Commission on Law Enforcement and the Administration of Justice. It immediately confirmed one suspicion: A sizable percentage of individuals in the sample who told interviewers that they had been harmed acknowledged that they had not reported the incident to the police. This additional proof of the existence of a "dark figure" of unreported crimes further undercut confidence in the accuracy of the FBI's *UCR* statistics for all offenses except murder, and underscored the importance of continuing this alternative way of measuring victimization rates and trends.

In 1972, the federal government initiated a yearly survey of businesses as well as residents in 26 large cities, but the project was discontinued in 1976. In 1973 the Census Bureau began interviewing members of a huge, randomly selected, nationwide, stratified, multistage sample of households (clustered by geographic counties). Until

1992, the undertaking was known as the National Crime Survey (*NCS*). After some revisions, it was retitled the National Crime Victimization Survey (*NCVS*).

The Issues It Addresses   *NCVS* respondents answer questions from a survey that runs more than 20 pages. They are interviewed every six months for three years. The questioning begins with a series of screening items such as, "During the last six months did anyone break into your home?" If the respondent answers yes, follow-up questions are asked to collect details about the incident.

When completed, the survey provides a great deal of data about the number of violent and property crimes committed against the respondents, the extent of any physical injuries or financial losses they sustained, and the location and time of the incidents. It also keeps track of the age, sex, race/ethnicity, marital status, income level, educational attainment, and place of residence of the people disclosing their misfortunes to survey interviewers. The survey records the victims' descriptions of the perpetrators and weapons, and accounts of self-protective measures they took before, during, and after the attack. Additional questions probe into any relationship between the victim and the offender, as well as reasons why the crime was or was not reported to the police.

The survey is person-centered. It is geared toward uncovering the suffering of individuals 12 years of age or older, and the losses experienced by entire households (but not of workplaces, such as burglaries of offices or robberies of banks). The questionnaire focuses on crimes of violence (forcible rape, robbery, and aggravated assault) like the *UCR*, plus simple assault, but not murder. It also inquires about two kinds of thefts from individuals (personal larceny with and without contact), and three types of stealing directed at the common property of households—burglary, larceny, and motor vehicle theft—again, just like the *UCR* (except that crimes against collectivities like organizations and commercial enterprises are not included). The list of offenses analyzed in the *NCVS* now includes identity theft but it is far from exhaustive.

For example, respondents are not quizzed about instances of kidnapping, swindling, blackmail, extortion, and property damage due to vandalism or arson.

The benefit of survey research is that it eliminates the futility of attempting the impossible: interviewing every one of the nearly 250 million people 12 years old or older living in nearly 118 million households in the entire United States in 2006 to find out how he or she fared in the past year. The combined experiences of the nearly 135,000 individuals over the age of 11 living in roughly 76,000 households randomly selected to be in the national sample can be projected to derive estimates of the total number of people throughout the country who were robbed, raped, or beaten, and of households that suffered burglaries, larcenies, or car thefts.

Shortcomings of the Data   At the survey's inception, the idea of asking people about their recent misfortunes was hailed as a major breakthrough that would provide more accurate statistics than those found in the *UCR*. But for a number of reasons the technique has not turned out to be the foolproof method for measuring the "actual" crime rate that some victimologists had hoped it would be. (For more extensive critiques of the methodology, see Levine, 1976; Garofalo, 1981; Skogan, 1981b, 1986; Lehnen and Skogan, 1981; Reiss, 1981, 1986; Schneider, 1981; O'Brien, 1985; Mayhew and Hough, 1988; Fattah, 1991; and Lynch and Addington, 2007).

First, the findings of this survey, like any other, are reliable only to the extent that the national sample is truly representative of the population of the whole country. If the sample is biased (in terms of factors connected to victimization, such as age, gender, race, class, and geographical location), then the projections made about the experiences of the roughly 250 million people who were not questioned in 2006 will be either too high or too low. Because the *NCVS* is household-based, it might fail to fully capture the experiences of transients (such as homeless persons) or people who wish to keep a low profile (such as illegal immigrants).

Second, the credibility of what people tell pollsters is a constant subject of debate and a matter of continuing concern in this survey. Under-reporting remains a problem because communication barriers can inhibit respondents from disclosing details about certain crimes committed against them (incidents that they also probably refused to bring to the attention of the police). Any systematic suppression of the facts, such as the unwillingness of wives to reveal that their husbands beat them, of teenage girls to divulge that they suffered date rapes, or of young men to admit that they were robbed while trying to buy illicit drugs or a prostitute's sexual services, will throw off the survey's projection of the true state of affairs. Furthermore, crimes committed against children under 12 are not probed (so no information is forthcoming about physical and sexual abuse by caretakers, or molestations or kidnappings by acquaintances or strangers). **Memory decay** (forgetting about incidents) also results in information losses, especially about minor offenses that did not involve serious injuries or expenses.

But over-reporting can occur as well. Some respondents may exaggerate or deliberately lie for a host of personal motives. Experienced detectives filter out from police statistics any accounts that do not sound believable. They deem the charges to be "unfounded" and decide that no further investigation is warranted (see Chapter 6). But there is no such quality control over what people tell *NCVS* interviewers. The police don't accept all reports of crimes at face value, but pollsters must. "Stolen" objects actually may have been misplaced, and an accidentally shattered window may be mistaken as evidence of an attempted break-in. Also, no verification of assertions takes place. If a person in the sample discusses a crime that was supposedly reported to the local police, there is no attempt to check to see if the respondent's recollections coincide with the information in the department's case files. **Forward telescoping** is the tendency to vividly remember traumatic events and therefore believe that a serious crime occurred more recently than it actually did (within the survey's reference period of "the previous six months"). It contributes to over-reporting because respondents think a

crime should be counted, when actually it was committed long before and ought to be excluded.

Because being targeted within the previous six months is a relatively rare event, tens of thousands of people must be polled to find a sufficient number of individuals with incidents worthy of discussion to meet the requirements for statistical soundness. For example, about 1,000 people must be interviewed in order to locate a handful who were recently robbed. Estimates derived from small subsamples (such as robbery victims who are elderly and female) have large margins of error. The *NCVS* therefore requires a huge sample and becomes very expensive to carry out.

Even with a relatively large number of participants, the findings of the survey can only describe the situation in the nation as a whole. The seriousness of the crime problem in a particular city, county, or state cannot be accurately determined because the national sample is not large enough to break down into local subgroups of sufficient size for statistical analysis (with a few exceptions). Furthermore, the projected absolute number of incidents (offenses committed and victims harmed) and the relative rates (victims per 1,000 people) are really estimates at the midpoint of a **range** (what statisticians call a **confidence interval**). Therefore, *NCVS* rates always must be regarded as approximate, plus or minus a certain correction factor (margin of error) that depends mostly on the size of the entire sample (all respondents) or a specific subsample, such as low-income young men, living in cities, who were robbed.

The *NCVS* has improved over the years as better ways have been devised to draw representative samples; to determine which incidents coincide with or don't fit crime definitions; and to jog respondents' memories. Beginning in 1986, questions probing several new subject areas were asked of victims: whether they thought the offender was high on drugs or alcohol at the time of the crime; how they behaved while under attack (self-protective measures); what they were doing when trouble struck (commuting, shopping, and so forth); and what contacts they had with agents of the criminal justice system (Taylor, 1989).

During the early 1990s, the survey was fine-tuned once again. An advisory panel of criminal justice policy makers, social scientists, victim advocates, and statisticians redesigned some questions to provide cues that could help victims recall events and details, especially about incidents involving nonstrangers. Also, more explicit questions were added about sexual assaults (involving unwanted or coerced sexual contact) that fell short of the legal definition of rape, and about outbreaks of domestic violence (simple assaults) (Hoover, 1994; and Kindermann, Lynch, and Cantor, 1997).

Over about 35 years, the survey's questions have been refocused, clarified, and improved. But the accuracy of the *NCVS* has suffered because of waves of budget cuts. To save money, the sample size has been trimmed repeatedly, and consisted of about 135,000 individuals in 76,000 households across the nation in 2006. Over the decades, expensive "paper and pencil interviews" (PAPI) carried out at people's homes have been replaced by follow-up phone calls (computer-assisted telephone interviews [CATI]) and mail-in questionnaires. The response rate for individuals who were invited to participate has slipped to about 86 percent; in other words, 14 percent of people chosen for the study declined in 2006 (Rennison and Rand, 2007; Rand and Catalano, 2007).

The sample used for the 2006 *NCVS* was adjusted to reflect demographic changes, but some highly technical corrections could not be implemented because of insufficient funding. The BJS cautioned that the overall findings from the 2006 survey were not strictly comparable with the findings from previous years due to differences in the samples of people living in rural areas.

Comparing the *UCR* and the *NCVS*

For victimologists, the greater variety of statistics published in the *NCVS* offer many more possibilities for analysis and interpretation than the much more limited data in the *UCR*. But both official sources have advantages and can be considered to complement each other.

The *UCR*, not the *NCVS*, is the source to turn to for information about murder victims because questions about homicide don't appear on the survey. However, two other valuable, detailed, and accurate databases for studying homicide victims are death certificates as well as public health records maintained by local coroners' and medical examiners' offices. These files may contain information about the slain person's sex, age, race/ethnicity, ancestry, birthplace, occupation, educational attainment and Zip code of last known address (for examples of how this non-*UCR* data can be analyzed, see Karmen, 2000).

The *UCR* is also the publication that presents information about officers slain in the line of duty, college students harmed on campuses, and hate crimes directed against various groups. The *UCR* is the place to go for geographically based statistics; it provides data about the eight index crimes reported to police in different towns and cities, entire metropolitan areas, counties, states, and regions of the country. *NCVS* figures are calculated for the whole country, four geographic regions, and urban/suburban/rural areas, but are not available for specific cities, counties, or states (because the subsamples would be too small to analyze). The *UCR*, but not the *NCVS*, calculates the overall proportion of index crime cases that are solved by law enforcement agencies. Incidents counted in the *UCR* can be considered as having passed through two sets of authenticity filters: victims felt what happened was serious enough to notify the authorities shortly afterward, and officers who filled out the reports believed that the complainants were telling the truth as supported by some evidence. Although limited information about arrestees is provided in the *UCR*, this annual report doesn't provide any descriptions of the people harmed by rapists, robbers, assailants, burglars, and other thieves (until the NIBRS replaces current record-keeping formats).

NCVS interviewers collect a great deal of information about the people who claim they were harmed by street crimes. The *NCVS* is the source to turn to for a more inclusive accounting of what happened during a given year because it contains information about incidents that were not reported to the police. The yearly surveys are not affected by any changes in the degree of cooperation—or level of tension—between community residents and their local police, by improvements in record keeping by law enforcement agencies, or by temporary crackdowns in which all incidents are taken more seriously. But the *NCVS* interviewers must accept at face value the accounts respondents describe. Also, the *NCVS* annual report has nothing to offer about murders, line-of-duty assaults and deaths of police officers, offenses committed against children under 12, robberies and burglaries directed at commercial establishments, and injuries from intentionally set fires.

Even when both of these official sources collect data about the same crimes, the findings might not be strictly comparable. First of all, the definitions of certain offenses (such as rape) can vary, so the numerators may not count the same incidents. The *UCR* keeps track only of rapes of women and girls, while the *NCVS* counts sexual assaults against males as well as females. The *UCR* includes robberies and burglaries of commercial establishments, but the *NCVS* does not.

In addition, the denominators differ. While the FBI computes incidents of violence "per 100,000 people," the BJS calculates incidents "per 1,000 people age 12 or older." For property crimes, the *NCVS* denominator is "per 1,000 households," not individuals (the average household has between two and three people living in it).

Therefore, it is difficult to make direct comparisons between the findings of the *UCR* and the *NCVS*. The best way to take full advantage of these two official sources of data from the federal government is to focus on the unique information provided by each data collection system.

USING DATA TO BRING THE BIG PICTURE INTO FOCUS

The two official sources of government statistics can yield useful information that answers important questions about everyday life, such as, "How often are people harmed by lawbreakers?"

Victimologists look at both raw numbers and rates. **Raw numbers** reveal the actual numbers of victims. For example, the body count or the death toll is a raw number. Just about 17,000 people were murdered in the United States during 2006. **Rates** are expressed as fractions or ratios that project the odds, chances, or risks of victimization in a year. The numerator of the fraction counts the number of individuals actually harmed, while the denominator reveals the total number of possible targets. Rates are usually presented with a standardized base (e.g., for every 1,000 people, per 1,000 households, or per 100,000 vehicles). Rates are the appropriate measurements to use when comparing the incidence of crime in populations of unequal size, such as the seriousness of the violence problem in different cities or countries, or at different periods of time.

The total population of the United States was close to 300 million in 2006. Dividing 17,000 slayings by 295 million people yields a tiny quotient that converts (move the decimal point five digits to the right) to a murder rate of about 5.7 killings per 100,000 inhabitants. That means that for every 100,000 people of all ages throughout the land, five or six perished from violence during that 12-month period. Giving the same statistic a more upbeat spin by accentuating the positive, that murder rate of less than six per 100,000 reveals that 99,994 out of every 100,000 Americans were not slain in 2006. (Note that when working with statistics and rounding off numbers such as body counts and murder rates, it is easy to forget that each death represents a terrible tragedy for the real people whose lives were prematurely terminated, and a devastating loss for their families.)

The BJS's *NCVS* doesn't generate data about murders, but it yields estimates (plus or minus some small correction factor because of sampling error) of the number of people who endure rapes, robberies, assaults, burglaries, motor vehicle thefts, and other larcenies each year. The standard definitions used by police departments for *UCR* purposes and by

NCVS interviewers appear side by side in Table 3.1. Also shown are estimated numbers of incidents and victimization rates for 2006 derived from both data collecting programs.

When reading Table 3.1, note that the definitions are parallel but not identical. Recall that the *NCVS* and *UCR* victimization rates are not directly comparable. The standard denominators for the *UCR*

TABLE 3.1 **Estimated Victimization Rates from the *UCR* and the *NCVS*, 2006**

Crime	*UCR* Definition	Incidents	Rate (per 100,000)
Murder	The willful (nonnegligent) killing of one human being by another; includes manslaughter and deaths due to recklessness; excludes deaths due to accidents, suicides, and justifiable homicides in self-defense.	17,000	5.7
Forcible Rape	The carnal knowledge of a female forcibly and against her will; includes attempts; excludes other sexual assaults and statutory rape.	93,000	31
Robbery	The taking of or attempting to take anything of value from the care, custody, or control of a person or persons by force or threat of force; includes commercial establishments and carjackings, armed and unarmed.	447,000	149
Aggravated Assault	The unlawful attacking of one person by another for the purpose of inflicting severe bodily injury, often by use of a deadly weapon; includes attempted murder and severe beatings of family members; excludes simple, unarmed assaults.	861,000	288
Simple Assault	No weapon used, minor wounds inflicted	not measured	not computed
Personal Larceny	Not a separate category	not measured	not computed
Burglary	The unlawful entry of a structure to commit a felony or theft; includes unlawful entry without applying force to residences and commercial and government premises.	2,184,000	729
Larceny-Theft	The unlawful taking, carrying, leading, or riding away of property from the possession of another; includes purse snatching, pocket picking, thefts from vehicles, thefts of parts of vehicles, and shoplifting; excludes the use of force or fraud to obtain possessions.	6,607,000	2,207
Motor Vehicle Theft	The theft or attempted driving away of a vehicle; includes automobiles, trucks, buses, motorcycles, snowmobiles, and commercially owned vehicles; excludes farm machinery and boats and planes.	1,193,000	398
Crime	***NCVS* Definition**	**Incidents**	**Rate (per 100,000)**
Murder	Not included in the survey	not measured	not computed
Rape	The carnal knowledge of a male or female through the use of force or threats of violence; includes attempts as well as verbal threats; excludes sexual contacts and statutory rape.	overall* 192,000	80
		completed 117,000	50
		attempted 76,000	30

TABLE 3.1   (Continued)

Crime	NCVS Definition	Incidents	Rate (per 100,000)
Sexual Assault	The imposition of unwanted sexual contact (grabbing, fondling) with or without force; includes attempts and threats; excludes molestations of children under 12.	overall 69,000	30
Robbery	The taking directly from a person of property or cash by force or threat of force, with or without a weapon; includes attempts; excludes commercial establishments.	overall 713,000	290
		completed 482,000	200
		attempted 230,000	90
Aggravated Assault	The attacking of a person with a weapon, regardless of whether an injury is sustained; includes attempts as well as attacks without a weapon that result in serious injuries; excludes severe physical abuse of children under 12.	overall 1,344,000	540
Simple Assault	The attacking of a person without a weapon resulting in minor wounds or no physical injury; includes attempts and intrafamily violence.	overall 3,777,000	1,530
Personal Theft	The theft of cash or possessions from any place other than the victim's home or its immediate vicinity without the use of force or threats; includes pocket picking and purse snatching as well as attempts.	overall 173,000	70
Household Burglary	The unlawful entry of a residence, garage, or shed, usually but not always for the purpose of theft; includes attempts; excludes commercial or governmental premises.	overall 3,561,000	3,020 (per 100,000 households)
		completed 2,848,000	2,420
		attempted 713,000	600
Theft	The theft of property or cash without contact; includes attempts to take unguarded possessions as well as larcenies committed by persons invited into the home.	overall 14,363,000	12,190
Motor Vehicle Theft	The driving away or taking without authorization of any household's motorized vehicle; includes attempts.	overall 992,000	840

NOTE: Subcategories may not add up to totals because of rounding errors.
All UCR and NCVS figures for incidents were rounded off to the nearest 1000.
All NCVS rates were rounded off to the nearest 10.
NCVS rates were multiplied by 100 to make them comparable to UCR rates.
*Overall = completed + attempted
Sources: FBI's UCR, 2006: BJS's NCVS, 2006; Rand and Catalano, 2007.

rates are per 100,000 individuals of any age; for NCVS rates are per 1,000 persons 12 years of age or older. Furthermore, NCVS property crime rates are calculated as per 1,000 households and therefore do not correspond neatly to the FBI's per 100,000 individuals. To facilitate rough comparisons, NCVS rates were presented in Table 3.1 as for every 100,000 simply by multiplying the published rate per 1,000 by 100.

Glancing at the data from the *UCR* and the *NCVS* presented in Table 3.1, the big picture takes shape. Note that the numbers of incidents and the victimization rates from the *NCVS* are consistently higher than the *UCR* figures for each type of offense. The main reason is that the *NCVS* numbers include crimes not reported to the police, and therefore not forwarded to FBI headquarters.

Both sources of data expose a widely believed myth. Contrary to any false impressions gained from news media coverage and television or movie plots, people suffer from violent crimes much less frequently than from property crimes. Every year, theft (a broad catch-all category) is the most common crime of all. Burglaries are the second most common form of victimization, and motor vehicle thefts rank third. According to *NCVS* findings, thefts of possessions—the stealing of items left unattended outdoors plus property or cash taken by someone invited into the home, such as a cleaning person or guest—touched an estimated 12,190 out of every 100,000 households, or roughly 12 percent, in 2006. Fortunately, this kind of victimization turns out to be the least serious; most of these cases would be classified as petty thefts inflicting expenses of less than $250. The *NCVS* finding about how common thefts are each year is confirmed by the *UCR*. Larcenies of all kinds (including shoplifting from stores in the *UCR* definition) vastly outnumber all other types of crimes reported to police. These everyday thefts when added together cost individuals and stores about $5.6 billion in 2006. Financial losses from burglaries of residences and commercial properties added up to $4 billion that year.

As for violent crimes, fortunately a similar pattern emerges: The most common is the least serious type. Simple assaults (punching, kicking, and slapping) are far more likely to take place than aggravated assaults, robberies, rapes, or murders. Aggravated assaults, which are intended to seriously wound or kill, ranked second in frequency on the *NCVS*. According to the *UCR*, aggravated or felonious assaults were the most common type of violent offense reported to the police, but that is because the *UCR* doesn't monitor the number of simple assaults committed. Only the number of arrests for simple assaults, not the number of incidents, appears in Part II of the *UCR*; NIBRS keeps track of both statistics but a nationwide tally is not yet possible.

Robberies take place much more often than rapes. The *NCVS* keeps track not only of rapes but also of other sexual assaults (fondling, grabbing, even verbal threats to do so). Unfortunately, more than half of the rapes disclosed to the *NCVS* interviewers were completed acts, and not attempts. The smaller *UCR* estimate of the total number of incidents indicates that many rape victims who disclosed their problems to interviewers were not willing to bring their plight to the attention of police. Also, the *UCR* only counts forcible rapes of girls and women but not sexual assaults against boys or men. Both sources of data agree that rapes take place much less often than nonsexual assaults or robberies.

An analysis of the "big picture" indicates that the most terrible of all violent crimes—homicide—is the least likely of all to be committed, according to *UCR* data. But because the consequences of killings are so devastating, murders (and robberies that potentially could escalate into slayings) will be the focus of the next chapter.

SUMMARY

Statistics can convey important information about crimes and their victims, but consumers of numerical data must ascertain exactly what was counted, how accurate the measurements are, and whether vested interests are promoting particular interpretations.

The two leading sources of data about crime victims published annually by the U.S. Department of Justice are the FBI's *Uniform Crime Report* and the BJS's *National Crime Victimization Survey*. The *UCR* draws on police files and is useful to victimologists who want to study murders, but it is of limited value for research into other kinds of victimizations. The *NCVS* contains information about a wider range of violent and property crimes and gathers data directly from members of a large national sample who answer questions about their experiences over the past six months. Victimization rates are expressed per 1,000 in the *NCVS* or per 100,000 in the *UCR* to facilitate fair comparisons between groups, cities, or countries of different sizes.

KEY TERMS

big picture, 52

statistics, 52

official statistics, 52

victimization rates, 52

patterns, 52

trends, 52

profiles, 53

spin, 53

Uniform Crime Report (UCR), 54

National Crime Victimization Survey (NCVS), 54

correlation, 54

Crime Clock, 55

index crimes, 58

hierarchy rule, 58

self-report survey, 60

memory decay, 62

forward telescoping, 62

range (confidence interval), 62

raw numbers, 64

rates, 64

QUESTIONS FOR DISCUSSION AND DEBATE

1. Choose some statistics presented in this chapter and interpret them in two ways: first, make them seem as alarming as possible; and second, portray them as reassuring as possible.

2. What kinds of data about crime victims can be found in the FBI's annual *Uniform Crime Reports*? What are the sources of inaccuracies in these statistics?

3. What kinds of data about crime victims can be found in the BJS's annual *National Crime Victimization Survey*? What are the sources of inaccuracies in these statistics?

CRITICAL THINKING QUESTIONS

1. What information about crime victims is *not* systematically collected by the *UCR* and the *NCVS*, or even the NIBRS? Why would this additional information be important? How could it be used?

2. Make up some hypothetical scenarios in which people with a vested interest in convincing the public that victimization rates are either going up or going down could "shop around" for *UCR* or *NCVS* statistics about robberies and burglaries to support their claim.

SUGGESTED RESEARCH PROJECTS

1. Find out the latest rates per 100,000 people for the index crimes for your home state by searching the FBI website that posts the *UCR* statistics. What crime rates are substantially higher or lower in your state than for the entire United States (as shown in Table 3.1)?

2. Find out the definitions and the precise wording of the questions that are asked in the *NCVS* by downloading the survey instrument from the BJS website. Discuss how the inquiries about aggravated assault, rape, and other sexual assaults are phrased, and how respondents might be confused or unclear about how to answer these questions.

4

Violent Crimes:
Murders and Robberies

FOCUSING ON MURDERS

This chapter focuses on people harmed by violent offenders, especially by murderers and robbers. (The plight of those who suffer at the hands of rapists will be examined in Chapter 10.) Data from the *UCR* and the *NCVS* will be used to answer a set of unsettling questions:

- What are the odds of being attacked during any given year? Annual incidence rates reveal the risks faced by large numbers of people.

- What are the chances that a person will be harmed by a criminal at least once during his or her lifetime (not just in a single year)? **Cumulative risks** estimate these odds by projecting current situations into the future. Does violent crime burden all communities and groups equally, or are some types of people more likely than others to be physically injured and killed? **Differential risks** indicate the odds of an unwanted event taking place for members of a social grouping (for example: urban, suburban, or rural residents).

- Is violence a growing problem in American society, or is it subsiding? **Trend analysis** provides the answer.

- Which dreaded event is an individual more likely to directly experience—an accident, an illness, or a crime? **Comparative risks** assess the relative threats posed by each kind of misfortune to members of their group (for example, the chances of being murdered versus the odds of dying in an automobile crash for teenagers).

- Is the threat of crime as serious a problem in other societies as it is in the United States? **International comparisons** enable researchers to rank countries according to their homicide rates.

Using the *UCR* to Analyze Murders

Murder is the most terrible crime of all because it inflicts the ultimate harm and the damage cannot be undone. The loss suffered by the departed person's survivors is total and irreparable. But the social reaction to the taking of a person's life varies dramatically. It is determined by a number of factors, among them the state's laws, the offender's state of mind, the deceased's possible contribution to the escalation of hostilities, the social standing of each party, where the crime was committed, how the person was dispatched, and whether the slaying attracted media coverage. Some murders make headlines, while others slip by virtually unnoticed except by the next of kin. Some killings lead to the execution of the perpetrator; others ruled to be justifiable homicides result in no penalty and possibly even approval.

Homicide is broadly defined as the killing of one human being by another. Not all homicides are punishable murders. All murders are socially defined: the determinations are carried out by legislators, police officers and detectives; prosecutors and defense attorneys; judges and juries; and even the media and the public's reaction to someone's demise. Deaths caused by carelessness and accidents are not classified as murders (although if the damage was foreseeable, they might be prosecuted as manslaughters). Acts involving the legitimate use of deadly force in self-defense whether carried out against felons by police officers or by private citizens under attack (see Chapter 13), are also excluded from the body counts, as are court-sanctioned executions.

The law takes into account whether a killing was carried out intentionally (with "express malice"), in a rational state of mind ("deliberate"), and with advance planning ("premeditation"). These defining characteristics of first-degree murders carry the most severe punishments, including (depending on the state) execution or life imprisonment without parole. Killing certain people—police officers; corrections officers; judges; witnesses; and victims during rapes, kidnappings, or robberies—may also be capital offenses.

A homicide committed with intent to inflict grievous bodily injury (but no intent to kill) or with extreme recklessness ("depraved heart") is prosecuted as a second-degree murder. A homicide committed in the "sudden heat of passion" as a result of the victim's provocations is considered a "voluntary" (or first-degree) manslaughter. The classic example is "the husband who comes home to find his wife in bed with another man." A negligent killing usually is treated as an "involuntary" (second-degree) manslaughter, or it may not be subjected to criminal prosecution at all.

Second-degree murder is not a capital crime and cannot lead to the death penalty. Offenders convicted of manslaughter are punished less severely than those convicted of murder. Some types of slayings have special names (see Holmes, 1994): infanticide (of a newborn by a parent), filicide (of a child by a parent or stepparent), parricide (of a parent by a child), domestic or intimate partner homicide (of a spouse or lover), serial killing (several or more victims dispatched one at a time over an extended period), mass murder (several people slaughtered at the same time and place), felony murder (committed during another serious crime, like robbery or rape), and contract killing (a professional "hit" for an agreed-upon fee).

The first criminologists who were attracted to victimology were drawn by the interaction between victims and offenders. They were especially intrigued by any prior relationships between the two parties in cases of interpersonal violence. For example, they wondered whether the killer and the mortally wounded person had known each other (as intimates, adversaries, or casual acquaintances), and whether those who were slain shared many common characteristics with their killers. They also wanted to find out what groups of people suffered the greatest casualties, how they perished, and what caused the confrontations that led to untimely deaths. In other words, they wanted to derive a **profile** or **statistical portrait** of the "typical" murder, killer, and victim.

NCVS interviewers ask no questions about murders of household members, so the *UCR* and the records of coroners or medical examiners are the official sources of information. *UCR* guidelines compel police officials to fill out a **Supplementary Homicide Report** (SHR) about each killing in their jurisdiction. The resulting SHR database provides information about the age, sex, and race of the victim and—if detectives solved the case and made an arrest—the accused person's age, sex, race, weapon, motive, and relationship to the deceased.

Data derived from the FBI's SHRs for 2006 sheds light on these issues. *UCR* statistics indicate that men die violently much more frequently than women. Year after year, at least three-quarters of the corpses are of boys and men (79 percent in 2006). Also, about 9 out of 10 of the known offenders were teenage boys or men (91 percent of the arrestees were males in 2006). Therefore, most murders can be categorized as male-on-male. When females get killed, the murderers usually turn out to be males (92 percent were in 2006). On the infrequent occasions when females kill, they tend to slay their own small children or the men in their lives, rather than other women.

As for the race of those who were slain, the *UCR* recognizes only these categories: "white," "black," and "other" (Asians) plus "undetermined or unknown." (Note that most Hispanics were counted as whites on the SHRs.) During 2006, half of all who perished (50 percent) were black, an almost equal proportion were white (46 percent), and the remaining 4 percent were of other races or of unknown background. Because about 14 percent of the population identifies itself as "black" on the latest Census surveys, violent crime is a disproportionally serious problem in African-American communities. Year after year, most murders turn out to be intraracial, not interracial (see Wood, 1990). Focusing solely upon lone-offender/single-victim killings carried out during 2006, the *UCR* documented that 92 percent of black victims were slain by black offenders, and 82 percent of white victims were killed by white perpetrators.

As for age, the typical victims were in their late teens, twenties, and thirties when they were killed. Almost two-thirds (63 percent in 2006) of those who died violently were between ages 17 and 39. An even higher proportion of perpetrators fall into this age range. As a result, many murders can be characterized as young men slaying other relatively young men.

For decades, the majority of killers have dispatched their adversaries with firearms—sometimes rifles and shotguns, but usually revolvers and pistols, which account for about three-quarters of all gun murders. Deaths due to bullet wounds rose from 64 percent in 1990 to just about 70 percent in 1993, before subsiding to 65 percent in 1998, inching back up to 70 percent in 2004, and dipping back down to 68 percent in 2006. Knives and other sharp instruments ran a distant second as the weapons of choice, accounting for less than 15 percent of all deaths. The rest were killed by blunt instruments; fists and feet; hands (largely via strangulation and smothering); and other ways (explosions, arson, poisons, by being pushed, and other less-frequent means).

Specific relationships connecting victims and offenders can be broadly categorized to shed light on certain patterns within slayings. Three main categories can be distinguished. The two were family members (nuclear or extended); acquaintances, neighbors, or close friends (including girlfriend or boyfriend); or complete strangers brought together by fate. According to data from police investigations from the 1990s to 2006, in the most common situation (ranging from 29 percent to 38 percent) the offender was a friend or acquaintance. Killings of one family member by another added up to an additional 12 percent to 14 percent each year. Slayings by strangers accounted for about 12 percent to 15 percent of cases for which the relationship could be surmised by detectives. Unfortunately, unsolved homicides "of unknown relationship" (at the time the SHRs were submitted) made up the largest category, hovering between 35 percent and 45 percent in recent decades.

If detectives could determine the victim—offender relationship in this residual grouping (which presumably contains many difficult-to-solve slayings by complete strangers), the percentages due to family quarrels and conflicts with friends and acquaintances probably would be much smaller. However, looking only at solved cases, the old adage remains true: that a person is more likely to be killed by someone he or she knows than by a stranger (only 23 percent of the known killers in 2006). But if the proportion of murders committed by strangers is rising, that would be a frightening development because it is more difficult to anticipate and guard against attacks by unknown assailants (see Riedel, 1987). (SHRs are filled out shortly after killings take place. Police departments do not send updated reports to the *UCR* for "cold cases" that they solve months or years later.)

As for the reasons for the confrontations that claimed lives (what police departments and the FBI

call "circumstances"), the 2006 SHRs expose some widely held myths arising from TV shows and movies. Of the more than 9,700 murder victims whose circumstances were known, only eight were labeled as prostitutes. "Gangland killings" of mobsters claimed 118 lives but amounted to barely 1 percent of all murders nationwide. Drug dealer turf battles and drug-fueled brawls added another 9 percent. Killings arising from clashes between rival street gangs accounted for less than 9 percent of all murders in which the motive was known—however, the nationwide death toll for "juvenile gang killings" (motivated by or related to the activities of a "youth gang") added up to 865 in 2006, making gang membership a risky business in many urban neighborhoods. Robbers stole more than 1,000 lives, comprising about 7 percent of the body count (see Box 4.1 below for a closer examination of these tragedies).

However, the largest category was "other arguments" (15 percent of all cases solved during 2006): heated disputes of all sorts, some trivial or based on misunderstandings. If that miscellaneous grouping of 15 percent is added to "unknown reasons" arising from unsolved cases (35 percent), then the motives for half of all killings can't be meaningfully analyzed.

In sum, it is difficult to generalize why killings typically take place. But the statistical portrait that emerges from *UCR* data is of young men shooting other young men during confrontations over some issue that seemed important to them at the time.

Searching for Crime Waves: Detecting Trends in Interpersonal Violence

Each annual report from the *UCR* or the *NCVS* presents the latest readings on the current state of America's crime problem. But these are just snapshots that depict what went on during a relatively short time period—one calendar year. Trends refer to changes that occur over longer stretches of time. Sharp increases in rates over several consecutive years are commonly known as **crime waves**. Downward trends indicating reduced levels of criminal activity can take place as well. Ironically, there isn't a good term to describe a sudden yet sustained improvement in public safety. Perhaps the term **crime crash** (see Karmen, 2000) captures the essence of such a profound and largely unexpected downturn (as a tumble in the price of shares on the stock market is called a crash). To bring the big picture into focus, a crucial question that must be answered is whether street crime is becoming more or less of a problem as years pass.

During the 1960s, a major crime wave engulfed the country, according to the FBI's *UCR*, which was the only annual source of nationwide data during that decade. Since 1973, the findings of the Bureau of Justice Statistics' (BJS) *NCVS* have provided an additional set of figures to monitor the upward and downward drifts in victimization rates. According to both these monitoring systems, crime rates "crashed" during the 1990s, as the graphs below demonstrate. Is the United States still in the midst of this crime crash? Few social scientists, politicians, or journalists would declare that the "war on crime" has been won. But what do the statistics derived from the two yearly

government reports reveal about the level of criminal activity in recent years? Are victimization rates rising once again, remaining steady, or dropping further?

Changes over Time in Murder Rates

Graphs are particularly useful for spotting trends at a glance. Trends in homicide rates can be traced further back than changes over time for the other crimes. The *UCR* has been monitoring murder since the beginning of the 1930s. But another source of data, drawn from death certificates and calculated by the National Center for Health Statistics, can be tapped to reconstruct what has happened since the start of the century. Graphing this data, as shown in Figure 4.1, facilitates the identification of steep increases and sharp decreases in the homicide rate over the decades. Long-term trends can then be considered against a backdrop of major historical events affecting the nation as a whole.

As the trend line in Figure 4.1 indicates, homicide rates climbed rapidly soon after the statistical reporting system based on records from coroners'

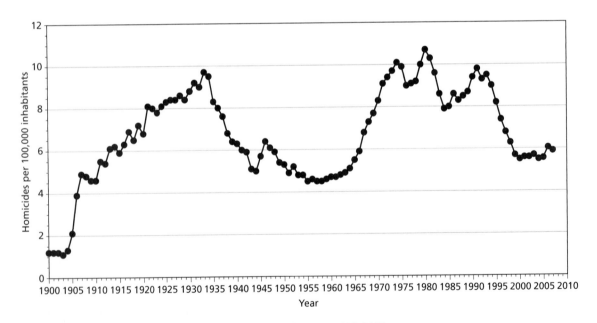

FIGURE 4.1 Trends in Homicide Rates in the United States, 1900–2007
SOURCES: National Center for Health Statistics, 1999; *UCR*, 2007.

offices was initiated at the outset of the 1900s. From 1903 to 1933 the murder rate soared from fewer than one person killed out of every 100,000 each year to nearly 10 per 100,000 annually. The number of violent deaths plummeted after Prohibition ended in 1933, even though the economic hardships of the "Great Depression" persisted throughout the 1930s. Only five slayings took place for every 100,000 inhabitants during the years of World War II. A brief surge in killings broke out after most of the soldiers returned home from the war, but then interpersonal violence continued to decline during the 1950s, reaching a low of about 4.5 victims per 100,000 people by 1958.

From the mid-1960s to the late 1970s, the number of slayings shot up again. This crime wave reflected the demographic impact of the unusually large baby-boom generation passing through its most crime-prone teenage and young-adult years, as well as the social turbulence that arose during the 1960s and lasted well into the 1970s. An all-time high was recorded in 1980, when the homicide rate hit 11 deaths per 100,000 people per year (BJS, 1988). After reaching that peak, murder rates dropped for several years until the second half of the 1980s, when the crack epidemic touched off another escalation of bloodshed. By the start of the 1990s, murder rates once again were close to their highest levels for the century. But as that decade progressed, the fad of smoking crack and toting guns waned, the economy improved, the proportion of the male population between 18 and 24 years old dwindled, and consequently the murder rate crashed (see Karmen, 2000; Fox and Zawitz, 2002). The death toll has remained rather stable during the first decade of the twenty-first century, as Figure 4.1 shows. With nearly 17,000 victims in 2007, the U.S. murder rate stood at 5.6 killings per 100,000 inhabitants, basically unchanged since the decade began.

Changes over Time in Aggravated Assault Rates

Murder and robbery are the two crimes that are the focus of this chapter, but a look at aggravated assault trends also would be appropriate. By definition, aggravated assaults result in serious injuries, or involve attacks or threats of harm with a deadly weapon. Therefore, some aggravated assaults are attempted murders in which the victims barely survived (a bullet missed its mark, a knife wound was not fatal, a severe beating almost claimed a life). To put it differently, homicides are aggravated assaults that inflict mortal wounds. With some bad luck or poor medical care, an aggravated assault easily could wind up as a murder. Conversely, with good fortune, a tragedy might be averted by ambulance crews and hospital emergency room personnel, and an act of violence that would have added to the body count remains a near-death experience and instead is officially recorded as an aggravated assault. Whether a victim of an aggravated assault lives or dies depends on several factors, including the weapon used, the severity of the wound, the injured party's pre-existing health condition, and the quality of medical care received. According to a nationwide study that analyzed the caliber of various counties' trauma care systems, a continuous drop in the lethality of assaults since 1960 can be primarily attributed to advances in emergency medicine (Harris et al., 2002). The policy implication is that the most important way to keep the murder rate down is to help critically wounded people stay alive by having competent ER doctors, nurses, and EMTs on call, ready to spring into action.

Both the *UCR* and the *NCVS* keep records of the annual number of aggravated assaults. Because two sources of official data can be tapped, a graph depicting changes over time in assaults with a deadly weapon can have two trend lines: one according to the *UCR* and the other according to the *NCVS*. The graph shown in Figure 4.2 displays the estimated rate for aggravated assaults committed across the United States from 1973 to 2006.

The *NCVS* trend line shows that close calls and near-death experiences of people shot or stabbed declined slightly in frequency from the early 1970s until the early 1990s. Then the *NCVS* was redesigned; the rate of aggravated assaults jumped in part because of the new measurement methods. However, by the end of the 1990s and for several

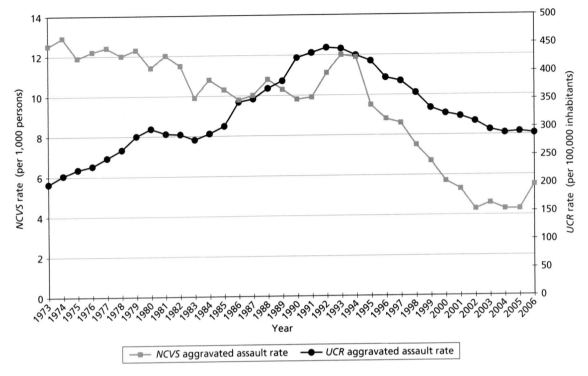

FIGURE 4.2 Trends in Aggravated Assault Rates in the United States, 1973–2006

NOTE: *NCVS* 1973–2006 findings adjusted for compatibility with redesigned 1992 survey.

SOURCES: FBI's *UCRs*, 1973–2006; BJS's *NCVS*, 1993–2006.

years into the new century, a dramatic improvement in the level of serious interpersonal violence became evident from *NCVS* figures. Between 1993 (when the survey was redesigned and the rate hit a peak) and 2006, aggravated assaults disclosed to *NCVS* interviewers "crashed" about 60 percent. *UCR* data show a different pattern. After years of rising numbers of reports about serious attacks, complaints to the police about aggravated assaults peaked in the early 1990s. After that, just as the *NCVS* line on the graph indicated, the level of violence subsided substantially during the second half of the 1990s and continued to diminish gradually through 2006. But unlike the *NCVS* figures, the *UCR* rates in 2006 were low—but not at their lowest levels in 30 years. During 2007, reports to the police about shootings, stabbings, and other aggravated assaults once again drifted downward (FBI, 2008).

Changes over Time in Robbery Rates   Robbery is often cited as the offense most people worry about when they discuss their fears about crime in the streets. Trends in robbery rates are displayed in Figure 4.3. The *UCR* trend line shows that robberies soared after 1977 and peaked in 1981, plunged until 1985, and then shot up again to record levels in the early 1990s. After that, reports of muggings and hold-ups plummeted impressively until 2001, and then leveled out during the first decade of the 21st century, rising a bit in 2006 and then falling back a little during 2007 (FBI, 2008).

The *NCVS* trend line tells a similar, but not identical, story. It indicates that the robbery rate fell between 1974 and 1978, rebounded until 1981 when it hit an all-time high, dropped sharply during the early 1980s, but then climbed back up from 1985 until 1994. After that, the robbery rate

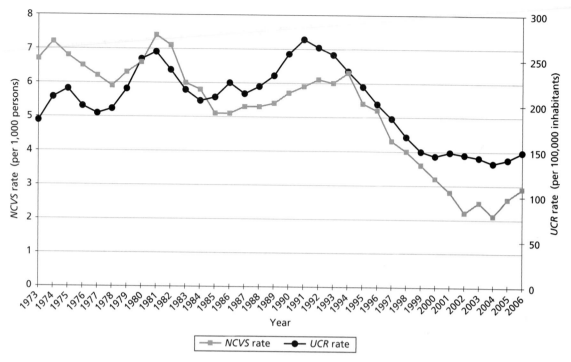

FIGURE 4.3 Trends in Robbery Rates in the United States, 1973–2006

NOTE: *UCR* includes reported commercial robberies. 1973–2006. *NCVS* findings adjusted for compatibility with the redesigned 1992 survey.

SOURCES: FBI's *UCR*s, 1973–2006; BJS's *NCVS*, 1993–2006.

tumbled from the second half of the 1990s until 2002. Robbery rates crashed an impressive 65 percent between 1993 and 2002, reaching their lowest levels since the *NCVS* surveys began, before creeping up a little by 2006.

The graphs depicted in Figures 4.1, 4.2, and 4.3 confirm the good news that violent crime rates have fallen dramatically, perhaps even "crashed," from their historically high (and politically intolerable) levels in the early 1990s. *UCR* figures for 2007 showed violent crime totals were down slightly after inching up in 2006 (FBI, 2008). To conclude from these graphs showing favorable trends in murders, robberies, and aggravated assaults that the "worst is over" might be overly optimistic, however. Certainly, interpersonal violence is not "getting out of hand" or "spiraling out of control" for the nation as a whole, although specific communities may be

rocked by sporadic spikes in lawlessness and bloodshed. No criminologist or victimologist knows for sure what the future holds.

Predictions about future crime waves or crashes must be based on projected changes in a number of underlying variables. Developments in some of these root causes are very hard to anticipate, like the emergence of new drug epidemics, perhaps involving methamphetamine. Other crucial variables are difficult to measure, such as the willingness of children of recent immigrants to maintain their parents' optimism about the American dream. And of course, the experts don't agree about the reasons why street crime rates rise and fall. Another crime wave could break out, or the dramatic improvement in America's crime problem that materialized as one century drew to a close and another one began just might continue after the current pause. But it is safe to conclude that the ranks of victims of violence are not growing as rapidly as they were in the "bad old days" of the 1960s, 1970s, 1980s, and early 1990s.

Uncovering Victimization Patterns

Recognizing Differential Risks   Victimization rates for the entire population indicate how frequently murders, rapes, robberies, and assaults are committed against "average" Americans and how often "typical" households suffer burglaries and motor vehicle thefts. It is reasonable to suspect that the chance of becoming a victim is not uniform for everyone but more likely for some and less likely for others, just as different categories of people do not face the same odds of getting hurt accidentally—say, from a skiing mishap—or of contracting a particular disease, such as HIV/AIDS. People with attributes in common such as sex and age may be affected by crime much more or much less often than others. If these suspicions can be documented, then any overall rate that projects a risk for all Americans might mask important variations by subgroups. In other words, victimologists must disaggregate, or break down, general victimization rates to reveal the **differential risks** faced by particular categories of people.

A pattern within a victimization rate is recognizable when one category suffers significantly more than another. The most obvious example is the incidence of rape: Females are much more likely to be sexually violated than are males. Searching for patterns means looking for regularities within a seemingly chaotic mass of information and finding predictability in apparently random events. To discover patterns, researchers must sort through data collected each year about various groupings of people and households that participated in the *NCVS* survey. Patterns can emerge when rates are calculated separately for each grouping, especially by sex, age, race, marital status, income class, and area of residence. Once a pattern has been established over the years, then the group's differential risks (as observed in the past) can be projected into the future. For example, because men historically have suffered assaults more often than women (according to the annual surveys),

it can be predicted that men will face greater risks of being attacked than women next year and in the foreseeable future, unless profound social changes affecting interpersonal violence take place.

The differential risks derived from victimization patterns will be investigated for the crimes of murder and robbery.

Differential Risks of Being Murdered   As was noted in Chapter 3, the murder rate in the United States in 2006 was 5.7 per 100,000. That means that between five and six people of all backgrounds were killed, and at least 99,994 survived out of every collection of 100,000 people. This statistic captures the odds of being slain for the fictitious "average" American, which is a useful social construct for certain purposes (for example, to compare risks faced by the average American to the average Canadian or Mexican). But this composite statistic conceals as much as it reveals. When the FBI compiles statistics from SHRs and publishes them in annual *UCRs*, a number of striking patterns within homicides emerge (which should be especially alarming for those who fall into some or all of the high-risk categories, and should be somewhat reassuring for members of other groups). The risks of being murdered vary greatly by region of the country, area of residence (urban, suburban, or rural), sex, age, and race.

As for different sections of the country, the highest homicide rates for many years have been found in the South (with 6.6 per 100,000 in 2006) and the lowest in the Northeast (at 4.5 per 100,000), with the Midwest and West falling between these two extremes. Residents of metropolitan areas (urban centers rather than suburbs) face higher risks of violent death than do inhabitants of rural counties or of small cities beyond the fringe of metropolitan areas. Risks can even be further finetuned by city. A closer look at the FBI's data from municipal police departments confirms that some cities were much more dangerous places to live in than others when size is taken into account, which is the only sound way to make such comparisons.

The map in Figure 4.4 indicates that among the largest cities in the country, homicide risks were much higher in Detroit, Philadelphia, Houston,

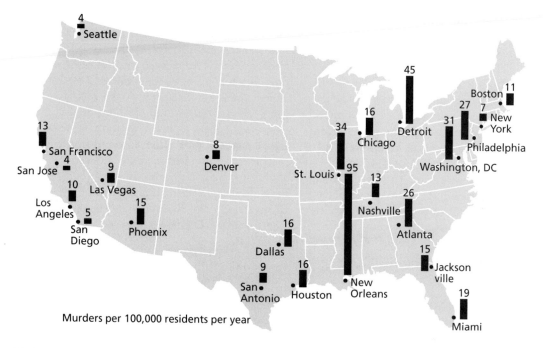

Murders per 100,000 residents per year

F I G U R E   4.4   Murder Rates in Major U.S. Cities, 2007

NOTE: Murder rates were calculated on the basis of the population living within city limits and not for the entire metropolitan area of surrounding counties. Also, the influx of commuters and tourists is not taken into account.

SOURCES: FBI's 2007 *UCR*.

and Dallas than in Denver, Las Vegas, New York and San Antonio. Other well-known cities with high murder rates per 100,000 residents include New Orleans—which became even more dangerous since the floods caused by Hurricane Katrina— St. Louis, and Washington, D.C.. Seattle, San Jose, and San Diego continue to be the safest cities, from 2006 right up through 2007.

The disparities are not a function of size but seem to be determined by conditions such as population density; the local economy (poverty and unemployment rates, wage scales, and the gap between rich and poor); special problems (the easy availability of illegal handguns, the extent of drug trafficking, and the ineffectiveness of police strategies); traditions and customs (including the persistence of a subculture that condones violence); and demographic factors (especially divorce rates, and the proportion of the population that is poor, male, young, and of marginalized minority group

background) (Tardiff, Gross, and Messner, 1986; Chilton, 1987; Land, McCall, and Cohen, 1990; Messner and Golden, 1992).

To complicate matters further, murder rates vary dramatically within the confines of a city. Homicides take place more often in low-income neighborhoods than in wealthy communities in the same city. Some upscale urban areas are rarely scenes of a slaying while the mean streets on the "wrong side of the tracks" are virtual battlefields between rival street gangs, drug dealing crews, or hostile factions of organized crime. Also, neighborhood homicide rates can flare up or die down substantially from year to year as local conditions deteriorate or improve (see Karmen, 2000).

Besides where one resides, one's sex is another crucial determinant of risks. More than three-quarters of those who are murdered annually are males—a proportion that has remained roughly the same since at least the early 1960s. Expressed as rates, boys and men are killed almost four times as often as girls and women.

Besides geographical location and sex, murder rates vary dramatically by age (see Akiyama, 1981). Ten-year-olds are the least likely age group to be slain. The risks of being murdered rise during the teenage years and peak during the early twenties, but then drop substantially as a person grows older.

Statistically, race turns out to be the most important demographic factor associated with differential risks and has been for many years (see Wood, 1990). African Americans confront much graver dangers of dying violently, and Asian Americans much lower risks. Recall that 50 percent of all the people slain in 2006 were African Americans. Because almost 14 percent of Americans identified themselves as people of African descent on the 2006 Census, these *UCR* calculations confirm that black communities across the country suffer from disproportionately high rates of lethal violence. This burden is underscored by another *UCR* statistic: although black males make up only a little more than 6 percent of the population, they suffered 42 percent of all violent deaths nationwide. Black females comprise roughly 7 percent of all Americans and nearly 8 percent of all victims, so those proportions were not out of line, statistically speaking. About 34 percent of those slain were white males, and roughly 13 percent were white females. The remainder were males and females of Asian descent, or the corpses could not be classified.

From this review of the demographic factors that are correlated with murder rates, a profile can be drawn of groups of people who run the greatest risks of suddenly dying from an act of violence. They are southerners, urban residents, males, teenagers and young adults between 18 and 24, and African Americans. Low-income people fall into this high-risk group as well, but police files and FBI compilations do not collect information about the social class of the deceased. Nevertheless, the high body counts in poverty-stricken neighbors underscore the connection between violence and economic status. Those who fall into the opposite groups face the lowest risks of all: northeasterners, residents of small towns in rural areas, females, children and the elderly, whites and Asians, and the wealthy.

Since World War II—and in particular between the mid-1980s and the mid-1990s—the most ominous change concerning homicides has been the trend of the decreasing age of both killers and victims. Criminologists attribute the escalation in lethal violence among teenagers to: the revival of street gangs and the formation of drug-dealing outfits, teens' willingness to resort to force to settle even minor disputes, their easier access to handguns, and their involvement with cocaine and alcohol. As the 1990s drew to a close and the new century began, these pressing problems subsided (Blumstein, 1995; Brownstein, 1996; Blumstein and Rosenfeld, 1998; Karmen, 2000; Lynch, 2002).

Making International Comparisons

When bringing the big picture into focus, it is important to remember that victimization rates vary dramatically not only from time to time and place to place within the United States, but also from society to society. Cross-national comparisons that reveal the magnitude of the crime problem in other countries can yield valuable clues about the causes of illegal behavior, as well as suggestions for innovative policies for prevention and control.

Two main sources of data about victimization rates in other countries are the United Nations, which periodically surveys its members, and the International Police Organization (Interpol), which has cooperative relationships with law enforcement agencies around the world. The European Union (EU) collects data from the criminal justice systems of its member states.

For a number of reasons, however, making **international comparisons** can be difficult, and hasty conclusions can be misleading. First of all, many governments do not routinely disclose reliable and up-to-date data about their crime rates, or they publish figures that seem unrealistically low, probably because they fear that high rates will damage their nations' public images and scare off potential tourists and investors. Even when governments make an effort to be cooperative and to carry out accurate measurements, problems arise because of differences in definitions (for example, of rape, robbery, and burglary) and in reporting and record-keeping practices. Researchers who studied cross-national crime data came to these conclusions: Compared to other nations providing trustworthy statistics, U.S. victimization rates for violent crimes were very high, those for auto theft were fairly high, and those for burglary were near the middle of the range (Kalish, 1988). Violence is more of a problem in the United States than in many other highly developed societies, but theft is not (Zimring and Hawkins, 1997).

The U.N.'s World Health Organization (WHO) keeps track of homicides in most countries across the globe. But its statistics on murder in various societies must be interpreted with great caution. Each country's definitions of wrongful killings reflect laws and local customs that govern the way deaths are classified. For international comparisons to be valid, definitions of the types of killings that constitute murder must be consistent. For example, certain countries may count attempted murders, but in the United States (and many other societies) cases in which wounded people survive are classified as aggravated assaults. Other inconsistencies result if a nation's body count includes deaths from legal interventions (such as the use of deadly force by police officers and executions), totally unintentional deaths (like negligent manslaughter and vehicular homicides), and self-induced deaths (suicides)—all of which are excluded from U.S. figures (Kalish, 1988).

The latest available credible and consistent data from Interpol (for 1999–2001), the WHO (for 2002), and the European Union (2004-2006) is presented in Table 4.1. The data indicate that residents of the United States have much more to worry about than people who live in Canada, Australia, New Zealand, Japan, and most of the industrialized countries in Europe. The exceptions are the three Baltic states and Russia. The extremely high rate of inter-personal violence in South Africa reflects the continuing turmoil resulting from colonization, impoverishment, and the racist apartheid policies that were finally dismantled during the early 1990s.

Some of the developing nations of Asia, Africa, and Latin America report low homicide rates while others suffer from very high levels of criminal violence, but these statistics are not listed in this table. Note that some of the killings that boost the body count in strife-torn societies across the globe are not the outgrowth of "ordinary" street crime but are the result of intense political polarization, expressed as vigilantism, terrorism, and low-intensity guerrilla warfare.

Because some societies are strikingly different from others in their economic systems, criminal justice systems, cultural traditions, and age distributions, it might make more sense to limit comparisons of murder rates to fairly similar, highly industrialized nations. Because a key determinant of the murder rate in any country is simply the proportion of the population that falls into the highest risk group (young males), one way to deal with variations is to calculate the homicide rate for every 100,000 teenage boys and young men in each society. Following this procedure and then restricting the comparison only to other highly industrialized societies, the United States stood out as having the worst murder rate during the late 1980s (Deane, 1987; Rosenthal, 1990).

When the murder rates in different nations were analyzed, higher rates tended to be associated with great economic inequality (huge gaps between the wealthy and the poor), limited government funding of social programs for the disadvantaged, cultural supports for "legitimate" violence by government officials and agencies (frequent executions and periodic warfare), family breakdown (high divorce rates), high rates of female participation in the labor force, and ethnic heterogeneity (see Gartner, 1990).

Clearly, geographic location—where a person resides—is a major factor that determines murder risks around the globe. Just as substantial variations emerged between different U.S. cities (refer back to Figure 4.4), so too do foreign cities vary greatly in the dangers their residents face. The wide range of murder rates in the world's leading cities is evident in Table 4.2. Note that cities, which have much smaller populations than entire countries, have the potential to show more volatility in homicide rates per 100,000 inhabitants over the years; the rampages of a relatively small number of offenders can have a noticeable statistical impact.

The reported rates assembled in Table 4.1 confirm that the leading city in each nation generally has a higher murder rate than in the rest of that country.

TABLE 4.1   Murder Rates across the Globe: Selected Countries

Country	Murder Rate per 100,000 Inhabitants, Three-Year Average, 1999–2001 Interpol	Murder Rate per 100,000 Inhabitants, 2002 WHO	Murder Rate per 100,000 Inhabitants, Three-Year Average, 2004–2006 EU*
Australia	2	2	1
Austria	1	1	1
Belgium	2	2	2
Bulgaria	4	3	3
Canada	2	2	2
Cyprus	1	0	2
Czech Republic	3	1	1
Denmark	1	1	1
Estonia	11	15	7
Finland	3	3	2
France	2	1	2
Germany	1	1	1
Greece	1	1	2
Hungary	2	2	1
Ireland	1	1	1
Italy	2	1	1
Japan	1	1	7
Latvia	6	13	7
Lithuania	11	11	10
Malta	1	2	1
Netherlands	2	1	1
New Zealand	3	1	1
Norway	1	1	1
Poland	2	2	1
Portugal	1	1	1
Romania	2	4	2
Russia	22	33	16
Slovakia	3	2	2
South Africa	56	43	47
Spain	1	1	1
Sweden	1	1	1
Switzerland	1	1	1
Turkey	3	3	6
United Kingdom	2	1	2
United States	6	6	6

NOTE: Figures for Australia, Canada, Czech Republic, Japan, and South Africa in column 4 are for 2006 only.
SOURCES: Barclay and Tavares, 2003 (Interpol); WHO, 2004 (UN); Tavares and Thomas, 2008 (EU).
* Also *UCR*, Statistics Canada (Juristat), national police websites, and newspaper reports.

New Yorkers have much more to fear (even after public safety improved in 2007, dipping down to six murders per 100,000) than the inhabitants of any other great city except Moscow. Tokyo, the largest city listed, was the most peaceful place of all.

As for trends over time, Table 4.2 indicates that there is no evidence of dramatic changes and certainly no signs of any alarming upsurge in urban violence worldwide. During the first years of the 21st century, most cities that are important to the global economy and to tourism experienced relatively stable murder rates. Those who are killed are almost always permanent residents of a city; travelers, individuals on business trips, conventioneers, and other visitors rarely get caught up in deadly confrontations far from home (see Karmen, 2000).

TABLE 4.2   Murder Rates across the Globe: Selected Cities

Country – City	Murder Rate per 100,000 Residents Three-Year Average, 1999–2001, Interpol	Murder Rate per 100,000 Residents Three-Year Average, 2004–2006, EU*
Australia – Sydney	2	1
Austria – Vienna	3	1
Belgium – Brussels	3	3
Canada –		
Montreal	2	1
Toronto	2	2
Czech Republic – Prague	4	na
Denmark – Copenhagen	2	2
Finland – Helsinki	2	2
France – Paris	2	1
Germany – Berlin	2	2
Greece – Athens	1	1
Hungary – Budapest	2	2
Ireland – Dublin	1	2
Italy – Rome	1	1
Japan – Tokyo	1	1
Netherlands – Amsterdam	3	3
Norway – Oslo	2	2
Poland – Warsaw	4	2
Portugal – Lisbon	2	1
Russia – Moscow	18	10
Spain – Madrid	2	1
Sweden – Stockholm	3	na
Switzerland – Geneva	2	na
Turkey – Ankara	3	5
New Zealand – Wellington	2	3
United Kingdom – London	3	2
United States – New York	8	7

NOTE: na = not available
SOURCES: Barclay and Tavares, 2003 (Interpol); WHO, 2004 (UN); Tavares and Thomas, 2008 (EU).
*Also *UCR*, Statistics Canada (Juristat), national police websites, and newspaper reports.

ASSESSING COMPARATIVE RISKS: PUTTING CRIME INTO PERSPECTIVE

Another important way to grasp the big picture involves weighing the relative threats posed by different types of misfortunes. The chance of being harmed by a criminal needs to be compared to the odds of being hurt in an accident or of contracting a serious illness. The study of **comparative risks** rests on estimates of the likelihoods of experiencing various negative life events. One purpose of studying comparative risks is to determine what kinds of threats (crimes, accidents, or diseases) merit greater precautionary measures by both individuals and government-sponsored campaigns. (A list of calamities could be expanded to include plagues, fires, and natural disasters such as floods, tornadoes, earthquakes, and hurricanes.) Once the chances of being stricken by dreaded events are expressed in a standardized way (as rates per 100,000 people) the dangers can be compared, as they are in Table 4.3.

TABLE 4.3   Comparing the Risks of Death Posed by Crime, Accidents, and Certain Diseases, 2006

Cause of Death	Death Rate per 100,000 All Americans	Death Rate per 100,000 Persons 15–24 years old
All causes	810	82
Heart Problems (cardiovascular disease)	210	2
Cancers (malignant neoplasms)	187	4
Strokes (cerebrovascular disease)	46	1
Lung Problems (pulmonary diseases)	42	Fewer than 1
Diabetes	24	Fewer than 1
Influenza, pneumonia	19	Fewer than 1
Motor vehicle accidents	15	26
Other accidents	25	12
Suicides ("intentional self-harm")	11	10
Homicides (including legal intervention) ["assault"]	6	13

SOURCES: Center for Disease Control and Prevention's National Center for Health Statistics, Vital Statistics Report, 2008.

The nationwide data assembled in the first column of Table 4.3 for people of all ages, both sexes, and varying backgrounds indicates that the number of deaths from natural causes greatly exceeded losses of life from external causes. In particular, heart disease, cancer, and stroke were by far the leading causes of death in the United States during the early twenty-first century, including 2006. As for other untimely demises, more people died from accidents than from homicide (murders plus deaths by "legal intervention"—justifiable homicides by police officers as well as executions of death row prisoners). In fact, more people took their own lives through suicides than lost them due to lethal violence, which ranked at the bottom of the list. Tentatively, it can be concluded that most people worry too much about being murdered.

However, dying violently is something for young adults to be concerned about, as the second column in Table 4.3 shows. The usefulness of comparing the death rates assembled in the first column of Table 4.3 to each other is limited because these figures describe the risks faced by the "average" American, a social construct that each person resembles to some extent. But the actual odds a specific individual faces may differ tremendously from this fictitious composite norm.

The most important determinants of mortality rates are age, sex, race/ethnicity, social class, and place of residence. To make more meaningful comparisons, some of these key variables, especially age, must be controlled, or held constant (see Fingerhut, Ingram, and Feldman, 1992a, 1992b). For example, for Americans between the ages of 15 and 24, homicide was the second leading cause of death, after car crashes. Accidents (not involving motor vehicles) and suicides claimed substantial numbers of lives too. But few teenagers and young adults died from heart attacks, cancer, strokes, influenza, HIV/ AIDS, or other diseases (NCHS, 2005), as the second column in Table 4.3 reveals. Whereas suicides outnumber homicides for "the average American," the opposite is true for people between the ages of 15 to 24. Also, although not shown in the table, within every age group, being murdered loomed as a greater danger to boys and men than to girls and women, and to racial minorities as compared to members of the white majority.

Another problem with risk comparisons is that the ranking represents a snapshot image of a fluid situation. Thus, Table 4.3 captures a moment frozen in time—the relative standing of dangers of accidents, diseases, and crime in 2006. But it cannot depict underlying trends.

For example, an encouraging downward trend in fatal accidents took place during the 1980s. Deaths due to plane crashes, falls, drownings, fires, and poisonings all dropped during that decade, probably as a result of greater safety consciousness, new devices such as smoke detectors and car seats for children, and new policies such as mandatory seat belt laws and tougher penalties for drunk driving. By 1990, the risk of dying in a car crash had fallen to its lowest level since the 1920s, according to a study by the National Safety Council (Hall, 1990). During the 1990s, the chances of being murdered diminished impressively, as did the odds of perishing shortly after contracting full-blown HIV/AIDS. As the chances of dying from a particular disease, a terrible accident, or a fatal assault rise or fall over time, listings of comparative risks must undergo periodic revision.

To further complicate the picture, occupation must be taken into account when comparing the risks of becoming a homicide victim to the risk of suffering a fatal injury at work. Risks are closely tied to tasks; some jobs are far more dangerous than others. Focusing on deaths in the workplace, studies conducted by the National Institute for Safety and Health and by the federal government's Bureau of Labor Statistics established that fatal accidents take place most often in jobs related to construction, farming and forestry, and transportation. Putting accidents aside, researchers discovered that certain lines of work, such as law enforcement and cab driving, carry much greater risks of being murdered on the job. (See Chapter 11 for a discussion of deaths at work.)

In sum, individuals face widely varying risks of being murdered, depending on which groups they fall into (who they are, where they live, and what they do on a daily basis).

FOCUSING ON ROBBERIES

Robbers usually are complete strangers on the prowl for suitable prey; therefore they are among the most feared and hated of all street criminals. The offense combines stealing with extortion or outright violence (often including the use of weapons), so it carries some of the stiffest prison sentences permissible under law. And yet, throughout history, bandits were considered much more interesting than their victims, and their exploits were often romanticized. The highwaymen of Robin Hood's band, pirates who plundered ships laden with treasure, frontier outlaws who ambushed stagecoaches and trains, and gangsters who held up banks during the Great Depression—all were the subjects of stories and songs sympathetic to, or at least understanding of, the impulses that drove their dramatic deeds. But the glitter has largely faded, and in its place is the image of the mugger or gunman as a vicious thug, a cruel predator, and an exploiter of weakness—one whose random violence casts a shadow over everyday life. This reversal in the imagery of robbers has sparked renewed concern for their victims.

Robbers and Their Victims

Completed robberies are face-to-face confrontations in which perpetrators take something of value directly from victims against their will, either by force or by threats of violence. Whether the hold-up is completed or just attempted, the law considers armed robberies more serious than unarmed ones (**strong-arm robberies**, **muggings**, or **yokings**). Successful robbers, armed or unarmed, are skilled at "target manipulation" or "victim management" (Letkemann, 1973). From a close-up, symbolic-interactionist perspective within sociology, victim-offender moves and responses can be analyzed as a set of complementary roles. Robbers are the initiators and aggressors; the people they are preparing to pounce upon are usually passive, at least at the start. But the individuals who discover that they are under attack can refuse to play their assigned role, reject the script, and struggle against the scenario imposed on them. The intended prey might even gain the upper hand, switch roles, and disrupt the final act, or end it in a way dreaded by the aggressors. In other words, the incident may or may not proceed according to the offender's game plan. When analyzed as a transaction based on **instrumental coercion** (applying force to accomplish a goal), a typical robbery proceeds through five stages or phases: planning, establishing co-presence, developing co-orientation, transferring valuables, and leaving (Best and Luckenbill, 1982).

1. During the planning stage the offenders prepare to strike by choosing accomplices, weapons, sites, getaway routes—and intended targets. They look for certain favorable characteristics, such as valuable possessions, vulnerability to attack, relative powerlessness to resist, and isolation from potential protectors. Strangers are preferred because they will have greater difficulty in providing descriptions to the police and in identifying suspects from pictures or lineups.

2. During the second phase of the interaction, the offenders establish **co-presence** by moving within striking distance. The robbers try not to arouse their intended prey's suspicion or to provoke either unmanageable opposition or fright and flight. Some offenders rely on speed and stealth to approach unsuspecting individuals. Others employ deceit to trick people into letting down their guard.

3. The third stage is developing **co-orientation.** At this stage the robbers announce their intentions to dominate the situation and exploit their advantages. They order their targets to surrender valuables, and they demand compliance. Their prey can either acquiesce or may contest the robbers' bid to take charge, depending on an assessment of the aggressors' **punitive resources** (ability to inflict injury). Robbers who fail to develop co-orientation (to secure cooperation and submission) through threats may resort to violence to intimidate or incapacitate their opponents.

4. If the robbers successfully gain and maintain the upper hand, the interaction moves into its fourth phase. Victims are searched and their valuables are seized. But the interaction is terminated prematurely (from the offenders' point of view) if the targets uncooperatively resist, have no valuables, are unexpectedly rescued, or escape.

5. The fifth stage is the exit. It is marked by the robbers' attempts to break off the relationship at a time and under conditions of their choosing. As they prepare to leave the scene, they may inflict injuries to prevent interference with the getaway, or they may issue threats about the dangers of pursuing them or reporting the crime to the authorities (Best and Luckenbill, 1982).

This breakdown of robbery transactions into distinct stages and discrete steps facilitates the recognition of possible outcomes. Targeted individuals may or may not suffer financial losses from stolen (or damaged) property. Robbers may or may not injure their victims at the outset or at the end. Their casualties may or may not need medical attention and hospital care. The prey may or may not be able to resist the aggressors' advances and may be able to prevent successful completions of the unwanted transference of valuables. Officers on patrol may or may not become involved. And a very small proportion who resist may be killed in tragic incidents that escalate from robbery to homicide (see below).

Using the *NCVS* to Analyze Robberies

Because nearly all robbery victims live to tell about their experiences, more details can be gathered about them than about people who were murdered. Some limited information about robberies that were reported to and solved by local police departments appears annually in the FBI's *UCR*; the data indicate the number of incidents and describe the people who were arrested—but not the people who were accosted. The *NCVS* and not the *UCR* is the source to tap to find out "how often, who, how, where, when," plus information concerning losses, injuries, stolen property recovery rates, and reactions during the confrontations.

Respondents in the sample who confided that they had been robbed within the past six months provided *NCVS* interviewers with a wealth of data. They described the assailants who robbed them and the weapons used against them, and they disclosed whether the robbers got what they were after, where and when the crimes took place, if they resisted, whether they got hurt, and if so, how seriously. The answers from these unfortunate individuals in the sample were used to derive projections about the experiences of all Americans over the age of 11 who were robbed. To simplify matters, only single victim/single offender incidents will be analyzed.

Interviewers for the BJS's *NCVS* discovered that in 2006, only a little more than half (57 percent) of the people they questioned who disclosed that they had been robbed during that year also had told the police about their harrowing experiences. Victims were more likely to inform law enforcement agencies about incidents that involved physical injuries and substantial losses. Blacks were much more inclined to report robberies (75 percent) than whites (53 percent) but Hispanics were far less willing (41 percent). Females were just about as likely to turn to the police for help (56 percent) as males (58 percent). Teenagers were reluctant to call upon the authorities for help (only 40 percent did) while senior citizens over age 65 readily did (75 percent), with other age groups falling between these extremes. Most (61 percent) of the confrontations took place in or near the victims' homes or within one mile of them, and most (58 percent) occurred at night (between 6 pm and 6 am).

The primary motive behind robbery is theft. But offenders did not always get what they wanted. Almost one-third (32 percent) of robberies ended up as unsuccessful attempts to steal cash and valuables. The average (median) loss in successful robberies was $175. Most often, victims were relieved of personal effects such as portable electronic or photographic gear, and jewelry, followed by purses and wallets containing credit cards and cash. Nearly 85 percent of these robbery victims never recovered any of these valuables on their own or after an investigation by the police. Over ten percent lost time (often several days) from work because of the crime.

The people who were robbed did not recognize their assailants in most cases (76 percent). However, males more often than females told survey interviewers that the assailants who used or threatened force were complete strangers they had never seen before. The overwhelming majority (83 percent) of robbers were males.

In about two-fifths (41 percent) of all the robberies that took place in 2006, the assailant was unarmed. Of the attackers (usually strangers) that brandished some kind of weapon, more than one-fifth (22 percent) had a firearm (almost always a handgun). In the remainder of the armed robberies, offenders most often used knives, followed by other sharp and blunt instruments, and then other assorted weapons to intimidate and subdue targets.

Robbers, armed or not, hurt their victims for a number of reasons. They may do so initially to intimidate the target into submission. They may become violent during the hold-up in reaction to resistance, lack of cooperation, or stalling. Offenders may relish taking advantage of a helpless person or may seize the opportunity to show off to accomplices. Injuring their targets may be a sign of panic, disappointment in the haul, anger, scorn, contempt, sadism, or loss of self-control. Unleashing violence may also be instrumental: Wounding individuals can render them incapable of later identifying the robbers, pursuing them, or even calling for help. Explosive outbursts at the end of the transaction may be intended to shock, stun, or preoccupy victims, their associates, and any bystanders so that they will hesitate to summon the police.

Despite all these possible motives for inflicting injuries, most robbers didn't wound their victims. Only a little more than one-third of those who suffered either completed or attempted robberies were wounded (34 percent of males, 39 percent of females; and 46 percent of blacks and 35 percent of whites). However, some who escaped injuries were grabbed, shoved, and otherwise roughed up. Among the wounded, most victims experienced minor injuries, such as cuts, scratches, bruises, and swellings. A small proportion suffered serious injuries, such as broken bones, lost teeth, loss of consciousness, or gunshot wounds that required medical care in a hospital emergency room. About one in 9 robbery victims incurred medical expenses, usually from visiting a hospital emergency room.

Whether to resist an attack is one of the most controversial and practical issues probed by interviewers carrying out the National Crime Victimization Survey. Different resistance strategies lead to different outcomes. People targeted by robbers must make a split-second decision—whether to flee, fight, or otherwise resist; or to surrender and cooperate.

NCVS interviewers ask about two sets of self-protective strategies: one embraces force to repel an attacker, including brandishing and using a gun, knife, or other weapon; or fighting back bare-handed to drive off or even capture the assailant. The other set centers on nonviolent strategies: trying to escape, screaming to frighten the offender and summon help, and threatening or reasoning with one's adversary. Of course, during a confrontation a person might resort to more than one of these strategies. By combining the different self-protective measures, most robbery victims tried to defend themselves in 2005: 56 percent of males, 64 percent of females; 58 percent of whites, 70 percent of blacks.

People were a little more inclined to put up resistance if the assailant was someone they knew or recognized (67 percent) as opposed to a complete stranger (56 percent). The most common protective strategy was trying to physically resist or even capture the offender, followed by an attempt to run away or hide, trying to reason with or scare off the offender, or shouting for help. Fighting back barehanded was also a common reaction, but drawing a weapon in self-defense was rarely tried or possible (Bureau of Justice Statistics, 2008).

Starting in 1986, questions were added to the National Crime Victimization Survey about how victims judged the consequences of the self-protective measures they undertook in the heat of battle. In 2006, most of the robbery victims (59 percent) told NCVS interviewers that their self-protective actions probably helped their situation; while only about 8 percent concluded their reactions hurt them. In the opinion of the remainder of the sample, their actions both helped and hurt, neither helped nor hurt, or had an unknown

effect on the offenders. Of those who believed their actions helped, the benefit was to minimize or prevent injuries to themselves, to ward off their attackers, to facilitate their escape, and to safeguard the items the robbers sought. As for unwanted outcomes, some victims who took self-protective measures reported that their actions made their assailants angrier and more aggressive.

One research project concluded that armed robberies that began with the brandishing of a gun or knife were less likely to escalate into bloodshed because the threat posed by the deadly weapon was sufficient to convince most victims to surrender without a struggle (Cook, 1987). A study of nearly 3,000 stranger-to-stranger incidents reported to NCVS interviewers between 1973 and 1979 yielded these observations: Nonforceful resistance—which included reasoning with, arguing with, and verbally threatening the offender, as well as yelling for help or trying to run away—was statistically linked to both lower monetary losses and reduced levels of physical attack and injury. Forceful resistance—fighting back barehanded or with a weapon—was also associated with lower property losses but higher injury rates (Block and Skogan, 1986). Similarly, an analysis of more than 4,500 incidents from 1979 to 1985 resulted in these conclusions: Any form of self-protective tactic reduced the chances that the robber would get away with valuables. Armed resistance was a much more effective form of self-protection than unarmed resistance. Drawing a gun was the most effective response for thwarting the robbers' intentions and avoiding injuries, but it was very rarely possible or attempted. Fighting back without a weapon, and calling for help to attract attention and scare off the attacker, tended to lead to injuries. Facing a gun inhibited resistance, but because robbers rarely fired, most stickup victims lost their possessions but escaped injury (Kleck and DeLone, 1993).

It is tempting but dangerous to offer advice based on the successes and failures reported to NCVS interviewers by people who confronted robbers. The outcomes of robberies in terms of both injuries and losses are determined by a complex web of interactions among offenders' initiatives: choice of weapon and target; victims' responses: unwillingness to cooperate; offenders' re-actions to resistance: willingness to escalate or to give up and disengage; bystanders' initiatives: will-ingness to intervene; and other situational factors—number of offenders, number of victims, location, time, value of property at risk. Consequently, no simple rules of thumb or foolproof stratagems can be derived from the data.

Some experts suggest that people who dread being robbed should always carry sums of money they feel they can afford to lose and should hand over these "crime taxes" immediately to appease robbers' demands. Others argue that victims can help deter crime by employing various strategies, depending on the circumstances, that make robbery attempts unprofitable, frustrating, and even danger-ous for aggressors (see Ziegenhagen and Brosnan, 1985; Kleck and DeLone, 1993).

Because some studies indicated that victims who complied with robbers' demands were more likely to escape injury, criminal justice officials rec-ommend trading valuables for personal safety (see Celona, Williams, and Greene, 2005). For exam-ple, one small-town police department proposed that during a confrontation, the victim should try to stay calm and do exactly as the robber com-mands. They advised not resisting or doing any-thing to upset the perpetrator, such as making sudden moves. Victims should give the bandit time to leave, but try to get a good description of him and his vehicle, and note the direction he takes as he flees. Do not try to be a hero, the department reminded its local citizens, because it is better to lose your money than your life (Police Department, Cary, NC, 2007).

Checking Out Whether More Robberies Are Turning into Murders

Because robbery is such a potentially devastating crime, the question arises, "How often do robberies escalate into murders?" In other words, what are the chances of being killed by a robber? Robbers may wound their victims (and perhaps inadver-tently kill them) to quell resistance or to prevent them from reporting the crime, pressing charges, and testifying in court.

Some people have the impression that robbers kill more readily "these days" than in the past. It is part of a gloomy perception that American society is falling apart, that civilization is collapsing, and that predators today are more depraved than ever before. In the aftermath of a vicious slaying, jour-nalists sometimes play up this theme. This is noth-ing new.

For example, during the "good old days" of the 1940s and 1950s, when street crime was not a major issue in electoral campaigns because it wasn't per-ceived to be a pressing problem, some people feared robbers would kill them even if they surrendered without a fight and cooperated. A reporter at the time (Whitman, 1951, p. 5) wrote: "The hoodlum will bash in your head with a brick for a dollar and ninety-eight cents. The police records of our cities are spotted with cases of 'murder for peanuts' in which the victims, both men and women, have been slugged, stabbed, hit with iron pipes, hammers, or axes, and in a few cases kicked to death—the loot being no more than the carfare a woman carried in her purse or the small change in a man's pocket."

Several decades later *Newsweek*'s cover story (Press et al., 1981, p. 48) titled "The Plague of Violent Crime," observed: "Another frightening difference in the crime picture is that life is now pitifully cheap. Law enforcement officials think they have witnessed a shift toward gratuitous slaughter. 'It used to be 'Your money or your life,' says a Bronx assistant district attorney.... Now it's 'Your money and your life.'"

Is it true, as some people suspect, that more and more robberies are escalating into murders (see Cook, 1985; and 1987)? Victimologists can com-bine *UCR* statistics on murders and *NCVS* findings about robberies to shed some light on this grisly question (see the data assembled in Table 4.4 inside Box 4.1).

BOX 4.1 "Your Money or Your Life!"

The number of people killed by robbers each year can be estimated from *UCR* figures of the numbers of murders and the motives of the killers, as established by the detectives who solved these cases. The number of robberies committed annually can be estimated from *NCVS* figures. *UCR* figures are smaller because they represent only the robberies known to the police. Because *NCVS* figures exclude robberies of establishments like convenience stores and banks, they also underestimate the actual but unknown combined total of personal and commercial robberies. Also note that a study of robbery-related homicides in Baltimore during 1983 revealed serious problems in the way deaths are classified. In a considerable proportion of all murders, detectives cannot figure out the motives for the slayings. And in some robbery-murders, the killer robbed the deceased person's corpse as an afterthought (see Loftin, 1986).

Acknowledging the problems of uncertainty and incompatibility cited above, rough calculations can be performed to derive ballpark estimates of how often targeted individuals—whether they are cooperating or resisting—are murdered by robbers (see Table 4.4).

Several tentative conclusions can be reached from this statistical evidence drawn from official sources: In

a declining proportion of all murders (11 percent in 1980; 7 percent in 2000 and 2006), the offender's motive was to use deadly force to take something of value and then escape. The nationwide annual death toll is disturbing. Nearly 2,500 people died at the hands of robbers in 1980, and more than 1,000 perished in 2006. But, thankfully, slayings committed during the course of hold-ups are rare, considering the huge numbers of confrontations (well over a million in 1980, roughly half a million in 2006) in which a life could have been taken along with money or possessions.

Hence, people who are killed constitute a tragic but tiny proportion—about one-fifth of 1 percent—of all who are accosted. That means that about 99.8 percent survive the ordeal. Furthermore, there is no consistent and pronounced upward trend, so no solid evidence supports the contention that as time passes, robbers are becoming more inclined to snuff out the lives of their targets.

A detailed study of more than 100 solved homicides that occurred in Chicago during 1983 concluded that when confronted by an armed offender who growls, "Your money or your life!" statistics confirm that the correct response is to hand over the money and hang on to your life (Zimring and Zuehl, 1986).

T A B L E 4.4   Yearly Estimates of Murders Committed During Robberies

	1980	1990	2000	2006
Number of persons murdered (from the *UCR*)	23,040	23,438	15,586	15,854
Percentage of murders where robbery was the motive (from the *UCR*)	11	9	7	7
Number of robbery victims killed (from the *UCR*)	2,488	2,156	1,077	1,041
Total number of robbery victims (from the *NCVS*)	1,179,000	1,150,000	732,000	484,000
Murdered victims as a percentage of all robbery victims	0.21%	0.19%	0.14%	0.22%

SOURCES: FBI's *UCR*, 1980, 1990, 2000, 2006; BJS's *NCVS*, 1980, 1990, 2000, 2006.

Differential Risks of Being Robbed

According to the *NCVS* for 2006, the robbery rate was 2.9 per 1,000. That means nearly 3 individuals out of every 1,000 residents over the age of 11 got robbed that year. But, just as with murder rates, sharp differences in robbery risks become evident when the odds facing the "average" American are disaggregated or deconstructed. Breaking down the

NCVS sample into subcategories, certain demographic groupings were robbed much more often than others, as Table 4.5 demonstrates.

To put the issue bluntly, some people have much more to fear than others. Starting with sex, the first pattern that stands out is that robbers target males more often than females. Males are held up nearly twice as often as females (3.9 compared to

TABLE 4.5   Robbery Rates for Various Groups, 2006

Victim Characteristics	2006 Rate
Overall rate	2.9
Sex	
Male	3.9
Female	2.0
Race and Ethnicity	
White	2.8
Black	3.8
Other	2.7
Hispanic	4.9
Age	
12–15	4.0
16–19	4.6
20–24	7.3
25–34	4.6
35–49	2.0
50–64	1.3
65 and older	1.1
Marital status	
Married	1.1
Widowed	1.1
Divorced or Separated	4.1
Never married	5.6
Family income	
Less than $7,500	7.2
$7,500–$14,999	6.5
$15,000–$24,999	4.2
$25,000–$34,999	5.3
$35,000–$49,999	1.5
$50,000–$74,999	2.2
$75,000 or more	2.0
Residence*	
Urban	4.4
Suburban	2.2
Rural	1.4*

*Rate for rural areas is not available for 2006; 2005 figures are provided.
NOTE: Rates are per 1,000 people with these characteristics per year.
SOURCES: BJS's *NCVS* of 2006; Rand and Catalano, 2007; BJS, 2008.

2.0 per 1,000). With regard to race and ethnicity, the rates suffered by Hispanics and blacks are substantially higher than the rates for whites and others (mostly Americans of Asian ancestry). As for age, the analysis of the survey's findings revealed that younger people (between the ages of 12 and 34) were accosted much more often than older people. Individuals in their early twenties faced the gravest risks of all in 2006. After those peak years, risks

decline steadily with advancing age. Contrary to the impression that robbers prey primarily upon the elderly and frail, senior citizens are singled out the least often of any age group.

Family income appeared to be negatively correlated with victimization rates. As income increased, the chances of being robbed generally decreased, with two exceptions. Ironically, the desperately poor were robbed of their meager possessions much more often than others. Residents of urban areas were targeted more often than suburbanites and inhabitants of small towns and rural areas (Rennison, 1999; Catalano, 2005; and NCVS, 2008).

In addition to sex, age, race/ethnicity, income, and area of residence, marital status made a big difference: Individuals who had never been married or who were separated or divorced endured much higher robbery rates than either married or widowed people, who generally were older and tended to be female. Chances are, most robbers don't check for wedding rings before striking. This pattern provides an important clue that will be used to explain differential risks.

To sum up the patterns gleaned from Table 4.5, higher risks were faced by men than women, minorities than whites, younger people than middle-aged or elderly people, single individuals than married couples, poor people than those who are better off financially, and city residents than those living in suburbs or small towns. Combining these factors, the profile of the person facing the gravest dangers of all is an impoverished, young, Hispanic or black man living in an inner city neighborhood. Affluent, elderly white ladies living in rural areas lead the safest lives.

Unfortunately, the *NCVS* does not calculate a victimization rate for comparison purposes for an individual who falls into all the high-risk or all the low-risk subcategories. However, the survey findings indicated that black teenage boys between the ages of 16 and 19 (falling into the higher risk groups for race, sex, and age) were robbed at a frighteningly high rate of 30 out of every 1,000 (for 2005; comparable figures for 2006 are not available). If these black teenage boys also live in low-income families that reside in big cities (thereby falling into all five of the high-risk categories), then they probably suffer a robbery victimization rate that is off the charts compared with people from other backgrounds.

One additional variable is worthy of consideration—occupation. Robbery rates differ substantially depending on the nature of a person's work. Statistics from the *NCVS* indicated that people holding the following (generally less desirable) jobs were much more likely to be robbed: taxi drivers, gardeners, busboys, dishwashers, carnival and amusement park workers, car wash attendants, messengers, newspaper carriers, peddlers, and certain construction workers. However, musicians and composers, painters and sculptors, and photographers also were victimized at above-average rates. Least likely to be accosted were inspectors, line workers, bank tellers, opticians, farmers, professional athletes, elementary school teachers, engineers, and psychologists (Block, Felson, and Block, 1985). A more recent study determined that retail sales workers, especially clerks at convenience stores and liquor stores, were robbed the most, along with cab drivers. College professors faced the lowest risks of being robbed (Warchol, 1998).

Differential risks also show up clearly when a particular kind of robbery—carjacking—is the focus of attention (see Box 4.2).

PROJECTING CUMULATIVE RISKS

Yearly victimization rates might lull some people into a false sense of security. Annual rates give the impression that crime is a rare event. Only a handful of people out of every thousand fall prey to offenders; most people get through a year unscathed. But fears about victimization do not conform to a January-to-December cycle. People worry that they might be robbed, raped, or murdered at some point during their lives.

Estimates of the **cumulative risks** of victimization, viewed over a span of 60 or more years (from age 12 into the 70s, the average life expectancy in the United States today), yield a very

different picture of the seriousness of the contemporary crime problem nationally. What appears to be a rare event in any given year looms as a real threat over the course of an entire lifetime (Koppel, 1987), according to the gloomy projections in Table 4.6.

Over a span of about 60 years, nearly everybody will experience at least one theft, and most people may eventually suffer three or more thefts, according to the projections made on the basis of rates that prevailed during the 1970s and 1980s, as presented in Table 4.6. Although the chance that a girl or woman will be raped in a given year is minuscule, it rises to a lifetime threat of 80 per 1,000, or 8 percent (about 1 female in every 12). For black females the risk is somewhat greater (at 11 percent, or nearly 1 in 9) over a lifetime. Robbery is a more common crime, so the projection is that about 30 percent of the population will be robbed at least once over a 60-year period. Of this group 5 percent will be robbed twice, and 1 percent will be robbed three or more times.

Taking differential risks by sex and race into account, males are more likely to be robbed at least once in their lives (37 percent) than females (22 percent), and blacks are more likely to be robbed one or more times than whites (51 percent compared to 27 percent). When it comes to assault, the terms **likelihood** and **probability** take on their everyday meanings as well as their special statistical connotations. Being assaulted at least once is probable for most people—roughly three out of every four people. (However, this alarming prediction includes failed attempts to inflict physical injury, threats of bodily harm that were not carried out, minor scuffles, and intrafamily violence.) Males face a greater likelihood of becoming embroiled in fights than females (82 percent compared to 62 percent).

However, the mathematical and sociological assumptions underlying these crude projections are very complex and subject to challenge. The calculations were based on constants derived by averaging victimization rates for the years 1975 to 1984 (Koppel, 1987). If crime rates drop substantially over the next 40 years or so, as they did during the 1990s, these estimates will turn out to be overly

BOX 4.2 Carjacked Drivers

In the movies, as well as in real life, motorists are yanked out of their cars and trucks by highwaymen who hop in behind the wheel and make a getaway. In the early 1990s, the catchy term **"carjacking"** was coined to describe the robbery of a motor vehicle directly from a driver, as distinct from a theft of a parked car. Once the crime had a name, the news media started to report the most outrageous cases (such as the death of a woman who, while trying to rescue her toddler from the back seat of her commandeered BMW, became entangled in her seat belt and was dragged more than a mile).

Police departments began to keep track of carjacking incidents separately from the general category of "robberies of all types", and state legislatures began to impose stiffer penalties for the crime. In 1993, Congress passed the Anti-Car Theft Act, which made robberies of motorists carried out with a firearm a federal offense, under the legal rationale that vehicles and guns are involved in interstate commerce (see Gibbs, 1993a). The 1994 Violent Crime Control and Law Enforcement Act made killings arising from carjackings punishable by death.

Although the probability of being robbed of an automobile or truck is low, the potential for disastrous consequences is high. With luck, occupants are forced out of their vehicles and left standing at the roadside shaken but uninjured. However, this frightening type of confrontational crime can easily escalate from a robbery into an aggravated assault, abduction, rape, and even murder.

Because this combination of circumstances is relatively uncommon, researchers have to merge the findings from a number of years of *NCVS* surveys to assemble a sufficient number of cases to analyze. During each of the 10 years from 1993 to 2002, the *NCVS* projected that roughly 38,000 carjackings took place nationwide. That worked out to about 0.17 incidents (some involved more than one person) per 1,000 people, or 17 per 100,000—making this kind of robbery about three times more common than murder. Almost 25 percent of these motorists were hurt; of these casualties, about 9 percent suffered gunshot or knife wounds, broken bones, or internal injuries.

According to the FBI's SHRs, each year up to 15 motorists were killed during carjackings. As for trends, this kind of hold-up, like other varieties of robberies, tapered off after the mid-1990s (Klaus, 2004).

Many of the differential risks surrounding carjackings paralleled the patterns for other robberies. Male motorists faced greater risks of being accosted than females. Cars driven by people from households with incomes less than $50,000 were seized more frequently than vehicles owned by more affluent families (which probably also means that robbers took less expensive cars more often than high-end vehicles). Higher risks were faced by black and Hispanic motorists, drivers between the ages of 25 and 49, people who were not married, and city residents (Klaus, 1999a, 2004).

In the vast majority of the incidents, the driver was alone; in almost half of all confrontations, the robber acted alone. Males committed more than 90 percent of these crimes and were armed in about 75 percent of the incidents (45 percent wielded a gun).

Two-thirds of the drivers put up resistance. About one-quarter used confrontational tactics such as fighting back against the assailant, trying to capture him, chasing him, or threatening him. About one-third tried nonconfrontational tactics like bolting out of the car and/or screaming for help. Nearly all motorists (98 percent) reported their losses to the police if the robber drove away with their vehicle, but only 58 percent of attempts were brought to the attention of law enforcement agencies. About one-quarter of the owners never recovered their vehicles, but about half suffered some financial losses (Klaus, 1999a; 2004).

Carjacking is very difficult to anticipate and defend against; there are no foolproof precautions, and drivers must be on the alert for many different scenarios when starting or stopping and while parking. Victims of this crime of opportunity sometimes are criticized for not being vigilant when loading or unloading packages, driving while preoccupied with music or cell phone conversations, traveling with their car doors unlocked, blundering through dangerous neighborhoods rather than taking safer routes, or falling into a trap by stopping after being bumped in a staged accident, by a vehicle full of robbers.

pessimistic. Conversely, if the crime problem intensifies during the first few decades of the twenty-first century, the real odds will be much greater than these percentages.

Lifetime likelihoods of being murdered also have been computed. Unlike the projections above, which are based on *NCVS* findings, murder risk estimates are derived from *UCR* data. Differential

TABLE 4.6   Chances of Becoming a Victim over a Lifetime

Type of Victimization and Person's Race, Sex, and Age	Percentage of Persons Who Will Be Victimized			
	Once or more	Once	Twice	Three times or more
Rape				
All 12-year-olds, females	8	8	—	—
Whites	8*	7	—	—
Blacks	11	10	1	1
Robbery				
All 12-year-olds	30*	25	5	1
Males	37	29	7	—
Females	22*	19	2	—
Whites	27	23	4	4
Blacks	51	35	12	15
Assaults				
All 12-year-olds	74	35	24	15
Males	82	31	26	25
Females	62	37	18	7
Whites	74*	35	24	16
Blacks	73*	35	25	12
Personal theft				
All 12-year-olds	99	4	8	87
All 40-year-olds	82*	31	19	33
All 60-year-olds	43	32	9	2

*Figures do not add up to total shown in "once or more column" because of rounding.
NOTE: Estimates are based on average victimization rates calculated by the National Crime Survey for the years 1975–1984; for rape, 1973–1982.
SOURCES: Adapted from Koppel, 1987.

cumulative risks can be presented as ratios, such as "1 out of every *x* people will be murdered." All the remaining individuals (*x* − 1) within this category are expected to die from diseases and other natural causes, accidents, or suicides. A small *x* indicates a grave danger. Overall, roughly one American alive today out of every 200 will die a violent death. But the risks vary tremendously, depending on personal attributes, especially sex and race. In general, males are more likely to be slain than females, and blacks are more likely than whites. But when data for both sex and race are included, black females turn out to be in greater danger of being murdered (1 out of every 171) than white males (1 out of every 241). White females have the least to fear, relatively speaking, of the four groupings (1 will be killed out of every 684). But the prospects facing black males are frightening. If the rates of the late 1990s

continue over the decades, 1 out of every 35 black males (about 3 percent) eventually will become a victim of homicide (FBI, 1999). In the early 1980s the projected threat was even greater: 1 out of every 21 black males (nearly 5 percent) was predicted to die violently (Langan, 1985).

The recognition of differential risks as an important feature of the big picture touches off another round of questions for victimologists to grapple with as they analyze *UCR* and *NCVS* data. Why does the burden of victimization fall so heavily on some groups of people and not others? Did crime victims do something to jeopardize their well-being, or were their misfortunes basically due to bad luck or fate? What can potential targets do to minimize risks? Are there policies the government or society can implement to help people lead safer lives?

THE SEARCH FOR RISK FACTORS

The data above from the *UCR* and the *NCVS* confirmed a long-held suspicion that certain groups of people are more likely than others to be murdered, robbed, assaulted, or to lose their valuables to burglars, car thieves, and other crooks. Why is that? What, if anything, did they do or fail to do that caught the attention of criminals? What differentiated them from the rest of the population? In general, what risk factors heighten dangers and make people and their possessions more vulnerable to attack? Answers to these questions can be of great use to criminal justice professionals, as well as to individuals in high-risk groups who face grave perils.

Although victimologists cannot agree among themselves about precisely which behaviors and practices increase susceptibility, being singled out definitely does not appear to be a random process, striking people just by chance. When individuals ask, "Why me?" victimologists suggest that the reason in most cases goes beyond simply being in the wrong place at the wrong time.

Theoretical explanations start as hypotheses that answer questions that begin with "Why?" After making an empirical generalization (an observation based on patterns or trends that emerged when the data were analyzed) theorists are inclined to ask, "What accounts for this?" For example, *NCVS* findings confirm earlier observations based on *UCR* statistics from police files that two types of crimes—unlawful entries (burglaries accomplished without using force to get in) and stranger rapes—occur more frequently during the warmer months. This empirical generalization about the seasonality of certain illegal activities requires an explanation. Why should burglary and rape exhibit a predictable cycle of increases and decreases during the course of a year? An offender-centered explanation might propose that burglars and rapists are more active during warmer weather. Another line of thought could be that something about their intended targets changes with the seasons. Perhaps warm weather behavior patterns create greater opportunities for

predators to stalk their quarry. During the summer, people spend more time outside and are more likely to leave windows open while they are away from home. As a result, strangers find more occasions to assault girls and women sexually, and prowlers find more unprotected homes to invade (Dodge, 1988).

One of the first victimologists (see Von Hentig, 1941) zeroed in on risk factors. He was convinced that certain personal attributes played a part in determining vulnerability. The mentally retarded, newly arrived immigrants, less-educated people, and very inexperienced people were pictured as attractive targets for exploitation by criminals employing deception and fraud. Con artists swindled the greedy, heartbroken, and lonesome with legendary ease. Physically handicapped people, the elderly and frail, the very young, and perhaps females in general were assumed to be easy prey for robbers. According to this early approach, a varied collection of psychological, biological, and social conditions set whole categories of people apart as particularly vulnerable.

Situational factors highlight how people and their possessions are more susceptible at certain times, periods, or stages than at others. For example, muggers might lie in wait as payday approaches or when Social Security checks arrive in the mail. Armed robbers might approach storekeepers at closing time.

Similarly, tourists are the preferred targets of robbers, thieves, and pickpockets. Career criminals figure that even if they are caught by the police, few travelers on business trips or vacations would be willing and able to spend time and money to return to the jurisdiction of the crime to press charges and take part in legal proceedings. A tourist's average length of stay is invariably too brief to see a case through to a conclusion. As a result, charges against defendants who harm people on business trips or vacations are usually dropped or drastically reduced because of the absence of the complainant.

To curtail the attractiveness of tourists as targets, extraordinary policies are needed. For instance, Waikiki Beach in Honolulu, Hawaii, was a haven for muggers and rapists until an apprehensive travel industry—convinced that crime was hurting business—began to pay for a victim-witness return project. Free airplane tickets, accommodations, and child care were furnished to visitors who flew back to Hawaii, pressed charges, and testified at trials. Government officials even interceded with the travelers' employers to assure them of the importance of the trip. As a result, prosecution and conviction rates went up, and tourists reportedly no longer suffered excessively high rates of robbery, theft, and assault ("Hawaii Return-Witness Program," 1982).

The Determinants of Differential Risks: Routine Activities and Lifestyles

Most victimologists are not satisfied with explanations that emphasize a single vulnerability factor that is biological (gender, age, or race), psychological (loneliness or greed), social (income or occupation), or situational (immigration or recreational travel). A number of more elaborate explanations attempt to account for differential risks.

From an offender's standpoint, potential targets (individuals, homes, and cars) can be rated along several dimensions. One dimension is **attractiveness**. Teenage muggers assault classmates to rob them of stylish shoes or coats, or the latest electronic devices. Some people and things appear "ripe for the taking," while others present more of a challenge to the robber of being thwarted or even captured. Certain prizes can easily be snatched, spirited off, and cashed in (such as car stereos and airbags), while others would take a long time and a lot of trouble to fence, and the net return might be minimal (such as used automobile tires).

Proximity describes whether the offender can get within range of the target, geographically (direct contact) and socially (interaction). Offenders might have great difficulty getting within striking distance of certain attractive targets, such as country mansions or millionaires. Proximity is a disadvantage to workers such as mental health attendants and corrections officers who deal with dangerous

people on a regular basis (see Garofalo, 1986; Siegel, 1998).

Certain individuals might be chosen simply because they are within striking distance, such as nonviolent inmates locked in with hardened convicts in prisons, jails, holding cells, or institutions for the criminally insane. Similarly, elderly people trapped in high-crime housing projects or well-behaved students stuck in troubled high schools also suffer grave dangers because they are readily available targets.

Vulnerability is a dimension that refers to a target's ability to resist and repel an attack, whether well-protected or largely undefended. For instance, at one extreme, rare coins in a museum are attractive to thieves and can be viewed up close, but usually are displayed in tightly guarded settings. At the other extreme, it can be a costly mistake to leave valuables in plain view in autos and vans. The same vulnerability factors apply to people: bodyguards may accompany corporate chieftains, but storekeepers walk home alone at night.

Taking factors such as attractiveness, proximity, and vulnerability into account leads to an explanation for differential risks that centers upon **routine activities**. This theory stresses the interactions of three variables: the presence of motivated criminals (for example, drug addicts desperate for cash), the availability of suitable targets (people or their possessions), and the absence of capable guardians (ranging from police officers to burglar alarms). Would-be offenders seize opportunities to strike whenever attractive targets are not well protected. Everyday living arrangements that can affect victimization risks include patterns of commuting, shopping, attending school, and going to work. In recent decades, vulnerability to robbery and burglary increased as routine activities shifted away from the home and toward greater interaction with nonfamily members. Daily routines govern the **social ecology of victimization:** the kinds of people who will be harmed and the manner, time, and location of the incidents. For example, people who spend most of their time at home are not in much danger of being murdered by strangers; if they do meet a violent end, it is likely to be at the hands of family members or close friends (Messner and Tardiff, 1985; Maxfield, 1987).

The routine activities explanation for differential risks links several major themes within criminology and victimology. One is that social conditions continuously generate criminally inclined individuals; another is that opportunities for committing thefts and robberies multiply as possessions proliferate. A third theme is that preventive measures in tandem with unofficial guardianship (informal mechanisms of social control in which relatives and neighbors assume responsibility for the well-being of others) may be more effective than stepped-up policing and punishment in discouraging would-be offenders from striking. The fourth theme is that certain activities and circumstances expose people and their possessions to grave dangers (see Cohen and Felson, 1979; Cohen, Kluegal, and Land, 1981; Felson, 1994; Finkelhor and Asdigian, 1996; and Siegel, 1998).

In addition to these factors, victimologists often point to the sociological term **lifestyle** as a concept to account for observed differences in susceptibility to violence and theft. Lifestyle refers to how people spend their time and money at work and leisure, and the social roles they play (such as business traveler, student, or homemaker). Lifestyles that place people in jeopardy may appear to be freely chosen but also are strongly influenced by structural constraints (such as the financial need to use public transportation) as well as role expectations (such as how teenagers "ought" to spend Saturday nights).

For example, *NCVS* findings presented in Table 4.5 indicate that single young men and women were robbed at much higher rates than their married counterparts. Surely muggers don't feel guilty about preying upon people sporting wedding bands. It could be the willingness of young singles to venture out alone at night to seek the company of acquaintances and even strangers that accounts for much of the difference in the dangers they face. The relatively low rates of robbery, rape, and assault by strangers for young married men and women with small children can also be understood as a function of lifestyle. In their daily routines of social companions, leisure activities, and family-centered obligations, young mothers and fathers are less exposed to dangerous people and places than their counterparts without spouses or youngsters (Skogan, 1981a; Felson, 1997).

The pursuit by single people of certain forms of amusement and excitement boosts risk levels. Evening activities such as cruising around, congregating in parks, drinking and partying with complete strangers, and frequenting bars and clubs late at night inject elements of uncertainty and volatility. Consequently, those who seek pleasure in daring and edgy activities run greater risks of being harmed.

At the other extreme from conventional routines, deviant lifestyles generally heighten risks. For example, prostitutes working the streets seem particularly prone to hold-ups, rapes, beatings, and even violent deaths (especially by serial killers). These young women are easy targets because they operate in the shadows, are willing to accompany complete strangers to isolated or desolate locations, and often abuse alcohol or other drugs that loosen their inhibitions, increase their desperation for money, and impair their judgment. Crimes committed against them are not taken very seriously by the public or the authorities, and witnesses on their behalf (usually other prostitutes, pimps, or johns) are often disreputable, unreliable, or uncooperative, and therefore ineffective protectors (see Boyer and James, 1983).

A related concept, the **deviant place factor**, calls attention to exact locations rather than the general lifestyle of particular individuals. Certain settings attract predators on the prowl and troublemakers looking for some action. **Hot spots** for crime tend to be concentrated in urban settings (Sherman, Gartin, and Buerger, 1989) and include crowded public spaces that serve as crossroads for a wide range of people (like downtown bus or train terminals), desolate areas where the police officers rarely patrol, or hangouts where heavy drinking and drug consumption regularly take place (perhaps seedy clubs or empty parking lots). Those who frequent these locations by necessity or choice expose themselves to greater risks.

In sum, lifestyles (including congregating at hot spots and spending time at deviant places) largely determine the quantity and quality of the contacts between potential targets and criminally inclined individuals. Differences in lifestyles lead to variations in exposure to risks. In the long run, **exposure** is the primary determinant of a group's victimization rate (for example, compare teenagers to senior citizens) (see Hindelang, Gott-fredson, and Garofalo, 1978; Garofalo, 1986; Jensen and Brownfield, 1986; Mustaine and Tewksbury, 1998b).

Reducing Risks: How Safe Is Safe Enough?

In general, it is safer to stay at home, especially at night; to travel in pairs or groups and use taxis; to avoid public spaces, unfamiliar places, and complete strangers; to steer clear of known hot spots and dangerous characters; and to not let down one's guard by becoming intoxicated or distracted. Those precautions are a price that many older people are willing to pay to avoid putting themselves in harm's way. But many teenagers and young adults reject such restrictions in their quest for entertainment and nightlife (see Felson, 1997; Mustaine and Tewksbury, 1998a).

It is difficult to evaluate the effectiveness of specific precautions to prevent victimization, such as keeping away from known hot spots and volatile people who engage in deviant lifestyles. It is hard to pinpoint particular instances when these strategies clearly have prevented a crime from taking place. These risk-reduction strategies do seem to work according to the differential rates of victimization for robbery and murder for entire demographic groupings discussed above, but not in ways that are readily quantifiable on the individual level. Even the most sheltered lives can be marred by unanticipated or dreaded events. Therefore, whether to sacrifice certain freedoms and pleasures for enhanced safety is a trade-off that each person must confront and weigh.

To illustrate the nature of the dilemma, take the relatively low robbery rates of the elderly compared to other age groups, even though senior citizens are presumed to be especially vulnerable to the young men who use force to steal. This apparent paradox can be explained by noting that older people usually incorporate many risk-reduction strategies into their lifestyles and routine activities to the point that these self-imposed restrictions become second nature. For instance, to find young adults out after midnight drinking in bars, nightclubs, and gambling casinos seems normal; to encounter elderly people in such settings at those hours is surprising. Teenagers and young adults ride home alone on public transportation late at night; old people rarely do.

When social scientists estimate risks, they are predicting how many people will experience unwanted incidents. Statistical concepts underlying risk estimates can be difficult to grasp. Only three distinct probabilities can be readily understood: "0," which signifies that an event is impossible; "1," which means that an event is inevitable; and "0.5," which indicates a toss-up, or a 50–50 chance (as in seeking "heads" when flipping a coin). But risks that are 0.1 (1 in 10) or 0.01 (1 in 100) or 0.001 (1 in 1,000) are harder to fathom or evaluate. If the odds of something happening were one in a million, statisticians would advise people not to worry about it (or count on it if the event is desirable, such as winning a lottery). But when two or three people in every thousand are robbed each year, how significantly should the risk of robbery be taken into account when planning one's daily schedule? How much preparation and anxiety would be rational in the face of these odds? What sacrifices would be appropriate in terms of forgoing necessary or welcomed activities (such as taking evening classes or watching the sun set on a deserted beach)? At what point does disregarding risks and ignoring precautions become foolhardy?

The proper balance between safety and risk is ultimately a personal decision. But it is also a matter of public debate. In general, more protection can be secured by greater expenditure. Dangers can be reduced if individuals and groups are willing to pay the price for more police patrols, improved lighting, surveillance cameras, and other security measures.

However, a demand for absolute safety (zero risk) is irrational in statistical terms. Probabilities of unwanted events can be reduced but never entirely eliminated. "How safe is safe enough?" is strictly a value judgment. At some point, it is reasonable for a person to declare that the odds pose an acceptable risk (Lynn, 1981).

In economics, a **cost-benefit analysis** can determine the point of diminishing returns, when additional outlays to attempt to achieve a goal exceed the value or return of that investment. **Risk-benefit analysis** might seem equally sound and precise, but on close inspection they hinge on questionable assumptions and debatable judgments. Obviously, the price of a second front-door lock is outweighed by its benefit if the door comes with a flimsy standard lock. Just as obviously, adding a third lock to a door that already has two imposes more costs than benefits.

But what about comparisons that are less clearcut? What about installing floodlights and a burglar alarm? How about stepped up police patrols in a neighborhood plagued by break-ins? At what point are there too many police officers to justify their salaries? Can the pain and suffering of victims or the public's fear of street crime (or terrorism) be converted by some formula into justifiable taxpayers' or consumers' expenditures? How much is a human life worth in monetary terms?

Ambivalence about Risk Taking

Contradictory messages permeate American culture on the subject of risk taking. On the one hand, the entrepreneurial ideology extols risk taking and generously rewards business ventures that defy conventional wisdom, survive financial hardships, and thrive in a highly competitive, adverse economic environment. Similarly, popular heroes are invariably risk takers who boldly take on daunting challenges: pioneers, explorers, inventors, private detectives, secret agents, soldiers of fortune, high-stakes gamblers, and other adventurers. Adolescence by definition is a period of experimentation, and risk-taking is part of growing up.

On the other hand, middle-age and middle-class values emphasize control over one's destiny and counsel prudence in the face of danger. Conscientious, responsible, "mature" adults plan, build, invest, and save to be prepared for adversity, illness, retirement due to old age, accidents, or devastating losses inflicted by criminals. They seek safety, peace of mind, insurance, and protective devices.

Scientific achievements contribute to the mastery of events and domination over nature. Technological progress is recognized as the reduction of uncertainty and the attainment of reliable, predictable performance. Autonomy (personal independence) and security are highly desired goals. Yet realizing many other goals and dreams requires individuals and groups to leave their comfort zones and strike out into the unknown, as when activists strive for reforms and rebels rise up in pursuit of sweeping changes.

The ambivalent attitudes toward risk taking in American culture are mirrored by contradictory responses to victimization. Some readily rush to the defense of victims while others impulsively criticize them as reckless people who have failed in their gambits. Their suffering evokes sympathy, but it also invites second-guessing about what might be altered in their attitudes and lifestyles to avoid future troubles.

From Crime Prevention to Victimization Prevention

Intense interest in the part played by lifestyle and daily behavioral routines has led to many new strategies to reduce risks. Victimologists and criminologists have coined terms to describe the ways people try to diminish their odds of being harmed by incorporating **risk-reduction activities** into their everyday routines.

Avoidance strategies (Furstenberg, 1972) are actions people take to limit personal exposure to dangerous people and frightening situations, such as not allowing strangers into their homes or ignoring passersby who attempt to strike up conversations on deserted streets.

Risk-management tactics (Skogan and Maxfield, 1981) minimize the chances of being harmed when exposure is unavoidable. Examples include walking home with other people rather than alone, or carrying a concealed weapon.

Crime prevention through environmental design (referred to by the acronym CPTED) stresses the importance of creating well-protected, defensible space (Newman, 1972) by **target hardening** (adding locks, erecting fences) and maintaining effective surveillance (limiting the number of entrances, improving visibility by trimming bushes and adding bright lights).

Crime resistance means making an offender's task more difficult through threat assessment and advanced planning.

Risk-reduction actions can be categorized as individual or collective (when arranged in cooperation with others) (Conklin, 1975), or as either private-minded or public-minded (Schneider and Schneider, 1978).

The term **crime prevention** in a practical sense means "the anticipation, recognition, and appraisal of a crime risk, and the initiation of some action to remove or reduce it" (National Crime Prevention Institute, 1978). It refers to proactive strategies that prevent the development of illegal activities, as opposed to reactive **crime control** measures taken in response to acts that have already been committed. Formerly, crime prevention strategies centered on government programs designed to eradicate the social roots of illegal behavior, such as desperation for money, job shortages, failing school systems, and racial discrimination. Community-based crime prevention campaigns focused on lowering the dropout rate in school systems, providing decent jobs for all those who want to work, and developing meaningful recreational outlets for otherwise idle youth. But since the 1970s, this approach, which relies upon social investments by government to ameliorate conditions that generate street crime, has fallen out of favor because the considerable expenses require substantial revenue from taxation.

Over the decades, a subtle shift has taken place in so-called crime prevention measures. A better term than crime prevention for some of these preemptive moves, like installing surveillance cameras, is **victimization prevention** (see Cohn, Kidder, and Harvey, 1978).

Victimization prevention is much more modest in intent than crime prevention. Its goal is to discourage criminals from attacking particular targets, such as certain homes, warehouses, stores, cars, or people. Like defensive driving, victimization prevention hinges on the dictum, "Watch the other guy, and anticipate his possible moves." The shift from crime prevention on a societal and governmental level to victimization prevention on a neighborhood, group (business, campus, office building), and personal level demands that potential victims become **crime conscious** (or "street smart). The responsibility for keeping out of trouble increasingly falls on the possible targets themselves, who must outmaneuver and keep one step ahead of would-be offenders. Crime-conscious individuals are compelled to follow victimization prevention tips, which are long lists of "dos and don'ts" compiled from observations of other people's misfortunes. The recommendation derived from routine activities theory is that cautious people should take measures that make them appear to be well protected and their property well guarded, so that criminally inclined prowlers will look elsewhere for easier pickings (Moore, 1985).

However, the **valve theory of crime shifts** predicts that the number of offenses committed actually will not drop when targets are hardened because criminal activity simply will be displaced. If one area of illegal opportunity is shut off (for example, if robbing bus drivers is made unprofitable by the imposition of exact fare requirements or prepaid cards), people desperate for cash will shift their attention to comparable but more vulnerable targets (such as cabdrivers or storekeepers) (National Commission on the Causes and Prevention of Violence, 1969a). When crime is displaced and criminals are deflected, the risk of victimization goes down for some but rises for others, assuming that offenders are intent on committing crimes and are flexible in terms of time, place, target, and tactics (Allen et al., 1981).

Victimization prevention strategies adopted by very crime conscious individuals actually might endanger other people who may be less cautious or less able to implement countermeasures. Victimization will be redistributed spatially, geographically, and socially—a far cry from genuine crime prevention, which would lower the risks everyone faces. For example, a pamphlet distributed by the country's largest police department frankly acknowledged that self-protective measures might merely redirect offenders elsewhere: "No vehicle is theft-proof. You must approach this problem with the attitude that it will not be my car that becomes part of the statistics. As selfish as it may sound, if the thief wants a car of your year, make, and model, let it be someone else's. If you follow these guidelines and take all the necessary precautions to protect your car, the chances are it will not be stolen" (New York Police Department, 1992).

The contention that victimization prevention methods simply shift the burden on to others, while alleviating the dangers faced by cautious people and their well guarded possessions, is a plausible hypothesis that researchers must examine. One thing is clear: Target-hardening strategies certainly lend themselves to commercial exploitation. Advertisements constantly proclaim that new, virtually foolproof, security-enhancing products are for sale. As these goods and services are purchased by a growing market share of people who desperately don't want to become statistics, victimologists can test the claims to see which devices work best, or if they have any appreciable impact at all.

How many anti-crime devices and precautions are sufficient? How safe is safe enough? Should each prudent person worry only about his or her own personal safety and take protective measures to chase away prowlers and fend off thieves, or should the entire community and the whole society, largely through government-directed strategies, take collective actions to drain the swamp that breeds street crime?

Criminals as Victims

As was pointed out in Chapter 1, people involved in illegal activities can become victims too.

The **equivalent group** explanation portrays victims who engage in certain high-risk deviant lifestyles in a less than sympathetic light. It emphasizes the possibility that certain pairs of victims and victimizers share the same interests, participate in the same activities, and are drawn from homogenous or overlapping lifestyle groups. According to this theory, offenders select their victims from their own circles of adversaries, acquaintances, and even former friends. Adherence to and participation in the norms of certain deviant subcultures can sharply raise the chances of becoming a casualty. Victims may be viewed as "fair game" or "easy prey" because their own involvement in criminal behavior discourages them from turning to the authorities for help (see Fattah, 1991; Siegel, 1998).

Many murders can be pointed to as illustrations of the explanation that both parties were drawn from overlapping social groupings. Most perpetrators and many of their victims had been in trouble with the law before their final showdowns, according to a survey of more than 8,000 prosecutions carried out in the nation's 75 largest counties during 1988. About 45 percent of the deceased turned out to have criminal records (arrests or convictions for misdemeanors or felonies) as did 75 percent of all defendants (see Dawson and Langan, 1994). Entire categories of killings are reminders that not all murder victims were totally innocent, law-abiding people minding their own business. The most obvious examples of overlapping lifestyles include victims and offenders engaged in racketeering, gang fighting, and drug-dealing.

As noted above in the analysis of murders based on data about "circumstances" from the *UCR*'s SHRs, of the approximately 9,770 slayings during 2006 in which the motive was determined by detectives, a considerable proportion could be characterized as "criminal-on-criminal." Clashes between rival juvenile gangs claimed more than 850 lives; nearly 120 slayings were gangland killings among mobsters; nearly 800 participants in the drug scene died while violating narcotic drug laws; and more than 20 inmates died from brawls behind bars ("institutional killings"). Taken together, just about 1,800 people (over 18 percent of the body count) were on the wrong side of the law when they died violently. (These are low-end estimates. Annual body counts due to mob hits, gangbanging, and drug-fueled conflicts would be larger if the circumstances surrounding thousands of unsolved killings each year could be determined by detectives, and if local police didn't submit thousands of SHRs with the reasons listed as "Other—not specified" or left blank, according to the FBI's *UCR* for 2006.

Perhaps the greatest source of misery for many families arises from pointless and preventable "gang related murders." The fratricidal slaughter of young gangbangers by neighborhood rivals amounted to between 5 percent and 7 percent of all killings nationwide, and between 8 percent and 10 percent of all gun murders between 1993 and 2003, FBI SHRs show (Harrell, 2005). About 5 percent of all homicides across the United States of blacks, and 7 percent of whites (many were young Hispanics), were deemed to be "gang-related" in 2005 (Harrell, 2007). Killings between feuding street gangs diminished slightly but steadily from 2002 to 2005 but rose in 2006, SHRs reveal.

Drug Scene Deaths Nationwide, a number of slayings that were deemed narcotics-related claimed many lives during the height of the crack epidemic in the late 1980s, and peaked in 1989 at about 1,400 (Timrots and Snyder, 1994). Several distinct scenarios can result in deadly drug-connected showdowns: cutthroat competition between rival dealers (turf battles), conflicts between buyers and sellers (quarrels over high prices, money owed, misrepresentation of the contents, and scams surrounding inferior quality), and robberies of dealers or customers. Drug-related murders incorporating these subcategories can soar to greater proportions in metropolitan areas at certain times (see Tardiff, Gross, and Messner, 1986; Spunt et al., 1993).

In Washington, D.C., drug-related murders boosted the homicide rate more strikingly than anywhere else during the late 1980s. About 20 percent of murders (in which the motive was known to the police) in 1985 were drug-related; either the coroner determined the victim was under the influence of drugs, traces of controlled substances or

paraphernalia were discovered at the crime scene, or the killing occurred in a drug hangout such as a "shooting gallery" or "crack house," according to the Office of Criminal Justice in the District of Columbia. This proportion rose to 34 percent the following year, jumped to 51 percent in 1987, soared to 80 percent in 1988, and crested at 85 percent during the first part of 1989 (Berke, 1989; Martz et al., 1989). In New York City, drug-related killings also peaked at over one-third of all slayings by the close of the 1980s, but dropped by half to less than 17 percent by the end of the 1990s as the crack epidemic waned (see Karmen, 2000).

The drug problem fuels a substantial amount of interpersonal violence. However, it is possible to manipulate impressions about its impact by either including or excluding certain subcategories of murders (such as robbers killing drug dealers). Another example is that the SHRs present a separate category for users high on drugs who kill ("brawls due to the influence of narcotics" claim between 50 and 100 lives each year). Should these killings be kept out or added into the working definition of "drug-related homicides" in order to inflate or deflate the death toll due to drug abuse? Larger or smaller estimates of the body count arising from the drug scene can be circulated by special-interest groups to prove or disprove claims about the scope of the problem to make it appear more or less serious, or about the "war on drugs" to present it as succeeding, failing, or causing more harm than good (see Brownstein, 1996).

The equivalent group explanation also helps to account for the carnage among teenage boys that intensified from the mid-1980s into the early 1990s. The overwhelming majority (about 85 percent) of these premature deaths were from gunfire. A cycle of aggression and retaliation developed as growing numbers of young men from poverty-stricken families in drug-ravaged communities armed themselves, both for self-protection and for prestige—whether or not they were directly involved in the crack, cocaine, or heroin trade that was thriving in their neighborhoods. When they fought each other with weapons, often over minor matters as boys tend to do, the body count soared. These young gunslingers did not "freely choose" their lifestyles, however. The root causes of this teenage arms race were economic hardships, failing schools, dwindling legitimate job opportunities, limited supervised recreational activities, family instability, and a pervasive subculture of violence (see Fingerhut, Ingram, and Feldman, 1992a; Blumstein and Rosenfeld, 1998).

The equivalent group explanation also sheds light on the connection between drinking and violence. Alcohol consumption has been implicated even more consistently than illicit drug use as a cause of interpersonal conflicts leading to fatal outcomes (see Spunt et al., 1994; Parker, 1995). For example, the FBI's SHRs for 2006 reveal that "brawls due to the influence of alcohol" claimed twice as many lives as "brawls due to the influence of narcotics" (107 compared to 51).

The first detailed analysis of urban murders (in Philadelphia around 1950) determined that the victim, the offender, or both were drinking before the killing took place in 64 percent of the cases (Wolfgang, 1958). Reports from medical examiners in eight cities in 1978 revealed that the percentage of corpses testing positive for alcohol ranged from a low of 38 percent to a high of 62 percent (Riedel and Mock, 1985). In New York City between 1973 and 1997, the proportion of victims who had been drinking before they were murdered was as low as 29 percent and as high as 42 percent, according to autopsies performed by the Office of the Chief Medical Examiner (Karmen, 2000). In a study of nearly 5,000 homicides committed in Los Angeles between 1970 and 1979, researchers reported that they detected alcohol in the blood of nearly half the bodies autopsied. The blood-alcohol content in about 30 percent of these 5,000 murder victims was high enough to classify the person as intoxicated by legal standards at the time of death. The typical alcohol-related slaying involved a young man who was stabbed to death in a bar on a weekend as the result of a fight with an acquaintance or even a friend (Goodman et al., 1986).

Binge drinking is a dangerous practice that some people have incorporated into their lifestyles. Two mechanisms explain the link between consuming large quantities of alcohol and violence. The **selective-disinhibition perspective** suggests that if one person binges—or worse yet, if both parties do—judgment will become clouded, and these individuals are likely to misinterpret each other's intentions, cues, and actions, and then behave in a less restrained manner. The **outlet-attractor perspective** proposes that at certain drinking locations (such as liquor stores, bars, and clubs) people gather with the expectation that they will seek "time out" from normal constraints and act "out of character" in an "anything goes" environment (Parker and Rebhun, 1995). These research findings raise the possibility that some casualties may have been partly at fault for the escalation of tensions and the outbreak of violence because their behavior "under the influence" was similar to the disinhibited actions of their attackers.

Some murders that arise from intense conflicts between people who are high can be viewed as the outcome of a sequence of events in a transaction. The initial incident might be a personal affront, perhaps something as minor as a slur or gesture. Both the offender and the victim contribute to the escalation of a **character contest**. As the confrontation unfolds, at least one party, but usually both, attempts to "save face" at the other's expense by not backing down. The battle turns into a fatal showdown if both participants are steeped in a tradition that favors the use of force as the way to settle bitter disputes (Luckenbill, 1977). Recall that the largest category in the listing of "circumstances" comprised people who were slain as a result of a dispute of some kind. Most of the deaths that resulted from these fights were unplanned and led to manslaughter indictments and convictions. But some mortal wounds were inflicted by drug-addled individuals who came armed to confront their adversaries. Through bad luck, poor judgment, or inadequate planning, some would-be killers wound up dead.

Controversies surround all of the explanations that center on deviant lifestyles and the membership of victims and offenders in equivalent groups. A blame-the-victim bias slips into the interpretations. Individuals who end up injured or mortally wounded are written off as troublemakers who "got themselves hurt or killed" while taking part in illegal activities. Branded as young gangbangers, mobsters, or drug abusers, they are demeaned as full-time lawbreakers who become part-time casualties (today's victim was yesterday's offender). Their entire lives are judged and stigmatized solely on the basis of the worst incidents that are known, assumed, or alleged about their prior behavior: their criminal records. The unmistakable implication is that their suffering is less deserving of compassion, support, and respectful treatment by the authorities who handle their cases.

Deterrence Theory as Applied to Victims

For more than two centuries, since the time of Cesare Beccaria and Jeremy Bentham, the originators of the **classical school of free will** or **rational choice theory**, a fierce debate has raged over whether would-be offenders are deterred by the prospects of apprehension, conviction, and punishment. Rarely, if ever, is the debate redirected to focus on past and potential victims.

Do victims learn a lesson from their bad experiences, and does the public profit from the mistakes made by others?

Simply put, **deterrence theory** holds that swift and sure punishment is the solution to the crime problem. According to the tenets of specific deterrence, punishing offenders teaches them a lesson they won't forget, so they will not repeat the forbidden act. According to the logic of general deterrence, publicly punishing offenders makes them into negative role models that serve as a warning to others to avoid committing similar misdeeds.

Proponents and opponents argue whether offenders really learn the intended lesson (especially in jails and prisons, which can serve as "graduate schools" that churn out individuals with advanced degrees in criminality). Do would-be lawbreakers really mull over their decisions rationally, think twice, and decide not to commit illegal acts? Or do they often act impulsively, disregarding the possible consequences in the heat of passion? Do others who hear about the crime and the punishment that followed truly make the connection, think "That could be me!" and become "scared straight" and dissuaded from violating the law?

Applying the principles of general deterrence to law-abiding people, do members of the public closely identify with victims who made mistakes? Do they also make the connection, "It could have been me!" and profit from someone else's misfortune? Does news media coverage of specific incidents strike fear in the hearts and minds of large numbers of would-be victims, making them think twice before engaging in similar risky behavior? Does the frightening prospect of becoming a victim lead to constructive responses, such as incorporating risk avoidance and risk management precautions into lifestyles?

When addressing the concept of specific deterrence, a parallel question arises. Do first-time victims learn their lessons? Do they realize their past mistakes, vow not to repeat these errors, take "dos and don'ts" tips more seriously, and change their ways? Or do they disregard the persistent threats, continue to take their chances, plow ahead stubbornly, and become repeat victims, suffering serial victimizations (two or more incidents during a relatively short time)?

The answers to these queries require careful research. A reasonable hypothesis is that some potential victims are more likely to be deterred than others. Specifically, individuals who are middle class, middle-aged or older, and female are probably more inclined than others to respond to the fear of being harmed ("punishment") by thinking twice and concluding that the risks outweigh the benefits. They exercise free will, rationally decide the activity isn't worth the risk, and choose a more prudent course of action. But what about the former victims who are not deterred from continuing to behave carelessly or recklessly, and get harmed again?

The discovery of repeat victims who have suffered from a series of offenses certainly draws attention to the possibility that some people are partly responsible for their own troubles. This line of inquiry leads to a close inspection of their specific motives and acts that immediately preceded the crime. As the victim-offender interaction is deconstructed, reconstructed, and scrutinized, exactly how the injured party behaved becomes the focus of attention. Victimologists have shown a keen interest in discovering the attitudes and actions that increase rather than reduce risks. Their constructs, explanations, and research findings are examined in the next chapter.

SUMMARY

This chapter focused on the people harmed by violent offenders, especially by murderers and robbers. Trends capture changes in victimization rates over time, while patterns indicate connections between the attributes of victims and the frequency with which they are targeted. Data from the *UCR* and the *NCVS* indicate that many types of victimization are taking place less frequently since their peak years in the late 1980s and early 1990s.

Cumulative risks indicate the odds of being victimized over the course of a lifetime: experiencing a theft someday is nearly a certainty. Comparative risks reveal which kinds of misfortunes are more or less likely than others: Homicide is not the leading cause of death for any group. International comparisons demonstrate that societal conditions and traditions greatly affect a country's crime rates: The United States stands out as suffering higher rates of violence than similar advanced industrialized societies. Differential risks underscore which categories of people are victimized more often than others. Studying the reasons for differential risks yields theories that explain why certain groups are more vulnerable to victimization than others.

Differential risks of being victimized are largely determined by routine activities and lifestyles that result in more or less exposure to dangerous individuals and hot spots for illicit behavior. Involvement in illegal activities surely heightens risks. Each person must perform a cost-benefit analysis about precautions in everyday life and expenditures for risk-reduction measures, and determine for himself or herself how safe is safe enough. Some people do not learn lessons from the misfortunes of others or from their own brushes with trouble and are not deterred from high-risk behaviors, so they become repeat victims.

KEY TERMS

differential risks, 71

cumulative risks, 71

comparative risks, 71

international comparisons, 71

homicide, 71

Supplementary Homicide Report (SHR), 72

profile, 72

statistical portrait, 72

crime waves, 74

crime crash, 74

exit, 76

differential risks, 78

strong-arm robberies, 85

muggings, 85

yokings, 85

instrumental coercion, 85

co-presence, 86

co-orientation, 86

punitive resources, 86

likelihood and probability, 92

carjacking, 93

attractiveness, 96

proximity, 96

vulnerability, 96

routine activities, 96

social ecology of victimization, 96

lifestyle, 97

deviant place factor, 97

hot spots, 97

exposure, 97

cost-benefit analysis, 99

risk-benefit analysis, 99

risk-reduction activities, 99

avoidance strategies, 99

risk-management tactics, 100

crime prevention through environmental design, 100

target hardening, 100

crime resistance, 100

crime prevention, 100

crime control, 100

victimization prevention, 100

crime conscious, 100

valve theory of crime shifts, 100

equivalent group, 101

selective-disinhibition perspective, 103

outlet-attractor perspective, 103

character contest, 103

classical school of free will, 104

rational choice theory, 104

deterrence theory, 104

QUESTIONS FOR DISCUSSION AND DEBATE

1. Identify an individual you know who falls into several high risk categories for being robbed. Explain the reasons for the well-documented fact that members of various groups face differential risks.

2. Describe some trends in violent victimization that became evident during the second half of the 1990s. Which of these trends continues today?

CRITICAL THINKING QUESTIONS

1. Review your own lifestyle and routine activities. What are the most dangerous things you do, in terms of exposure to criminals and entering hot-spot zones? What could you do to reduce your risks? What changes would be impractical or unworkable?

2. Argue that undertaking crime prevention on a governmental level is a more socially responsible approach than simply encouraging individuals to incorporate victimization prevention strategies into their everyday lives.

3. Try to explain why murder rates are so stable and predictable from one year to the next. Why was last year's rate for the entire United States so close to this year's rate?

SUGGESTED RESEARCH PROJECTS

1. Monitor this year's murders in your hometown by carefully searching through local newspapers for articles that provide the necessary details. Assemble a database that includes: profiles of the victims and the offenders, breakdowns of the victim-offender relationship, weapons used, and circumstances categorizing of the killings. How do these slayings compare statistically to the national averages presented in this chapter?

2. Develop a table that lists the same cities from the map in Figure 4.4. But instead of murder rates, assemble robbery rates from the FBI's *UCR*. Does the ranking of these large U.S. cities by robbery rates come out the same as for murder rates?

3. Develop a brief questionnaire about high-risk activities and survey people you know. Ask whether they feel these activities are too dangerous to undertake in terms of being robbed. See if the willingness to take precautions (adopt victimization prevention strategies) is connected to age, sex, or past misfortunes.

5

Victims' Contributions to the Crime Problem

The first few criminologists drawn to the study of victims were enthusiastic about the concept of **shared responsibility** as a possible cause of crime. By raising questions previous researchers had overlooked about victim proneness, individual vulnerability, and personal accountability for one's misfortunes, they believed they were developing a more complete explanation about why laws are broken and people get hurt. But they also touched off a controversy within victimology that still rages today.

Throughout this chapter, arguments from both sides of the debate over shared responsibility will be presented in a balanced manner. First, the concepts of facilitation, precipitation, and provocation will be introduced. Then, evidence from research into the issue of shared responsibility will be examined. After a general discussion of "victim blaming" and "victim defending," the debate between these two schools of thought will be explored in two specific areas: whether certain motorists whose cars were driven away thoughtlessly facilitated the thefts, and whether some individuals whose identities were "stolen" carelessly contributed to their own financial troubles.

Next, the strengths, weaknesses, and limitations of the victim-blaming and victim-defending perspectives will be underscored by the presentation of a third approach, "system-blaming." The chapter will conclude with a discussion of the importance of the question of shared responsibility within the legal system.

THE QUESTION OF SHARED RESPONSIBILITY

Until victimology emerged, mainstream criminology had consistently ignored the role that injured parties might play in setting the stage for lawless behavior. Victimologists have pledged to correct this imbalance by objectively examining all kinds of situations to determine whether people who were harmed might have played a part in their own downfall.

Thus, victimologists have gone beyond offender-oriented explanations that attribute lawbreaking solely to the exercise of free will by the wrongdoer. Victimologists suggest that certain criminal incidents be viewed as the outgrowths of a process of interaction between two parties. What has emerged is a dynamic model that takes into account initiatives and responses, actions and reactions, and each participant's motives and intentions.

Several expressions coined by the pioneers of victimology capture their enthusiasm for examining interactions: the "**duet frame of reference**" (Von Hentig, 1941), the "**penal couple**" (Mendelsohn, 1956), and the "**doer-sufferer relationship**" (Ellenberger, 1955). Reconstructing the situation preceding the incident can provide a more balanced and complete picture of what happened, who did what to whom and why, and thereby represents an improvement over earlier one-sided, static, perpetrator-centered accounts (Fattah, 1979).

A well-known line of inquiry (albeit a controversial one) within criminology centers on the differences, if any, between lawbreakers and law-abiding people. Criminologists ask, "What is 'wrong' with them? Are there physical, mental, or cultural differences that distinguish offenders from the rest of us?" Why are some groups of people (for example, young men from impoverished families) at a greater risk of getting caught up in street crimes than other groups (say, wealthy elderly women) are? In a similar vein, victimologists ask, "What distinguishes victims from non-victims? Do individuals who get targeted think or act differently from those who don't?" Furthermore, why are some groups of people (again, poor, young men) much more likely to be victimized (killed, shot, stabbed, beaten, or robbed) than other groups (once more, wealthy elderly women)?

Just posing these questions immediately raises the possibility of shared responsibility. Victimologists have borrowed the terminology of the legal system, traditionally used to describe criminal behavior, to describe the motives and actions of victims as well. The words *responsibility, culpability, guilt,* and *blame* crop up routinely in studies based on a dynamic, situational model of interactions between two people. In the broadest sense, the concept of shared responsibility implies that certain victims along with their offenders did something wrong. Just adopting this framework contends that some—but certainly not all—of the individuals who were hurt or experienced losses did not do all they could to reduce their odds or limit their exposure to dangerous individuals or threatening circumstances.

In retrospect, certain victims can be criticized for failing to heed warning signs or take precautions:

- A motorist shows no concern about where he parks his car, even though he knows that it ranks high on the list of most frequently stolen vehicles.

- An elderly person tosses out bank statements and credit card bills without worrying whether personal information in them will end up in the wrong hands.

- A woman gets drunk at a party even though she is among complete strangers.

- A young man receives death threats from an adversary yet refuses to turn to the authorities for help.

- A wife separates from her ill-tempered and violence-prone husband but fails to seek an order of protection to ward off further contact.

Some injured parties might be faulted for overlooking signs of an impending attack:

- A resident hears sounds of a prowler in the backyard but disregards the threat of home invasion.

- A car owner is awakened by the wail of an alarm but doesn't check to see if his vehicle is being broken into.

- A drunk in a bar is staring at a patron who recklessly stares right back.

Certain victims surely bear some responsibility for the assaults directed against them: mobsters, drug dealers, and street gang members readily come to mind. Because their conduct antagonized their rivals, they are largely to blame for their troubles. But what about the vast majority of innocent victims who lived law-abiding lives before they were targeted? Perhaps some behaved foolishly and later regretted their recklessness. For others, their only shortcoming was that they acted carelessly and paid a price for their negligence. They failed to abide by well-meaning advice and decided to take their chances. In sum, instead of minimizing the risks they faced, certain individuals maximized them by making bad choices. Following this line of thought many victims can be faulted to some degree. The circumstances under which they were harmed were partly of their own making. The unfortunate events that befell them could have been avoided—at least in hindsight.

The quest for evidence of shared responsibility captivated the first criminologists who became interested in victim behavior. Leading figures encouraged colleagues to focus upon the possibility of shared responsibility in their research and theorizing. Some of their statements excerpted from studies that appeared decades ago are assembled in Box 5.1.

Researchers looking for clear-cut cases of shared responsibility often focus on individuals who have suffered a series of thefts or attacks: "repeat victims." They seem to make the same mistakes over and over again. But perhaps it is not entirely their fault, according to crime analysts working on behalf of police departments who look for patterns that may indicate where offenders will strike next and precisely whom they might target. These analysts have come up with two primary reasons to account for repeat victimizations: a **boost explanation** that focuses on offender talents, and a **flag explanation** that emphasizes target vulnerability.

Boost explanations of repeat victimizations point out that career criminals gain important information about the people and places they strike repeatedly from the successful perpetration of the initial illegal act. They use this knowledge to plan their next attack against the same target. For example, burglars learn when a particular home is unoccupied, or how to circumvent a certain warehouse's alarm system. Car thieves figure out how to open the door of a specific make and model of car without a key. Robbers discover where a storekeeper hides his cash right before closing time. In contrast, flag explanations of repeat victimizations are victim-centered. They point out that unusually vulnerable or attractive targets suffer the depredations of a number of different offenders as opposed to the same criminal over and over. For example, apartments with

B O X 5.1   Expressions of Support for Inquiries into the Victim's Role

- A real mutuality frequently can be observed in the connection between the perpetrator and the victim, the killer and the killed, the duper and the duped. The victim in many instances leads the evildoer into temptation. The predator is, by varying means, prevailed upon to advance against the prey. (Von Hentig, 1941, p. 303)

- In a sense, the victim shapes and molds the criminal. Although the final outcome may appear to be one-sided, the victim and criminal profoundly work upon each other, right up until the last moment in the drama. Ultimately, the victim can assume the role of determinant in the event. (Von Hentig, 1948, p. 384)

- Criminologists should give as much attention to "victimogenesis" as to "criminogenesis." Every person should know exactly to what dangers he is exposed because of his occupation, social class, and psychological constitution. (Ellenberger, 1955, p. 258)

- The distinction between criminal and victim, which used to be considered as clear-cut as black and white, can become vague and blurred in individual cases. The longer and the more deeply the actions of the persons involved are scrutinized, the more difficult it occasionally will be to decide who is to blame for the tragic outcome. (Mannheim, 1965, p. 672)

- In some cases, the victim initiates the interaction, and sends out signals that the receiver (doer) decodes, triggering or generating criminal behavior in the doer. (Reckless, 1967, p. 142)

- Probation and parole officers must understand victim-offender relationships. The personality of the victim, as a cause of the offense, is oftentimes more pertinent than that of the offender. (Schultz, 1968, p. 135)

- Responsibility for one's conduct is a changing concept, and its interpretation is a true mirror of the social, cultural, and political conditions of a given era . . . Notions of criminal responsibility most often indicate the nature of societal interrelationships and the ideology of the ruling group in the power structure. Many crimes don't just happen to be committed—the victim's negligence, precipitative actions, or provocations can contribute to the genesis of crime . . . The victim's functional responsibility is to do nothing that will provoke others to injure him, and to actively seek to prevent criminals from harming him. (Schafer, 1968, pp. 4, 144, 152)

- Scholars have begun to see the victim not just as a passive object, as the innocent point of impact of crime on society, but as sometimes playing an active role and possibly contributing to some degree to his own victimization. During the last thirty years, there has been considerable debate, speculation, and research into the victim's role, the criminal-victim relationship, the concept of responsibility, and behaviors that could be considered provocative. Thus, the study of crime has taken on a more realistic and more complete outlook. (Viano, 1976, p. 1)

- There is much to be learned about victimization patterns and the factors that influence them. Associated with the question of relative risk is the more specific question (of considerable importance) of victim participation, since crime is an interactional process. (Parsonage, 1979, p. 10)

---

sliding glass doors are easily broken into, convenience stores that are open around the clock are always accessible to shoplifters, and taxi drivers and pizza deliverers are particularly easy to rob (Weisel, 2005).

The Controversy over Shared Responsibility

A man double-parks in front of a convenience store, leaves the engine running, and goes inside to buy cigarettes and a cup of coffee. When he comes back outside, he spots a teenager driving off in his car. Is he partly to blame for the theft of his vehicle? What proportion of auto theft victims might also be subjected to criticisms for losing their vehicles to juvenile joyriders and professional thieves?

***

A woman leaves her purse unguarded at her table in a club while she is dancing.

- Victimology also postulates that the roles of *victim* and *victimizer* are neither fixed nor assigned, but are mutable and interchangeable, with continuous movement between the two roles…. This position, understandably, will not be welcomed by those who, for a variety of practical or utilitarian reasons, continue to promote the popular stereotypes of victims and victimizers, according to which the two populations are as different as black and white, night and day, wolves and lambs. (Fattah, 1991, p. xiv)

Calls for Research into the Victim's Role in Specific Crimes

- *Murder:* In many crimes, especially criminal homicide, which usually involves intense personal interaction, the victim is often a major contributor to the lawless act…. Except in cases in which the victim is an innocent bystander and is killed in lieu of an intended victim, or in cases in which a pure accident is involved, the victim may be one of the major precipitating causes of his own demise. (Wolfgang, 1958, pp. 245, 264)

- *Rape:* The offender should not be viewed as the sole "cause" and reason for the offense, and the "virtuous" rape victim is not always the innocent and passive party. The role played by the victim and its contribution to the perpetration of the offense becomes one of the main interests of the emerging discipline of victimology. Furthermore, if penal justice is to be fair it must be attentive to these problems of degrees of victim responsibility for her own victimization. (Amir, 1971, pp. 275–76)

- *Theft:* Careless people set up temptation-opportunity situations when they carry their money or leave their valuables in a manner which virtually invites theft by pocket picking, burglary, or robbery. Carelessness in handling cash is so persistently a part of everyday living that is must be deemed almost a national habit …. Because victim behavior today is conducive to criminality, it will be necessary to develop mass educational programs aimed at changing that behavior. (Fooner, 1971, pp. 313, 315)

  Victims cause crime in the sense that they set up the opportunity for the crime to be committed. By changing the behavior of the victim and potential victim, the crime rate can be reduced. Holders of fire insurance policies must meet fire safety standards, so why not require holders of theft insurance to meet security standards? (Jeffrey, 1971, pp. 208–209)

- *Burglary:* In the same way that criminologists compare offenders with non-offenders to understand why a person commits a crime, we examined how the burglary victim and non-victim differ in an attempt to understand the extent to which a victim vicariously contributes to or precipitates a break-in. (Waller and Okihiro, 1978, p. 5)

- *Auto theft:* Unlike most personal property, which is preserved behind fences and walls, cars are constantly moved from one exposed location to another; and since autos contain their own means of locomotion, potential victims are particularly responsible for varying the degree of theft risk by where they park and by the occasions they provide for starting the engine. The role of the victim is especially consequential for this crime; many cases of auto theft appear to be essentially a matter of opportunity. They are victim facilitated. (McCaghy, Giordano, and Henson, 1977, p. 369)

When she returns to her seat, she discovers her wallet is missing. Over the next few weeks, she gets replacements for her stolen credit cards, driver's license, and other identification cards, and assumes her inconveniences have ended. But a few months later, she begins to get phone calls from bill collectors about falling behind in payments for loans she never took out. Is she partly at fault for succumbing to identity theft? How many victims of ID theft might also be criticized for failing to adequately guard their important personal documents?

Since the 1970s, some criminologists and victimologists have expressed concern over the implications of studies into mutual interactions and reciprocal influences between the two parties. Those who raised doubts and voiced dissent might be seen as loosely constituting a different school of thought. Just as criminology (with a much longer, richer, and stormier history than victimology) has recognizable orientations and camps within it (for example, adherents of labeling theory and conflict models), so, too, does victimology have its rifts and factions. To put it bluntly, a victim-blaming tendency clashes repeatedly with a victim-defending tendency over many specific issues. However, victimologists cannot simply be divided up into victim blamers and victim defenders. The situation is complex, as the following discussion indicates.

Victim Facilitation, Precipitation, and Provocation

The notions of victim facilitation, precipitation, and provocation come from the broad theme of shared responsibility to describe the specific, identifiable, blameworthy actions taken by certain individuals immediately before they were harmed. Unfortunately, these three terms have been used somewhat loosely and inconsistently by criminologists and victimologists to the point that important distinctions have been blurred or buried.

Victim Facilitation The term **facilitation** ought to be reserved for situations in which victims carelessly and inadvertently make it easier for a thief to steal. Those who negligently and unwittingly assist their offenders share a minor amount of blame. They increase the risks of losing their own property by their thoughtless actions. If it is assumed that many thieves were already on the prowl, looking for opportunities to grab and run, then facilitation is not a root cause of crime. Facilitation is more like a catalyst in a chemical reaction that, given the right ingredients and conditions, speeds up the interaction. Facilitating victims attract criminally inclined people to their poorly guarded possessions and thereby influence the spatial distribution of crime but not the number of incidents.

Auto theft and burglary are the two property crimes most often cited in studies of the problem of facilitation. A motorist who leaves keys dangling in the car's ignition is considered blameworthy if a juvenile joyrider impulsively hops behind the wheel and drives off. Similarly, a ransacked

home is the price a person might pay for neglecting to follow standard security measures. A residential burglary can be considered facilitated if the intruder did not need to break into the premises because a homeowner or apartment dweller left a door or window unlocked or wide open. By definition, these burglaries are not break-ins; they are acts of trespass by intruders seeking to commit thefts.

Details about victim-facilitated burglaries appear in the *National Crime Victimization Survey*. The *NCVS* keeps track of three categories of household (not commercial) burglaries: forcible entries or break-ins, attempted forcible entries, and unlawful entries without force. Attempted, unsuccessful no-force invasions are not counted because survey respondents usually would be unaware of these close calls.

Throughout the 1990s and into the early years of the twenty-first century, 50 percent or more of all completed burglaries reported to *NCVS* interviewers were unlawful entries without force. A reasonable implication is that the number of successful burglaries could be cut in half if residents would take greater care to lock up their homes. If they did, burglars would have to work harder, and in some cases would be deterred, thwarted, scared off, or caught red-handed.

Some kinds of people are more likely to be "guilty" of burglary facilitation than others, according to the breakdowns about no-force entries presented in recent *NCVS* annual reports. The age of the head of the household turned out to be an important determinant of whether or not someone would be so thoughtless as to facilitate a burglary. Younger people were much less careful than senior citizens.

Another key factor was financial: the lower-income families in the survey suffered much higher rates of no-force entries. The number of people in the household mattered a great deal: The more people living under the same roof, the more likely carelessness would take its toll. Individuals living alone experienced fewer facilitated burglaries; households with six or more people suffered rates that were almost three times as high. As for the race and ethnicity of the head of the household, black and Hispanic families suffered higher rates of no-force entries. Victims reported less than 40 percent of all no-force entries to the police, according to the *NCVS* for 2006 (BJS, 2008).

Elderly folks often talk fondly about the "good old days" when they left their doors unlocked. That practice wouldn't be prudent these days; such risky behavior would be considered blameworthy. More and more people are crime-conscious, according to the findings from the *NCVS* as well as the *UCR* for the years 1973 to 2006 (see Figure 5.1). Unlawful entries without force dropped sharply, from a little more than 40 per 1,000 households down to only 16 per 1,000 over that interval. Apparently, concerns and precautions about residential security are more widespread these days. Burglars must work harder because fewer people are making it easy for intruders to invade homes and spirit off possessions. The trend line shows that the rate of no-force entries has remained low and basically flat during the early years of the twenty-first century.

Figure 5.1 also shows a trend that the sellers of homeowner's insurance and expensive alarm systems would not want publicized: The risk of burglary has dropped substantially over the decades according

to both the NCVS and the *UCR*. The number of completed forcible entries tumbled by more than 67 percent, from about 30 per 1,000 dwellings in 1973 to a little less than 9 per 1,000 in 2006. The *UCR* trend line also shows a parallel decline in reported burglaries from the early 1980s until the late 1990s, and then a leveling out. In sum, the preventable problem of victim facilitation has subsided, and burglaries of all types are not as common as they used to be.

Victim Precipitation and Provocation

A husband-and-wife team, each with a history of robbery arrests and drug abuse, embark on a dangerous course of action to solve their financial problems. Armed with a sub-machine gun, they barge into storefront social clubs operated by organized crime families and seize the mobsters' ill-gotten gains. After hitting four Mafia social clubs in different neighborhoods over three months, their highly provocative and predictably short-lived crime spree comes to a

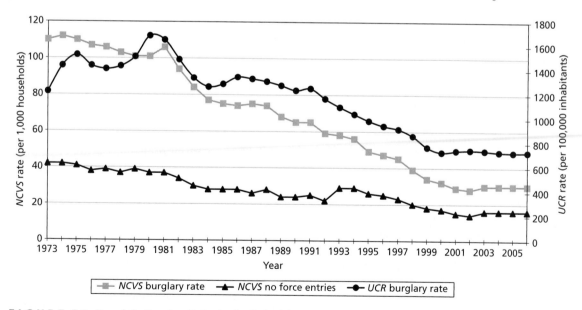

FIGURE 5.1 Trends in Burglary Rates in the United States, 1973–2006

NOTE: *NCVS* burglary rate measures attempted as well as completed burglaries, including forced entries.

SOURCES: *BJS' NCVS* 1973–2006; FBI's *UCR* 1973–2006.

sudden end on Christmas Eve. As the couple sits in their car at a traffic light on a congested street, a man walks up and shoots each robber in the head several times. Rival mob factions both claim credit for arranging the rubout until the police finally arrest one of their gangsters a dozen years later (Rashbaum, 2005).

Victim facilitation is a possibility in burglaries, motor vehicle thefts, and other larcenies. Charges of precipitation and provocation are hurled at victims of murder, robbery, assault, and rape. The accusation embedded in the term **precipitation** is that the individual who gets hurt contributed significantly to the outbreak of violence.

Provocation is stronger than precipitation; it means the loser is more responsible than the victor for the fight that ensued. The injured party instigated an attack that would not have taken place otherwise. Someone accused of provocation goaded, challenged, or incited a generally law-abiding person into taking defensive measures in reaction to forceful initiatives. When the battle ended, the aggressor was the one who was wounded or killed. (Unfortunately, over the years, victimologists and criminologists have used the terms *precipitation* and *provocation* loosely, and even interchangeably, obscuring the distinction between lesser responsibility for precipitation and greater responsibility for provocation.)

The first in-depth investigation of what was termed victim precipitation centered on homicides committed in Philadelphia from 1948 to 1952 (Wolfgang, 1958). Precipitation was the label applied to those cases in which the person who was killed had been the first to use force by drawing a weapon, striking the first physical blow during an argument, or in some way initiating violence to settle a dispute. Often, the victim and the offender knew each other; some had quarreled previously. Situations that incited them to violence included charges of infidelity, arguments over money, drunken brawls, and confrontations over insults or "fighting words."

Victim-precipitated cases differed in a number of statistically significant ways from homicides in which those who were slain did not bring about their own demise. Nearly all the precipitative victims were men; a sizable minority of the innocent victims were women. Conversely, few women committed homicide, but a substantial proportion of those who did so were provoked by violent initiatives by the men they killed. Alcohol was consumed before most killings, especially prior to precipitated slayings—usually, the victim had been drinking, not the offender.

In cases of precipitation, the one who died was more likely to have had a previous run-in with the law than in other murders. More than a third of the precipitative victims had a history of committing at least one violent offense, as opposed to one-fifth of the blameless victims.

Overall, about one murder of every four in Philadelphia from 1948 to 1952 could be labeled as victim-precipitated. Hence, in a quarter of the cases, widely held images of victims (as weak and passive individuals shrinking from confrontations) and of offenders (as strong, brutal aggressors relentlessly pursuing their prey) didn't fit the facts as reconstructed from the police department files. In many of the victim-precipitated homicides, the characteristics of the victims closely resembled those of the offenders. In some cases, two criminally inclined people clashed, and chance alone determined which one would emerge as the winner or the loser in their final showdowns (Wolfgang, 1958).

Petty quarrels escalate into life-and-death struggles through a sequence of stages, or a series of transactions. The initial incident might be a personal affront, perhaps something as minor as a slur or gesture. Both offender and victim contribute to the unfolding of such a "character contest." As the confrontation escalates, each party attempts to "save face" at the other's expense by hurling taunts, insults, and threats, especially if onlookers are pressuring them to fight it out (Luckenbill, 1977).

Those who lost the showdowns didn't welcome their fate. What might be misinterpreted as a death wish was really an adherence to the norms of a **subculture of violence** (see Curtis, 1974; and Wolfgang and Ferracuti, 1967). In many serious assaults, detectives often discover that both the injured party and his assailant were mutual combatants immersed in lifestyles that championed a willingness to use force to resolve disputes (Singer, 1986). This readiness to resort to combat to settle arguments is not a sign of psychopathology but is instead learned behavior. Lifestyles that require people to fight it out and not back down are reported to be most prevalent among Southerners (Butterfield, 1999) as well as among young men in poor, urban neighborhoods who conform to a "code of the streets" to prove their manhood and gain their peers' respect (Anderson, 1999).

The term **subintentional death** is applied to situations in which those who got killed played contributory roles in their deaths by exercising poor judgment, taking excessive risks, or pursuing a self-destructive lifestyle (Allen, 1980). This charge— that some people want to end their emotional suffering and consciously or unconsciously enter risky situations or engineer tragic events—is leveled most commonly at repeat victims. In homicide cases, the argument rests on a record of several "near misses" preceding the final violent outburst. If the deceased person's outright dares and subliminal invitations are interpreted within this framework, victim-provoked homicide is tantamount to suicide (Mueller, in Edelhertz and Geis, 1974); it is as if a mentally disturbed individual had a death wish but could not quite carry it through without help (Wolfgang, 1959; Reckless, 1967). This assumption of hidden motives is unsympathetic to the dead people who allegedly manipulated others to kill them, and it fosters a tendency to view some victims in a harsh light—as troublemakers whose demise is not a real tragedy.

Provocation is worse than precipitation. In extreme cases, the crime would not have occurred if a victim had not instigated or incited an otherwise law-abiding person into committing an illegal act, as the following example illustrates.

A 23-year-old teacher befriends a 17-year-old high school student. She implores him to kill her because she is dying from a painful illness and is distraught over divorcing her husband. Reluctantly, he agrees to shoot her, but she

survives the botched job with a bullet to the shoulder. From her hospital bed she tries to turn the incident into an example of the need for greater school security, but detectives figure out what really happened, and the student is arrested for weapons possession and attempted murder. (Mitchell, 1992)

Note that according to the law, not all people wounded or killed by shootings are classified as crime victims. For example, an armed robber slain in a gun battle with a bank guard would be classified as a dead offender, not a provocative victim. His demise would not be a murder but an act of **justifiable homicide** if the security officer acted in self-defense. Similarly, some casualties of justifiable homicides apparently committed "suicide by cop" (see Klinger, 2001) by provoking police officers to shoot them—for example, advancing in a menacing manner while brandishing an unloaded gun.

Arrestees who are hurt by police officers using excessive force (beyond what the law allows when subduing a suspect while making an arrest) qualify as crime victims. However, these casualties of unlawful retaliatory violence dished out on the spot by infuriated agents of the law are often condemned for having provoked the officers into using excessive force to subdue them and take them into custody. The image of an instigator is reinforced in a person who was injured during a beating, if at first he was openly defiant and charged with resisting arrest or assaulting an officer. The accused's allegations are difficult to prove in criminal court (and in civil lawsuits) because any officers who witnessed key events might abide by a code of silence and take part in a coverup of misconduct. Also, intense pressures to drop the brutality complaint are brought to bear on an injured person during plea negotiations.

Consequently, it is difficult to assess the extent of the problem of police brutality as well as the problem of victim provocation of officers (incitement in the form of resisting arrest). Reliable nationwide data and monitoring systems don't exist. Yet charges of police brutality and countercharges of arrestee provocation must be taken seriously and investigated carefully because these divisive incidents can polarize the public, strain police-community relations, and even touch off riots.

The Frequency of Shared Responsibility in Violent Crimes

The issue of the victims' roles in cases of street crime was systematically explored for the first time in the late 1960s by the National Commission on the Causes and Prevention of Violence (NCCPV). As its name suggests, the blue-ribbon panel was searching for the roots of the problem and for practical remedies. If large numbers of people were found to be partly at fault for what happened to them, then changing the behavior of the general public might be a promising crime-prevention strategy. Social scientists working for the commission took a definition of victim precipitation derived from previous studies by criminologists and victimologists, and they applied it to four types of crimes: murders, aggravated assaults, forcible rapes, and robberies. Then they drew a sample of reports from police files from seventeen cities and made a judgment in each case about whether the person who was attacked shared any responsibility with the assailant.

Victim-precipitated homicides (defined as situations in which the person who died was the first to resort to force) accounted for 22 percent of all murder cases in the 17 cities: 26 percent in Philadelphia (Wolfgang, 1958), and 38 percent in Chicago (Voss and Hepburn, 1968). About 14 percent of aggravated assaults were deemed to be precipitated (in which the seriously injured person was the first to use physical force or offensive language and gestures). Armed robberies were committed against precipitative individuals "who clearly had not acted with reasonable self-protective behavior in handling money, jewelry, or other valuables" in 11 percent of the hold-ups in the 17 cities, about the same as in a study conducted in Philadelphia (Normandeau, 1968). Only 4 percent of the forcible rapes that led to arrests were designated as precipitated, in which the woman "at first agreed to sexual relations, or clearly invited them verbally and

through gestures, but then retracted before the act." However, as many as 19 percent of all sexual assaults in Philadelphia were deemed to be precipitated by females (Amir, 1967). (This controversial notion of victim-precipitated rape will be explored in Chapter 10.)

The commission concluded that instances of victim complicity were not uncommon in cases of homicide and aggravated assault; precipitation was less frequent but still empirically noteworthy in robbery; and that the issue of shared responsibility was least relevant as a contributing factor in rapes (National Commission on the Causes and Prevention of Violence, 1969b; Curtis, 1974).

Recognizing Complete Innocence and Full Responsibility

A **typology** is a classification system that aids in the understanding of what a group has in common and how it differs from others. Over the decades, victimologists have devised many typologies to try to illustrate the degree of shared responsibility, if any, that victims might bear in particular incidents. Some of the categories of people identified in typologies include who are "ideal" (above criticism), "culturally legitimate and appropriate" (seen as fair game, outcasts), "deserving" (asking for trouble), "consenting" (willing), and "recidivist" (chronic) (see Fattah, 1991; also Mendelsohn, 1956; Fattah, 1967; Lamborn, 1968; Schafer, 1977; Sheley, 1979).

Up to this point, the degree of responsibility a victim might share with an offender has ranged from facilitation through precipitation to provocation. But the spectrum of possibilities extends further in each direction. A typology of shared responsibility must include two more categories in order to be exhaustive. At one extreme is complete innocence. Then, after facilitation, precipitation, and provocation, the final category at the other endpoint can be labeled as full responsibility.

Completely innocent individuals cannot be blamed for what happened to them. As crime-conscious people, they tried to avoid trouble. They did what they reasonably could to reduce the risks they faced. (After the fact, it can always be argued that they did not do enough.) In cases of property crimes, these victims took proactive steps to safeguard their possessions in anticipation of the possibility of burglary, larceny, or some other form of theft. They cannot be faulted for negligence or even passive indifference. In order to deter attacks, they sought ways to make the criminals' tasks more difficult. To protect their possessions, they hardened their targets by purchasing security devices (not guilty of facilitation). To avoid violence, they did nothing to attract assailants to themselves (not guilty of precipitation) and nothing to instigate otherwise law-abiding people to attack them (not guilty of provocation).

If taking precautions and adopting risk-reduction strategies qualifies as the basis for blamelessness and complete innocence, then at the other extreme, total complicity becomes the defining characteristic for full responsibility. Logically, a victim can be solely responsible only when there is no offender at all. Individuals who bear total responsibility for what happened are, by definition, really not victims at all. They suffered no harm from lawbreakers and actually are offenders posing as victims for some ulterior motive. Phony complainants usually seek either reimbursement from private insurance policies or government aid for imaginary losses. They file false claims and thereby commit fraud. For instance, someone who falls down a flight of steps might insist he was pushed by a robber. Fake victims may have motives other than financial gain. Some people may pretend to have been harmed in order to cover up what really occurred. For example, a husband who gambled away his paycheck might tell his wife and detectives that he was held up on the way home.

VICTIM BLAMING VERSUS VICTIM DEFENDING

Arguments that victims of crime might share responsibility with their offenders for what happened due to facilitation, precipitation, and provocation have been characterized as **victim blaming**. **Victim defending** counters this approach by challenging whether it is accurate and fair to try to hold the wounded party accountable for injuries and losses that a wrongdoer inflicted.

Two opposing ideologies might imply that there are two distinct camps, victim blamers and victim defenders, but most people are inconsistent when they respond to criminal cases. They criticize specific individuals but defend others, or they find fault with certain groups of victims (for example, abusive husbands who are killed by their wives) but not other groups (such as women who are raped by their dates).

Victim blaming assumes that the offender and the victim are somehow partners in crime, and that a degree of mutuality, symbiosis, or reciprocity may exist between them (see Von Hentig, 1948). To identify such cases, both parties' possible motives, reputations, actions, and records of past arrests and convictions must be investigated (Schultz, 1968).

Victimology, despite its aspirations toward objectivity, may harbor an unavoidable tendency toward victim blaming. It is inevitable that a careful reconstruction of the behavior of a victim before, during, and after a crime will unearth rash decisions, foolish mistakes, errors in judgment, and acts of carelessness that, with 20-20 hindsight, can be pointed to as having brought about the unfortunate outcome. Step-by-step analyses of actions and reactions are sure to reveal evidence of what injured parties did or failed to do that contributed to their suffering.

Victim blaming follows a three-stage thought process (see Ryan, 1971). First, the assumption is made that there is something wrong with these individuals. They are said to differ significantly from the unaffected majority in their attitudes, their behaviors, or both. Second, these presumed differences are thought to be the source of their plight. If they were like everyone else, the reasoning goes, they would not have been targeted for attack. And third, victims are warned that if they want to avoid trouble in the future, they must change how they think and act. They must abandon the careless, rash, or provocative patterns of behaviors that brought about their downfall.

Arising from a close-up and personal interactionist analysis of a particular sequence of events, victim blaming is a widely held view for several reasons. It provides specific and straightforward answers to troubling questions such as "Why did it happen?" and "Why him and not me?" Victim blaming also has psychological appeal because it draws upon deep philosophical and even theological beliefs concerning why bad things happen to seemingly good people. In addition, victim blaming readily comes to mind because it is a familiar theme, often voiced spontaneously by wrongdoers and presented even more convincingly by defense attorneys.

The widely held doctrine of personal accountability that underlies the legal system also encourages victim-blaming explanations. Just as criminals are condemned and punished for their wrongdoing, so, too, must victims answer for their behavior before, during, and after an incident. In retrospect, they may be credited for clever responses that minimized the harm they experienced, or faulted for errors in judgment that only made things worse. Such assessments of praise or blame are grounded in the belief that individuals exercise a substantial degree of control over events in their lives. They may not be totally in command, but they are not powerless or helpless pawns and are not resigned to their fate, waiting passively to become a statistic. Just as cautious motorists should implement defensive driving techniques to minimize accidents, crime-conscious individuals are obliged to review their lifestyles and routines to enhance their personal safety. By following the advice of security experts about how to keep out of trouble, those who are cautious and concerned can find solutions to the social problem of street crime.

Fervent believers in a **just world outlook**—people get what they deserve before their lives end—find victim blaming a comforting notion. Bad things happen only to evil characters; good souls are rewarded for following the rules. The alternative—imagining a world governed by random events where senseless and brutal acts might afflict anyone at any time, and where wrongdoers go unpunished—is unnerving. The belief that victims must have done something neglectful, foolish, or provocative that led to their misfortunes dispels feelings of vulnerability and powerlessness, and gives the blamer peace of mind about the existence of an orderly and just world (Lerner, 1965; Symonds, 1975; Lambert and Raichle, 2000).

Victim blaming is also the view of offenders who are devoid of empathy and pity. Evidently, they are so desensitized that they do not feel the guilt, shame, remorse, or moral inhibitions that otherwise would constrain their behavior. By derogating and denigrating the victim, juvenile delinquents or adult criminals can validate their hurtful acts as justifiable. Outbursts of stark cruelty and savagery become possible when the injured party is viewed as worthless, less than human, an appropriate object for venting hostility and aggression, or as an outcast deserving mistreatment (Fattah, 1976, 1979). To neutralize pangs of conscience, delinquents frequently disparage intended targets as having negative traits ("He was asking for it," or "They are a bunch of crooks themselves"). In extreme cases, youthful offenders believe the suffering they inflict is retaliatory justice that deserves applause ("We deserve a medal for doing that") (Sykes and Matza, 1957; Schwendinger and Schwendinger, 1967).

Defense attorneys may persuasively articulate the victim-blaming views of their clients, especially in high-profile murder cases. A "trash-the-reputation" (demonization of the deceased) approach, coupled with a "sympathy" (for the accused) defense, might succeed in swaying a jury and securing an acquittal or in convincing a judge to hand down a lesser sentence. For example, in cases where children slay their parents, the dead fathers and mothers may be portrayed as vicious abusers and perverse molesters, and their offspring are portrayed as the helpless objects of adult cruelty (see Estrich, 1993b; Hoffman, 1994).

Victim defending rejects the premises of victim blaming (those who suffer are partly at fault) and challenges its recommendations (people who were targeted must change their ways to avoid future incidents). First of all, victim blaming is criticized for overstating the extent to which facilitation, precipitation, or provocation explains the genesis of an illegal act. Motivated offenders would have struck their chosen targets even if the victims had not made their tasks easier, called attention to themselves, or aroused angry reactions. Second, victim blaming is condemned for confusing the exception with the rule and overestimating the actual proportion of cases in which facilitation, precipitation, or provocation took place. Shared responsibility is unusual, not common. A few people's mistakes don't justify placing most victims' attitudes and behaviors under a cloud of suspicion. Third, exhorting people to be more cautious and vigilant is not an adequate solution. This advice is unrealistic because it overlooks the cultural imperatives and social conditions that largely shape lifestyles. Most people lack the opportunities and resources to alter their means of travel, their hours of work, the company they keep, the schools their children attend, or the neighborhoods in which they live. Many risk-reduction suggestions and stern admonitions about do's and don'ts are impractical, unrealistic, and unproven.

Over the past several decades, many victimologists have embraced the tenets of victim defending, and have sharply denounced crude expressions of victim blaming as examples of muddled thinking and confused reasoning about the issue of shared responsibility (see the excerpts of their arguments in Box 5.2).

Victim defending is clear about what it opposes, but it is vague about what it supports. Two tendencies within victim defending can be distinguished concerning who or what is to be faulted. The first can be called **offender blaming**. Offender blaming resists attempts to shift the burden of full responsibility off of lawbreakers' backs and onto victims' shoulders. Unfortunately, victim defending coupled with offender blaming represents an inconsistent and one-sided application of the doctrine of personal accountability because only the aggressor, not the target, is held responsible for the misdeed.

The second tendency is to link victim defending with **system blaming**, wherein neither the offender nor the victim is the real culprit. To

varying degrees both parties are largely products of their culture and social environment. The attitudes and behaviors of both individuals have been influenced by the agents of socialization—parental input, peer group pressures, subcultural prescriptions about do's and don'ts, school experiences, media images, religious doctrines—along with criminal justice practices, economic imperatives, and many other social forces. Victim defending/system blaming is a more complex and sophisticated outlook than victim defending/offender blaming. According to this more sociological type of analysis, the roots of the crime problem are to be found in the basic institutions upon which the social system is built (among many others, see Franklin, 1978; and Balkan, Berger, and Schmidt, 1980).

To illustrate the differences in 1. victim blaming, 2. victim defending coupled with offender blaming, and 3. victim defending linked to system blaming, two problem areas will be explored. First, explicit charges of victim facilitation in automobile theft will be examined. Then the focus will shift to implicit accusations that certain victims of the white-collar crime of identity theft facilitated the thieves' tasks.

VICTIM FACILITATION AND AUTO THEFT: IS IT THE CARELESS WHO WIND UP CARLESS?

Stealing Cars for Fun and Profit

Nearly one million households in metropolitan areas suffered a vehicle theft (or an attempted vehicle theft) during 2006, according to the *NCVS*. That volume of incidents translated to a rate of more than eight vehicle thefts for every 1,000 households. Similarly, the *UCR* for 2006 indicated that police departments across the country received roughly 1.2 million complaints about completed or attempted thefts of cars, vans, trucks, buses, and motorcycles from households and businesses, for a rate of nearly 400 thefts for every 100,000 inhabitants. Therefore, both official sources confirm that vehicle

---

B O X 5.2   Criticisms of the Notion of Shared Responsibility

- The concept of victim precipitation has become confused because it has been operationalized in too many different, often incompatible ways. As a result, it has lost much of its usefulness as an empirical and explanatory tool. (Silverman, 1974, p. 99)

- The study of victim precipitation is the least exact of the sociological approaches; it is part *a priori* guesswork and part "armchair detective fun and games" because the interpretation rests, in the final analysis, on a set of arbitrary standards. (Brownmiller, 1975, p. 353)

- A tendency of investigators to assign responsibility for criminal acts to the victims' behavior reinforces similar beliefs and rationalizations held by most criminals themselves.... Scientific skepticism should be maintained regarding the concept of victim participation, especially for crimes of sudden, unexpected violence where the offender is a stranger to the victim. (Symonds, 1975, p. 22)

- Victims of crime, long ignored but now the object of special scholarly attention, had better temper their enthusiasm because they may be more maligned than lauded, and their plight may not receive sympathetic understanding. Some victimologists have departed from the humanitarian, helping orientation of the founders of the field and have turned victimology into the art of blaming the victim. If the impression of a "legitimate victim" is created, then part of the burden of guilt is relieved from the perpetrator, and some crimes, like rape for example, can emerge as without either victims or offenders. (Weis and Borges, 1973, p. 85)

- Victim precipitation explanations are plagued by the fallacy of circular reasoning about the cause of the crime, suffer from oversimplified stimulus-response models of human interaction, ignore incongruent facts that don't fit the theory, and

inadequately explore the victim's intentions. (Franklin and Franklin, 1976, p. 134)

- An analytical framework must be found that salvages the positive contributions of the concept of victim precipitation, while avoiding its flaws—its tendency to consider a victim's provocations as both a necessary and sufficient condition for an offense to occur; its portrayal of some offenders as unrealistically passive; and its questionable moral and legal implications about who is the guilty party. (Sheley, 1979, pp. 126–27)

- Crime victimization is a neglected social problem in part because victim precipitation studies typically fail to articulate the distress of the victims and instead suggest that some may be to blame for their own plight. The inferences often drawn from these studies—that some individuals can steer clear of trouble by avoiding certain situations—suffer from the *post hoc ergo propter hoc* fallacy of treating the victims' behavior as both necessary and sufficient to cause the crime. (Teevan, 1979, p. 7)

- To accept precipitation and provocation as legitimate excuses for attenuating responsibility for violent crime is false, illogical, psychologically harmful to victims, and socially irresponsible.... Victim-blaming has been injected into the literature on crime by well-meaning but offender-oriented professionals. It becomes the basis and excuse for the indifference shown to supposedly "undeserving" victims. (Reiff, 1979, pp. 12, 14)

- The eager acceptance of arguments about victim responsibility by scholars and the public alike is undeserved; these accounts of why the crime occurred often lack empirical verification, can lead to cruel insensitivity to the suffering of the victim, and tend to exonerate or even justify the acts of the offenders, especially rapists. (Anderson and Renzetti, 1980, p. 325)

---

theft takes place much less often than larceny or burglary but is much more common than any of the serious violent crimes in the FBI's crime index.

This problem is certainly not new—it emerged more than 100 years ago, at the dawn of the

automobile age. As long ago as 1919, Congress passed the Dyer Act, which authorized the FBI to investigate organized theft rings that drove stolen vehicles across state borders to evade local police forces with limited jurisdictions. Then, as now, cars were taken for a number of reasons.

Professional thieves steal cars for profit; joyriders take cars for a spin just for fun. Juvenile joyriding (which the law calls "unauthorized use of a motor vehicle" and treats as a delinquent act) has been a craze among teenage boys ever since cars were marketed with the message that owning one is a sign of manhood and a basis for independence. These amateurs—who seek the status, thrills, and challenge of "borrowing" cars to impress their friends—often prey upon careless motorists who leave their keys handy.

Professional thieves don't need to rely on negligent drivers. It takes them just a few minutes with the right tools to disarm alarm systems and defeat standard security hardware such as door, ignition, and steering wheel locks. Working in league with commercial theft rings, these pros steal cars either to sell or to strip for parts. Steal-to-sell (**retagging**) operations alter the registration and title documents and vehicle identification number, and then pass off the car as used. Steal-to-strip operations (**chop shops**) dismantle vehicles and sell the sheet metal crash replacement parts (such as the hood, trunk lid, fenders, and doors) as if they came from legitimate salvage and recycling pipelines to auto body repair shops.

Another motive for stealing a vehicle is to use it for temporary or short-term travel, often as a getaway car after committing some other crime, such as a bank robbery. The fifth variety of auto theft is provided as a "service" to the "victim" as part of a conspiracy to commit insurance fraud. Some owners pay to have their cars disposed of without a trace so that they can collect insurance reimbursement for vehicles they no longer want or no longer can afford to run or repair.

Collectively, these thefts cost owners nearly $8 billion, with losses averaging about $6,650 per stolen vehicle in 2006, the UCR reported. Yet some commentators mistakenly portray auto theft as the "happy crime" in which no one loses and everyone gains (see Plate, 1975). The argument goes that the thief makes money; the owner is reimbursed by the insurance company and then enjoys the pleasure of shopping for a new car. Meanwhile, the manufacturer gains a customer who wasn't due back in the showroom for another couple of years,

and the insurance company gets a chance to raise comprehensive fire and theft loss premiums and invest that money in profitable ventures.

But in actuality, most victims of auto theft are quite upset for a number of reasons. Many motorists devote a great deal of time, effort, and loving care to keeping their vehicles in good shape. Second, the shock of discovering that the vehicle vanished touches off a sense of violation and insecurity that lingers for a long time. Third, not all owners purchase theft coverage, usually because they cannot afford it. Even those who are insured almost always must suffer a hefty deductible out of their own pockets, and they might owe more on the car loan than the vehicle is worth, so the insurance payoff does not cover the money owed. Personal items left in the vehicle are gone, as are any expensive add-ons. The loss is always unanticipated, necessitating emergency measures such as taking cabs, renting cars, canceling important appointments, and buying a more expensive replacement. Finally, motorists who collect insurance reimbursement might find that either their premiums are raised or their policies cannot be renewed.

Changes in motor vehicle theft rates over the past few decades are shown in Figure 5.2. One trend line, based on NCVS findings, portrays yearly rates of thefts of noncommercial vehicles disclosed to survey interviewers, whether successful completions or failed attempts, for every 1,000 households. The other trend line, from the UCR, depicts yearly rates of completed or attempted thefts of all motorized vehicles, per 100,000 people, reported to police departments across the country. Both of these sets of statistics indicate that rates of auto theft rose during the late 1980s, reached an all-time high at the start of the 1990s, subsided as the twentieth century drew to a close, and then remained relatively constant, perhaps dipping a bit more (according to the UCR) during the early years of the twenty-first century.

By contrast, however, theft rates are soaring for one type of vehicle: motorcycles. In 1998, about 27,000 were stolen, but that number doubled to more than 55,000 by 2003, then soared to 71,000 in 2004, and remained at that record level in 2005.

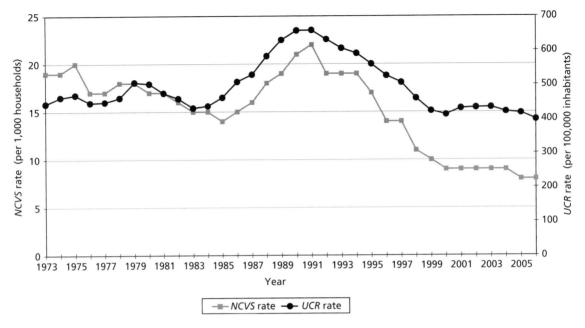

FIGURE 5.2   Trends in Motor Vehicle Theft Rates in the United States, 1973–2006

NOTE: *UCR* figures include thefts of taxis, buses, trucks and other commercial motor vehicles.

SOURCES: BJS' *NCVS* 1973–2006; FBI's *UCR* 1973–2006.

As more motorcycles fill the roads, and as they become more expensive, their attractiveness to thieves rises. Law enforcement agencies have not yet developed adequate responses to the surge in stealing. Motorcyclists lavish great attention on their cherished possessions by installing high-performance engines and exhaust systems, chromed parts, and specialized frames. Most of the stolen vehicles—from 70 percent to 75 percent—are never returned to their owners, according to the National Insurance Crime Bureau (which issued a press release with a victim-blaming headline: "Be an easy rider—not an easy target!") (Scafidi, 2006a).

Unfortunately, stolen car recovery rates also have dropped, from more than 90 percent in the 1940s and 1950s to only about 62 percent in 2005, according to insurance industry sources (Scafidi, 2006b). The situation is not quite as bleak according to the findings of the *NCVS*. A car is the one kind of stolen property that is most likely to be returned to its rightful owner. About 70 percent of all motorists got their vehicles back in 2006.

However, about one-fifth of the owners probably were dismayed. What the police retrieved, or what the motorists relocated by themselves, and what the *NCVS* counted as a partial recovery of what was formerly a source of pride and joy, might have been just an irreparable, stripped hulk.

Which Motorists Should Be Most Concerned When Parking?

As with all crimes, risks vary dramatically. In the case of auto theft, the chances of becoming a victim depend upon the make, model, and year of the vehicle. A prime consideration centers on the appeal or black market value of the various cars, SUVs, vans, and pickup trucks to those who make a living by repeatedly stealing vehicles. Professional thieves prowl the streets looking for specific makes and models on their shopping lists. Which parked cars do they enter and drive away most often?

The answer, in the form of a ranking of vehicles, should be fairly straightforward. Consumers

TABLE 5.1   Which Vehicles Were Stolen Most Frequently During 2005?

Rank	From the NICB Year/Make/Model	From CCC Services Year/Make/Model	From NHTSA Year/Make/Model	Total Stolen Nationwide 2005	Rate Per 1,000
1	1995/Honda/Civic	2001/BMW/M Roadster	2005/Nissan/Altima	1,035	3
2	1991/Honda/Accord	1998/Acura/Integra	2005/Chevrolet/Malibu	908	4
3	1989/Toyota/Camry	2004/Mercury/Marauder	2005/Toyota/Corolla	864	2
4	1997/Ford/150 Series Pickup	1999/Acura/Integra	2005/Dodge/Neon	783	5
5	2005/Dodge/Ram Pickup	1995/Acura/Integra	2005/Toyota/Camry	732	3
6	1994/Chevrolet/ 1500 Pickup	2002/Audi/S4	2005/Chevrolet/Impala	701	3
7	1994/Nissan/Sentra	1996/Acura/Integra	2005/Ford/Focus	637	3
8	1994/Dodge/Caravan	1997/Acura/Integra	2005/Honda/Civic	577	2
9	1993/Saturn/SL	2001/Acura/Integra	2005/Honda/Accord	576	2
10	1990/Acura/Integra	2000/Jaguar/Xjr	2005/Ford/Taurus	527	3
			All 2005 models		1.8

NOTES: Number of stolen cars is drawn by NHTSA from the FBI's NCIC. Theft rate is per 1,000 vehicles manufactured and sold to the U.S. public during 2005. Theft rates are rounded.off to the nearest integer.
SOURCE: First list: from NICB (Scafidi, 2008b); second list: from CCC (2006); third list: from NHTSA, 2008.

need to know this information when shopping for used cars (brand-new models do not yet have track records) if they are concerned about the chances of losing their vehicles or about the costs of insuring them against theft—premiums usually cover "comprehensive theft and fire damage". In other words, crime-conscious motorists ought to be aware of how desirable or undesirable their prized possessions are to thieves cruising around. But each year, several listings that bear little resemblance to each other are published by agencies that analyze different databases and use different criteria (see Gibson, 2004). (See Table 5.1).

For vehicles stolen during 2005, the second column in Table 5.1 presents the ranking derived from the nearly 1.3 million thefts reported to police departments across the country and stored in the FBI's National Crime Information Center (NCIC) database. Relatively inexpensive Hondas and Toyotas filled the upper ranks on this list of "hot cars" compiled by the National Insurance Crime Bureau (NICB). The same three passenger cars topped the 2007 rankings too, but the 2007 Toyota Corolla shot up to the tenth spot.

Note that most of these top 10 vehicles "most attractive" to crooks were rather old; some had been on the road for more than 10 years. This pattern is surprising at first until it is realized that the older cars are stolen to be stripped of their parts, which are then used to repair crash-damaged newer cars—unless the manufacturer changes the dimensions of the later models (Scafidi, 2008b). But a distinctly different ranking of the 10 most wanted makes/models/years emerges when an alternative database is analyzed, compiled by more than 350 insurance companies but including only the vehicles that their member companies insured against theft and that were never recovered. This list of total losses, from CCC Information Services, Inc., appears in the third column of Table 5.1.

Acura Integras manufactured years ago hold the top spots on this ranking based on the number of policyholders' claims for reimbursement from insurance companies. But what if a theft rate is calculated by taking into account not only the number of reported stolen vehicles of a given make, model, and year, but also the number of these cars on the road that served as potential targets? The resulting list from the National Highway Transportation and Safety Administration (NHTSA) of yearly theft rates—only for 2005 models that were reported stolen during 2005 to police departments and entered into the FBI's NCIC database—appears in the fourth column of Table 5.1 and looks quite different from the other two. Cars that were stolen the most frequently top the list, but their theft rates are not necessarily high if huge numbers were sold. In fact, some cars driven around by hundreds of thousands of motorists have rates that are essentially the same as the national average (1.8 reported thefts for every 1,000 new cars on the road during 2005).

Table 5.1 demonstrates that a key risk factor is the make, model, and year of the car. Certain types are more prized by thieves, in greater demand in the market for parts, and are easier to steal. Insurance records of thefts confirm the pattern that for several reasons, as cars age they are more likely to be targeted, especially during their fourth, fifth, and sixth years on the road. If the model lines are not substantially redesigned, then stolen sheet metal crash parts from the older cars can be used by illicit collision body shops to repair damaged newer ones. Also, middle-aged cars are less likely to be equipped with the latest state-of-the-art anti-theft devices that thieves have not yet learned how to defeat. Another reason is that as cars wear out and depreciate, their owners have less incentive to maintain security devices in good working order and to vigilantly observe precautions about where they park their less-valuable vehicles. Because most cars have a "life expectancy" of seven to 10 years, security experts warn owners never to let their guard down (see Clark and Harris, 1992; "NICB Study," 1993; Krauss, 1994).

Finally, to make matters more complex, the desirability of particular vehicles on the black market varies around the country. For example, thieves concentrated on Japanese models in Los Angeles, pickup trucks in Dallas, and American sedans in Chicago, reflecting the preferences of consumers in those metropolitan areas (Sparkman, 2003). The insurance industry generates detailed lists annually of the most frequently targeted cars that are tailored for every state and even each large city (see NICB, 2008b), so that companies can maximize their profits by fine-tuning premiums to reflect payouts to their local customers for theft losses.

Differential risks are determined by a number of factors besides the attractiveness of the target in the stolen car market. Another set of determinants of risk must be the number of professional thieves and chop shops operating in a given area, as well as the effectiveness of the efforts by local police departments to put them out of business. The importance of the geographic factor is illustrated in Table 5.2.

TABLE 5.2   Vehicle Theft Rates in U.S. Cities, 2007

Metropolitan Area	Rank	Rate of Thefts per 100,000 Residents
Modesto, CA	1	1050
Las Vegas, NV	2	1035
San Diego, CA	3	945
Stockton, CA	4	840
San Francisco, CA	5	830
Laredo, TX	6	820
Albuquerque, NM	7	820
Phoenix, AZ	8	820
Yakima, WA	9	815
Tucson, AZ	10	805
Seattle, WA	16	740
Detroit, MI	18	700
New Orleans, LA	21	665
Miami, FL	27	590
Los Angeles, CA	28	575
San Jose, CA	32	545
Atlanta, GA	36	530
Dallas, TX	50	480
Orlando, FL	52	465
Washington, D.C.	56	450
Denver, CO	59	445
Jacksonville, FL	62	440
San Antonio, TX	69	420
St. Louis, MO	76	410
Chicago, IL	84	395
Philadelphia, PA	110	340
Nashville, TN	145	285
New York City, NY	224	200
Boston, MA	225	200
Pittsburgh, PA	257	165
Boulder, CO	299	130
Madison, WI	353	75
Ithaca, NY	359	40
State College, PA	361	40

NOTE: The boundaries of metropolitan statistical areas are defined by the U.S. Census and often include nearby counties and suburban towns. Rankings were calculated by the NICB based on *UCR* rates. Rates are rounded to the nearest 5.

SOURCE: NICB, 2008a.

This listing of vehicle theft rates for the nation's metropolitan areas is based on data assembled by insurance companies from police reports maintained in the FBI's *UCR*. From a motorist's point of view, this ranking indicates the most dangerous places to park a car. Drivers in many Western states, and especially in California cities, have the most to worry about when they walk away from their cars. Those who find parking spaces on New York City's reputedly mean streets have far less to be apprehensive about than motorists in any other big city in America. Drivers who park in the university towns of Madison, Wisconsin; Ithaca, New York; and State College, Pennsylvania, can rest assured (statistically speaking) that their vehicles will still be there when they return.

Tables 5.1 and 5.2 show that motorists who drive vehicles that are on thieves' "hottest cars" list and who park them on the meanest streets of the most dangerous cities face unusually high risks. Victim-blamers would argue that these owners are on notice that their cars are likely targets and they ought to take extra precautions (provided that they are aware of the odds and of their options).

Besides vehicle attractiveness and geographic location, two other factors surely influence the vulnerability of a parked car: the effectiveness of factory-installed and after-market add-on antitheft devices, and the immediate micro-environment—such as traffic patterns, passing pedestrians, the intensity of lighting at night—surrounding the street, driveway, or lot where the vehicle sits unguarded. These two factors are under the control of individuals to some degree, except that many motorists cannot afford secure but expensive parking arrangements and costly antitheft hardware.

As previously noted, different categories of people do not face the same risks of harm from criminals. According to an analysis of a database of more than 12 million attempted and completed vehicle thefts disclosed to *NCVS* interviewers between 1973 and 1985, people who faced the greatest dangers of losing their cars were apartment dwellers, residents of inner-city neighborhoods, African Americans and Hispanic Americans, low-income families, and households headed by people under the age of 25. The people whose cars were least likely to be stolen were residents

of rural areas, homeowners, and those over age 55 (Harlow, 1988). Could it be that a motorist's spending priorities, lifestyle choices, and routine driving and parking patterns—in other words, their attitudes and behaviors—determine, to some degree, the fate of their vehicles?

Blaming the Victim for Facilitating the Crime

No intelligent person would put from $1,000 to $5,000 in good money in the street and expect to find it there an hour later, yet that is exactly what a large number of people do when they leave an automobile in the street without locking it. Even more, not only are they leaving money at the curb but they are also putting four wheels under it to make it easier for the thief to take it.

AUGUST VOLLMER, POLICE CHIEF, BERKELEY, CALIFORNIA (VOLLMER AND PARKER, 1936: 65)

Yet through all this practical, emotional, and monetary attachment to the automobile, there emerges convincing evidence that it is one of the motorist's most carelessly neglected possessions.

J. EDGAR HOOVER, FBI DIRECTOR (HOOVER, 1966)

People need to apply more common sense to protect their vehicles.

DONNA DRISCOLL, V.P. FOR MARKETING, LOJACK, INC. (2003) (QUOTED IN LISI, 2003)

Who or what is to blame for the theft and attempted theft of more than a million vehicles a year?

If motorists fail to do all they can do to protect their vehicles, then they might be faulted for negligence. Car stealing seems to be the only crime for which there is an organized victim-blaming lobby, a peculiar situation that developed long ago. Composed of representatives of automakers, insurance companies, and law enforcement agencies, this lobby has castigated motorist carelessness since the dawn of the automobile age. As the statements above demonstrate, victim-blamers are quick to scold negligent drivers for facilitating thefts by leaving their vehicles unlocked, or, even worse, for leaving keys in the ignition locks.

The contribution of victim facilitation to auto theft has usually been measured as the percentage of recovered stolen cars in which there was evidence that the thieves had used the owners' keys. Although this methodology has limitations, surveys based on it show a trend that casts doubt on the continued relevance of negligence as a factor. Data from insurance company records from the 1940s through the 1960s indicate that between 40 percent and 90 percent of all thefts were facilitated by victims through carelessness about locks and keys. During the 1970s, police, FBI, and insurance industry records showed that facilitation was a factor in 13 percent to 20 percent of all thefts (Karmen, 1979; National Institute of Justice, 1984). In the early 1990s, an insurance industry publication reported that only 13 percent of all vehicle thefts were still victim facilitated (National Insurance Crime Bureau, 1993).

These estimates support the following analysis: At one time, when the public was less conscious about crime, facilitation may have contributed substantially to joyriding escapades. But teenage amateurs no longer are responsible for most car thefts in cities and suburbs. Professionals—often working for commercial rings that may be affiliated with organized crime syndicates—now represent the greater threat. As the years roll by, key facilitation is declining in significance.

Even though the proportions of car thefts that are facilitated by motorists have been dropping over the decades, the absolute number remains high. For example, if 13 percent of roughly 1 million thefts in 2006 were made easier by the thoughtless behavior of drivers, that means about 130,000 acts of car stealing were preventable. According to a poll of 1,000 motorists commissioned by insurance companies, evidence persists that drivers are still not doing all they can to safeguard their cherished possessions. Nearly 40 percent said they were "not at all concerned" about having their cars stolen. As for precautions, about 75 percent of car owners had not installed an alarm or other antitheft device. As many

as 30 percent conceded that they did not always lock their car doors, and roughly 10 percent admitted that there were occasions when they left their keys in their vehicles (National Insurance Crime Bureau, 1995). A more recent survey of 930 drivers commissioned by a company selling recovery devices established that the proportion of motorists who had not purchased antitheft devices had dropped to 43 percent. However, more than one-third of respondents (and half of the 18- to 24-year-olds) confessed that they routinely left their vehicles unattended while the engines were running to either warm up or cool off the interior or to accomplish a quick errand (Lisi, 2003).

The clash in outlooks between victim blaming and victim defending is an example of a half-empty/half-full debate. Victim blaming focuses on the proportion of motorists who have bad habits. Victim defending emphasizes that the overwhelming majority of people whose cars were stolen did nothing wrong; these drivers don't have self-defeating attitudes and don't act carelessly. According to victim defenders, the image of the absentminded owner that is frequently conjured up by victim-blaming arguments is an outmoded stereotype that no longer fits (Karmen, 1980).

Up to this point, the focus of victim-blaming arguments has been placed on motorist negligence. But some who lose their cars to thieves might be even more blameworthy. Besides facilitation, it is possible to devise scenarios to illustrate precipitation, provocation, and even total responsibility for a theft. A typology of different kinds of victims of a single crime, such as auto theft, can be useful to illustrate the differences between complete innocence, facilitation, precipitation, provocation, and full responsibility. Such a typology also makes it possible to determine estimates of relative proportions of various types or groupings of owners—what, if anything, they do wrong and how stealing might be prevented.

Conscientiously resisting victims are blameless. They bear no responsibility because they tried to protect their autos by scrupulously following the crime prevention tips suggested by security specialists and by purchasing antitheft devices.

Auto security experts advise motorists to sharpen their crime awareness and then adopt a "layered approach" to "harden their targets." The first layer involves taking standard precautions: rolling up windows, locking doors, and removing the key from the ignition. The second layer relies on a presumed deterrent effect of visible or audible devices that broadcast the message that the vehicle is protected by an extra line of defense: car alarms, decals warning intruders to keep away, VIN numbers etched into the window glass, microdot marking, tire deflators, tire locks, steering column collars, brake pedal locks, and wheel locks. The third level takes advantage of sophisticated technology to immobilize the vehicle against attempts to bypass the ignition and hotwire the car: fuse cut-offs; hidden kill switches; starter, ignition, and fuel pump disablers; wireless ignition authentication; and smart keys with embedded chips. The fourth and most expensive layer consists of a tracking device, perhaps with remote monitoring using GPS technology, that will send signals to enable the police to recover the vehicle and perhaps catch the thieves red-handed (see Scafidi, 2008).

If the defensive measures adopted by conscientiously resisting victims proved futile, then they must have been preyed upon by professional thieves who knew how to disarm or circumvent the most resistant locks and sophisticated alarm systems.

Conventionally cautious victims relied on the antitheft features provided by automobile manufacturers as standard equipment. They took the precautions of removing all valuables from sight, rolled up their cars' windows, locked all doors, and pocketed the keys. Even though they did all they were supposed to do, experienced thieves with the proper tools had no trouble driving their cars away. These victims did nothing wrong but did not undertake additional theft-resistance efforts, so they can be faulted for not taking the threat of car stealing seriously enough. Thus, they can be considered largely blameless, although they are not above criticism.

Carelessly facilitating victims set the stage for crimes of opportunity through gross negligence. Their vehicles were taken by inexperienced thieves or joyriders. They made the criminals' tasks easier by leaving the car doors unlocked, the windows open, or worst of all, the keys in the ignition. They can be considered partly responsible precisely because their indifferent attitudes and thoughtless behavior contributed to their own losses. However, they were unintentional, unwilling, inadvertent victims who bear no guilt legally.

Precipitative initiators were knowing and willing victims who deliberately singled out their vehicles for trouble. They wanted their cars to be stolen because they figured that they would be better off financially if they received the blue-book value (a standard guide of used vehicle prices) as reimbursement from the insurance company rather than if they maintained, repaired, or sold their vehicles.. So they took steps that went beyond carelessness. They intentionally left their cars unlocked with the keys in the ignition and parked invitingly in high-crime areas. By maximizing the vulnerability of their autos, they incited would-be thieves to strike. But the relationships between the precipitating victims and the criminals were impersonal. They never met, despite the symbiosis between them. If challenged or investigated, these substantially responsible victims could conceal their dishonest motives and contend that they were merely negligent motorists who had left their keys in their cars accidentally.

Provocative conspirators are largely responsible for the loss of their cars. They are scam artists who pretend to be injured parties but actually were the accomplices of the thieves they hired to get rid of their unwanted vehicles. Without their instigations, the thefts would not have taken place. As part of a conspiracy to commit insurance fraud, these unscrupulous owners arranged to have their cars "splashed" (driven off a bridge or pier into deep water), "squished" (compacted, crushed, and then shredded beyond recognition), or "torched" (set on fire) to collect insurance reimbursement. Provocative conspirators share the same financial motives as precipitative initiators, but they leave nothing to chance; they know and pay off the criminals who work with them (see Behar, 1993) in what police and insurance claims investigators call "owner give-ups" (see Scafidi, 2006b).

Fully responsible **fabricating simulators** are not victims at all because they never even owned cars. They insured a nonexistent vehicle (a "paper" or "phantom" car) and later reported it stolen to the authorities so that they could collect money by defrauding insurance companies. These con men pretend to be victims and concoct a story for their own dishonest purposes.

The relative mix of these six types of auto theft victims can be roughly estimated. Carelessly facilitating victims who leave their keys in their cars made up, at most, 20 percent of all victims in the 1990s but constituted a higher proportion decades ago. Another 10 percent to 25 percent were suspected of engaging in insurance fraud (Baldwin, 1988; Sloane, 1991; Kerr, 1992). The percentage of conventionally cautious and conscientiously resisting motorists is more difficult to operationalize and measure, but it is growing as more cars are protected by alarms and other built-in or after-market antitheft devices like smart keys and immobilizers. If as many as 25 percent of all victims wanted their cars to be stolen (precipitative initiators, provocative conspirators, and fabricating simulators combined) and another 20 percent were careless facilitators, then conventionally cautious and conscientiously resisting motorists together add up to the remaining 55 percent.

Victim defenders would reject the argument made by victim blamers that emphasizes shared responsibility and would instead point out that the majority of motorists whose vehicles were driven away were totally or largely innocent and should not be criticized for suffering these losses.

STOLEN IDENTITIES: WHICH THEFTS ARE VICTIM-FACILITATED, AND WHICH PRECAUTIONS ARE REASONABLE?

The crime of identity theft undermines the basic trust on which our economy depends. When a person takes out an insurance policy or makes an online purchase or opens a savings account, he or she must have confidence that personal financial information will be protected and treated with care. Identity theft harms not only its direct victims, but also many businesses and customers whose confidence is shaken. Like other forms of stealing, identity theft leaves the victim poor and feeling terribly violated.

PRESIDENT GEORGE BUSH, 2004 (REMARKS WHEN SIGNING THE IDENTITY THEFT PENALTY ENHANCEMENT ACT)

The Nature of the Problem

Throughout history, people seeking to evade capture have used disguises, false papers, and aliases to pass themselves off as someone else. Spies, saboteurs, infiltrators, terrorists, and fugitives from justice used fictitious histories, documents, and résumés to fool authorities. But now computer databases and high-tech devices provide incentives for impersonators for a different reason: monetary gain.

The relatively new, increasingly sophisticated, and surprisingly common white-collar crime of **identity theft** arises from the illegal appropriation of someone's personal information—such as the individual's name, address, date of birth, Social Security number, and mother's maiden name. Unscrupulous impostors use these identifiers to max out existing charge accounts and obtain new credit cards in their target's name and then run up huge bills that are ignored. ID thieves empty people's savings accounts and pass bad checks. They secure car loans that will never be repaid based on another person's credit history, and enjoy gas heat, electricity, cell phones, and landlines but disregard the costs and consequences of becoming delinquent. They drive around and get tickets with a license that has their picture but someone else's name, apply for government benefits they don't deserve, are hired for jobs by pretending to be an employee with better credentials, and may even get arrested under an assumed name before disappearing while on bail.

This summarizes the range of swindles and scams impersonators use to harm their victims. Table 5.3 shows the relative frequency of each of these forms

T A B L E 5.3   How Victims of Identity Theft Were Harmed, Nationwide, 2006

Crime	Percent of Complaints
Credit Card Fraud	
Charging items to existing accounts	11
Opening new accounts in their names	15
Bank Frauds	
Draining existing accounts	6
Receiving electronic fund transfers	8
Opening new accounts in their names	3
Utilities Fraud	
Getting a new cell phone in their names	7
Getting a new telephone in their names	4
Getting gas, electric service in their names	6
Loan Fraud	
Taking out business/personal/student loans in their names	3
Taking out auto loans/leases in their names	2
Taking out mortgages in their names	1
Employment-Related Fraud	
Working under their victims' names	14
Government Document Frauds	
Filing false tax returns for refunds in their names	6
Obtaining drivers licenses in their names	1
Other Purposes and Ways, including attempts	24

NOTE: Figures are based on 246,000 complaints received by the Federal Trade Commission (FTC) from individuals and participating agencies in 2006. Percentages exceed 100% because some victims were harmed in more than one way and due to rounding.

SOURCE: Federal Trade Commission Identity Theft Data Clearinghouse, February 2007.

of fiscal exploitation as the percentage of complainants who suffered losses in a particular way. Credit card fraud was the most common category, afflicting about one-quarter of all victims; loan fraud was the least likely swindle exposed that year.

As many as 8 million Americans suffer from identify theft each year, the Federal Trade Commission (2008) estimates. That figure is much greater than the number of homes burglarized annually (about 3.5 million), and of motor vehicles stolen per year (nearly 1 million) in cities and suburbs, according to the *NCVS* (Baum, 2007).

Identity theft is often characterized as America's fastest-growing crime, but that may no longer be accurate. Different databases about trends over recent years yield contradictory impressions. One survey found a 50 percent increase in ID theft over the three years ending in 2006 and attributed the rise to the emergence of organized cybercrime rings operating overseas (Gartner, Inc., in Kaplan, 2007). Yet no statistically significant change was found in the number of people reporting they were victimized in 2005 (3.7 percent) compared to 2002 (4.6 percent), according to another small telephone-based survey commissioned by the federal government to detect changes over the years (Synovate, 2006). Another small-sample annual poll detected a slight downward drift (from 4.7 percent in 2003, to 4.3 in 2004, then 4.0 in 2005, slipping to 3.7 percent in 2006) (Javelin Strategy and Research, Inc., cited in Leland, 2007). Researchers suspect that the type of outreach—randomly telephoning, sending questionnaires via the mail, or collecting data online—might account for the discrepancies in the trend data.

Questions about identity theft were added to the *NCVS* in 2004. The 2005 *NCVS* estimated that 5.5 percent of the nation's households suffered an incident that year. Unauthorized use of an existing credit card was the most widespread problem, more common than draining an existing savings or checking account or using personal information to open a new credit card account or to secure a loan. A small decline was detected in the number of households experiencing identity theft incidents during the second half of 2005 (2.8 percent) compared to 2004 (3.1 percent), according to an analysis of the relatively large sample, but the difference was not statistically significant (Baum, 2007).

Another source of estimates about how many people have had their identities "hijacked by privacy pirates" is from the Federal Trade Commission (FTC), which operates an Identity Theft Data Clearinghouse that receives information from about 150 law enforcement agencies and collects details from online complaint forms and calls to its hotline (877-IDTHEFT). Incident reports have been pouring in to the FTC's Consumer Sentinel monitoring system since it was set up in 1997. During 2002, details about roughly 160,000 incidents were logged. The number rose to about 215,000 by the end of 2003. By the close of 2004, more than 245,000 identity theft complaints had been received. The next year, 10,000 more incidents were reported, but in 2006 the total dropped by about 10,000 cases, so identity theft no longer was growing in volume with each passing year (FTC, 2007).

As with most crimes, many cases go unreported, so these statistics are underestimates of the problem. An FTC-sponsored survey in 2003 of more than 4,000 randomly selected Americans uncovered that most who had been financially harmed conceded that they did not report the incident to local police or to any of the three major credit bureaus. The average victim did not discover the misuse of identifiers for about a year, although nearly half detected that something was wrong in some account within the first month. In most cases (over 70 percent), the person who suffered the loss could not figure out how the theft took place. (FTC, 2003; Synovate, 2003).

Differential Risks of Becoming a Victim of Identity Theft

Several obstacles hamper attempts to derive accurate estimates of the frequency of these thefts and the profile of those who are targeted most often. First, some people do not yet know that impostors have assumed their identities. Second, some victims are not aware that the FTC has been designated as the national clearinghouse for complaints. Third, certain individuals and businesses are unwilling to report their personal financial problems to law enforcement agencies and government hotlines.

Finally, confusion persists over definitions of the crime and its victims. Consumer and privacy groups use more inclusive definitions to dramatize the seriousness of the problem and the weaknesses of anticrime efforts undertaken to date by government agencies and businesses. Representatives of financial services companies insist that cases involving a forged check or an unauthorized credit card transaction should not be counted as full-blown identity theft (Katel, 2005).

Individuals in their late teens and early 20s were the most likely to report that they had suffered an incident, yet they were least likely to observe

risk reduction precautions (shredding documents and setting up computer firewalls), according to a 2006 survey (Javelin Strategy and Research, Inc., cited in Leland, 2007).

NCVS findings yielded more details about differential risks. Rates did not vary significantly by race and ethnicity, or by marital status. But families earning $75,000 or more were targeted more than those in lower income brackets, Senior citizens were taken advantage of less often than others, and inhabitants of rural areas less frequently than city dwellers or suburbanites, according to the 2005 *NCVS* (Baum, 2007).

As with other types of crimes, Table 5.4 indicates that where people live plays a major role in shaping differential risks. Many more reports of being impersonated per 100,000 residents have been filed at the FTC clearinghouse from Arizona, Nevada, California, and Texas than from other states. The risks by geographic locale can be fine-tuned

T A B L E 5.4 **States Where Residents Faced the Highest and Lowest Risks of Identity Theft, 2006**

Rank	State	Victimization Rate per 100,000 Inhabitants
1	Arizona	148
2	Nevada	120
3	California	114
4	Texas	111
5	Florida	98
6	Colorado	93
7	Georgia	86
8	New York	85
9	Washington	83
10	New Mexico	83
	Lowest risks	
46	West Virginia	39
47	Iowa	35
48	South Dakota	30
49	North Dakota	30
50	Vermont	29

NOTE: Based on 246,000 complaints received by the FTC from individuals and participating law enforcement agencies during 2006.
Many incidents are not reported.
SOURCE: Federal Trade Commission Identity Theft Data Clearinghouse (FTC, 2007).

further by focusing on cities. During 2006 metropolitan-area residents faced the greatest dangers of identity theft in: Brownsville, McAllen, Laredo, Corpus Christi, and Dallas-Fort Worth, Texas; Phoenix, Scottsdale, and Tucson, Arizona; Napa, Madera, Yuba City, Hanford, Vallejo, Stockton, Bakersfield, Fresno, Modesto, Ventura, Riverside, San Bernardino, and Sacramento, California; Vero Beach, Miami-Fort Lauderdale, Port St. Lucie-Fort Pierce, and Lakeland, Florida; Las Cruces and Las Vegas, Nevada; and Dunn, Durham, and Goldsboro, North Carolina. Clearly, identity stealing is a greater problem in the West than in other regions of the country, according to both the FTC's city and state rankings, which vary substantially from year to year.

Losses and Suffering

Just as the findings of different studies yield confusion about general prevalence, yearly incidence, and twenty-first century trends, so too are there widely varying estimates of the actual costs of this crime. The scams and swindles exact a serious toll on society as a whole, adding up to billions of dollars in losses annually. New account fraud is more costly but less frequent. Depletion of existing accounts is less common but more expensive to recover from. Businesses sustain most of the financial losses because individuals usually are not held responsible for charges that turn out to be fraudulent.

But individuals collectively spend billions in their efforts to repair their credit worthiness. Individuals also suffer indirect costs in the form of businesses' expenses for fraud prevention and lost revenue that are passed on to them as higher fees; for legal bills to pay for civil litigation initiated by creditors over disputed purchases; and for time lost and aggravation they endure while undoing the damage inflicted by the impostor (President's Task Force, 2007:11).

ID theft was estimated to cost $48 billion during the early years of the twenty-first century. The average thief was thought to gain about $10,200 from setting up phony accounts and about $2,100 in credit card abuse. The mean amount of time that

a thief exploited a target's name was three months. Typical out-of-pocket expenses victims suffered averaged $500; businesses lost about $4,800 per theft (Sherman, 2005; National Criminal Justice Reference Service [NCJRS], 2005). Fraudulent new accounts cost consumers an average of $1,180 and required about 60 hours of time to repair credit histories. Thefts from existing accounts led to average losses of $160 and took 15 hours to remedy during 2002. Harm to individuals in out-of-pocket expenses and time spent on paperwork depended on how long it took to discover the fraud (Synovate, 2003).

However, a series of estimates of cumulative losses imposed by all ID thefts since 2001 (Synovate, 2006:5-6) using a small sample derived from random-digit dialing were much more modest in size because median rather than mean values were calculated, thereby greatly reducing the mathematical impact of a relatively small number of cases of severe financial harm. The median value of goods and services obtained by ID thieves was a mere $500. The median amount of out-of-pocket losses victims suffered was $0 (however, 10 percent of victims suffered losses greater than $1,200 in the form of lost wages, fraudulent bills, and legal expenses). The median number of hours spent to repair the damage was just four (although 10 percent spent more than 50 hours straightening out their financial affairs).

Identity theft goes through a lifecycle. People discover they have been preyed upon when they get a call from a credit card fraud division, or when a purchase is declined at the point of sale because a card's limit has been exceeded. Others find out when they are contacted by a bill collector demanding payment on a delinquent account, or when a monthly statement marked "overdue" arrives in the mail. Others notice unauthorized charges on credit card statements, peculiar and costly long-distance calls on phone bills, cashed or bounced checks they never wrote, or suspicious withdrawals from their bank accounts. In extreme cases, they discover they have been targeted when the police take them into custody as a fugitive on an outstanding warrant, and then it becomes clear that a lawbreaker was released after showing false documents and posting bail. It can take weeks, months, maybe even years before individuals become aware that they have been targeted because the crooks want to get away with the charade for as long as possible. Some don't discover the extent of the damage until they are denied new credit cards, turned down for student loans, or charged extra high interest rates for mortgages and car loans (Collins and Hoffman, 2004).

Once the surreptitious destruction of a good credit rating is discovered, victims must file complaints with their local police and the FTC. They must cancel all their compromised credit and identification cards, close existing savings and checking accounts, and begin the time-consuming, aggravating, and somewhat expensive process of contacting and sending notarized notifications to fraud units of the three national credit bureaus.

Next, victims might notify the FBI, IRS, U.S. Postal Inspection Service, Social Security Administration, Secret Service, Passport Office, and their departments of motor vehicles. Counselors at an FTC hotline offer advice about the steps to be followed and how to use their standard ID Theft Affidavit to simplify the process of settling disputed charges with defrauded creditors (FTC, 2002 and 2008; U.S. General Accounting Office, 2002; Slosarik, 2002; and Lee, 2003a).

The emotional toll of trying to restore their financial reputation can cause some victims to become highly suspicious of other people's motives and profoundly distrustful of officials and agencies they had counted upon to help them. Victims can experience a wide range of reactions, from denial to humiliation to outrage. Their distress is compounded if the crime is never solved and the real name of the thief never becomes known. Some feel overwhelmed and powerless, as well as ashamed and embarrassed for appearing to be spendthrifts and deadbeats. Others join self-help groups that have websites to share advice and facilitate mutual support with those who know firsthand what it is like to repair a lifetime record of creditworthiness (Busch-White, 2002; and Savage, 2003).

Laws and Law Enforcement

Victims of identity theft were "discovered" during the 1990s when nearly all state legislatures criminalized the unlawful possession of personal identification information for the purposes of committing fraud. In 1998, Congress passed the Identity Theft and Assumption Deterrence Act, which not only imposed stiff sentences and fines on those who committed this new federal offense, but also stipulated that the impersonated individual was a crime victim deserving of financial protection and reimbursement. Prior to this act, only the grantors of credit who suffered monetary losses were considered to be the actual victims entitled to receive court-ordered restitution from convicted thieves.

The FTC was given the task of compiling the details about fraudulent transactions from complainants and issuing annual reports from its Identity Theft Data Clearinghouse and its Consumer Sentinel database. A provision of the Fair and Accurate Credit Transactions Act of 2003 enabled consumers to get one free credit report each year so they can check for any suspicious activity in their accounts. Congress authorized the Department of Homeland Security to get involved when it passed the REAL ID act in 2005. The Social Security Administration also is charged with devising ways for federal agencies and the private sector to reduce the unnecessary use of Social Security numbers, because those identifiers are the keys to unlocking many confidential accounts. It also educates consumers how to avoid and recover from identity theft. Some local police departments and prosecutors' offices are setting up special units. A National Identity Theft Law Enforcement Center to improve the effectiveness of training, coordination, investigation and prosecution remains in the planning stage (NCJRS, 2005; Kelleher, 2006; President's Task Force, 2007).

Several problems continue to undermine the effectiveness of efforts by law enforcement agencies to come to the aid of identity theft victims. First, many officers lack necessary training, and their departments lack the needed resources to provide an adequate response. Second, multijurisdictional complications undercut an agency's commitment to follow through on a complaint. When a victim in one city reports to a local police department that a thief has stolen personal information and is carrying out fraudulent financial transactions in another city, state, or country, which law enforcement agency bears primary responsibility for seeing the investigation through to completion?

Furthermore, many victims of identity theft do not bring their monetary troubles to the attention of local police. An FTC survey carried out in 2003 found that only 38 percent of the respondents who informed financial institutions such as banks and credit card companies also filed complaints with the police. In 8 percent of these cases where individuals sought help, the police refused to fill out a report (FTC, 2005). However, the more financially serious acts of fraud involving setting up a new account in a victim's name were reported to law enforcement agencies at a somewhat higher rate, 43 percent. This reporting rate for the white-collar crime of identity theft mirrors the findings of the *NCVS* for comparable street crimes: a 44 percent reporting rate for personal thefts and a 38 percent rate for all other property crimes that same year (NCJRS, 2005).

Some victims are understandably upset if authorities seem unsympathetic, show skepticism at their protestations of innocence, and appear reluctant to officially file their complaints and take action. Victims may sense that *they* are assumed to be guilty of wrongdoing as they fill out notarized forms, telephone merchants who are demanding payment, fend off collection agencies, and write lengthy explanations to credit rating bureaus. Victims realize that they bear the burden of proof: They are held financially responsible unless and until they can establish their innocence and clear their names.

Because law enforcement countermeasures are not yet effective, identity snatchers know that the risks of apprehension, conviction, and punishment are relatively low, while the returns are potentially high. These crimes are difficult, time-consuming, and expensive to investigate, especially when multiple jurisdictions are involved. In fact, offenders exploit these problems by misusing the stolen information far from the original crime scene preferably another county, state, or country (Collins and Hoffman, 2004).

Blaming Victims for Ignoring Risk-Reduction Strategies

Protect your Social Security number and other personal information. [Addressing college students:] Don't let identity thieves rob you of your educational future!

INSPECTOR GENERAL JOHN HIGGINS OF THE U.S. DEPARTMENT OF EDUCATION (2005)

The first line of defense against identity theft often is an aware and motivated consumer who takes reasonable precautions to protect his information. Every day, unwitting consumers create risks to the security of their personal information. From failing to install firewall protection on a computer hard drive to leaving paid bills in a mail slot, consumers leave the door open to identity thieves. Consumer education is a critical component of any plan to reduce the incidence of identity theft.

(PRESIDENT'S TASK FORCE ON IDENTITY THEFT, 2007: 39)

Awareness is an effective weapon against many forms of identity theft. Be aware of how information is stolen, and what you can do to protect yours, monitor your personal information to detect any problems quickly, and know what to do when you suspect your identity has been stolen. Armed with the knowledge of how to protect yourself and take action, you can make identity thieves' jobs much more difficult.

FEDERAL TRADE COMMISSION (2008), "WHAT CAN YOU DO TO HELP FIGHT IDENTITY THEFT?"

We're all vulnerable to identity theft—that's the bad news. The good news is that you can protect yourself.

FBI AGENT JEFF LANZA, 2006 (FBI, 2008)

As the threat of identity theft mushrooms, a victim-blaming versus victim-defending debate is emerging. Victim blaming accentuates the many ways careless people can make the thieves' tasks easier—facilitation—and even call attention to their vulnerability and single themselves out for trouble—precipitation. Victim defending points out the many opportunities that thieves can seize to purloin information that are beyond the ability of individuals to control or counter.

Thieves can steal information from their unsuspecting prey during a range of routine activities. Personal identifiers can be intercepted in technologically sophisticated ways while victims are engaged in banking transactions online or when they are buying merchandise or tickets over the Internet. Cell phone transmissions can also be monitored to hijack information. Birth certificates can be obtained under false pretenses from records maintained by county governments. Crooks posing as landlords or employers conducting background checks can get other people's credit reports (Office of the Inspector General, 2005).

As for the victim-offender relationship, the criminal is usually but not always a complete stranger. Thieves can resort to a range of methods to get the information they need to become effective impostors. They can employ old-fashioned methods such as grabbing wallets and purses during burglaries and robberies or by breaking into parked cars to find personal papers and laptops. Identity crooks can commit a federal offense by sorting through a person's mail for bank and credit card statements, pre-approved credit card offers, new checkbooks, telephone bills, or tax receipts. Patient criminals can even file a "change of address" form at a post office to divert a target's mail to a location of their choosing. Gutsy thieves can pry loose secrets by "pretexting:" posing as representatives of a government agency or business with a legitimate need to know personal information. They can pilfer records kept by an employer, or they can bribe an employee who has access to confidential files. They can engage in **"dumpster-diving"** by rummaging through an individual's garbage or the trash thrown away by businesses or hospitals, searching for discarded receipts and bank statements.

Besides these low-tech means, some thieves have mastered sophisticated high-tech methods. **"Shoulder surfers"** find out passwords by watching their marks at ATMs. Corrupt employees can use **"skimmers"** to scan and capture crucial information during credit card transactions at restaurants and other stores. Others obtain what they need to know via the Internet by searching agency records (especially about births, marriages, and deaths). Cyber-thieves, perhaps operating on some other continent, can engage in **"phishing"** and **"pharming."** "Phishermen" try to fool, entice, or frighten e-mail recipients into disclosing account numbers, user names, and passwords on authentic-looking fake websites; they write that they need to update an existing account or repair a security breach with a bank or other financial institution. Pharmers attack legitimate websites with malicious codes that steer traffic to look-alike sites that "harvest" (intercept and decode) encrypted online transactions. "Keystroke logging" spyware, planted inside a computer with a malicious code or virus, betrays everything an unsuspecting user types. "Screen-scrapers" can snatch and transmit whatever is on a monitor of an infected PC. Cell phone transmissions and instant messaging are current targets for a new wave of attacks (FTC, 2002; Slosarik, 2002; Collins and Hoffman, 2004; NCJRS, 2005; Shanahan, 2006).

Clearly, the victim-offender relationship can range from trusted employees, former intimate partners, and estranged relatives to casual acquaintances (like dishonest bank tellers or postal workers), to total strangers like "electronic intruders" (hackers) who break into files maintained by supposedly secure websites.

Arguments that implicitly or explicitly blame identity theft victims have been voiced by government officials and representatives of the financial services industry. This point of view proceeds from the assumption that people determine their own fate and that carelessness is the most frequent cause of the problem. The individual whose identity was stolen probably failed to take adequate measures to protect his personal data. His inattention to details attracted Dumpster divers and shoulder surfers and made their illegal information-gathering tasks much easier to carry out. A foolish lapse in judgment can set up a "mark" to be defrauded (such as giving a stranger personal information over the phone when falling for a scam about entering a contest or claiming a prize). Just carelessly losing a wallet can lead to serious trouble. Indeed, the implicit victim blaming underlying theft-prevention educational campaigns is that those who don't observe precautions will be sorry someday when impostors misappropriate their identities. Victims who accept blame often obsess over how they inadvertently may have given their secrets away.

Most victims never figure out, "Why me?" A study commissioned in 2005 by a credit card company, an online check-clearing company, and a bank focused on the relatively small proportion that did discover how their personal identifiers were stolen. The survey provided ammunition to the victim-blaming view; it concluded that the failure of the victims to safeguard documents was the single most frequent cause of trouble. Lost or stolen wallets, credit cards, and checkbooks were the source of the problem in nearly 30 percent of all identity theft cases in which victims thought they knew why it happened to them (Katel, 2005).

College students might be especially vulnerable to identity theft for several reasons. They store personal data in shared, largely unguarded dormitory rooms. Many undergraduates might not take precautions because they do not have much money or assets. They do not realize that they could be targeted for their unblemished "good names and reputations," and not the limited amounts of cash in their bank accounts.

Advocates of victim-blaming cite a recent survey that documents lax attitudes toward handling personal identifiers on campus. That survey established that almost half of all college students received unsolicited credit card applications but many did not properly destroy this junk mail. Nearly one-third of student respondents conceded that they rarely, if ever, carefully reviewed the entries on their credit card and checking account statements. About half did not object to posting their grades by Social Security number (Office of the Inspector General,

2005). Many universities are now holding workshops on identity theft awareness, and are striving to safeguard their massive files on their students. But as many as half of all personal information breaches reported in 2006 involved campus databases. (President's Task Force, 2007:40).

A virtual cottage industry has sprung up to sell identity-theft prevention and self-help guidebooks (see May, 2001; Vacca, 2002). Government agencies do their part by warning the public to manage personal information "wisely and cautiously" by observing lengthy lists of dos and don'ts, such as these from the FTC (2008):

- Keep important documents such as bank books and tax returns under lock and key, as well as computers and laptops.

- Stash personal records so they aren't readily available to roommates, domestic employees, party guests, or repair workers.

- Use a paper shredder to destroy unsolicited pre-approved credit card invitations, as well as unneeded receipts, bills, and account statements, to thwart Dumpster divers who pick through trash for items revealing personal information.

- While away from home, discard paperwork from financial transactions at restaurants, banks, ATMs, and gasoline stations.

- Promptly remove incoming letters from a mailbox, and take outgoing bills and checks directly to post office collection boxes.

- Devise clever (rather than easily remembered but also easily guessed) passwords and creative substitutes for a birth date or a mother's maiden name for electronic accounts.

- Scrutinize bills and account statements for unauthorized transactions.

- Carefully review activity reports from each major credit bureau annually to check for unauthorized applications and accounts.

- Pay attention to each card's billing cycle, and quickly get in touch with creditors if monthly statements don't arrive on time.

- Request information about security procedures at one's workplace, such as who has access to databases, whether records are kept in a safe location, and how old files are disposed of by clerks.

- When a Social Security number is requested in a business transaction, ask: "Why is it needed? How will it be used? What law requires that it be divulged? What will happen if I refuse to provide it?"

- Go to the trouble of opting out of telephone solicitations, direct mail lists, and pre-approved credit card offers.

Similar advice comes from the Fraud Division of the U.S. Department of Justice (2008), which summarizes four ways of minimizing risks by using the acronym SCAM.

- Be "Stingy" about giving out personal information.

- "Check" your financial records regularly.

- "Ask" to see free credit reports each year.

- "Maintain" careful records of financial accounts.

Anyone intent on avoiding trouble can purchase an ID theft package plan. It consists of a monitoring service that sends out real time e-mail and cell phone alerts to subscribers whenever a change in information about them is detected in public records, credit reports, and commercial files. It may also take proactive steps of imposing fraud alerts and freezes on new accounts. If, despite these preventive measures, a customer suffers identity theft, the company provides an advocate who is an expert in designing and carrying out a personalized recovery plan. In addition to the early warning system and the assistance of an advocate, the plan also offers an insurance policy that reimburses policyholders for out-of-pocket recovery costs such as fees and time off from work (PR Newswire, 2005).

In sum, victims of identity theft sometimes are blamed—explicitly or implicitly—for failing to take this threat seriously. They ignored the long and growing lists of do's and don'ts, did something wrong, and singled themselves out for trouble (see Kelleher, 2006). They did not incorporate into their routines the many new suggestions for reducing risks. Because of carelessness (such as tossing away bank statements), neglect (like not buying a shredder), or foolishness (by falling for a scam) they facilitated the ruination of their creditworthiness.

Victim Defending: Facilitation Is Not the Heart of the Problem

It has been said that the theft of one's identity and personal information is not a matter of "if" but a matter of "when."

ELIOT SPITZER, NEW YORK STATE ATTORNEY GENERAL, 2005 (QUOTED IN KATEL, 2005: 534)

Firewalls and virus protection programs are routinely penetrated by sophisticated hackers seeking ID information.

BRUCE HELLMAN, SUPERVISOR OF THE FBI'S NEW YORK COMPUTER HACKING SQUAD (QUOTED IN SHERMAN, 2005:24)

Even if you take all of these steps, however, it's still possible that you can become a victim of identity theft.

U.S. DEPARTMENT OF JUSTICE, FRAUD DIVISION, 2008

The victim-defending perspective concedes that consistently following theft prevention recommendations would reduce a person's risks by making a thief's tasks more difficult to carry out. But the victim-defending viewpoint insists that even the most scrupulous observance of all these suggestions at all times still might prove ineffective. Experts warn that no one can stop a determined identity snatcher from achieving his goal. Therefore, it seems unfair to blame most victims because sophisticated identity pirates can overcome any obstacles cautious individuals place in their paths.

More and more people have sharpened their "cyber-streetwise" skills. They routinely shred unsolicited pre-approved credit card offers and financial documents that periodically fill their mailboxes. They immediately delete bogus e-mails from fake websites without opening any attachments, and regularly update their antivirus, firewall, and spam-blocking software. They resist giving up their Social Security numbers unless disclosure is mandatory (as on federal tax forms), and monitor their credit reports annually for free. And yet even as they foil attempted scams, ID crooks devise clever new ways to rip them off (Shanahan, 2006).

Furthermore, many people would consider the long lists of dos and don'ts to be unreasonable (such as workers grilling their employers about ways of safeguarding personnel files); impractical (customers refusing to provide Social Security numbers to creditors); burdensome (like changing their passwords containing many letters and numbers every six months); or unworkable (emptying home mailboxes at midday). Victim defenders point out that it is an emotional burden for most people to live the way victim blamers urge them to do: to regularly visit safe deposit boxes in banks to store all their documents with identifiers; shred all their financial statements; pick up their mail at secure boxes they rent at post offices; encrypt their routers for home wireless networks; periodically update security software and stay current by installing the latest patches; keep a lookout for skimmers, shoulder surfers, and Dumpster divers; and pay monthly fees for unlisted telephone numbers and commercial monitoring services that place fraud alerts with the three major credit bureaus and impose freezes on requests for new accounts.

Because the bulk of ID thefts go unsolved, it is not known how impostors are able to pilfer the confidential information they are seeking. According to the survey cited above, of the relatively small proportion of victims who found out how their personal data was compromised (FTC, 2005), many of the thefts were beyond their ability to prevent or thwart. It might be fair to blame most of the 29 percent of those who lost their wallets, but it would be unfair to fault some of them for surrendering their valuables to robbers or for leaving unsecured papers at home or at the office that were carted off by burglars. Victims can be criticized for falling for e-mail phishing scams (2 percent of all cases where the thieves' modus operandi were determined), and for tossing unshredded documents into the trash (3 percent). But they can't be held responsible if

their personal identifiers are intercepted during a transaction with an online seller's unsecure website (13 percent of all cases), or are purloined by a dishonest employee at the office or behind the counter (9 percent), or are swiped from their daily mail deliveries (8 percent). It is debatable whether they can they be condemned for unscrupulous actions by friends and relatives (11 percent) who had access to their personal information.

TRANSCENDING VICTIM BLAMING AND VICTIM DEFENDING

The analysis above of auto theft and identity theft, uncovered some strengths and weaknesses of both victim blaming and victim defending. Contrary to sweeping characterizations made by some victimologists, victim blaming is not inherently an exercise in scapegoating, an example of twisted logic, or a sign of callousness. It depends on which crime is the focus of attention, who the victims are, and why some people condemn that behavior. Similarly, victim defending is not always a noble enterprise engaged in by those who champion the cause of the downtrodden.

Victim blamers are not necessarily liberal or conservative, rich or poor, young or old, or male or female. Sometimes they switch sides and become victim defenders—depending on the facts of the case, the nature of the crime, and the parties involved. Individuals are not consistent; nearly everyone blames certain victims and defends others.

The strengths of victim blaming and victim defending lie in their advocates' willingness to address specific criminal acts and real-life incidents. The two clashing perspectives dissect in great detail who said and did what to whom and under what circumstances. Victim-blaming and victim-defending arguments bridge the gap between theoretical propositions and abstractions on the one hand, and how people genuinely think and act on the other.

The most serious drawback of both perspectives is a tendency to be microscopic rather than macroscopic. Victim-blaming and victim-defending arguments get so caught up (or bogged down) in the particularities of each case that they tend to ignore the larger social forces and environmental conditions that shape the attitudes and behaviors of both criminals and victims. Thus, whenever partisans of the two perspectives clash, they inadvertently let the system—with its fundamental institutions (established ways of organizing people to accomplish tasks) and culture (way of life, traditions)—off the hook. Yet these outside influences compel the actors in the drama to play the well-rehearsed roles of offender and victim and to follow a well-known script in an all-too-familiar tragedy.

In the case of car theft, victim-blaming and victim-defending arguments nearsightedly dwell on the actions of motorists and thieves. What is excluded from the analysis is as important as what is included. A comprehensive battle plan must take into account how sophisticated and organized commercial thievery has become, and how profitable the black market for "hot" cars and stolen parts continues to be. It must also grasp how the practices of insurance companies provide incentives for thieves to steal cars for parts, and how salvage yards make it easier for thieves to infiltrate stolen items into the flow of recycled parts to auto body repair shops. An effective anti-crime strategy must also come to grips with the inadequacies in record-keeping and in the stamping of serial numbers on crash parts. These shortcomings make it difficult for law enforcement officers to detect and prove thievery (see Karmen, 1980; NIJ, 1984).

Even more important, it is necessary to go beyond victim blaming and victim defending to realize that the manufacturers bear responsibility for the ease with which their products are taken from their customers. Pros brag that they need just a minute or two (and an ordinary screwdriver or some shaved-down keys) to defeat standard antitheft locks on the doors and ignitions of many makes and models (see Kesler, 1992; Behar, 1993; "Auto Theft Alert," 1994; S. Smith, 1994; and McKinley, 2006).

Perhaps blaming victims for auto theft serves to distract attention from engineering issues. The most virulent victim blaming has emanated from automobile industry spokespersons, insurance company representatives, and top law-enforcement officials. Who or what are they protecting? Certainly, they are not apologists for the lawbreakers, either the joyriding juveniles or the professional crooks. Apparently, condemning the motorists who left their cars vulnerable to thieves is intended to divert attention away from the automobile manufacturers who design and sell cars that are so easily stolen! Considerable evidence exists to substantiate the charge that until recently vehicle security (like passenger safety) was assigned a low priority by automakers, probably because thefts stimulate new car sales (see Karmen, 1981a). Vehicle security is likely to remain a problem until manufacturers are compelled by law to post theft-resistance ratings from an independent testing bureau or government laboratory on new-car showroom stickers.

As for identity theft, the system-blaming perspective proceeds from the assumption that most impersonations and counterfeit cards cannot be traced back to some act of carelessness. Consequently, effective prevention strategies cannot be predicated on efforts to transform thoughtless individuals into crime-conscious customers one at a time. Government must do more to compel organizations with databases (especially "data-brokers" who sell personal information for commercial purposes) to take additional measures to protect the public from raids on files by cyber-crooks and fraudsters across the globe who seek credit, debit, and ATM card account information (like PIN codes), Social Security numbers, and birthdates. For example, from January 2005 up to the first six months of 2008, more than 234 million records containing sensitive personal information were exposed in security breaches within the U.S. alone. That means that millions of people were put at high risk of identity theft when government agencies, banks, other commercial enterprises, and a number of universities (especially during 2008) reluctantly were compelled to admit that intruders broke into their record-keeping systems, office files, and computer databases (Privacy Rights Clearinghouse, 2008). Even though most victims are not able to determine how and why they were targeted, it seems likely that a great many must be totally innocent because their identities were stolen due to a security breach, and not because of carelessness on their part.

Many law enforcement agencies still lack experts in forensic computing and remain far behind the curve when it comes to detecting intrusions, figuring out who did it, and gathering evidence that will stand up in court. The odds are in the thieves' favor. Convictions take place in only one out of every 700 to 1,000 reported identity theft cases (Katel, 2005).

Most federal and state legislation passed to date focuses on deterring and punishing offenders. It offers little protection or relief in the form of government compensation or restitution by offenders for those who lose money, and fails to hold accountable the commercial ventures whose careless practices enable thieves to periodically swipe long lists of confidential data. Most state governments (38 plus the District of Columbia, as of 2007) have passed laws to compel organizations that maintain databanks to notify people put at risk when a breach of security takes place. But Congress must also pass stricter regulations that would impose uniform higher internal security standards on the operations of agencies and companies that suffer breaches with infuriating regularity. Thefts of personal data from supposedly secure computer files can endanger hundreds of thousands of consumers at a time (editors, *The New York Times*, 2005; Sherman, 2005; President's Task Force, 2007; and Consumer's Union, 2008).

The system-blaming approach also questions the sincerity of the efforts made by the giant corporations (especially banks and credit card companies) that seem to suffer losses when their customers fall prey to identity thieves. Even though this kind of fraud initially costs them billions of dollars annually, ultimately they pass along most of these expenses to their customers by raising rates and fees, just as large stores charge higher prices to cover "inventory shrinkage" due to shoplifting and employee theft. Any remaining losses can be written off at tax time. It appears that top executives have calculated that it is better for their businesses' bottom line to recoup money from honest customers than it is to spend more on fraud prevention or to pay more to pursue and help bring to justice impostors masquerading as someone else.

The three major credit bureaus suffer no direct losses, and even gain additional revenues when fearful consumers sign up for credit monitoring services or purchase personal activity reports (May, 2002). Sensing that this problem has become a deeply entrenched feature of the financial landscape, companies have discovered that the "crisis" presents an opportunity to make money by marketing services to detect suspicious activity and by selling a new form of insurance that repays policyholders for expenses arising from misappropriations of their good names.

Clearly, transcending the analytical confines of both victim blaming and victim defending requires that the researcher go beyond criminology and victimology and into the broader realm of social science: sociology, anthropology, psychology, economics, and political science. Only then can the effects of the social system on shaping the thoughts and actions of specific offenders and their victims be appreciated and understood. Doling out the proper mix of exoneration and blame to just two people is of limited value because the influences of outside forces are eliminated from consideration.

THE LEGAL IMPORTANCE OF DETERMINING RESPONSIBILITY

A wife returns home late at night after having a tryst with her landscaper at a motel. Her husband, a former professor and executive, becomes enraged and slams her face into the floor of the garage, splitting her head open. The police find her blood-soaked body behind the wheel of her SUV in a creek, but when they determine that the apparent driving accident was staged, the husband is arrested. He is prosecuted for her murder, but the jury finds him guilty of the lesser charge of passion/provocation manslaughter. The judge sentences him to eight years in prison, and he will be eligible for parole after five and a half years (Miller, 2005).

The process of fixing responsibility for crime unavoidably rests on judgments that are subject to challenges and criticisms. These judgments are based on values, ethics, allegiances, and prejudices concerning the crucial question of whether (and to what degree) the victim shares responsibility with the offender for a violation of the law. A number of important decisions that affect the fate of the offender, the plight of the victim, and the public's perception of the crime hinge on this issue of victim responsibility.

Whether or not the victim facilitated, precipitated, or provoked the offender is taken into account by police officers, prosecutors, juries, judges, compensation boards, insurance examiners, politicians, and crime control strategists. Victim responsibility is an issue at many stages in the criminal justice process: in applications for compensation; in demands for restitution and compensatory damages; in complaints about how crime victims are treated by family, friends, and strangers at home, in hospital emergency rooms, in court, and in the newspapers; and in the development of crime prevention programs and criminological theories.

At every juncture in the criminal justice process, judgments must be made about the degree of responsibility, if any, the victim bears for what happened. The police confront this issue first. For example, when called to the scene of a barroom brawl, officers must decide whether to arrest one or both or none of the participants and what charges to lodge if they do make arrests. Often the loser is declared the victim, and the combatant still on his feet is taken into custody for assault.

When prosecutors review the charges brought by the police against defendants, they must decide if the complainants were indeed totally innocent victims. If some degree of blame can be placed on them, their credibility as witnesses for the prosecution becomes impaired. A district attorney may decide that the accused person would probably be viewed by a jury or a judge as less culpable and less deserving of punishment and therefore has less of a chance of being convicted. Because relatively few cases are brought to trial, the prosecution will engage in plea bargaining (accepting a guilty plea to a lesser charge) if a blameworthy victim would be an unconvincing witness. Such cases might even be screened out and charges dropped. For instance, a study of files in the District of Columbia during the early 1970s revealed that evidence of victim blameworthiness halved the chances that a case would be prosecuted (Williams, 1976).

Killings that resulted from extreme provocations by the deceased are likely to be considered justifiable homicides and won't be prosecuted. Jurisdictions use different standards to determine what constitutes provocation and justification. For example, a study of slayings in Houston, Texas, determined that 12 percent were justifiable, but in Chicago only 3 percent of all killings were considered justifiable by local authorities. It appears that the legal definition of justification was broader in Texas than in Illinois (Block, 1981).

If the provocation by the person who died is considered insufficient to render a homicide justifiable, it might be treated as an extenuating circumstance. Evidence of victim provocation can persuade the district attorney to charge the defendant with manslaughter instead of murder. In a homicide or assault case, the victim's provocation must have been "adequate" in order for the charges to be reduced or for the defendant to be acquitted on the grounds of justifiable self-defense. In most states, that means that the defendant's violent responses to the victim's provocations must have occurred during the heat of passion, before a reasonable opportunity for intense emotions to cool (Wolfgang, 1958; Williams, 1978).

If the defendant is convicted, the judge may view the victim's provocation as a mitigating factor that makes a lesser sentence appropriate. In

---

B O X 5.3   Prof Calls for Crackdown on Crime Victims

There is so much talk about crime in the streets and the rights of the criminal that little attention is being paid to the victims of crime. But there is a current of opinion that our courts are being too soft on the victims, and many of them are going unpunished for allowing a crime to be committed against them. One man who feels strongly about this is Professor Heinrich Applebaum, a criminologist who feels that unless the police start cracking down on the victims of criminal acts, the crime rate in this country will continue to rise.

"The people who are responsible for crime in this country are the victims. If they didn't allow themselves to be robbed, the problem of crime in this country would be solved," Applebaum said.

"That makes sense, Professor. Why do you think the courts are soft on victims of crimes?"

"We're living in a permissive society and anything goes," Applebaum replied. "Victims of crimes don't seem to be concerned about the consequences of their acts. They walk down a street after dark, or they display jewelry in their store window, or they have their cash registers right out where everyone can see them. They seem to think that they can do this in the United States and get away with it."

"You speak as if all the legal machinery in this country was weighted in favor of the victim, instead of the person who committed the crime."

"It is," Applebaum said. "While everyone is worried about the victim, the poor criminal is dragged down to the police station, booked and arraigned, and if he's lucky he'll be let out on bail. He may lose his job if his boss hears about it and there is even a chance that if he has a police record, it may prejudice the judge when he's sentenced."

"I guess in this country people always feel sorrier for the victim than they do for the person who committed the crime."

"You can say that again. Do you know that in some states they are even compensating victims of crimes?"

"It's hard to believe," I said.

"Well, it's true. The do-gooders and the bleeding hearts all feel that victims of crimes are misunderstood, and if they were treated better, they would stop being victims. But the statistics don't bear this out. The easier you are on the victim, the higher the crime rate becomes."

"What is the solution, Professor?"

"I say throw the book at anybody who's been robbed. They knew what they were getting into when they decided to be robbed, and they should pay the penalty for it. Once a person has been a victim of crime and realizes he can't get away with it, the chances of his becoming a victim again will be slim."

"Why do people want to become victims of crime, Professor?"

"Who knows? They're probably looking for thrills. Boredom plays a part, but I would think the biggest factor is that victims think they can still walk around the streets of their cities and get away with it. Once they learn they can't, you'll see a big drop in crime statistics."

"You make a lot of sense, Professor. Do you believe the American people are ready to listen to you?"

"They'd better be, because the criminal element is getting pretty fed up with all the permissive coddling of victims that is going on in this country."

SOURCE: From "Victim Precipitation," by Art Buchwald, copyright © *The Washington Post*, February 4, 1969. Reprinted by permission.

---

jurisdictions where restitution by offenders to victims is permitted or even mandated, the culpability of victims can be a cause for reducing the amount of repayment that criminals must undertake. Similarly, the judge or the jury in civil court is likely to consider a victim's blameworthy actions as a reason for reducing the monetary damages a defendant must pay for causing loss, pain, and suffering. Parallel considerations arise when victims of violent crimes apply to a criminal injury compensation board for reimbursement. If the board members determine in a hearing that the

victim bears some responsibility for the incident, they will reduce the amount of the award or may, in extreme cases of shared guilt and provocation, entirely reject the victim's claims (see Chapter 12).

In some conflicts that erupt after extensive interaction between two mutually hostile parties, the designations "offender" and "victim" simply do not apply. When both people behaved illegally, adjudication under the adversary system may not be appropriate. Neighborhood justice centers have been set up to settle these shared responsibility cases through mediation and arbitration. Compromises are appropriate when both disputants are to some degree "right" as well as "wrong" (see Chapter 13).

In sum, widely held beliefs and stereotypes about shared responsibility can profoundly shape the way a case is handled within the criminal justice process. Given the limited choices of strategies derived from victim blaming versus victim defending, policymaking swings back and forth between attempts to control the behavior of either would-be predators or their potential prey—but not their larger social environment, which is what a system-blaming analysis of social institutions would recommend.

The frustrations of trying and failing to deter or rehabilitate criminals periodically propels public safety campaigns in the opposite, presumably easier, direction toward crackdowns on victim facilitation, precipitation, and provocation. What follows is a satire, in which a fictitious professor of victimology puts forward preposterous proposals to solve street crime (see Box 5.3).

SUMMARY

When victims ask, "Why me?" victimologists suggest explanations that range far beyond the notions of being in the wrong place at the wrong time, fate, or just plain bad luck. Explanations that raise the possibility that the victim, along with the offender, shares some degree of responsibility for what happened are the subjects of bitter debate.

Victim-blaming arguments focus on facilitation through negligence, precipitation due to recklessness, and provocation because of instigation. Victim blaming insists that injured parties must change their ways if they want to live safer lives. Victim defending either places the entire blame for what happened on lawbreakers (offender blaming) or finds fault with social institutions and cultural values that shape the lives of both offenders and victims (system blaming).

KEY TERMS

doer-sufferer relationship, 108

duet frame of reference, 108

penal couple, 108

shared responsibility, 108

boost explanation, 109

flag explanation, 109

facilitation, 112

precipitation, 114

provocation, 114

subculture of violence, 114

conscientiously resisting victims, 115

justifiable homicide, 115

subintentional death, 115

typology, 116

victim blaming, 117

victim defending, 117

just world outlook, 118

offender blaming, 119

system blaming, 119

chop shops, 121

retagging, 121

conventionally cautious victims, 126

carelessly facilitating victims, 127

precipitative initiators, 127

provocative conspirators, 127

fabricating simulators, 128

identity theft, 128

dumpster diving, 134

phishing, 134

pharming, 134

shoulder surfing, 134

skimming, 134

QUESTIONS FOR DISCUSSION AND DEBATE

1. Compare and contrast victim facilitation, victim precipitation, and victim provocation. Cite examples to illustrate the differences.

2. Explain victim blaming step by step, and then argue that people whose cars and whose identities are stolen may have made thieves' tasks easier. How can they avoid revictimization?

3. Describe the victim-defending point of view, and then apply it to both vehicle theft and identity theft.

4. Explain system blaming in general, and then apply this perspective to both vehicle theft and ID theft.

CRITICAL THINKING QUESTIONS

1. Is it possible to be too crime conscious—too concerned about being victimized? Defend your point of view by providing examples of risk reduction strategies that demand sacrifices that might be considered to be unreasonable.

2. Review the statements for and against scrutinizing the victim's role that appear in Boxes 5.1 and 5.2. Select quotes from victimologists with whom you strongly agree and several with whom you strongly disagree, and explain your views.

3. Although it is impossible to prevent victimization, it is possible to reduce risks—but it will cost individuals, companies, and governments much more. Explain and give examples.

SUGGESTED RESEARCH TOPICS

1. Find out from insurance companies' websites the makes, models, and years of vehicles stolen most often in your state and in your nearest metropolitan area. See if your vehicle is on the list of most wanted by thieves.

2. Find out from the FTC website the seriousness of identity theft in your state and in your nearest metropolitan area.

3. Find more examples of victim-blaming accusations for various crimes by searching through databases of newspaper and magazine articles.

6

Victims and the Criminal Justice System: Cooperation and Conflict

Part 1: The Police

Criminologists study the operations of the criminal justice system, which is made up of law enforcement agencies, prosecutors' offices, defense attorneys, judges, juries, probation and corrections departments, and parole authorities. They investigate how the system handles offenders—specifically, suspects, defendants, convicts, probationers, inmates, and parolees. Victimologists explore how the system handles victims: how the police respond to complainants; how prosecutors, defense attorneys, and judges treat these witnesses for the state; and how corrections, probation, and parole officials react to victims' special requests.

Sociologists who analyze social institutions from a functionalist perspective point out that the criminal justice system is supposed to serve as the first line of defense for innocent, law-abiding people against the depredations of the "criminal element." In other words, the system ought to work to help victims recover from harm inflicted by offenders. But those who adopt a conflict perspective see the legal system in a different light. Agencies and officials act to some extent on their own behalf and follow policies that are in their own self-interest, as well as to the advantage of more powerful interest groups that dominate society (see Reiman, 2005). Therefore, it is not surprising from the conflict perspective to discover that certain issues place victims at odds with the agencies and officials whose ostensible mission is to protect and assist them.

VICTIMS VERSUS THE CRIMINAL JUSTICE SYSTEM

The criminal justice system is one branch of government that comes under scathing attack from all political quarters. Conservative crime control proponents, treatment-oriented liberals, civil libertarians, civil rights activists, feminists, and victim advocates—all find fault with its procedures and principles. Over the past few decades, even some officials who run its agencies and shape its daily operations have joined the chorus of critics calling for change. However, they sharply disagree over how to reform the system.

The consensus among the experts who focus on victim issues is that the criminal justice system does not measure up to expectations. It fails to deliver what it promises. It does not meet the needs and wants of victims as its clients or consumers of its services. Serious problems persist, and the indictments of the system voiced over the years still stand today (see Box 6.1).

Suppose a person is robbed and injured. What could and should the system do to dispense justice in this case?

Law enforcement agencies are at the intake end of the legal system and are the criminal justice professionals that victims initially encounter. Police officers could rush to help the victim and provide whatever physical and psychological first aid might be needed. They could catch the culprit and properly collect evidence that will stand up in court. They could recover any stolen goods taken by the robber and speedily return these items to the rightful owner. The prosecutor could make sure the defendant is indicted and then press for a swift trial. After conviction, the victim's views about a fair resolution of this case could be fully aired. The judge could hand down a sentence that would balance the victim's wishes with the community's desires and the robber's needs. Correctional authorities could see to it that the probationer, prisoner, or parolee doesn't harass or harm the person whose complaint set the machinery of criminal justice into motion. If the offender was ordered by the judge to reimburse the victim for his losses and expenses, then correctional authorities could insure that these payments or services are delivered in a timely fashion, as promised.

But this "best-case scenario" frequently does not materialize. Instead of enjoying the cooperation of officials and supportive services from agencies as the system handles "their" cases, victims might find themselves sorely disappointed or even locked into conflicts with the police, prosecutors, judges, wardens, and parole boards.

WHAT DO VICTIMS WANT: PUNISHMENT? TREATMENT? RESTITUTION?

A serial killer terrorizes a small city by binding, torturing, and killing his victims. He taunts the local police for three decades by sending them clues, but they fail to figure out his identity until finally they trace a disk he sent them to his church's computer. After a court hearing, the son of his tenth and final victim denounces him to reporters as "a rotting corpse of a wretch of a human hiding under a human veneer.... I'm spiteful, I'm vengeful, and I

B O X 6.1 Notable Criticisms of How the Criminal Justice System Handles Victims

---

If there is one word that describes how the criminal justice system treats victims of crimes and witnesses to crimes, it is "badly."

JAMES REILLY, DIRECTOR OF THE VICTIM/WITNESS ASSISTANCE PROJECT OF THE NATIONAL DISTRICT ATTORNEY'S ASSOCIATION (1981, P. 8)

Crimes that terrorize take many forms, from aggravated assault to petty thievery. But one crime goes largely unnoticed. It is a crime against which there is no protection. It is committed daily across our nation. It is the painful, wrongful insensitivity of the criminal justice system toward those who are the victims of crime.... The callousness with which the system again victimizes those who have already suffered at the hands of an assailant is tragic.

SEN. JOHN HEINZ, SPONSOR OF THE OMNIBUS VICTIMS PROTECTION ACT PASSED BY CONGRESS (1982, P. A19)

Without the cooperation of victims and witnesses in reporting and testifying about crime, it is impossible in a free society to hold criminals accountable. When victims come forward to provide this vital service, however, they find little protection. They discover instead that they will be treated as appendages of a system appallingly out of balance. They learn that somewhere along the way the system has lost track of the simple truth that it is supposed to be fair and to protect those who obey the law while punishing those who break it. Somewhere along the way, the system began to serve lawyers and judges and defendants, treating the victim with institutionalized disinterest.... The neglect of crime victims is a national disgrace.

LOIS HERRINGTON, CHAIR OF THE PRESIDENT'S TASK FORCE ON VICTIMS OF CRIME (1982, PP. VI–VII)

For too long, the rights and needs of crime victims and witnesses have been overlooked in the criminal justice system.... we have begun to address this problem [through federal legislation passed in 1994 and 1996]. But those important measures are not enough.

PRESIDENT BILL CLINTON (1996, P. 1)

[According to a recent survey] victims often feel that they are treated as a piece of evidence, helpful only when they help prove the prosecution's case and when they help a police officer find the bad guy. But they often feel disrespected and ignored and that their interests and concerns are irrelevant.

SUSAN HERMAN, DIRECTOR OF THE NATIONAL CENTER FOR VICTIMS OF CRIME (1999)

In the year 2000, Americans were victims of millions of crimes. Behind each of these numbers is a terrible trauma, a story of suffering and a story of lost security. Yet the needs of victims are often an afterthought in our criminal justice system. It's not just, it's not fair, and it must change. As we protect the rights of criminals, we must take equal care to protect the rights of the victims....
But too often our system fails to inform victims about proceedings involving bail and pleas and sentencing and even about the trials themselves. Too often, the process fails to take the safety of victims into account when deciding whether to release dangerous offenders. Too often, the financial losses of victims are ignored.... When our criminal justice system treats victims as irrelevant bystanders, they are victimized for a second time.

PRESIDENT GEORGE BUSH (2002)

---

relish the thought that he knows that he'll walk into that prison but he'll be carried out." (Wilgoren, 2005:A20)

***

The mother of a small-time gangster who was rubbed out by a major mob figure sneers at the killer just before the judge sentences him to life behind bars, and warns him: "You will burn in the infernal fires of

hell, where you will hang out with your friend Lucifer!" (Cohen, 2008:19)

***

A man whose wife was killed when a terrorist blew up a federal building undergoes a long and painful journey through anger, hate, and ultimately forgiveness. When the killer is first captured and brought to court, he confides to a reporter, "I wanted to grab my rifle, go sit by the highway and give him a proper greeting."

But now he acknowledges that he has reached a surprising conclusion: that the execution of the bomber is wrong. "It is not about justice—it is about revenge. It's blood lust. And if I don't stand up now and say this, well, it's just cowardice," he declares. (Goodell, 2001)

Why should victims bring their problems to the attention of the legal system? What do they want? What would be best for them? What does "justice" mean to them?

Rather than answer these questions that others must decide, the victims' rights movement has sought empowerment. That means the ability to have some input into important decisions at every step in the criminal justice process, from initially filing a complaint with the police up to the release of the offender from custody, or probation, or parole. Empowerment would enable the injured parties to exercise their "agency"—taking actions in pursuit of outcomes that embody their sense of fair play, self-interest, and desire for closure.

But why demand inclusion? Why insist on having chances to participate at key junctures in the criminal justice process?

Victims can pursue one or even a combination of three distinct goals. The first is to see to it that hard-core offenders who act as predators are punished. The second is to use the justice process as leverage to compel lawbreakers to undergo rehabilitative treatment. The third possible aim is to get the court to order convicts to make restitution for any expenses arising from injuries and losses.

Punishment is what comes to most people's minds first, when considering what justice entails. Throughout history, people have always punished one another. However, they may disagree about their reasons for subjecting a wrongdoer to pain and suffering. Most deliberations in court concern questions of punishment: who, why, when, where, and how much?

Punishment is usually justified on utilitarian grounds as a necessary evil. It is argued that punishing transgressors curbs future criminality in a number of ways. The offender who experiences unpleasant consequences learns a lesson and is discouraged from breaking the law again—assuming that the logic of specific deterrence is sound. Making an example of a convicted criminal also serves as a warning to would-be offenders contemplating the same act, provided that the doctrine of general deterrence really works. Punishment in the form of imprisonment has been defended as a method of enhancing public safety by incapacitating dangerous predators so that they can no longer roam the streets preying upon innocents. Another rationale for punishment by the government is that it satisfies the thirst for revenge of angry victims and their supporters who otherwise may harbor an urge to engage in vigilantism and get even on their own. Finally, punishment also has been justified on the grounds of "just deserts" as a morally sound practice, regardless of any value it has in deterring or incapacitating criminals. According to this theory of punishment as retribution, it is fair to make offenders suffer in proportion to the misery they inflicted on others. Since biblical times, people have believed in the formula of retaliation in kind: *lex talionis*, or "an eye for an eye." According to this point of view, retribution evens the score, rights a wrong, and restores balance to the moral order, as long as the severity of the punitive sanction is in proportion to the gravity of the offense.

The quest for retribution has shaped history. Incorporated into the customs and consciousness of entire groups, classes, and nations, it is expressed in simmering hatreds, longstanding feuds, ongoing vendettas, and repeated wars. Revenge fantasies can sustain individuals and even give purpose and direction to their lives. For example, former victims can be found in the forefront of campaigns to deprive inmates of whatever comforts and privileges they enjoy behind bars so they will be even more miserable in bleak "no-frills" prisons (see Hanley, 1994a).

However, the thirst for vengeance undercuts recovery if it becomes an obsession. Even when fulfilled, acts of revenge are rarely as satisfying as had been imagined. Yet for victims to feel a sense of fury and rage toward those who have abused them is entirely human. In the hours and days following a crime, it is psychologically useful and even cathartic for victims to dream of inflicting pain on those who wronged them. But a chronic preoccupation with striking back needlessly prolongs angry memories and painful flashbacks about the incident.

Individuals consumed by a desire to get even never break free of the pernicious influence of their victimizers. Survivors learn that the best revenge of all is to transcend their offender's grip, put the experience behind them, and lead a fulfilling life (Halleck, 1980).

Despite the current popularity of punishment as the antidote to victimization and the cure for crime, the punitive approach remains controversial. Uti-litarian opponents have documented how impractical, expensive, ineffective, and even counterproductive high rates of imprisonment can be. Civil libertarians have condemned such harsh punishments as a tool of domination and oppression used by tyrants and totalitarian regimes to terrorize their subjects into submission (see Menninger, 1968; Wright, 1973; Prison Research, 1976; Pepinsky, 1991; Elias, 1993; Mauer, 1999; Dubber, 2002).

But some victims do not look to the criminal justice system to exact revenge by tormenting the lawbreaker in their names. Instead, they want professionals and experts to help wrongdoers become decent, productive, law-abiding citizens. Victims are most likely to endorse treatment and rehabilitation services if their offenders are not complete strangers. They realize that it is in their enlightened self-interest to try to salvage, save, rescue, and cure troubled family members, other loved ones, friends, neighbors, classmates, or close colleagues at work. Rehabilitation might take the form of counseling, behavior modification, intense psychotherapy, detoxification from addictive drugs, medical care, additional schooling, and job training. "Helping" offenders remains as much a part of the justice system's mission as making them sorry for what they did, despite the temporary ascendancy of a pessimistic, "nothing works" disenchantment with the ideal of rehabilitation popularized because of a mistaken interpretation of a major study (Martinson, 1974).

Rehabilitation followed by reintegration into the community is a long-term strategy that benefits both victims and society. Incapacitating unrehabilitated predators is a short-term strategy that merely buys time and promotes a false sense of security. Angry and frustrated inmates may pose even greater threats to public safety when they are released from custody. Victims who overcome their initial emotional outrage over what offenders did to them might become equally infuriated about heavy-handed punitive policies that backfire and drive offenders to new heights of antisocial conduct. Victims also could become dismayed by inept efforts to rehabilitate inmates in jails or prisons, or convicts on probation or parole.

As a third alternative, some victims seek restitution rather than retribution or rehabilitation. They want the legal system's help to recoup their losses and pay their bills—a necessary prerequisite for full recovery. Restitution collected from offenders can help to restore victims to the financial condition they were in before the crimes occurred. Once offenders make amends monetarily, reconciliation becomes a possibility (see Chapters 12 and 13).

Whether they desire that something be done to the offender (punishment), for the offender (treatment), or for themselves (restitution), victims want the professionals who run the criminal justice system—police, prosecutors, judges, wardens, probation officers, parole officers—to take effective actions in response to violations of law. What they don't want is inaction, lack of interest, neglect, abuse, empty promises, or attempts at manipulation.

VICTIMS AND THE POLICE

Law enforcement agencies are the first representatives of the criminal justice system that victims encounter in the immediate aftermath of crimes. If their cases are not solved with an arrest, then police officers in metropolitan areas and sheriff's deputies in rural areas will be the only criminal justice professionals with whom victims will have contact.

These first responders can help out in many ways. The police can arrive quickly when summoned and can provide on-the-spot first aid. Detectives can launch thorough investigations and solve crimes by taking suspects into custody, recovering stolen property, and gathering evidence that will lead to convictions in court.

Victims are the primary consumers of police services. Their opinions based on their direct experiences can greatly influence police–community relations. Unfortunately, these "clients" or "customers" can become bitterly disappointed with the performance of law enforcement agencies ostensibly committed to "serve and protect" them if officers are slow or reluctant to respond, don't believe their accusations, conduct superficial investigations, don't solve their cases by making arrests, and fail to recover their stolen property.

Whether victims expect too much or receive too little, their grievances against the police can contribute to community relations problems. Administrators of departments have proposed police professionalism as the solution. This involves upgrading the caliber of academy recruits, using psychological tests to weed out potentially brutal or corrupt members of the force, devising regulations and procedures to cover every kind of anticipated emergency, monitoring on-the-job performance, and offering in-service training and specialized squads to handle problems inadequately addressed in the past.

Satisfaction with a police department's services is greater if officers act in a professional manner, if they arrive faster than expected, and if they make a serious effort to investigate property crimes, according to a survey of more than 400 victims in a Midwestern city (Brandl and Horvath, 1991). However, a survey carried out in 12 cities during 1998 revealed that a problem persists. Among those who had never called t the cops for help, 86 percent described themselves as satisfied with the performance of their local police force. But only 69 percent of the victims of violent crimes who had dealt with the police in the aftermath of their incidents expressed satisfaction with the way the officers and detectives hired to serve and protect them had acted in response to their calls for assistance (Smith et al., 1999). Given the commitment to forging partnerships as the foundation for **community policing** that has developed in recent years, victims and their self-help organizations as well as service providers must be permitted to become more involved in devising solutions to neighborhood problems (see Ready, Weisburd, and Farrell, 2002).

Reporting Incidents

Criminal justice authorities want people to "report, identify, and testify" and have launched periodic campaigns to promote this theme ("Crime Control Needs," 1985). Officials fear that if would-be offenders believe that their intended victims won't complain to the authorities about their depredations, then the deterrent effect of the risk of getting caught and punished will be undermined. Furthermore, if the public provided more complete information about where and when crimes were committed, then crime analysts working for the police could more effectively anticipate where predators will strike next.

Victims who fail to report incidents forfeit important rights and opportunities, such as eligibility for services and reimbursement of losses through compensation plans, tax deductions, and insurance policies. Despite these appeals to self-interest incentives and civic responsibility, most individuals still do not tell the authorities about incidents in which they were harmed. *NCVS* findings document the existence of differential reporting rates. That means that certain types of incidents are more likely to be reported than others, that particular groups of people are more inclined to bring their troubles to the attention of the police than others, that entire departments are more likely to be informed about lawless behavior within their jurisdictions than others, and that reporting rates slowly change over time. Several overall patterns are worth noting (see Table 6.1 for a summary of reporting rates since the *NCVS* began in 1973). Acts of violence are reported more often than thefts. Victims are more inclined to tell the authorities about incidents in which they are confronted by offenders brandishing weapons, and/or sustain physical injuries, and/or suffer considerable financial losses. Also, completed acts are brought to the attention of the police more often than mere attempts (according to figures not presented in Table 6.1).

T A B L E 6.1   Trends in Reporting Crimes to the Police, Selected Years, 1973–2006

	Percentage of Victimizations Disclosed to *NCVS* Interviewers That Also Were Reported to the Police			
	1973	**1978**	**1983**	**1988**
All crimes	32	33	35	36
Rapes	49	49	47	45
Robberies	52	51	53	57
Aggravated assaults	52	53	56	54
Simple assaults	38	37	41	41
Burglaries	47	47	49	51
Household larcenies	25	24	25	26
Motor vehicle thefts	68	66	69	73
	1994	**1998**	**2002**	**2006**
All crimes	36	38	39	41
Rapes	32	32	54	41
Robberies	55	62	71	57
Aggravated assaults	52	58	57	59
Simple assaults	36	40	43	44
Burglaries	51	49	58	50
Household larcenies	27	29	33	32
Motor vehicle thefts	78	80	86	81

NOTE: Figures include reports of both attempts and completed acts. Survey redesign influenced rape reporting rates after 1992.
SOURCES: Bastian, 1993; BJS's *NCVS, Criminal Victimization in the United States,1990–2006.*

Of all the crimes inquired about on the *NCVS*, completed auto theft emerges each year as the category with the highest reporting rate (about 89 percent, as compared to 49 percent of attempts, in 2006). Most vehicle owners notify law enforcement agencies about their loss for several sound reasons: There is a good chance their missing cars, SUVs, and trucks will be recovered if officers are aware of the disappearance; filing a formal complaint is required for insurance reimbursement; and motorists do not want to be held responsible for any accidents or crimes involving their vehicles. (For example, detectives will assume that the owner was behind the wheel of a getaway car used in a bank robbery.)

The lowest reporting rates were registered for thefts of household property worth less than $50. As for the category of violent crimes, robberies and aggravated assaults were reported most frequently, and simple assaults and rapes least often. The only reporting rate that changes substantially from year to year is for rapes and other sexual assaults.

Sometimes it approaches one half of all incidents disclosed to *NCVS* interviewers, but during other years the reporting rate tumbles to less than one-third of all known rapes. Overall, the police tend to find out about half of all the violent crimes committed in a community but do not learn about most (roughly 60 percent) of the property crimes perpetrated against its residents (Harlow, 1985; Rennison, 1999; Catalano, 2005).

As for trends, a government publication accentuated the positive by emphasizing how reporting rates, particularly for acts of violence, rose modestly over the years, up to 2003 (Hart and Rennison, 2003; Catalano, 2005). But there was no official acknowledgement when reporting rates for certain crimes slipped during 2006 (see the last column in Table 6.1 above).

Furthermore, a victim advocacy group (National Center for Victims of Crime, 2003) argued that the public should be shocked—rather than reassured—by these statistics. Their interpretation accentuated the negative, pointing out that the millions of incidents that victims decide not to bring to the attention of the authorities each year reflect a continuing and widespread lack of confidence in the criminal justice system. The persistence of this underreporting problem can be taken as evidence that police forces across the country have had only limited success over the decades in enlisting the public to cooperate more closely with law enforcement.

Victimologists have long suspected that reporting rates vary from department to department, depending on the closeness of the working relationships between local law enforcement agencies and the residents they are supposed to protect and serve. Those suspicions were confirmed when the *NCVS* carried out a comparative study of reporting rates in 12 cities during 1998. Fewer victims of violence called the cops in Spokane, Washington (31 percent) and New York City (32 percent) than in Washington, D.C. (50 percent) or Springfield, Missouri (58 percent). A smaller percentage of the people who suffered property crimes filed complaints in San Diego, California (28 percent), and New York City (29 percent), than in Kansas City, Missouri (45 percent), and Savannah, Georgia (47 percent) (see Smith et al., 1999).

Note that these differential reporting rates from department to department undercut the accuracy of making city-to-city comparisons of crime rates based on the FBI's *UCR* compilation of crimes "known to the police." Police forces that successfully cultivate closer ties to their communities learn about a greater proportion of the crimes committed within their jurisdiction. "User-friendly" departments that have won the trust of their clients (for example, by devising ways to file complaints online, and by providing translators for those who don't speak English sufficiently) wind up penalized in the form of rising crime rates because of improving reporting rates. A department that suddenly becomes victim-oriented might appear to be engulfed by a crime wave. Ironically, departments that alienate their local residents look better in comparison—they may seem to be effectively suppressing criminal activities (when the actual reason for the low numbers of reported incidents is that a smaller proportion of the inhabitants within their jurisdictions turn to

them for help). (City-by-city rankings of murder rates don't depend on voluntary reports by victims, of course.)

Different groups of victims are more or less likely to bring their problems to the attention of the authorities. During the 1990s, females were more inclined to report violent incidents than were males, and older people were more willing than younger ones (especially teenagers). Those who had never been married were less inclined to file complaints than their married or divorced counterparts. Urban residents notified their local police a little more often than suburbanites. In general, reporting rates were higher for victims of violence who were injured (especially shot), confronted by an armed assailant, attacked by a stranger, or harmed by someone who seemed high on drugs or alcohol. Reporting rates were relatively lower for incidents involving offenders thought to be gang members. Despite public misimpressions, lower-income people were somewhat more willing to call the police than higher-income individuals, and black victims reported attacks more readily than white or Asian victims (Hart and Rennison, 2003).

During 2006 these group differences in willingness to notify the authorities sharpened. Asian girls and women were the most reluctant of all to turn to officials for help (reporting just 35 percent of all violent incidents) Hispanic girls and women only reported 41 percent of the assaults, robberies, and rapes they suffered. White females informed the police of 51 percent of the violent acts committed against them. But black females were even more inclined to call the cops (63 percent of the time). Differences in reporting rates among males of various racial and ethnic groups were relatively minor (BJS, 2008).

NCVS interviewers ask victims to explain why they did or did not report to the police the incidents they disclosed to survey interviewers. Different reporting rates reflect rational calculations about advantages and disadvantages that can vary from group to group (see Biblarz, Barnowe, and Biblarz, 1984; Greenberg and Ruback, 1984; Gottfredson and Gottfredson, 1988). When victims reported violent crimes, their leading reasons were "to prevent future violence," "to stop the offender," and "to protect others." Smaller percentages of respondents told interviewers their motivations were "to catch and punish the offender" and "to fulfill their civic duty." When people did not file complaints, their most common explanations were that the incidents were "a private/personal matter," "not important enough to involve the police," or "some other officials were notified;" and that the offenders were unsuccessful in achieving their intentions. Insurance coverage was not a significant factor in deciding whether or not to report incidents (Hart and Rennison, 2003; BJS, 2008).

In most jurisdictions, victims are not legally obliged to inform authorities about violations of law committed against them or their property. But if they go beyond silence and inaction, and conspire or collaborate in a cover-up to conceal a serious crime (like a shooting), they can be arrested themselves and charged with **misprision of a felony**. The failure of witnesses to report certain kinds of offenses, especially the abuse of a child or an elderly person, is a misdemeanor in many jurisdictions (Stark and Goldstein, 1985).

Responding Quickly

When victims call for help, they expect officers to spring into action immediately. To meet this challenge, police departments have 911 emergency systems. But incoming calls have to be prioritized by dispatchers who determine each one's degree of urgency. Obviously, reports about immediate danger—such as screams for help in the night or concerns about prowlers or shots fired—merit a higher priority than calls about cars that have disappeared from parking spots. If officers reach crime scenes quickly, they have a better chance of rescuing someone who is in grave danger, catching the culprit, recovering stolen property, gathering crucial evidence, and locating eyewitnesses.

For at least 50 years police departments have been experimenting with ways to reduce response times to emergency calls. But *NCVS* findings fuel suspicions that a substantial proportion of victims might be dissatisfied with the amount of time it took officers to arrive at crime scenes. In roughly 90 percent of all calls for help in the midst or aftermath of a violent incident, an officer came within 60 minutes, but in certain explosive confrontations that response certainly was not fast enough. Furthermore, no positive trend materialized during the 1990s, even though crime rates fell sharply across the nation, and many police forces grew in patrol strength. Table 6.2 shows average nationwide response times, as estimated by people caught up in violence who called for help, from 1990 through 2006. (Note that questions about

T A B L E 6.2   Trends in Police Response Times to Violent Crimes, Selected Years, 1990–2006

| Year | Police Response Times | | | |
	Within 5 Minutes	Within 6 to 10 Minutes	Within 11 to 60 Minutes	Total within One Hour
1990	28%	31%	32%	91%
1994	31%	29%	31%	91%
1998	26%	29%	32%	86%
2000	28%	26%	31%	85%
2003	31%	29%	29%	89%
2006	27%	32%	30%	89%

NOTE: Percentages refer to proportion of incidents.
Some victims each year could not recall police response times.
Percentages rounded to nearest integer.
SOURCE: BJS's *NCVS, Criminal Victimization in the United States, 1990–2006.*

this aspect of police performance were not part of the *NCVS* until 1990 [Whitaker, 1989].)

Travel time is only one reason for delays. Precious moments are lost most often and more importantly when victims and witnesses hesitate before reporting a crime in progress. There are several reasons for such citizen delay: Onlookers and even participants might be confused about whether an illegal act really occurred; victims and witnesses might want to first cope with emotional conflicts, personal trauma, and physical injuries, and then regain their composure before informing the authorities of what happened; or (less frequently) they couldn't locate a telephone (Spelman and Brown, 1984). However, with the proliferation of cell phones since the 1990s, the amount of time lost until someone calls 911 ought to become less of a problem. And yet, reducing the time elapsed on the police's end remains a matter of life and death and ought to be a priority for pro-victim organizations to tackle.

Handling Victims with Care

Detectives need ongoing cooperation from individuals who have reported crimes, for without their help the cases are more difficult to solve. But two areas of conflict between victims and the police can arise at the complaint investigation stage. First, the uniformed officers and detectives who respond to the calls might seem remote, uninvolved, even unconcerned about the victims' plight. Second, the police may conclude that the complainants' charges lack credibility and as a consequence may discontinue their hunt for clues and suspects.

Some victims might be deterred from seeking assistance by their fear of a type of psychological police brutality. After the first injury (the suffering inflicted by the criminal), victims are particularly susceptible to a **second wound**. Expecting the police to comfort them and help with their problems, they sometimes find that officers unwittingly make them feel worse. These slights also can be delivered by care providers such as emergency room personnel, or by friends and relatives.

In the aftermath of a street crime, victims are likely to feel powerless, disoriented, and infuriated.

Fear, guilt, depression, and revenge fantasies engulf them. They expect authority figures to calm and console them, to help them restore their sense of equilibrium, and dispel lingering feelings of helplessness. But if officers and detectives act callously and prolong suffering needlessly, victims feel let down, rejected, and betrayed by those they counted on for support (Symonds, 1980b).

Studies of police work suggest that what victims are encountering is the protective coating of emotional detachment that officers develop to shield themselves from becoming overwhelmed by the misery they routinely see around them. If they seem distant and disinterested, it is part of a "working personality" they must develop because of the potential for danger in a hostile environment and the need to maintain objectivity in the face of complicated situations and conflicting witness accounts. A frighteningly unusual event for the victim can be a rather unexceptional incident for a seasoned officer (Ready, Weisburd, and Farrell, 2002). To avoid **burnout**, law enforcement officers (like others in "helping" professions) sense that they must inhibit their impulses to get deeply involved in their cases. The paramilitary nature of police organizations and the bureaucratic imperatives of specialization and standardization reinforce the inclinations of officers to deal with tragedies as impersonally as possible. In addition, the "macho" norms of police subculture—with its emphasis on toughness, camaraderie, suspicion of outsiders, insider jokes, graveyard humor, and profound cynicism—put pressure on members of law enforcement agencies to act businesslike when dealing with profoundly upsetting situations (Ahrens, Stein, and Young, 1980).

If officers appear unmoved by the suffering that surrounds them, it also might be that they fear "contamination" (Symonds, 1975). People who regularly come into close contact with the casualties of natural and social disasters tend to isolate and ostracize the victims as if they had a contagious disease. Such "distancing" is a defense mechanism to preserve the helper's faith that ultimately justice prevails: Misfortunes happen only to those who somehow deserve them.

Many departments have initiated training programs to prepare at least a portion of their force to act sensitively when they deal with victims with acute needs. Officers and detectives are taught how to administer "psychological first aid" to people in distress. They are instructed to respond swiftly, listen attentively, show concern, and refrain from challenging the victims' versions of events or judging the wisdom of their reactions while the crime was in progress. Officers are told to not show any skepticism because a rape victim is not badly bruised or bleeding, a child did not report a molestation immediately, an elderly person has trouble communicating, or a blind person offers to assist with the identification of a suspect. At the conclusion of training sessions, officers should be informed that responsiveness to victims carries a high priority within the department and has become a criterion for evaluating performance and a consideration in granting promotions (Symonds, 1980b; President's Task Force, 1982; National Sheriff's Association, 1999). By 2000, more than 70 percent of all big-city police departments (serving more than 250,000 residents) had set up special victim assistance units, and more than 90 percent had officers on call who were trained to handle cases of child abuse, missing children, and domestic violence (Reaves and Hickman, 2002).

One of the most emotionally draining tasks in police work is notifying the next of kin of people who have been murdered. Anecdotal evidence indicates that many officers are inept at delivering bad news in plain language and with compassion. To rectify this problem, some departments have developed guidelines and manuals so that survivors are not further traumatized by memories of clumsy and uncaring behavior by officers carrying out these most unpleasant death notification obligations (Associated Press, 1994d).

Challenging the Victim's Version of Events

When people fill out a complaint form in a police station, they want officers to accept without question their versions of what transpired. From a

detective's point of view, however, it may be a necessary part of the job to maintain some healthy skepticism and handle complainants as "presumptive" victims until they pass a credibility test to weed out those whose stories are bogus.

It is always possible that the person alleging to be a bona fide victim is making a fraudulent claim for some ulterior purpose. People might falsely swear they were harmed by criminals for a number of reasons. An angry individual may exact revenge against an enemy by getting him in trouble with the law. A person who did something improper may want to cover up the true circumstances surrounding an event (for example, when a husband claims he was robbed to account for the loss of his pay, which he actually spent on a prostitute or gambled away). Another motive is to commit insurance fraud. For example, tourists may dishonestly claim that they were robbed of their cash-filled wallets or expensive cameras as part of a scam to get reimbursement for nonexistent losses from insurance policies sold to travelers (Associated Press, 1999b).

The following examples demonstrate that occasionally individuals who appear to be victims may attempt to manipulate the authorities and mislead investigators to conceal their roles in a serious offense or for another sinister or self-serving reason.

***

A man and his estranged girlfriend are sitting in a car arguing over visitation arrangements concerning their 14-month-old son, who is in the back seat. A robber comes up to them, shoots her fatally and then shoots him in the leg. When he tells slightly different versions of events to detectives, they become suspicious. When he is visited in the hospital by a cousin who closely fits the description of the gunman, they are both arrested and charged with murder. (Baker, 2008)

***

A 20-year-old Army private tells detectives at a hospital that he was shot in the knee during a robbery. But the police investigators determine that he arranged to be wounded to avoid having to return to combat duty in Iraq. He pleads guilty to the misdemeanor of falsely reporting an incident, and receives a sentence of one year in jail. He also is ordered to return to his military base where he may be subjected to a court martial. His wife and the accomplice who shot him for a fee of $500 also face conspiracy, assault, false reporting, and illegal gun possession charges. (Chan, 2007)

***

The founder and leader of a nationwide civilian anticrime patrol receives favorable coverage when he tells reporters that he was injured when he tried to capture three rapists at a subway station. Years later, after nearly dying from a shooting, he admits that he conspired with other members of the newly formed group to stage a series of publicity stunts to further the organization's reputation for courage and effectiveness. About a dozen years after that, this acknowledged fabrication is used by a defense attorney to undermine his credibility with a jury when he testifies against a mob boss who, the prosecution alleges, ordered his assassination for mocking and taunting the Mafia on a radio program. (Gonzalez, 1992; Preston, 2005)

***

A woman recounts how she escaped the inferno of the World Trade Center after terrorists crashed two hijacked airplanes into the skyscraper hundreds of times to journalists, fellow survivors, and college audiences. But investigative reporters discover that none of the details of her account can be verified. Members of the nonprofit survivors' network for which she served as president cannot fathom why a person who did not go through that ordeal would make false claims and then lead visitors on tours to Ground Zero, and take part in numerous fundraising efforts. (Fernandez, 2007)

Two categories of errors are possible in handling complaints from people insisting they are innocent victims. The first type, illustrated above, occurs when detectives initially believe a person who later is exposed as a liar. The other type of mistake, illustrated below, is to disbelieve the account of someone who really is telling the truth.

A 26-year-old mother of two accepts a ride from a stranger who kidnaps her. For the next two months, this retired handyman with an ailing wife holds her captive in a concrete bunker in his backyard and repeatedly rapes her. When he finally releases her, she runs to the police and tells of her ordeal as a sex slave. They don't take this kidnap and rape victim's story seriously, finding it hard to believe. Eventually, four additional young runaways and drug abusers recount horrific tales that are similar. Finally, the police launch an investigation, locate the bunker, and arrest the man who quickly pleads guilty to these vicious crimes. (Jacobs, 2003; Smalley and Mnookin, 2003)

Unfounding, illustrated above, is a process in which the police reject a person's claim about being harmed by a criminal as unbelievable or at least unprovable in court. **Defounding** means that detectives believe an offense really did take place, but it was not as serious as the complainant described (Lundman, 1980). For example, what was initially reported as a burglary might upon further investigation be classified as merely an instance of criminal trespass—which is a misdemeanor rather than a felony—if nothing of value was stolen.

Just as individuals might have a motive to lodge a false charge, police investigators might have an incentive to declare a report of a crime completely unfounded or to defound it down to a lesser offense. By defounding and unfounding complaints, detectives can reduce the number of serious crimes recorded in their precincts, perhaps because their supervisors want to convince the public that the crime rate is decreasing impressively. Scattered instances of this kind of statistical manipulation, particularly the defounding of initial charges by precinct commanders under great pressure to produce "results," have been exposed in New York

City since the mid-1990s (see Levitt, 2004). If they are under pressure to meet departmental performance targets, some detectives might cut down the number of difficult cases they must try to solve by abusing their discretion and writing off legitimate pleas for help. For example, for more than 20 years, Chicago detectives dismissed about 21 percent of their complaints about serious crimes as unfounded; the average rate for other big-city departments was less than 2 percent, according to the FBI. Detectives were inclined to dismiss victims' accounts as unfounded because they would receive higher ratings and faster promotions if they "closed" more cases. Auditors reviewing these police files concluded that as many as 40 percent of the rape, robbery, burglary, and theft reports disregarded as unfounded probably did take place as the victims claimed. The kinds of cases that were prime candidates for official disbelief involved victims who were difficult to contact, knew their assailants, or did not lose much money ("Chicago Police," 1983; "Burying Crime in Chicago," 1983).

In Oakland, California, overworked detectives in the late 1980s dismissed 24 percent of the rape complaints they received as unfounded. At that time, the FBI reported that other departments across the country disbelieved about 9 percent of all rape charges. After a newspaper article questioned why there was such a disparity in the unfounding rate, the police chief conceded that perhaps 200 cases were tossed aside too quickly and merited re-examination. But detectives in this California city advanced several arguments in their own defense. First, they asserted that the nationwide figure of 9 percent was a misleading standard for comparison, since many departments keep the unfounding rate artificially low by classifying cases as "filed pending further investigation" (not officially closed) rather than "closed due to baseless or false charges." Second, they pointed out that because of budget constraints, the sexual assault unit's six investigators were so swamped with cases that they had to prioritize their workload. They felt pressured to disregard complaints from women who would appear uncooperative, untruthful, or unsympathetic in court, such as prostitutes and

drug abusers who would be inclined to lie about the circumstances surrounding the sexual assaults for fear of getting in trouble for solicitation or possession of controlled substances. Finally, the detectives insisted that many of the complainants refused to agree to medical examinations and failed to appear for follow-up interviews, making the investigation of their charges difficult, time consuming, and unlikely to lead to convictions (Gross, 1990).

People who knowingly fill out false complaints are breaking the law in most states if they "gratuitously" volunteer unsolicited, incorrect information to the police. The laws that make it a misdemeanor to file a false instrument (statement) are intended to deter perjury and thereby protect innocent individuals from the embarrassment and hardships caused by untrue accusations. A lying complainant who instigates a wrongful arrest for an improper motive such as revenge also can be sued in civil court for malicious prosecution.

However, to encourage citizen cooperation with law enforcement, most jurisdictions have adopted a doctrine of witness immunity that shields complainants who furnish information to the police "in good faith" from any subsequent lawsuits by innocent individuals they mistakenly identified as suspects (Stark and Goldstein, 1985). But those who waste the time and money of law enforcement agencies by filing patently false accusations can get into legal trouble, as the following example demonstrates.

A young woman mysteriously disappears while jogging just four days before her elaborate wedding. Hundreds of neighbors, wedding guests, and police officers search the area and pass out missing person flyers, while bloodhounds scour the banks of a nearby river and media outlets across the country broadcast her description. Her fiancé, the last person to see her, comes under suspicion but resists pressures by the police to take a lie detector test. Several days later and hundreds of miles away she reappears, calls 911 and tells the authorities that she just was released by a Hispanic man and a white woman who had kidnapped her. A few hours later, the "runaway bride" admits she had gotten "cold feet" and had taken a long bus ride. Her friends, family, and neighbors are both relieved and furious that she was not a victim of foul play. Their views and her problems become the fodder for talk shows and tabloid headlines. In court, she pleads no contest to one felony count of making a false statement to the police, and the judge imposes a sentence of two years on probation, 120 hours of community service, plus a fine. (Johnston, 2005)

Police departments do not want to be manipulated or deceived. Even though lie detector tests are not admissible in court because their findings are not considered reliable, NYPD detectives received authorization in 2005 to use polygraphs during the early stages of an investigation to test their suspicions that a suspect, a witness, or a complainant was lying to them (Celona, 2005).

Investigating Complaints and Solving Crimes

Victims who report crimes expect their local police and sheriff's departments to launch investigations that successfully culminate with the apprehension of suspects and the seizure of solid evidence pointing to their guilt. But the question arises, "How often do law enforcement agencies fail to figure out who did it?" By the conclusion of most movies and television shows, the wrongdoer has been captured, reinforcing the message that crime doesn't pay. But in real life, statistics in the FBI's *UCR* reveal a shocking conclusion: during the twenty-first century, police departments are having more trouble than ever in solving cases despite breakthroughs in forensic science (like DNA identification), the proliferation of surveillance cameras, and the establishment of computerized databases of known offenders and their fingerprints. Taken collectively, the nation's 17,000 federal, state, county, and municipal law enforcement agencies have never before had such a disappointing track record. This means that after fruitless searches for clues and leads, most victims of property crimes and many who suffered interpersonal violence will

wind up feeling defeated by the lack of closure in their cases.

Some widely publicized homicides that remain unsolved to date serve as a reminder that family members and close friends can suffer endless frustration if a killer gets away with murder:

> The parents of a little girl who wins beauty contests wake up early one morning to prepare for a family vacation—and discover a ransom note on the staircase inside their home. The kidnapper demands $118,000, exactly the amount that the father had just received as a bonus from his company. Shortly after they summon the police, the father discovers the child's body in the basement. She had been sexually abused and then strangled. Because inexperienced officers do not conduct an effective investigation and no one is ever arrested for the murder, a cloud of suspicion hangs over the grieving parents and her brother. Years later, a new, highly sensitive test is performed on traces of DNA on the murdered child's clothing and her father, younger brother, and mother (now deceased) are officially eliminated as suspects in her slaying. These secondary victims, who suffered additional emotional turmoil as the subjects of conspiracy theories for over a decade, receive a note from the district attorney's office, stating, "No innocent person should have to endure such an extensive trial in the court of public opinion." (Ramsey and Ramsey, 2000; Bellamy, 2005; and Johnson, 2008)

***

> A young woman serving as a federal intern leaves her apartment building to go off jogging and then disappears. Under unrelenting pressure from the media and her parents, the police search for her fruitlessly for a year, until a man stumbles upon her remains in a nearby park. Accusations are hurled at her hometown congressman, with whom she was having a secret affair, but he vehemently denies any involvement, and no one is ever arrested for slaying her. (Lengel and Dvorak, 2004)

***

Four letters contaminated with anthrax bacteria are mailed to high-profile persons and organizations in the weeks following the crashes of hijacked airplanes on September 11, 2001. Seventeen people are stricken with the disease, and five die from this apparent terrorist act. A scientist is vilified in the press as a potential suspect, but no one is ever arrested for the murders. Years later, this former Army biodefense researcher wins a multimillion dollar lawsuit against the U.S. Department of Justice because the FBI wrongfully identified him as a "person of interest." "Solving this case is a top priority for the FBI and for the family members of the victims who were killed," a Bureau spokesman insists. When another scientist at the same lab is about to be arrested, he commits suicide. The FBI declares that the case is closed and that the dead scientist acted alone, but a senator who was one of the recipients of an anthrax-laced letter disagrees and believes accomplices remain at large. (Shane, 2008)

Half of all closed homicide cases are solved within a week, and 93 percent are solved within a year, according to a study of nearly 800 cases in four large cities during 1994–1995 (Wellford and Cronin, 2000). Therefore, despite the establishment of **cold case squads** to re-examine old unsolved serious crimes, the prognosis is not promising if no one has been identified as a suspect after one year. However, there is no statute of limitations for murder, so on rare occasions a victim's relatives are elated to learn that a killer who thought he had escaped the long arm of the law has been brought to justice, as this example demonstrates:

The mother of an 18-year-old woman is sexually assaulted and then strangled in her apartment. Twenty-five years later an ex-convict is arrested when his DNA matches evidence found at the crime scene. The woman's 43-year-old daughter tells reporters, "I've called these guys so many times to try and keep this case alive. If there are any other families

out there, they need to do whatever it takes." After a sleepless night, she declares, "This was the happiest and saddest day of my life." (Charkes, 2008)

The FBI's annual *Uniform Crime Report* (see Chapter 3) calculates and publishes average **clearance rates** for each of seven index crimes for police departments across the country. In general, clearing crimes means making arrests. FBI guidelines instruct police departments to consider a case to be solved when it is closed by an arrest. Exceptional clearances take place when the suspect cannot be arrested because he has died or is otherwise beyond reach (for example, can't be extradited). Old cases that are closed by an arrest count toward this year's clearance rate. From a victim's point of view, the police have successfully completed their mission when, acting on solid evidence, they determine the identity of a suspect, locate him, and take him into custody. Note that the police consider the crime solved at that point even if the arrestee is not ultimately convicted of the original charge or any lesser charge. If the accused is found not guilty after a trial, the case usually is not reopened. Police departments routinely compile the percentages of cases that are closed by arrests because this indicator of effectiveness must be calculated and submitted to the FBI's Uniform Crime Reporting division. These clearance rates are used to evaluate the performance of individual detectives, specialized squads (such as those concentrating on homicide, burglary, and sex crimes), and the department as a whole.

But these same statistics can be interpreted from a different angle and for a different purpose. The proportion of cases that are solved can indicate the percentage of complainants who have a solid basis for being satisfied or dissatisfied with the investigatory services provided by local police forces. Victims want their cases to lead to arrests because taking suspects into custody symbolizes that "justice has been served." An arrest means that their misfortunes have been considered significant enough to warrant official action, and their request for assistance has been taken seriously by those in authority. Victims who report crimes and cooperate with investigations want someone to be held directly accountable for the injuries and losses they have suffered. That person might be ordered by the judge to make restitution to repay expenses. Besides restitution, injured parties might demand retribution in order to gain solace from the knowledge that the government is punishing the wrongdoer in behalf of the victim. Also, victims with a sense of civic responsibility might want to see the offender removed from society and incapacitated behind bars in order to make the streets safer for others.

For these reasons, solving cases by making arrests can be considered a high-priority issue from the standpoint of victims who report crimes and cooperate with law enforcement authorities. However, because the FBI and local departments do not track what happens to these cases at later stages of the criminal justice process, clearance rates tend to be overestimates of the proportion of criminals who are "brought to justice" and made to "pay" for their crimes. The actual outcome for each of the seven index crime categories is even worse than these clearance rates imply. Just because a suspect is arrested doesn't mean that this individual is ultimately found guilty. Some charges are dropped by prosecutors or dismissed by judges, freeing those arrestees. Of those who are prosecuted, many engage in negotiations via their defense attorneys and plead guilty to lesser charges, or are not convicted by a jury after a trial (see the leaky net diagram in Chapter 12).

Data from selected years over the past five decades appear in Table 6.3. These statistics summarize the overall accomplishments of roughly 17,000 law enforcement agencies during the second half of the twentieth century and the first few years of the twenty-first.

Accentuating the positive, the figures for 2006 reveal that police forces nationwide were more successful at solving violent crimes, which are more serious and threatening than property crimes. Accentuating the negative and looking at these numbers from the victims' point of view, it is clear that the vast majority of people who go to the trouble to report thefts to the police will not be pleased with the outcome of their cases; the investigations will be discontinued before any arrest is made. Put another way, in 2006, 83 percent of larceny complainants, 87 percent of vehicle theft victims, and 87 percent of burglary complainants were frustrated because their offenders escaped the long arm of the law. Similarly, 75 percent of those who reported robberies also experienced the aggravation of learning that no one was apprehended for accosting them.

More than half (59 percent) of females who had the courage to tell the authorities in 2006 that they had been raped did not experience the comfort of knowing that their attackers had been arrested. Presumably, these assailants who remain at large were mostly strangers and not the perpetrators of acquaintance rapes. Only a little more than half

T A B L E 6.3   Trends in Clearance Rates, Selected Years, 1953–2006

Type of Crime	Percentages of Cases Solved							
	1953	1963	1973	1983	1993	1998	2003	2006
Murder	93	91	79	76	66	69	62	61
Rape	78	69	51	52	53	50	44	41
Aggravated assault	75	76	63	61	56	59	56	54
Robbery	36	39	27	26	24	28	26	25
Burglary	27	27	18	15	13	14	13	13
Larceny	20	20	19	20	20	19	18	17
Vehicle theft*	26	26	16	15	14	14	13	13

*Since the 1970s, this category of the *Uniform Crime Report* has included the theft of all motorized vehicles, including trucks, vans, motorcycles, and buses.
SOURCE: FBI, *UCRs*, 1954–2006.

(54 percent) of those who endured an aggravated assault were relieved to find out that arrests were made in their cases (FBI, 2008).

The highest clearance rates of all are achieved by homicide squads, but even the best detectives who devote considerable time and effort to selected cases can't manage to figure out who did it in nearly two-fifths of all slayings (39 percent in 2006). To put it dramatically, that means that almost two out of every five killers each year don't get caught. Thousands of killers annually join the ranks of those who have gotten away with murder and are roaming the streets.

The *UCR* clearance rates compiled in Table 6.3 reveal a disturbing trend. For every one of the seven index crimes, a general downward drift is evident from the early 1950s to the early years of the twenty-first century. (Arson, the eighth index offense, is excluded from this compilation because the FBI considers these numbers incomplete and unreliable; many fires of suspicious origin may have been intentionally set.) During the 1950s, police departments were able to solve practically all murders and most rapes and aggravated assaults. Clearance rates for these three violent crimes as well as for robberies dropped sharply during the crime wave of the late 1960s. During the 1970s and 1980s, the solution rates for rapes and serious assaults remained stable, while the ability of the police to solve murders continued to decline.

Burglaries and auto thefts were closed by an arrest roughly twice as often in the 1950s as in the 1990s. Grand and petit larcenies (major and minor thefts of all kinds) have always been difficult to solve. During the early 1990s, clearance rates hit new lows across the board, but then improved slightly by 1998 (for murders, serious assaults, and robberies), as crime rates and consequently detectives' caseloads fell throughout the nation. Disappointingly, solution rates (especially for murder and rape) dipped again at the beginning of the twenty-first century. By 2006, the overall ability of police departments to solve a reduced volume of street crime cases of violence and theft had sunk to an all-time low.

Translating these statistical trends into human terms, most victims have good reasons to be dissatisfied with the performance of their local police and sheriffs' departments. Because property crimes vastly outnumber violent offenses, and relatively few thieves are caught, most victims will be disappointed if they count on law enforcement agencies to arrest somebody for harming them. Ironically, decades ago, long before the victims' rights movement began to demand improved services, local law enforcement agencies were much more effective at accomplishing their basic mission of catching culprits.

UCR statistics reveal the existence of differential rates for solving crimes from department to department. As Table 6.4 indicates, some urban police forces were able to solve a much greater percentage of murder cases than their counterparts in other large cities. Some departments caught killers at rates substantially above the national average for cities of a quarter of a million inhabitants or more (which was 60 percent in 2003 but slipped to 54% in 2006). The families and close friends of people killed in these cities were more likely to experience the relief of learning that someone was charged with the slayings of their loved ones. On the other hand, the kin of murder victims in cities with subpar performance records were likely to remain tormented by the inability of their local police departments to arrest any suspects.

According to the data in Table 6.4, the clearance rate for murders achieved by police departments in certain cities remained remarkably consistent from year to year (for example, in Los Angeles, Seattle, and Washington, D.C.), while in other jurisdictions the proportion of solved cases was quite volatile (such as in Oklahoma City, Boston, and San Diego). As for trends, average homicide clearance rates have slipped steadily throughout the twenty-first century in "Group 1" cities with populations over 250,000 residents. In a number of cities, dramatic changes in solution rates took place over the years (for example, improving in Las Vegas while tumbling ominously in Baltimore and Detroit).

TABLE 6.4 Clearance Rates for Homicide Cases in Major U.S. Cities, 2003–2006

City and State	2003	2004	2005	2006
All cities of 250,000 or more	60	58	57	54
Phoenix, AZ	41	34	41	40
Los Angeles, CA	57	56	57	57
San Diego, CA	58	92	88	56
San Francisco, CA	39	42	38	50
San Jose, CA	79	83	96	62
Denver, CO*	49	51	—	—
Washington, D.C.	60	61	61	64
Jacksonville, FL	61	54	62	65
Chicago, IL*	—	—	—	—
Indianapolis, IN	82	87	80	74
Baltimore, MD	76	59	54	53
Boston, MA	64	28	29	47
Detroit, MI	50	37	30	28
Las Vegas, NV	38	54	74	68
New York, NY*	—	—	—	—
Columbus, OH*	—	37	56	—
Oklahoma City, OK	63	97	63	64
Portland, OR	44	45	45	60
Philadelphia, PA	65	65	63	56
Memphis, TN	80	79	72	66
Dallas, TX	64	59	74	81
Houston, TX	57	60	59	70
San Antonio, TX	67	78	70	—
Seattle, WA	78	71	72	70
Milwaukee, WI	80	82	63	59

*The FBI's Uniform Crime Reporting Division had not received statistics from the police departments in Chicago, New York City, Denver, and Columbus for certain recent years.
SOURCE: "Return A Record Cards," 2002–2006, FBI's Uniform Crime Reporting Division, released to the author by special request.

A number of factors might account for the wide range of clearance rates. The ability to solve homicide cases depends in part on practices and policies that a department can control, such as ensuring that the first officer who arrives at the crime scene is trained to follow proper procedures, assigning a sufficient number of detectives to a case, having them respond quickly, and devoting a substantial amount of resources to homicide investigations. Clearance rates also depend on factors beyond a department's control, such as the particular mix of difficult versus easy-to-solve cases in its jurisdiction (Wellford and Cronin, 2000). For example, murder/suicide cases virtually solve themselves, such as when a husband kills his wife and then himself and leaves a note behind. "Smoking gun" cases are also cleared on the spot. On the other hand, murders among mobsters, rival street gangs, or drug dealers are much more difficult to successfully close because of the lack of cooperation of witnesses and other knowledgeable people. Even the best departments find murders of robbery victims by complete strangers to be tough to solve.

Furthermore, victims and witnesses who are immersed in the "code of the streets" that prevails in poverty-stricken neighborhoods generally view helping the authorities to solve crimes as "snitching." Consequently, one strategy to boost clearance rates would be to improve police-citizen interactions in a way that restores the legitimacy of the police (see Steward, et al., 2008). However, several factors widely assumed to be crucial—who the victim was, where the slaying took place, and the detective's workload and degree of experience—actually may not affect homicide clearance rates, according to a study of more than 800 killings between 1984 and 1992 (Puckett and Lundman, 2003).

In sum, if more departments were more effective at catching culprits, a higher proportion of residents would be satisfied with the performance of their local police on this most fundamental aspect of a law enforcement agency's mission.

Arresting Suspects and Seizing Evidence

A registered sex offender kidnaps and rapes a 9-year-old girl who lives near him. He then ties up the third-grader and buries her alive in a shallow grave. When the police interrogate him, he quickly confesses to these horrific crimes. But his confession was not admissible in court because a detective mistakenly did not honor the suspect's request to consult with a lawyer. However, a jury convicts the little girl's killer on the basis of forensic evidence, and the judge imposes the death penalty. (AP, 2007c; and Goodnough, 2007).

When victims formally lodge complaints, they expect action in the form of thorough investigations and the collection of evidence culminating in an arrest—in a legal, proper manner that will hold up in court. When police professionalism falls short of expected standards, judges might rule that crucial evidence should be excluded because government officials violated constitutional safeguards concerning the rights of the accused. When that happens, offenders benefit, police officers and their superiors are embarrassed, and victims suffer needless frustration.

When police officers make arrests, they have a legal obligation to inform suspects of their Miranda rights to remain silent and to be represented by a lawyer. When victims file complaints, they immediately discover that the police are under no comparable constitutional pressure to read them their "rights" about their obligations and opportunities. To start with, victims need to know the names and badge numbers of the officers and the detectives

handling their cases, where and when they can be reached, case identification numbers, whether or not suspects have been apprehended, and if so, whether they are being detained in jail or are being released on bail. To guarantee these elemental rights endorsed by a presidential task force in 1982, a number of states have passed statutes that specify that police departments must keep victims posted on the status of their cases. In the other states, victims must depend on departmental policies and the good will of individual officers.

When victims report crimes, they expect that detectives will keep them posted about anyprogress toward solving their cases. But findings from the *NCVS* indicated that a large percentage of victims during the 1980s never were informed whether their cases were solved and arrests were made. Even when police were successful in closing a case with an arrest, they might not have shared this news with these most interested parties. For example, in 1986 only 15 percent of robbery victims eventually learned that a suspect was arrested for robbing them. Yet police departments averaged a clearance rate of 25 percent for robberies that year. Similarly, only 34 percent of aggravated assault victims who reported the crimes to the police were informed about resulting arrests, although police departments solved about 59 percent of all aggravated assault cases brought to their attention that year. The neglect on the part of the police to tell burglary victims that someone was arrested for breaking into and stealing from their homes was even more dramatic: Only 7 percent of all victims were notified, although about 14 percent of all reported burglaries were solved. Motor vehicle theft victims were better informed. About 15 percent of all cases were solved, and 11 percent of all victims found out about an arrest (FBI, 1987; Whitaker, 1989).

Dissatisfaction also can arise when detectives deem a complainant's misfortunes to be too minor to merit official action. It is difficult to justify the expenditure of the department's limited human resources, time, and money to solve minor cases. Some departments issue directives that specify cutoff points below which no action will be taken beyond simply making a formal note of the complaint. For example, in Dade County, which includes Miami, Florida, reports about stolen cars were taken solely over the telephone and only during certain hours (Combined News Services, 1993). In New York City during the 1980s, a detective from the burglary squad was assigned to a case only if the reported loss exceeded a figure of several thousand dollars (Gutis, 1988). Sometimes the police might be reluctant to expend much effort if victims are likely to receive insurance reimbursement.

Many complainants discover that with the passage of time their cases have been closed even though they remain unsolved. How long an investigation remains open depends on the workload in the jurisdiction and the seriousness of the offense. If the police are unable to establish the identity of a suspect or cannot obtain sufficient evidence to justify an arrest, then they can exercise their discretion to discontinue any active effort to solve the crime. Victims have no formal means of compelling law enforcement agencies to continue to work on unsolved mysteries. Dissatisfied complainants have been unable to convince judges to intervene in matters of police discretion unless a pattern of non-investigation reflects racial or religious discrimination on the part of government officials sworn to serve and protect the public (Austern, 1987).

Even when a trail of evidence leads to a suspect, an arrest is never automatic. Police officers exercise a great deal of personal and departmental discretion in deciding whom to take into custody and book, and whom to let go, especially for misdemeanors. The factors that influence these decisions include pressures from colleagues and superiors, the individual predilections of officers, the nature of the offense, and the relationship of the victim to the suspect. Victims can become angry when officers don't arrest these suspects.

One solution for victims is to convince judges to issue arrest warrants based on their sworn complaints which officers then must then carry out. A second solution is to exercise the dangerous do-it-yourself option known as a **citizen's arrest**. Private citizens are empowered to use whatever force necessary to prevent a suspect from escaping until the police arrive to take charge of the situation. Civilians must apprehend their suspects immediately after a crime is committed and must turn their captives over to the authorities without delay. Police officers are generally obligated to accept custody of suspects taken prisoner by victims or bystanders.

But citizen's arrests are risky undertakings. Suspects are likely to resist capture and endanger victims or bystanders who intervene. In cases of mistaken identity, even victims who acted with probable cause and in good faith can be sued in civil court for false arrest and false imprisonment. Police officials generally discourage civilians from thinking of themselves as deputized to make arrests. They point to the lengthy training sworn officers receive in self-defense tactics, the use of firearms, and the application of laws governing arrests, the seizure of evidence, and suspects' rights. Because attempts to make citizen's arrests can easily devolve into acts of vigilantism, law enforcement officials encourage activist-oriented civilians to become involved in police auxiliary units or neighborhood anticrime patrols instead (Hall, 1975; Stark and Goldstein, 1985).

Recovering Stolen Property

Besides catching culprits, the police can satisfy victims' needs by recovering their stolen items. Just as clearance rates indicate the approximate percentage of victims who receive optimum service in terms of arrests, recovery rates show how often the police succeed in retrieving stolen goods. Unfortunately, unlike clearance rates, recovery rates are not routinely tabulated and published by police departments or the FBI. (The *UCR* merely notes the overall dollar value of recovered stolen goods for all reported incidents of a particular index crime.) However, recovery rates are available from the *NCVS*.

Interviewers ask respondents whether all or part of the money and property taken from them was returned to them (not counting insurance reimbursement). Police recovery rates can then be estimated. But the figures will be biased upward because some victims are able to get back their stolen property through their own efforts. Unfortunately, this statistic cannot be refined further to determine the

T A B L E 6.5   Trends in Stolen Property Recovery Rates, Selected Years, 1980–2006

Type of Victimization	1980	1984	1988	1992	1996	2000	2003	2006
Robberies	24	27	21	18	20	18	21	16
Burglaries	12	10	9	10	8	8	8	12
Household larcenies	12	9	8	8	9	10	9	11
Motor vehicle thefts	65	70	73	72	71	67	65	70

NOTES: Percentages represent the proportions of all cases in which victims get back stolen items. Recovery may be total or partial.
An unknown proportion of the recoveries were accomplished by victims without police assistance.
Figures were calculated from *NCVS* data on theft losses. Only incidents that resulted in theft losses were considered.
SOURCE: BJS, *Criminal Victimization in the United States, 1980–2006.*

percentage of victims who recovered items by themselves and what percentage was retrieved by police. Therefore, these rough approximations overestimate the ability of the police to return stolen goods to their rightful owners. Furthermore, these estimates combine partial and full recoveries, again biasing the statistics upward and presenting the abilities of police departments across the nation as more effective than they really are. Partial recoveries might not satisfy victims; a discarded wallet emptied of any cash or credit cards, for example, or a badly stripped automobile with a traceable vehicle identification number would count as partial recoveries. With these reservations in mind, Table 6.5 shows estimated police recovery rates from 1980 to 2006.

The data reveal that this aspect of police work will leave most people who suffered robberies, burglaries, and household larcenies dissatisfied with the outcomes of their cases. The recovery rates are very low. Furthermore, these percentages are overestimates because some recoveries are only partial and some should be credited entirely to victims who did not receive help from the police. Only owners of stolen vehicles are likely to get back some or all of what was taken from them. But these statistics don't indicate the condition the vehicles were in when found—the recovered cars may have been severely damaged or stripped.

As for changes over time since the start of the 1980s, the data show considerable stability, perhaps with some slight trends in a disappointing downward direction. Even though crime rates fell substantially during the 1990s across the nation, and detectives had more time to investigate the remaining

cases, the ability of police departments to retrieve stolen goods apparently did not improve. Some slight upticks in recovery rates for property crime (but not robbery) took place during the early years of the 21st century, according to the statistics compiled in Table 6.5.

Even if the police recover stolen property, some victims might not get it back for a while. Law enforcement agencies have the authority to hold seized items if they are of value in continuing investigations. Prosecutors are allowed to maintain custody of pieces of evidence until after the trial or even until those convicted have exhausted all appeals. Victims frustrated by that delay are now assisted in some states by statutes that compel the police to return stolen property "expeditiously"—as soon as it is no longer needed for law enforcement purposes. In a growing number of jurisdictions, laws direct the police and prosecutors to promptly photograph the evidence and then return the actual item whenever it is feasible. But in states without these kinds of procedural directives, the release of property seized as evidence requires the explicit approval of the police department property clerk or the prosecutor's office or even the judge hearing the case. Victims who are denied prompt repossession might have to appeal the decision of the official maintaining custody of the property to some higher criminal justice authority. If the items are damaged, destroyed, or lost by the police property clerk's office or the prosecutor's office, victims can go to civil court to file claims for monetary compensation (Stark and Goldstein, 1985).

Scattered studies suggest that many victims encountered this problem decades ago, before new procedures were mandated as the result of the rise of a victims' movement. In a Wisconsin jurisdiction, 31 percent of complainants who had been seriously harmed reported difficulties in getting back stolen property held as evidence (Knudten, Knudten, and Meade, 1978). In California a survey of victims determined that in 30 percent of the cases in which stolen property was recovered by the police and used in court as evidence, the items were never returned to their owners (Lynch, 1976). Follow-up studies are needed to establish whether this problem persists.

Measuring Progress toward a Victim-Oriented Police Department

The adoption of "community policing" by many departments symbolizes a commitment to granting residents a larger say in guiding the operations and policies of their local law enforcement agencies. Community policing also has opened the door to a more victim-oriented approach within law enforcement. What would a "consumer-centered" or "user-friendly" model entail? What **performance measures** indicate that a department is effectively carrying out its mission to protect and serve the residents of its jurisdiction?

First of all, a victim-oriented department would extend outreach efforts to neighborhood residents to build their confidence that they will be appropriately received when they bring their problems to a police station. A user-friendly department would facilitate the process for lodging complaints, making it as painless and as streamlined as possible. Complaints about very minor matters might even be taken over the phone or by filling out a form online. If crime victims become encouraged to come forward, an indicator of success would be a temporary rise in the crime rate because a greater proportion of incidents would be reported and recorded. Also, a localized version of the National Crime Victimization Survey could be used to discover what percents of victims still are not reporting various types of crimes, and why.

When victims come forward, they expect to be handled with care. To achieve this goal, a

department would have to train its officers to handle death notifications with compassion, to better comfort traumatized victims, to provide physical and psychological first aid, and to avoid delivering a second wound because of insensitivity or victim-blaming accusations. The special needs of victimized children, battered women, rape victims, and disabled persons also would be addressed effectively (see Chapters 9 and 10). Officers could also be trained to spot a complainant who is making a false charge, so that all complainants would not be greeted with skepticism as possible fakers and liars, and detectives would not subject them to needless, accusatory questioning. Customer-satisfaction surveys could be an appropriate way to measure whether victims felt departments were handling their cases with care.

A victim-oriented department would dispatch officers quickly to 911 calls for help. Statistics showing downward trends in response times to emergencies would indicate progress along this front. Presumably, police forces constantly work to solve as many crimes as possible. But victim-oriented forces would not only seek to make arrests in high-profile cases that merit intense media coverage, but also the minor cases that revolve around property crimes. Clearance rates should rise in departments that are becoming more user-friendly, indicating that victims and witnesses are cooperating with investigations to a greater degree, sharing all they know, looking through books of mug shots, and picking suspects out of lineups. Similarly, such local law enforcement agencies should make greater efforts to recover stolen property and return it to its rightful owner after it is no longer needed for court proceedings. Officers and detectives must gather evidence properly so that it can be entered as a prosecution exhibit against the accused. Court records about the percent of charges at the time of arrest that are later dropped or dismissed under the exclusionary rule because of improperly obtained evidence can be examined to monitor progress along this front.

In sum, police departments have to revamp their operations and reconsider their priorities, and do all they can do to provide the same high-quality services to victims that they would provide to injured fellow officers and members of their own families.

SUMMARY

In their pursuit of justice—whether they seek punishment or treatment for the offender, or restitution for their losses—victims might find themselves in conflictual rather than cooperative relationships with police officers and detectives.

If they report crimes, victims want the police to respond quickly, administer psychological and physical first aid effectively, believe their accounts, apprehend suspects, gather evidence that is admissible in court, and get back any property that was taken from them. However, uniformed officers and detectives might be slow to arrive, handle victims insensitively, consider their versions of events unbelievable or exaggerated, fail to solve their cases, and be unable to recover their stolen goods. Various statistical measures collected by the *NCVS* and the *UCR* (such as reporting rates, response times, and clearance rates) can be used as performance indicators to provide some rough estimates about how often victims receive the services and assistance they seek from their local police and sheriff's departments.

KEY TERMS

community policing, 149

misprision of a felony, 152

second wound, 153

burnout, 153

unfounding, 155

defounding, 155

clearance rates, 158

cold case squads, 158

citizen's arrest, 163

performance measures, 165

QUESTIONS FOR DISCUSSION AND DEBATE

1. Make up some details about robbery or burglary incidents, and then decide whether it is in their best interest for victims to seek punishment, treatment, or restitution in these particular cases.

2. Make up some details about robbery or burglary incidents, and then discuss what an ideal police department could do for the victims in these cases. Then reverse the outcomes, and highlight every problem with the local police that could further compound the suffering of victims in these particular cases.

CRITICAL THINKING QUESTIONS

1. From the viewpoint of police chiefs, argue that victims have unrealistically high expectations and make unreasonable demands in terms of the department's priorities, resources, and personnel.

2. Speculate about the causes of the falling clearance rates for solving crimes of violence.

SUGGESTED RESEARCH PROJECTS

1. Interview local residents who have been victims of crimes such as robbery and burglary, and find out whether or not they reported the incidents to the police. Question them about why they did or did not. Ask those who reported crimes whether they know if their cases were solved by an arrest.

2. Meet with local police officials and discover what your department's clearance rate is for the seven index crimes, its response time to 911 calls, the percentage of auto theft or robbery complaints that were determined to be unfounded, and the recovery rate for stolen motor vehicles. See if this information is contained in a publicly available annual report or on a departmental website.

3. Draw up a comprehensive checklist of all the victim-oriented services that could and should be offered by a user-friendly police department. Rate your local department on how well it provides each form of assistance and support to crime victims.

7

Victims and the Criminal Justice System: Cooperation and Conflict

Part 2: Prosecutors, Defense Attorneys, Judges, and Corrections Officials

This chapter examines what might happen in cases police solve by making an arrest. As the fate of the accused person is determined by the criminal justice system, victims will interact with prosecutors, defense attorneys, judges, and—if the defendant is convicted—corrections officials. Cooperation is the desired outcome, but conflict might erupt over certain divisive issues with these criminal justice professionals and the agencies that employ them. One key question that will be addressed throughout this step-by-step walk through the system is: Are all victims treated the same way, or are some groups handled much better than others?

Note that this chapter does not explore how victims fare within the juvenile justice system. This separate system, dating back to the early 1900s in most states, resolves cases in which minors are accused of committing crimes of violence against people of all ages, as well as property crimes and status offenses (such as curfew violations). It operates according to other principles and does treat victims differently: generally worse because they are not permitted to play much of a role and can exercise fewer options and rights. In 13 percent of the violent crime cases that police solved, the arrestees were under the age of 18. In 19 percent of the solved property crimes, only juveniles were taken into custody, according to the FBI's *UCR* for 2006. Therefore a considerable number of victims will discover that "their" solved cases will be handled in a system that is supposed to prioritize rehabilitation over punishment. Victims harmed by these delinquents face a separate set of problems that are beyond the scope of this chapter.

VICTIMS AND PROSECUTORS

Prosecutors are the chief law enforcement officials within their jurisdictions. They represent the interests of the county, state, or federal government. But their agencies also supply the lawyers that deal directly with victims. Therefore, prosecutors' offices can be viewed as public law firms offering free legal services to complainants who are willing to cooperate and testify as witnesses. To a great extent, victims are on the "same side" as the government; prosecutors and victims therefore are "natural allies" who ought to cooperate with each other. However, county prosecutors, usually referred to as **district attorneys**, are elected officials. Besides wanting to do what is best for victims, they also are concerned about their careers and political futures, the well-being of their agencies, and the general good of the entire community and society. Attending to these concerns and addressing these interests can cause conflict between prosecutors and victims.

Prosecutors' offices can and should serve victims in a number of different ways. First, the lawyers who handle criminal cases and personally work with victims, **assistant district attorneys** (ADAs), can keep their clients informed of the status of their cases, from the initial charges lodged against defendants to the release of convicts on parole. Second, ADAs can help the individuals they represent to achieve justice by conveying to the attention of judges their clients' views on questions of bail, continuances, dismissed cases and dropped charges, negotiated pleas, sentences, and restitution arrangements. Third, they can take steps to protect their clients from harassment, threats, injuries, and other forms of intimidation and reprisals. Fourth, ADAs can try to resolve cases as quickly as possible without unnecessary delays and help their clients to minimize losses of time and money by notifying them of required court appearances and scheduling changes. Fifth, ADAs can assist victims in retrieving stolen property recovered by police and seized as evidence (President's Task Force, 1982).

Sometimes prosecutors are able to balance the interests of the government, their own bureaucracies, and their clients without much conflict. But in certain cases, prosecutors cannot do what is best for all of their constituencies simultaneously. Conflicts can arise between the aims of the government and the outcome desired by those who were harmed. Conflicts also can emerge between the bureaucracy that employs prosecutors and injured parties who are the "consumers" of their services. Finally, prosecutors advancing their careers may not follow unpopular courses of action favored by their clients.

In all of these potential conflicts, if prosecutors must sacrifice the interests of any party, it is most likely to be those of the victim, and not of the government, their bureaucracy, or their careers. Victims can feel betrayed if "their" lawyers do not look after their needs and wants. Or to put it another way, a lawyer—assigned without choice by the government and for no fee—might not do a satisfactory job from a client's standpoint.

Assisting Victims and Other Witnesses for the State

The difficulties, inconveniences, and frustrations faced by people serving as witnesses for the prosecution have been well-known for decades (see McDonald, 1976). In 1931, the National Commis-sion on Law Observance and Enforcement commented that the administration of justice was suffering because of the economic burdens imposed on citizens who participated in trials. In 1938, the American Bar Association noted that witness fees were deplorably low, courthouse accommodations were inadequate, intimidation went unchecked, and witnesses' time was often wasted. In 1967, the President's Commission on Law Enforcement and Administration of Justice reached similar conclusions. In 1973, the Courts Task Force of the National Advisory Commission on Criminal Justice Standards and Goals noted that the failure of victims and witnesses to appear at judicial proceedings when summoned was a major reason for cases being dismissed. Noncooperation was attributed to the high personal costs of involvement incurred by citizens trying to meet their civic obligations.

In the past, victims serving as prosecution witnesses often were mistreated in a number of ways. They would be summoned by subpoena to appear at a courtroom, grand jury room, or prosecutor's office. They would wait for hours in dingy corridors or in other grim surroundings. Busy officials would ignore them as they stood around bewildered and anxious. Often, they wouldn't be called to testify or make statements because of last-minute adjournments. Accomplishing nothing, they would miss work and lose wages, be absent from classes at school, or fail to meet their responsibilities at home. In most jurisdictions they would receive insultingly low witness fees for their time and trouble. In certain metropolitan areas, they would receive no compensation at all because no official informed them of their eligibility and of the proper application procedures. Their experiences could thus be characterized as dreary, time consuming, depressing, exhausting, confusing, frustrating, and frightening (Ash, 1972).

In 1974, the National District Attorneys Association (NDAA) commissioned a survey to determine the extent to which victims and other witnesses for the prosecution encountered these problems. Conducted in Alameda County, California, the survey documented that about 12 percent of victims were never notified that an arrest had been made in their case. Nearly 30 percent never got their stolen property back, even though it had been used as evidence. About 60 percent of injured victims who were eligible for financial reimbursement were not informed of their right to file a claim. Roughly 45 percent reported that no one had explained to them what their court appearance would entail. About 27 percent of witnesses, including victims, called to court were not asked to testify. Even though 78 percent lost pay to appear, about 95 percent received no witness fees. As a final insult, 42 percent were never notified of the outcome of the case (Lynch, 1976).

To address these problems, the Law Enforcement Assistance Administration funded the first Victim/Witness Assistance Projects (VWAPs) through the NDAA. Pilot programs were set up in prosecutors' offices in California, Illinois, Utah, Colorado, Kentucky, Louisiana, Pennsylvania, and New York during the mid-1970s (Schneider and Schneider, 1981; Geis, 1983). Since then, most prosecutors' offices have followed suit.

Several assumptions underlie the growth and development of these programs. One is that providing services will elicit greater cooperation from victims and witnesses. Presumably, well-briefed, self-confident witnesses who have benefited from such programs will be more willing to put up with the hardships of testifying in court, leading to lower dismissal rates and higher conviction rates, the standards by which prosecutors' offices are judged. Also, offering services to a group perceived to be highly deserving of governmental aid will be good for community relations. Public confidence and faith in the criminal justice system will thus be restored, resulting in higher levels of cooperation within jurisdictions that have assistance programs (Rootsaert, 1987).

Most VWAPs are charged with the laudable but loosely defined mission of helping victims, aiding witnesses, and furthering the goals of law enforcement. In the best programs, agency personnel intervene as soon as possible after an offense is committed, providing immediate relief to the injured parties through services that include hotlines; crisis counseling; emergency shelter, food, and transportation; and immediate lock repairs. Some projects provide translators, forms for replacing lost documents, and assistance in getting back stolen property recovered by the police. Most make referrals to social service and mental health agencies for those needing long-term care and counseling. All programs furnish information about opportunities for reimbursement of losses and eligibility for compensation benefits (see Chapter 12). A few offer mediation services for victims who seek to reconcile their differences with their offenders (see Chapter 13). To encourage witness cooperation, pamphlets about the adjudication process (with titles like "What Happens in Court?" and "Your Rights As A Crime Victim") are prepared and distributed. Through a case-monitoring and notification system, the staff keeps victims and other witnesses advised of indictments, postponements and continuances, negotiated pleas, convictions, acquittals, and other developments. Linked to the notification system is a telephone alert or on-call system to prevent unnecessary trips to court if dates are changed on short notice, which also avoids wasting the time of police officers who are needed as witnesses.

Some programs also have set up reception centers exclusively for prosecution witnesses in courthouses to provide a secure waiting room free from last-minute opportunities for intimidation by offenders and their families and friends. Transportation to and from court, escorts, and child care are frequently available. Help in obtaining witness fees also is provided. The staff in some programs may go as far as to intercede with employers and landlords and other creditors who might not appreciate the stresses and financial difficulties faced by witnesses (Schneider and Schneider, 1981; Geis, 1983; Weigend, 1983; Rootsaert, 1987).

Some signs that VWAPs are reducing the mistreatment of victims are evident. In 1974, only 35 percent of the offices of district attorneys routinely notified victims of felonies of the outcomes in their cases; 97 percent of these offices did so by 1992, according to the National Prosecutor Survey Program (Dawson, Smith, and DeFrances, 1993). By 2005, about 6 percent of the personnel working in state prosecutors' offices were classified as victim advocates. Large offices in big cities employed 13 advocates on average, although the median nationally in all offices, large and small, was just one person (Perry, 2006).

The establishment of VWAPs has raised some constitutional and ethical questions, however. To deny services to a victim whose cooperation is not needed (or who desires to pursue a case that the prosecutor's office wants to drop) would be unfair but not illegal, since the aid is granted as a privilege rather than as a right. To deny similar services (free parking, child care, last-minute phone calls canceling a scheduled appearance) to witnesses for the defense would violate notions of fairness within the adversary system. As long as the defendant is presumed innocent unless proven guilty, evenhanded treatment of all witnesses should prevail. Rapport between victims and VWAP personnel that becomes too close can cause another problem: The testimony given in court can be considered coached or rehearsed if it departs from the original statements the complainant and witnesses made and covers up contradictions in order to make the most convincing case against the defendant.

Protecting Victims Who Serve as Witnesses for the Prosecution

A man is robbed of $550 by three gunmen. He reports the stick-up to officers and they round up three suspects. After he identifies them as the men who stole his money, he begins to receive death threats. The prosecutor suggests various measures to protect him, but he declines the offer. One night his doorbell rings, and when he answers it, a stranger pulls out a gun and shoots him in the head. ("Warned Not to Testify," 1991)

Chilling tales like this one could dissuade people who are unsure whether to report crimes, press charges, and testify in court. Victims who agree to serve as prosecution witnesses need to be protected from intimidation and reprisals. The gravest dangers are faced by defectors from street gangs and mob syndicates, people harmed by drug-dealing crews, and battered women trying to break free from abusive mates. Intimidation can range from nuisance phone calls, stalking, and explicit threats of physical attacks to actual property damage (stone throwing, fire bombings) and assaults. The fear of reprisals can cause a victim to ask that charges be dropped, or to not show up to testify, or to recant earlier testimony when cross-examined. When intimidation succeeds, prosecutors are forced to drop charges; judges dismiss cases; or juries fail to convict, and guilty parties go free (Gately, 2005).

Because complainants' perceptions of the risks of cooperation determine whether they will testify in court, the primary responsibility for safeguarding the well-being of witnesses for the state falls to the ADA handling the case. When prosecutors don't react to acts of intimidation by providing police protection, one of the victim's worst fears is confirmed—namely, that the criminal justice system can't provide security from further harm and that the only way to avoid reprisals is to stop cooperating. Anonymous nighttime calls or acts of vandalism are difficult to trace. But if left unaddressed, these incidents convey the message that complainants are on their own, and they signify to offenders that intimidation is worth a try. It may have the desired effect, and it carries little risk of additional penalties (see Docksai, 1979; President's Task Force, 1982; Healy, 1995).

Just how serious is the problem of intimidation? The rates of nonreporting due to fear of reprisal are presented in Table 7.1. Each year only a very small percentage of respondents admit to NCVS interviewers that worries about retaliation stopped them from informing police about violent crimes. Therefore, this issue appears to be of minor concern. Fears about the offender getting even inhibit a small percentage of rape victims from trying to get their attackers in trouble with the law. Worries about offender retaliation are even less of a deterrent to reporting in cases of simple assault and robbery. The major exception is that a considerable

TABLE 7.1   Trends in Fear of Reprisal as a Cause of Nonreporting, Selected Years, 1980–2005

| Type of Crime | Percentage of Nonreporting Victims Who Feared Reprisals | | | | | | |
	1980	1984	1988	1992	1996	2001	2006
Rape	12	11	10	7	12	8	17*
Robbery	6	3	7	6	4	6	6*
Aggravated assault	6	7	5	6	6	6	11
Simple assault	3	4	4	3	3	4	6

NOTE: Percentages represent the proportions of respondents citing "fear of reprisal" as the primary reason for not reporting a crime to police that they did disclose to NCVS interviewers.

*indicates that this figure is based on a small number of cases and might be unreliable.

SOURCE: BJS, *Criminal Victimization in the United States, 1980–2006.*

proportion of the victims of aggravated assaults like shootings and stabbings told interviewers in 2006 that they feared reprisals. (The percentages fluctuate considerably from year to year because the number of survey respondents who were harmed in these specific ways is extremely small, statistically speaking.) As for changes over time, the intimidation problem apparently intensified during 2006.

But these statistics might yield false impressions. The actual number of non-reporting victims is not known. Measuring intimidation is difficult, in part because would-be complainants (and witnesses) who are "successfully" intimidated might be afraid to disclose their plight to NCVS interviewers as well as detectives. Various studies have yielded contradictory findings about how often injured parties are effectively intimidated by the people they accuse. In one survey, about 13 percent of all victims confided that their offenders or the defendants' friends or relatives had attempted to scare them, most commonly by threatening them verbally during face-to-face confrontations. Some would-be complainants had property vandalized, but not even 1 percent were actually assaulted. The incidents occurred in police stations and courthouses, as well as in the neighborhoods and homes of the victims.

The willingness of complainants to cooperate with prosecutors was not seriously undermined by attempts at intimidation, and these attempts did not influence conviction rates to any statistically significant extent, according to a sample of about 1,000 New Yorkers interviewed at the start of the 1980s (Fried, 1982). But when the same agency conducted another study about 10 years later, the researchers came to a different conclusion: Attempts to intimidate often succeeded. New Yorkers who were threatened were more than twice as likely to ask that charges be dropped as those who were not contacted by defendants. Individuals who had close prior relations (romantic involvements or family ties) with defendants were more likely to receive menacing looks, to be warned about bodily harm or damage to property, or to be assaulted than those who lodged complaints against complete strangers ("Study Shows Intimidation," 1990). Between 1980 and 2003, at least 19 witnesses to serious

crimes, some of whom were warned to "lie or die," were permanently silenced by lethal attacks in New York City (Glaberson, 2003). Police departments and prosecutors' offices certainly have not eliminated fear of reprisals as a genuine concern, and that continuing threat holds down cooperation rates, solution rates, and conviction rates.

The problem of intimidation goes beyond direct threats. Would-be complainants may experience strong pressures from families and friends not to come forward and tell police what happened. Subjected to this "cultural intimidation" by their community to not "snitch," they may be forced to either settle the score privately or let the matter rest. But that only perpetuates a cycle of attacks and retaliatory strikes as part of a culture of violence that adds to the level of danger and misery in high crime areas, especially in inner city neighborhoods. Government officials and community activists need to counteract this drift toward "do-it-yourself" acts of revenge that pass as street justice by developing creative ways to protect those who are urged by officials to cooperate with law enforcement agencies and the prosecution (America's Most Wanted, 2008; NY1, 2008).

Much of the intimidation problem can be traced to officials who have shirked their responsibilities to victims. Police officers might con victims into cooperating by making empty promises of added protection, knowing full well that their precincts don't have the resources to provide such special attention. Because attrition lightens their workload, ADAs might allow cases to collapse when key witnesses and complainants fail to appear after being subpoenaed—perhaps due to intimidation. Judges may not be vigilant for the same reason: intimidation leads to nonappearances and ultimately dismissals, which reduces caseloads. To reduce fears about reprisals, the American Bar Association's Committee on Victims (1979) put forward five recommendations:

1. Legislatures should make attempts at intimidation a misdemeanor.

2. Police forces ought to set up victim/witness protection squads.

3. Judges should issue orders of protection and consider violations as grounds for contempt-of-court citations and revocations of bail.

4. Judges should grant continuances rather than drop all charges against defendants if complaining witnesses mysteriously fail to appear when subpoenaed.

5. Prosecutors must avoid carelessly revealing information concerning the whereabouts of victims, even after cases are resolved.

Prosecutors always have had to coax victims and other witnesses to cooperate by offering them protective services until the trial is over, or even longer. Victims need assistance to change their phone numbers and door locks, obtain orders of protection, move to new homes, hide out in safe houses or hotels, and in extreme cases, get around-the-clock armed guards (Kleinfield, 1995).

However, inadequate funding limits the ability of prosecutors' offices to offer these protective measures to all who need them (New York State Law Enforcement Council, 1994). The most extensive governmental response to the threat of reprisals has been the establishment of witness-protection programs on the state and federal level. They provide tight security to victims, witnesses, and their immediate families. These services primarily are intended to safeguard witnesses willing to testify against criminal organizations like mob families, street gangs, and drug trafficking networks. Many of the beneficiaries are not really victims but former lawbreakers like mob turncoats, former drug dealers, and defectors from street gangs. The federal Witness Security Program promises relocation, new identities, new jobs, and payment of moving expenses (Associated Press, 1994f).

One other type of intimidation needs to be addressed, in the name of balance and fairness. Defense lawyers, defendants, and reluctant defense witnesses can face intimidation in the form of fears of unfavorable media exposure and harassment by authorities, especially in highly publicized and controversial "must-win" cases. One-sided formulations of the intimidation problem imply that it is improper for anyone other than law enforcement

agents to contact witnesses and victims. But an important principle of the adversary system is that defense attorneys must be allowed to interview witnesses and compel them to testify truthfully because a person accused of a crime has a constitutional right to confront his or her accusers (American Bar Association Committee on Victims, 1979).

Dismissing Charges and Rejecting Cases

Crime victims, police officers, and prosecutors are all supposed to be on the same side within the adversary system. Yet their alliance—based in theory on a common commitment to convict people guilty of crimes—often unravels. Victims may feel rebuffed and abandoned when prosecutors dismiss or reduce charges and counts against suspects. A decision not to go forward means no further official action will be taken, and victims will not achieve the goals they sought when they reported the crime, whether they were looking for maximum punishment as revenge, compulsory treatment of the offender, or court-ordered restitution.

To prosecutors, these decisions, even if they infuriate victims, are unavoidable. It is impossible for prosecutors to fulfill their legal mandate to enforce every law and to seek the conviction of all lawbreakers. When evaluating the cases brought before them by police and deciding whether to go forward, ADAs must take into account other considerations besides the victims' wishes: What are the chances of conviction over acquittal? Are there serious doubts about the guilt of the accused? How credible and how cooperative are the victim and other witnesses? Does the complainant have any improper motives for pressing charges? Was the evidence obtained according to constitutional guidelines, or will it be tossed out of court under the exclusionary rule? Is the effort worth the state's limited resources? How much will it cost in time and money to resolve the matter? Would indictment, prosecution, and conviction of the defendant serve as a general deterrent to others who are contemplating committing the same type of offense? Would punishing the offender discourage him or her from repeating this illegal act? Would pressing charges and seeking conviction enhance the community's sense of security and confidence in the criminal justice system? Could the accused serve as a police informant or as a key witness for the prosecution in other cases if his or her cooperation were secured by lenient treatment? Would pressing or dropping charges set off protests from powerful interest groups in the community? If the ADA's office declines to prosecute, would the case be pursued by another branch of government or in a different jurisdiction? Are there appropriate pretrial diversion programs in this jurisdiction that provide treatment to wrongdoers as an alternative to adjudication? How are cases of this kind usually handled in this jurisdiction? And, finally, would a victory in this case substantially advance the careers of the ADA handling the case and of the prosecutor heading the office? (See the National Advisory Commission, 1973; Sheley, 1979; and Boland and Sones, 1986.)

When all these factors are taken into account, it is clear that the victim is only one of several key players who influence the decisions of prosecutors. Police officials, other colleagues in the prosecutor's office, defense attorneys, judges, community leaders, journalists covering the story, and vocal interest groups all affect prosecutorial decision making.

Cases that have been "solved" by arrests might not be pursued for a number of reasons. Prosecutors might screen them out because of perceived weaknesses that undercut the chances of conviction. Judges might dismiss charges on their own initiative if they feel that the evidence is weak. In general, jurisdictions in which prosecutors weed out many cases before going to court have low case-dismissal rates at later stages of judicial proceedings. Where prosecutors toss out few cases, judges throw out many more. Periodic nationwide surveys of overall felony case processing revealed that nearly half of all cases that were "solved" by arrest were not carried forward (either rejected at screening by prosecutors, dismissed in court by judges, or diverted out of

the system) (Boland and Sones, 1986; Boland, Mahanna, and Sones, 1992). Clearly, the outcomes of these decisions could cause a great many victims to become dissatisfied with the adjudication process.

Negotiating Pleas

The vast majority of cases that are carried forward (not diverted to treatment programs, screened out by prosecutors, or dismissed by judges) are resolved in out-of-court settlements known as **plea negotiations**. Plea negotiation is the process in which the ADA and the defense counsel meet in private to hammer out a compromise and avoid holding a public trial. The typical outcome of the "bargaining" (as most observers and participants derisively refer to the offers and counter-offers) is that the defendant agrees to confess in return for some **consideration** from the government, such as dropping certain charges (often the more serious ones carrying the most severe penalties), or the dismissal of particular counts (accusations of harm against specific victims). Often, the consideration is a promise or recommendation for a lesser punishment: a suspended sentence, probation, a fine, or incarceration for an agreed-upon time period that is less than the maximum permitted by the law. An overwhelming 97 percent of all convictions were secured by the accused admitting guilt (possibly just to a misdemeanor instead of the original felony charge) rather than by a jury rendering a guilty verdict, according to a study of cases adjudicated in the 75 busiest urban U.S. counties during 2004 (Kyckelhahn and Cohen, 2008).

The expression **plea bargain** gives the erroneous impression that defendants who "**cop a plea**" invariably get a break or good deal that permits them to escape the more severe punishment they deserve. Actually, police officials and prosecutors routinely engage in **bedsheeting** and **overcharging** so that they will have more bargaining chips in anticipation of the negotiations that will follow. Bedsheeting is the practice of charging a defendant with every applicable crime committed during a single incident. For example, an armed intruder captured while burglarizing an occupied home could face charges of criminal trespass, breaking and entering, burglary, attempted grand larceny, and carrying a concealed weapon, in addition to the most serious charge of all, robbery. Overcharging means filing a criminal indictment for an offense that is more serious than the available evidence might support (for example, charging someone with attempted murder after a fistfight). Some of these charges could not be proven in court, but defendants and their lawyers might be too cautious to gamble and call a prosecutor's bluff. For these reasons and others, most accused individuals who plead guilty in return for concessions receive the penalties that they probably would have received if convicted after a trial (Rhodes, 1978; Beall, 1980; Katz, 1980). Plea negotiation, even though it has been widely condemned for decades, appears to be the only practical way of handling a huge volume of cases. If all the defendants detained in a jail demanded their constitutional right to be judged by a jury of their peers after a trial, the local courts would be paralyzed by gridlock.

Because doing away with deals and inducements is unrealistic, some victims want to play active roles in the plea negotiations that resolve their cases. They justify their quest for empowerment by emphasizing that they were the ones directly involved and personally harmed, and thus it is "their" case. But this demand and formulation of the issue has evoked considerable resistance from prosecutors.

It is often presumed that the adversarial model characterizes the actual workings of the adjudication process. In the hard bargaining between prosecution and defense, the ADA must be able to produce a cooperative witness eager to testify in order to convince the defendant to cave in, negotiate a plea, and confess guilt to at least some of the charges. But the reality of the situation might be that the **courtroom work group** (composed of the judge, ADA, and defense counsel) shares a mutual interest in processing large numbers of cases expeditiously. Victims serving as witnesses for the prosecution are outsiders whose presence and involvement is often unwanted by these insiders because it will slow down their assembly-line practices that resolve cases quickly. Victims see their situations as unique events that deserve careful

consideration, not as routine occurrences to be rapidly **disposed of** according to some formula based on that jurisdiction's current **going rate** (typical penalty or sentence for the type of crime in question, routinely agreed upon by the insiders) (see Walker, 2006).

Predictably, prosecutors, defense attorneys, and judges make dire predictions about what would happen if victims (and police officers and defendants as well) joined them at the table at pretrial conferences. These insiders contend that the candid discussions necessary to foster settlements would be inhibited by the presence of outsiders, and that volatile confrontations between victims and defendants would break out. Furthermore, both victims and defendants could misconstrue the role of judges and accuse them of improper conduct, and as a result the dignity of judges would be diminished by their open involvement in negotiations in front of outsiders (Heinz and Kerstetter, 1979). Prosecutors in particular feel threatened by the inclusion of victims (whom they supposedly represent, in addition to the state) at such meetings. They object because victims might try to use the administrative machinery as an instrument of revenge and might put forward unreasonable demands for the imposition of maximum penalties. Deals would fall through, and risky and costly trials would result (McDonald, 1976).

In general, victims do not have a right to participate in or even be consulted during the process of plea negotiation. Few jurisdictions grant victims a clearly defined role, and most state laws still do not provide them with any formal mechanisms to challenge the decisions of the prosecuting attorneys who act in their names as well as on behalf of "the people." The Supreme Court has issued several rulings that specifically deny complainants the right to challenge the decisions prosecutors make about handling their cases. (See box 7.1 below.)

One reason why victim/witness assistance programs have had little success in improving appearance and conviction rates is that they do not encourage injured parties to be the active participants in negotiations that some would like to be (Davis, 1983).

Nevertheless, most victims are convinced that criminals are getting away with something when they accept plea bargains offered by the prosecution. Actually, resolving cases by negotiating pleas rather than by holding full-scale trials might be in the best interests of certain victims. Besides ensuring a conviction, plea bargaining spares victims the ordeal of testifying in court and undergoing hostile questioning during cross-examination by defense attorneys. For some victims, testifying in painful detail means reliving the horror of the crime, as in this trial:

> A tearful victim tells a jury how she had fallen asleep cuddling her toddler while her husband was working late. She awoke when she heard a prowler enter through a kitchen window, but remained still. Unfortunately he spotted her, pulled out a knife, and put the blade to her daughter's throat. Faced with a nightmare choice, she quietly submitted and was raped. "It was disgusting," she testifies. On cross-examination, she admits that she can't identify the accused (whose DNA was lifted from the bedding) because the intruder covered her head with a sheet. (Ginsberg, 2005)

Concerns about emotional distress suffered by a victim on the stand are voiced most often in cases of forcible rape and child molestation. Other types of complainants also may be particularly reluctant to undergo cross-examination if the facts of the case portray them in a negative light or reveal aspects of their private lives that they do not want exposed to the world via media coverage (especially in jurisdictions where trials can be televised, which includes most states).

VICTIMS AND DEFENSE ATTORNEYS

Victims and defense attorneys are on opposite sides and therefore are natural enemies within the adversary system. Whether hired privately for a fee or provided free to indigents, these lawyers have a duty to advise suspects, defendants, and convicts about legal proceedings and the options they can exercise. Defense lawyers have an obligation to zealously represent their clients' best interests, which usually translates to getting out of trouble with the law entirely, or at least being sentenced to less than the maximum punishment.

Conflicts often break out between victims and defense lawyers over two matters: how long the process takes and the number of court appearances needed, as well as the line of questioning directed at victims who testify in court when they appear as prosecution witnesses. From a victim's view, defense attorneys might engage in two abusive practices: asking judges for postponements of their clients' cases to wear victims down, and using unfair tactics to undermine the credibility of complainants when they appear as prosecution witnesses.

Postponing Hearings

The Sixth Amendment to the Constitution guarantees the accused the right to a speedy trial. Hence, problems of congested court calendars and needless delays usually have been approached from a defendant's standpoint. Many states and the federal courts have set limits on the amount of time that can elapse between arrest and trial (not counting continuances requested by defense attorneys). But complainants serving as government witnesses also suffer from the uncertainty that envelops unresolved cases, and they share a common interest with defendants in having legal matters settled in as short a time as possible.

If accused people have been released on bail, however, defense lawyers may have an incentive to stall proceedings to "buy time on the streets" and to wear down witnesses for the prosecution. As delays mount and complainants appear in court unnecessarily, they and other crucial prosecution witnesses may lose patience with the protracted deliberations of the legal system. Their commitment to see the case through to its conclusion may erode. Stalling succeeds when a complainant or another key witness gives up in disgust and fails to appear in court as required. For example, a victim who lost her handbag to an unarmed bandit might miss so many days from work that the lost wages far exceed what the robber took, so she may eventually drop out. Stalling for time might also pay off if victims or other witnesses for the prosecution forget crucial details, move away, become ill, or die in the interim. At that point, the defense attorney can move for a dismissal of charges (Reiff, 1979). Prosecutors can also manipulate continuances for their own ends. If defendants are in jail rather than out on bail, then government attorneys may stretch out proceedings to keep them behind bars longer and as a way to pressure them to give in and accept unfavorable plea offers. In the process, the defendant's right to a speedy trial could be violated.

Postponements can prolong and intensify the suffering of complainants. In order to be available if called to testify, they might have to arrange repeatedly for child care, miss school or work, cancel vacations, and break appointments, only to discover (often at the last minute) that the hearings have been rescheduled. To defeat this wear-the-victim-down strategy, some defense motions for postponements could be opposed more vigorously by prosecutors. Similarly, requests for a postponement should be rejected by judges if they suspect the defense's call for a continuance is a stalling tactic (President's Task Force, 1982). To prevent complainants and police officers from showing up in court on days when hearings have been postponed, victim/witness assistance programs in prosecutors' offices operate last-minute notification systems.

As a general rule, the more serious the charges against the defendant are, the longer it takes to resolve the case. Cases resolved by negotiated pleas don't take as long as cases resolved by trials (Boland, Mahanna, and Sones, 1992). Researchers determined that murder cases in state courts took an average of more than one year to be resolved, rape cases required 176 days, and robbery cases went on for 140 days from arrest to sentencing, according to a study of more than 50,000 felonies processed in the nation's 75 largest counties during 2004 (Kyckelhahn, 2008). However, in some high-crime areas, huge backlogs cause even greater delays, prolonging the anxiety of both complainants and defendants waiting for the final outcome of their conflicts.

Cross-Examining Witnesses during Trials

If they can't wear down victims by stalling, defense attorneys might try to discredit them on the stand, along with other prosecution witnesses, during the trial so that the jury won't give much weight to their testimony.

Trials are relatively rare events, so most victims are not called to testify and undergo cross-examination. Because the outcomes of trials are uncertain and involve risks, attorneys for both sides usually prefer to strike a deal out of court. However, statistically, most trials are successful from the point of view of victims and prosecutors: Defendants usually are found guilty.

The percentage of criminal indictments that result in trials before juries or in bench trials before judges varies according to two factors: the jurisdiction and the nature of the charges. Some prosecutors are more willing to put defendants on trial. Serious felonies such as murder, rape, aggravated assault, and robbery go to trial more often than cases involving lesser crimes such as burglary or auto theft. Rape complainants are the most likely to be subjected to hostile cross-examination by defense attorneys. But only about 5 percent of rape cases were resolved through trials with the help of the complainants' testimony in the nation's largest prosecutorial jurisdictions in 2000 (Rainville and Reaves, 2003).

Because defense attorneys are obliged to be vigorous advocates for their clients, they may advance arguments at a trial or during plea negotiations that the defendant is in fact innocent. In casting doubt on the version of events cobbled together by police and the prosecution, defense attorneys draw upon their skills and training to undermine the accusatory testimony of victims. Under the adversary system, each side puts forward its best case and assails the version of events presented by the opposition. Cross-examination is the art of exposing the weaknesses of witnesses. The intent is to impugn the accusers' credibility by trapping them into revealing hidden motives, lapses of memory, unsavory character traits, embarrassing indiscretions, prejudices, or dishonest inclinations.

Cross-examinations can be ordeals for witnesses. But if defense attorneys were not allowed to sharply question prosecution witnesses, then the right of defendants to try throu~~gh~~ their lawyers to refute the charges against them ~~would be~~ undermined. The concerns of com~~plaining~~ witnesses (including defense ~~witnesses~~ cross-examined by prosecu~~tors and har~~rassed on the stand under ~~the law~~ against the public humili~~ation of defen~~dants who are arrested ar~~nd charged).

In addition to a ~~Sixth~~ Amendment to the C~~onstitution grants~~ the right to confront ~~the accuser. The burden of~~ proof falls on the pro~~secution. The defendant is~~ considered innocen~~t until proven guilty. The~~ accuser must be ~~believed beyond a reasonable doubt about~~ his or her credib~~ility. Testimony must meet a rea~~sonable doubt. ~~The testimony~~ against a form~~er defendant may require a~~ witness for the gove~~rnment to be an expert in forensic~~ science or forensic psycho~~logy, or an experienced law~~ enforcement officer (although the ~~reliability of~~ police testimony has become the subject ~~of~~ debate). But when the full brunt of the defense's well-honed counterattack is directed at a novice complainant, the potential for adding insult to injury reaches disturbing proportions. At its best, the confrontation in the courtroom puts the victim-as-eyewitness to the test. At its worst, the victim is a target to be injured again by being made to look like a liar, a fool, or an instigator who got what he or she deserved.

Because defense attorneys have a duty to vigorously represent the best interests of their clients, these courtroom tactics might seem harsh. To rattle a witness, discredit damning testimony, and sow seeds of doubt and confusion among jurors, they may have to resort to theatrics and hyperbole. The Code of Professional Responsibility that guides legal strategies permits a zealous defense to gain an acquittal or a lenient sentence, but it prohibits any line of questioning that is intended solely to harass

or maliciously harm a witness. Experts and the public often disagree over whether a defense attorney or prosecutor crossed the line and acted unethically by badgering a witness during a cross-examination. Cases that provoke the greatest controversy are those in which defense attorneys cast aspersions on the character of victims or blame them for their own misfortunes (Shipp, 1987).

In murder trials, families and friends of the de~~cea~~sed find it particularly upsetting if defense attor~~neys attack~~ the attitudes and actions of the dead ~~to~~ justify or exonerate the behavior ~~of the defendant. U~~nlike cross-examinations, ~~attacks on~~ the reputation (or "trash~~ing") of mur~~der victims are peculiarly ~~unfair because t~~he insinuations cannot rebut ~~them. The~~se cases show:

~~A woma~~n is strangled late at night in a ~~car by~~ a young man she was dating. ~~He argues~~ that she died accidentally as he ~~and hi~~mself during "rough sex play." ~~The defense~~ subpoenas her diary, in which she ~~allegedly g~~raphically described aggressive ~~sexual ex~~ploits with other men—later, it ~~turns ou~~t that the diary doesn't contain such ~~informa~~tion. Some members of the jury are ~~swayed~~ by the defense's arguments. The jury ~~remai~~ns deadlocked for days. Before it can ~~deliv~~er a unanimous verdict, a last-minute plea is negotiated that permits the defendant to admit guilt to the lesser charge of manslaughter instead of murder. At a press conference, the father denounces the defense's portrayal of his dead daughter, and calls it a bizarre pack of lies. (Hackett and Cerio, 1988; Lander, 1988)

***

An actor who played a detective on television is on trial for shooting his wife, whom he referred to as a "pig" and said he wanted to "snuff." The defense raises doubts about each of the prosecution's specific charges, and portrays the murdered woman as a "sleazy grifter" who recruited rich and famous men by sending them form letters attached to nude pictures of herself. The defense claims she told friends that she always wanted to marry a celebrity. Calling her a "scam artist," the defense tells the jury that she used at least a dozen aliases and left behind 10 former husbands. She allegedly pressured the 71-year-old star into a loveless marriage by getting pregnant in order to get at his money. The jury decides he is not guilty of murder and is deadlocked over the charge that he sought to hire a TV stuntman to kill her. (LeDuff, 2005; Riley, 2005)

VICTIMS AND JUDGES

Judges are supposed to act as referees within the adversary system. Defendants often consider them to be partisans representing the state and favoring the prosecution. Angry victims, however, frequently see judges as guardians of the rights of the accused rather than protectors of injured parties. Victims who have been mistreated by the offender, police officers, the prosecutor, and the defense attorney expect that the judge will finally accord them the justice they seek. But conflicts between victims and judges can erupt over bail decisions and sentencing.

Granting Bail

Police officers often resent the granting of bail as a repudiation of their hard work and the risks they took to apprehend perpetrators. To them, releasing defendants on bail is tantamount to turning dangerous criminals loose. Victims also can be outraged by judges' decisions to grant bail to defendants whom they see as the culprits who harmed them.

The Eighth Amendment to the Constitution prohibits the setting of excessive bail. Whether it establishes a chance to be bailed out as an affirmative right, however, is a subject of scholarly debate and considerable public concern. State and federal courts routinely deny bail to defendants accused of first-degree murder. In noncapital cases, bail can be denied to jailed suspects who have a history of flight to avoid prosecution or who have tried to interfere with the administration of justice by intimidating a witness or a juror. Otherwise, defendants generally are given the chance to raise money or post bond to guarantee that they will show up at their hearings and trials.

The amount of bail is usually determined by the judge and is set according to the nature of the offense and the record of the defendant. The prosecutor usually recommends a high figure while the defense attorney argues for a sum that is within the defendant's reach. Making bail is a major problem for defendants who are poor and have no prosperous friends or relatives. Across the country, houses of detention are crammed with people unable to raise a few hundred dollars to purchase their freedom until their cases are resolved. Nationwide, a little more than half of all victims of violent crimes faced the prospect that the person accused of harming them would be let out on bail in the 75 largest counties in 2004 (Kyckelhahn and Cohen, 2008).

The question of bail versus jail raises a number of troubling issues. When accused people are denied bail and subjected to preventive detention, or are unable to raise the necessary amount, they are sent to jail and thereby immediately undergo punishment before conviction. The living conditions in houses of detention are usually far worse than in prisons, which hold convicted felons. Yet the release of a defendant who is genuinely guilty and may strike again poses an immediate danger to the entire community and a direct threat to the complainant who will serve as a witness for the state. One partial resolution of this dilemma is for the judge to impose and enforce as a condition of bail that the defendant must avoid all contact with the complainant and other prosecution witnesses or else forfeit the privilege of pretrial release.

Sentencing Offenders

After a defendant—by an admission of guilt as part of a negotiated plea or by a jury verdict after a trial—is convicted, the judge has the responsibility of imposing an appropriate sentence. Judges can exercise a considerable amount of discretion when pronouncing sentences unless there are mandatory minimums or explicit guidelines. Sentences can involve incarceration, fines, enrollment in treatment programs, community service, and obligations to repay victims. The particular objectives that guide sentencing are specific deterrence, general deterrence, incapacitation, retribution, rehabilitation, and restitution.

The substantial variation among judges in the severity of punishment they mete out in comparable cases is termed **sentence disparity**. Civil libertarians find great disparities troubling because judges might be expressing their social prejudices, to the extent that they deal more harshly with certain groups of offenders. Convicts might view sentence disparities as a sign of unjustifiable arbitrariness. Crime control advocates consider wide ranges as evidence that judges on the low end are too "soft" or "lenient" toward offenders. Activists in the victims' rights movement find the spectrum of possible punishments as a motivation to press for greater input in sentencing.

Historically, excluding victims from the sentencing process has been justified on several grounds. If the purpose of punishing offenders is to deter others from committing the same acts, then sanctions must be swift, sure, and predictable, and not subject to uncertainty and modification by injured parties. If the objective is retribution, then lawbreakers must receive the punishments they deserve and not the penalties their victims request. If the goal of sentencing is to rehabilitate offenders, then the punitive urges of the people they harmed cannot be allowed to interfere with the length and type of treatment prescribed by experts (McDonald, 1979).

The potential impact of victims' desires on sentencing is limited because so many other parties already shape those decisions. Victims who want to help determine their offenders' sentences have to compete for influence with other individuals and groups that routinely affect judicial discretion. State legislatures pass laws that set maximum and minimum limits for periods of confinement and for fines. Prosecutors make recommendations based

on deals arrived at during plea negotiations and draw upon the courtroom work group's mutual understandings about appropriate penalties for specific crimes in that jurisdiction at that time ("the going rate"). Defense attorneys use whatever leverage they have on behalf of their clients. Defendants determine their own sentences to some degree by their demeanor, degree of remorse, prior record of convictions, and other mitigating or aggravating personal characteristics and circumstances. Probation officers conduct pre-sentence investigations and make recommendations to guide judges. Parole boards determine the actual time served when they release convicted felons from prison ahead of schedule or keep them confined until their maximum sentences expire. Corrections officers influence whether or not convicts earn "good-time" reductions and parole by filing reports about cooperative or troublesome behavior. The news media can shape case outcomes by their coverage or lack of it. The public's reactions also can affect the handling of cases, prompting harshness or leniency. And ultimately, state governors can shorten terms of imprisonment and even stop executions by issuing pardons or commuting sentences. Therefore, the victim's notion of what would be an appropriate sentence is just one of many.

If victims want to compete against this constellation of forces and play a role in shaping sentences, they can make their wishes known in two ways: by conveying their requests to judges in writing or by expressing their views orally (**allocution**) at sentencing hearings. Written **victim impact statements** enable judges to learn about the actual physical, emotional, and financial effects of the offense on the injured parties and their families. Questionnaires ask (under the threat of penalties for perjury) about wounds, medical bills, counseling costs, other expenses, insurance reimbursements, and lifestyle changes resulting from the crime. Statements of opinion ask victims what they would consider to be fair and just. In most jurisdictions, the victim impact statement is incorporated into the **pre-sentence investigation report** (PSIR) prepared by a probation officer.

The invention and adoption of impact statements and granting the allocution privilege were important gains for the victims' rights movement. Prior to their acceptance and implementation, victims had to rely on prosecutors to present their views and to fully describe their plights. Direct appeals to judges were thought to undermine the judiciary's professional objectivity by injecting inflammatory emotional considerations into the proceedings. But advocates of victims' rights argued that the situation was unbalanced. Convicted persons did not have to depend solely on their lawyers to speak for them. They were permitted to directly address the court before their sentences were handed down. Yet two lives—the injured party's as well as the wrongdoer's—were profoundly shaped by the sentence, which represented an official evaluation of the degree of harm inflicted. Judges couldn't make informed decisions if they heard from only one side: the defendants themselves and their lawyers, families, friends, and other character witnesses. Notions of fairness dictated that suffering individuals also be allowed to write or speak about their experiences before sentences were determined (President's Task Force, 1982).

A nationwide study of how criminal justice officials find out about the harm offenders inflicted on their victims concluded that for judges, the most important source of information was the PSIR, not the prosecutor or the trial testimony. However, the probation officers who prepared that report usually obtained much of their information from second-hand sources, such as police reports and medical records, and not directly from interviewing the injured parties or reading their impact statements (Forst and Hernon, 1984).

Just because activists in the victims' rights movement succeeded in securing the right to submit an impact statement or to speak in person at a sentencing hearing does not mean that these practices have become widespread and effective. On the contrary: A study carried out in California in 1982 concluded that very few victims took advantage of these opportunities, and when they did their participation had very little influence (Villmoare and Neto, 1987).

When a sentence is handed down, it is possible that the victim is misled into thinking that it is more severe than it actually is. Therefore, the victims' rights movement has urged states to impose a truth-in-sentencing rule that would require judges to calculate and announce the earliest possible date (actual time served) that a convict could be released from confinement, taking into account time off for good behavior behind bars and parole immediately upon eligibility (Associated Press, 1994b). For example, during the 1980s, felons sent to prison by state court judges across the country served an estimated 38 percent of their maximum sentences. A federal truth-in-sentencing law, passed in 1987 and adopted since then in most states, requires felons to serve at least 85 percent of their court-imposed sentences (Langan, Perkins, and Chaiken, 1994). A study of more than 300 victims of felonies in eight jurisdictions across the country established that most victims were dissatisfied with the sentences judges handed down in their cases. Eighty-six percent agreed with the statement that "guilty offenders are not punished enough" (Forst and Hernon, 1984). This perception that many judges are too lenient is shared by the public at large. Nationwide polls periodically ask, "In general, do you think the courts in this area deal too harshly or not harshly enough with criminals?" In 1972, 66 percent of those polled answered "not harshly enough." By 1976, the number had risen to 81 percent. In 1986, the figure peaked at 85 percent, but then declined to 81 percent in 1993 (Maguire and Pastore, 1994). By 2002, the proportion of the public who perceived that judges were not dishing out appropriately harsh punishments had dropped back down to 67 percent, just about the same level as in 1972 (NORC, 2004).

The persistence of this widespread impression raises a crucial question: Just how much punishment is enough? Victims might feel that the offenders convicted of harming them don't stay in prison long enough. But no formula or equation exists to calculate the gravity of an offense and translate this rating into the "proper" amount of time a perpetrator should be incarcerated. Profound disagreements divide people over the issue of whether certain murders should carry the death penalty or life imprisonment without parole. Usually overlooked, however, are the dramatic differences in maximum penalties from state to state for lesser crimes such as rape, robbery, or burglary. Clearly, legislators who have the authority to set the upper limits for penalties can't agree on the maximum length of prison time that one person who harms another really deserves. It is impossible to conclude with any degree of objectivity that a particular offender "got off too lightly" when the maximum sentences differ so sharply from one jurisdiction to another (see Katz, 1980).

A bitter controversy erupted over whether or not members of the immediate family of a murder victim should be permitted to try to influence the jury's sentencing decision in **bifurcated capital trials** during the penalty phase (after the defendant has been convicted and faces the possibility of execution). The following case brought before the Supreme Court was at the core of the debate over the admissibility of highly emotional information from victim impact statements or via allocution.

> In a drug-induced frenzy, a man stabs to death the mother of two toddlers, as well as her two-year-old daughter. During the penalty phase of the trial, the grandmother describes to the jury how the three-year-old boy who survived the attack still cries mournfully for his mother and little sister. The jury sentences the convict to die in the electric chair. (Clark and Block, 1992)

Victims' rights groups and prosecutors' organizations argued that it was illogical to demand that a jury focus all of its attention on the defendant's difficult circumstances and other mitigating factors and then ignore the suffering of the survivors of the deceased. But civil rights and civil liberties groups argued that the introduction of impact statements could be highly inflammatory and prejudicial in capital cases, diverting the jury's attention toward the victim's character (how much or how little the dead person would be missed and mourned) and away from its duty of evaluating the defendant's blameworthiness and the circumstances of the crime. The first time the high court considered a case that raised the issue, it voted to exclude impact statements. But when the issue came up a second time, the majority of justices ruled that survivors could testify during the penalty phase of a capital case (Clark and Block, 1992).

Appealing to the Supreme Court

On rare occasions, a case involving a crime victim raises significant legal issues that have not yet been addressed and resolved by an earlier judicial ruling. In these instances, victims and their supporters, or prosecutors, or even defense attorneys, have turned to the U.S. Supreme Court to make a wise and fair decision that will serve as a precedent for future cases to follow.

The Supreme Court is the highest appellate body in the judicial system. It hears only those cases on appeal from federal and state courts that appear to raise important principles of constitutional law. Its nine justices are appointed by the president (who must secure the approval of the Senate) for life so that they can make decisions without fearing repercussions from powerful outside pressure groups. When a majority of Supreme Court justices (five or more) agree on a decision, that ruling sets a precedent that must be followed in all lower courts throughout the nation. These landmark decisions also guide the procedures followed by police departments, prosecutors, trial judges, corrections officials, and other agencies within the criminal justice system.

Over the past several decades, a number of decisions handed down by the Supreme Court have affected the rights and interests of crime victims (see O'Neill, 1984). Some of these far-reaching rulings are summarized in Box 7.1. In most of these landmark decisions, the Court rejected arguments raised by victims and their supporters.

B O X 7.1 **Supreme Court Decisions Directly Affecting Victims**

Decisions Advancing Victims' Interests and Rights

Victimized Children Can Testify via Closed-Circuit Television
In 1990 in a 5–4 decision (*Maryland v. Craig*), the Supreme Court held that it was constitutional for a state to pass a law that shields a child who accuses an adult of sexual abuse from a face-to-face confrontation during a trial. The child's testimony and the defense attorney's cross-examination can take place in another room and can be shown to the jury over closed-circuit television if the prosecutor can convince the judge that the young witness would be traumatized by having to testify in the defendant's presence. The majority felt that the state's interest in the physical and psychological well-being of the abused child may outweigh the defendant's Sixth Amendment right to face his or her accuser in person (Greenhouse, 1990).

Rape Victims' Past Experiences Can Be Kept Out of Court
In 1991 the Supreme Court ruled by a 7–2 vote that the rape shield laws passed in all 50 states were constitutional. The laws allow judges to suppress as irrelevant attempts by the defense to introduce allegations about past sexual experiences of rape victims (Rauber, 1991).

Victim Impact Statements Can Be Used in Capital Cases
In 1987 (*Booth v. Maryland*), the Supreme Court overturned a death sentence because the jury during the penalty phase of the trial heard a particularly heart-rending impact statement about how the murder of an elderly couple shattered the lives of three generations of their family. The majority ruled that the use of such "inflammatory" impact statements created a constitutionally unacceptable risk that juries might impose the death penalty in an arbitrary and capricious manner, swayed by the social standing and reputation of the deceased person. The majority believed that the victim's "worth" was not an appropriate factor for a jury to consider when weighing the killer's fate—imprisonment or execution—because it would undermine the guarantee of equal protection (Triebwasser, 1987b). But in 1991 (*Payne v. Tennessee*), the Court reversed itself and ruled that prosecutors could

introduce victim impact statements and that the survivors of murder victims could testify. The majority held that courts have always taken into account the harm done by defendants when determining appropriate sentences (Clark and Block, 1992).

People Concerned About Crime Have a Right to Own Guns In Their Homes
In 2008 (*District of Columbia, et al., v. Heller*), five justices interpreted the Second Amendment as granting the right to keep a loaded handgun for self-protection at home to individuals who fear that criminals might invade their residences, even in large cities with very strict handgun control laws (Greenhouse, 2008).

Decisions Opposing Victims' Interests and Rights

Government Has No Constitutional Duty to Protect Individuals
In 1989 (*De Shaney v. Winnebago County Dept. of Social Services*), six of the nine justices decided that a government agency could not be sued for failing to intervene (on behalf of a child repeatedly beaten and permanently injured by his father) because the state does not have a special obligation to protect individuals from harm by other private persons ("U.S. Supreme Court," 1989).

Victims Can't Sue Police Departments for Failing to Enforce Orders of Protection
In 2005 (*Gonzales v. Castle Rock Police*), the Supreme Court by a 7–2 margin ruled that a victim of domestic violence did not have the right to sue her local police department for failing to enforce a restraining order against her husband who subsequently murdered their three children. The court upheld the principle that police departments are not liable to lawsuits challenging the way officers exercise discretion in the performance of their duties, unless there is evidence of extreme negligence (Bunch, 2005).

Victims Cannot Compel Prosecutors to Take Action Against Suspects
A number of decisions handed down in 1967, 1973, 1977, 1981, and 1983 have established that attorneys

general and district attorneys have absolute discretion over whether to charge defendants with crimes and what charges to press or drop. Victims cannot compel prosecutors to take particular actions, and courts cannot intervene in this decision-making process (see Stark and Goldstein, 1985).

Victims of Rape and Domestic Violence Can't Sue Attackers in Federal Court

In 2000 (*United States v. Morrison*), the Supreme Court by a 5–4 margin struck down a provision of the 1984 Violence Against Women Act which had granted injured parties in domestic violence and rape cases the additional option of suing their assailants for monetary damages in federal court. The majority voted to uphold the doctrine of state sovereignty over gender-based violence rather than extend federal authority via the interstate commerce clause (Biskupic, 2000).

Newspapers Can Publish the Lawfully Obtained Names of Rape Victims

In 1989, a majority of six justices argued that the First Amendment's guarantee of freedom of the press protected a newspaper from liability for printing the name of a woman who already was identified as a rape victim in publicly available police reports. However, the decision did not declare unconstitutional state laws in Florida, Georgia, and South Carolina that prohibit the publishing of a rape victim's name as an invasion of privacy (Greenhouse, 1989).

Offenders Can Escape Paying Restitution to Victims

In 1989 (*Pennsylvania Dept. of Public Welfare v. Davenport*), the Court ruled 7–2 that if convicts declare bankruptcy, they can avoid paying court-ordered restitution because restitution obligations are dischargeable debts. In 1990 (*Hughey v. United States*), the Court ruled that a federal judge cannot order a defendant to pay restitution to a victim if the charge involving that victim was dropped as part of a negotiated plea. The Court based its ruling on a provision of the federal Victim and Witness Protection Act of 1982 (Eddy, 1990).

Victims Can't Easily Claim Income Gained by Notorious Offenders

In 1991 (*Simon & Schuster v. New York Crime Victims Board*), the Supreme Court struck down New York's

1977 "Son-of-Sam" statute, which served as a model for 41 other state laws. The law confiscated fees and royalties offenders gained from selling their inside stories to book publishers or moviemakers and permitted victims to claim that money. The unanimous opinion held that the state's worthwhile goals of ensuring that criminals do not profit from their crimes, and of transferring the proceeds to victims, did not justify infringements on the First Amendment right of free speech (Greenhouse, 1991).

Victims of Identity Theft Can't Have Extra Time to Sue Credit Bureaus

In 2001 (*TRW v. Andrews*), the Supreme Court ruled that people who find out that impostors have ruined their financial reputations have only two years from the time the mistake about their real creditworthiness was made to file damage lawsuits against the major credit bureaus that generate ratings, even if they don't discover these errors in sufficient time (Savage, 2003).

The Statute of Limitations on Child Sexual Abuse Charges Cannot Be Extended

In 2003, the Supreme Court struck down a California law that had lengthened the state's statute of limitations to enable criminal prosecutions of alleged molesters whose accusers came forward many years after the events took place. However, the decision did not block victims from pursuing lawsuits in civil court (Garvey and Winton, 2003).

Insufficient Proof that the Lives of Murdered Black People Count for Less

In 1987 (*McCleskey v. Kemp*), in upholding a death penalty conviction, the Supreme Court rejected a statistical analysis that seemed to show that the deaths of black victims were not taken as seriously as the deaths of white victims by criminal justice decision makers—prosecutors, juries, and judges. The court ruled that a pattern—in which offenders convicted of killing white people were 11 times more likely to be sentenced to die than those found guilty of murdering black victims—was not compelling evidence of intentional discrimination in violation of the Eighth and Fourteenth Amendments (Triebwasser, 1987a).

VICTIMS AND CORRECTIONS OFFICIALS

Corrections officials include jail and prison wardens and guards, and probation and parole officers. Victims whose cases led to successful prosecutions occasionally seek their cooperation but may find themselves in conflict over issues of safety and money.

Keeping Track of Offenders and Receiving Reimbursement from Them

Victims are more likely to have contacts with county probation departments than with county jail, state prison, or state parole authorities. Of those found guilty in state courts, more felons are sentenced to probation for up to several years than are sent to jail for up to a year or to prison for longer stretches (Brown and Langan, 1998).

Victims want two things from probation and parole officers. When offenders are placed on probation or are released on parole after serving time in prison, victims want to be protected from harassment and further harm. They can feel especially endangered by a vengeful, violent ex-offender if their cooperation and testimony was a crucial factor leading to conviction. And if making restitution is a condition of probation or parole, victims want to receive these payments right on schedule. Probation and parole officers share these goals but often find their caseloads so overwhelming that they cannot enforce these requirements effectively.

According to legislation in most states, corrections officials must safeguard the well-being and best interests of victims by keeping them notified of the inmates' whereabouts, parole board appearances, and release dates. Correctional agencies can go further and develop victim safety plans that make sure prisoners on temporary leave (on furlough, work release, or educational release) or who escape from an institution do not threaten, track down, stalk, and attack the people they injured earlier (see National Victim Center, 1990; Gagliardi, 2005).

When victims discover from other sources that their offenders (especially those guilty of aggravated assault, armed robbery, rape, or sexual molestation) are back on the streets, conflicts can erupt with corrections officials who did not meet their notification obligations. A widely used computer-based notification system now allows corrections officials to alert registered victims to a jail or prison inmate's whereabouts, including his release on bail; attendance at classes or work outside the institution; fulfillment of his sentence, probation, or parole obligations; or his escape from custody (Harry, 2002).

Influencing Parole Board Decisions

Statistically, few victims ever deal with members of parole boards because small percentages of offenders are caught, convicted, and sent away to prison for years. However, this group of corrections officials has received a great deal of attention from the victims' rights movement because it determines the fates of inmates who have inflicted serious harm.

By definition, parole means an early release for a felon before the maximum or upper limit of the judge's sentence has been served. Prisoners become eligible for parole after serving a specified proportion of their sentences, but parole is not automatic. After hearings, parole boards turn down most convicts, keeping them incarcerated for many more years. (However, even without parole, early release is still possible because most correctional institutions subtract time off for good behavior.)

The board grants conditional liberty to convicts who have earned the privilege of parole. They may return to their communities but must abide by restrictions on their conduct. Parolees who violate the rules can be reimprisoned for the remainder of their unexpired full sentences at the discretion of administrative judges after revocation hearings.

Victims with a punitive outlook will want parole boards to vote to keep convicts behind bars for their entire sentences. Victims seeking reimbursement will want boards to grant parole to convicts but impose strict restitution obligations on them. Victims concerned about offender rehabilitation will want boards to impose treatment obligations as a condition of parole.

Because many parolees commit additional crimes after serving time, boards granting early release have come under intense criticism and scrutiny. Even though parole's origins date back to the mid-1800s, convicts are finding it much more difficult to earn early release. Traditionally three rationales justify setting up boards to grant the privilege of a shortened sentence to selected prisoners. The first is that ex-convicts can make smoother transitions from a tightly controlled prison regimen to civilian life with the guidance of parole officers. Second, corrections officers can control the behavior of inmates more effectively if a possibility of early release looms as a reward for continuous good behavior. The third justification is that parole enables correctional authorities to better manage the flow of prisoners into and out of institutions, ensuring that sufficient cell space is available for new arrivals.

Prisoners' rights groups have rejected the notion that parole is a form of benevolence that serves as an incentive for rehabilitation. They have criticized the practice as a way of extending the length of time ex-convicts are under governmental control, as a device to prolong punishment, and as a source of anxiety and uncertainty for prisoners. These groups have called for the abolition of the practice of parole and have suggested determinate or fixed sentences of shorter duration as a replacement for indefinite sentences with widely varying minimums and maximums (Shelden, 1982).

Crime control organizations and think tanks also have demanded an end to the parole system but for different reasons. They perceive parole boards as granting undeserved breaks and unwarranted leniency because dangerous criminals are let out prematurely. They want parole ended and replaced with definite sentences of longer duration (President's Task Force, 1982). Victims, too, may bitterly resent the practice of parole if it reduces sentences of incarceration that they originally considered too short. If parolees harass victims or fail to pay them restitution in a timely manner, then parole board decisions will be resented.

As a result of the widespread dissatisfaction with parole, the federal prison system and a number of state systems have phased it out. In other jurisdictions parole is granted less often. The reliance on parole reached its peak in 1977, when as many as 72 percent of prisoners returning to society were granted conditional liberty with community supervision. By 1986, the proportion of released prisoners who were let out on parole had dropped to 43 percent (Hester, 1987), and by 1990 the figure stood at 41 percent (Jankowski, 1991). Of the inmates released from state prisons in 1998, only about 35 percent had been granted discretionary parole (as opposed to mandatory supervision after serving their entire term) (see Beck and Mumola, 1999; and Bonczar and Glaze, 1999). The proportion of inmates achieving discretionary early release crept back up to 39 percent during 2003 (Glaze and Palla, 2004) but then slipped back down to 35 percent in 2006 (Glaze and Bonczar, 2007). In sum, trends in the data reveal that more than one-third of prisoners still do not serve their maximum terms, so victims retain an interest in exercising their rights before parole boards.

Board members can serve victims by inviting them to participate in decision-making processes, by warning them in advance that the persons they helped send to prison are being let go, and by ordering the convicts to pay restitution as a condition of release. In some states, restitution is a mandatory requirement for parolees unless the board excuses them from it. In most states, legislation expressly grants victims the right to attend parole hearings (usually held inside prisons in remote locations) and personally inform board members of their views. Alternatively, they can submit written or videotaped impact statements (National Victim Center, 1990).

As with sentencing, the potential impact of victim input on decision making about parole is limited. The boards receive statements not only from victims, but also from prosecutors, judges, and other concerned parties. They interview the inmates and review their criminal records and the prison files describing their behavior behind bars. Most of the time, the decisions arrived at by boards are not determined by the wishes of victims but rather by intense political pressures to keep convicts confined longer or by pragmatic administrative considerations to let some out ahead of schedule to make room for new arrivals.

AND JUSTICE FOR ALL?

The Fourteenth Amendment to the Constitution promises **equal protection under the law** for all citizens: Federal and state criminal justice systems ought to regard social factors such as class, race, nationality, religion, and sex as irrelevant to the administration of the law. Traditionally, criminologists and political activists have applied this important principle of equal protection and "**blind justice**" to the way suspects, defendants, and convicts are treated by officials and agencies. The main focus of concern has been whether poor or minority offenders are subjected to discriminatory treatment. Whether certain kinds of victims are handled in a discriminatory manner is an equally significant concern that has escaped notice.

It is often said that the United States is a country "ruled by laws not men." This maxim implies that the principles of due process and equal protection limit the considerable discretionary powers of criminal justice officials. "Due process" means procedural consistency and equal protection requires that different categories of people be treated similarly. Yet enough discretion remains at each step in the criminal justice process to generate unequal outcomes. Of course, those who do exercise discretion can and do justify their actions. Explanations range from practical considerations about time and money to philosophical rationales about the true meaning of justice. Nevertheless, the actions they take generate, maintain, and reveal double standards, or more accurately (because sometimes more than two groups are involved) **differential handling**, ranging from exemplary service and support for some to **second-class treatment** for others.

Recognizing "Second-Class" Treatment

The wife of a wealthy doctor disappears while walking her dog. The police launch a massive search, hold a press conference, assign two dozen detectives to work full time to canvass the affluent neighborhood, circulate flyers, and use a bloodhound. Her body later is found floating in the river, but it cannot be determined if she fell in, jumped in, or was pushed. Less than two months later, a shy and studious African American college student never returns from an errand in a working-class immigrant neighborhood. Her mother calls 911 the next morning, and two officers fill out a missing persons report—reluctantly, saying that because she is 21 years old, they really are not supposed to. Once 24 hours have elapsed, a detective marks the case closed. The family appeals to local elected officials, and after a few days the police department reopens the case. But it is too late—during that time two kidnappers who torture and rape her in a dingy basement a few blocks away decide to kill her. A federal judge permits the victim's mother to file a lawsuit alleging bias in the police department's response, based on the race, class, and age of the missing person. (Gardiner, 2008)

Many social institutions have two or more tracks and deliver unequal services to their clients or consumers. For instance, the health care system does not treat patients the same; some get higher-quality medical attention than others. Similarly, the school system does not provide students with equal educational opportunities. Some are challenged, nurtured, and as a result excel, while others are discouraged, neglected, and consequently fail to reach their academic potential.

A systematic examination of how cases are processed by the criminal justice system must address a crucial question. Now that victims have rights and are no longer routinely overlooked, do some get better service than others?

Criminologists have documented the discrepancy between official doctrines and actual practices. For example, race and class ought to be extraneous factors in a system of "blind justice," but, in reality, they are useful predictors of how officials respond to offenders. When victimologists pieced together

---

BOX 7.2 Which Victims Get Better Treatment?

Arrests

Suspects are more likely to be taken into custody if the victims:

- Request that officers make an arrest in a deferential, nonantagonistic manner (Black, 1968)
- Convince the police that they themselves were not involved in any illegal activity before the incident (La Fave, 1965)
- Prove to officers that they are not a friend, relative, or neighbor of the suspect (Black, 1968; Giacinti, 1973; Goldstein, 1960; La Fave, 1965; Reiss, 1971).

Prosecutions

Charges are more likely to be lodged against defendants if the victims:

- Are middle-aged or elderly, white, and employed (Myers and Hagan, 1979)
- Have high status in the community ("Prosecutorial discretion," 1969)
- Are women and the offender is a male stranger (Myers, 1977)
- Are women without a reputation for promiscuity (Newman, 1966)
- Are not known to be homosexual (Newman, 1966)
- Are not alcoholics or drug addicts (Williams, 1976)
- Have no prior arrest record (Williams, 1976)
- Can establish that they weren't engaged in misconduct themselves at the time of the crime (Miller, 1970; Neubauer, 1974; Williams, 1976)
- Can prove that they didn't provoke the offender (Neubauer, 1974; Newman, 1966; Williams, 1976)
- Can show that it wasn't a private matter between themselves and a relative, lover, friend, or acquaintance (McIntyre, 1968; Williams, 1976)
- And the offender are not both black and are not viewed as conforming to community subcultural

norms (McIntyre, 1968; Miller, 1970; Myers and Hagan, 1979; Newman, 1966).

Convictions

Judges or juries are more likely to find defendants guilty if the victims:

- Are employed in a high-status job (Myers, 1977)
- Are perceived as being young and helpless (Myers, 1977)
- Appear reputable and have no prior arrest record (Kalven and Zeisel, 1966; Newman, 1966)
- Had no prior illegal relationship with the defendant (Newman, 1966)
- In no way are thought to have provoked the offender (Kalven and Zeisel, 1966; Newman, 1966; Wolfgang, 1958)
- Are white and the defendants are black (Allredge, 1942; Bensing and Schroeder, 1960; Garfinkle, 1949; Johnson, 1941)
- And the offender are not both black and are not viewed as acting in conformity to community subcultural norms (McIntyre, 1968; Miller, 1970; Myers and Hagan, 1979; Newman, 1966).

Punishments

Judges will hand down stiffer sentences to defendants if the victims:

- Are employed in a high-status occupation (Myers, 1977; Farrell and Swigert, 1986)
- Did not know the offender (Myers, 1977)
- Were injured and didn't provoke the attack (Dawson, 1969; Neubauer, 1974)
- Are white and the offenders are black (Green, 1964; Southern Regional Council, 1969; Wolfgang and Riedel, 1973; Paternoster, 1984)
- Are females killed by either males or females (Farrell and Swigert, 1986).

---

scattered research findings about how different categories of victims were treated, a comparable picture emerged. Certain victims were more likely to be given **red carpet** or **VIP treatment**, while others tended to be neglected, abused, and treated as second-class complainants by the same agencies

and officials. In other words, how a case was handled was determined by the victim's as well as the offender's social standing, in addition to the circumstances surrounding the crime.

The findings of many independent studies carried out decades ago are summarized in Box 7.2.

They yield a profile of the groups of people who in the past tended to be treated far better or much worse than others. Victims who were innocent and from "respectable" backgrounds and privileged strata were more likely to receive better service from police officers, prosecutors, juries, and judges. Individuals whose backgrounds were "tarnished" or who came from disadvantaged groups were less likely to get favorable treatment.

Many social handicaps that have held people back in life also impede their ability to receive fair treatment as crime victims. The same discretionary powers that result in overzealous law enforcement in some communities contribute to lax enforcement in others. Apparently, calls for help from members of groups that traditionally have suffered discrimination were not perceived as entirely legitimate or as compelling by some at the helm of the criminal justice system. The credibility of complainants from disadvantaged backgrounds often was eroded by a belief that these same people were the wrongdoers in other incidents. Such stereotypical responses by the authorities poisoned relations between the two camps.

From bitter experience, victims from "out groups," the lower strata, and marginal lifestyles have anticipated that their requests for intervention would be greeted with suspicion or even hostility. They expected perfunctory treatment at best. As a consequence, they have turned to the criminal justice system only under the most desperate circumstances (Ziegenhagen, 1977).

The manner in which police and prosecutors respond to homicides provides some clear examples of differential handling. When an "important" person is murdered, the police department comes under tremendous pressure from the media, elected officials, and powerful constituencies within the public to arrest someone quickly. To give an illustration, a highly publicized robbery and murder of a foreign visitor was so threatening to Florida's multibillion-dollar tourist trade that local business interests and the Chamber of Commerce generated tremendous pressure to apprehend whoever was preying upon vacationers (see Rohter, 1993b; Boyle, 1994). But when an "undesirable" is slain, overworked and understaffed homicide detectives may carry out only a superficial, routine investigation. For example, the fatal shooting of a street-level prostitute or drug peddler would attract little public notice or official concern and certainly wouldn't merit the establishment of a task force of detectives (see Simon, 1991; Maple, 1999).

On the other hand, when a member of the police force is slain, a team of homicide detectives will work day and night to follow up every possible lead in order to catch the killer and reinforce the message that the death of an officer will not go unpunished. To illustrate how law enforcement agencies assign capturing the killer of "one of their own" the highest priority, consider this comparison: In 1992, police departments across the country solved 65 percent of murders and 91 percent of the killings of fellow officers (FBI, 1993). Similarly, during 1998, 93 percent of line-of-duty officer killings were cleared, compared to 69 percent of civilian murders across the nation (FBI, 1999). And in 2007, right after homicide solution rates sank to an all-time low of 61 percent, 50 out of 51 murders of police officers were cleared by the arrest of a suspect or by exceptional means (the perpetrator was justifiably killed by the dying officer or by other officers, or the assailant afterwards committed suicide or died under other circumstances) (FBI, 2008).

Most of the research uncovering evidence of differential handling was conducted before the victims' rights movement scored sweeping legislative victories. Therefore, victimologists need to carry out a new round of investigations to discover whether the past inequity of differential handling noted in Box 7.2 persists to this day, or whether the lofty goals of "equal protection under the law" and "justice for all" are becoming a reality in state criminal justice systems across America.

SUMMARY

Whether they want to see their attacker punished via incarceration, given effective treatment in some rehabilitation program, or ordered to make restitution, victims might find themselves in conflict rather than in cooperative relationships with prosecutors, judges, and corrections officials.

Victims want prosecutors' offices to provide them with lawyers who will represent their interests faithfully, but they may be disappointed if the assistant district attorneys assigned to handle their cases don't take steps to protect them from reprisals, don't consult with them during plea negotiations, or fail to gain convictions from juries after trials. Victims are not surprised if defense attorneys try to wear them down by stalling tactics and try to impeach their testimony by asking hostile questions during cross-examinations at trials. Victims hope that judges will be evenhanded but can become upset if judges set bail low enough for defendants to secure release and then threaten them, and if judges impose sentences that do not reflect the gravity of the offenses that harmed them. Victims want corrections officials to keep them posted concerning the whereabouts of convicts, protect them from reprisals after release, and effectively supervise restitution arrangements that might have been imposed as conditions of probation or parole.

Several decades ago, before the rise of the victims' movement, insensitive mistreatment by agencies and officials within the criminal justice process was common. Victims from privileged backgrounds clearly were treated much better than others. Researchers need to document whether the system now delivers equal justice for all or if the problem of differential handling persists.

KEY TERMS

district attorneys, 169

assistant district attorneys, 169

plea negotiations, 175

consideration, 175

plea bargain, 175

cop a plea, 175

bedsheeting, 175

overcharging, 175

courtroom work group, 176

disposed of, 176

going rate, 176

sentence disparity, 181

victim impact statements, 181

allocution, 181

pre-sentence investigation report, 182

bifurcated capital trials, 183

equal protection under the law, 188

blind justice, 188

differential handling, 188

second-class treatment, 188

red carpet, 189

red carpet or VIP treatment, 189

QUESTIONS FOR DISCUSSION AND DEBATE

1. Argue that victims should not be allowed to participate in plea negotiations.

2. Argue that victims should have much more of a voice in determining sentences.

3. Argue that victims should not be allowed any input into parole board decisions.

4. Review how decisions by the Supreme Court have had an effect on the rights and best interests of victims.

CRITICAL THINKING QUESTIONS

1. Identify a group of victims who do not, in your opinion, deserve red carpet or VIP handling by prosecutors.

2. In what ways could probation officers, corrections officials, and parole boards do even more for crime victims?

SUGGESTED RESEARCH PROJECTS

1. Draw up a checklist of all the ways a prosecutor's office can provide assistance and support to victims of violent crimes. Find out what services are offered by the district attorney's office in your jurisdiction.

2. For each of the landmark decisions of the U.S. Supreme Court listed in Box 7.1 that had an impact upon victims, find out the facts of the case, the legal reasoning that was accepted by the majority of justices, and the arguments that were put forward in the dissenting minority position.

3. See if there is any evidence in articles in newspapers and magazines that the differential handling outlined in Box 7.2 either persists or has been rectified in recent years.

4. See if you can find out whether victims harmed by delinquent youth are handled more or less favorably in juvenile court compared to adult court in your local jurisdiction.

8

Children as Victims

The previous two chapters looked at the way the criminal justice system handles "ordinary" victims—adults harmed by street crimes such as robberies, assaults, burglaries, and car thefts. This chapter will analyze the special vulnerabilities and needs of a group that is particularly susceptible to victimization: children. The focus of attention will be how the criminal justice system gives, or is supposed to accord them additional considerations and extra-sensitive treatment.

Infants, toddlers, children, and even teenagers are vulnerable to physical and sexual abuse by their caretakers: parents, older siblings, other family members such as stepparents, as well as babysitters, teachers, and acquaintances. Youngsters are also highly desirable targets for kidnappers and pedophiles that may be relatives, acquaintances, or complete strangers.

If their offenders are arrested, children face special problems when their cases are processed by the legal system. If they are very young and/or if the accused wrongdoers are parents or guardians, they need someone to advocate on their behalf. They must be questioned with great care, and they face special difficulties in establishing the credibility of their testimony. Courtroom procedures and cross-examinations can be intimidating, if not traumatizing. For these reasons, children face problems that require imaginative solutions that do not violate the constitutional rights of the adult suspects, arrestees, and defendants accused by investigators and prosecutors of harming them.

THE ONGOING DEBATE BETWEEN MAXIMALISTS AND MINIMALISTS

One line of inquiry that arises repeatedly when special problems of particular groups are examined is, "How many people are suffering in this way?" An ongoing debate rages between the maximalist alarmist point of view and the minimalist skeptical perspective over the seriousness of each problem because the two official sources of data, the FBI's *Uniform Crime Report (UCR)* and the Bureau of Justice Statistics's *National Crime Victimization Survey (NCVS)*, do not furnish accurate statistical estimates.

In general, the **maximalist** position argues that an overlooked problem is reaching epidemic proportions. Dire consequences will follow unless drastic steps are taken. This outlook can be characterized as maximalist because it assumes the worst—large numbers of people are experiencing the problem, and the widespread suffering is not receiving sufficient attention. Maximalists try to mobilize people and resources to combat what they believe is a growing crisis.

Frightening claims about dangerous situations spiraling out of control provoke a predictable opposite reaction that can be termed the **minimalist** position. It is marked by a skeptical stance that tends to minimize the scope and seriousness of the problem. Minimalists consider maximalist estimates to be grossly inflated for either a well-intentioned reason or perhaps for a self-serving purpose. The minimalist assessment that massive expenditures and emergency measures are not warranted sparks bitter clashes with maximalists. These sharp differences take the form of acrimonious debates at conferences and hearings, strident denunciations in reports and books, and angry letters to the editors of newspapers and magazines that publish articles espousing the views of the other side.

Estimates that have generated the most heated exchanges concern the fates of missing children, the extent of physical child abuse, and the prevalence of incest and child molestation. Victimologists can enter into these controversies as objective "claims investigators" and apply the tools of social science research to determine where the truth lies—which is usually between the high-end estimates of maximalist alarmists and the low-end estimates offered by minimalist skeptics.

Like victim blaming and victim defending, maximalist and minimalist viewpoints are ideologies. Individuals accepting these views are alarmists or skeptics. But people who are alarmists on one issue might be skeptics on another, so, as with victim blaming and defending, it is best not to personalize the matters as disputes between individuals. It is more constructive to view the controversies as outgrowths of the opposing assumptions and outlooks of groups with different sources of information, political beliefs and socioeconomic interests.

MISSING CHILDREN

A six-year-old boy wanders over to the toy counter in a department store. A few minutes later, his mother realizes he has disappeared. The police launch an intensive search. Two weeks later and 100 miles away, a fisherman discovers the boy's severed head. The boy's father sets up a group to help locate missing children and becomes a host of a television show about tracking down wanted persons. But his son's murder is never solved because the local police misplace crucial evidence implicating a serial killer as the prime suspect. (Spitzer, 1986; Reuters, 1996)

***

A man rings the doorbell of a home on the pretext of looking for a lost dog. He barges in, pushes a babysitter aside, and drives off with a seven-year-old girl. Even though her hands are taped together, she manages to put on her seat belt. After a 100-mile ride and a high-speed chase, the kidnapper's car flips over. Inside the overturned vehicle, he holds a gun to her head for over an hour while he negotiates with the police. A sharpshooter kills him and rescues the little girl. (Associated Press, 1996c)

***

An intruder kills a mother and two other members of her household and spirits off an eight-year-old girl and her nine-year-old brother. A manhunt is launched by 40 detectives, and the pictures of the missing children are widely circulated. Six weeks later in the same small town, a waitress and a customer at a restaurant late at night recognize the little girl in the company of a 42-year-old man. They both call 911, and the police arrive quickly. She is reunited with her frantic father, her brother's body is recovered, and a registered sex offender with a history of

convictions for rapes and molestations is arrested. (CNN, 2005)

Tragedies like these periodically rivet the nation's attention. How often do such shocking kidnappings take place? How should parents react to this threat? And what is being done to prevent abductions and recover hostages before it is too late?

Hundreds of years ago, kidnapping was outlawed as a vicious crime under English common law. In the United States, news reports of abductions began to appear in the late 1800s. During the 1920s, several cases embodied a parent's worst nightmares (Gado, 2005). Ever since the early 1930s, if the kidnapper demands a ransom or transports the hostage across state lines, a federal crime has been committed and the FBI can enter the manhunt. In state and federal statutes today, force is not a necessary element of the crime of taking and holding a person of any age against his or her will. The abductee can be detained through trickery or manipulation (**inveiglement**). Besides extorting a ransom, the kidnapper might intend to rob the captive (for example, compel an adult to withdraw money from an ATM), exploit a victim as a sex object, steal and raise a very young child, or cruelly snuff out a life for some other nefarious reason.

At the start of the 1980s, the agony suffered by kidnapped children and their families was rediscovered by crusading members of the victims' movement, reporters, and government officials. The problem was subsumed under the broader catchphrase **missing children**, which referred to youngsters whose whereabouts were unknown to their parents and caretakers. At any given time, some children who are missing might be in the clutches of kidnappers, but others could have been whisked off by an angry ex-spouse. Some might be runaways, and others "throwaways" (cast-outs). Children could be lost, or just in a safe but unknown place because of miscommunication and misunderstandings. In essence, the designation missing child refers to the lack of knowledge of a frightened caretaker, and does not necessarily establish that a youngster is in danger. But many people immediately assume the worst, and fear foul play, when a child is missing. It was no coincidence that the recognition of this age-old parental nightmare took place at the same time that widespread concerns were intensifying that the traditional family structure for raising children was disintegrating in America because of divorce and daycare.

Highlights of major recent developments that address the problem of missing children appear in Box 8.1.

Heightened Fears about the Problem in the Absence of Data

Statistics about kidnappings measure one of the most heinous crimes imaginable. Yet no organization or government agency was monitoring the scope of this problem at the beginning of the 1980s when renewed fears arose. No systematic and comprehensive records were kept about the number of cases in which a distraught parent told police officers that a child was missing, the number of arrests of hostage-takers by local departments and state prosecutions for kidnapping, or the number of youngsters that were murdered. Because no one knew how many innocent, helpless children were seized and carried off each year, wild estimates circulated, and public fear levels soared.

The official source of data about crimes known to the police, the *UCR*, was of little use because kidnappings were not a Part 1 index offense. Furthermore, arrests for kidnappings were combined with lesser crimes under the headings "offenses against family and children" and "all other offenses" in Part 2. In the other official source, the *National Crime Victimization Survey*, respondents were not asked about kidnappings of members of their households. In fact, the interviewers did not inquire about any crimes committed against youngsters under 12. The only estimates about the number of missing children presumed to be victims of foul play were derived from very limited studies of police files or projections from surveys based on small samples. Insufficient record keeping and monitoring remains a vexing problem to this day.

As a result, a heated debate has periodically erupted over the decades between maximalist alarmists and minimalist skeptics over what has happened to youngsters whose whereabouts are not known to their parents. Starting in the early 1980s, maximalists argued that kidnapping had become frighteningly common and that a complacent public needed to become aroused and mobilized. Assuming the worst about the disappearances, alarmists called for emergency measures to halt the apparent surge in abductions by strangers. They warned that child snatchers were everywhere, no youngster was ever completely safe, and parents could never be too careful about taking precautions and restricting their children's activities. Two remarks illustrate the near-hysteria of the times: a Congressman offered "the most conservative estimate you will get anywhere" that 50,000 children were abducted by strangers each year (see Best, 1988; 1989a); and a father of a murdered child told a congressional hearing, "This country is littered with mutilated, decapitated, raped, and strangled children" (see Spitzer, 1986).

Minimalists suspected that the true scope of problem was blown out of proportion by well-meaning maximalists whose overestimates unduly alarmed parents. The public's fears were stoked by businesses that sought to profit from selling products and services to panicky adults; by journalists willing to sensationalize stories to attract larger audiences; by politicians looking for a get-tough issue that no one would dare oppose and would gain them publicity and votes; and by child-search organizations seeking recognition, private contributions, and government funding. Minimalists charged that maximalists were using the most inclusive definitions to generate the largest possible numbers (see Schneider, 1987). A child welfare advocate summed up the minimalist position when he charged that inflated statistics were being circulated by "merchants of fear" and "proponents of hype and hysteria" who "have foisted on a concerned but gullible American public" what he termed "one of the most outrageous scare campaigns in modern American history" (Treanor, 1986).

BOX 8.1   Highlights of the Rediscovery of the Missing Children Problem

1932   The child of a famous aviator is kidnapped and killed. A man caught with some of the ransom money is executed. State and federal laws are strengthened.

1955   The National Child Safety Council is established as the first private and voluntary organization in the field.

1974   Congress passes the Juvenile Justice and Delinquency Prevention Act, which mandates that runaways be sheltered but not arrested and confined.

1977   California becomes the first state to make violating a child custody agreement a felony.

1980   Congress amends the Juvenile Justice and Delinquency Prevention Act to permit police departments to hold chronic runaways under court order until they return home. Congress passes the Parental Kidnapping Prevention Act, which prohibits state courts from modifying original custody decrees issued after divorces and establishes a locator service that tracks down "fugitive parents" by tracing Social Security numbers.

1981   A Senate subcommittee holds the first hearings on the problem of missing children.

Child safety groups form a Child Tragedies Coalition.

Mysterious disappearances of 28 youngsters in Atlanta over a two-year period are solved when a young man is convicted of murder.

1982   Congress declares May 25 National Missing Children's Day and passes the Missing Children's Act, which grants searching parents new rights in their dealings with law enforcement agencies.

1983   A TV docudrama about the abduction and murder of a boy named Adam is viewed by an estimated 55 million people (about 1 of every 4 Americans).

1984   Congress passes the Missing Children's Assistance Act, which sets up a National Center for Missing and Exploited Children as a resource base and establishes an advisory board to guide, plan, and coordinate federal efforts.

1985   After a televised documentary, President Reagan appeals to viewers to help find missing children; 60 photos are broadcast and three youths are quickly reunited with their families.

1986   The first annual National Conference on Missing and Exploited Children is held.

1987   A National Association of Missing Child Organizations is formed to share information and maintain professional standards.

A National Resource Facility is opened for public use.

1988   Congress amends the Missing Children's Assistance Act to allocate money for establishing and operating clearinghouses on the state level to coordinate local law enforcement, social services, and educational activities.

1990   Congress passes the National Child Search Assistance Act, which requires officers to immediately enter information about disappearances into police computer networks.

1991   Congress enacts the International Parental Child Kidnapping Act.

1993   In response to the kidnap-murder of a 12-year-old girl by a parolee, federal and state lawmakers pass "three strikes and you're out" provisions to incarcerate repeat offenders for life.

1996   The Department of Justice sets up the Victim Reunification Travel Program to assist parents whose children have been unlawfully abducted to other countries by non-custodial family members.

2001   The National Center for Missing and Exploited Children sets up a cold case unit to investigate disappearances going back to 1947.

2003   Congress passes a bill that assists states to set up a national kidnapping "Amber Alert" broadcasting system to enlist the public in the hunt for an abducted child.

SOURCE: Davidson, 1986; National Center for Missing and Exploited Children, 1987; Howell, 1989; Aunapu et al., 1993; Jones, 2003; OJJDP, 2008).

As concerns escalated during the 1980s, strikingly different estimates were disseminated from maximalist as compared to minimalist sources (see Best, 1988, 1989a; Forst and Blomquist, 1991; Kappeler, Blumberg, and Potter, 1993). Several factors having to do with police department practices, vague definitions, and opposing assumptions account for the sharp divergence. Some departments were less inclined than others to request outside assistance and federal intervention. Consequently, the FBI did not investigate some kidnapping cases in which a stranger might have been involved. The definitions police forces used in classifying crimes determined the number of stranger-abduction cases in their files. For example, if an incident occurred in which a child was lured into a car, sexually molested, and then abandoned hours later, it might be categorized as a sexual assault for record-keeping purposes, inadvertently obscuring the fact that an abduction took place, albeit for a relatively short time.

Assumptions about unsolved cases colored the estimates as well. The disappearance of a teenager might be the tragic result of a stranger abduction. But a more likely explanation is that a missing adolescent is a runaway who will eventually return home voluntarily. (Such youth may be victims in a different sense—of parental sexual or physical abuse. Furthermore, while out on their own, they are very vulnerable to sexual exploitation.) Other missing teens are not runaways but **throwaways** expelled from their homes by angry or neglectful parents. Finally, some children were not snatched by strangers but were whisked away by an angry parent who disregarded a court order after a bitter custody battle following a separation or divorce. (Seizures by noncustodial parents obviously can be ruled out in most disappearances.) In some remaining cases, especially those involving very young children, the missing youth may simply be lost for a while. Minimalists suspect that many missing children are merely temporarily lost, were spirited off by an angry ex-spouse, are runaways or throwaways, or are in the clutches of molesters who will soon release them. Maximalists assume that many missing children are victims of foul play and will never be reunited with their distraught parents.

This debate demonstrates how important statistics are in bringing social problems to the attention of the media, the public, and policy makers, and in assessing the seriousness of some aspect of criminal activity.

Many worthy causes compete for media coverage, public concern, and governmental action. The first few crusaders to alert people to the danger of kidnappings by strangers issued press releases with shockingly huge estimates that generated widespread fears. They were the only experts on the subject because no officials or agencies were authorized to analyze mysterious disappearances of children across the country. But some journalists and social scientists became skeptical of these statistical projections. Soon, members of the media adopted misleadingly low official estimates with the same uncritical enthusiasm with which they had earlier accepted the activists' overestimates. This capsule history of the controversy confirms these suspicions: Large numbers call attention to neglected social problems more readily than small numbers; figures from official sources carry greater weight than unofficial estimates; and large official estimates are the best of all to galvanize public support and governmental action (Best, 1988, 1989a).

Estimates of the Incidence and Seriousness of the Problem

In an effort to try to resolve the maximalist–minimalist debate, the Department of Justice, as mandated by the 1984 Missing Children's Assistance Act, funded a five-year National Incidence Study of Missing, Abducted, Runaway, and Throwaway Children (NISMART). Researchers collected data in several ways: by conducting a telephone survey of nearly 35,000 randomly selected households; by analyzing FBI homicide records and the case files about nonfamily abductions in 83 law enforcement agencies in 21 randomly selected counties across the nation; and by interviewing runaways and the professionals who dealt with them in social service agencies and juvenile facilities. The social scientists clarified definitions, consulted with experts, and generated numbers that led them to the conclusion that the term "missing children" caused endless confusion by mixing five distinct problems that had very different victims, causes, dynamics, and remedies.

The first was the worst-case scenario that fit the stereotype of a kidnapping by a stranger with evil intentions. Thankfully, it turned out to be a rare occurrence. The second type, family abductions, was found to be a much bigger problem than policy makers had realized. Many missing children turned out to be runaways, but some of these homeless youngsters had actually been "cast out," and therefore throwaways constituted the fourth type of missing child. The fifth and final category were children who were missing because they got lost, were injured and couldn't reach their parents, or innocently failed to tell their caretakers where they were going and when they would return home. The report's findings indicated that adherents of the maximalist position were overestimating the real scope of the stranger-danger threat to young people, and those who took the minimalist approach were underestimating its true dimensions (Finkelhor, Hotaling, and Sedlak, 1990).

A follow-up NISMART study was carried out 10 years later but used different data collection methods. The pool of cases of missing children was assembled by a national telephone survey of adult caretakers in about 16,000 households and a mail survey of law enforcement agencies serving 400 counties throughout the nation. In addition, 74 juvenile facilities were contacted to find out how many of the youngsters in their care had run away during 1997. By combining the statistics gathered from these three sources, the researchers were able to address the question of what happened to missing children during the late 1990s and how many really were crime victims. The findings of NISMART–1 and NISMART–2 are summarized in Box 8.2.

Although the two comprehensive NISMART studies shed much-needed light on many emotionally charged issues, several other key questions were answered by an intensive study of police department records for 1984 in Houston, Texas, and Jacksonville, Florida: What kinds of children are typically the targets of nonfamily abductions? Are

they lured or captured by force? When and where are they approached, and where are they taken? How long are they held? What additional crimes are committed against them?

According to the researchers who analyzed more than 200 cases reported to the police in those two cities that year, girls are targeted much more often (in 88 percent of the cases) than boys (although many young males may not tell their parents about the abduction and subsequent molestation, and their parents may not report the incidents to the police). The typical captive was between 11 and 14 years old. A little more than half (57 percent) of the youngsters were forced to go with their captors (perhaps intimidated by the sight of a weapon or physically overpowered); the remainder were lured or tricked into accompanying their abductors. Most of the victims were taken to secluded spots, either indoors (empty apartments, garages) or outdoors (woods, fields), but a sizable number were kept in a vehicle. Nearly all (98 percent) were released within 24 hours. In the majority of the cases (72 percent), the abductor molested the child; in most of the remaining cases (22 percent), the child escaped unharmed from an attempted kidnapping. About 4 percent were simply held and let go; and, sadly, 2 percent were murdered after being sexually assaulted. The researchers discovered that only 15 percent of the cases involving an abduction were primarily classified by the police as a kidnapping. Most of the cases were filed under the heading of sexual assault and were so categorized in the *UCR* (NCMEC, 1986).

Other research that zeroed in on kidnappings of children under 18 that tragically resulted in homicides yielded an estimate of about 100 stranger killings a year (about 0.5 percent of murders nationwide in the mid-1990s). More than 7 of every 10 victims were white girls. Their average age was 11. The typical assailant was a single white man about 27 years old, often with a history of past sexual assaults and abductions. Roughly three-fifths of the abductions were characterized as crimes of opportunity by strangers; the rest were carried out by friends or acquaintances of the youngster's family. About 7 out of 10 had been sexually assaulted or

---

B O X   8.2   How Often Are Children Kidnapped, and What Happens to Them?

The NISMART–2 study analyzed nearly 800,000 cases across the country that were reported to police departments and child-search organizations in the late 1990s. Statistically, about 11 children out of every 1,000 were reported missing during 1999. The analysis yielded the following estimates of the number of victim–offender relationships and the characteristics of abducted children:

90–115 Life-threatening Kidnappings of Children by Adults per Year
These cases fit the stereotype of a kidnapping: A child is detained overnight or longer and/or is transported 50 miles or more. The abductor intends to permanently keep the child, extort a ransom, or commit some other crime, including murder. In most of these extremely serious offenses, the kidnapper is not a complete stranger to the youngster and could be a disgruntled former boyfriend of the child's mother, a friend of the family, a neighbor, or a babysitter.

Most of these 115 captives grabbed by strangers or acquaintances during 1999 were teenagers. Nearly 70 percent were females, and more than 70 percent were white. Unfortunately, in 40 percent of these 115 cases, the child was murdered before the authorities could find her or him. In an additional 4 percent, the

victim's body was never recovered (Finkelhor, Hammer, and Sedlak, 2002).

Between 1976 and 1987, as few as 50 and as many as 150 children were murdered by kidnappers each year. There was no discernible trend over the 12-year period. The victims tended to be older (aged 14 to 17), female, and from racial minority groups. Overall, a teenager's chances of being kidnapped and murdered during this period were calculated to be 7 out of every 1 million; the chances for younger children were 1 out of 1 million per year.

The NISMART–1 study, with data based on different collection methods, yielded a larger estimate of 200 to 300 kidnappings in 1988.

12,000 Short-Term Abductions by a Non-Family Member per Year
These cases meet the legal elements of kidnapping: A crime by an acquaintance or by a stranger who takes the child by force, or by threats, or by deceit into a building, vehicle, or other place and/or detains the child for more than an hour, perhaps to commit a sexual assault or molestation.

The NISMART–1 study yielded an estimate of 3,200 to 4,600 short-term abductions in 1988. About half the abductees were at least 12 years old, and three-quarters were girls. In more than two-thirds of

---

raped before they were slain. Almost half of the youth had been dispatched within the first hour, and within four hours, almost three-quarters had been murdered, according to an analysis of 562 child killings carried out in 44 states between the late 1970s and the mid-1990s ("Study Puts Facts," 1997).

Hunting for Children Who Have Vanished

A 12-year-old girl and her two friends are enjoying a slumber party when they hear a knock on the bedroom door. The girl opens the door, and a tall, bearded man wielding a large knife barges in. As her two friends giggle, thinking it is a practical joke, the intruder ties them up and carries the

12-year-old off into the night. The kidnapping galvanizes a sleepy community into action. Waves of volunteers flock to a storefront command center. Thousands of people beg to be assigned some task, like answering telephones or circulating posters with a picture of the victim and a police artist's sketch of the suspect. Shopkeepers close their stores, and workers give up their vacations to assist the search. A well-known actress donates a huge reward for information leading to an arrest or the safe return of the abducted child ("Kidnapping Summons City to Action," 1993). The kidnapper is questioned by the police for trespassing in a rural area, but they do not know the victim is in the trunk of his vehicle. Two months

the cases, the youngsters were abducted for sexual purposes. The majority of incidents began in a street setting, involved the use of force (often the brandishing of a weapon), and the ordeal lasted less than a day. Black and Hispanic children were disproportionately victimized in these ways. About 11,500 attempted abductions by strangers per year were reported to survey interviewers by caretakers. In most of these attempts, a passing motorist tried to lure a child into a car, without the use of coercion and without inflicting physical injuries. Most attempts—and probably a substantial number of completed abductions for the purpose of sexual assault—were not reported to police, generally because the children were ashamed or intimidated.

56,500 Long-Term Abductions by a Family Member per Year

In these cases a family member, usually a parent, takes the child in violation of a decree from family court and tries to conceal the taking and/or the whereabouts of the child and/or moves the child to another state and/or intends to keep the child permanently or alter custodial arrangements.

The NISMART–1 study based on different data-collection methods generated an estimate of 163,000 child snatchings in 1988. These abductions were most likely to occur during January and August, when school vacations and parental visits end. Most incidents lasted from a few days to up to a week. In about 60 percent of these unlawful detentions, the parent with custody rights did not inform the police; lawyers were contacted in 50 percent of the cases. In about 50 percent of these power struggles, the caretaking parent knew where the child was being held but was unable to recover the child from the lawbreaking ex-partner.

Accounting for the Remaining Cases of Children Reported as Missing

The NISMART–2 study concluded that of the nearly 800,000 children who were reported missing to police or child-search agencies, almost 360,000 (45 percent) turned out to be either runaways or throwaways (driven out of their homes). A roughly equal amount, 340,000 (43 percent), were considered missing by their alarmed parents because of "benign explanations"—misunderstandings and miscommunication about where the children were going and when they would return. The remaining youngsters, almost 62,000 (8 percent), did not return home on time because they were lost or injured.

SOURCE: NISMART–1: Finkelhor, Hotaling, and Sedlak, 1990; Forst and Blomquist, 1991. NISMART–2: Sedlak, Finkelhor, Hammer, and Schultz, 2002.

---

later he is arrested. A crowd gathers for a vigil outside the jail, chanting "Tell the truth and set your conscience free." Shortly afterward the middle-aged man, who was out on parole after spending 15 of his last 20 years behind bars for abductions, assaults, and burglaries, confesses that he strangled the girl and leads police to her body. He is sent to death row. An outraged community demands that a "three strikes and you're out" law be passed to prevent hardened convicts like him from ever being released. (Gross, 1993; Noe, 2005)

Kidnapping a youth symbolizes the ultimate clash between good and evil: innocent and defenseless little children in the clutches of ruthless adults. No other group of crime victims has so captured the attention and hearts of the public. Rarely has citizen involvement been solicited and supplied on such a grand scale as in campaigns to prevent abductions and recover stolen children. Few victims' rights organizations have been so instrumental in drafting new laws and reforming criminal justice procedures as the child-search movement. Even though the platitude "children are our most precious resource" was frequently voiced in the early 1980s, only a few groups were prepared to help locate missing children. They were staffed by a handful of people with an annual budget of less than $30,000. But by the late 1990s, a federally sponsored national center operated a network linking 30 federal agencies, 50 state clearinghouses, and more than 60 private and nonprofit organizations (Gill, 1989; Aunapu et al., 1993; Office of Juvenile Justice and Delinquency Prevention, 1998a).

Before child-search organizations were set up, parents were totally dependent on police departments. Unfortunately, working relationships between frantic parents and the law enforcement agencies that were supposed to be carrying out the manhunt frequently became strained. The issues that divided them were delays in police response, restricted access to law enforcement information, and a reluctance by local authorities to call for nationwide assistance.

When distraught parents turned to missing persons bureaus for help, they expected officers to spring into action by issuing all-points bulletins describing the child who had disappeared and by launching an intensive search. But many departments followed procedures that dictated that a youngster had to be missing for 24, 48, or even 72 hours before an official investigation could be initiated. These mandatory waiting periods were based on experiences that indicated the overwhelming majority of cases were not life threatening and would "solve themselves." The missing youths would turn out to be runaways who would soon return home tired, hungry, and broke. But infuriated parents condemned such arbitrary delays as endangering the lives of their children. They claimed that it enabled abductors to escape from the local area to other jurisdictions, where any call for a manhunt would receive an even lower priority, and interest in the case would be difficult to sustain. The crux of the problem for parents was that the burden of proof fell on them to somehow demonstrate that their children were victims of foul play (see Collins et al., 1988).

In 1990, responding to parental appeals for reform, Congress passed the National Child Search Assistance Act. The legislation prohibited law enforcement agencies from imposing waiting periods before entering the child's description into computer networks linking the FBI's National Crime Information Center, police departments, and state clearinghouses (Girdner and Hoff, 1994). Parents of formerly missing children who volunteer to undergo training have formed teams that provide emotional support and logistical advice to parents in distress (OJJDP, 2008). A family survival guide written by parents who have been through this ordeal suggests that immediate steps include putting out a "Be On the Look Out" (BOLO) bulletin to other police departments, faxing a photo to the National Center for Missing and Exploited Children (NCMEC), and searching with bloodhounds. Many states now require police officers to take in-service training courses on how to investigate missing children cases, to interact with their families, and to follow the FBI's Child Abduction Response Plan (OJJDP, 1998a). The NCMEC's "Adam" program faxes missing-child posters to police departments, news media outlets, schools, and medical facilities where the search is taking place. From its inception in 2000 until mid-2008, the Adam program helped recover 100 children (Nuwar, 2008).

During the late 1990s, **Amber Alert** systems were set up in many states and received support from the federal government in 2003 to help searchers enlist the cooperation of the public. Amber stands for "America's Missing: Broadcast Emergency Response," but the system is named after a nine-year-old girl who was kidnapped while riding her bicycle in Texas in 1996. A neighbor was able to describe to the police the vehicle into which she was lured, but without an effective system to widely disseminate that information, law enforcement agencies were unable to find the car in time. Community residents were outraged four days later when her body was discovered, and demanded the establishment of some way to broadcast emergency bulletins so that more people could be rapidly enlisted to hunt for a missing or abducted child. Using the same arrangements as for severe weather warnings, a voluntary rapid-response network of radio and television stations broadcasts descriptions of the suspect, the victim, and other clues like a vehicle's license plate to a huge audience in the immediate area.

The goals are to deter kidnappings by scaring would-be offenders with the prospect of being swiftly apprehended and severely punished; and failing that, to rescue children quickly, before they are injured or killed. The system sends out a message whenever a law enforcement agency has a reasonable belief that a child under 18 has been abducted and is in imminent danger of severe bodily harm or death. By 2005, all 50 states and an additional 64 localities had set up Amber Alert systems. During 2006, about 260 alerts were issued nationwide in an effort to recover almost 315 children. Most of the cases were either family child snatchings (mostly by noncustodial parents) or non-family abductions (but not necessarily by strangers); a small number concerned lost children. Ten alerts turned out to be based on hoaxes, and another 25 reports later were deemed unfounded. Issuing the alert directly led to saving the child in one-quarter of the more than 200 recoveries. Unfortunately, nine of the children were murdered before they could be located (OJP, 2008). During 2007, all the active Amber Alert cases were resolved by the year's end. The alerts made 57 of the 268 recoveries possible, but the authorities arrived too late in six tragic cases (OJJDP, 2008).

The importance of an immediate mobilization—"the more eyes, the better"—in order to "beat the clock" was underscored by a study of 600 kidnappings that ended in tragedies. About three-quarters of the children were killed within the first three hours, and nine-tenths within the first 24 hours (Jones, 2003; Zgoba, 2004; NCMEC, 2005).

The Possibility of the Stockholm Syndrome

Some hostages are held for a long period of time before they are rescued. During the later stages of their captivity, they might pass up chances to escape. For example, they may appear in public with their captors, and might not reveal to people who talk to them (even including police officers) that they are being held against their will (for a description of the missed opportunities of a teenage girl, see Grady, 2003; and CNN, 2003; for details about the case of a teenage boy, see AP, 2007a). The children's resignation about their plight underscores the need to develop effective and sensitive treatment procedures to help "debrief" hostages so that they can fully recover from their ordeals.

Cases in which a captive appears to have grown attached to the captor raise the possibility that a victim can suffer from the "Stockholm Syndrome." The phrase was coined by a psychologist who studied a siege in which four strangers seemed to bond with the two bank robbers who held them as bargaining chips for six days. It is defined as a temporary mental state in which captives of any age develop close emotional ties with their captors during the ordeal. The prisoners pass up chances to escape, resent the risky actions by the authorities to free them, and begin to see the situation through the kidnapper's eyes. This survival strategy may arise from a sense of hopelessness and helplessness, a loss of identity, isolation from the outside world, trauma, and terror. The hostage is seeking acceptance, meaning, security, and physical and psychological safety.

In addition to hostages, these tendencies might be observed among true believers in cults, battered women, and others who are subjected to prolonged physical and psychological isolation and abuse (Wong, 2003). However, it is likely that this type of coping mechanism by captives has been over-emphasized and inaccurately diagnosed. Identifying with the aggressor and seeing rescuers as adversaries is the exception to the rule. An analysis of narratives contained in the FBI's Hostage/Barricade database turned up evidence of Stockholm Syndrome symptoms in only 8 percent of more than 1,200 incidents handled by local, state, and federal law enforcement agencies during the 1990s (Fuselier, 1999).

Protecting Children

As parents and their children have become more conscious of stranger-danger, they have incorporated preventive steps into their daily routines in a myriad of ways. Youngsters are instructed by police officers, teachers, and parents—as well as through comic book characters, board games, songs, and books—"What to do if ..." The training that the children receive in recognizing and rejecting **child lures**—deceitful tricks abductors use to entice them—far exceeds the old warning of "Don't accept candy from strangers." They are taught to distinguish between good touches and bad touches, to be wary of certain situations and behaviors, as well as specific kinds of people. The aim is to build self-confidence rather than to instill unreasonable fears.

Some risk-reduction strategies involve planning, products, and services. At the height of the social panic that gripped many families during the mid-1980s, so many new products flooded the market that department stores set up child safety displays. Today, high-tech outlets sell homing devices that trigger alarms when children stray or are taken beyond a certain range. Dentists offer to bond microchips containing identifying information to children's teeth. Graphic designers can be hired to create images that project what a missing child might look like at different ages. Shopping centers attract crowds by offering fingerprinting for infants and toddlers. Playgrounds, schoolyards, and large stores are designed to limit access and close down escape routes. Tens of thousands of stores have set up **Code Adam** responses (named after a child who was abducted from a store and murdered; see the first real-life example, above) that lock down all doors and notify customers and employees that a child has just been reported missing on the premises. The shadow cast by the ominous stranger has eclipsed the mushroom-shaped cloud that haunted the imaginations of previous generations (Wooden, 1984; "Teaching Children," 1999; Verhovek, 2001).

Understandably, child-safety campaigns have provoked a backlash. Skeptics dismiss as "urban legends" most of the accounts that circulate via the Internet and in e-mails about children of inattentive parents who are whisked out of stores and malls and other public places by kidnappers who quickly alter the youngsters' appearances by changing their clothes or slipping wigs on them. These cautionary tales that urge parents to be vigilant and to not let youngsters out of their sight, even for a moment, reflect widespread fears about predatory strangers that apparently well up in people who reside in increasingly impersonal and anonymous urban and suburban settings and who regret the loss of close-knit communities ("What a way … " 2008).

Some skeptics worry about the potential social and psychological costs of certain victimization prevention measures. They wonder whether an anxious, suspicious, and dependent generation will be cheated out of a carefree childhood and grow up obsessed by security considerations and burdened prematurely by adult's fears. Other critics are concerned about the questionable performance of

expensive products and services. They take a dim view of commercial outfits that charge for information, devices, and forms of assistance that can be obtained free from nonprofit child-find organizations or police departments. Other minimalists are suspicious of the motives of the many corporations that have made tax-deductible contributions to child-search projects; amid the hoopla over staged events, they get free publicity and cultivate good public relations. Civil libertarians fear that the intense concern about stranger-danger will erode the public's healthy reluctance to allow government bureaucracies to maintain fingerprints and photographs on file, which could be another step toward a "big brother" police state. Victimologists can carry out research to determine whether certain widely touted child safety measures really work as intended, fail to be effective, or, worse yet, have unanticipated negative social and emotional side effects (see Karlen et al., 1985; Andrews, 1986; Gill, 1987, 1989; Adler, 1994; Brody, 2003).

PHYSICALLY AND SEXUALLY ABUSED CHILDREN

The Rediscovery of Child Abuse

A telephone call for help triggers a military-style raid on the ranch of an insular fundamentalist sect that practices polygamy—grown men marry teenage girls who are too young to give consent under state law. A total of 462 youngsters, ranging in age from infants to 17 year-olds, are seized from their parents to determine whether they have been victims of sexual abuse. The children, who have been cut off from the outside world, are placed in large group shelters rather than foster homes by a state child welfare agency that is so chronically understaffed and underfinanced as to be almost dysfunctional. A judge orders that each child be assigned a lawyer, as their mothers, some of them teenagers, seek to be reunited with their sons and daughters. Arguing that the state has an obligation to protect child-brides who are forced into arranged marriages and compelled to submit sexually to adults, the governor pledges that this form of victimization won't be tolerated, warning the men in the sect, "If you are going to conduct yourself that way, we are going to prosecute you." But a state court rules that local officials overstepped their authority and orders the return of the children to their families because the Child Protective Services agency produced very little evidence that the youngsters were endangered. Although the leaders of the religious group announce that they have changed their doctrine to forbid marriages of females under the age of legal consent, child welfare and state criminal investigations continue into a subculture in which girls are forced into "plural marriages," unconditional obedience to their husbands, and compulsory childbearing. (Johnson and Frosch, 2008; Garrett, 2008; and Corbett, 2008)

Definitions of child abuse—both physical and sexual—remain the subject of much debate. For centuries, parents were permitted to beat their children as they saw fit in the name of imposing discipline. Legal notions of progeny as the property of their parents, as well as religious traditions ("honor thy father and mother" and "spare the rod and spoil the child") legitimized corporal punishment of youngsters as a necessary, even essential, technique of child rearing. Only if permanent injury or death resulted were adults in danger of being held responsible for going too far, a problem labeled **cruelty to children**. The **House of Refuge movement** of the early 1800s intervened on behalf of beaten and neglected children. Its priority was to prevent abused children from growing up to be delinquents. Youngsters were removed from their dysfunctional homes, but unfortunately they were then thrown into environments where they mingled with young vagrants and lawbreakers. During the late 1800s, the Society for the Prevention of Cruelty to

Animals expanded its mission and began to take responsibility for rescuing children from uncaring foster parents and heartless employers. Its offshoot, the Society for the Prevention of Cruelty to Children, used the police powers it was granted to place abused youngsters from big-city slums into rural juvenile institutions in a misguided attempt to head off delinquency. During the early 1900s, the "child savers" movement was motivated by the same fear: that neglect and abuse caused lawbreaking later in life. It designed a special court system and developed reform schools strictly for juveniles (see Platt, 1968; and Pfohl, 1984). The concern that abused children grow up to become abusers and victimizers themselves continues to inspire a great deal of theorizing and research (see for example, Gray, 1986; Wyatt and Powell, 1988; Barringer, 1989; Widom, 1989.)

In the early 1960s, pediatric radiologists (doctors who study X-rays of childhood injuries) sparked the rediscovery of physical abuse. Apparently, the pledge of confidentiality inhibited physicians such as pediatricians and emergency room doctors from exposing the consequences of severe beatings, as did their reluctance to get embroiled in the criminal justice process. Pediatric radiologists, on the other hand, had little direct contact with parents and desired greater recognition within the medical profession. Therefore, they were willing to set the rediscovery process into motion, exposing brutality labeling it as deviant behavior, and encouraging legislation against it by alerting colleagues and the public to the **battered child syndrome** (Pfohl, 1984). This syndrome was identified as a cyclical pattern in which excessive physical punishment was perpetrated by parents who had been beaten themselves as children. In the typical case, the child was younger than three years of age and suffered traumatic injuries to the head and limbs, and the caretakers claimed that the wounds were caused by an accident and not a beating. News media coverage of horror stories that described particular viciousness, severe injuries, and disturbing circumstances evoked strong condemnations and helped to galvanize a social movement. Initially, journalists focused on battering, but they soon broadened their inquiries to include cases of gross neglect, emotional cruelty, and eventually sexual exploitation and incest.

Coverage of these human-interest stories fit the organizational needs not only of the news media to attract readers and viewers but also of professional and occupational groups and private and nonprofit agencies seeking increased funding and more recognition for their missions (Johnson, 1989). Social workers, women's organizations, public health associations, and law enforcement groups joined doctors to help raise public consciousness about the suspected dimensions of the problem. Between 1962 and 1966, legislatures in all 50 states passed laws forbidding parents from abusing their children (Pfohl, 1984). Because the victims usually were too young or too frightened to complain, requirements for reporting cases of apparent abuse to child welfare and protection agencies were imposed on doctors, teachers, and others who routinely came into contact with youngsters.

In 1974, Congress passed the Child Abuse Prevention and Treatment Act and amended it in 1978. The law prohibited maltreatment in all its guises (acts of omission as well as commission), including neglect, physical abuse, sexual abuse, and emotional abuse. Neglect ranged from abandonment to failure to meet a child's basic requirements in three areas: physical needs (including inadequate supervision and medical care); emotional needs (denial of nurturing and affection, tolerance of a child's drug or alcohol abuse, or fierce fighting in the child's presence); and educational needs (tolerance of chronic truancy). Physical abuse involved assaults (punching, kicking, scalding, suffocating, shaking, and extended confinement, even if unintended as the consequence of excessive punishment). Sexual abuse was recognized as incest, fondling, sodomy, intercourse, rape, and commercial exploitation (impairment of morals, use for pornographic purposes or prostitution). In addition, maltreatment could take the form of emotional abuse (leading to serious behavioral or mental disorders) (see Irwin, 1980; National Clearinghouse, 1997). During the 1980s, the focus of researchers, practitioners, and an indignant public shifted from physical maltreatment to sexual abuse (Milner, 1991).

How Children Suffer

A woman who is about to serve a prison sentence leaves her three children with relatives. But the relatives have no room for them so the children are forced to stay in a basement with a mattress to sleep on and a bucket for a toilet. The boys are routinely beaten and burned while the family is investigated 10 times over a span of 10 years by overburdened caseworkers. When one of the boys dies from horseplay and his mummified remains are discovered, the caretakers are sent to prison and public indignation forces the state government to overhaul the operations of its child welfare agency. (Jones, 2005)

The persistence of child abuse always has been of great concern to victimologists. They ask, What are the short-term and long-term consequences of suffering maltreatment? What percentages of cases go unreported and unattended? Are existing mandatory reporting requirements and compulsory treatments effective? How are abused youngsters handled by the authorities?

To anticipate and thereby prevent future cases of abuse, victimologists want to discover the risk factors that indicate which children face the gravest dangers. For example, an inquiry carried out by the National Center on Child Abuse and Neglect verified the suspicion that children with physical, emotional, and mental disabilities are maltreated by their primary caretakers, generally their mothers, at an unusually high rate. Disabled children are physically abused at twice the rate of other youngsters, sexually abused nearly twice as often, and emotionally neglected almost three times as frequently (Associated Press, 1993a). Research into the backgrounds of physically abused children indicates that beatings are more likely to occur in dysfunctional families racked by a combination of symptoms of marital discord: where the parents fight viciously (partner abuse); one or both of the parents are currently drug abusers and/or alcoholics; the mother was raised by a substance-abusing parent; and the mother was often beaten while she was growing up (Salzinger, Feldman, and Hammer, 1991). As for sexual abuse (which is imposed most often on boys and girls between the ages of 7 and 13) poor parent–child communication, parental un-availability, and intense father–mother conflict seem to be risk factors (Finkelhor, 1994).

It is widely believed that children from poverty-stricken families face the greatest risk of neglect, physical abuse, and sexual abuse (DeConcini, 1989; Garbarino, 1989). However, official statistics and agency files that indicate abuse cases seem con-cerntrated in lower socioeconomic neighborhoods might be misleading because the problems of poor families are more likely to come to the attention of social welfare agencies and police departments. Therefore, some researchers have concluded that there is no substantial difference in victimization rates among children of different social classes or races (Finkelhor, 1994).

However, a study of how police officers ex-ercised their discretion about whether to report suspected cases of child abuse concluded that under-reporting actually may be a bigger problem in poor neighborhoods. Officers were more likely to overlook signs of possible abuse in low-income minority families because of prejudicial beliefs that violence and promiscuity are "normal" among the poor and that minority youths need sterner disci-pline (Willis and Wells, 1988).

The consequences of being abused greatly con-cern victimologists. Studies of sexually exploited youngsters indicate that they may suffer complicated, far-reaching, and long-lasting problems. A review of the literature written by therapists turned up seven groupings of adverse effects. Affective pro-blems were evidenced by guilt, shame, anxiety, fear, depression, anger, low self-esteem, concerns about secrecy, feelings of helplessness, and an inordi-nate need to please others. Physical repercussions in-cluded genital injuries, unwanted pregnancies, venereal diseases, loss of appetite, sleep disruptions, and bed-wetting. Cognitive effects took the form of shortened attention spans and trouble concentrating. Behavioral symptoms materialized as hostile-aggressive acting out, tantrums, drug taking, delin-quency, withdrawal, and repetitions of the abusive relationship. Self-destructive impulses were mani-fested as suicidal thoughts, high risk behavior, and self-mutilations. Psychopathological repercussions showed up as neuroses, character disorders, psychotic thought patterns, and multiple personalities. Finally, sexual disorders took the form of age-inappropriate sexual knowledge, talk, and involvements. Because sexual abuse can range from a single molestation to an ongoing incestuous relationship, each youngster might exhibit a different mix of symptoms, and no specific problem or repertoire of behaviors definitively and conclusively indicates that a child has been abused (Yapko and Powell, 1988; Whitcomb, 1992).

Many women who are on public assistance be-cause of multiple problems—addiction to alcohol or drugs, disabling bouts of anxiety and depression, and injuries from violent mates—were sexually abused when they were girls (de Parle, 1999). Worse yet, experiencing neglect, physical abuse and sexual abuse as a youngster becomes a risk fac-tor for entering a cycle of delinquency, crime, and violence later in life. Those who were physically abused face the gravest risks of becoming law-breakers, more than those who were sexually abused or grossly neglected. However, illegal be-havior as a grown-up is not an inevitable side effect; most adults who were abused as children don't have arrest records (Widom, 1989, 1995; Turman, 1999; Widom and Maxfield, 2001). An intergenerational transmission of poor parenting skills takes place when abused children grow up and harm their own children in the same ways that they were mis-treated. Children socialized into a subculture of vi-olence that is very much on display in their homes are taught to use force to settle disagreements in the same imitative manner they learn other behaviors.

Estimates of the Incidence, Prevalence, and Seriousness of Child Abuse

It is difficult to determine the true depth and breadth of the problem because reliable information is difficult to obtain. The two official sources of crime statistics, the FBI's *UCR* and the BJS's *NCVS*, contain no data about child maltreatment's **incidence** (new cases that come to light each year) and **prevalence** (proportion of youth in some population that is being studied who have ever suffered this form of victimization). The *UCR* monitors the age of murder victims, but not all homicides against youngsters were carried out by abusive parents or caretakers. The *NCVS* does not ask respondents younger than 12 about any illegal acts committed against them. Therefore, another source of official statistics must be tapped: the reports collected from child protection services (child welfare agencies) in the 50 states.

The maximalist and minimalist perspectives disagree sharply over interpreting these official statistics (see Gardner, 1990, 1994; Mash and Wolfe, 1991; Feher, 1992; de Koster and Swisher, 1994). The maximalist view contends that the time has come to reject the reluctance of earlier generations to face the facts and to recognize the enormity of the crisis. Parents are abusing and neglecting their children in record numbers, and pedophiles, sadistic adolescents, and other abusers are preying on youngsters as never before. This alarmist perspective puts forward strong arguments to support its case that child abuse is all too common and must be taken much more seriously (see Finkelhor, 1990; Whitcomb, 1992; Ceci and Bruck, 1993).

Maximalist Arguments The maximalist perspective assumes that statistics from official sources are gross underestimates of the true depth of the emergency.

- Presumably, a great (but unknown) number of episodes are never reported to the authorities—not by the child, the other parent, another relative, neighbor, doctor, or teacher. Underreporting is a serious problem because many victimized children are too young to know their rights or to be believed, or are too terrorized to tell anyone. Most abuse and neglect takes place behind closed doors without witnesses, and tangible evidence is lacking unless obvious physical injuries or venereal

diseases appear. Many professionals who are supposed to err on the side of caution fail to file mandatory official reports when they suspect abuse, preferring instead to pressure adults in troubled families to enter counseling, drug treatment, or other programs. The professionals responsible for intervening in child abuse cases hold cherished beliefs about family privacy and parental rights and are therefore reluctant to become enmeshed in court cases. This overshadows their concerns about the well-being of very young children.

- Many reports of abuse are mistakenly screened out and dismissed by child welfare agencies that simply do not have sufficient time, money, and staff to do the thorough investigations necessary to verify the charges. Just because a report is deemed to be "unsubstantiated" (due to a lack of sufficient evidence to meet stringent legal standards of proof) does not mean it is untrue; classifying a report as "unfounded" certainly does not mean it is completely baseless or intentionally and maliciously false.

- Alarmists cite additional statistics from unofficial sources that reveal shocking incidence and prevalence rates. Violence against children (minor acts that range from throwing an object at them to extreme outbursts like using a knife or gun against them) seems to be the norm, occurring in more than 60 percent of intact (two-parent) American families each year, according to the findings of a telephone survey of more than 1,400 parents (Straus and Gelles, 1986). As for physical abuse prevalence rates, as many as 30 percent of very poor children are beaten or grossly neglected at least once (and often chronically) while they are growing up (Garbarino, 1989).

- As for sexual abuse prevalence rates, the percentage of girls who are molested during their childhoods might be as high as 38 percent, if peer exploitation by siblings is included (Russell, 1984), or even 62 percent (when counting being subjected to male exhibitionism) (Wyatt, 1985). Between 4 percent and 16 percent of women in various surveys reported a childhood sexual experience with a relative, and about 1 girl in every 100 endured sexual contacts with her father or stepfather (Herman, 1981; Russell, 1986). As many as 31 percent of boys may have been sexually abused (see Peters, Wyatt, and Finkelhor, 1986).

- There has been a disturbing rise in recent years in the most reliable statistic of all: deaths due to extreme abuse and neglect (as determined in many jurisdictions by a child fatality review team made up of coroners, detectives, prosecutors, and social workers). Deaths of children from maltreatment dropped slightly, from about 1,260 during 1992 to just under 1,200 in 1997. Unfortunately, the number of deaths known to child protective services in 44 states rebounded to around 1,300 in 2001. It climbed to about 1,500 fatalities attributed to abuse and neglect during 2003, a rate of 2 deaths per 100,000 children (Gaudiosi, 2004), and remained at that level (1,530 deaths) in 2006 (ACF, 2008). (Skeptics contend that the increase can be attributed to improvements in state reporting systems that now provide more complete coverage—see McCurdy and Daro, 1994; U.S. Department of Health and Human Services, 1999; NCCANI, 2003.)

The first Child Fatality Review Teams were set up in the mid-1980s to keep better records about these cases that fuel maximalist–minimalist debates. A National Center on Child Fatality Review has been established as an information clearinghouse for the findings of each state's child death review studies (Langstaff and Sleeper, 2001). Perhaps because of more comprehensive record keeping, the United States (along with Mexico and Portugal) had the highest death rate from child abuse among the world's 27 richest nations, according to UN statistics (Dowdy, 2003).

Minimalist Views   The minimalist point of view makes the following arguments to back up its contention that child abuse is less widespread than the maximalist alarmist perspective would have the public believe (see Besharov, 1990; Wexler, 1990; Ceci and Bruck, 1993):

- The definition of child maltreatment has been expanding and diluting over the years. Minor instances of bad parenting that were justifiably overlooked in the past are now being routinely reported. All forms of physical discipline (slaps, spankings) should not automatically qualify as child abuse. Various ethnic and religious subcultures have dramatically different notions of where to draw the line between appropriate parenting and maltreatment, but some protection agencies blindly apply a rigid "one standard fits all" approach. No state prohibits parents from using "reasonable corporal punishment" when disciplining their children; in fact, five states expressly permit it (see Pagelow, 1989). In a 1977 ruling (*Ingram v. Wright*), the Supreme Court held that corporal punishment in school (within reasonable limits, by designated personnel, and with parental approval) is permissible under the Constitution. In many studies it is not clear which definition is being applied to real-life cases—the law's, the reporter's, the researcher's, or the child's (especially once they have grown up). Yet some research applies the label "abuse" to acts that most consider normal discipline involving corporal punishment instead of reserving it for clearly inappropriate and excessive force.

- Child abuse actually may not be increasing; it is just that reports of abuse are going up, skeptics charge. Heightened public awareness and mandatory reporting regulations are producing this apparent crime wave. Professionals face civil and criminal penalties if they cover up or are grossly negligent in overlooking abuse. In many states, mandatory reporting requirements are imposed on adults—not just those who routinely come into contact with children as part of their occupation—leading to many baseless charges. Furthermore, in all jurisdictions, any person can file a report (often anonymously) to a "tip" hotline. Large numbers of honestly mistaken allegations, as well as maliciously false ones, are mixed in with true disclosures, making the problem seem worse than it is. When failure to report occurs, children face grave dangers; but when unwarranted allegations are entered into files, the reputations of innocent parents are called into question, and agencies waste their limited resources. Caseloads from official sources yield grossly inflated estimates because many allegations are never validated conclusively. **Unfounded reports** (unsubstantiated or "not indicated" cases) are dismissed or closed when, after an investigation, there is insufficient legally admissible evidence on which to proceed. Unproven allegations about child abuse should not be counted in official statistics. The public's emotionally driven desire to "do something," coupled with sensational media coverage about a formerly taboo topic, plus the "take no chances" zeal and defensiveness of professionals subjected to mandatory reporting requirements, accounts for the rise in unproven complaints. The high rate of unsubstantiated claims (more than half of allegations) recorded by many child protection agencies is due, in part, to a lack of screening of calls to hotlines. The inflated figures also result from a willingness to follow up anonymous tips, some of which may be deliberately false and vengeful acts intended to get an adult in trouble (estimated at 3 percent), and an acceptance of complaints from estranged spouses locked in custody battles. Other unsubstantiated cases arise from a reliance on "behavioral indicators" as possible symptoms of abuse (in the absence of corroboration in the form of statements by the victim or eyewitnesses, or physical evidence) (Besharov, 1987; Snyder and Sickmund, 1995).

- As for incidence rates, skeptics point out that fewer than 1 percent of all children in the United States were reportedly sexually abused in 1991 (Robin, 1991). As for prevalence rates, the percentage of females who suffer sexual abuse during their childhood could be as low as 7 percent (Siegel et al., 1987), and for males, it might be as low as 3 percent (see Peters, Wyatt, and Finkelhor, 1986).

- The label *child sexual abuse* covers a wide range of forbidden activities. The long-term consequences of adults forcing children to submit to sexual demands may be severe for the victims, but the willing sexual involvement of adolescents with adults, although exploitative, may not be as harmful, according to an analysis of studies of college students who disclosed that they had been sexually involved with grownups while in their early teens (see Goode, 1999).

- Concerning trends, data from official sources furnish some evidence that the rising tide of reports from the 1970s to the early 1990s actually may have reversed during the late 1990s and the early years of the twenty-first century. The 2002 victimization rate of 12 cases of neglect and abuse per 1,000 children was down by nearly 20 percent from the 1993 peak rate of 15 per 1,000 (McDonald, 2004). That maltreatment rate of 12 per 1,000 remained stable through 2006 (ACF, 2008).

- Substantiated cases of child sexual abuse decreased over 40 percent during the 1990s, from its peak in 1992 (at about 150,000 cases) to 2000 (less than 90,000 cases). By 2006, that figure had dropped even further (to just over 78,000) (Finkelhor and Jones, 2004; Crimes Against Children Research Center, 2005; ACF, 2008).

- The frequency of parents resorting to force may have been diminishing during a decade when the maximalist position thought it was growing. Researchers carrying out a National Family Violence Re-Survey in 1985 noted a substantial decline from 1975 in disclosures of "very severe violence" (biting, kicking, punching, beating up, using weapons like a knife or gun) by parents against their children. The incidence rate dropped from 36 cases of "very severe violence" to 19 cases for every 1,000 families in the 10-year period, a nearly 50 percent drop (Straus and Gelles, 1986).

- In general, the social factors that contribute to child abuse are alcohol and drug problems among adults, teenage motherhood, and impoverishment ("Child Abuse Reports," 1988). The social conditions that decrease maltreatment are upturns in the nation's economy, a trend toward marrying later in life and having fewer children, greater public awareness and condemnation of abuse, improved treatment and prevention programs, and more shelters for battered women and their offspring (Jennings, 1986; and Straus and Gelles, 1986).

The maximalist-minimalist debate continues over whether abuse is growing or subsiding as a problem. Statistically speaking, the number of maltreatment cases (especially child sexual abuse) substantially declined during the 1990s and into the new century, but no one knows for sure why this trend materialized. The leading explanations are that child protection agencies in various states adopted stricter guidelines that eliminated questionable reports and excluded cases that did not involve primary caretakers; and that these agencies simplified their definitions of charges to either "substantiated" or "unsubstantiated," and dropped the in-between category "indicated." Also, reporting rates may have declined, especially by professionals. But if abuse really did diminish in American society, the improvement may have been due to stepped up prevention efforts, increased prosecutions and jailings of offenders, and more profound cultural changes in parental attitudes and behaviors toward children (Finkelhor and Jones, 2004).

More Controversies Surrounding Childhood Sexual Abuse

Intense controversies have broken out over the real extent of sexual abuse during childhood. One area of contention surrounds charges of parent–child incest, especially allegations of father–daughter sexual contacts. These accusations usually arise during divorce proceedings or shortly afterward. Also, molestation charges sometimes are leveled by children many years later against their parents or other trusted adults (see MacDonald and Michaud, 1995; Beckett, 1996).

The incest taboo, which prevails in nearly all societies, forbids reproductive sexual relations between members of the same family other than husband and wife. Incest (whether father-daughter, mother-son, or brother-sister) was traditionally viewed as an activity so repulsive and heinous that it must be extremely rare, occurring perhaps in one family out of a million (Weinberg, 1955). But a careful review of records maintained by child protection agencies in Boston from 1880 to 1930 revealed that in 10 percent of the troubled families, incest was taking place. Almost all the perpetrators were older male relatives, usually fathers but also stepfathers, uncles, and older brothers; nearly all the victims were young girls (Gordon, 1988). Ever since the 1980s, adult–child incest (and, in particular, man–girl sexual contact) has been rediscovered as a problem and acknowledged to be more widespread than was ever thought or feared.

Accusations Made During Divorce Proceedings and Custody Battles When allegations of sexual abuse surface in the midst of a divorce and a tug-of-war over a child, two camps quickly emerge. One side argues that since there are no outsiders who witness violations of the incest taboo within the home, these "family secrets" usually are not exposed unless the parents break up. The other side contends that baseless allegations are being taken too seriously, and the resulting investigations ruin the lives of innocent parents, usually fathers. In the mid-1980s an organization was formed to provide support to adults who insisted that they were falsely accused. They nicknamed their predicament the **SAID syndrome**: sexual allegations in divorce ("False Accusations," 1989). Their contention was that in most of these cases, a spiteful mother pressured her daughter to echo a fictitious story about molestations that never occurred. Spreading this vicious lie was a wife's vindictive ploy to discredit her former husband so that the court would issue an order to prevent the girl's father from having further contact with her as she grew up (Fahn, 1991; Sheridan, 1994).

Charges are deemed "unsubstantiated" in these civil proceedings if the bulk of the evidence is insufficient to confirm that the girl was sexually molested by the defendant. The investigators for the child protection agency who interview the girl and her parents in order to evaluate the family dynamics and home environment often feel a need to resolve the matter quickly and minimize the strain on all three parties. Many jurisdictions are too overburdened by huge caseloads to carry out a thorough investigation. Some caseworkers lack the assessment skills and interviewing techniques necessary to elicit crucial testimony. Faced with a father who vehemently denies everything, an intimidated and confused child torn by divided loyalties, and a lack of corroboration by witnesses, the investigators may have little choice but to conclude that it was unlikely that abuse occurred. However, their verdict might be attributed more to the constraints of time, money, and training than to the merits of the case. An unproven charge is not necessarily untrue (Fahn, 1991).

Although feelings run high on both sides of this controversy, it is usually not an issue in divorce proceedings. In a study of more than 6,000 cases in 7 family court jurisdictions, allegations of sexual abuse lodged by one parent against the other were raised in only 2 percent to 10 percent of disputes over custody and visitation rights (Nicholson, 1988).

The Furor over Recalling Repressed Memories of Childhood Sexual Abuse

A prosecutor cross-examining a man accused of molesting his three-year-old daughter suddenly becomes nauseated and dizzy. Fragmented memories flash before her. She begins to pound on the witness stand and screams, "These men just get away with it! The law never does anything!" After the judge jails her for two days for contempt, she enters therapy. She begins to remember being repeatedly molested by both her older brother and her father, although they deny it. To break the conspiracy of silence around childhood

incest, she teams up with several other lawyers to draft new legislation to enable grown children to sue their molesters many years after the alleged incident occurred. (Mithers, 1990)

***

A therapist who is also a sociologist writes a memoir in which she claims that she can now remember how her father abused her when she was a little girl. She believes she has finally figured out why she suffered pain and bleeding between her thighs when she was 5, and endured depression, anorexia, despair, and suicidal tendencies while growing up. But her 91-year-old father, a prominent religious leader and retired professor of ancient scripture, denies the charges, and her seven siblings also dispute her recollections. (Wyatt, 2005)

Sigmund Freud, the founder of modern psychology, originally believed in the early 1900s that many female adults diagnosed as suffering from "hysteria" were desperately trying to repress memories of childhood sexual abuse. But after several years of psychoanalyzing women with this diagnosis, he arrived at the conclusion that his female patients' suspicions about being molested when they were very young were actually just fantasies of incestuous desires, which were strictly taboo. Ever since then, the question of memory loss and recovery (amnesia and delayed recall) has been controversial, and grown-ups who claim they were molested as infants, toddlers, or very young children generally have not been believed.

During the 1980s, a memory-recovery movement emerged to support adult "survivors" (as they prefer to be called) of childhood incest and molestations. The movement forged a coalition of victims, support groups, authors of self-help handbooks, and therapists who practiced memory-retrieval techniques. This movement took a maximalist stance. It proclaimed that new treatment methods made it possible for many sufferers of certain common symptoms to discover that they actually had been incest and molestation victims. Their efforts to repress the traumatic events were burdening them with deep-seated emotional problems. The possibility of repressed memories was addressed in incest support groups, the recovery movement, confessions and revelations by well-known figures, tabloid items, talk show conversations, made-for-television movies, magazine cover stories, popular psychology best sellers, family therapy journals, websites, and the testimony of expert witnesses during civil lawsuits. The thousands recalling childhood sexual abuse (including celebrities and other public figures) represented just the tip of the iceberg, according to alarmist assumptions. Unfortunately, maximalists predicted, many sexual abuse victims will never become aware of the true source of their misery and anguish, and will go through life blaming themselves for their emotional distress (Maltz and Holman, 1986; Bass and Davis, 1992; Herman, 1992).

The aftershocks of childhood incest can be devastating. Youngsters reportedly suffer from clinginess, loss of appetite, nightmares, bed-wetting, inappropriate sexual preoccupations and knowledge, and posttraumatic stress disorder. As they grow older, they are more prone than others to experience reckless promiscuity, sexual dysfunctions, eating disorders, depression, guilt, self-hatred, self-mutilation, alcoholism and drug abuse, and suicidal impulses. However, there is no single symptom that crops up in a majority of sexually abused children. Also, although these symptoms are consistent with abuse, they don't constitute legal proof that incest definitely occurred; other problems can bring about these same disorders (Kendall-Tackett, Williams, and Finkelhor, 1993).

Maximalists believe that when adults suspect unspeakable acts were foisted on them as children, these unsettling hunches are usually well-founded. They have been expending great mental energy to unconsciously block, blot out, or deny any recollection of their "terrible secrets." But with the help of new therapeutic techniques, a flood of these submerged memories eventually can be unleashed. The therapy involves hypnosis, psychoactive drugs that serve as truth serums, age regression, guided fantasy,

and automatic writing. Successful patients progress through several stages, proceeding from initial denial, to suspicions, to realization (after considerable self-examination, probing, dredging up, and digging). Survivors come to recognize that many others have shared their fate, speak openly about their past tribulations, and join self-help support groups to further the healing process (Bass and Davis, 1992; Terr, 1994).

Incest is always difficult to prosecute because usually the case lacks eyewitnesses or tangible evidence and therefore hinges entirely on a child's contentions against an adult's denials. When children grow older, it is usually too late to bring criminal charges. In most states the statute of limitations for felonies runs out five to seven years after the crime is committed. Therefore, adults who think they can recall memories of incest seek to punish their tormentors in a different arena—civil court—via lawsuits for monetary damages for pain and suffering.

Many state legislatures have recognized the possibility of "delayed discovery" and the legitimacy of the demands by incest survivors for some avenue of redress. In these jurisdictions, the lawmakers lengthened the statute of limitations for filing civil lawsuits (which previously expired a few years after the youth reached the age of majority, generally at 18) to several years after the victim recalls the abuse (which could be as long as 20 or 30 years or more). This reform can be considered pro-plaintiff (pro-victim, but anti-defendant) because the purpose of a statute of limitation is to protect accused persons from having to fight allegations from the distant past. Defendants might not remember where they were and what they did—and witnesses in their defense may have moved away or died (Mithers, 1990). Thousands of lawsuits have been filed, encouraged by a national center for prosecuting cases of child sexual abuse in civil court. Some suits arise from claims that boys were molested by men other than their fathers. But typically the plaintiff is a woman who believes she was forced to endure incestuous acts imposed by her father. In about one-quarter of these suits, both parents stand accused of wrongdoing and complicity.

In reaction to the emergence of the repressed memory movement and its maximalist outlook, a countermovement has emerged that takes a minimalist position. Its skeptical perspective concedes that until the 1980s the sexual abuse of children, particularly by parents, went largely underreported and unprosecuted. But this movement questions whether a genuine medical breakthrough and a new, sound method of psychological diagnosis really have been developed.

The suspicion is that certain intervention techniques do not unearth buried memories but actually invent **pseudomemories** that are delusions arising from the therapist's repetition of persuasive suggestions. As a result, certain practitioners who are so intent on unlocking repressed memories are misguiding some of their highly vulnerable and confused patients.

This minimalist perspective charges that the maximalist alarmist definition of the kinds of behaviors that constitute childhood sexual abuse is much too inclusive (for example, unwanted kisses and hugs, or a lack of respect for personal privacy). Similarly, too many vague symptoms on lengthy checklists in self-help manuals are interpreted as likely signs of childhood sexual abuse—everything from ordinary physical ailments (headaches, stomach pains, dizziness) and common emotional problems (general malaise, alienation, low self-esteem, and phobias) to widespread attitudes and behaviors (like feeling powerless or having difficulties in maintaining long-term relationships). As a result of these overly broad definitions as well as unwarranted assumptions about the origins of these symptoms, many therapy patients end up deceiving themselves. They come to believe that they remember awful events that never really happened (Goldstein, 1993; Ofshe and Watters, 1993; Loftus and Ketcham, 1994; Pendergrast, 1994; Yapko, 1994).

The debate over claims of therapeutic breakthroughs on the one hand versus charges of planted suggestions and intense coaxing on the other became unusually acrimonious during the early 1990s. Maximalists denounced skeptics who questioned the authenticity of some claims as "enemies" of incest survivors. Minimalists dismissed the many testimonies about long-forgotten episodes of childhood sexual abuse as part of a modern witch hunt reflecting a jump-on-the-bandwagon phenomenon and a passing fad. Some psychologists and psychiatrists voiced concerns that the furor surrounding symptom-producing traumatic memories was undermining the reputation of the entire profession of clinical therapy and causing patients who had genuinely suffered to be scoffed at as misguided souls.

Some feminists supported the memory recovery movement as a sociopolitical force that could help put an end to the sexual exploitation of children, especially girls, and the subordination of women. They interpreted the resistance as a backlash, just another tactic in the long-standing tradition of silencing, denying, dismissing, belittling, and deriding what women say about their oppression within the family. But others argued that the tendency of the incest survivor movement to blame so many problems that crop up in women's lives on some clearly identifiable villain who might have committed sexual offenses long ago has the counterproductive political consequence of shifting the focus of activism from seeking sweeping social changes to pursuing individual recovery and personal retribution (see Darnton, 1991; Chira, 1993; Horn, 1993; Tavris, 1993; Ofshe, 1994; Sivers, Schooler, Freyd, 2002).

Parents and others targeted by these suits organized a foundation to defend themselves against what they branded a "false memory syndrome" or a "parent alienation syndrome." In family courts, this defense is successful if the judge discounts the youngster's allegations and grants custody of the child to the accused parent. In criminal courts, some convictions based on recalled memories have been overturned. In civil courts, some defendants have filed countersuits against their accusers for defamation of character. Some former patients who recanted their exhumed memories have brought malpractice suits against the therapists who persuaded them to view themselves as incest survivors (see Horn, 1993; Sugarman and McCoy, 1997; Achimovic, 2003). A website supporting people who insist they have been subjected to "false allegations" asserts that questionable accusations about sexual abuse, physical abuse, and acquaintance rape have a great deal in common.

Sexual Abuse of Children by Clerics Starting in the 1970s, reports began to circulate about religious figures who took advantage of their positions of authority and trust to sexually exploit members of their flock. The worst offenders appeared to be "gurus" who told the followers of their cults that religious teachings required that they should submit to the leader's sexual demands.

During the 1980s, a number of adults identified themselves as survivors of sexual abuse carried out by pedophile priests within the Roman Catholic Church. By the early 1990s, a sufficient number of people had come forward to form self-help groups, which then linked up to become a nationwide support network. Most members were grown men who said they had been molested when they were altar boys during their preteen and teenage years; some were women who recounted tales of exploitation during their adolescence.

In the absence of reliable data about the true scope of the problem, a maximalist-minimalist debate erupted. Spokespersons for the two major victims' self-help organizations tended to adopt a maximalist stance. They predicted that the actual number of molested youngsters was probably far greater than just the hundreds who received monetary settlements from civil lawsuits and the several thousand members who had joined the two major self-help groups. They pointed out that many victims were reluctant to go public because of shame and self-blame. In fact, the degree of denial could be so great that some adults continued to insist that abusive conduct never took place even after a molester confessed in court to sexually exploiting them. They argued that a single pedophile could cause a great deal of suffering, and cited the case of one defrocked priest who was believed to have molested between 80 and 130 youngsters during a period of about 30 years. Furthermore, they warned that a steady stream of innocent youth was unwittingly being set up for victimization on a continual basis.

These maximalists contended that since the late 1960s, church officials had covered up the true proportion of the scandal by transferring priests accused of sexual abuse to other parishes as a way of hiding the wrongdoing, and by financially rewarding victims with hush money to remain silent. Reformers urged state legislatures to adopt stringent mandatory reporting requirements that specifically added clergy to the list of occupations, such as teachers, daycare workers, and doctors, who must bring cases of suspected child abuse to the attention of state protection agencies. Victim advocates also urged lawmakers to extend the statute of limitations for prosecuting sexual offenses because many survivors don't come forward until they are well into adulthood, due to intense guilt as well as desires to suppress memories of childhood molestations.

Victims and their advocates wanted clerics whom they accused of being pedophiles to be prosecuted on charges of sexual assault, indecent exposure, and endangering the welfare of a child. Self-help groups also encouraged their members to pursue civil lawsuits, even though the testimony, depositions, and formal inquiries dealt with matters that were intensely personal to reveal and painful to relive. Activists also demanded more effective counseling and psychotherapy services, to be paid for by the clerics' employers. They called upon the church's hierarchy to permit greater openness and accountability around decision making; to cooperate fully with law enforcement investigations; and to acknowledge publicly that the victims' plight had been ignored or dismissed (see Lobdell, 2002; Pfeiffer, 2002; Serbin, 2002; U.S. Conference of Catholic Bishops, 2002; Ostling, 2003; Stammer, 2003; Wakin, 2003; and Jones and Goodnough, 2008).

Minimalists within the hierarchy of the church and its most loyal parishioners wondered if some who claimed they were abused years ago simply were seeking money by filing lawsuits in civil court about matters that could no longer be prosecuted and either proven or disproven in criminal court. Minimalists also questioned whether the extent of exploitation and wrongdoing by employees of this very large organization was of any greater proportion, statistically speaking, than for any other similar-sized group that dealt with children, such as teachers or therapists. They expressed concerns that the entire priesthood was being unfairly maligned.

Minimalists cited a study that estimated that only 866 (not even 1.5 percent) of the more than 60,000 men who had served as priests over four decades ever had been accused of sexual improprieties. The minimalist position accepted the assurances of church authorities who insisted that they had taken the allegations seriously over the years and had implemented reforms that would ensure greater transparency of operations, improved responsiveness, and enhanced protection of children from further harm.

Recommendations by the U.S. Conference of Catholic Bishops (USCCB) in 1992 for programs to promote safe environments had been adopted in most jurisdictions: All credible allegations of abuse were quickly responded to; if sufficient evidence was presented, the accused clergyman was promptly relieved of his ministerial duties. Church officials complied with the obligations of civil law by reporting incidents and cooperating with investigations. They reached out to the children and their families and demonstrated sincere commitment to their spiritual and emotional well-being, minimalists asserted. However, when defending against liability lawsuits by victims concerning charges of negligent hiring and retention of abusive employees, lawyers for the church argued that outside interference into the tenets, canons, policies, and practices of their organization would be an unconstitutional intrusion by government in violation of the First Amendment's guarantee of religious freedom (see Pfeiffer, 2002; Serbin, 2002; USCCB, 2002; Wakin, 2003).

In 2003, in an extensive study authorized and paid for by the USCCB, researchers circulated questionnaires to 195 dioceses and eparchies. The anonymous responses indicated that nearly 4,400 of the roughly 110,000 deacons and priests (4 percent) who served during the period from 1950 to 2002 may have committed sexual offenses against minors. Approximately 10,670 individuals were known to

have made allegations of child sexual abuse against priests. About 17 percent of these complainants contended that their siblings also were sexually abused. Nearly 60 percent of the complainants alleged that the abuse lasted for more than one year. Two-thirds of the accusations had been voiced since 1993. Most (81 percent) of the complainants were males; the most frequent (40 percent) age range when the abuse took place was between 11 and 14. Almost 90 percent of the allegations concerned sexual acts that went beyond unwanted touching over the youngster's clothing (John Jay College Research Team, 2004; see also Perillo, Mercado, and Terry, 2008).

The Roman Catholic Church disclosed in 2007 that during the 5 years since its sexual abuse crisis erupted, it had received about 13,000 credible accusations against its clergymen, dating back to 1950. Because Protestant denominations are less centralized than the Catholic Church, an indirect way to measure the number of youngsters molested by its clergymen was to monitor the number of claims received by the three companies that insure nearly all Protestant congregations, religious schools, and camps. One insurance company logged about 100 reports of sexual abuse of minors per year over a ten-year period ending in 2007. Another processed an average of 100 reports per year for 20 years. A third handled almost 75 reports per year over a 15-year time span. However, not all the claims were credible, adjudicated in civil court, or led to financial settlements (Associated Press, 2007b). In New York City, an elected official invited the Orthodox Jewish listeners of his radio program in 2007 to send him accounts of sexual abuse in their tight-knit community. Shortly thereafter, more than 1,000 alleged victims came forward and provided the names of 60 individuals accused of predatory behavior in religious schools and troubled homes. Those who made these allegations had sworn the elected official to secrecy because they feared they would become stigmatized as "troublemakers" and would end up as outcasts. When he received a subpoena for his files to bolster a civil lawsuit by students against a teacher, he vowed that he would rather "go to jail for 10 years" because in his estimation "99 percent [of the victims] would not go to the police under any circumstances" due to cultural taboos and prohibitions against turning to secular authorities for help (Vitello, 2008).

Strange Allegations of Ritualistic Abuse by Satanic Cults

Four members of a family that runs a preschool, plus three teachers who work there, are accused of subjecting 42 children to satanic rituals that involved sexual abuse. Charges are quickly dropped against five of the defendants. The mother is kept in jail for two years but is acquitted after a lengthy trial. After five years in detention and two trials, charges are dismissed against her son. Jurors are divided over the issue of whether the overzealous officials who interviewed the children in fact suggested much of their testimony. (Goldberg, 1998)

***

A deputy sheriff is arrested and charged with sexually abusing his two daughters, now 18 and 22. Soon the charges emanating from the devoutly religious 22-year-old (who has a history of making unsubstantiated complaints about sexual abuse) grow to alarming proportions: She claims to have attended 850 satanic rituals and to have watched 25 babies being sacrificed and then cannibalized. Eventually, both daughters, the mother, and then even the father, can visualize being present at these ceremonies where members of a sadistic devil-worshiping cult forced the women to perform sexual acts with goats and dogs. The father is grilled by his police department colleagues and quickly confesses, but then hires a new lawyer and tries to withdraw his guilty plea. However, it is too late, and he is convicted of six counts of child molestation. His older daughter demands that he receive the most severe

punishment possible, and the judge sentences him to 20 years in prison. (Wright, 1994)

One of the most peculiar debates between the maximalist and minimalist viewpoints reached a feverish pitch that resembled what sociologists call a "moral panic" during the late 1980s and early 1990s. It incorporated several elements of great concern at the time: child abuse, sexual exploitation, kidnapping, and repressed memories.

The maximalist position was that thousands of people disappeared each year because they were dispatched by secret cults. Believers in the existence of a satanic conspiracy circulated frightening accounts about bizarre "wedding" ceremonies in which covens of witches and devil worshipers chanted, wore costumes, took drugs, sacrificed animals, and even mutilated, tortured, and murdered newborn infants or kidnapped children. In its most extreme form, the charge was that satanic cults engaged in baby breeding and in kidnapping in order to maintain a supply of victims for human sacrifices and cannibalism.

The people who came forward and said that they survived ritual abuse were often young women who made these claims after undergoing psychotherapy. They told tales of being fondled, raped, sodomized, and exploited as objects in sexual games and pornographic films. Usually, the scenarios they recalled involved groups of adults, sometimes including members of their own families, abusing very young children. Although the alleged victims complained that they encountered resistance or even outright disbelief when they reported the crimes to officers, some law enforcement agencies took their charges seriously. Newsletters, conferences, and training sessions were organized for detectives, social workers, child welfare investigators, and therapists. Responding to a public outcry, several state legislatures outlawed the "ritual mutilation" of innocents during religious initiation rites (see Bromley, 1991; Richardson, Best, and Bromley, 1991; Lanning, 1992; Shapiro et al., 1993; Sinason, 1994).

The minimalist position pointed out that the scare developed after bizarre charges about teachers practicing witchcraft at a California preschool generated one of the longest and costliest trials in American history (but no convictions). To investigate the deluge of claims about ritual abuse, researchers sponsored by the National Center on Child Abuse and Neglect surveyed more than 11,000 psychiatrists, psychologists, clinical social workers, district attorneys, police executives, and social service agency administrators during 1993. The respondents told the survey interviewers that more than 12,000 accusations of ritual abuse had been brought to their attention, but that not a single case had been proven in which a well-organized, intergenerational ring of satanic followers had sexually molested, tortured, or killed children in their homes or schools. The study only could find some cases in which lone individuals or couples carried out abusive rituals or perpetrated crimes in the name of religion (Goleman, 1994).

The minimalist view attributed the panic to sensationalism by the tabloid press and irresponsible talk shows that fed a climate of rumors and fears. The time was ripe because of widespread and deep-seated anxieties concerning new brainwashing techniques of mind control; the growth of cult-like religious groups; the breakdown of traditionally structured families; the redefinition of male and female roles; youthful experimentation with sex and drugs; increased conflict over abortion as "babykilling"; and greater reliance on daycare services for preschoolers. Fears about well-financed, hidden cells of satanic infiltrators seemed to replace "communist subversives" as the forces of an "evil underworld" in these versions of conspiracy theories (see Bromley, 1991; Richardson, Best, and Bromley, 1991; Lanning, 1992; Sakheim and Devine, 1992; Nathan and Snedeker, 1995; LaFontaine, 1997).

Although many people claimed to have witnessed, participated in, and survived these "devilish activities," minimalist skeptics conclude that their credibility was as questionable as the truthfulness of the hundreds of people who swore they had been abducted by aliens from outer space (see Schemo, 2002; Clancy, 2005) or who said they remembered events from their "past lives" as different people.

ABUSED CHILDREN AND LEGAL PROCEEDINGS

Children who survive kidnappings or endure physical and sexual abuse need to bring their problems to the attention of the authorities. Detectives and prosecutors must test the veracity of their accounts in a sensitive manner. If their charges seem credible and adults are arrested on the basis of their complaints, then their cases must be handled with care by the legal system.

Cases revolving around allegations of abuse within a family traditionally are dealt with by child welfare protective services, family courts, and the juvenile justice system. Cases involving very serious charges are brought to criminal court. But by trying to protect the child from further harm, the judicial proceedings can inadvertently compound the youngster's suffering. It has become clear that the adult-oriented criminal justice system is not designed to address the emotional and physical needs of traumatized children. As key witnesses for the prosecution, youngsters often find the setting hostile and the proceedings confusing, hard to fathom, and frightening (Munson, 1989).

Taking into Account the Best Interests of the Child

A victimized child needs an advocate who will provide support and advice during legal proceedings, especially when the alleged offender is a parent. The law has recognized the inability of the government's prosecutor to play this role and created a special position, the **guardian** *ad litem* (GAL), to look after "the best interests of the child." The Child Abuse Prevention and Treatment Act passed by Congress in 1974 required that youngsters be provided with GALs if their cases were heard in family court. The Victims of Child Abuse Act of 1990 went further and recommended the provision of GALs to young complainants when their serious accusations channeled their cases to criminal court. By 1997, nearly 650 advocacy programs operated in jurisdictions across the country.

Usually, these court-appointed advocates are attorneys, but in some states they can be specially trained volunteers. Their duties include accompanying the child to legal proceedings and helping him or her get needed social, mental health, and medical services. In criminal proceedings against an abuser, the GAL is supposed to serve as counselor, interpreter, defender against system-induced trauma (insensitive handling), monitor, coordinator, advocate (of rights to privacy and protection from harassment), and spokesperson (about wishes, fears, and needs). In some states, GALs assist the child in preparing a victim impact statement and can submit their own recommendations to the court about what would be best for the child's welfare (Whitcomb, 1992; Lawry, 1997). Because youngsters in foster care can suffer from additional acts of physical and sexual abuse and neglect, some states have set up an independent child advocate's office to serve as a watchdog and intervene on behalf of these children (Smothers, 2003).

The creation of the role of guardian *ad litem* dramatized the importance of a much larger question: What are the injured party's best interests? When victims are too young to be able to explain for themselves what would be to their advantage, it is up to GALs to advocate in their behalf. But what are the options, opportunities, perils, and pitfalls of various courses of action?

Two official responses are possible in cases of physical or sexual abuse. One is to view parental wrongdoers as dysfunctional people in need of treatment and rehabilitation. The other is to react to them as criminals who deserve incapacitation and punishment.

These two alternatives reflect opposing philosophies. Mental health professionals (psychiatrists, psychologists, counselors, and social workers) tend to see criminal proceedings as unproductive, inhumane, damaging to both victims and perpetrators, and inappropriate in all but the most horrendous cases. Police officials and prosecutors tend to resent therapeutic approaches that, in their view, coddle offenders and excuse their antisocial conduct. But in recent years the alternatives have become intertwined, as criminal proceedings have been used to compel abusers to undergo court-mandated and supervised treatment programs as a condition of pretrial diversion or probation (see Berliner, 1987; Harshbarger, 1987; Newberger, 1987).

The Credibility of Children as Witnesses

A 15-year-old boy testifies that a famous rock singer invited him to his mansion for sleepover parties, got him drunk, and then molested him on several occasions two years earlier while he was undergoing treatment for cancer. The boy's younger brother takes the stand and claims he saw the singer fondle his brother in two additional incidents. But the defense argues that the brothers and their mother are "con artists, actors, and liars" who had taken advantage of the bout with cancer to wheedle money from celebrities. After a three-month trial, the jury finds the pop star not guilty of molestation and not guilty of providing alcohol to minors. (Broder and Madigan, 2005)

An estimated 20,000 children are called upon each year to testify in legal proceedings stemming from allegations of sexual abuse, and as many as 80,000 more are questioned by investigators annually about possible molestations (Goleman, 1993). As a result, whether children tend to tell the truth or are prone to concoct stories has become an emotional issue with significant legal repercussions.

Historically, when children were drawn into the adult court system as prosecution witnesses, the proceedings were inherently biased against their participation. Their testimony was automatically suspect, and their unique and legitimate needs were routinely overlooked. Now it is widely recognized that young complainants have unique problems that require special handling.

Should youngsters have an automatic credibility problem simply by virtue of their age? Would children lie about important matters? Is there a kernel of truth to most revelations, whether spontaneously volunteered or coaxed out of children, or do hysterical parents and overzealous investigators set off witch hunts and fall for hoaxes? Researchers estimate that around 500 studies have examined the issue of children's "suggestibility" ever since a bitter controversy erupted during the late 1980s (Goldberg, 1998).

> Nineteen children between the ages of three and five testify at the trial of their nursery school teacher. They tell the jury that over a period of seven months, during nap time, this 22-year-old woman (who had received an excellent evaluation and a promotion) inserted knives, forks, spoons, and Lego blocks into them. Some testify that they played games naked and she made them drink urine, eat feces, and defecate on her. Although no staff members saw, heard, smelled, or suspected anything suspicious, and no parent ever detected any evidence of strange behavior, the jury believes the children. Three years after the alleged incidents, the 10-month trial ends, and the teacher is convicted on 115 counts of sexual abuse and sentenced to 47 years in prison. But five years later, the conviction is overturned on appeal when a three-judge panel rules that prosecution interviewers pressured the little complainants to confirm the charges with bribes and threats. Also, the judge was faulted for violating his impartiality when he coaxed the young witnesses to testify against the teacher over closed-circuit TV in his chambers while sitting on his lap. The prosecution decides not to retry the case, in part because some parents conclude that putting their now teenage children back on the witness stand would be too stressful. (Manshel, 1990; Nieves, 1994)

The testimony of children has been viewed with skepticism ever since the Salem witch trials of 1692, when a number of girls made fantastic claims that they publicly recanted several years later after the "witches" were executed. Now, social scientists are conducting experiments to determine the accuracy of the memories children acquire, retain, and retrieve. Because of their immaturity, very young children suffer from cognitive limitations that can undermine their credibility. They think in very concrete terms and have trouble understanding generalizations. They do not organize their thoughts logically or recount stories sequentially. They may be unable to properly locate events in space, distance, and time, making it difficult for them to be sure about where and when something happened. They tend to assume that adults know the whole story, and think that their partial answers are satisfactory. They also have short attention spans. Finally, they might be uncomfortable confiding in strangers who intimidate them (Whitcomb, 1992).

Two distinct points of view characterize the debate over the issue of credibility (see Ceci and Bruck, 1993; Lewin, 2002). At one extreme is the pro-prosecution/pro-victim "believe the children" position that says that youngsters are generally competent witnesses about events that happened to them weeks or months earlier, are resistant to suggestions, and do not make up charges about abuse, especially sexual molestations and assaults that didn't happen. In fact, children might even retract accusations that ring true if the social reaction to their disclosure threatens to cause chaos. For example, a girl who reveals an incestuous relationship might recant her original testimony if she fears that she will be rejected and branded as a liar by her father, who faces disgrace and imprisonment; that her mother will become hysterical and enraged; that her siblings will be furious about the disruption of their family life; and that caseworkers and detectives will become more intrusive. The girl could feel she is being blamed for provoking the crisis and might back down in a vain attempt to restore some semblance of normality (Whitcomb, 1992).

At the other extreme is the pro-defendant position that questions the trustworthiness of the testimony of children who serve as witnesses for the prosecution. Children's versions of events should be viewed with skepticism because they are extremely vulnerable to coaching and manipulation by adults. The testimony of very young witnesses loses credibility once they have been subjected to intensive questioning by caseworkers, detectives, prosecutors, and parents who strongly believe that abuse has taken place. If authority figures attempt to "validate" their preconceived notion of what may have happened, the youngsters might keep repeating the "right answers" to the leading questions adults ask. Then the youngsters might eventually be swayed and regurgitate the adults' suspicions back to them, as if these events actually occurred. When a high-pressure interviewing technique is imposed upon a hyper-suggestible youngster, the result can be the creation of a false memory. A baseless charge against an innocent adult ultimately could lead to a wrongful conviction.

Contradictory findings about the reliability of children's claims have filled forensic literature since the mid-1970s. Some studies conclude that youngsters can be swayed only about minor details, but others indicate that repeated interrogations can coerce children to make up tales that they believe are memories.

Professionals who look into and report instances of suspected maltreatment must be scrupulous about carrying out two legal obligations simultaneously: promoting the best interests of their young clients while safeguarding the legal rights of the adults they investigate (Ceci and Bruck, 1993; Hewitt, 1998).

Ever since the landmark decision of the Supreme Court in 1895 (*Wheeler v. United States*), children have had to pass pretrial competency tests before testifying (unless they were over the age of 14). Nearly 100 years later, the Victims of Child Abuse Act of 1990 reversed that presumption; now children are considered competent witnesses unless there is evidence to the contrary. However, in most state courtrooms across the country, before a trial begins, the judge evaluates whether a youngster understands the difference between truth and falsehood, appreciates the seriousness of the oath to swear to tell the truth, and can remember details of past events. Child welfare advocates welcome these reforms because they believe most children in abuse cases don't lie (Whitcomb, 1992). But civil libertarians are concerned that the presumption of competency might undermine a defendant's right to a fair trial (Austern, 1987; Dershowitz, 1988).

Devising Child-Friendly Practices

Besides credibility, another special problem requires a special solution: testifying in legal proceedings can add to the suffering of victimized children. To avoid further traumatizing these youngsters, the idea of developing a child-friendly courtroom setting and protocol quickly caught on (see Libai, 1969).

The right to a public trial always has protected defendants against judicial misconduct and governmental persecution behind closed doors. However, the prospect of testifying in front of a crowd of strangers can deter a youthful complainant from pressing charges. In particular, the spectacle of describing in intimate detail what happened during an episode of sexual abuse is so potentially disturbing to a sensitive youngster that exceptions to the public nature of a trial have been legislated. Some states grant judges the authority to bar spectators from the courtroom during the testimony of a child who claims to have been sexually abused. In more than half of the states, the release of identifying information by the news media about a complainant in a sexual abuse case is severely limited (Whitcomb, 1992).

The Sixth Amendment guarantees defendants in criminal trials the right to confront their accusers. In theory, looking the defendant in the eye in court as an accusation is repeated has traditionally been considered a test of a complaining witness's truthfulness. But when very young children are the complainants, they often dread seeing the defendant in person. For many years, to avoid last-minute intimidation when the youngster took the stand, prosecutors would position themselves to block the small witness's view of the defendant. Other prosecutors simply instructed the child to look at someone in the spectator section during the testimony, preferably toward a supportive, familiar person. More obvious methods of shielding frightened complainants from the direct gaze of defendants, such as using a screen or one-way glass, or having the children turn their backs, were deemed to violate the face-to-face requirement of the confrontation clause.

With the advent of closed-circuit television and videotaping, more options developed. To avoid intimidation and anxiety caused by the presence of jurors and other courtroom personnel, nearly all states allow youngsters to be questioned in another room using two-way, live closed-circuit television. To spare the child the ordeal of reliving unpleasant experiences in front of strangers, most of these states permit testimony and cross-examination previously videotaped at depositions, grand jury proceedings, or preliminary hearings to be used in trials. In 1990 the Supreme Court ruled (in *Maryland v. Craig*) that these alternatives to direct confrontation were constitutionally permissible under certain circumstances (Whitcomb, 1992).

Hearsay is usually not admissible during trials because statements uttered outside the courtroom are not made under oath and are not subject to cross-examination. Yet in child abuse cases, what the youngster said before legal proceedings were initiated may be very compelling evidence. For example, a casual remark by a very young and immature girl might be a surprisingly graphic description of a sexual act that should be unfamiliar to her. Therefore, in the "interest of justice" in more than half the states, special exceptions to the hearsay rule enable witnesses to tell the court what allegedly sexually abused children have told them. In 1980, the Supreme Court ruled (in *Ohio v. Roberts*) that a statement made by a complainant who does not testify at the trial can be used as evidence if it falls under one of the rules for hearsay exceptions or meets a reliability test (Whitcomb, 1992).

In the late 1970s, investigators began to use anatomically detailed dolls (with prominent genitalia) to facilitate and enhance interviews with children who might have been sexually abused. The rationale was that the presence of a doll would make the interview seem less formal and stressful, enable children with limited vocabularies or overwhelming emotions to demonstrate what happened to them, and permit the information to be disclosed without any reliance on leading questions. The Victims of Child Abuse Act of 1990 endorsed the use of dolls as demonstrative aids during interviews and court proceedings, and some states have followed suit. But critics point out that experiments have shown that even children with no suspected

history of abuse play with the anatomically intriguing dolls in a suggestive way that could falsely imply an inordinate interest in sexuality based on personal experiences (see Whitcomb, 1992).

Other reforms that are less controversial and more often implemented include allowing children to use drawings to describe what happened to them, interviewing them in decorated playrooms at police stations rather than in dingy, bare-walled interrogation rooms, and modifying the courtroom's protocol and seating arrangements to make the setting less imposing. Additional child-friendly practices include giving young witnesses an orientation tour of the courthouse, enrolling them in brief "court schools" that explain the role of key figures and the procedures that will be followed, permitting them to have a supportive person at their side, and using just one trained interviewer to elicit all their testimony. To limit the length of the ordeal of going to trial, some jurisdictions give child abuse cases a high priority in scheduling and try to avoid continuances that cause upsetting delays. To minimize stress, the medical, mental health, treatment, and legal aspects of abuse cases are now coordinated by child protection teams of professionals from different disciplines. Information-sharing procedures eliminate unnecessary interviews. Public funds cover the costs of physical and mental health examinations. Caseworkers from protective services agencies and law enforcement officers are empowered to take children endangered by their situations into emergency custody. Because confused and intimidated youngsters often do not inform anyone of their plight for years, many states have extended their statutes of limitations so they do not begin to run until the complainant reaches a more mature age (see Whitcomb, 1986; "Child Abuse Victims," 1989; Howell, 1989; Myers, 1998).

A survey revealed that the following percentages of judges have used these approaches to minimize the stress on youngsters who testified in their courtrooms:

Adjust questions to the child's comprehension level (88 percent); Exclude the public during the child's testimony (55 percent); Allow the child to testify in the judge's chambers (46 percent); Have only the judge ask the questions (45 percent); Permit the child to testify while sitting on an adult's lap (41 percent); Rearrange courtroom furniture (31 percent); Videotape the child's testimony (27 percent); Remove the defendant from the child's view (16 percent); Have a therapist ask the questions (13 percent);Allow the child to testify over closed-circuit television (11 percent); Install a one-way mirror (3 percent) (Hafemeister, 1996).

The **funnel model** of the criminal justice system best describes what typically happens to child abuse cases. Although the legal system starts with a huge workload, cases are "removed" or "lost" at each stage in the proceedings (arrest, prosecution, indictment, plea negotiation, trial) until there are very few left at the end of the process—leading to incarceration in jail or prison. Children testifying and being cross-examined, and adults getting convicted and locked up turns out to be a relatively rare event (see Chapman and Smith, 1987; Whitcomb, 1988, 1992).

PROACTIVE VERSUS REACTIVE STRATEGIES

Strategies to prevent children from being abused take many forms. Proactive approaches attempt to prevent abuse from taking place. They range from screening potential child care workers to weed out known molesters, setting up "help lines" and crisis nurseries where parents can drop off their children if they feel they are about to lose control of their emotions, organizing Parents Anonymous support groups for abusers, and offering child-rearing courses for new parents (Irwin, 1980). To prevent infanticides (and neonaticides within 24 hours of birth), 47 states have passed "Safe Haven" laws that allow parents to leave unwanted newborns at sites like hospitals or firehouses, anonymously and without fear of prosecution. However, the effectiveness of this drop-off, no-questions-asked legislation is difficult to determine because few states keep records of the number of unwanted babies (some resulting from rapes) that are abandoned, dead or alive. The existence of the law and the locations of the places prepared to receive newborns generally are not well-publicized. In the New York City area, six discarded babies were found dead during 2006, twice as many as in the preceding year, even though the state's Safe Haven law went into effect during 2000 (Buckley, 2007).

The problem of child maltreatment touches on many profound issues. Although proactive and preventive strategies are as important as reactive criminal justice responses, sharp differences of opinion surface over the proper role of government in the balance between social nurturance and social control. In reply to the question, "Whose children are they?" one long-standing answer is that children belong to, or are the property of, their parents.

Another way of looking at youngsters is to see them as "junior" citizens: Parents have custody of them, but the larger community has "visiting rights." In extreme cases, the community might even assert "joint custody" and violate the privacy of the family and the rights of parents. Government agencies step in as the parents of last resort when children face a clear and present danger. Yet in an age when the social conditions experienced by children are generally deteriorating (in the form of reduced parental involvement and support, increased exposure to violence, and persistent poverty during childhood in female-headed households), stepped-up efforts to criminalize the maltreatment of children might not do much to stem the growth of the problem (Garbarino, 1989). On the other hand, the price for inaction or minimal reaction in the name of family preservation on the part of child protection agencies and family courts is heightened risks of serious injury or death.

ADDITIONAL FORMS OF EXPLOITATION AND MISTREATMENT OF YOUNG PEOPLE

Besides the maltreatment of children by their parental caretakers, several other victim–offender relationships fall within the realm of physically abusing and sexually exploiting young people.

Sibling Abuse

When brothers and sisters fight each other, their roughhousing is often dismissed as "kids will be kids" or disregarded as a normal expression of sibling rivalry. Sons are more violent than daughters, and all-boy families are the most violent of all. The use of force to resolve quarrels breaks out more often between siblings than between parents or between parents and children. Older youths might not only physically assault but also sexually abuse younger male and female siblings. The younger child generally does not tell anyone about the incidents for fear of being blamed, of not being believed, or of suffering reprisals (see Straus, Gelles, and Steinmetz, 1980; Pagelow, 1989; Wiehe, 1997; Caffaro and Caffaro, 1998).

Sibling-on-sibling violence stands out because it is the most frequent yet least studied type of assault, which evidently reflects the difference between the priorities of researchers and the concerns of youngsters. In terms of a typology of victimization during childhood, violence between siblings can be classified as pandemic: occurring in the lives of a majority of children as they grow up. It is more common than the incidence of robbery, theft, vandalism of a possession, assault by a peer, and physical punishment by a parent (Finkelhor and Leatherman, 1994). Sibling abuse can set the stage for other expressions of violence. For example, victimized boys might grow up to become abusers of their dates during courtship (Simonelli et al., 2002).

Abuse of Adolescents by Parents

The fact that even teenagers can be abused by their parents used to be overlooked entirely or subsumed under the heading "child abuse" and then neglected in favor of a focus on the very young and totally helpless. Attempts to define and measure abuse become confusing because of cultural ambivalence about the thin line between physical abuse and physical discipline (see Jackson et al., 2000). Many adults consider venting parental wrath justifiable when there is "sufficient provocation"—if a teenager is argumentative, defiant, incorrigible, or out of control. Adolescents are not viewed as particularly vulnerable or defenseless, as are infants, toddlers, and children under 12. The same force that could injure a little child might not seriously wound a teenager. The overt consequences of psychological abuse and emotional neglect become less detectable as adolescents mature into independent young adults (see Lourie, 1977; Libbey and Bybee, 1979; Pagelow, 1989).

Attempts to measure the frequency of adolescent abuse have yielded estimates that from one-fifth to almost one-half of all cases of child maltreatment known to social service agencies involved youths between 12 and 17 (measurements were taken at various times during the 1970s and 1980s). Parents tend to use greater force against their older children. As a result, battered teenagers can suffer serious wounds just like younger children. Their injuries usually come to light when the adolescents are reported by parents or teachers to the authorities for disobedience or "acting out" behavior, or when they are referred to counselors for emotional problems. Girls are more likely than boys to be physically, sexually, and emotionally abused; boys are more often emotionally and educationally neglected (Pagelow, 1989).

As boys grow older, the power differential between parents and their sons decreases and physical abuse declines. As girls become sexually mature and seek greater independence, the power differential between parents and their daughters diminishes more incrementally, leading to conflicts as parents attempt to impose restraints backed up by force. Sons who strike back get into legal trouble for assault. Girls generally do not fight back physically, but they seek to escape a repressive household by running away, acting promiscuously, or taking drugs. The majority of abused teenagers are white and from low-income families where they are either the only child or one of four or more children. The abusive parents tend to be middle-aged, are often stepparents, and are going through their own mid-life crises. Excessive parental force takes the form of hair pulling, slapping, choking, beating, threatening with a knife or gun, and assault with a weapon (see Pagelow, 1989).

Statutory Rape of Minors

Statutory rape has been largely overlooked by criminologists and victimologists because of the absence of reliable data and the presence of a willing "victim." But information contained in the FBI's NIBRS database for 21 states during the years 1996–2000 sheds some light on about 7,500 cases that were reported to police departments, either by the minor or by the boy or girl's parents or caretakers. The police kept track of these complaints when an older wrongdoer (of any age) engaged in sexual relations with a younger person (between age 7 and 17) who is not mature enough in the eyes of the law to willingly grant consent. In other words, these cases of nonforcible sexual intercourse would not be illegal if both partners were old enough to make responsible decisions.

A few high-profile cases of female teachers carrying on affairs with underage male students have challenged the prevailing stereotype of exploitative older males taking advantage of teenage girls. But the NIBRS data confirms that this stereotype is based on facts: the overwhelming majority (95 percent) of the complaints centered on allegations by female minors. Very few adult male homosexuals were involved in these NIBRS reports. In the relatively rare cases in which boys were considered victimized (5 percent), the overwhelming majority (94 percent) of their sex partners were older females, not older males. The average age difference between the older males and the girls was six years, while the average gap between older females and boys was nine years. About 30 percent of the wrongdoers considered themselves boyfriends or girlfriends; 60 percent were classified as acquaintances; 7 percent were members of the victims' families; and the remainder were strangers. The police made an arrest of the older sex partner in a little over 40 percent of the cases (Troup-Leasure and Snyder, 2005).

SUMMARY

The true extent of the victimization of children cannot be accurately measured. As a result, maximalist alarmists assume the worst and call for drastic crime control measures to head off a crisis. Minimalist skeptics disagree and believe that the incidence, prevalence, and seriousness of the indisputably real problems of physical child abuse, sexual molestation, and kidnappings are not spiraling out of control.

Although children are highly desirable targets for kidnappers and pedophiles, analyses of reports about missing children yield the somewhat reassuring finding that abductions by strangers that result in murders are relatively rare. Efforts to recover kidnapped children are much more organized and effective than they used to be when the problem first surfaced at the start of the 1980s.

Infants, toddlers, children, and even teenagers are especially vulnerable to physical and sexual abuse by their caretakers: parents, older siblings, and other family members such as stepparents, as well as babysitters, teachers, and acquaintances. Maximalists and minimalists differ over whether these twin problems of physical and sexual abuse are intensifying or subsiding. Bitter controversies surround charges of retrieved memories of molestations during childhood, accusations about parental sexual abuse voiced during divorces, and claims of abuse by priests or during satanic rituals.

The legal system's handling of young witnesses for the prosecution has improved dramatically in recent years. Children harmed by their parents are assigned a guardian *ad litem* to advocate on behalf of their best interests. They are questioned with greater care, but still face special difficulties in establishing the credibility of their testimony. Courtroom procedures and cross-examination practices have been reformed so that they are less intimidating and less stressful to youngsters serving as witnesses for the prosecution. However, these new practices must not violate the rights of the defendant who may be falsely accused, civil libertarians insist.

KEY TERMS

maximalist, 194

minimalist, 194

inveiglement, 195

missing children, 195

throwaways, 198

Amber Alert, 202

child lures, 203

Code Adam, 204

cruelty to children, 205

House of Refuge movement, 205

battered child syndrome, 205

incidence, 208

prevalence, 208

unfounded reports, 210

SAID syndrome, 211

pseudomemories, 214

guardian *ad litem*, 219

funnel model, 223

QUESTIONS FOR DISCUSSION AND DEBATE

1. Why are the views of maximalists and minimalists so far apart on the fate of missing children?

2. Why are the views of maximalists and minimalists so different on the question of whether the problem of the physical and sexual abuse of children is intensifying or subsiding?

CRITICAL THINKING QUESTIONS

1. Suggest a set of procedures concerning the testimony of children serving as witnesses for the prosecution against adults that allegedly molested them that would surely violate the constitutional rights of the defendants.

2. Speculate why stories about people who claim that they survived satanic rituals have largely disappeared from the news.

SUGGESTED RESEARCH PROJECTS

1. Perform a content analysis of stories about repressed memories of childhood sexual abuse that appeared in the press over the last few decades. Pick a newspaper and magazine database and do keyword searches to see what kinds of accounts made the news and how the cases were resolved.

2. From the list in Box 8.1, choose a program or legislation to help find missing children, and see

if there is evidence about the effectiveness of these measures.

3. Evaluate the accomplishments of the Amber Alert system by collecting data and accounts from websites that monitor its operations in various states.

4. Investigate safe-haven provisions in your area: When was the law passed, how well publicized is it, where can distraught mothers hand over unwanted newborns, and how many babies have been rescued from abandonment this way?

9

Victims of Violence by Lovers and Family Members

VIOLENCE BETWEEN INTIMATES

This chapter begins by focusing upon another aspect of family violence—not the abuse of children by parents, but the abuse of one intimate partner by another. **Intimate partners** are those people with whom the victim has had a romantic relationship, and therefore includes a spouse, ex-spouse, boyfriend, ex-boyfriend, girlfriend, or former girlfriend. This kind of domestic violence mars the lives of millions of Americans, and yet it was a taboo topic until the start of the 1970s. Now violence between intimates has come out from the shadows and is the most thoroughly studied victim-offender relationship of all—and for several good reasons. The consequences of these beatings can be severe for the injured party (physical wounds, depression, posttraumatic stress, loss of job, homelessness, even death from homicide or suicide), for the offender (arrest, prosecution, probation, incarceration, mandatory therapy), for their children (emotional scars, divorce, custody battles), and for the entire society (costs of medical care and social services, lost productivity, and criminal justice expenses).

These victims of violence by assailants who are close to them face a host of special problems that require special solutions that are creative, thoughtful, and effective.

THE REDISCOVERY OF WIFE BEATING

In her autobiography, the daughter of a prominent political figure reveals that she endured many vicious beatings by her first husband, a police officer, shortly after they married. During fits of jealous rage, he punched and kicked her in the head so brutally that she fantasized about killing him. But when she picked up his service revolver, she found she was incapable of pulling the trigger. She told her coworkers, friends, and parents that her cuts and swellings were due to her clumsiness. Her father, a famous actor and former president of the United States, finally discovers the truth about her "bruises from accidents" when he reads her book. (Bruni, 1989)

The rediscovery of the plight of battered wives during the 1970s shattered the illusion of **domestic tranquility**—the image that women were safe

from harm as long as they remained at home, protected by their husbands from the vicious dog-eat-dog world raging outside. Once it was realized that a "silent crisis" marred the lives of many women and that the perpetrators were not menacing strangers but the men they married, the "look-the-other-way," "mind-your-own-business," and "hands-off" policies toward "lovers' spats" that took place "behind closed doors" could no longer be justified (see Straus, 1978; Pagelow, 1984a, 1984b; Gelles and Cornell, 1990; Straus and Gelles, 1990; Dobash and Dobash, 1992).

For centuries, legal traditions granted the man, as "head of the household" whose home was "his castle," the "right" to "discipline" his wife and children "as he saw fit" because they were regarded as his "property" or "chattel." This convention became a basis of English common law (which was accepted into American jurisprudence) for a nonintervention stance that denied women equal protection under the law. Such institutionalized indifference was legally permissible because it was a wife's duty to "love, honor, and obey" her husband. Indeed, many battered wives did not even define their beatings as crimes and did not consider themselves to be victims because they accepted the prevailing ideology echoed by authority figures, friends, and parents that they had "stepped out of line" and "had it coming" and therefore "got what they deserved." Such traditional thinking made the marriage license into a hitting license for husbands (Dobash and Dobash, 1979).

A mistaken impression prevails that the issue of spouse abuse was raised for the first time during the 1970s, primarily by feminists intent on exposing the injustices and cruelties of **patriarchy**, the traditional system of male dominance. Actually, there have been two previous periods of concern about family violence in American history (Pleck, 1989).

As early as the mid-1600s, the Pilgrims who settled in New England officially recognized the possibility that wives could be assaulted by their husbands, that husbands could be brutalized by their wives, that children could be harshly mistreated by their parents, and that incestuous sexual relations could be imposed on youngsters. Guided by religious teachings about the virtues of harmonious family life and the sins of disobeying authority, the Puritans in Plymouth Colony and Massachusetts Bay Colony passed the first laws in the world forbidding verbal or physical abuse between family members. Wife beating was punishable by a fine or a whipping; however, the sentence for husband abuse was up to the judge. Child abuse (called **unnatural severity**) carried a fine, but if incest was discovered it could result in execution by hanging, according to the interpretation of the Bible at that time.

Even though conformity to all laws was insisted upon and intervening into a neighboring family's affairs was expected, none of these laws were vigorously enforced. Only on rare occasions were wives brought to court for verbally abusing ("nagging") their husbands. Husbands rarely were fined and almost never whipped for beating their wives, and charges were dropped if judges decided wives had provoked their husbands' wrath. Wives who complained that their husbands beat them often recanted their accusations when they got to court. No case of child abuse was ever prosecuted, and no one was ever put to death for incest, according to court records from these New England colonies. Apparently, these laws merely served a symbolic function, outlining rights and responsibilities and setting limits.

Puritan teachings held that God ruled the state, the state supervised the family, and the husband headed the household. The occasional use of force to discipline a wife (what they called **moderate correction** within **domestic chastisement**) was permissible "within reasonable limits"—as long as the beating caused no permanent damage. In those days, the expression **rule of thumb** actually was a guideline that prohibited men from using sticks thicker than their thumbs to beat their wives, whose "provocations" included "passionate language" (scolding) or refusing to engage in sexual relations. The desire to reinforce patriarchal control, uphold parental rights, and shore up the nuclear family necessitated that laws criminalizing abuse within families would be rarely enforced and that "sinners" would receive lenient sentences. The

most effective restraints on male violence were informal social controls: community disapproval, pressures from the wife's parents, and in extreme cases, divorce (Rhode, 1989; Pleck, 1989).

As the agricultural way of life gave way to industrialization and urbanization, a second wave of concern about family violence developed in the late 1800s. Reformers argued in favor of the principle that the government had a responsibility to enforce morality as codified in law. Fears about immigrants, drifters, and the growing "dangerous classes" of criminals and delinquents in the large cities fueled this movement for change. Temperance advocates hammered at the evils of drinking by emphasizing how wives and children were abused by drunkards who wasted their time and money in saloons. Offshoots of the Society for the Prevention of Cruelty to Children (SPCC) were set up across the country. Some women's rights activists contended that fines and jail terms were insufficient to deter wife beating and called for the restoration of the whipping post. (Public flogging had been abandoned in most states about 100 years earlier as an uncivilized and barbaric form of corporal punishment.) Other feminists sought ways to help battered wives get orders of protection and divorces (Pleck, 1989).

The third wave of reform focused on victim-support activities and was championed by feminists in the women's liberation movement of the early 1970s. Wife beating symbolized women's oppression within the family, and the lack of responsiveness on the part of the men who ran the criminal justice system demonstrated how women faced institutionalized discrimination in everyday life. Projects such as shelters for battered women exemplified the self-help, tangible aid, and empowerment that women could achieve if they acted collectively. A movement to support battered women developed from this concern about family violence.

Before the 1970s, wife beating received very little attention in the journals read by counselors, social workers, and others in the helping professions. This "silent crisis" did not merit much press coverage, either. Now entire conferences, organizations, college courses, websites, journals, books, readers, handbooks and even an encyclopedia are devoted to reducing the violence that breaks out between intimates (for examples, see Barnett, Miller-Perin, and Perin, 2005; Hines, 2005; Loseke, Gelles, and Cavanaugh, 2005; Payne and Gainey, 2005; Roberts, 2002, 2005; Roberts and Roberts, 2005; Sokoloff and Pratt, 2005; and Jackson, 2007).

Blaming Her for His Violent Outbursts

The battered women's self-help movement initially encountered resistance and opposition because of the widespread acceptance of victim-blaming arguments that portrayed beaten wives unsympathetically. Many people, including some counselors and family therapists, believed that a high proportion of beatings were unconsciously precipitated or even intentionally provoked. The wives who were said to be responsible for inciting their husbands' wrath were negatively stereotyped as "aggressive," "masculine," and "sexually frigid." Their husbands were characterized as "shy," "sexually ineffectual," "dependent and passive," and even as "mothers' boys". The dynamics of a pair's conflict were set into motion whenever a badgered husband tried to please and pacify his querulous and demanding wife. Eventually, her taunts and challenges would provoke an explosion, and he would lose self-control (see Snell, Rosenwald, and Robey, 1964; Faulk, 1977).

Victim blaming emphasized the wife's alleged shortcomings: her domineering nature, her coldness, and her secret masochistic cravings for suffering. It placed the entire burden of change on the woman—not the man, the community, or the culture that encouraged male dominance. Activists in the battered women's movement rejected this outlook because it failed to condemn the violence and implied that it was not a matter to be addressed by police departments and courts. The husband's main problem appeared to be his weakness rather than his resort to force to get his way (see Schechter, 1982; Beirne and Messerschmidt, 1991).

The battered women's movement succeeded in replacing this victim-blaming outlook with a victim-defending one. This husband-blaming/wife-defending point of view quickly gained adherents, as journalists depicted wife beating in ways surprisingly favorable to a feminist pro-victim perspective. Abusers generally were depicted in these media accounts as "super-macho" types who felt that following conventional sex-based roles gave them a right to discipline and control their wives and to beat back any challenges to their manly privileges. The targets of their wrath were pictured as stereotypically feminine women who believed that a wife's place was in the home and that she should be selflessly devoted to her husband, dependent upon him as a breadwinner, and deferential to his rightful authority.

Several progressive themes ran through most of the articles. One was that wife beating was a social problem afflicting millions and not just a personal trouble burdening only a few unfortunate women. Another was that the women did not deserve or provoke the abuse heaped upon them, and that the consequences were serious, even life-threatening. Many articles concluded that this crisis in a fundamental social institution, the family, should be of concern to everyone because domestic violence broke out at all levels of society, even if it was harder to detect in affluent families. Governmental action could bring it under control through social programs coupled with more vigorous criminal justice responses. Most articles identified the root causes as unjust gender relations, buttressed by an ideology that proclaimed that males were superior to females. Male supremacy was perpetuated by socialization practices that exhorted boys to be aggressive, tough, and powerful while teaching girls to be passive, submissive, and supportive, according to a content analysis of stories and reports appearing in widely read magazines during the 1970s and 1980s (Loseke, 1989).

Therapists working with victims and couples began to recognize a cycle of violence accompanied by learned helplessness, which they termed the **battered-woman syndrome**. Beatings often follow a pattern and escalate in frequency and intensity unless the couple receives help. Three phases make up a cycle that repeats itself periodically in their relationship: tension building; the violent explosion; and the tranquil, loving aftermath (Walker, 1984).

During the tension-building phase the aggressor hurls insults and even breaks objects while his docile target tries to appease him in a vain attempt to stave off a blow-up and preserve their relationship. She attempts to cope with her mate's bad behavior and conceals it from others, isolating herself from potential rescuers. When her sacrifices fail, the second stage of acute violence erupts. He goes on a rampage and savagely assaults her. Feeling trapped, she acts submissively as part of a defense mechanism to avoid his wrath. The injuries that he inflicts shock and confuse her. When he becomes fearful of driving her away, he begins to show shame and remorse, and the third stage—the reconciliation or "honeymoon" phase—commences. He apologizes, pledges it won't happen again, and acts tenderly. Still seeking marital bliss and unwilling to confront the seriousness of her plight, she blames herself for his loss of control and forgives him. Believing she can head off his next round of assaults, she becomes protective of him, covers up what happened, and decides not to seek outside help or try to leave him. An illusion of normalcy prevails for a while. But nothing has been resolved or corrected, and soon tensions rise and the cycle repeats itself. But his next round of attacks increases in ferocity. He expresses less contrition and she feels less confident about being able to defuse his anger. He ratchets up his efforts to dominate her life, and she finds herself more isolated, trapped, vulnerable, and endangered than before (Walker, 1984).

Estimates of the Incidence, Prevalence, and Seriousness of Spouse Abuse

"I never reported it. … I was intimidated, ashamed. I had nowhere to go. I had five children to raise. I was told that if I ever left, he would find me and kill me," said the police chief of a small rural department, who suffered broken bones, burns, and stab wounds in a series of beatings that began two weeks after she married. ("Police Chief …" 1993)

As the terms spouse abuse, wife beating, and woman battering became part of everyone's vocabulary, a number of questions arose; the most basic was: "How widespread is the problem?" The myth that few husbands beat their wives was hard to dispel because official statistics had no such breakdown under the general heading of assault. When the battered women's movement organized **speakouts**, where wives disclosed their situations to sympathetic audiences, these true confessions revealed that violence between lovers was all too common. But anecdotal evidence would not suffice to document the genuine dimensions of the problem. The maximalist perspective was that the visible victims were just the tip of the iceberg. Fierce fighting poisoned many outwardly loving relationships, and battering constituted a low-profile epidemic. However, a minimalist reaction arose to challenge maximalist assumptions. The opposing viewpoints sharply disagreed in part because of complexities surrounding efforts to estimate the seriousness of the problem.

The first and most basic methodological issue concerns which victim–offender relationships should be included and which excluded. Several terms with similar and overlapping but not identical meanings can cause confusion and create inconsistencies from one study to another. Choosing one definition over another can make the scope of the problem seem much larger or much smaller. Restricting attention to wife abuse (beatings of married females) will yield the lowest estimates. Measuring the frequency of spouse abuse (which includes male as well as female victims who are legally married) will lead to medium-size estimates. The highest estimates will be generated by counting all instances of intimate partner violence (IPV). The broadest term, it refers to all male- and female-initiated physical abuse in romantic relationships, including couples who are dating, living together, or legally separated, whether heterosexual or homosexual. Woman battering focuses on female victims, married or not. Hunting for statistics about

domestic disturbances (a police expression) only will turn up cases known to authorities, but involving any members of the same household, including grandparents and siblings, not just intimates. The phrase domestic violence refers to the largest grouping of all because it embraces physical fights, which may or may not be reported to the police, between parents, siblings, elders, children, unmarried lovers, and other relatives living under the same roof.

Additional fuel for the maximalist–minimalist debate arises from vague notions of which specific behaviors constitute abuse, violence, battering, or beatings. There are distinctions among these terms and different shades of meaning, connotations, and ambiguities that permit observers to draw very different conclusions. First of all, it must be noted that although verbal and emotional abuse (including intimidating and controlling behaviors motivated by extreme jealously, humiliating insults, name calling, and other forms of harassment) is psychologically harmful, it is not a criminal matter (but it can be grounds for divorce). Sexual abuse (withholding affection, refusing sexual relations, rejecting birth control devices) is also cruel but not criminal, whereas physically subjugating a partner to submit could be considered forcible rape.

Resorting to acts of interpersonal violence is clearly illegal, but complications abound when researchers try to measure its occurrence. For example, should credible threats about using force be counted? If **abuse** is recognized only when a person is physically injured and not just attacked, then very different estimates of the incidence rate can result. Because most physical assaults do not bring about visible injuries, partners may attack each other but not inflict tangible injuries sufficient to be labeled abuse. If physical injury is taken to be the defining criterion, then domestic violence is overwhelmingly a male-on-female crime. But if all kinds of attacks are counted, then females act aggressively against their male partners almost as often as males assault female lovers. Put succinctly, many men who are attacked by women are not wounded; assaults by males inflict injuries more often than assaults by females (Straus, 1991). Clearly,

the definition used by the researcher profoundly shapes the findings and the interpretation of these numbers.

Social workers, family therapists, feminists, psychologists, criminologists, victimologists, police officers, and prosecutors have tried but failed to reach a consensus about where to draw the line between inclusion and exclusion of actions labeled abusive, violent, or assaultive. Many people approve of, tolerate, or are resigned to some "normal" level of quarreling and fighting among partners in romantic relationships.

Although there is no standard definition, a good working definition would take into account the severity of the assault, the assailant's intentions, the actual physical injury inflicted, the depth of psychological trauma, and the nature of the threat. These behaviors can cover the gamut of specific acts of simple and aggravated physical assaults, including pushing, shoving, pulling, dragging, shaking, ripping clothing, hitting with an open hand, punching with a closed fist, choking, kicking, stomping, throwing an object, threatening with a weapon, and wounding with a weapon such as a knife or gun. The full continuum of physical injuries ranges from bruises and swellings, cuts and scratches, sprains, and burns to dizziness, loss of vision or hearing, fractures, concussions, and even more serious internal wounds. Emotional harm, on the other hand, is not so easily classified (see Loseke, 1989; Rhodes, 1992).

A related issue concerns whether minor violence constitutes criminal violence. Beating one's partner with a baseball bat surely is criminal violence; using a lesser object (stick, belt) is also criminal by most definitions; but what about punching with a closed fist, or slapping with an open hand? The lack of public consensus can be called **normative ambiguity** (Straus, 1991), and it reflects the distinction some would make between conflicts that occur within the family and fights between strangers. The cultural support that still exists for using force to settle family quarrels has important policy implications. If all physical attacks between spouses were criminalized—judged by the same standards (rules, expectations) as those used to recognize assaults between nonfamily members—many more angry outbursts between husbands and wives, if reported, would trigger arrests.

Reliable sources of data about the incidence and prevalence of intimate partner violence are difficult to find. For cases of child abuse, compulsory reporting laws have been passed in every state, and data-gathering clearinghouses have been established. But for partner abuse no comparable reporting and compiling systems yet exist. The FBI's *Uniform Crime Report (UCR)* is of little use because assaults between intimates are not recorded in a separate category from other assaults (until the transition to NIBRS is completed). The BJS's *National Crime Victimization Survey (NCVS)* attempts to measure disclosures by household members of assaults committed against them by partners. But it produces a serious undercount because most victims don't consider themselves to have been "unlawfully" harmed by an "offender" in the legal sense, unless they were seriously injured or the perpetrator was a former partner (after separation or divorce).

Researchers studying *NCVS* findings from 1978 to 1982 determined that only about half of all batterings were reported to police departments. (Of course, many incidents are not disclosed to the *NCVS* if the assailant is present when the injured party is interviewed.) The main reasons cited for informing the authorities were to end the attack, to keep it from happening again, and to get the offender in trouble so that he would be punished. The leading reasons for not calling for help were the women's beliefs that the incidents were private and personal matters, that the crime wasn't important enough, that the police wouldn't or couldn't assist them, and that they would be subject to reprisals if they dared to seek outside protection. *NCVS* data indicate that women who report being assaulted by a mate are likely to report being physically abused again when they are interviewed in later years. Police files confirm fears that the cycle of violence tends to escalate in frequency and severity over time (Langan and Innes, 1986).

Given the limitations of these two official sources of crime statistics, researchers have had to devise their own measurement scales and carry out

their own surveys or turn to fragmentary sources, such as records kept by hospital emergency rooms. However, using a biased source can strongly skew the results of a study. For example, findings based on files about women seeking treatment cannot be generalized (the **clinical fallacy**) because the sample is not representative of the entire population (Straus, 1991).

Maximalist Arguments   Despite these methodological problems, a number of statistical findings support the maximalist contention that domestic violence remains a deeply hidden but extremely serious problem.

- A consistent finding running through years of research is that women are much more likely to be harmed by an intimate than by a stranger. For most women, statistically speaking, the most dangerous places they frequent are their homes, and the most dangerous people they surround themselves with are family and friends (Bernstein and Kaufman, 2004; Schwartz, 2005).

- At least 6 million women were physically abused one or more times each year (using the criterion of even just one incident of minor violence, such as being slapped) during the mid-1980s. Using a more restrictive definition of serious assaults (being kicked, punched, choked, or attacked with a weapon), at least 1.8 million women were targets of severe male aggression annually. An average victim was assaulted six times during the year, according to projections from a 1985 national family violence survey (Straus, 1991). Although simple assaults are most common, about one-third of the violent outbursts described to *NCVS* interviewers would be classified by law as more serious felonies—aggravated assaults, rapes, and even robberies (Langan and Innes, 1986).

- More than 25 percent of all women will be physically assaulted and/or even forcibly raped by a current or former spouse, cohabiting partner, or date within their lifetimes. About 1.5 percent suffer these kinds of attacks by an intimate during the course of a single year, according to disclosures by respondents in a National Violence Against Women Survey (Tjaden and Thoennes, 2000). Projecting these findings to the whole population, up to 4 million women experienced a serious assault by an intimate partner each year as the 1990s drew to a close (Washington Crime News Service, 2003).

- About half of all incidents of battering are not reported to police departments, partly because of fear of reprisals and previous negative experiences with officers answering domestic disturbance calls. About one-third of all these nonreporting victims suffered more than one violent attack during the six months preceding their *NCVS* interview during the mid-1990s (Fleury et al., 1998; Greenfeld et al., 1998).

- About 1 million women each year seek medical attention for wounds inflicted by a male partner—husband, ex-husband, boyfriend, or former lover. Somewhere between 22 percent and 35 percent of visits by women to hospital emergency rooms are to treat injuries resulting from a partner's assault. Domestic violence poses the greatest threat of injury to women between the ages of 15 and 44, taking a greater toll than automobile accidents, robberies, and cancer combined (Gibbs, 1993b). Violence may be the source of an even greater proportion of injuries, but women tend to be reluctant to disclose to doctors that they were physically abused, and physicians often shy away from the subject ("Screening ... " 2006).

- A little more than one-tenth of all solved murders turn out to be committed by intimates. For female murder victims, that proportion is about 33 percent and has been rising since 1995. But for male murder victims, only about 3 percent were slain by intimates, and that figure has been falling (BJS, 2008b).

- For African-American women between the ages of 15 and 45, homicide by an intimate partner is the leading cause of death, and IPV is

the seventh most frequent cause of death for all women in the United States. Actually, as many as 40 percent to 50 percent of murdered females may have been killed by intimates (spouses, former husbands, current boyfriends, or ex-lovers). The complete death toll due to IPV is undercounted because definitions in the FBI's *Supplementary Homicide Report (SHR)* do not include ex-boyfriends, plus some deaths of homeless women and some suicides can be traced to IPV. In 70 percent to 80 percent of intimate partner homicides (of men and women), the man had physically abused the woman before one of them, usually the woman, died (Campbell et al., 2003).

- The total social costs of domestic violence—for health care (including mental health), social services (including aid to homeless women fleeing abusive relationships), lost productivity, and criminal justice outlays—add up to between $5 billion and $10 billion a year (Senate Committee on the Judiciary, 1993; Max et al., 2004). Domestic violence is a leading cause of female homelessness, according to a survey sponsored by the U.S. Conference of Mayors (Washington Crime News Service, 2003).

- Some violent men continue to beat their mates even when the women are pregnant. Between 6 percent and 8 percent of women queried in various studies conceded to interviewers that they were injured by their husbands or partners during their pregnancy. The prevalence rate of assaults during pregnancy is perhaps as low as 3 percent but may be as high as 21 percent, depending on the sample used in the study (Goldstein and Martin, 2004). Beatings that pregnant women receive cause more birth defects than all diseases for which children are immunized. The greatest risks are faced by young women who are poorly educated, not married, living in crowded households, and unable to get prenatal care (Hilts, 1994). For women of childbearing age, homicide by an intimate partner is the leading cause of death (Gibbs, 1993b).

- The rate of domestic violence in military families is much higher than it is among civilians. In 1990, physical fighting between spouses was estimated to affect 19 out of every 1,000 military families. That figure rose to 26 per 1,000 married couples in 1996 but declined to 14 per 1,000 in 2004—but that was still far above the estimated civilian rate of 3 per 1,000. The military concedes it has a "spousal aggression issue," as the Pentagon calls it, but points out that many soldiers are young and come from poverty-stricken families, and these two factors are correlated with high rates of reported domestic violence. However, the armed forces might actually have a more serious domestic violence problem than the figures indicate because the Department of Defense keeps records only of substantiated attacks against a current legal spouse living on a military base. Incidents that take place off-post might not be entered in the Pentagon's statistics, and assaults against ex-partners, live-in lovers, or dates do not count as "spousal aggression" (Schmitt, 1994; Houppert, 2005).

Minimalist Views   The minimalist position is that violence between intimates, while serious, is not the dire threat to women's physical and mental well-being as alarmists' calls to action make it seem.

- Even though young women face the highest risks, only about 20 of every 1,000 (1 in 50) females in their early 20s are victimized by an intimate in a year, according to the *NCVS* (Greenfeld et al., 1998).

- In 2001, current or former spouses or boyfriends were responsible for only about 20 percent of all nonfatal violent offenses inflicted upon women. Most of these attacks were only simple assaults (Rennison, 2003). Many minor assaults that are registered on surveys don't lead to physical injuries and should not be lumped in with aggravated assaults that inflict severe bodily harm. Some incidents that are counted in studies were just threats or attempted assaults that failed. Furthermore, some researchers use an expanded definition of abuse that includes vicious name-calling, which may cause psychological damage but not physical wounds. Finally, some of the fighting is initiated by women or can be considered acts of retaliation, so women are not automatically the passive recipients of aggression (see Straus, 1999).

- Intimate partner violence negatively affects the work victims perform for organizations via absenteeism, tardiness, and distraction, but productivity losses might not be as serious and direct as originally assumed (Reeves and O'Leary-Kelly, 2007).

As for trends, minimalists point out that domestic violence seems to be declining in frequency. In fact, the problem may have begun to subside shortly after it was rediscovered at the start of the 1970s.

- Researchers found in a 1975 survey that about four of every hundred couples admitted engaging in at least one serious outbreak of violence within the year. A decade later, however, researchers using the same definitions in interviews (this time with a larger representative sample of married and cohabiting couples) uncovered evidence that the rate had dropped to about three couples per hundred per year. Serious incidents were defined as those involving kicking, hitting with a fist, biting, and beating up, or using or threatening to use a gun or knife during a dispute. The overall incidence rate, which included less serious instances of slapping, shoving, pushing, and throwing things, was estimated to be about 16 percent of married and cohabiting couples per year. The prevalence rate was only 33 percent for one or more incidents involving any degree of violence during the entire marriage or cohabitation (Straus and Gelles, 1986).

- *NCVS* data also indicate that intimate partner violence against women is diminishing. About 1.1 million offenses were carried out in 1993, but by 2001 only about 600,000 such incidents were estimated to have taken place nationally, a drop of about 45 percent (Rennison, 2003). By 2005, simple as well as aggravated assaults against women by their intimate partners had declined further, by about 67 percent, compared to 1993 levels (BJS, 2008a).

- Deaths arising from IPV have been falling significantly since the late 1970s, according to the *UCR*'s *SHR* breakdowns (see Table 9.1 below). The diminishing risk of being killed by a lover has been especially pronounced for African-Americans, married people, and men. The number of men murdered by women they had been romantically involved with dropped a dramatic 75 percent from 1976 to 2005. The number of women slain by the men in their lives remained steady until 1993, but then it began to fall and reached a record low in 2004. Focusing on specific groups, over the three decades the number of black males killed by intimates dropped by 83 percent, white males by 61 percent, black females by 52 percent, and white females by 6 percent (BJS, 2008b). Because most homicides take place between married couples, the drop is due in part to a decline in marriage rates over the decades and enhanced selectivity among those who decide to wed, as well as a greater willingness for couples embroiled in bitter conflicts to divorce. Also, the improving economic situation of women, in terms of greater employment opportunities and rising incomes, enables more wives to leave abusive mates (Dugan et al., 2003).

Recognizing Warning Signs

Besides seeking answers to the question of how many, victimologists also wonder, "What kinds of families are wracked by these problems?" At first there were only media images and personal revelations (true confessions), but this kind of anecdotal evidence might be very unrepresentative and misleading. Atypical cases make the news, but what kinds of women are usually objects of their lovers' wrath?

The statistical profile of a couple in which the woman is at risk for a severe beating is as follows,

(the more factors that fit, the higher the risk): The family income is low. She is young, unemployed, poorly educated, and lives with but is not married to a man of a different religious or ethnic background. He is between the ages of 18 and 30, is unemployed or working in a blue-collar job, did not graduate from high school, beats his children, and abuses alcohol and illicit drugs. His parents were violent toward each other, and he grew up in a rough neighborhood. She suffers from anxiety and depression, low self-esteem, passivity, dependence, and an inordinate need for attention, affection, and approval. She lives in isolation from family and friends, and also may be especially vulnerable due to physical disabilities. He is impulsive, jealous, possessive, and verbally domineering. He too suffers from a low sense of self-worth and dreads rejection and abandonment. Her threats to move out to escape his clutches provoke fears that he is losing control of her (Ingrassia and Beck, 1994; Healy and Smith, 1998; "Domestic Abusers," 1999; and Tjaden and Thoennes, 2000).

The highest-risk groups for intimate partner violence, as identified by their disclosures on the *NCVS*, are women who are between the ages of 16 and 24, black, living in low-income households, and residing in urban areas (Greenfeld, Rand, and Craven, 1998).

Battered women may be in very grave danger of severe or fatal injuries if a number of these "red flags" are evident: He owns a gun, threatens to kill her, chokes or strangles her during fights, is exceedingly jealous and possessive, compels her to submit to sex, controls most of her daily activities, is a substance abuser and goes on drug-taking or drinking binges, disregards restraining orders and stalks her, and acts violently towards others as well. Social service agencies working with abused women often estimate their clients' level of risks by asking about these warning signs listed on a "danger assessment tool" (Campbell et al., 2003).

Researchers also have discovered that a substantial age discrepancy raises the risks that one spouse will kill the other. The chances of lethal violence are much higher if the man is at least 16 years older than the woman, or if the woman is at least 10 years older than the man, according to a study of intimate partner homicides that took place in Chicago from the mid-1960s to the mid-1990s (Breitman, Shackelford, and Block, 2004).

Aiding Victims Who Feel Trapped

Before women who are trapped in abusive relationships can be helped, they must begin to recognize that they genuinely are crime victims. They must reject the illusions that they can prevent or maintain control over future outbursts and that the beatings are their fault. They must stop minimizing the extent of the physical and emotional injuries their partner inflicts, and they must resist shifting the blame to his drinking problem or other external triggers. Also they must reverse their impulses to isolate themselves to hide their troubles and avoid embarrassment (Arriaga and Capezza, 2005).

A nagging question often asked is: "If he is so brutal, then why does she stay with him?" Until the 1970s, this complicated situation was dismissed with the victim-blaming rejoinder that being regularly beaten must somehow fulfill a pathological need of hers. For example, battered wives have been accused of being masochistic and of enjoying feeling miserable or of looking forward to the passionate lovemaking that supposedly follows when a repentant husband asks her for forgiveness (see Paglia, 1994).

Researchers have discovered a number of plausible reasons why women stay with their violent mates and repeatedly endure the cycle of battering/reconciliation/battering. Some feel dependent, dread being alone, and despair that they have nowhere to go and no one to turn to for aid and comfort. They are intimidated, even terrorized, and fear reprisals if they dare to try to escape their possessive and controlling husbands who are obsessed with a "You belong to me!" and "If I can't have you, no one can!" mentality. They worry about their children's welfare (psychological damage, loss of financial support, and custody and visitation issues). Some still love their tormentors and invoke higher loyalties (a commitment to the institution of marriage and to the vows they took "for better or worse, in good times and in bad").

Because of cultural and religious traditions, they are ashamed of the stigma of "abandoning" or "deserting" a husband and of a "failed marriage." Many believe they should stand by their men and try to help to cure them—attributing the whole "mess" to external causes such as alcoholism, unemployment, or stress at work. Finally, trying to escape from a batterer is a risky course of action. Some find themselves stalked and beaten more viciously when they try to break up or after they separate from their abusive partners (Frieze and Browne, 1991; Steinman, 1991; Barnett and LaViolette, 1993; Kirkwood, 1993; Hampton, Oliver, and Magarian, 2003).

From its inception, the highest priority of the battered women's movement has been to provide tangible aid at a time of great need. To offer immediate support to victims during a crisis, activists established **shelters** as places of refuge. In 1974, following the lead of feminists in England a few years earlier, a self-help group in St. Paul, Minnesota, transformed an old meetinghouse into the first of many women's shelters in the United States (Martin, 1976). These "safe houses" offer a number of services to their temporary residents. First and foremost, they provide short-term room and board in a secure setting for women, and often their children, who are in continuing physical danger. Most also furnish emergency clothing and transportation. By bonding together in self-help groups, the women can give one another emotional support when grappling with transitional issues, particularly about whether to try to sever or to salvage their relationships with abusers. Counselors discuss legal issues (such as pressing charges; obtaining court orders of protection; and navigating the complexities of separation, divorce, child custody, and alimony), educational matters (such as, for displaced homemakers, returning to school and retraining), and job hunting. Hotline staffers instruct victims where to go because the addresses of shelters are kept secret to protect the residents from being stalked. Through outreach activities, staff members raise public awareness about the needs for empowering these otherwise dependent women and for reforming the criminal justice and social service systems (Warrior, 1977; Neidig, 1984; Dutton-Douglas and Dionne, 1991; OJP, 1998).

Although the first safe houses were set up initially as independent self-help projects staffed by volunteers, many people quickly agreed that local governments had a responsibility to establish permanent shelters run by social service agencies. By 1987, about 1,200 battered women's shelters were operating across the country. By the end of the 1990s, about 1,900 shelters were operating around the nation ("Domestic Abusers," 1999). The first temporary shelter run by a police department opened in Virginia during 2000 (Ellis, 2000). Most were overcrowded, underfunded, and understaffed, according to the National Coalition Against Domestic Violence (Abrams, 1987). Victims who are turned away from overcrowded facilities or whose time runs out face the same limited choices that battered women confronted before there was a movement to shelter them: return home and face renewed attacks or seek temporary respite with friends, relatives, or parents.

As government-sponsored shelters spread during the 1980s, a backlash against them emerged. "Pro-family" organizations sought to limit local, state, and federal funding for shelters, and police referrals of victims to them. These critics contended that shelter workers tended to be home-wreckers who contributed to the breakup of marriages by encouraging battered wives to divorce abusive husbands (see Stone, 1984; Pleck, 1989). Actually, most women who took refuge in a shelter did return to live with their mates again, and many of them suffered additional beatings, according to limited follow-up studies by researchers attempting to assess the effectiveness of this method of intervention (Dutton-Douglas and Dionne, 1991). As might be anticipated, women who flee violent mates and seek refuge in government-sponsored shelters tend to be the poorest and most desperate. Two surveys of women seeking emergency housing estimated that they were suffering between 60 and 70 beatings per year, whereas the average victim endured 6 per year. They also differed from the "norm" in another way: These targets of routine beatings rarely dared to fight back (see Straus, 1991).

In recent years, service providers and scholars have begun to recognize the importance of being sensitive to racial, ethnic, and cultural differences in order to design effective outreach strategies, therapeutic intervention programs, and criminal justice policies (Bent-Goodley, 2005; Sokoloff and Pratt, 2005).

Battered Women and the Criminal Justice System: Violence Is Violence, or Is It?

A woman is beaten by her husband hundreds of times. She divorces him and then testifies against him in court. He is sent to prison and vows to get even with her some day. A note is placed in his file that she must be warned before he is released from custody. One day he is let out for a brief furlough, but she is not contacted. He catches her by surprise at home and murders her. (Pollitt, 1989)

Historically, battered women seeking help from the criminal justice system were regularly maltreated, discouraged, disappointed, and repeatedly injured as the authorities stood idly by because a double standard prevailed. Battering was treated as special (in a negative sense) by police departments, prosecutors, and courts. The assaults were not considered as real crimes because the violence was not carried out by strangers. The dominant noninterventionist ideology recommended that the long arm of the law shouldn't reach into the sanctuary of the home and intrude into private family squabbles between spouses unless the fighting approached life-threatening levels. Otherwise, battered women were urged to endure their lot and preserve their marriages by forgiving and forgetting.

The consciousness-raising efforts undertaken by activists in the battered women's movement have successfully convinced many people that a hands-off policy endangers wives who feel trapped in abusive relationships. Women in distress needed, and were entitled to, the Constitution's pledge of "equal protection under the law." The marriage license did not grant husbands a license to hit their wives. Fights between partners could have grave consequences when left to fester and smolder. Instead of fading away, the conflicts could escalate in intensity and lead to severe injuries—usually for the woman, less often for the tormentor (see Schechter, 1982).

Once the public as well as criminal justice officials became convinced that intervention was the proper course of action, a question arose: "What type of response would lead to the desired results—that the violent men would change their ways?" Three long-standing options were explored: separate the combatants, arrest the assailant, or refer the couple to marital counseling. Each choice had its possibilities and shortcomings. Battered women, their advocates, and victimologists are still divided over how best to respond to the problem: whether to pursue a legal course of action that depends on a quick resort to criminal justice solutions or to follow a social service approach that relies on counseling and reconciliation (see Sherman, 1986; Fagan, 1988; Gondolf, 1988; Ohlin and Tonry, 1989; Pleck, 1989; Buzawa and Buzawa, 1990; Roberts, 1990; Bouza, 1991; Bowman, 1992; Hilton, 1993; Klein et al., 1997; Healy and Smith, 1998; Jasinski and Williams, 1998; Malefyt et al., 1998; Maxwell, Garner, and Fagan, 2001; Sontag, 2002).

The preserve-the-family way of handling domestic violence was the favored approach during the 1950s and 1960s. It proposes that the objective of outside intervention should be to restore harmony to the marriage. That means salvaging the relationship, keeping the family intact, healing its wounds, and fostering its nurturing potentials. Couples locked in ongoing bitter conflicts need to see counselors who could mediate disputes and build on the underlying strengths of their relationship. Advocates of this therapeutic, nonadversarial, pro-reconciliation approach presume that many battered women are partly to blame for being the first to resort to force, or at least for provoking their husbands' ire. Such cases of shared responsibility are not well-handled by the courts with their emphasis on total guilt or complete innocence, conviction or acquittal, and victory or defeat. But seeking professional assistance is a long-term approach that seems promising only if a strong underlying bond persists, the women are not afraid to be candid during therapy sessions, and the aggressors are motivated and committed to voluntarily participating and to reforming their behaviors. Also, this reliance on social service agencies and mediation has been criticized for trivializing or condoning what might be serious criminal violence, for assuming shared responsibility, and for disregarding glaring inequalities in power relations between the two parties in their negotiations. Because their instability is deemed to be individual, personal, and peculiar, the approach downplays the seriousness and pervasiveness of wife beating as a social problem inextricably connected to family life, contemporary culture, and gender relations.

The rely-upon-the-legal-system approach has been in favor since the 1980s. It argues that "violence is violence," regardless of who the offender is and what his relationship with the target of his wrath might be. Criminalizing spouse abuse entails arresting the wrongdoer, and, if he is convicted, following up with a fine and/or a jail term, coupled with compulsory treatment in a batterers' anger management therapy group during a period of probation. The approach rests on these tenets: Separate the parties, rescue and protect the injured, and punish but also rehabilitate the aggressor. The philosophical underpinnings of the legalistic approach are that the state has a responsibility to enforce public morality as codified in law, and that the government has a duty to intervene when vulnerable individuals are in danger and they reach out to the authorities for help. Adherents of this approach fault the criminal justice system for not taking violence between intimates as seriously as violence between strangers. Too often assailants are not arrested; or if the police take them into custody, charges are not filed or are later dropped; or if prosecutors achieve convictions, judges impose very lenient sentences.

Proponents of the legalistic approach advocate reliance on the civil remedy of an **order of protection** (also called a **restraining order**) backed by criminal penalties to discourage a batterer from harassing, stalking, and striking again until he has undergone a cure or accepted separation and divorce. Arresting the aggressor might serve as a deterrent to further abuse, provided that the man learns the intended lesson from a night in a police holding cell and a day in court. But it is considered a risky strategy that could turn out to be counterproductive. When he returns home infuriated, he might escalate the ferocity of his attacks against his partner who, he feels, has gotten him in trouble. Prosecution could be a waste of precious resources and court time, especially if the woman changes her mind about pressing charges, forgives her mate, and bails him out of jail. Incarceration can be self-defeating because locking up the breadwinner means he cannot provide a steady income for his economically dependent wife and children. Just temporarily separating the two parties might not have any lasting impact. If officers summoned by the neighbors or by the victim simply demand of the aggressor that he leave the premises and not return until he has calmed down, nothing much might come out of this brush with the law. Only if the man was acting out of character (perhaps due to unusual disinhibition from heavy drinking) would a brief cooling-off period resolve matters (see Davies, Lyon, and Catania, 1998).

Traditionally, strategies intended to address the problem of domestic violence have been focused on ways of helping females recognize warning signs that they are becoming involved with violence-prone males, aiding them to disengage from existing relationships with abusers, and devising means of physically protecting them. New criminal justice policies aimed at abusers signal a social commitment to take the problem more seriously and to try to break the cycle that perpetuates the use of violence within families from parents who are negative role models to their imitative children. But criminal justice strategies that rely on arresting abusers and compelling them to surrender their firearms and enter into treatment often are ineffective because of a lack of coordination, close supervision, vigorous enforcement, and follow-through by service providers, police forces, prosecutors' offices, judges, probation departments, and parole authorities (Kennedy, 2004).

The Police Response Police officers always have found breaking up fights between husbands and wives to be an unpleasant, thankless, and dangerous assignment. In the past, departmental policies governing domestic disturbances stressed preserving the peace. The preferred course of action for officers who responded to calls about lovers' quarrels was to pressure the participants to call a halt and then "kiss and make up." If that failed, the officer might have insisted that the enraged man vacate the premises until he regained his composure. If the household was known to have been the site of a ruckus in the past, the couple might have been referred to counseling. Officers routinely failed to advise victims of their rights to file complaints because they identified with their male counterparts and assumed that the females either provoked the fights or subconsciously enjoyed the beatings. Only as a last resort—if the women's injuries were so severe as to require surgical sutures (the "stitch rule")—would officers make an arrest (Rhode, 1989).

A field experiment conducted in Minneapolis, Minnesota, during the early 1980s aimed to find out which course of action produced the lowest recidivism rate. Officers followed a randomly selected option—either compel the batterer to take a walk and cool off, refer the couple to counseling, or arrest the aggressor—before they rang the doorbell (unless they discovered clear evidence of a felonious assault). For the next six months, researchers surveyed the victims by telephone about any further fighting and monitored that address for additional domestic disturbance calls. The social experiment's findings indicated that arrested offenders were about half as likely to assault their partners again (13 percent did during the follow-up period) as those men who only were forced to leave their homes to cool off (26 percent of them were recidivists). Those couples who were referred to counseling suffered a relapse rate in-between these two extremes (18 percent had another violent fight). These results led the researchers to conclude that police departments should adopt a "presumption of arrest" policy unless good reasons convinced the officers at the scene that taking the assailant into custody would be counterproductive (Sherman and Berk, 1984).

As the findings of this social experiment became widely publicized, many police departments shifted away from their past practice of selective enforcement based on the officers' exercise of discretion toward an officially announced policy of full enforcement without discretion. They issued mandatory, or **pro-arrest**, **directives**, even though the researchers had recommended a presumptive or preference-for-arrest stance. Furthermore, the same lower recidivism rate for arrested men did not materialize when the experiment was replicated in other cities (as it must be in social science to establish **external validity**, which means that the findings can be generalized with confidence to other situations). In fact, the results from five replication sites suggested that arresting certain men (who were poor, unemployed, and without much of a stake in conforming to societal standards) may cause them to behave worse toward their mates in the future. Only batterers who were employed, well educated, and married to their partners (not just living together) seemed to be shaken and deterred by being arrested (see Sherman, Berk, and Smith, 1992; Berk et al., 1992).

The widespread adoption of pro-arrest policies required retraining officers and a change in state laws. Police officers are empowered to make a probable cause warrantless arrest for a domestic violence misdemeanor not committed in their presence only if: there are visible signs of injury, a dangerous weapon was involved, the officers believe the violence will continue after they depart, the police have prior knowledge of the offender's predilection for violence, or an order of protection was violated (Bouza, 1991).

In many states, officers must write a complete report, transport wounded people to a nearby hospital, supervise the eviction of abusers from their strife-torn homes, and inform the injured parties of their legal rights by reading or presenting a written list. In most places, the victim does not have to be married to the offender to receive these forms of protection (Hendricks, 1992). Some police departments have appointed special domestic violence prevention officers who are responsible for assisting victims with safety planning in general, and in particular increasing their security in the vicinity of their homes and workplaces.

Although the law is now supposed to be on the side of battered women, in some jurisdictions glaring problems might remain. Evaluations of actual practices showed that the local police often were not arresting the men accused of violence (Bouza, 1991; Steinman, 1991; Ferraro, 1992; Miller, 1992; Senate Committee on the Judiciary, 1993).

The Prosecutorial Response After deciding whether to call the police, the next dilemma a battered woman faces concerns prosecution: Should she keep up the pressure and get him into further trouble, thereby jeopardizing the relationship? Or should she withdraw her complaint and permit her violent mate to come home?

Historically, prosecutors have discouraged women from pressing charges because they are concerned about their office's conviction rates and don't want to pursue cases that are likely to fall apart. Also, they have traditionally viewed domestic violence cases as private matters that don't merit expenditures from their tight budgets. Lovers' quarrels ought to be diverted into mediation, assuming that both parties share responsibility for these ugly disputes and want to salvage their relationship.

In many jurisdictions, most domestic violence cases are dismissed. Of the remainder, most are negotiated down to lesser offenses, and these convictions usually result in a sentence of probation, perhaps coupled with mandatory participation in an anger management or aggression control program. In other jurisdictions where spouse abuse is handled more seriously, prosecutors have simplified procedures for filing complaints, set up special units staffed with trained assistant district attorneys, provided supportive victim–witness assistance programs and advocates, and devised more sentencing options. The goal is to better deal with "flip-flopping" victims whose frantic 911 calls about a drunken abuser on a Friday night give way to a Monday morning's reconsideration about the batterer as a breadwinner (Hubbard, 2006).

A woman might bail out the man the police arrested because she fears punishing her mate would be counterproductive, resulting in further harm to her and their children in the long run. Also, she may fear his fury when he is ultimately released, or she may prefer that he receive treatment at a social program rather than punishment from the criminal justice system. The following example of a murder/suicide illustrates the gravity of this decision:

> A single mother unwittingly seals her fate by bailing out her abusive boyfriend who is in jail for violating an order of protection. After the freed prisoner argues with his parents over the phone, he goes on a rampage. When he barges into their apartment, she tries to flee in their car with her four-year-old daughter in tow. But as she puts the key into the ignition, he shoots her in the face. Then while her daughter screams, he fires a bullet into his own head. (Livingston and Fagen, 2007)

Because many women change their minds about pressing charges or are manipulated or intimidated by their violent mates to drop the charges, prosecutors in some jurisdictions have established procedures to go forward without the complainant's testimony by relying on evidence such as 911 tapes of calls for help, eyewitness accounts, hospital reports, and incriminating statements by the defendants. Certain jurisdictions adopting this **no-drop** approach (also referred to as victimless prosecutions) have gone as far as mandating cooperation and threatening complainants with contempt-of-court proceedings if they set the legal machinery into motion and then decide they don't want to follow through and testify. However, the absence of the accuser in court usually results in dropped charges, dismissed cases, or acquittals (Bouza, 1991; Cahn and Lerman, 1991; Ferraro, 1992; Davis and Smith, 1994; Ford, 2003).

The Judicial Response   The final set of obstacles facing victims arises from their attempts to get the courts to act in their best interests. Judges seeking to dispose of cases and clear their calendars are reluctant to clog up their courtrooms with long and drawn-out spouse abuse cases. But judges can take several steps to assist those who were hurt: accede to their wishes that bail either be made low, kept high, or revoked if reprisals occur; speed up case processing by avoiding continuances; and issue orders of protection or restraining orders, which are intended to shield injured parties from further attacks. These court orders are supposed to grant immediate relief by enjoining abusers from entering the battered women's sphere of activity. A judge's order can evict and bar an assailant from their shared residence; prohibit contacts, threats, harassment, or stalking; limit supervised child visitation rights; require him to pay child support; and compel him to enter treatment. In the interest of the complainant's immediate safety, a temporary order of protection can be handed down in the defendant's absence if there is insufficient time to grant notice and hold a hearing. (After a proceeding where both parties have an opportunity to present their versions of events, the temporary order might be extended for up to a year.)

Because the orders are issued in civil court, the aim is separation of the disputants and not punishment. The standard of proof is a preponderance of the evidence, not guilt beyond a reasonable doubt. Violating a court order of protection can be a civil or criminal offense that subjects the trespasser to immediate arrest. However, criminal justice officials and advocates for battered women have serious doubts whether orders of protection currently are, or can ever be, truly effective. In theory, stay-away orders straddle the middle ground between inaction (no arrest, dropped charges) and overreaction (incarceration that results in escalating tensions, a criminal record, diminished job opportunities, and reduced financial support for the family).

In practice, the greatest problem is that civil orders are not vigorously enforced by many police departments, especially in high-crime urban areas (Finn, 1991; Ferraro, 1992; Buzawa and Buzawa, 1996). A restraining order is often disparaged by critics as nothing more than a piece of paper that can not guarantee security. However, the overwhelming majority of women who had received a temporary or permanent order of protection reported that they felt better about themselves and felt safer. After obtaining the order, they also were less likely to have experienced unwanted contact from the abuser and less likely to have suffered injuries, according to a survey conducted in the mid-1990s (Keilitz et al., 1997; Heisler, 2004).

To facilitate the application process, domestic violence protective order packets are provided to battered women, victim advocates, prosecutors' offices, and private attorneys, and are online at various websites, too. The simple instructions in the kits are written in a number of languages (Lippincott, 2006). The stay-away stipulation of restraining orders is enforced using cell phones, electronic ankle bracelets, and alarm systems in some jurisdictions (Herszenhorn, 1999). The Violence Against Women Act, passed in 1994 and renewed in 2000, requires that every state fully recognize and enforce protective orders issued in a different state.

About 300 specialized domestic violence courts have been set up in 23 states since the 1990s to encourage battered women to call the police, file complaints, press charges, testify as witnesses for the state, seek orders of protection, and see cases through to completion. Judges in these integrated services courts preside over domestic violence cases exclusively and are authorized to allow cases to go forward using 911 calls and police reports in place of the testimony of reluctant victims. Civil libertarians and defense attorneys are concerned that in proceedings involving these forms of hearsay evidence, the defendant is not permitted to ask questions of the accuser, in apparent violation of the Sixth Amendment's confrontation clause. Dismissal rates reportedly have fallen, and conviction rates have risen due to increased guilty pleas from batterers, who are often compelled to enter anger management programs as a condition of probation. Every complainant is assigned an advocate in these experimental specialized courts, so that more victims will have faith in the effectiveness of the criminal justice system (Gettleman, 2005b).

The Legislative Response: Over the decades since the "silent crisis" was rediscovered, lawmakers at federal, state, county, and municipal levels have passed numerous statutes that provide special solutions to the unique problems faced by victims of domestic violence. For example, during custody battles in family court, husbands accused of abuse claim that their former wives poison the minds of their children against their fathers. The use of this argument, known as "parental alienation syndrome," has been restricted by law in custody cases in several states (Childress, 2006).

Also, in many states, a person—even a law enforcement officer—restrained by a domestic violence court order is prohibited from possessing a firearm while the order is in effect (Heisler, 2004). Civil orders of protection are no longer restricted to victims who are legally married or who have a child in common with their abuser. These stay-away orders are now available in some places for unmarried couples involved in domestic partnerships, whether heterosexual and homosexual. When abusers are locked up, the targets of their wrath are entitled to be kept posted about their whereabouts within the correctional system and to get advance notice if their assailants are about to be released from custody (on bail, from jail, or on probation). Another new regulation stipulates that landlords cannot penalize a battered woman who breaks her lease before the rental arrangement expires if she must quickly move away to a new address unknown to the abuser.

THE REDISCOVERY OF BATTERED HUSBANDS

The attention paid to wife beating led inevitably to the rediscovery of husband beating. Starting in the late 1970s, several social scientists began to challenge the stereotype that men virtually always were the initiators and the victors in lovers' quarrels. They reported that their data on family violence had uncovered an overlooked problem—husband battering. Survey findings revealed that there was some truth to the old cartoon images of women slapping men's faces, or wives chasing husbands with rolling pins or throwing dishes at them.

Some studies indicated that women attacked the men in their lives (by slapping, kicking, biting, punching, throwing something, or threatening with a weapon) about as often as men assaulted women they professed to love (see Steinmetz, 1978a; Straus and Gelles, 1986; Mignon, 1998; Straus, 1999). Researchers referred to the possibility that women were the offenders in intimate partner abuse about as often as men as gender symmetry (see Belknap and Melton, 2005). But that contention set off a debate. Skeptics argued that the full story or entire sequence of events, and the social context surrounding the history of violence in tumultuous relationships, was not recorded in these surveys and studies. Much of the self-reported violence acknowledged by these women was probably unleashed in response to male provocations or carried out in self-defense, and did not qualify as aggressive initiatives. Because men tend to be bigger and stronger than women, their use of physical force is far more likely to be intimidating and injurious.

Perhaps for every battered woman there exists an abused man when it comes to minor uses of force (pushing and shoving). But many of these female perpetrators were previously victims. And the overwhelming majority of instances of severe aggression in which someone winds up in an emergency room are male-on-female offenses. Therefore, husband abuse should not be mistakenly equated with wife abuse, and a recognition that men can be injured too should not be used to undercut the urgency of tackling the much more pressing issue of women battering (see Pleck et al., 1978; Lewin, 1992; Cose, 1994; and Belknap and Melton, 2005).

As a result of gender-neutral mandatory arrest policies targeting the "primary physical aggressor," women make up one quarter or more of all arrestees for domestic violence in some jurisdictions (see Goldberg, 1999; Young, 1999). Yet when women perpetrate violence that goes beyond self-defense, their resort to physical force usually is a means of releasing pent-up anger and resentment, and constitutes an act of retaliation to avenge past abuse (Langhinrichsen-Rohling, 2005). Women don't use physical methods to control or intimidate their partners, as men try to do. But pro-arrest policies hurt the same individuals the criminal justice system is supposed to protect. Mistakenly condemned as aggressors, some women are compelled to attend batterer-intervention programs originally designed to rehabilitate violent men. This is an unintended consequence of relying too heavily on arrest and prosecution as a means of quelling intimate partner violence. The superficial gender neutrality of the criminal justice process actually leads to "gendered injustices" when women who really are not belligerent are treated the same way as violence-prone men (Miller, 2005).

Genuinely innocent battered men face several unique problems. First of all, most are reluctant to report their plight to the authorities. If they call the police, they face either disbelief or mockery and scorn. The disbelief can cause officers to act on the basis of negative stereotypes, presume these males actually were the initiators, and arrest them. They face ridicule for not being able to "control" their mates (unless the battered men are elderly or physically infirm). Because males traditionally are supposed to be physically adept and to "take charge of situations," for battered husbands to publicly admit their wives won the family fights is to confess that they are not living up to "manly" standards. Their failure to measure up to the prescription to be the "head of the household" might add to their confusion and distress. This special stigma might inhibit them from seeking help and can only contribute to their sense of isolation.

Second, if they overcome their feelings of inadequacy, self-loathing, and shame, and dare to come forward, they do not have access to the same resources now available to battered women, especially support groups, professional counseling, and temporary shelters. The first sanctuary for battered men was established in 1993 in St. Paul, Minnesota, where the first women's shelter had been set up more than 20 years earlier. It housed at least 50 men in its first six months. In most cases, however, battered husbands have one crucial advantage over battered wives: Their ability to support themselves financially encourages many of them to leave their troubled relationship. Furthermore, when they separate, they are rarely stalked, brought back, and beaten again (Chavez, 1992; Lewin, 1992; Cose, 1994; Straus, 1999).

Some battered men perish from their wounds. When that happens, the slaying often touches off an intense debate over whether the dead man provoked his own demise. Victim-blamers often become victim-defenders, and vice versa, when the fatally injured party is a man.

VICTIM PROVOCATION AND MURDER: WHEN IS THE SLAYING OF A WIFE BEATER JUSTIFIED?

A sergeant in a crime scene unit, known as a "nice guy" and "family man" who coached Little League and was active in his church, retires from the police department after 20 years of service. Neighbors and friends are stunned when his wife, a secretary, shoots him 11 times with his own guns in their home. Although police records do not show any history of domestic disturbances at their address, she says she tried many times to get help through friends and via a hotline. She claims she suffered "horrible abuse" for 18 years, and that he threatened to kill their children and her parents. Viewing that situation as "very dangerous," and fearing for her own life, she took drastic measures. She feels "relieved yet remorseful" at the tragic and terrible outcome, her lawyer says, after she is arrested for murder. (O'Shaughnessy, 2008)

***

A woman is raped on her way home from work. Twenty years later she marries a wealthy widower, but soon discovers he served two years in prison for murdering his first wife. For 10 years, this jealous, possessive man controls her every movement, beats her, makes unreasonable sexual demands, and mocks her

lingering rape trauma by repeatedly sneaking up from behind and grabbing her. One day he threatens to do to her what he did to his first wife. When he falls asleep, she shoots him in the head. She is convicted of second-degree murder and sentenced to five years in prison. But with a new lawyer, she appeals, is granted a second trial, and presents a defense of extreme psychological impairment. After the jury becomes deadlocked, she pleads guilty to manslaughter and the judge sentences her to probation. (Abramson, 1994)

At first it seems hard to fathom: A significant part of the victims' rights movement is deeply concerned about the plight of "murderers." The movement has raised money to pay the fees of defense attorneys, packed courtrooms to demonstrate solidarity with the accused, and held rallies outside prison gates demanding new trials, parole, pardons, or clemency for some of the killers within (Schechter, 1982; Johann and Osanka, 1989; Gross, 1992). This strange twist of events can be easily explained: The specific cases that cause grave concerns for these otherwise pro-victim activists involve battered women who slay their violent mates.

From the standpoint of the law, the dead man is the victim, and the woman who took his life is the offender. But from the perspective of groups advancing the interests of battered women, the official designations of offender and victim are misleading. The people behind bars are not really criminals and don't deserve confinement. The mortally wounded husbands are not bona fide victims but actually are dead aggressors. The battered women who ended these vicious men's lives are not the wrongdoers but the genuine victims.

Victim-blaming and victim-defending viewpoints lead to opposite conclusions regarding the tragic ends of these tortured love affairs. In such cases, victim defending means siding with the dead man and arguing that his provocations, outrageous as they might have been, were not sufficient to justify the woman's overreaction, and that what she did cannot be condoned. Victim defending leads to offender blaming: She must be punished for the terrible crime she committed. Conversely, blaming the deceased male means excusing and justifying the actions of the female survivor: He incited her to slay him.

Intimate Partner Homicides:
A Closer Look

Wives might kill their husbands for many reasons; to put an end to physical abuse is just one possibility. Similarly, men may have various motives for slaying their wives. Table 9.1 presents the yearly death toll for all murders between "lovers"— whether out of fury, revenge, jealousy, or financial gain—compiled from SHRs submitted to the *UCR* by police departments nationwide. (Each year, in more than one-third of all murders, homicide detectives could not determine a motive or the relationship between the victim and the offender, so this listing of body counts are minimal estimates.) It is not known how many homicides fall into the pattern of battered women slaying their violent mates, but intimate partner killings must be put into perspective. When it comes to lethal disputes between lovers, male-on-female violence remains the much more serious problem: Many more husbands and boyfriends kill their wives and girlfriends than the other way around, regardless of the specific motives.

During the 1990s and the early 2000s, the ratio of female deaths to male deaths widened from two-to-one to more than three-and-one half to one. For example, during 2006, detectives determined that 567 wives were murdered by their husbands, and 450 girlfriends by their boyfriends (for a total female death toll of 1,017), while only 123 husbands were slain by their wives and 150 boyfriends by their girlfriends (adding up to a male body count of 273, yielding a ratio of 3.7 female deaths for every one male death). Considering that it is estimated that millions of women are beaten each year by the men who profess to love them, only a tiny portion of these battered women are slain, and an even smaller proportion (far less than 0.1 percent annually) react by killing their abusive mates.

One positive trend shown in Table 9.1 is that the number of cases of lethal violence between intimates subsided impressively during the 1990s. However, killings of females by male intimates inched back up during the first six years of the new century. Murders by females of the males they once loved generally have been dropping steadily since the early 1980s. Although the body count has leveled off in recent years, the death toll of men killed by the women they were romantically involved with dipped to a record low in 2006.

Similar to the extensive investigations that take place after airplane crashes, in more than half of all states fatality review boards conduct post mortems to determine what went wrong and what could have been done differently to prevent sexual relationships from turning deadly. The fatality review team delves into the way the criminal justice system and social service agencies responded to the first signs of trouble, if any, and how early intervention efforts could have been more effective in protecting the victim (Websdale, 2003).

Arguments Stressing That the Brutal Man Did Not Deserve to Die

Victim-defending arguments on behalf of the dead man are put forward most directly by the detective who arrests the battered woman and by the prosecutor who presses charges against her. Their reasoning goes as follows: His fits of temper and violent outbursts were wrong, even criminal in nature, but so was her escalation of the level of conflict. She went too far, using criminal violence to halt criminal violence. She did not explore and exhaust all other options open to her before she chose to resort to deadly force. In particular, she should have fled their home, escaped his clutches, and dissolved their relationship. The battered woman did not fulfill her legal duty to retreat (and flee) but instead stood her ground and engaged in mutual combat. Cases in which brutal men were shot while asleep or unconscious from too much drinking were clearly acts of vengeance, motivated more by fury than fear. Such actions in retaliation for alleged wrongs cannot be stretched to fit an expanded definition of

TABLE 9.1   Murders by Intimates, 1977–2006

Year	Wives Killed by Husbands and Girlfriends Killed by Boyfriends	Husbands Killed by Wives and Boyfriends Killed by Girlfriends	Ratio of Female to Male Victims
1977	1,396	1,185	1.2 to 1
1978	1,428	1,095	1.3
1979	1,438	1,137	1.3
1980	1,498	1,129	1.3
1981	1,486	1,149	1.3
1982	1,408	1,008	1.4
1983	1,487	1,043	1.4
1984	1,420	897	1.6
1985	1,480	835	1.8
1986	1,525	866	1.8
1987	1,508	824	1.8
1988	1,592	765	2.1
1989	1,441	817	1.8
1990	1,524	797	1.9
1991	1,528	714	2.1
1992	1,510	657	2.3
1993	1,531	591	2.6
1994	1,348	574	2.3
1995	1,214	458	2.7
1996	1,103	369	3.0
1997	1,109	339	3.0
1998	1,078	372	2.9
1999	974	300	3.2
2000	1,015	315	3.2
2001	1,034	295	3.5
2002	1,045	287	3.6
2003	1,037	283	3.7
2004	1,034	295	3.5
2005	1,055	287	3.7
2006	1,017	273	3.7

NOTE: Relationships were often left blank by police departments on the SHRs.
SOURCES: Zavitz, 1994; FBI's *UCRs*, 1994–2006.

self-defense predicated upon standards of a reasonable response to an imminent threat. In the final confrontation that ended their stormy relationship, the battered woman retaliated in kind, getting even with her husband for past abuses. She struck back to settle old scores and to punish her husband for tormenting her. Such attempts by a woman to be the judge, jury, and executioner of an abusive husband, by "taking the law into her own hands" to deliver a dose of "vigilante justice" cannot be permitted. His death must not go unpunished, and she must not get away with murder (see Rittenmeyer, 1981; Dershowitz, 1988).

Victim defending asserts that the truth about their relationship will never be known. The dead man's side of the story cannot be told, and the woman's version of the events stands largely unchallenged. Her account of what happened between them over the years is self-serving: He is depicted as uncontrollably, irrationally, chronically, and savagely violent. In her view, the couple's problems were entirely his fault. This impression is reinforced by her use of the terms *batterer, initiator,* and *aggressor* to describe him, and *target, object,* and *victim* to refer to herself. The explanations of the survivor unrealistically place the burden of responsibility solely on the deceased party (see Neidig, 1984).

Victim defending concludes with several observations. First of all, courtroom testimony should focus on the woman who did the killing. The dead husband whose reputation is being vilified is not on trial and cannot counter the negative portrait she is painting. Second, there must be better ways for a decent society to express its outrage at the brutality some wives are forced to endure than to symbolically condone revenge killings and excuse lethal preemptive strikes. Not prosecuting wrongdoers, or acquitting defendants who clearly broke laws to retaliate for past beatings, or granting clemency to convicts only encourages others to pursue these same drastic courses of action (see Caplan, 1991; Bannister, 1992; Frum, 1993; Gibbs, 1993b).

Arguments Emphasizing That the Brutal Man Provoked the Lethal Response

Victim-blaming arguments proceed from the premise that the husband was responsible for his own demise. The wife who emerged as the victor was reluctant to fight at the outset. In his final moments, however, the husband became a casualty because he incited his law-abiding mate through inflammatory insults, challenges, threats, gestures, and physical assaults that no longer could be ignored, endured, or evaded. Under attack and facing serious bodily harm, the wife repelled his aggression with self-protective measures. The husband expired as a result of an act of self-defense and not revenge. In these incidents, the party that should be faulted is the dead man who was the loser in a battle he started. He drove her to kill him in order to save her own life at a point when he was on the verge of murdering her. In a sense, the man got what he deserved by setting up a life-and-death struggle from which the woman could extricate herself only by resorting to lethal force. The killing should be classified by the police and prosecutor as a justifiable homicide and not a murder. He is not a genuine victim but an offender who died during his final assault.

Victim blaming asserts that these slain husbands are different from other married men and that their extreme attitudes and behaviors are the causes of their demise. If they had changed their ways when they had a chance, they never would have met such a fate. Specifically, the men who provoke their spouses to slay them are more abusive than the typical batterer. They attack their partners more often and more viciously and are more likely to carry out sexual assaults (that today are recognized by law as marital rapes). They tend to drink more heavily and to use illicit drugs more frequently than other batterers. Also, they are more inclined to threaten to kill their wives and to drive them to harbor suicidal fantasies and self-destructive impulses, according to an analysis of 41 cases (Browne, 1987).

In a study of 100 battered women who killed their violent mates compared to 100 who didn't, those who struck back were more isolated socially and economically. They had suffered more severe beatings, their children were more likely to have been physically abused, and their partners were heavier drinkers and drug takers (Ewing, 1987). Additional recent studies confirm that compared to other battered women, abused women who kill their tormentors have suffered more severe attacks; have experienced an escalation in the level of violence; felt trapped because they had fewer resources to be independent, in terms of education and employment; were involved in more traditional relationships (legally married, together for many years, raised children); and had turned to the police for help after assaults (Block, 2003).

In courtroom proceedings as well as in everyday discussions, the question often arises, "Why didn't she leave him before that terrible fatal showdown took place?" As discussed above, victimologists have documented how battered women who want to escape abusive relationships confront many obstacles. Some of these barriers arise from specific personal limitations (such as unrealistic fears or dreams), and others stem from the shortcomings of criminal justice operations (such as ineffective enforcement of restraining orders) or from larger social problems (for example, unequal pay for equal work, and high costs of child care and housing).

Husband-blaming arguments point out that for many battered wives, escape was not a realistic option, or they tried to leave but failed. The question presupposes that fleeing her home would put an end to the dangers she faced. But in many cases the possessive husband would not tolerate her departure. Although she felt she could no longer live with him, he felt he couldn't let her live with someone else. He became infuriated by what he perceived to be rejection, abandonment, or desertion. With that mind-set, he was likely to stalk his wife, track her down if she was hiding, and use force to bring her back. As a result, the battered woman actually was held captive, trapped in a no-win situation she couldn't end.

Practical considerations might also have deterred her from trying to escape. Abruptly severing an intimate relationship is difficult when a couple has children, property in common, and intertwined families, friends, daily routines, and jobs. A woman who separates from an abusive mate with a good job may lose custody of her children (Catania, 2005). Shelters for battered women are few and far between, filled to capacity and with waiting lists and time limitations, and are just temporary havens at best. The woman may feel terrified at the thought of having to live on the run like a fugitive and of uprooting her children, and might be outraged at the "solution" of abandoning her home to the guilty party. Furthermore, she may know of women who are separated or even divorced but still get beaten by their former husbands (Browne, 1987; Mechanic and Uhlmansiek, 2000).

An understanding of the battered-woman syndrome helps to explain why some women seem stuck in destructive relationships. The assaults inflict a type of posttraumatic stress disorder of learned helplessness that undermines her self-esteem and sense of control. Gripped by fear, with beatings following a predictable pattern, the woman can believe she is in constant danger even when the man is not on the offensive (Walker, 1984). As a result, the demoralized and terrorized woman might choose to fight back at a moment when he is not acting in a threatening manner. This can explain why she might seize the element of surprise and strike with whatever weapon is at hand when he is distracted, asleep, or has passed out from drinking or drug taking.

The battered-woman syndrome is becoming recognized as a legitimate defense in court proceedings. Presenting this cycle of tension, conflict, and temporary reconciliation as an explanation of her reactions is explicitly permitted by laws passed in nine states and by Congress and is admissible subject to the judge's discretion elsewhere. Expert testimony during a trial about the cumulative psychological consequences of periodic beatings can help to explain why a woman killed a violent mate who was not advancing menacingly at the time of his death (Kristal, 1991; Sargeant, 1991; Gibbs, 1993b; Stevens, 1999; Schneider, 2000).

Legal Questions If the battered woman is believed by authorities to have acted in self-defense in a kill-or-be-killed showdown, then no charges will be pressed against her. However, if she appears to have shot or stabbed him after deliberation or premeditation at a time when she was not in imminent danger, then she can be indicted for first-degree murder. If there was no evidence of advance planning, but she did act with malicious intent at the crucial moment, then she may be indicted for the lesser crime of second-degree murder. If the prosecution believes that the dead man's provocations caused her to kill him in a spontaneous fit of rage or in sheer terror, then she could face the less serious charge of voluntary manslaughter. If the death of the man appears to be merely the outgrowth of her reckless disregard for his well-being, then the charge will probably be involuntary manslaughter, which carries the lowest penalty, perhaps just probation (Austern, 1987; Bannister, 1992).

The possible outcomes in these cases range from no arrest, to no indictment, to an acquittal by a jury of all charges, to conviction for murder or manslaughter and a lengthy term of imprisonment. Usually, the case is resolved when the woman's lawyer strikes a deal with the prosecutor to allow her to plead guilty to a lesser charge, with the understanding that the judge will hand down a reduced sentence. In a small proportion of cases, the women elect to stand trial; of those, most argue that they suffered from diminished capacity or temporary insanity at the time of the confrontation. But a growing number raise an affirmative defense against the murder or manslaughter charges and assert that they were compelled to lash out in self-preservation and should not be punished (Browne, 1987).

When female defendants claim they are "not guilty by reason of diminished capacity or temporary insanity," they are offering an excuse for the act. By using such a defense, the woman concedes that taking the man's life was wrong. But she argues that she should not be punished for killing him because her mental state was so impaired at the time that she was unable to form criminal intent. Temporary insanity pleas seem most appropriate in cases involving defendants who cannot recall their actions and who are found to be dazed and confused in the aftermath of the confrontation. If acquitted, she need not be confined in a mental institution because she poses no danger to the community or to herself; the irritant that provoked her out-of-control response has been eliminated (see Bernat, 1992). However, legal strategies that rely on convincing a jury of the woman's irrational and pathological behavior shift attention away from the man's provocations and her right to self-protection (Schneider, 1980).

A plea of self-defense is the alternative to one of temporary insanity. A victim-blaming argument interprets her resort to deadly force as defensive, even if it does not appear so by traditional standards. The legal doctrine of self-defense was developed by men to apply to fights between men and is usually debated and interpreted by men. The classical model posits a clash between two males of roughly equal strength who are strangers. Self-defense is accordingly defined as the justifiable use of an appropriate amount of force against an adversary by an individual who reasonably believes that he is in imminent danger of unlawful bodily harm, and that the use of such force is necessary to prevent serious injuries from being inflicted.

But this highly subjective male-oriented model, with its assumptions and prescriptions, needs to be modified when applied to clashes between males and females. For example, a woman can be considered to be acting in self-defense if she uses a weapon like a knife or gun against a man who is unarmed. The rationale is that his hands and feet can be viewed as deadly weapons because women—especially battered wives—have been beaten to death by unarmed men. Because women are generally less skilled in combat and tend to be smaller in stature, the use of a lethal weapon is a way of matching but not necessarily exceeding his level of violence. A battered woman who resorts to deadly force during the phase of the cycle when the husband is threatening harm but not yet physically attacking can also be considered to be acting in self-defense. Unlike a person confronted by a stranger, she is in a position to know from bitter past experience that his threats are real and will be carried out. The battered woman learns to recognize the cues signaling that a beating is imminent, such as subtle changes in the man's voice or facial expressions. Similarly, the wife who strikes out against her assailant during a lull in the ordeal or after an outbreak has peaked can also be considered to be acting in self-defense because she knows the patterns of his attacks (see Jones, 1980; Schneider, 1980; Bochnak, 1981; Thyfault, 1984; Kuhl, 1986; Saunders, 1986; Browne, 1987; Ewing, 1987; Gillespie, 1989; Bannister, 1992; Richie, 1996; Leonard, 2001).

Victim-blaming arguments are most convincing to detectives, prosecutors, and juries when many of the following elements are present: The battered woman had been threatened many times, beaten repeatedly, rescued by the police from his wrath on several occasions, and granted an order of protection. She had testified in court after pressing charges, sought marital counseling, attempted to escape, separated from him, and filed for divorce. Also, she had visible and severe injuries at the time of her arrest, and suffered permanent damage from the wounds he inflicted during their final confrontation. If a "psychological autopsy" or courtroom reconstruction of the tormentor is presented effectively by a defense attorney using an expert witness, the jurors could become so inflamed that they will want to "dig up the bully's corpse and kill him all over again" (see Sargeant, 1991).

The clash between victim-blaming and victim-defending perspectives illustrates, among other things, that all crimes are socially defined. No act is inherently criminal, even the taking of a life. Each killing of one person by another must be examined and interpreted within its context and cultural framework by detectives, prosecutors, defense attorneys, judges, jurors, the media and the general public. Indeed, some slayings of wife beaters by the targets of their wrath might be deemed justifiable homicides.

THE REDISCOVERY OF OTHER VICTIMS OF BEATINGS

When violence in intimate relationships began to be recognized as pervasive, several other rediscoveries became inevitable. First, battering can emerge during dating and courtship, when the ties that bind are not so strong. Second, violence by adolescents can be directed at their parents. Third, adults can become physically and psychologically abusive toward frail, elderly people. Finally, partner abuse is not limited to heterosexual couples; violence can also break out in intimate relations between members of the same sex.

Young Women Battered during Courtship

A high school senior begins dating a classmate who is known to have a bad temper. At first, she is so thrilled to have a boyfriend who seems to really care for her that it doesn't bother her that he constantly checks up on her and gets angry when she spends time with other teens. But one night when she announces she is going away for the weekend with her friends, he flies into a rage, grabs her by the arm, and throws her against a wall. He warns her never to make

arrangements without his permission. She is stunned and terrified to find out he is so controlling. (Joyce, 2004)

Now that the plight of battered women is well-known, as is the problem of date rape (see the next two chapters), a growing number of researchers are exploring the phenomenon of physical violence during courtship (see Makepeace, 1981; Laner and Thompson, 1982; Allbritten and Allbritten, 1985; Stets and Pirog-Good, 1987; Demaris, 1992; Follingstad et al., 1992; O'Keefe and Trester, 1998; Joyce, 2004).

Prevalence estimates include the survey findings that about 20 percent of female high school students report being abused by a boyfriend, that 33 percent of teenage girls concede that a dating partner has become physically abusive, and that the violence escalates as the relationship becomes more serious. The *NCVS* has established that teenagers in general are less likely to report any category of crimes committed against them, so dating violence is surely severely underreported. Most teenage girls tell no one; if they do talk about the incident, they are more inclined to share their secrets with a peer than with a parent (see Joyce, 2004). However, young women are the first to use force during arguments in a surprising proportion of cases (see Langhinrichsen-Rohling, 2005).

Courtship is considered to be the training ground for marriage, so controlling behaviors (like slapping, grabbing, shaking, kicking, choking, threatening with a weapon, and throwing things) that begin during dating may persist, and perhaps escalate, after a couple weds. But in several crucial ways, violence during courtship differs from violence within marriage. First of all, less force is used over shorter periods of time. Second, young women are more likely to initiate violence against their dates/boyfriends/fiancés than wives are against their husbands (or unmarried women against their live-in lovers). Perhaps the young women feel they can assert themselves more freely because they are not trapped in a day-after-day cohabitation situation and can break off the relationship if the spiral of violence gets out of hand. Of course, much of the physical force exerted by females can, in all fairness, be classified as examples of fighting back—acts of immediate self-defense, of retaliation for earlier male aggression, or even as pre-emptive strikes to forestall impending assaults.

When young women are severely victimized, the question: "Why does she stay?" arises. Clearly, some reasons married women cite as most important do not apply to dating: remaining together for the sake of the children, depending on the husband financially, or believing that a failed marriage is shameful and divorce is wrong. So other explanations need to be tested. Perhaps some young women tolerate abuse because rules and behavioral limits in romantic relationships currently are in a state of flux as traditional norms are challenged and rejected. Other women battered during courtship may interpret fits of jealous rage as signs of his intense feelings and deep devotion. Still others may consider violence within intimate relationships to be normal because they were mistreated as children or their parents behaved abusively toward each other. A small percentage might even feel comfortable being dominated by a "virile" young man.

Even when the female is the aggressor and the male is the target, or when mutual combat breaks out, the adversaries are not evenly matched, and it is not a fair fight. Young men have several advantages—larger size, greater strength, and better hand-to-hand combat skills—that protect them from serious harm and endanger their girlfriends' well-being. Because male-initiated violence is more frequent and more serious, it is not the female's problem alone. Prevention and education programs involving discussions, role-playing, and decision-making exercises are presented in high schools and teen centers. Serious incidents caused by dysfunctional behaviors lead to group counseling for troubled couples and ultimately problems with the authorities for the aggressors (see Makepeace, 1981; Laner and Thompson, 1982; Allbritten and Allbritten, 1985; Stets and Pirog-Good, 1987; Demaris, 1992; Follingstad et al., 1992; O'Keefe and Trester, 1998; Joyce, 2004).

Abuse of Parents by Adolescents

When teenagers batter their parents, the fathers and mothers tend to feel ashamed and usually wish to keep the matter private, so severe underreporting confounds attempts to estimate the scope of the problem. In many cases, the use of force directed at parents can be seen as retaliation for the violence these caretakers previously visited upon their children. In that sense, an intergenerational cycle of violence has been set into motion.

Mothers and stepmothers are more likely to be injured than fathers or stepfathers. But male parents are more likely to be the targets of extreme violence, perhaps as revenge for previous abuse or in self-defense as the attack escalates. Physically aggressive fathers with drinking problems are the most common victims of severe injuries or even lethal force by sons who view themselves as protectors of their mothers and siblings. In the rare cases in which a daughter is involved in the murder of a parent, the actual killer is usually a male she recruited to carry out the deed (see Steinmetz, 1978b; Straus, Gelles, and Steinmetz, 1980; Lubenow, 1983; Pagelow, 1989; Mones, 1991; Ewing, 1997).

Elder Abuse

According to *NCVS* data, elderly people are the least likely of any age group to become victims of violence, personal theft, and household crimes, largely because of the precautions they take (BJS, 1994c; Klaus, 1999b). But starting in the 1970s, victimologists and advocates for senior citizens began to delve into other ways that older people are made to suffer by younger people (see Goldsmith and Goldsmith, 1976; Boston, 1977; Center, 1980; Hochstedler, 1981). As a result, **elder abuse** was rediscovered as another expression of conflict within families, along with child abuse and spouse abuse. Many obvious parallels facilitated the rediscovery process. Once the term was coined, the problem began to receive the attention it merited from geriatric social workers, care providers, and law enforcement professionals, as well as researchers (see Quinn and Tomita, 1986; Breckman and Adelman, 1988; Steinmetz, 1988).

Definitions of elder abuse vary but usually include both acts of commission (assaults, unreasonable confinement, financial exploitation in the form of outright theft, extortion, fraud, embezzlement, or misuse of income or savings) as well as acts of omission (failure to provide medical care, food, clothing, and shelter; failure to protect from health and safety hazards; and failure to assist with personal hygiene) by caretakers responsible for the older person's well-being. Therefore, abuse encompasses gross neglect as well as acts of intentional harm (House Subcommittee, 1992).

Domestic elder abuse is perpetrated by people who provide care to elderly people who live at home. The offender is most commonly a close relative, especially a grown child, spouse, or sibling. Less often, the abuser is a son- or daughter-in-law, grandchild, niece, nephew, friend, or neighbor. The typical target is a frail, ailing woman more than 70 years old. In most cases, the victim and the abuser live in the same household in social isolation from friends, neighbors, and kin who might otherwise informally deter the wrongdoing. The abusers usually are overburdened caregivers who become depressed and hostile at the long-term prospects of tending to a mentally and physically impaired, isolated, and dependent individual. When homebound parents are physically beaten or financially exploited, sons are the most likely culprits. When daughters and daughters-in-law are abusive, their maltreatment usually takes the form of emotional and physical neglect. Mistreatment by home health aides is also suspected to be common (Pagelow, 1989). Institutional elder abuse is committed by nonrelatives, such as employees of nursing homes, who have a contractual obligation to tend to the needs of older people (McGrath and Osborne, 1989). Allegations of physical and even sexual abuse against the roughly 1.6 million residents of 17,000 nursing homes across the United States are not promptly reported or acted upon, and arrests and prosecutions are rare. Nursing home operators, fellow staff members, and relatives of the victim have self-serving reasons to be reluctant to bring charges about abusive employees to the attention of authorities (Pear, 2002).

An estimated 1.5 million older Americans (about 5 percent of senior citizens) were subjected to physical, psychological, or financial abuse or suffered serious, even life-threatening, neglect in 1992 (House Subcommittee, 1992). Up to 5 million cases of elder abuse, neglect, or exploitation may occur yearly, according to a 1998 study commissioned by the U.S. Department of Health and Human Services (McMillion, 2003). Depending on the definition, the problem might be even more serious—according to a maximalist perspective—because of severe underreporting. . Congressional investigators estimated that only about 16 percent of abused elders dared to bring their plight to the attention of the proper authorities.

Many reasons explain the reluctance of victims to complain about their predicaments.. The offender is most likely a family member who is depended upon for daily care. Abused elders might see their situations as cause for shame or as private family matters. Some might feel they provoked the abuse; others may not even be aware of the wrongdoing—particularly financial exploitation. Mandatory reporting laws similar to those that require disclosure of suspected child abuse have been imposed on health care professionals, especially doctors, generating upwardly spiraling statistics and overwhelming caseloads for geriatric social workers. However, as in child abuse cases, many allegations are never substantiated (Wolf and Pillemer, 1989; Editors, *The New York Times* 1991; Tatara, 1993).

Investigation, arrest, and prosecution are important strategies, but they only address part of the problem. Abusers need to be educated about how to care for the elderly, and victims need social services and medical assistance. Older people who are mistreated can suffer from severe emotional distress, especially depression, and are likely to die more quickly. Because the number of reported cases of elder abuse is increasing, and the Bureau of the Census predicts the population of Americans older than 65 will triple by 2030, it is likely that the problem will intensify in coming years (Davis and Medina-Ariza, 2001). The U.S.

Administration on Aging has set up a national clearinghouse of information about the many ways the nation's elders may suffer physical, psychological, sexual, and financial abuse ("Elderly crime victims," 2003).

Battering within Same-Sex Relationships

With greater openness about homosexuality, a predictable rediscovery was that physical fighting can mar the intimate relationships between gay men and between lesbians. Partner abuse in gay and lesbian couples is suspected to occur about as frequently as within heterosexual relationships, afflicting between 25 percent and 35 percent of same-sex couples (McClennen, 2005). However, gay men and lesbians who are abused by their partners have fewer options and legal rights than their married heterosexual counterparts. As a result, they often turn to programs intended to assist victims of hate crimes such as gay bashings committed by strangers. Understandably, the homosexual community initially was reluctant to publicly concede that partner abuse took place for two reasons. Some feared that revealing the problem would fuel homophobia. Others were concerned that the discovery of violence in male–male and female–female relationships would force reconsiderations about the causes of wife-beating. Domestic violence would no longer be viewed as strictly the result of patriarchal male dominance over females. Battering would have to be considered to be an outgrowth of the way power and privilege are exercised in any and all intimate relationships (see Island and Letellier, 1991; Renzetti, 1992; King, 1993; Haugrud, Gratch, and Magruder, 1997; Burke, 1998; Cruz and Firestone, 1998; Jackson, 1998; McClennen, 2005).

PREVENTING BATTERING

Preventing battering means halting further abuse of people who have already suffered beatings, as well as heading off the eruption of violence before it starts.

To prevent further abuse, it is necessary to diagnose whether the injured woman is caught up in a situation that can be characterized as common couple violence or trapped in a more serious, possibly life-threatening, situation called intimate patriarchal terrorism. Common couple violence is more widespread, and involves occasional outbursts of physical abuse by husbands, and sometimes by wives, amid ongoing hostilities. To quell this type of relationship aggression, **secondary prevention programs** attempt to teach high-risk couples negotiation and anger management techniques.

To rescue women from men who consistently use force to maintain patriarchal control is more difficult and dangerous, and requires much more than couples counseling. Battered women's shelters and orders of protection are needed for the victims, and arrest and prosecution are necessary interventions to restrain the assailants. As always, reliance on criminal justice solutions may bring about temporary relief in certain abusive relationships and might even solve particular conflicts within some families. But working to cure abusers one at a time and helping each of their victims to recover does not address the root causes of the problem. **Primary prevention programs** are intended to head off a resort to physical force by refuting myths, challenging stereotypes, and changing the attitudes held by large numbers of potential victimizers and victims, such as high school students (see Arriaga and Capezza, 2005; Rhatigan, Moore, and Street, 2005). Unfortunately, many existing prevention programs, as well as other apparently pro-victim measures such as mandatory arrest policies and aggressive prosecution, have not been effective, according to the many evaluations carried out by criminologists and victimologists (Mears and Visher, 2005).

According to activists in the battered women's movement, it is a mistake to attempt to "pathologize" spouse abuse as a problem that burdens merely a limited number of emotionally unstable couples. But it is also incorrect to try to normalize family violence as a byproduct of unavoidable conflicts that occasionally arise in every intimate relationship.

Social scientists have developed a variety of competing explanations to account for partner abuse (see Gelles, 1987; Hotaling et al., 1988). Those who apply exchange theory start with the explanation that in every couple each partner supplies the other with valued services and benefits. The problem arises when a domineering person employs force to obtain his goals and discovers that the gains outweigh the losses (rough treatment pays off). In nuclear families where couples live in isolation from the scrutiny and support of others, the benefits of violence can exceed the costs because authorities are reluctant to violate the privacy of intimates. Similarly, a resource theory analysis proposes that decision-making power within a family flows from the income, property, contacts, and prestige that each partner contributes to the relationship.

Because men have advantages in the outside economy, they command much more power in most families, leaving women in a subordinate and therefore vulnerable position. According to the subculture-of-violence theory, battering occurs more often in poverty-stricken families where resorting to physical force to settle disputes is more acceptable than among the middle classes, who purportedly believe in negotiation and compromise.

The problem of male violence arises because acting aggressively is generally taught and encouraged, as is female passivity and resignation, as part of sex-role socialization, according to social learning theory. Intergenerational transmission of wife beating occurs when boys grow up watching their fathers beat their mothers in times of stress or during bouts of heavy drinking. The root causes lie in the traditions of patriarchy according to feminist theory. The division of domestic labor in families places the husband in the dominant role and assigns him male prerogatives; the wife is compelled to accept a subordinate position burdened by female duties. These distinctions are legitimized by religion and the state, as symbolized by the wife's marriage vows to "love, honor, and obey" her husband.

Some couples are on a collision course whenever the head of the household feels that his wife's assertions of independence threaten his privileges and social status as protector and provider, and he may hit her in order to regain control.

In other couples, overly dependent, passive, and submissive wives serve as inviting targets for displaced aggression and misplaced blame. The women seem resigned, crushed, and defeated and have learned to feel helpless and trapped because attempts to escape seem emotionally destructive to the children, economically disastrous, and likely to trigger even more violence. In a society controlled by giant corporations and large government bureaucracies, some men seize upon domination over their wives and children as a substitute for real autonomy in their personal lives. As long as women with children are financially dependent on men, and both sexes are raised to expect male aggression and tolerate female passivity, woman battering will persist as a serious social problem (see Dobash and Dobash, 1979; Schechter, 1982; Walker, 1984; Yllo and Bograd, 1988; Rhode, 1989; Viano, 1992; Healy and Smith, 1998).

When battered wives become widows by their own deeds, parceling out blame should not be limited to just one spouse or the other. If domestic disturbances are to be prevented from escalating to such explosive levels, then effective outside intervention is necessary. Murders within marriages reflect failures of both criminal justice and social service agencies: to provide adequate protection for the victim who ultimately becomes the perpetrator and to provide timely treatment for the abuser who eventually loses his life. Some responsibility for these tragedies also falls on those officials who assign a low priority to cases of "lover's quarrels," who cling to a "hands-off, settle it yourselves" doctrine, and who discourage the development of adequate refuges for battered women and the establishment of sufficient therapy programs to rehabilitate abusive men. In addition, members of each succeeding generation need to re-examine and reconsider for themselves both prevailing and alternative views about gender roles, independence and dependence, romantic relationships, marriage, decision making in families, and intervention into intensely personal matters by the government and other outsiders (see Yllo and Bograd, 1988; Websdale and Johnson, 1997; Chornesky, 2000).

SUMMARY

Victims of domestic violence face many special problems that require special solutions. They still have to contend with old-fashioned views that what goes on behind closed doors between lovers is nobody else's business. The most obvious special problem is that they are exposed to constant danger because they live in the same homes as their attackers, are usually emotionally and financially dependent upon them, and are raising children together. Assailants are often viewed as otherwise law-abiding and upstanding members of the community, so victims are likely to be blamed or to fault themselves for the ugly flare-ups. If they have children in common, battered women run the risk of losing parental control of them if the violence takes place in front of them, or if the estranged father is better off financially and seeks joint custody or even sole custody. If the violence festers, it may escalate to the point that one partner or the other gets seriously injured or killed.

Reliable statistics about the incidence and prevalence of being beaten by a lover are lacking, so a maximalist-minimalist debate rages over the true extent and seriousness of the problem. The debate has become politicized because so much is at stake: relations between the sexes, courtship practices, ideas about romance and marriage, and clashing perspectives about which policies are genuinely "pro-family."

Special problems always require special solutions. To reduce domestic violence, shelters have been set up across the country as places of refuge for women and their young children. Specialized domestic violence courts have been established in some jurisdictions. The judges who work there are experts in diagnosing the problems and are familiar with the available range of protective and treatment options. Courts can issue restraining orders, and physically abusive mates can be arrested and sent to anger management programs. Special problems faced by parents harmed by their adolescent children, elderly people abused and exploited by their grown children, and gay or lesbian victims assaulted by their lovers require even more creative solutions.

Primary prevention and secondary prevention programs are intended to help reduce outbreaks of violence between intimates.

KEY TERMS

Intimate partners, 228

domestic tranquility, 229

patriarchy, 229

unnatural severity, 230

moderate correction, 230

domestic chastisement, 230

rule of thumb, 230

battered-woman syndrome, 231

speakouts, 232

domestic disturbances, 233

abuse, 233

normative ambiguity, 233

clinical fallacy, 234

shelters, 238

order of protection, 240

restraining order, 240

pro-arrest, directives, 242

external validity, 242

no-drop, 243

elder abuse, 253

secondary prevention programs, 255

primary prevention programs, 255

QUESTIONS FOR DISCUSSION AND DEBATE

1. Discuss the pros and cons of officers following a mandatory arrest-the-aggressor policy at the scene of domestic disturbances.

2. Explain why many battered women do not leave their abusive mates.

3. Under what circumstances, if any, could the killing of a vicious wife-beater by his victim be ruled a justifiable homicide, in your opinion?

CRITICAL THINKING QUESTIONS

1. If beatings take place in same-sex relationships as well as among heterosexual couples, and during courtship as well as during marriage, then what is the root cause of violence between intimates?

2. Give possible reasons why the number of murders of husbands by wives and of boyfriends by girlfriends has dropped so sharply over recent decades.

SUGGESTED RESEARCH PROJECTS

1. Compile a comprehensive list of the policies (such as mandatory arrest of the aggressor) and the opportunities for assistance (such as shelters) that can be offered by government, nonprofit, self-help, and charitable organizations to ease the plight of battered women. Find out from local criminal justice officials, women's organizations, and others in the helping professions what is currently available in your hometown.

2. Locate some recent cases in databases of newspaper and magazine articles in which women were prosecuted for killing their abusive mates. Gather details about the slayings, the couples' lives together before the final confrontation, and the outcomes of these cases in court.

10

Victims of Rapes and Other Sexual Assaults

A paradox surrounds the crime of rape. On the one hand, a victim's allegations sometimes are sneered at and can become the subject of crude jokes. On the other hand, some rapists are punished so severely that sexual assault ranks as one of the most terrible and strictly forbidden interpersonal crimes. Today, who the offender is, who the injured party is, and how the female acted before and during the sexual assault determine the criminal justice system's response to the crime. Public reactions are shaped by social attitudes as much as by legal codes, and both attitudes and laws have been changing in recent decades.

Even the language used to describe this type of victimization matters and has been evolving. If the formulation is that "a woman got raped..." the implication is that it is the woman's problem and perhaps even her fault. If the phrasing is more active and direct, that men rape women or that it is a crime of males against females, then the onus shifts and falls on the aggressors—not their targets—and on those aspects of the culture that encourage coupling violence with sexuality.

The word rape comes from the Latin *rapere*, which means "to take by force." In English common law, the crime was called unlawful **carnal knowledge**. By definition, the unwanted intrusion could be committed only by a male against a female who was not his wife. But the old common law definition has been updated by new legislation in each state. First of all, the crime is now gender-neutral, which means that males also can be targets (almost always of other men). Second, intercourse is not the only punishable activity. Other unwanted invasions of the body and forced submission to sexual acts are outlawed as well, by statutes prohibiting sexual assaults and sexual battery.

One element of the crime remains the same: forcible rape implies that the objectified person reasonably fears bodily harm if she or he refuses to acquiesce. Lack of consent therefore remains the key factor that distinguishes a sexual assault from an unpleasant sexual experience by an overly aggressive partner. Aggravated rape is penalized more severely because it involves more than one assailant, and/or the use of a weapon, and/or the infliction of additional wounds besides unwanted penetration. Sexual assaults short of rape (for example, unwelcome sexual contacts like fondling) carry a lesser penalty. Taking sexual advantage of a person

who is mentally retarded or unable to give meaningful consent because she or he is drugged, drunk, or unconscious (whether or not this altered state was induced by the offender) also is illegal. Besides forcible rape, **statutory rape** also is against the law, but the penalties are not as severe. When a minor below the legal age of consent voluntarily engages in sexual intercourse, the act automatically is considered to be exploitative because a young person is considered not mature enough to to make such an important decision. By definition, statutory rapes do not involve violence or the threat of force, and sex acts are not imposed on minors against their will (refer back to Chapter 8).

THE REDISCOVERY OF THE PLIGHT OF RAPE VICTIMS

Forcible rape is surely one of the most heinous violent crimes imaginable, and yet for centuries the social reaction to this offense showed little regard for the well-being of the victim. In the distant past, rape was handled as an offense that harmed the interests of a man—either a father or husband—rather than a violation of personhood that threatened the emotional and physical health of the daughter or wife. Some rapists were punished severely, but others went unprosecuted, depending on the status of both the accused offender and the female he harmed. In biblical times, a man could be put to death for the rape of an innocent virgin. But if a married woman was raped, she could be executed too because she was considered blameworthy (unless her husband intervened on her behalf). During medieval times a man seeking upward mobility might engage in **heiress stealing**—abducting and then raping a young woman from a wealthy family in order to compel her or her family to agree to be his bride. As feudalism evolved, only the rape of a noblewoman was punishable; forcing a peasant woman to submit was not considered a crime. During warfare, over the ages, the enemy's women were taken by conquering soldiers as spoils of victory; rapists in military units were rarely arrested, prosecuted, or punished.

Rapes involving people of different races are particularly controversial and polarizing. From the days of slavery up until the 1950s, black men who merely were accused of raping white women were in danger of being lynched by angry mobs before being put on trial, especially in the Deep South. Between 1930 and 1968, 455 convicted rapists were executed in the United States (most were black men found guilty of sexually assaulting white women). However, in 1977, the Supreme Court (in *Coker v. Georgia*) ruled that capital punishment was an excessive penalty for rape. Consequently life imprisonment became the maximum sentence (see Brownmiller, 1975; Siegel, 1998). In 2008, the Supreme Court struck down capital punishment for the forcible rape of a child.

These examples illustrate the point that the wishes and well-being of the injured party were not taken into account by the men who determined a rapist's fate in the past. Clearly, when a rape took place, the offender became the focus of attention while his victim's best interests largely were overlooked.

At the start of the 1970s, feminists fighting for the rights of women to control their own bodies (particularly reproductive rights via contraception and abortion) called attention to the plight of rape victims. Instead of being regarded as some man's "damaged goods," feminists insisted that these girls and women should be recognized as individuals suffering from terrible violations of their personhood who deserved respect, support, assistance, empowerment, and protection from further harm. This pro-victim, anti-rape movement exposed a legacy of injustice, institutionalized neglect, and routine abuse. Because of class, race, and gender discrimination, most women did not report such offenses to the authorities, and of the incidents that were reported most went unpunished.

Feminists argued that rape was more than a personal tragedy: It was a social problem and a political issue. They interpreted sexual assaults as skirmishes in what had been referred to traditionally as the unending battle of the sexes. Forcible rapes functioned as acts of terrorism that intimidated all women and served to keep them in their "proper place"—subordinate to males (dependent upon "good" men for protection against "bad" men), and outside of male territorial preserves. A sexual assault symbolized how a male could exploit his power differential (his superior physical force) to have his way in a man's world.

How rape cases were handled dramatized how the men who ran the criminal justice system could not be trusted to act on behalf of victimized girls and women. Invariably, when accusations about rape were lodged, the all-male police, prosecution, judiciary, and juries scrutinized the relationship between the two parties (especially their social class, race/ethnicity, prior contacts, and her alleged blameworthiness). These men often lost sight of the violence inflicted upon the target during the sexual assault (see Russell, 1975; Griffin, 1979; Rhode, 1989; Muehlenhard et al., 1992).

Through books, articles, dissertations, discussions at consciousness-raising groups, demonstrations at trials, and public "speakouts," the anti-rape movement and feminist legal scholars worked to redefine the prevailing image of the crime and to rediscover its victims. Their outreach campaigns triggered public and private discussions about previously unnamed types of violations like date rape, acquaintance rape, marital rape, serial rape, and male rape. Their aim was to shatter the myths surrounding the crime (see Koss, 2005).

Over the ages, rape had been pictured as an act of lust and an outpouring of uncontrollable sexual urges. This old view seems plausible only if the vicious physical injuries and devastating emotional pain sustained by the "objects of desire" are ignored. Threats of violence and the use of force surrounding the sexual assault—before, during, and after—betrays its true nature: an attack upon the victim's dignity and personhood for the purpose of domination and subjugation. The assailant reveals his hatred and contempt for all females—certainly not "passion" or "love" for a particular girl or woman. According to this new view, rape is really all about power and control.

"REAL RAPES" COMPARED WITH "DATE RAPES"

A woman is driving with her boyfriend. When they stop at a red light, a man wearing a stocking mask and wielding a gun forces them out of the car. He orders the boyfriend to lie down in the trunk, and compels her drive to a deserted spot. After he rapes her, he throws her in the trunk too and makes his escape. This serial rapist, who has been in and out of prison repeatedly, is captured and convicted years later, after sexually assaulting a girl near her school bus stop. (Shifrel, 2007)

***

A young man convinces a young woman to go to his apartment after a date. They begin to kiss, but when he makes further sexual overtures, she politely whispers no. He persists, believing that the dating ritual requires the male to be the aggressor and the female to respond with ladylike token resistance, at least at first. He assumes from past experience that no means maybe, and maybe means yes, unless he gets a slap in the face. When she says she's not ready for "that" yet, he misinterprets her protestation as an invitation to be even more assertive. As he climbs on top of her, she becomes petrified that further resistance will be met with violence. The evening ends with the young man perceiving that ultimately he "seduced" her, and the young woman feeling that she was violated against her will. She has him arrested. (Dershowitz, 1988)

Sexual crimes involve coercion of an unwilling person, according to the law. But not all sexual assaults qualify as "real" rapes, according to public opinion (see Estrich, 1986). The first case cited above surely constitutes a real rape. But controversy still surrounds the handling of certain incidents, such as the second one cited. Many people have trouble distinguishing imposed intercourse from "willingly engaging in sex." As a result, when a woman claims to have been penetrated against her will, some people might conjure up images of "lovemaking" rather than "forcible bodily invasion."

Real rapes or "classic rapes" (in the language of sociology, **ideal types** in the sense that they are the clearest examples) are readily identifiable and raise few legal questions or moral doubts. Real rapes have several defining features: They are perpetrated against unsuspecting females who are ambushed in blitz attacks. The offender is a complete stranger. He is armed with a weapon and pounces out of the darkness to surprise his quarry. The injured party is virtuous and above reproach—she is too young, too old, or too inexperienced to be faulted for attracting his attention and arousing his desires. At the time of the attack, she is engaged in a "wholesome" activity that is above criticism. Even though she faces grave dangers, she dares to fight back, resists to her utmost, and suffers severe injuries in a futile attempt to fend him off. Eyewitnesses glimpse parts of the struggle and hear her cries for help. As soon as she escapes from his clutches, she reports the crime to the police. Detectives find forensic evidence that backs up all her charges of being caught off guard, confronted with a weapon, brutally assaulted, overpowered, and compelled to submit to his demands. Finally, the assailant, who is obviously a deeply disturbed predator, quickly confesses when captured.

Few people would have any difficulty conceding that a rape that mirrors many of these characteristics is one of the worst experiences that a woman can suffer. Today, detectives, prosecutors, juries, and judges agree that girls or women harmed in such heinous attacks deserve to be treated with dignity and sensitivity within the criminal justice process and that the vicious assailants must be removed from society and severely punished (see Estrich, 1986).

The problem for most rape victims is that the facts in their cases usually fall short in one way or another of the unambiguous standards that characterize a brutal real rape between strangers. As a result, the accusers' versions of events are likely to be questioned when essential elements are missing. Perhaps the woman had been hitchhiking, or drinking in a bar, or attending a party. The most controversial cases arise out of forced sex as the culmination of a date.

The following headline-generating story was not considered a "real rape" by many people, including the jurors who acquitted the alleged assailant:

> A young man from a politically prominent family meets a woman late at night at a fashionable cocktail lounge. They share some drinks, dance, and flirt. She accompanies him back to the oceanfront home where he is vacationing and they take a walk on the deserted moonlit beach at three in the morning. They embrace, he sheds his clothes, takes a brief swim, and then ... throws her down on the sand, overpowers her, and violates her, she insists. (Gibbs, 1991)

During the 1980s, victims of sexual assaults by men they knew were rediscovered. Since then, federal and state laws have been rewritten and victimization surveys have been reworded to take into account the possibility that the attacker was not a stranger (see Fisher, Cullen, and Daigle, 2005). **Acquaintance rapes** (by relatives, neighbors, classmates, colleagues from work, casual dates, and intimate partners) might be quite distinct from real rapes by complete strangers, depending on the nature of the victim-offender relationship and their interactions. In cases of acquaintance rape, doubts about her recitation of the facts quickly surface if some other crucial defining features of real rapes are missing. Perhaps she fails to meet the old-fashioned criterion of being "virtuous," or she does not report the attack promptly. Maybe the assailant did not brandish a weapon, or he did not inflict serious physical injuries.

If there was no ferocious struggle or she did not scream for help, some will reject her contention that she was unwilling. If there is no corroboration by eyewitnesses or from forensic tests, the case may boil down to her word against his. As a consequence of any of these ambiguities, the acquaintance or non-stranger she accuses is less likely to be arrested, prosecuted, and convicted (see Estrich, 1986).

Until the late 1980s, most prosecutors were reluctant to move forward, press charges, and go to trial when the accused man was not a complete stranger if there were no eyewitnesses, no bruises from a beating, and no signs of a fierce struggle. Yet forced sex arising out of a romantic encounter meets the legal definition of rape—the use of physical coercion against a non-consenting person—and does not depend on the prior relationship of the accuser and the accused (see Estrich, 1993a; Spears and Spohn, 1997). But a victim of rape by a date, or especially by a former intimate, surely still will have trouble convincing a detective, prosecutor, judge, and jury that the man she willingly accompanied (and even engaged in sexual intercourse with on previous occasions) imposed himself on her against her will in this instance—unless she has visible wounds.

Some would argue that if forced intercourse is preceded by a series of consensual acts with sexual overtones, her "contributory behavior" makes the nature of the crime less serious, and it should be penalized less severely than an ambush of an unsuspecting and depersonalized target. Others insist that it makes no difference if the victim and the offender knew each other and interacted warmly, even passionately, before the incident. The encounter cannot be written off as a case of miscommunication, a terrible misunderstanding, or an instance of a woman having regrets for the way she behaved the night before. What counts is that she was stripped of control, denied the right to make a crucial decision, and compelled to submit to someone else's sexual demands (Gibbs, 1991). These sharply contrasting interpretations lead to a victim-blaming versus victim-defending debate over who or what is at fault and what should be done.

VICTIM PRECIPITATION AND RAPE: DID SHE SINGLE HERSELF OUT FOR TROUBLE?

Late one night, a 22-year-old mother of two enters a bar filled with men. She has a few drinks and flirts with some of the patrons. Suddenly, she finds herself held down on a pool table. Six young men force themselves on her as onlookers cheer and she screams and curses. The six men are arrested and put on trial for aggravated rape. Their defense is that she acted seductively and "led them on." The prosecution argues that a sexual assault begins whenever a man continues after a woman has said no. The jury concludes that she did not consent to what they did to her and convicts four of the six defendants. The judge sentences them to terms of 6 to 12 years in prison. At a rally held on behalf of the victim, speakers hail the outcome as a symbol that gang rape will not be tolerated as a spectator sport. But at a demonstration protesting the verdicts and sentences, speakers sympathetic to the young men contend, "She got herself raped," and "She should have known what she was getting herself into." They hold her largely responsible for enabling the men "to take advantage of her." (Schanberg, 1984, 1989)

***

A man is on trial for rape. His lawyer points out that the alleged victim was wearing a tank top, a lacy miniskirt, and no underpants. The defendant is found not guilty because, as one juror explains, "We felt she asked for it." The failed prosecution inspires the state legislature to amend the laws governing rape trials to bar defense attorneys from asking complainants about the clothes they were wearing at the time of the assaults. (Merrill, 1994)

The clash between victim blaming and victim defending is particularly bitter when it comes to rape. If auto theft provided a clear illustration of a crime for which there are well-organized interests with a stake in promoting motorist blaming, then rape serves as the best example of a crime for which there is a vocal and deeply committed victim-defending community. The controversy erupts over whether certain instances of rape should be viewed as victim-precipitated acts of uncontainable male sexual desire or whether all instances of forced sex are inexcusable acts of brutal domination always imposed upon unwilling, objectified targets.

A great deal is at stake in the battle for public support between victim-blaming and victim-defending viewpoints. The problem of rape forces people to choose between two distinct courses of action. Who or what has to change: how women behave in the company of men, as victim blaming contends; or how boys and men treat girls and women, as victim defending emphasizes? Accepting victim-blaming arguments might lead to the acquittal of certain defendants, but the more socially significant consequence is that this line of thought "excuses" institutions and traditions that are under attack for demeaning women. According to victim defenders who blame the system, to reduce the threat of rape it is necessary to root out anti-female biases found within rigid sex roles, prevailing definitions of masculinity and femininity in popular culture, the job market, and the economy, as well as existing laws and criminal justice practices (see Hills, 1981).

Victim-Blaming Views

The victim-blaming viewpoint contends that some rape victims differ in their attitudes and actions from other females who are able to avoid sexual assault. Allegedly, there are certain kinds of women who go around "asking for trouble" and eventually "get themselves raped." Such harsh condemnations rest on two premises: that the male was overwhelmed by sexual desire and lost his self-control; and that the female somehow facilitated the assault (perhaps by weakening herself by taking drugs or alcohol); thoughtlessly precipitated it (by making rash decisions that put her in a temptation-opportunity situation); or even provoked his over-powering response (by suggestive and seductive utterings or deeds) (see Gibbs, 1991).

Victim blaming chastises women who suffer sexual assaults for acts of omission (not being cautious) as well as acts of commission, such as hitchhiking (Amir, 1971). Sometimes the female is castigated for secretly harboring fantasies of being ravished, and then enabling such scenarios to take place (MacDonald, 1971). The victim-blaming interpretation of date rape characterizes the incident as a terrible misunderstanding in "he said/she said" terms: He says she wanted to and didn't really object, while she says he intimidated her and forced her to yield. "Miscommunication" results when a female sends mixed messages, fails to make her true intentions clear, and doesn't protest unwanted sexual advances vehemently enough—a common problem during this period of rapid changes in the rules of the "dating game," with its courtship rituals and shifting sexual mores (see Warshaw, 1988; Muehlenhard et al., 1992).

The most widely cited (and most heavily criticized) study of victim precipitation in rape was based on data drawn from the files of the Philadelphia police concerning cases reported in 1958 and 1960 (Amir, 1971). The researcher considered "precipitation" to have occurred whenever a girl's or woman's behavior was interpreted by a teenage boy or man either as a direct invitation to engage in sexual relations that was later retracted (she agreed and then changed her mind, according to him); or when she signaled that she would be amenable if he persisted in his demands (she was saying no but meant yes, in his opinion). Included in this researcher's working definition of a precipitated rape were acts of commission such as drinking alcohol, hitchhiking, or using what could be taken as indecent language or gestures. Acts of omission, such as failing to object strongly enough to his sexually charged overtures, also counted against her. The offender's interpretation was considered to be the crucial element in recognizing instances of precipitation. Even if the male was mistaken in his beliefs about her intentions, his perceptions led to actions, and that was what really mattered.

In the police department's files, specific indicators of precipitation were statements by the offender, witnesses, or detectives claiming that "she behaved provocatively," "she acted seductively," "she was irresponsible and endangered herself," or "she had a bad reputation in the neighborhood." Using these criteria, the researcher deemed 19 percent of Philadelphia's forcible rapes to be precipitated. Comparing precipitated rapes with non-precipitated ones, it was found that alcohol consumption was more likely to have taken place, and that the offender was more inclined to sexually humiliate his victim. Precipitating victims included higher percentages of females who were white, teenagers, and casual acquaintances of the males they first met at bars or parties (Amir, 1971).

The victim-blaming perspective contends that some young women precipitate rapes because of their lifestyles. They do not understand (or choose to ignore) the risks involved in certain situations, such as going to bars unescorted or accepting rides home with men they hardly know. They are unaware, naive, or gullible in their dealings with males. They wear clothing or use language that men stereotype as signaling sexual availability. They ignore the dangers that might arise if they are suddenly confronted with a weapon or are overpowered while under the influence of alcohol or some other drug. For some teenage girls, their reckless behavior is considered a form of acting out. These adolescents—especially if they come from poverty-stricken homes and suffer parental rejection—are said to be seeking protection, attention, love, intimacy, and status through precocious sexuality. As a result, they get involved with older male casual acquaintances and find themselves in situations in which they are forcibly exploited (see Amir, 1971; Dean and de Bruyn-Kops, 1982).

Two sets of consequences follow from the acceptance of victim-blaming arguments. First, if the female shares some responsibility, then the male can be considered less culpable and less deserving of severe punishment. Second, girls and women must be educated to behave more cautiously and avoid any miscommunication about their real desires.

If the victim's behavior can be criticized, then the "tragic misunderstanding" is not entirely the offender's fault. The legal principle involved is that the female assumed the risk of attack when she voluntarily participated in potentially dangerous events that led up to the rape, such as drinking heavily or agreeing to enter an isolated room. Even though the male remains subject to arrest, her contributory behavior can provide grounds for granting him the benefit of the doubt. This line of reasoning can influence every stage of the criminal justice system's handling of these cases.

Anticipation of harsh interrogation might discourage a victim from bringing her problem to the attention of the authorities. If, after thoroughly questioning the complainant to determine her background, reputation, actions, and possible motives, the police believe that she contributed to her own victimization, charges might not be pressed. If the police do make an arrest, the prosecutor might decide that the case is unwinnable and therefore might drop the charges. If the case is brought to trial, jurors may exercise their discretion in interpreting the facts and may find the assailant guilty of a lesser charge than forcible rape (sexual assault, for example). If the defendant is convicted, the judge may hand down a lenient sentence in view of the mitigating circumstances—her misleading seductiveness might have been taken as a sign of **implied consent** (for additional references, see Schur, 1984; Marciniak, 1999).

The other major consequence of accepting the victim-blaming point of view is that the burden of preventing rape is shifted away from aggressive males, the police, or the prevailing culture, and onto the potential targets. Girls and women are admonished that they might unwittingly be courting disaster and that it is their obligation to constantly review their lifestyles and do what they can to minimize their risks and maximize their safety. Because controlling the actions of offenders is so difficult, victim blaming seeks to reduce the incidence of rape by constraining the behavior of the potential targets. Females are warned to be careful whom they associate with, what they say in conversations, where they go, and how they dress. They are urged to communicate clearly, to signal their true intentions, and to avoid teasing or taunting males. They are held personally accountable for their own security and are pressured to follow crime-prevention tips derived from the mistakes made by other females. Just as the threat of punishment is intended to make would-be rapists think twice before breaking the law, the public humiliation of victim blaming is meant to pressure females to think twice before stepping out of traditional, sheltered, family-centered roles and activities.

Teenagers and young adults are especially likely to hold these traditional beliefs about the female's responsibility for precipitated rapes. Surveys reveal that between one-quarter and one-half of all adolescents express agreement with some statements that pin blame on victims because of their demeanor, clothing, or prior actions (see Marciniak, 1999). A sizable proportion of female college students also hold victims accountable for their "mistakes" (Cowan, 2000; Bondurant, 2001; Carmody and Washington, 2001).

In many acquaintance rape cases, the male, the female, or both were drinking alcohol or taking drugs before the confrontation. Several studies have generated the finding that about half of all men arrested for rape disclosed that they had been drinking before the crime, and about half of all women who were raped concede they had been drinking preceding the assault. (However, these figures don't indicate how much they drank or how intoxicated either party was [see Abbey et al., 2004].) Girls and women who voluntarily get drunk and consequently become easy to subjugate often are singled out for particularly harsh condemnations. They are faulted for recklessly getting so high that they became unaware of developments taking place around them, unable to think clearly enough to give meaningful consent or to vehemently object, and incapable of physically warding off unwanted advances. Whereas males may use alcohol as a way to erode their "partner's" will to resist, females are condemned for getting drunk enough to dissolve their inhibitions and provide themselves with a convenient excuse afterward (see Corbin, Bernat, and Calhoun, 2001; Falck, Wang, and Carlson, 2001).

Victim-Defending Perspectives

Victim-blaming views have become controversial since the 1970s. Victim-defending arguments, originally developed by feminists in the women's rights movement, challenge this conventional wisdom handed down from generation to generation and provide alternative explanations for why some men force themselves upon women.

Victim defending rejects as a myth the notion that rapes are acts of lust or outpourings of uncontrollable passion. Sexual assaults are reinterpreted as outbursts of aggression fueled by hatred and anger. Through sexual acts, assailants express their intentions to dominate, subjugate, conquer, and humiliate. Their violence is not triggered by arousal and frustrated desires but instead is motivated by contempt for females in general and their target in particular. Nothing suggestive or erotic that the victim said, wore, or did could justify such hostile and degrading reactions from a stranger, acquaintance, intimate, or spouse (Russell, 1975; Clark and Lewis, 1978; Griffin, 1979).

Using force to compel an unwilling partner to submit and be controlled as a depersonalized object should never be confused with "making love" or even "engaging in sex." Victim defending questions the applicability of the concept of precipitation, which was originally developed to describe the blameworthy, aggressive initiatives taken by men who start and then lose fights. Although some homicides might be deemed justifiable (cases of self-defense), there is no such thing as justifiable rape (Amir, 1971). In victim-precipitated homicides, the person who died was the first to escalate the level of conflict by resorting to physical strength or a weapon; then the survivor reacted to the assault by fighting back with deadly force. Violence incited retaliatory violence.

Because the woman does not physically assault the man before he attacks her, the only way to apply the concept of precipitation to rape is to consider the incident as primarily a sexually charged encounter. Only then can real or presumed sexual advances by the female be considered triggering mechanisms. But there is no justification for his resort to force, no matter what she wore, did, said, or promised. Furthermore, there is great confusion over what constitutes a sexual overture. Because the female's behavior can be subjected to a wide range of interpretations, whose perceptions should be accepted when deciding if there was precipitation on her part: his, hers, the police's, the jury's, or the researcher's? (See Silverman, 1974; Chappell, Geis, and Geis, 1977; McCaghy, 1980.)

Therefore, the belief that certain rapes are precipitated has been dismissed as a personification and embodiment of rape mythology, cleverly stated in academic-scientific terms (Weis and Borges, 1973); as a scholarly endorsement of the rapist's point of view that provides an excuse for blaming the injured party (Clark and Lewis, 1978); and as an *ex post facto* interpretation that fails to take into account the female's version of events (LeGrande, 1973).

As for date rapes, victim defending asserts that whenever compulsory intercourse occurs, a real rape has been committed, and not a seduction as the culmination of a romantic courtship ritual. Nor is the rape a terrible misunderstanding stemming from miscommunication. The boy or man has used coercion to take from her what he wanted and intended to get all along, while violating her personhood in the process (Estrich, 1986; LaFree, 1989). If she was silent and passive and yielded without a struggle, this behavior should not be taken to mean acquiescence. Such an interpretation overlooks the paralyzing effects of the aggressor's overwhelming physical strength, his use of force at the outset, his tactics that caught the victim by surprise, or the implied threat posed by the presence of a weapon (see Estrich, 1986; LaFree, 1989).

Victim defending also rejects, as ideologically tainted, the crime-prevention tips endorsed by victim blaming that girls and women are supposed to follow to survive in a "man's world." Females who did not scrupulously observe these precautions are unfairly set up for blame and even berate themselves ("If only I had... "). A woman who abides by the long and rapidly growing list of recommended self-protection measures (given heightened concerns about drug-facilitated date rape—see Chapter 11) ends up resembling the proverbial "hysterical old maid armed with a hatpin and an umbrella who looks under the bed each night before retiring." For years a laughable stereotype of prudery, she has become a model of prudence (Brownmiller, 1975). Adhering to crime-prevention tips means forgoing many pleasures and privileges to which men are accustomed, such as taking a walk alone on a deserted beach or strolling through the park at night. Warding off would-be rapists requires women to engage in an extraordinary amount of pretense and deception (pretending a boyfriend, husband, or father is nearby). Furthermore, seeking the protection of "trustworthy" men to fend off unwanted advances by predatory males undermines the efforts of women to develop their own strengths, self-confidence, self-reliance, and independent networks of mutual support.

Victim defenders do not portray females as naive, gullible, helpless, dependent, and vulnerable targets who require strict supervision to keep them out of trouble. Women, like men, exercise **agency** and ultimately are responsible for their own choices and fate. But victim defenders insist that rape prevention campaigns should not solely be aimed at females, but should educate and enlighten potential male aggressors too, as well as to pressure and threaten them to do the right thing when relating to the "opposite sex." In sum, victim defending aims to dispel victim-blaming "rape myths" (see Box 10.1).

B O X 10.1   The Controversy Surrounding Widely Held "Rape Myths"

From a victim-defending standpoint, certain victim-blaming arguments about acquaintance rapes are deemed to be "rape myths." These widely held and frequently voiced points of view about the female, the male, and the nature of their sexual encounter tend to dismiss the seriousness of the violation of the woman's dignity and personal integrity, or even deny that anything illegal took place.

Six familiar beliefs, four that blame the victim and two that defend the perpetrator, have been labeled as myths that reinforce narrow stereotypes, distort reality, and interfere with the process of separating fact from fiction (see Burt, 1980; Lonsway and Fitzgerald, 1994; Frankiuk et al., 2008).

Researchers adopting a victim-defending stance measure how many people believe:

1. "She is lying" for some ulterior purpose.
2. "She asked for it" by doing things that seemed to imply consent, such as drinking alcoholic beverages or accompanying the man to his home.
3. "She wanted it at the time" but changed her mind and then altered the story line and cried "rape!"
4. "She is the kind of female who gets raped." Only "certain" women get raped, promiscuous ones who place themselves at great risk.
5. "He didn't mean to cross the line." The whole incident arose from miscommunication and a terrible misunderstanding; he thought her "no" meant "yes" so his behavior is excusable.
6. "He is not the type to commit a rape." The accusations must be unfounded because only

sex-crazed psychopaths use physical force to have their way.

One of the most serious obstacles to reducing sexual assault is the failure to recognize it and condemn it when it happens, and minimizing a case involving acquaintances as merely another unprovable "he said/she said" impasse. Acceptance of rape myths is not necessarily a sign of malicious intent but rather an example of internalizing traditional cultural stereotypes that may cause men to excuse or even justify their own sexually aggressive behavior.

The widespread acceptance of rape myths creates a vicious cycle that deters women from reporting, pressing charges, and testifying at trials. Victim defenders say that clinging to stereotypical thinking perpetuates the problem in how acquaintance rape victims are treated by hospital personnel, detectives, prosecutors, judges, and juries (see Franiuk et al., 2008).

A high-profile case is often tried in the court of public opinion, based on selective leaks of "evidence" presented in media accounts, long before the accused and the accuser actually appear before a judge (see Chancer, 2005). Usually, pretrial publicity biases potential jurors against defendants, but in certain widely covered cases of prominent men accused of acquaintance rape, journalists often present the defense attorney's arguments as well as the prosecutor's indictment. People who embrace rape myths, usually males more than females, tend to be reluctant to label an incident as a sexual assault even when it meets the legal criteria for a violation of an existing law.

THE CONSEQUENCES OF BEING SEXUALLY ASSAULTED

Victimologists have studied the plight of rape victims intensively for several decades. Researchers aim to assess the nature of the suffering and to discover ways to speed the recovery process (see McCahill, Williams, and Fischman, 1979; Girelli et al., 1986; Burt and Katz, 1987; Allison and Wrightsman, 1993; Wiehe and Richards, 1995; Giannelli, 1997).

Being raped is almost always a life-altering experience, and may haunt the survivor for the rest of her life. The ordeal itself and the turmoil that follows challenges and may even transform her identity and the assumptions she makes about the world. The emotional impact is manifested largely as fear, anxiety, depression, sexual dysfunction, and feelings of isolation. The mental toll shows up as the loss of illusions about invulnerability and immortality; the destruction of a sense of predictability within her environment and of the meaning of events in her life; and a diminution in her sense of self-worth. Other terrible consequences can include chronic physical pain, a substance abuse habit, an unwanted pregnancy, and the contraction of a venereal disease or, in rare instances, HIV/AIDS (Campbell and Wasco, 2005; Marx, 2005).

The distress from being treated as an object instead of a person may plunge her into a **rape crisis syndrome**. The acute initial phase lasts for two or three weeks immediately following the sexual attack. Typical short-term reactions include revulsion, shock, anger, fury, self-recrimination, fear, sorrow, and total disorientation. Victims often suffer nausea, tension headaches, and an inability to sleep. The second phase, in which the survivor's personality reintegrates, can last much longer and is characterized by recurring nightmares, defensive reactions, and strains in relationships with men. Many victims try to reorganize their daily lives by changing jobs, moving to a new location, dropping out of college, and limiting personal contacts. Lingering effects often include loss of sexual desire and the development of fears: of being confined indoors, about going outdoors among strangers, of being alone as well as being in crowds, and of people stealthily approaching from behind (Burgess and Holmstrom, 1974; Giannelli, 1997; Resick and Nishith, 1997).

Like others who are stunned by an unexpected, life-threatening ordeal, survivors of rape can suffer from **posttraumatic stress disorder** (PTSD) during the crime's immediate aftermath. They may re-experience the attack repeatedly in daydreams, flashbacks, or nightmares. Other symptoms include feeling different; wanting to avoid things that serve as reminders of the trauma; and suffering a general lack of interest or enthusiasm, an inability to concentrate, and increased irritability (Williams, 1987). A recognition of the severe consequences of the crime for the person abused as someone else's sex object should dispel any notions that rape is an act of passion rather than of subjugation, and ought to demolish any beliefs that the unwilling target somehow secretly desired or enjoyed such violent handling.

Even though most rapes are not completed (according to the yearly *NCVS* surveys, about two-thirds are not), females who thwart their assailants' intentions still suffer serious psychological scars. In fact, women who endured attempted rapes were more likely to contemplate suicide and to try to kill themselves than women who suffered completed rapes, according to the results of a telephone survey (Kilpatrick, 1985).

The devastating consequences of sexual assault do not burden the victim alone. The survivor's family members and friends, and even the care providers she turns to for help may suffer emotionally from vicarious trauma (Campbell and Wasco, 2005).

Women who survive gang rapes by multiple offenders generally suffer more than victims of single offenders, in the form of physical injuries, PTSD, and suicide attempts. Females subjected to gang rapes were more inclined to disclose their problems to the police, medical providers, and mental health programs but shockingly reported that they frequently received negative social reactions from these people to whom they turned for help (Ullman, 2007).

ESTIMATES OF THE INCIDENCE, PREVALENCE, AND SERIOUSNESS OF RAPE

About 92,000 girls and women across the country notified the police that they had been forcibly raped during 2006 (about 61 females for every 100,000 inhabitants), according to the FBI's *UCR* (about 8 percent were attempted rapes; the remaining 92 percent were completed acts). About 260,000 people (of whom a small percentage were males) living in urban and suburban areas disclosed to *NCVS* interviewers that they had been raped or sexually assaulted in some other way during 2006 (a rate of about 1 for every 1,000 residents).

But victimologists and criminologists routinely point out that official statistics usually do not accurately indicate how many crimes of a specific kind are committed each year, mainly because many people do not report incidents to the police. When it comes to rape, it is likely that even the most carefully collected data could yield undercounts. Figures from both government sources, the FBI's *UCR* and the BJS's *NCVS*, are indisputably incomplete. The *UCR* statistics are gross underestimates because a large percentage of sexual assault victims do not tell the authorities what happened. Each year, BJS findings confirm that less than half of the victims who were willing to discuss incidents with *NCVS* survey interviewers did not inform the police.

The problem of underreporting has not been resolved. Of the people who told *NCVS* interviewers that they had been raped or sexually assaulted during 2004, only about 36 percent also reported the crime to their local police or sheriff's department, which was one of the lowest rates in many years (see Catalano, 2005). The reporting rate rebounded to 41 percent during 2006 (Rand and Catalano, 2007). Of course, each year some

unknown proportion of victims do not reveal to anyone—including *NCVS* interviewers—that they had suffered a rape, attempted rape, or other type of sexual assault.

The interviewing approach adopted by the *NCVS* at the start of the 1970s was supposed to reduce nonreporting. All incidents disclosed to interviewers were counted, whether or not they were also brought to the attention of the local police. The manner in which the data were gathered for the *NCVS* before 1992 discouraged some individuals from discussing the embarrassing details about what had happened to them. Although confidentiality was pledged, anonymity was compromised by face-to-face questioning.

Surely, some girls and women were very reluctant to speak openly and frankly about such incidents, especially in the presence of other family members. Some respondents might feel uncomfortable delving into such a sensitive subject with any stranger, especially a male interviewer, particularly if his age, class, or ethnicity differed from that of the respondent. Some incidents that could be classified legally as rapes might not be defined as crimes by the females who experienced them, especially if the aggressor was an acquaintance, and he issued threats but was not brutally violent. Screening questions were worded in roundabout ways; the term *sexual attack* was used but was not spelled out sufficiently in graphic detail, and respondents were not given clear-cut examples. The survey's working definition excluded marital rapes; acts of forcible sodomy to other parts of the body; and incidents in which the perpetrator took advantage of a person's intoxicated state, mental illness, or mental retardation. Finally, **series victimizations**—repeated rapes, generally by an intimate or acquaintance—were not counted as separate incidents (Koss, 1992; Bachman, 1998).

In 1992, the BJS redesigned the survey's questionnaire and changed the project's name from the *National Crime Survey* to the *National Crime Victimization Survey*. The original set of questions never bluntly asked about rapes because the subject was considered too personal, delicate, and sensitive to address directly. Interviewers found out about these incidents only if the respondent volunteered the information while thinking about physical attacks and threatened assaults.

In the redesigned questionnaire, the interviewer asks, "Has anyone attacked or threatened you in any of these ways ... any rape, attempted rape, or other type of sexual assault?" The interviewer follows up by saying, "Please mention it even if you are not certain it was a crime. ... Incidents involving forced or unwanted sexual acts are often difficult to talk about. Have you been forced or coerced to engage in unwanted sexual activity by someone you didn't know before, or a casual acquaintance, or someone you know well?" Once this battery of questions was implemented (used on half of the sample), the *NCVS* estimate of the number of rapes and other sexual assaults suffered during 1992 jumped more than 150 percent (Kindermann and Lynch, 1997).

To address some of the methodological criticisms leveled by researchers against the way the FBI's *UCR* measured rape, its data-collecting systems were changed. In 1991 a National Incident Based Reporting System (NIBRS) definition of rape replaced the narrow *UCR* guideline of "carnal knowledge of a female forcibly and against her will." The FBI's NIBRS now counts sexual assaults directed against males and broadens the definition to keep track of incidents in which the person was not violated by force but was unable to give consent because of either a temporary or permanent mental or physical incapacity (for example, alcohol-induced unconsciousness). In addition, the NIBRS counts acts of forcible sodomy other than vaginal intercourse, sexual assaults carried out with an object, and forcible fondling. However, most police departments across the country had not switched to NIBRS by the first six years of the twenty-first century, so the older way of recording rape incidents solely against females is still retained in annual *UCRs*.

However, rape continues to be one of the most underreported of serious crimes, despite well-intentioned efforts to persuade more victims to come forward for help. Police detectives and emergency room personnel have received sensitivity training, sexual assault nurse examiners have been certified, hotlines have been set up, crisis centers have been established (including on college campuses), court advocates have been hired, and laws have been reformed—yet many victims still are reluctant to disclose the facts about sexual assaults they have endured.

Girls and women told *NCVS* interviewers that they did not report sexual assaults to the authorities because: They lacked proof that they were violated against their will; the incident was not serious enough; they are not sure the perpetrator intended to harm them; they fear they will be stigmatized because of widely held victim-blaming rape myths; and they anticipate a "second wound" if they are demeaned, belittled, or entirely disbelieved by people who are supposed to assist and support them. If they tell anyone, that individual is more likely to be a friend than an authority figure, family member, or lover (see Fisher, Daigle, and Cullen, 2008).

Even if the official figures are surely undercounts, what changes over time can be discerned? When annual estimates of rapes, as measured by the *NCVS* and the *UCR*, are plotted on the same set of axes, the trend lines on the graph diverge and become a source of confusing and contradictory impressions (see Figure 10.1). According to the *UCR*, an alarming, fairly steady upward trend in reported rapes can be seen from the early 1970s (actually, but not shown, the number of reported rapes began to rise in the mid-1960s) until the early 1990s. Reports of sexual violence unleashed by men against women reached a record high in 1992 (43 rape complaints for every 100,000 females), but after that the trend reversed. For the remainder of the 1990s, the rape rate declined, as did the rate of all other index crimes, including murder, robbery, assault, burglary, and motor vehicle theft. In sum, after worsening for several decades, this problem peaked in the early 1990s and then subsided during the rest of the 1990s. The number of reported rapes remained stable at this lower level during the first six years of the new century, according to *UCR* figures based on formal complaints to the police.

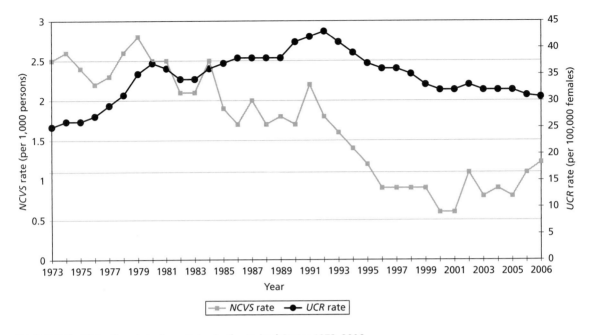

FIGURE 10.1 Trends in Rape Rates in the United States, 1973–2006

NOTES: UCR counts female victims only. 1973–1991 NCVS rates adjusted for compatibility with redesigned 1992 survey.

SOURCES: FBI's UCR, 1973–2006; BJS's NCVS, 1973–2006.

According to the *NCVS*, however, the number of rapes disclosed to survey interviewers, as opposed to local police departments, varied from year to year in a rather choppy and unpredictable way from 1973 until 1992, although the direction of drift was clearly downward. Therefore, prior to 1992, the impressions from the two sources were exactly opposite. Rapes were becoming more frequent according to police reports and less frequent according to disclosures to survey interviewers. After 1991, *NCVS* rape rates generally trended downward during the remainder of the 1990s, mirroring the decline indicated by *UCR* figures (compare the two lines in Figure 10.1). Therefore, both government-run monitoring systems indicated that sexual violence was becoming less of a threat to girls and women by the turn of the new century. During the first six years of the twenty-first century, the number of rapes and other sexual assaults disclosed to *NCVS* interviewers fluctuated a bit but remained roughly stable at the lowest levels in 30 years, as the graph in Figure 10.1 shows.

The discrepancy between *NCVS* and *UCR* trends until 1992 puzzled criminologists and

victimologists. Some suspected that *UCR* statistics showed an upward trend because more women were coming forward to report rapes that in the past would not have been brought to the attention of the police. In particular, public attitudes toward women raped by non-strangers were improving, so the police were learning about more assaults by dates and acquaintances (Orcutt and Faison, 1988). However, rape reporting rates did not increase steadily from the early 1970s until the early 1990s, according to *NCVS* figures (refer to Table 6.1, which presents for selected years the percentages of rapes revealed to interviewers that were also reported to the police). Perhaps police departments were hiring female detectives who took allegations of rape complainants more seriously and were investigating, documenting, and recording these kinds of incidents more carefully than had been done in the past (Jensen and Karpos, 1993).

As for prevalence estimates, studies since the 1950s indicate that incidents involving aggressive, forceful, and offensive sexuality are disturbingly common (see Abbey, 2005). About 15 percent of women reported they had endured a completed rape and an additional 3 percent had suffered an attempted rape, according to a government-sponsored survey of 8,000 women and 8,000 men during the mid-1990s (Tjaden and Thoennes, 1998). A prevalence rate of about 18 percent was much higher than the 8 percent lifetime likelihood projected during the mid-1980s (Koppel, 1987). Therefore, based on current rates, about 20 million females residing in the United States will be subjected to sexual violence at some point in their lives. Teenage girls and young women are the prime targets, although women of all ages face some risk of attack until they reach 65 (see Marx, 2005; and Fisher, Daigle and Cullen, 2008).

DIFFERENTIAL RISKS OF BEING SEXUALLY ASSAULTED AND RAPED

Even though the NCVS figures are underestimates, the differential risks derived from yearly surveys are worth analyzing. The findings confirm the suspicion that various categories of girls and women face lower or higher levels of risk. The statistical portrait painted by a large database collected between 1973 and 1987 indicates that the gravest risks of being raped are faced by females in their late teens or early 20s, unmarried, living in low-income families, unemployed, black, and residing in large cities (see column 2 of the victimization rates in Table 10.1). Females who face the smallest risks are over age 50, white, married or widowed, affluent, and living in rural areas (Harlow, 1991). Figures from 1998, 2004, and 2006 reveal that these risk factors have not changed much over the decades (see columns 3, 4, and 5 in Table 10.1). However, the differences between the rates suffered by women of various races have narrowed, as well as between urban and suburban females. In general, the risks of being sexually assaulted have declined for all groups (see Rennison, 1999; Catalano, 2005; and BJS 2008).

One issue that concerns many people also has received attention from victimologists—whether strangers or non-strangers pose a greater threat to girls and women. The answer is not clear from official statistics, largely because so many victims do not want to discuss the incidents with anyone—not detectives and not survey interviewers. The attacker was a stranger more than half the time (55 percent), according to an analysis of attempted and completed rapes disclosed to NCVS interviewers from 1982 to 1984 (Timrots and Rand, 1987). However, a comparable analysis of NCVS data from 1987 to 1991 yielded a somewhat lower figure of 44 percent for sexual assaults by strangers (Bachman, 1994). Strangers were responsible for 25 percent of all attacks disclosed in 1998, 30 percent in 2001 and 2005, and 39 percent in 2006 (BJS, 2008). The post-1992 redesigned NCVS survey might be eliciting more responses about illegal behavior by acquaintances and intimates (Rennison, 1999; 2002a; Rand and Catalano, 2007).

According to another recent survey that focused on violence against women, the overwhelming majority of perpetrators (more than 80 percent) were not strangers. Most (more than 60 percent) were a current or former intimate partner; many other assailants were an acquaintance (more than 20 percent). Complete strangers committed the remainder of the sexual assaults (about 17 percent) (see Fisher, Daigle and Cullen, 2008). As for incidents reported to the police, in only 28 percent of the cases did the girl or woman not recognize the rapist, according to the NIBRS database of 3,800 reports to the police from three states in 1991 (Reaves, 1993).

The apparent trend in NCVS findings of a declining percentage of stranger rapes (except for 2006) and the growing proportion of non-stranger rapes may reflect an increasing willingness of females to disclose these kinds of incidents and not a genuine rise in acquaintance rapes. And yet, for a number of reasons, women who have been assaulted by someone they know still may be more reluctant to report the crime to the police or discuss the matter with survey interviewers. They might experience a greater sense of shame, guilt, embarrassment, and self-blame, and might feel that they should have been able to head off the attack. Others might fear reprisals for going to the authorities and dread that their account will not be believed or that

TABLE 10.1   Which Females Face the Gravest Risks of Rape and Sexual Assault? Selected Years, 1973 to 2006

	Annual Rape Rate per 1,000 Females 1973–1987	1998 Annual Rape Rate per 1,000 Persons	2004 Annual Rape Rate per 1,000 Persons	2006 Annual Rape Rate per 1,000 persons
All Females	1.6 for every 1,000	1.5 for every 1,000	1.6 for every 1,000	1.1 for every 1,000
Age				
12–15	2.3	3.5	2.2	3.4
16–19	4.8	5.0	2.5	2.5
20–24	4.1	4.6	2.5	1.8
25–34	2.3	1.7	0.7*	1.4
35–49	0.6	0.7	0.5	0.7
50–64	0.2	0.2	0.3*	0.5
65 and over	0.1	0.0	0.1*	0.0
Race and ethnicity				
White	1.5	1.5	0.8	1.1
Black	2.7	2.0	1.7	1.1
Other	1.8	0.7	0.0*	0.7
Hispanic	1.5	0.8	0.6*	0.9
Marital status				
Married	0.5	0.5	0.2*	0.2*
Widowed	0.4	0.3	0.0*	0.2*
Divorced or separated	4.3	2.6	2.3	2.6
Never married	3.5	3.1	1.6	2.1
Income				
Low	2.7	2.7*	2.0*	2.3*
Middle	1.2	1.5*	0.9*	1.1*
High	0.8	1.2*	0.6*	0.4*
Area of residence				
Urban	2.5	1.7	1.5	1.2
Suburban	1.4	1.4	0.8	1.0
Rural	1.1	1.5	0.3*	na

NOTE: Rates in Column 1 were derived from an analysis of 2,515,200 rapes (832,200 completed and 1,683,000 attempted) reported by respondents to *NCVS* interviewers from 1973 until 1987. After 1992, sexual assaults are included. 1998, 2004, and 2006 rates include small numbers of male victims.

* = *NCVS* estimate is based on a very small number of cases within the sample.

na = not available.

SOURCES: Harlow, 1991; Rennison, 1999; Catalano, 2005; and BJS, 2008.

others will condemn them for encouraging the male's forceful response. Some may even wish to protect the identity of the assailant if he is a relative, former friend, boss, or a powerful community figure (Klaus, DeBerry, and Timrots, 1985).

In sum, the preponderance of the available evidence indicates that intimates, dates, and acquaintances seem to be offenders much more often than sinister stalkers, intruders, and other assailants whose identities were unknown to the girls and women they ambushed.

HOW THE CRIMINAL JUSTICE SYSTEM HANDLES RAPE VICTIMS

Before public consciousness was raised by the anti-rape movement, complainants who courageously reported sex crimes frequently found themselves socially stigmatized. An old-fashioned notion prevailed—"Good girls don't get raped"—so those who do must have done something to deserve their fate. Even if an unquestionably innocent victim was taken against her will, she was callously looked down upon as being "defiled" and "devalued" by the experience. Those who dared to press charges were often told that their cases were unprosecutable or unwinnable, given the unreasonably stringent legal standards required for conviction.

The laws passed over the centuries and amended by judges' case-by-case decisions were not intended and never functioned to guarantee women's safety, freedom of movement, and peace of mind. The use of terms such as "fallen," "ravaged," and "despoiled" to describe rape victims betrayed antiquated attitudes of men toward girls and women: that they were the "property" of their fathers or husbands who lost "market value" and became "damaged goods" if they were "violated." Rape laws reflected and reinforced prevailing double standards regarding appropriate forms of sexual conduct and sex-based roles for females and males (LeGrande, 1973).

The account presented in Box 10.2 illustrates how the system routinely mistreated survivors in the "bad old days" before the victims' rights movement raised objections and brought about meaningful reforms. This fictional composite sketch illustrates everything that possibly could go wrong. It was compiled by the President's Task Force on Victims of Crime from testimony about real-life ordeals brought to their attention at the start of the 1980s. Because this "worst-case scenario" provides a virtual checklist of nearly all the possible problems, frustrations, and abuses that can arise, it can serve as a standard for comparison with current case handling to identify how much progress has been made and exactly what remains to be accomplished.

The narrative follows one woman's plight as her case is processed. The presidential task force pinpointed why victims find themselves pitted against the police, the prosecuting attorney working for the government, the defense lawyer acting on behalf of the accused, the judge presiding over the case, the jury sitting in judgment, and the parole

board determining the convict's future. This excerpt accentuates the negative by emphasizing the mishandling of rape cases at every level because victims of sexual assaults were—and still are—the most mistreated of all those who seek help from the criminal justice system (see Box 10.2).

The account presented in Box 10.2 identified and dramatized all the anti-victim practices and procedures that had accumulated within the criminal justice system over the centuries. One by one, they have been addressed by the anti-rape movement. Many policies and practices have been reformed over the past few decades, including the basic legal statutes that govern court procedures.

And yet 25 years after the President's Task Force issued recommendations for reform (based on the horror story below), a coalition against sexual assault released a report that concluded that rape victims often still suffer mistreatment in New York City. The study, based on interviews with 65 male and female victims, determined that only one-third were asked whether they had a safe place to return to in the aftermath of the attack; less than half were told about opportunities for counseling; and only half were informed about the availability of a vaccine to reduce the risks of contracting HIV/AIDs (Boyle, 2007). The report included a real-life experience that bore a disturbing resemblance to the worst-case scenario compiled by the President's Task Force two and a half decades ago:

> An intruder creeps into a 40-year-old librarian's bedroom and rapes her. She runs to a neighbor's home, wearing nothing but an overcoat. When the police arrive, they do not immediately race next door to investigate the crime scene. Eventually, she is transported to a hospital, but is left alone in a room because no victim's advocate is on duty. Two male detectives ask her to recount the series of events in great detail three times. After being tested for traces of DNA, she is totally naked because her coat was taken as evidence. After being released, she has to track down a male orderly to get something to wear, and has to plead with the hospital's staff to arrange for a taxicab to take her home. (Boyle, 2007)

B O X 10.2 The System's Shortcomings from a Victim's Point of View

---

The Crime

You are a 50-year-old woman living alone. You are asleep one night when suddenly you awaken to find a man standing over you with a knife at your throat. As you start to scream, he beats you and cuts you. He then rapes you. While you watch helplessly, he searches the house, taking your jewelry, other valuables, and money. He smashes furniture and windows in a display of senseless violence. His rampage ended, he rips out the telephone line, threatens you again, and disappears in the night.

At least you have survived. Terrified, you rush to the first lighted house on the block. While you wait for the police, you pray that your attacker was bluffing when he said he'd return if you called them. Finally, what you expect to be help arrives.

The police ask questions, take notes, dust for fingerprints, and take photographs. When you tell them you were raped, they take you to the hospital. Bleeding from cuts, your front teeth knocked out, bruised and in pain, you are told that your wounds are superficial, that rape itself is not considered an injury. Awaiting treatment, you sit alone for hours, suffering the stares of curious passersby. You feel dirty, bruised, disheveled, and abandoned. When your turn comes for examination, the intern seems irritated because he has been called out to treat you. While he treats you, he says that he hates to get involved in rape cases because he doesn't like going to court. He asks if you "knew the man you had sex with." The nurse says she wouldn't be out alone at this time of night. It seems pointless to explain that the attacker broke into your house and had a knife. An officer says you must go through this process, and then the hospital sends you a bill for the examination that the investigators insist upon. They give you a box filled with test tubes and swabs and envelopes and tell you to hold onto it. They'll run some tests if they ever catch your rapist.

Finally, you get home somehow, in a cab you paid for and wearing a hospital gown because they took your clothes as evidence. Everything that the attacker touched seems soiled. You're afraid to be in your house alone. The one place where you were always safe, at home, is a sanctuary no longer. You are afraid to remain, yet terrified to leave your home unprotected.

You didn't realize when you gave the police your name and address that it would be given to the press through police reports. Your friends call to say they saw this information in the paper, your picture on television. You haven't yet absorbed what's happened to you when you get calls from insurance companies and firms that sell security devices. But these calls pale in comparison to the threats that come from the defendant and his friends.

You're astonished to discover that your attacker has been arrested, yet while in custody he has free and unmonitored access to a phone. He can threaten you from jail. The judge orders him not to annoy you, but when the phone calls are brought to his attention, the judge does nothing.

At least you can be assured that the man who attacked you is in custody, or so you think. No one tells you that he is released on his promise to come to court. No one asks you if you've been threatened. The judge is never told that the defendant said he'd kill you if you told or that he'd get even if he went to jail. Horrified, you ask how he got out after what he did. You're told the judge can't consider whether he'll be dangerous, only whether he'll come back to court. He's been accused and convicted before, but he always came to court, so he must be released.

You learn only by accident that he's at large; this discovery comes when you turn a corner and confront him. He knows where you live. He's been there. Besides, your name and address were in the paper and in the reports he's seen. Now nowhere is safe. He watches you from across the street; he follows you on the bus. Will he come back in the night? What do you do? Give up your home? Lose your job? Assume a different name? Get your mail at the post office? Carry a weapon? Even if you wanted to, could you afford to do these things?

You try to return to normal. You don't want to talk about what happened, so you decide not to tell your co-workers. A few days go by and unexpectedly the police come to your place of work. They show their badges to the receptionist and ask to see you. They want you to look at some photographs, but they don't explain that to your co-workers. You try to explain later that you're the victim—not the accused.

The phone rings, and the police want you to come to a lineup. It may be 1:00 a.m. or in the middle of your work day, but you have to go; the suspect and his lawyer are waiting. It will not be the last time you are forced to conform your life to their convenience. You appear at the police station and the lineup begins. The suspect's lawyer sits next to you, but he does not watch the stage; he stares at you. It will not be the last time you must endure his scrutiny.

Charges Are Pressed Against a Defendant

You have lived through the crime and made it through the initial investigation. They've caught the man who harmed you, and he's been charged with armed burglary, robbery, and rape. Now he'll be tried. Now you expect justice.

You receive a subpoena for a preliminary hearing. No one tells you what it will involve, how long it will take, or how you should prepare. You assume that this is the only time you will have to appear. But you are only beginning your initiation in a system that will grind away at you for months, disrupt your life, affect your emotional stability, and certainly cost you money; it may cost you your job, and, for the duration, will prevent you from putting the crime behind you and reconstructing your life.

Before the hearing, a defense investigator comes to talk to you. When he contacts you, he says he's "investigating your case," and that he "works for the county." You assume, as he intends you to, that he's from the police or the prosecutor's office. Only after you give him a statement do you discover that he works for the man who attacked you.

This same investigator may visit your neighbors and co-workers, asking questions about you. He discusses the case with them, always giving the defendant's side. Suddenly, some of the people who know you seem to be taking a different view of what happened to you and why.

It's the day of the hearing. You've never been to court before, never spoken in public. You're very nervous. You rush to arrive at 8 a.m. to talk to a prosecutor you've never met. You wait in a hallway with a number of other witnesses. It's now 8:45. Court starts at 9:00. No one has spoken to you. Finally, a man sticks his head out a door, calls out your name, and asks, "Are you the one who was raped?" You're aware of the stares as you stand and suddenly realize that this is the prosecutor, the person you expect will represent your interests.

You speak to the prosecutor for only a few minutes. You ask to read the statement you gave to the police, but he says there isn't time. He asks you some questions that make you wonder if he's read it himself. He asks you other questions that make you wonder if he believes it.

The prosecutor tells you to sit on the bench outside the courtroom. Suddenly you see the man who raped you coming down the hall. No one has told you he would be here. He's with three friends. He points

you out. They all laugh and jostle you a little as they pass. The defendant and two friends enter the courtroom; one friend sits on the bench across from you and stares. Suddenly, you feel abandoned, alone, afraid. Is this what it's like to come to court and seek justice?

You sit on the bench for an hour, then two. You don't see the prosecutor; he has disappeared into the courtroom. Finally, at noon he comes out and says, "Oh, you're still here? We continued that case to next month." You repeat this process many times before you actually testify at the preliminary hearing. Each time you go to court, you take leave from work, pay for parking, wait for hours, and finally are told to go home. No one ever asks if the new dates are convenient to you. You miss vacations and medical appointments. You use up sick leave and vacation days to make your court appearances. Your employer is losing his patience. Every time you are gone his business is disrupted. But you are fortunate. If you were new at your job, or worked part-time, or didn't have an understanding boss, you could lose your job. Many victims do.

The preliminary hearing was an event for which you were completely unprepared. You learn later that the defense is often harder on a victim at the preliminary hearing than during the trial. In a trial, the defense attorney cannot risk alienating the jury. At this hearing there is only the judge—and he certainly doesn't seem concerned about you. One of the first questions you are asked is where you live. You finally moved after your attack; you've seen the defendant and his friends, and you're terrified of having them know where you now live. When you explain that you'd be happy to give your old address the judge says he'll dismiss the case or hold you in contempt of court if you don't answer the question. The prosecutor says nothing. During your testimony, you are also compelled to say where you work, how you get there, and what your schedule is.

Hours later you are released from the stand after reliving your attack in public, in intimate detail. You have been made to feel completely powerless. As you sat facing a smirking defendant and as you described his threats, you were accused of lying and inviting the "encounter." You have cried in front of these uncaring strangers. As you leave no one thanks you. When you get back to work they ask what took you so long.

You are stunned when you later learn that the defendant also raped five others; one victim was an eight-year-old girl. During her testimony she was

(Continued)

B O X 10.2   (Continued)

---

asked to describe her attacker's anatomy. Spectators laughed when she said she did not understand the words being used. When she was asked to draw a picture of her attacker's genitalia, the girl fled from the courtroom and ran sobbing to her mother, who had been subpoenaed by the defense and had to wait outside. The youngster was forced to sit alone and recount, as you did, each minute of the attack. You know how difficult it was for you to speak of these things; you cannot imagine how it was for a child.

Now the case is scheduled for trial. Again there are delays. When you call and ask to speak with the prosecutor, you are told the case has been reassigned. You tell your story in detail to five different prosecutors before the case is tried.

Months go by and no one tells you what's happening. Periodically you are subpoenaed to appear. You leave your work, wait, and are finally told to go home. Continuances are granted because the courts are filled, one of the lawyers is on another case, and the judge has a meeting to attend or an early tennis match. You can't understand why they couldn't have discovered these problems before you came to court. When you ask if the next date could be set a week later so you can attend a family gathering out of state, you are told that the defendant has the right to a speedy trial. You stay home from the reunion and the case is continued. The defense attorney continues to call. Will you change your story? Don't you want to drop the charges?

Time passes and you hear nothing. Your property is not returned. You learn that there are dozens of defense motions that can be filed before the trial. If denied, many of them can be appealed. Each motion, each court date means a new possibility for delay. If the defendant is out of custody and fails to come to court, nothing can happen until he is re-apprehended. If he is successful in avoiding recapture, the case may be so compromised by months or years of delay that a successful prosecution is impossible.

For as long as the case drags on, your life is on hold. You don't want to start a new assignment at work or move to a new city because you know that at any time the round of court appearances may begin again. The wounds of your attack will never heal as long as you know that you will be asked to relive those horrible moments.

No one tells you anything about the progress of the case. You want to be involved, consulted, and informed, but prosecutors often plea bargain without consulting victims. You're afraid someone will let the defendant plead guilty to a lesser charge and be sentenced to probation. You meet another victim at court who tells you that she and her family were kidnapped and her children molested. Even though the prosecutor assured her that he would not accept a plea bargain, after talking with the attorneys in his chambers, the judge allowed the defendant to plead guilty as charged with the promise of a much-reduced sentence. You hope that this won't happen in your case.

The Trial

Finally the day of trial arrives. It has been 18 months since you were attacked. You've been trying for a week to prepare yourself. It is painful to dredge up the terror again, but you know that the outcome depends on you; the prosecutor has told you that the way you behave will make or break the case. You can't get too angry on the stand because then the jury might not like you. You can't break down and sob because then you will appear too emotional, possibly unstable. In addition to the tremendous pressure of having to relive the horrible details of the crime, you're expected to be an actress as well.

You go to court. The continuances are over; the jury has been selected. You sit in a waiting room with

---

The Controversy over Unfounded Accusations

Rape always has been in a class by itself in one peculiar way: The complainant immediately confronts a credibility issue. Both the law and public opinion reflect great concern about the danger of false accusations against innocent men. Knowingly and maliciously filing a false complaint with the police and testifying dishonestly are punishable acts no matter what the crime, but fears about baseless charges arise almost automatically in rape cases.

Special safeguards to protect male defendants—which female accusers had to surmount—were built into the law (see MacDonald and Michaud, 1995). Two errors are possible: honest mistakes the defendant's family and friends. Again you feel threatened, vulnerable, and alone.

You expect the trial to be a search for the truth; you find that it is a performance orchestrated by lawyers and the judge, with the jury hearing only half the facts. The defendant was found with your watch in his pocket. The judge has suppressed this evidence because the officer who arrested him didn't have a warrant.

Your character is an open subject of discussion and innuendo. The defense is allowed to question you on incidents going back to your childhood. The jury is never told that the defendant has two prior convictions for the same offense and has been to prison three times for other crimes. You sought help from a counselor to deal with the shattering effect of this crime on your life. You told him about your intimate fears and feelings. Now he has been called by the defense and his notes and records have been subpoenaed.

You are on the stand for hours. The defense does its best to make you appear a liar, a seductress, or both. You know you cannot relax for a moment. Don't be embarrassed when everyone seems angry because you do not understand. Think ahead. Be responsive. Don't volunteer. Don't get tired.

Finally you are finished with this part of the nightmare. You would like to sit and listen to the rest of the trial but you cannot. You're a witness and must wait outside. The jury will decide the outcome of one of the major events of your life. You cannot hear the testimony that will guide their judgment.

The verdict is guilty. You now look to the judge to impose a just sentence.

The Sentence

You expect the sentence to reflect how terrible the crime was. You ask the prosecutor how this decision is reached, and are told that once a defendant is convicted he is interviewed at length by a probation officer. He gives his side of the story, which may be blatantly false in light of the proven facts. A report that delves into his upbringing, family relationships, education, physical and mental health, and employment and conviction history is prepared. The officer will often speak to the defendant's relatives and friends. Some judges will send the defendant to a facility where a complete psychiatric and sociological work-up is prepared. You're amazed that no one will ever ask you about the crime, or the effect it has had on you and your family. You took the defendant's blows, heard his threats, and listened to him brag that he'd "beat the rap" or "con the judge." No one ever hears of these things. They never give you a chance to tell them.

At sentencing, the judge hears from the defendant, his lawyer, his mother, his minister, and his friends. You learn by chance what day the hearing is. When you do attend, the defense attorney says you're vengeful, and it's apparent that you overreacted to being raped and robbed because you chose to come and see the sentencing. You ask permission to address the judge and are told that you are not allowed to do so.

The judge sentences your attacker to three years in prison, less than one year for every hour he kept you in pain and terror. That seems very lenient to you. Only later do you discover that he'll probably serve less than half of his actual sentence in prison because of good-time and work-time credits that are given to him immediately. The man who broke into your home, threatened to slit your throat with a knife, and raped, beat, and robbed you will be out of custody in less than 18 months. You are not told when he will actually be released, and you are not allowed to attend the parole release hearing anyway.

SOURCE: Excerpted from the report of the President's Task Force on Victims of Crime, 1982, pp. 3–11.

and deliberate acts of perjury. A complainant acting in good faith may identify the wrong person—an innocent stranger—as the perpetrator (this would not be a problem in acquaintance and date rapes). DNA tests make it possible to eliminate some male suspects and even to rectify some recent miscarriages of justice by overturning convictions and freeing innocent prisoners from their cells. Cases in which a victim misidentifies the assailant crop up periodically.

Fraudulent accusations are more of a concern than honest mistakes. A girl or woman could attempt to deceive authorities by lodging a fake charge against an innocent boy or man for one of many ulterior purposes: perhaps to arouse sympathy and gain attention, to punish a former lover, to provide a "don't blame me" explanation for contracting an embarrassing venereal disease or for becoming pregnant, or to hide the truth for another reason. Widely held negative stereotypes and suspicions about manipulative or vengeful women fuel these fears. Cases like the ones that follow are often cited to justify the skepticism that many complainants encounter in press accounts, police stations, prosecutors' offices, and courtrooms:

> A junior high school teacher is arrested, jailed, and suspended from his job because a 12-year-old girl tells detectives that he raped her at least seven times over the past few months. But the prosecutor's office drops the charges when the special education student, who has the mental ability of a six-year-old, confesses that she concocted the story on the advice of a young friend. The child admits that she told the lie because she feared her parents would discover that she was engaging in sex acts with a boy her own age. (Lenkowitz and Messing, 2003)

***

> A secretary working for a prominent law firm goes to the sex crimes squad and tells detectives in a calm and forthright manner that a senior partner raped her when they were working alone in the office late one night. When questioned, the attorney denies he raped her but admits to carrying on a discreet affair with her, telling his wife he was working late or traveling overnight on business trips. He claims that when she demanded that he leave his family and move in with her, his refusal provoked her to threaten to kill herself, or kill his wife, or kill him. Confronted by detectives with his version of events—that a "scorned woman" was making up terrible accusations to get even with him for dashing her dreams of upward mobility—she denies the charges. But when the police find hotel bills and airline ticket receipts documenting their secret trysts, she confesses that her vengeful claim was intended to cost him his prestigious job and his marriage. (Fairstein, 1993)

The 1931 "Scottsboro Boys" case stands out in history as the most notorious example of a false accusation of rape for a malicious purpose. The apparently trumped-up charges, that eight young black men gang raped two white women riding with young white men in a boxcar of a freight train, were made for political reasons. In the Old South, white women were often pressured by white men to accuse black men of rape so that the alleged suffering of the victims could be seized upon to justify the execution or lynching of the accused individuals, and by extension to legitimize the segregation and repression of all black men (Sagarin, 1975). The controversy surrounding the way the defendants in this case of Southern "racial justice" were ""railroaded in a kangaroo court" without lawyers and sentenced to die led to a Supreme Court decision (*Powell v. Alabama*, 1932). This landmark ruling established the right of indigent people accused of capital crimes to be represented by competent counsel provided by the government at no cost (later decisions extended this right to all defendants).

The task confronting detectives and prosecutors is to weed out the very small number of false claims (about a consensual act that is later characterized as forced, or about a totally fabricated incident that never took place) from the overwhelming majority of genuine charges. The dishonesty of a few does not justify routinely mistreating all complainants as possible liars (Fairstein, 1993). The task for criminologists and victimologists is to determine how often baseless charges are lodged and whether false accusations really are more of a problem in rape cases than in other crimes such as robberies or car thefts (see MacDonald and Michaud, 1995).

Credible statistics about the percentage of complaints that turn out baseless are hard to find. Pro-complainant advocates point out that social workers at a hospital and a police sex crime unit estimated their false complaint rates to be less than 2 percent (Bode, 1978). Pro-defendant advocates cite study results that concluded that 40 percent of more than 100 complaints turned out false—the woman recanted her original charges when told that she faced a stiff fine and a jail sentence—according to records from 1978 to 1987 of a police department in a small Midwestern city (Kanin, 1994).

The FBI's *UCR* reported that in 1966, after a preliminary investigation, police forces across the country had declared 20 percent of all rape complaints unfounded. Ten years later, the *UCR* stated that 19 percent had been closed as unfounded. The *UCR*s for 1996 and 1997 stated that about 8 percent of all rape complaints were classified as unfounded by local police departments, compared to 2 percent of complaints about other index crimes. No such figures have appeared in the *UCR*s since then. Note that the designation *unfounded* is not synonymous with "patently false." Some cases in this category were deemed unsubstantiated after an inconclusive investigation or unprovable in court in the opinion of detectives. But that doesn't mean the allegations were baseless or that accusers were deliberately committing perjury or imagining things (Archambault, 2005).

Detectives often have presumed, in the past, that false cries of forcible rape were the rule and not the exception. They were especially suspicious if the woman did not report the attack immediately, or didn't seem upset by her injuries. Her credibility was questioned if she was either extremely vague about the details or extremely precise, or was reluctant to describe the assailant or the exact location. Their disbelief of her story escalated if she was intoxicated at the time, had filed complaints before, or had a history of emotional problems (Jordan, 2004; and Archambault, 2005).

Consequently, many police departments routinely administered lie detector tests to check a complainant's credibility. Unfortunately, submitting to the questionable reliability of a polygraph loomed as an added indignity and served as a further deterrent to reporting crimes and pressing charges. Groups in the anti-rape movement—who are convinced the problem of false allegations is greatly exaggerated—went to court to get injunctions against the practice. The President's Task Force on Victims of Crime (1982) recommended that procedures that reflected automatic distrust of complainants be abandoned, and a number of states have specifically outlawed polygraph testing of complainants. However, reports surface periodically that police departments still administer polygraphs and other truth-verification tests such as computerized voice-stress analyzers to certain categories of sexual assault victims ("Report exposes lie detector tests …" 2003).

False accusations of sexual assault lodged by dishonest complainants posing as victims send shock waves within the criminal justice process and threaten to undermine much of the progress made by the anti-rape movement. Highly publicized instances like the ones that follow give renewed life to traditional doubts that cast a cloud of suspicion over the credibility of all genuine victims who demand to be taken seriously:

> A 15-year-old black girl is discovered in an apparent state of shock curled up in a plastic garbage bag. She does not say much to police officers or doctors but according to her relatives and her advisors, she had been kidnapped and repeatedly raped for several days by four white men who appeared to have law enforcement affiliations. Her explosive charges divide the public along racial lines. A special grand jury is impaneled by the state's attorney general to look into the inflammatory accusations and to explore the possibility of an official cover-up. It concludes that there is insufficient evidence to charge anyone with a crime. Months later, the girl's boyfriend claims that she told him that she and her mother made up the whole story so that her violence-prone stepfather would not beat her for staying out late. Unfortunately, an aunt who believed the story contacted the news media, which sensationalized the concocted allegations into headlines for months. Years later, one of the maligned men, an assistant district attorney, sues the supposed victim and her advisors in civil court for defamation of character and wins a monetary judgment against them. (Payne, 1989; Taibbi and Sims-Phillips, 1989; Schaye, 1998)

***

Two women are hired to strip at a party for the young men of a university lacrosse team. One of the dancers says she was hustled into a bathroom and sexually assaulted by three players. Three members of the team are arrested and indicted for rape, sexual offense, and kidnapping, even though highly sensitive genetic tests do not reveal any DNA trace evidence from them, and she is unable to identify her attackers from team pictures. The university president cancels the remainder of the lacrosse season, the coach resigns, and the three players are suspended pending a trial. The highly publicized case touches off scathing commentaries about the sense of entitlement privileged young white men feel toward exploiting poor young black women. But then the case unravels, the mentally troubled exotic dancer becomes uncertain about what really happened, and the veteran prosecutor who was just re-elected resigns in disgrace and is disbarred. The young men who were falsely accused, publicly humiliated, and traumatized by the prospects of 30-year sentences, file lawsuits against the former prosecutor, the police department, the DNA lab, and the city, charging them with premeditated police, prosecutorial, and scientific misconduct. (Brooks, 2006; Nizza, 2007; and Wilson, 2007)

The belief that the woman's word alone is not enough to secure a conviction in court is based on several legitimate concerns: that the male is entitled to the presumption of innocence; that certain females might somehow gain something by committing perjury; that defendants charged with rape are immediately—and possibly permanently—stigmatized even if they are later acquitted of all charges; and that conviction carries very severe penalties including, until the 1970s, execution.

Because of the credibility issue, very stringent standards of proof were crafted into rape laws to make it particularly difficult to secure convictions. The men who wrote the laws and administered the legal system considered these difficult-to-surmount hurdles to be safeguards against miscarriages of justice. But from the standpoint of a genuinely innocent victim, the safeguards loomed as major obstacles that discouraged and thwarted her pursuit of justice. From a feminist perspective, truth tests represented a clear case of institutionalized discrimination against female complainants. The exceptionally high standards of proof took several forms: demands for evidence that the accuser did not willingly consent to engage in sex; a requirement that her testimony be corroborated (backed up independently); and a tradition that she undergo particularly vigorous cross-examination by a defense attorney at the trial. At the end of a trial, a judge often delivered a "cautionary instruction" to the jurors before they began their deliberations, paraphrasing an English jurist's warnings from 1671 that it is easy to accuse a man of rape but hard to prove the charge, but it is even harder for an innocent man to defend himself and clear his name.

The Accuser versus the Accused

Rape prosecutions directly pit the rights of the accused male against the rights of the female complainant. He has the Sixth Amendment right to wage a vigorous defense through his attorney. She has a right to be taken seriously and treated with respect on and off the witness stand, according to recent victims' rights legislation and rewritten rape laws. Observing the rights of both parties requires a delicate balancing act that has yet to be resolved.

Advocates for rape victims argue that when the rights of one party are pitted against the other, her needs trump his. For example, a victim can contract HIV/AIDS from an assailant, especially if the intrusion is violent and bloody. Therefore, state laws mandating that accused rapists must quickly undergo HIV testing would seem to be "pro-victim" at the expense of the privacy of males who are suspects but not yet indicted or convicted. If court-ordered testing determines that he is not infected, this news might allay some of her fears.

However, experts insist that a genuinely "pro-victim" approach would not necessarily involve a loss of the arrested person's privacy rights. What if he is actually within the window period during which a person recently infected with the virus tests negative? What if he is not the assailant? What if no one is quickly apprehended? A safer course of action would be to guarantee that victims of sexual assaults be informed immediately about the availability of a treatment called post-exposure prophylaxis—which involves taking retroviral medications for 28 days—and be entitled to this urgent care at no cost (Hofmann, 2007). Criminal transmission of the AIDS virus is a separate punishable offense, but it also can be the reason for sentencing an attacker who knows he is infected more harshly (Myers and Jacobo, 2006).

Criminal court is the arena where the two parties will be pitted against each other. The accused man can pursue one of several possible defense strategies. The first is to argue that the complaining witness has made a terrible but honest error, picking an innocent man out of a lineup (the "mistaken identity" defense). The second is to deny that he engaged in sexual acts with her (the "it-never-happened" defense). This requires a direct attack on the alleged victim's credibility and motivation by charging that she made up the false story for some deceptive reason. The third defense is to concede that he had sexual intercourse with her but that she agreed at the time; afterward, she changed her mind, considered it a rape, and had him arrested (the "consent" defense) (see Toobin, 2003).

Built-in anti-victim biases that shaped the way cases were investigated and prosecuted were most evident in the corroboration rule, the resistance requirement, and the practice of inquiring into the complainant's sexual history in order to discredit her testimony. However, as public alarm grew about an apparent upsurge in sexual violence, legislators became more willing to change sexist practices that reflected the moralistic assumptions of the distant past. Beginning with Minnesota and Michigan in 1974, statutes were rewritten state by state as the analysis put forward by feminists gained acceptance and as more women became lawyers and legislators and reformed the legal system from within as well as pressuring it from without (Largen, 1987).

The issue of consent is central to any rape complaint because "willingness" or at least "voluntary compliance" is what distinguishes "making love" or "engaging in sexual relations" from being sexually assaulted. The injured party must convince the police, the prosecution, and ultimately a jury that she did not agree freely to participate in sex acts but was forced to submit by her attacker. The burden of proof shifts to the woman, who must present a compelling account that she was "violated against her will." The prosecution must establish beyond a reasonable doubt that she was forced—hit, knocked down, pinned down, overpowered, or threatened with serious bodily harm. The prosecution must also show that she is a woman of integrity and good character, who has no motive to distort the truth and ought to be believed. To stir up reasonable doubts, the defense will pursue a strategy of impeaching her credibility by attacking her virtue. The goal is to sow the seeds of doubt among jurors by asserting that she consented at the time but later regretted her decision and then lodged false charges. To undermine her credibility as the key prosecution witness, the defense attorney often pursues a "nuts and sluts strategy," portraying her as a mentally unstable liar and/or a sexually promiscuous, willing partner.

To counter such personal attacks, the prosecution must argue that the defense attorney is turning the tables and is putting the victim on trial and humiliating her once again, this time in front of the jury. From the complainant's point of view, some reasonable limits should be placed on the defense's cross-examination so it doesn't become a degrading spectacle. But from the defendant's point of view, it is only fair that she answer probing questions about her sexual involvements in the past and her mental health. Only then can he have a fighting chance to clear his name and expose the falseness of her charges against him in this credibility contest (see Estrich, 1993b; Vachss, 1993).

Unwanted Publicity and Negative Media Portrayals

Fears about intrusive press coverage, unwanted publicity, and victim-blaming accusations discourage some people who were sexually assaulted from turn-ing to the criminal justice system for help.

Since the middle of the 1800s, newspapers have regularly featured stories about violent crimes, but they rarely covered rapes until the two trials of the Scottsboro Boys in the 1930s. For a number of years, the only cases that aroused media interest were those that resulted in lynchings, when a black man accused of raping a white woman was murdered by a white mob. To this day, mainstream media outlets remain preoccupied with the rape of white women, con-tinue to sensationalize interracial cases involving a black defendant and a white victim, and rarely de-vote attention to sexual assaults committed against black women. Journalists tend to stereotype victims as either "virgins" (pure and innocent who are rav-aged by bestial males) or "vamps" (wanton and sex-ually provocative temptresses who arouse male lust). The victim is likely to be portrayed as a vamp if the defendant is an acquaintance and no weapon was brandished, if they are both from the same ethnic group and social class, and if she is young, attractive, and doesn't live with her family. By assigning blame to one party or the other, crime reporters improperly take on the responsibilities of judges and juries, ac-cording to a content analysis of the way the news media covered several highly publicized rape cases (Benedict, 1992).

The following case became a media spectacle that confirmed all the observations listed above:

A 19-year-old college student working in a hotel meets a famous 24-year-old professional basketball player and willingly goes to his room. She claims that after they flirted and kissed, the athlete used force to bend her over and to make her submit to sex acts. She has him arrested for felony sexual assault. The married man reluctantly concedes the acts took place but insists they were consensual. News accounts do not mention the accuser's name. But the press coverage describes her appear-ance, reveals her e-mail address, discloses her hometown and the college she attends, and recounts salacious stories about her sex life told by people describing themselves as her friends.

After a while, her name and picture circulate on the Internet. She is vilified by his fans, re-ceives threats, and several potential assailants are arrested. The prosecution's case falls apart when the young woman declares she will not testify because she anticipates that many of the dis-tortions that were leaked will be used to dis-credit her during cross-examination. Her civil lawsuit is settled amid threats from both sides about disclosing damaging information—about her medical, psychological, and sexual history, and about his sexual past. The famous athlete offers a public apology to his accuser, ac-knowledging that he understood how she might have had a different interpretation of their encounter. (Zernike, 2003; Johnson, 2005; Franiuk et al., 2008)

When a girl or woman lodges charges of sexual assault against a man, like any other complainant of any other crime, her name appears in police files and court documents. The question then arises as to whether her identity should be revealed in media accounts. Laws prohibit the press from publishing the name of the victim of a sex crime in a number of states. Elsewhere, most newspapers, magazines, and radio and television stations have adopted a policy of self-restraint that shields the injured per-son from unwanted public exposure.

The arguments in favor of keeping the com-plainant's name out of the media center on the potential for inflicting additional suffering on a per-son who is already hurt and on the chilling effect the unwanted publicity surrounding her case will have on other victims who are considering going to the authorities for help. The longstanding ethical norm of concealing a complainant's name devel-oped from a realization that rapes are not like other crimes. Victims are more likely to be emotionally fragile and afflicted by posttraumatic stress, nervous breakdowns, and suicidal impulses. Publicly identi-fied rape victims have always been discredited, stig-matized, scandalized, mocked, scorned, and even harassed. Harsh victim-blaming accusations are particularly likely and especially painful. Revealing a complainant's name is a humiliating second violation that is likely to prolong her suffering. Furthermore, other rape victims who see how powerless she was to prevent her name and intimate details about her life from being circulated might be discouraged from reporting similar incidents to the police. Media self-censorship is a way to respect a victim's privacy rights unless she chooses to go public and speak out about the attack (Pollitt, 1991; Young, 1991).

Arguments in favor of disclosing victims' names appeal to the principles of the public's right to know, the defendant's right to a fair trial, and the news media's right to be free from censorship. Media outlets have an obligation to disseminate all relevant and newsworthy facts. Accusations from anonymous sources are contrary to American jurisprudence. The accused, who must be presumed innocent unless proven guilty, endures humiliation from the publicity surrounding the arrest. The accuser's name should be revealed as well to deter untrue allegations. Potential witnesses with knowledge about her credibility might come forward with information about her background and character that could aid in the defense of a falsely accused man. Finally, shielding complainants from exposure implies that being forced to submit to a sexual act is a shameful, "dirty secret", when it actually should not be a cause of public humiliation. In the long run, routinely giving faceless victims a human identity might diminish the stigma that still surrounds being raped (see Dershowitz, 1988; Cohen, 1991; Kantrowitz, Starr, and Friday, 1991).

Rape Shield Laws

During the mid-1970s to the mid-1980s, the anti-rape movement successfully convinced legislatures in almost every state to pass laws prohibiting improper cross-examinations. Generally, **shield laws** stipulate that the defense cannot introduce evidence about an accuser's past sexual conduct unless the woman has been convicted of prostitution, has had consensual sex before with the defendant, or has an obvious incentive to lie. Procedural guidelines provide for a hearing to be held in the absence of the jury, spectators, and the press. The aim is to permit the judge to determine whether the defense

counsel's allegations about the woman's past are relevant and should be aired in open court.

Staunch supporters of shield laws want more restrictions placed on the ability of defense attorneys to assassinate the complainant's character as a way of impeaching her credibility. They cite several justifications: to encourage survivors to go to the authorities for help by assuring them their privacy will be respected; to spare complainants the embarrassment of having intimate details of their sex lives made public and used against them in court; to dispel the fallacy that "if she consented in the past she probably consented this time, too"; and to prevent juries from being distracted by allegations about the complainant's past affairs when they should be focusing on the issue of the defendant's use of force.

Critics of shield laws want fewer restrictions on the line of questioning a defense attorney can pursue. Limitations impair the ability of the accused to confront his accuser effectively, and therefore to have a fair trial on a "level playing field" (Stark and Goldstein, 1985; Austern, 1987; Lewin, 1992). Higher-court decisions generally have upheld shield laws, concluding that most inquiries into an accuser's reputation for "chastity" have little relevance for determining consent. However, shield laws may not actually be working to protect the privacy concerns of rape victims. During trials prosecutors may not object strenuously enough about what they consider irrelevant questions by defense attorneys that merely damage their clients' reputations, and judges may err on the side of the defendants in order to prevent subsequent convictions from being overturned on appeal (Spohn and Horney, 1992).

Force and Resistance

In the not-so-distant past, in order to convict a rapist, a woman had to convince a jury that she forcefully resisted to her utmost and ceased struggling only because she feared she would be killed or seriously injured. The justification cited for requiring such proof of fierce resistance was that signs of a struggle indicated the victim's state of mind (unwillingness) and refuted the defendant's claims that he reasonably believed his partner was feigning reluctance and was agreeing to engage in sex. Most state laws no longer require that the woman who wants to press charges must prove that she risked her life to fend off her attacker. A **reasonableness standard** stipulates that the degree of resistance that expresses lack of consent can depend on the circumstances. A strong verbal statement or an unambiguous physical act is sufficient to show lack of consent in the face of overwhelming force or an intimidating weapon. The woman does not have to fight back, scream, or try to flee. Evidence that the accused possessed a weapon or that the complainant was physically injured also is sufficient to establish non-consent (Robin, 1977; Stark and Goldstein, 1985; Austern, 1987).

Although they may be emotionally devastated, most survivors of sexual assaults were not physically wounded, according to a survey of 4,000 women. About 70 percent of those who endured completed rapes reported no additional physical injuries; nearly 25 percent said they suffered minor injuries; and the remaining 4 percent sustained serious wounds in addition to being penetrated against their will (Kilpatrick, 1992). Similarly, an analysis of the one-million-plus disclosures to *NCVS* interviewers between 1992 and 2000 about rapes and other sexual assaults yielded an estimate that between 3 percent and 5 percent of the respondents were seriously wounded (Rennison, 2002b). Nationally, FBI *SHRs* indicate that a declining proportion (from 2 percent in the mid-1970s to less than 1 percent in the mid-1990s) of murder victims were raped or sexually assaulted before they were killed (Greenfeld, 1997). In California, an analysis of female homicide victims revealed that 7 percent of the deceased had been sexually assaulted before they were murdered during 1988 (Sorenson and White, 1992).

How a victim reacts during the sexual assault can profoundly influence the outcome in terms of her injuries. Her behavior—either submission or resistance—affects the attacker's decisions whether to try to complete the act and about how much force to use to subdue her. Most assailants were

unarmed (about 21 percent had guns, knives, or other sharp instruments), according to an analysis of *NCVS* data from 1987 until 1992. Most women who took some type of self-protective action, such as yelling for help or fighting back, told survey interviewers that they believed it helped their situation (61 percent) rather than made it worse (17 percent) (Bachman, 1994). Women who resisted improved their chances of thwarting the rapists' aims of completing the act, but unfortunately they also increased their risks of suffering injury. One-third of the non-resisting victims were wounded in addition to being sexually assaulted. In contrast, two-thirds of victims who applied self-defense measures were physically hurt—bruised, cut, scratched, even stabbed or shot—according to a study of *NCVS* data from the late 1970s (McDermott, 1979). The best strategy turned out to be a **dual verbal defense** of calling out for help while simultaneously attempting to reason with, plead with, or threaten the attacker, a study of 125 victims concluded. However, nearly all of the women who resisted their assailants physically reported that their actions made the men angrier, more vicious, and more violent (Cohen, 1984).

Studies assessing the relative effectiveness of various responses have generated mixed, confusing, and perhaps impractical recommendations. It is impossible to predict the outcome of a particular assault, given the complex web of factors involving the offender, his intended victim, and their situation at that moment.

Criminologists report that different types of rapists react to resistance differently. Girls and women under attack and rape defense strategists face an unavoidable dilemma: Resistance may foil a rape but may further endanger their physical well-being. But at least one factor in the equation has changed to the advantage of survivors. Whether or not fiercely resisting "within reason" is the best strategy under all circumstances, it is no longer required to justify an arrest and prosecution.

The apparent acquiescence of some victims can be readily explained. The primary reaction of nearly all survivors is to fear for their lives, according to interviews conducted at a hospital emergency room

(Burgess and Holmstrom, 1974). Therefore, some females are simply immobilized by terror, shock, and disbelief. Faced with the prospect of death or severe physical injury, many conclude that their only way out is to strike a bargain or work out a tacit understanding with the attacker and trade submission for survival (that is, to endure sexual violation in return for some sort of pledge that they won't be killed, savagely beaten, or cruelly disfigured). There is, of course, no guarantee that compliance will minimize physical injury. Rapists do not have to keep their promises (Brownmiller, 1975).

Corroboration

In the past, one aspect of the law that made rape charges very difficult to prove beyond a reasonable doubt in most states was the **corroboration** requirement, which demanded that the prosecution discover independent evidence to back up the key elements of the complainant's account. Derived hundreds of years ago from the evolution of English common law, the corroboration requirement assumed that a woman's accusations alone were not credible without some other substantiation. Corroboration could take the form of obvious physical injuries; medical and forensic evidence gathered by a doctor; torn clothing; other signs of a struggle; or the testimony of an eyewitness or a third party such as a police officer, family member, or friend who had been promptly told about the assault. But the corroboration requirement was criticized as being patently unfair for putting survivors of sexual assaults in the unique position, compared to complainants of other kinds of assaults, of being automatically distrusted without additional "real proof." To strike a balance, most state laws have been reformed and no longer require corroboration unless the victim is a minor, was previously intimate with the accused, did not promptly report the crime to the authorities, or provides a version of events that is inherently improbable and self-contradictory (Robin, 1977; Stark and Goldstein, 1985; Austern, 1987).

Forensic evidence can corroborate a woman's claim that sexual intercourse took place and that the assailant injured her during the assault. Hospitals have standardized the practice of collecting evidence such as traces of blood, semen, hairs, and other sources of DNA as part of a "rape kit." At some hospitals, specially trained sexual assault nurse examiners are ready to accompany victims throughout the evidence-gathering medical procedures (Little, 2001).

But three problems can arise. First, at most hospitals in the United States, women are not routinely offered emergency contraceptive pills, which are most effective if taken within 72 hours, and this omission won't be corrected because new federal guidelines no longer specify that victims should be informed of this option (Editors, *New York Times*, 2005). Second, the costs of collecting and testing the forensic evidence (about $1,000) might unfairly be imposed on victims, even though federal funding is supposed to cover these expenses (Graves, 2002). Third, the biological evidence collected in the **rape kit** may never be used. Because of inadequate government financing, unanalyzed rape kits with untested DNA samples accumulate in police or prosecutorial storage areas or at understaffed crime labs, enabling assailants to escape apprehension and preventing victims from achieving closure (Herbert, 2002). A national forensic DNA study determined that the average time it took to process the DNA in a rape kit in an unsolved case ranged from 24 to 30 weeks. However, once it is processed, the DNA profile can be used by the prosecution to get a "John Doe" warrant that can keep the manhunt going until the statute of limitation expires ("Study points to reasons ... " 2005). As of 2005, 20 states had abolished the statute of limitations on unsolved rapes, but in four states it remained at five years or less (Sullivan, 2005).

Arrest, Prosecution, and Adjudication

In order for a crime to be solved, it must first be reported. But most rapes are not reported to the police, according to the annual findings from the *NCVS*. Each year, at least half of all girls and women who tell *NCVS* interviewers about sexual assaults never inform the police. The reasons females cite most often for not alerting authorities are that they fear reprisals, consider the incident to be a private or personal matter, or feel that they lack proof to make the charges stick. Women who report offenses to the police most often say that they do so to be rescued, to prevent the rapist from harming them again or from attacking someone else, and to get him in trouble so that he will be punished. Women are more likely to go to the authorities if the assailant used a weapon or if they are physically wounded and require medical care for their injuries. Surprisingly, whether or not the offender was a complete stranger, an acquaintance, or an intimate does not seem to affect the decision whether to report the crime, according to *NCVS* findings (BJS, 1994b). No pronounced upward trend toward higher rates of reporting appears in annual surveys (see Table 6.1), despite many public relations campaigns to encourage victims to come forward (such as poster campaigns and special hotline numbers) and several reforms (such as safeguarding a woman's privacy by not publicly identifying her, and providing intermediaries and advocates at rape crisis centers at hospitals and on college campuses).

Similarly, rape clearance rates for police departments across the nation show a disturbing decline over the past few decades (see Table 6.3). This lack of progress in boosting the solution rate is surprising and disappointing, considering that more acquaintance rape cases (in which the suspect's identity and whereabouts are known) presumably are being brought to the attention of the local authorities (see Kanin, 1984; Estrich, 1986). Also, to prevent victims from being deterred from pressing charges by the prospect of insensitive handling, some police departments have set up sex crimes squads with specially trained female detectives. Despite these new measures, the percentages of cases that were solved each year were much higher in the past, even though most of the reported rapes in those days involved attacks by strangers.

Although acquaintance rape cases are easily "solved" because the accused person is known to the accuser, convictions are more difficult to secure than in cases of stranger rapes. Attrition rates for acquaintance rape cases are substantially higher. Victims are more inclined to ask that charges be

dropped. Also, prosecutors are less willing to press forward because they fear the jury will find "reasonable doubts" about her insistence that she did not consent, and therefore will not convict the defendant (Mansnerus, 1989; LaFree, 1989; Bachman, 1998).

To increase the conviction rate, some district attorneys have established sex crimes prosecution units with specially trained lawyers. Traditionally, prosecutors whose performance was judged on the basis of their won/lost records preferred offering lenient pleas rather than risking defeat by going to trial. Prosecutors prefer to negotiate an out-of-court settlement unless the complainant fits the narrow stereotype of the kind of victims who are believed by jurors and elicit their sympathy: wives and mothers who are well educated, articulate, visibly upset but not hysterical while testifying, and attractive but not too sexy (Vachss, 1993). Even though more rape cases go to trial than any other type of charge except murder and aggravated assault, the overwhelming majority of cases are still resolved through plea negotiations. The percentage of rape cases that go to trial varies greatly by jurisdiction (Boland and Sones, 1986). About 10 percent of all rape cases were resolved by a trial, with the prosecution victorious about 70 percent of the time, in the 75 largest counties during 1994 (Reaves, 1998).

A negotiated plea is often justified on the grounds that it spares the accuser from having to recount under oath with great specificity exactly what happened to her. If she serves as a witness for the prosecution, she also faces the prospect of a tough cross-examination intended to undermine her credibility. It is widely assumed that testifying at a trial months or years later would lead to retraumatizing the victim. But a study of the experiences of nearly 140 women who had testified about rapes and other sexual assaults committed against them did not turn up clear evidence that symptoms of PTSD burdened them once more (Orth and Maercker, 2004).

Besides creating special investigation and prosecution squads, a number of other reforms have been enacted to improve arrest, prosecution, conviction, and incarceration rates. In most jurisdictions, the chances of conviction in sexual assault cases have been enhanced by new legal codes and sentencing structures that specify graded levels of seriousness from improper sexual contact to forcible rape, each carrying a corresponding penalty (Bienen, 1983; Largen, 1987). In many courtrooms, evidence of rape trauma syndrome can be introduced during trials to account for any questionable behavior on the victim's part (concerning reporting delays or failure to actively resist) that in the past would have undermined her credibility.

And yet despite many reforms and attempts at improving the criminal justice system's handling of rape cases, most attackers are never arrested, prosecuted, convicted, and certainly not incarcerated (see Lisefski and Manson, 1988; Senate Judiciary Committee, 1993). According to one nationwide study (Reaves, 1998), 35 percent of all defendants find the charges against them dropped; 3 percent are acquitted at a trial; and only 61 percent are convicted, mostly of felonies (but 3 percent of merely a misdemeanor). By the end of the adjudication process in state courts, only 35 percent of all accused rapists were sentenced to prison and another 10 percent ended up jailed for up to one year, and a slightly larger percentage were placed on probation. The following example illustrates the contention that convicted rapists still might receive lenient sentences:

A 15-year-old girl is lured to the home of an 18-year-old young man on the pretext of helping him work on his MySpace page. Suddenly, his 17-, 18-, and 19-year-old friends barge in, encircle her, and take turns raping her. All four assailants plead guilty to first-degree rape, but only the ringleader who masterminded the plot gets a sentence of four years in prison. The three others will each serve a year in jail. The prosecution justifies the negotiated plea as a way of sparing the high school sophomore the ordeal of being subjected to four separate cross-examinations at the trial. But the girl tells reporters that the one

year jail sentences are "nothing" as she is escorted by police from the courtroom amid catcalls, taunts, and threats from the young convicts' relatives. (Bode, 2007)

Optimists emphasize how much progress has been made over the past several decades by the pro-victim, anti-rape movement. It has tried to eliminate these unfair roadblocks on the path to justice by dismantling the institutionalized expressions of discrimination that put victims at such an unusual disadvantage in the not-too-distant past (see Fairstein, 1993). Pessimists, however, point out how many anti-victim traditions persist within the justice system.

The degree of success achieved by the anti-rape movement can be evaluated with reference to a number of criteria. One criterion concerns improvements in public attitudes respecting a woman's right to sexual autonomy free from coercion. Other signs of success are gains in the willingness of complainants to report the crimes and to press charges. Additional indicators of progress are decreases in the number of complainants who conclude that the entire fact-finding and decision-making process is emotionally painful and degrading; and increases in the rates of arrest, prosecution, conviction, and incarceration of rapists (see Goldberg-Ambrose, 1992; Spohn and Horney, 1992; Bachman and Paternoster, 1993).

CRISIS CENTERS: PROVIDING EMERGENCY ASSISTANCE

No matter how poorly (or how well) the criminal justice system handles rape cases in the long run, sexual assault victims need immediate aid.

Starting in 1972, feminist activists began to provide emergency assistance to women who had just been raped. The first crisis centers, also known as distress or relief centers, were set up in Berkeley, California, and Washington, D.C. These independent self-help projects were intended to provide an alternative to the very limited services available from the police, at hospital emergency rooms, and through mental health centers. These centers also became bases to organize support for the nation-wide anti-rape movement.

Rape crisis centers provide a variety of services. Usually, a 24-hour telephone hotline puts victims in contact with advocates who are standing by to help. The center's staff members are available to accompany women to emergency rooms where forensic evidence is collected and first aid is received, and to police stations or prosecutor's offices where complaints are filed and statements are made. Individuals may receive peer counseling and are invited to participate in support groups. Complainants are referred to other community agencies that provide social services. Some centers conduct in-service training to sensitize doctors, nurses, police officers, and assistant district attorneys about the needs and problems of the survivors they encounter. Most undertake educational campaigns to raise public consciousness about the myths and realities surrounding sex crimes and the victims' plights. Frequently, centers offer self-defense courses for women and children.

Many staff members at the original crisis centers are former victims who shared a commitment to themes embodied in the protest movements of the 1960s and early 1970s. Feminist activists put forward the analysis that rape was primarily a women's issue, best understood and more effectively dealt with by women than by men in positions of authority. A distrust of remote bureaucracies and control by professionals who claim to know what is best for their clients was derived from the youthful counterculture with its "crash pads" (emergency shelters), drop-in centers (for counseling and advocacy), and free clinics (for drug-related health crises) in "hippie" neighborhoods. The New Left's emphasis on egalitarianism, volunteerism, and collective action led to grassroots, community organizing projects stressing self-help and peer support, and to symbolic confrontations with the power structure: protest demonstrations at police stations and courtrooms.

With the passage of time, however, rifts developed within many rape crisis centers. More pragmatic and less ideological staffers softened the staunch stands taken by these nonprofit, nonbureaucratic, nonhierarchical, nonprofessional, and nongovernmental organizations. They pressed for a more service-oriented approach that would avoid militancy and radical critiques, improve chances for funding, increase referrals from hospitals and police departments, and permit closer cooperation with prosecutors. To the founders of the centers, such changes represented a cooptation by the establishment and a retreat from the original mission (see Amir and Amir, 1979; Largen, 1981).

For the staff members and volunteers at crisis centers and at domestic violence shelters too, the biggest problems in their emotionally exhausting jobs are vicarious traumatization, secondary traumatic stress, and burnout from constant exposure to the adverse reactions and suffering of their clients (Baird and Jenkins, 2003; Campbell and Wasco, 2005).

THE REDISCOVERY OF MORE RAPE VICTIMS

Because of the renewed attention paid to sexual assault by the anti-rape movement over the past three decades, the plight of two other groups soon was rediscovered: wives raped by their husbands and males subjected to sexual assaults by other men.

Wives Raped by their Husbands

The anti-rape movement argued that all forced sex should be outlawed, without regard for who the aggressor is and what his relationship to the victim might be. This recognition of sexual assault within intimate relationships led to the realization that rape can occur even between husbands and wives. A wife retains the right to say "no" to her husband despite the license issued by the government, the wedding vows to "love, honor, and obey," and religious teachings about submitting and performing wifely duties.

Raped wives also are battered wives in most cases. They are beaten periodically and sexually assaulted repeatedly over years, and many of the physical attacks symbolize domination and subjugation as well (Peacock, 1998).

Rape within marriage was considered impossible, by definition, under English common law. For centuries, the leading figures in jurisprudence contended that under the marriage contract, a wife consented to yield to her husband's desires wherever and whenever he wished. When activists in the feminist movement challenged this reasoning and sought to change the law, they met considerable resistance from traditionalists. The forcible rape of a spouse first became recognized officially as a crime in 1975, when South Dakota legislators rewrote the state's statutes and rejected the common-law exception that exempted husbands from arrest and granted them the "right" to unlimited sexual access (Russell, 1982). By 1990, in every state, that immunity no longer applied if his wife had separated from him and filed for divorce. In many states a sexually assaultive husband could be arrested and prosecuted even if the couple was living together—if he used a weapon, or took advantage of a mentally or physically incapacitated wife who was unable to give meaningful consent (Russell, 1990).

Estimates about the incidence and prevalence of marital rape do not rest on a solid empirical foundation because the problem is still shrouded in secrecy. According to projections from a telephone survey more than 1 million then-married women had been forced to perform unwanted sexual acts one or more times by their husbands (Crime Victims Research and Treatment Center, 1992). The prevalence rate of marital rape during the course of a marriage is thought to range from as low as 8 percent (Russell, 1990) to as high as 25 percent (Bergen, 1998). A troubling proportion of women, ranging from 15 percent to 25 percent, reported that they were raped by an estranged or ex-husband or former live-in lover (Finkelhor and Yllo, 1985).

Raped wives endure problems similar to women who were sexually assaulted by non-intimates. They are physically injured, psychologically scarred, and personally humiliated (Bowker, 1983). Wives whose husbands force them to submit to unwanted degrading acts are the least likely sexual assault victims to report incidents, to be believed by the authorities, to have their cases adjudicated, and to secure convictions. Between 1978 and 1985, only 118 husbands were prosecuted across the country, although 104 of them (90 percent) were convicted, according to a report by a national clearinghouse on marital rape (Barden, 1987). Researchers suspect that reports of forced sexual participation in marriage would be about as frequent as reports of rapes by dates, acquaintances, and strangers if there were ways to convince victims to fully disclose their plight (see Beirne and Messerschmidt, 2000).

Sexually Assaulted Males

The rape of a male by a female (or of a female by a female) is presumed to be rare, and the imagery usually arouses smirks rather than alarm. When women are arrested in sexual assault cases, they usually were acting as the accomplices of domineering men. But the molestation of little boys by men (see Chapter 8) has been of great concern for a long time (see Maghan and Sagarin, 1983; Porter, 1986).

More recently, the rape of a teenage boy or a young man by another male or by a gang of males was recognized as more than just a theoretical possibility. Yet this had been such a taboo subject that many state laws had ignored this possible victim–offender relationship and had defined rape strictly as a crime perpetrated by males against females. In 1986, however, Congress passed a bill revising federal rape statutes (governing the handling of sexual assaults committed on federal property). Among other changes, the law redefined rape as a gender-neutral offense, so both victims and perpetrators could be of either sex ("Federal Rape Laws," 1986). This official recognition that males also could be rape victims paved the way for their rediscovery, including efforts to estimate the scope of the problem and to devise effective ways of easing their suffering.

The first rough estimates about sexual assaults attempted or completed against males (teenagers and adults) were derived from the findings of annual *NCVSes*. Between 1973 and 1982, the number of male rape victims was projected to be almost 125,000, corresponding to about one-twelfth of the problem females faced (Klaus et al., 1985). In 1998, males suffered about the same proportion of all rapes (about one-thirteenth, or nearly 8 percent; a rate of 0.2 per 1,000), as reported to interviewers for the redesigned *NCVS* (which probed respondents' memories rather than in the old questionnaire for all kinds of sexual assault incidents) (Rennison, 1999). Similarly, about 9 percent of rapes reported to the police in three states during 1991 were male-on-male (0.8 percent were female-on-female and 0.2 percent were female-on-male), according to an analysis of more detailed data in the FBI's NIBRS (Reaves, 1993). As for lifetime prevalence, about 3 percent of all males probably have suffered a sexual assault, most occurring before age 18 (Tjaden and Thoennes, 2006).

Records kept by rape crisis centers indicated that about one caller of every 10 was a male. But these measures of the incidence of male-on-male rapes are probably gross underestimates because they exclude the sexual assaults committed in dangerous institutional settings such as jails, prisons, and reform schools.

Sexual violence among inmates was rediscovered and documented as a serious problem decades ago (see Lockwood, 1980) (see Chapter 2). In the late 1990s, an advocacy group charged that the authorities showed deliberate indifference to systematic abuse and exploitation that stronger prisoners imposed on weaker ones. The report called for a greater emphasis on prevention strategies, including more carefully classifying inmates to cellblocks and cells by risk levels, and increasing the size of the custodial staff. Other recommendations focused on improving means of redress, including safer reporting procedures, and stepped up arrests and prosecutions (Mariner, 2001).

When Congress passed the Prison Rape Reduction Act of 2003, it imposed a zero-tolerance policy and put prison officials on notice that they would be held responsible for failures to detect, prevent, and punish sexual assaults behind bars ("What sheriffs need to know…" 2004). However, most correctional institutions still have not set up secure and effective ways for inmates to report sexual assaults; nor are victims able to access adequate and timely medical and mental health services behind bars (National Sheriffs Association, 2008).

Prison rapes are more than abuses of human rights and personal dignity. They are routinely pictured in movies about prison life—sometimes mockingly—and are tacitly condoned as an additional form of punishment in "Scared Straight"-type warnings. Older and stronger "wolves" compel younger and weaker inmates to be their sex slaves in return for protection from gang rapes that would stigmatize them as easy pickings and as the "girl" of the institution. In the pumped-up, heavily tattooed, hyper-masculine world of prison life, males who are stripped of autonomy and compelled to obey orders as if they were little boys, try to regain their sense of manhood by forcing weaker inmates to submit to sexual demands as if they were females. Ironically, anti-rape education programs have discovered that the specter of being taken forcefully by another man might be an effective way to reach and sensitize domineering males who otherwise belittle or justify their sexual aggression toward females (Sabo, 1992; Beirne and Messerschmidt, 2000; and One in Four, 2008).

Male rape victims are subjected to the same disbelief, scorn, and insensitive treatment today that female victims routinely endured in the not-so-distant past. They are often blamed for their misfortunes, stereotyped as homosexual (the majority are exclusively heterosexual), disparaged as not being "real men" for not resisting to the utmost and for not thwarting their attackers, and accused of secretly enjoying the experience. Although males and females suffer in similar ways, experiencing bouts of depression, flashbacks, recriminations, nightmares, and an overwhelming sense of vulnerability, males are more visibly angry and more preoccupied with fantasies of revenge. A few large cities have set up support groups for these men. The available evidence indicates that male rape victims experience more force and brutality, are held captive longer, and are subjected to more acts of sexual humiliation.

Evidently, sexual assaults against both males and females are expressions of culturally induced drives toward domination and subjugation within a society that prizes exercising power over other people (Krueger, 1985; White and Wesley, 1987).

PREVENTING RAPE

Over the years, three approaches have been developed to address the problem of sexual assault. The oldest (now subject to vehement denunciation) is the blame-the-victim approach, which faults the attitudes, words, and actions of the person attacked. Following the logic of this approach, females must stop precipitating rape through careless, reckless, or even provocative behavior. Instead, these high-risk targets must learn to take precautions to reduce the threats they face in a dangerous, male-dominated world.

An alternative perspective is the blame-the-offender approach, which views sexual assaults as pathological acts by mentally disturbed individuals. If deranged sexual predators are the source of the problem, then the solutions lie in criminal justice strategies that remove these dangerous deviants from circulation (incapacitation via incarceration, followed by treatment, compulsory if necessary during civil commitment). Because the public can't be sure a released sexual predator has been cured completely, community notification laws are needed to alert neighbors whenever an ex-convict moves nearby, so that female family members can remain vigilant and take defensive measures. Various technological devices are now used to monitor the whereabouts of former sex offenders.

Deterrence through punishment attempts to teach the offenders who are not mentally deranged a lesson they won't forget, and to make transgressors into negative role models to serve as warnings to other men so they will think twice, consider the likelihood of imprisonment, and decide not to act out their vicious fantasies. But the effectiveness of deterrence and incapacitation strategies are undermined when many rapists are not caught and convicted, thereby escaping the sentences they deserve. At best, an efficient criminal justice system weeds out

assailants and brings them under control one at a time, after they have struck and harmed the objects of their wrath. At most, criminal justice "solutions" can only keep a lid on potentially explosive situations.

Because teenage girls and young women are more likely to be targeted than others, risk reduction strategies should focus on behaviors and situations that researchers have been identified as heightening their vulnerability to attack. Consuming alcoholic beverages to the point of intoxication, associating with males who are heavy drinkers, and spending large amounts of time in bars, clubs, fraternities, and parties raise the odds of being sexually assaulted. Resisting advances verbally and then physically if necessary can reduce the chances of a completed rape. Interventions proven to be effective include rape awareness programs; campaigns against binge drinking; self-defense, assertiveness, and resistance training; establishing support networks among friends; and providing health care services such as medical treatment and psychological counseling (see Fisher, Daigle, and Cullen, 2008).

In the debate over the causes of forcible rape, victim blaming, victim defending, and offender blaming focus too narrowly on the attitudes and actions of the male aggressors and their female targets. In the process, these points of view tend to ignore crucial insights about prevailing cultural themes surrounding appropriate sex roles, romance, eroticism, seduction, domination, sadism, and masochism. The possibility that the roots of forced sex lie in the economic, political, and social inequalities between males and females gets lost when the analysis is limited to a deconstruction of the "he said/she said" interaction.

Anti-rape activists have sought not only to defend victims but also to place the burden of blame for recurring outbreaks of male "sexual terrorism" on key social institutions, especially the family, the economy, the military, religion, and the media. Asserting that "the personal is political," they have stressed that apparently private troubles need to be seen as aspects of larger social problems besetting millions of people.

Therefore, the third approach is institution blaming. It is more sociological because it emphasizes the variety of offenders, motives, targets, and victim-offender relationships, and it considers sexual assault to be an outgrowth of the social environment. Collective solutions that get at the social roots of male-against-female violence hold greater promise in the long run than any reliance on individual strategies of risk reduction and self-defense.

The institution-blaming approach contends that heightened risks arise from patriarchy; exploitative cultural themes about females as sex objects for male gratification; traditional gender roles emphasizing male sexual aggressiveness and female passivity; and prevailing patterns of socialization (how children are raised). If social conditions breed generation after generation of sexually exploitative males, then the only viable long-run strategy is to eradicate the root causes of the problem. That means doing something about the encouragements to commit rape that pervade contemporary culture, such as pairing sex with violence in popular music lyrics, movies, pornography, and other forms of entertainment. The association of domination with eroticism also must be discouraged when it appears in advertising (promoting violence as "sexy" and portraying sexual desire as something to be expressed forcefully rather than tenderly). Cultural traditions and expectations that encourage young men to take the offensive and act aggressively in the "battle of the sexes" must be rejected, especially on the streets in youth gangs but also on campuses in fraternities and sports teams. Attitudes and myths that tacitly belittle, normalize, or excuse date rape and acquaintance rape must be countered. And more men must realize that rape is a problem they too should be concerned about and strive to solve (see Buchwald, Fletcher, and Roth, 1993; Smith and Welchans, 2000; Ottens and Hotelling, 2001; Price and Sokoloff, 2004; Abbey, 2005; Koss, 2005; Sanday, 2007; and Fisher, Daigle, and Cullen, 2008).

SUMMARY

Rape and sexual assault victims face a host of special problems. The nature of the attack can be emotionally devastating, with severe consequences that can spoil any future enjoyment of sexuality. Because of long-standing attitudes toward sexuality, public airing of details is embarrassing. Due to old ideas and traditional cultural themes, a woman's violation will be widely regarded as a loss of status. The victim is likely to be blamed, even if all the circumstances point to being at the wrong place at the wrong time. Her accusations may be disbelieved as entirely unfounded (it never happened) or exaggerated (she gave consent at the time but later cried rape). Filing a complaint and pressing charges will cause the most intimate aspects of a victim's life to become an open book. She will feel as if she, and not the male she accuses, is on trial. Even a conviction will not bring closure if she is emotionally scarred and suffers from lingering phobias and recurrent flashbacks or anxiety attacks.

Special solutions have been devised to address these problems. Starting in the 1970s, feminists in the anti-rape movement brought about significant changes in the way the criminal justice system and society respond to these attacks. The complainant can seek immediate solace and advice at a rape crisis center. The victim's name is not publicized. Trained detectives and prosecutors, many of them females, handle sex crimes cases. The collection of forensic evidence is carried out by the police and medical personnel more scientifically and thoroughly. The laws of evidence have been changed to make corroboration less difficult, and arguments smearing her as a willing participant based on her past sexual experiences are less likely to be admissible in court because of shield laws. She does not have to struggle to her utmost to prove that what happened to her was against her will.

And yet, serious problems persist: reporting rates, clearance rates, prosecution rates, conviction rates, and incarceration rates remain stubbornly low.

Strategies to reduce rape include focusing on educating girls and women to take precautions, on controlling known offenders, and on eradicating what are believed to be institutional supports for male sexual aggression.

KEY TERMS

carnal knowledge, 260

statutory rape, 260

heiress stealing, 260

ideal types, 262

acquaintance rapes, 263

implied consent, 266

agency, 268

rape crisis syndrome, 269

posttraumatic stress disorder, 269

series victimizations, 270

shield laws, 285

reasonableness standard, 286

dual verbal defense, 286

corroboration, 287

rape kit, 287

QUESTIONS FOR DISCUSSION AND DEBATE

1. Compile a list of all the ways rape victims were handled insensitively and improperly in the past, as described in Box 10.2. Determine whether each problem is being addressed adequately today.

2. Explain why the concept of victim precipitation is so controversial when it is applied to sexual assaults and rapes.

3. Under what circumstances, if any, should the identity of a woman who has been raped be made public?

4. Discuss the pros and cons of trying to reduce rape risks by convincing girls and women to alter their behavior.

CRITICAL THINKING QUESTIONS

1. If rapes take place in jails and prisons among men, then what are the root causes of sexual violence?

2. Speculate about the possible reasons why the proportion of rapes reported to the police has not improved over the decades, according to *NCVS* figures.

3. Speculate about the possible reasons for the decline in rape clearance rates over the decades, according to *UCR* figures.

4. What should pre-adolescent boys be told about rape victims? Should pre-adolescent girls be told the same information about rape victims?

5. Go over each of the six rape myths in Box 10.1 and argue that these beliefs are not myths but realities.

SUGGESTED RESEARCH PROJECTS

1. Compile a list of policies (such as setting up a sex crimes squad) and opportunities for assistance (such as establishing a rape crisis center) that can be offered by government, nonprofit, self-help, and charitable organizations to ease the plight of sexual assault victims. Check with local criminal justice officials, women's organizations, and others in the helping professions to see what services are available in your hometown.

2. Search databases of newspaper and magazine articles and find accounts of recent trials in which a woman testified against her alleged rapist. For each one, gather details about the incident (including time, place, weapon used); the prior relationship, if any, between the assailant and target before the sexual assault; how the defense challenged her accusations during cross-examination; and the outcome of the case.

11

Additional Groups of Victims with Special Problems

This chapter examines additional groups of victims whose plights have been rediscovered in recent years: students harmed in schools and on college campuses; individuals menaced by stalkers or targeted by hate-filled offenders; workers injured or murdered while doing their jobs; police officers wounded or slain in the line of duty; and people within the United States harmed by terrorist attacks. To some unavoidable extent, these categories overlap. For example, some of the individuals injured by workplace violence were women stalked by ex-lovers, police officers slain in the line of duty, or office staff killed by an act of terrorism. Now that these groups are receiving the long overdue attention they deserve, the criminal justice system needs to improve how it handles their cases and addresses their needs.

VICTIMS OF CRIMES COMMITTED AT SCHOOL

Threats Facing College Students

In the not-so-distant past, the ivy-covered towers of academia were pictured as sanctuaries that were shielded from the problems of the "real world." But a growing stream of stories about college students killed, raped, and robbed on campus has shattered that myth. Undergraduates and graduate students can be hurt by other students, or by outsiders who enter the buildings and grounds, or by local residents when students venture outside their gated communities. An abundance of bicycles, electronic devices, and computers in an open, unguarded environment attracts burglars and thieves to dormitories and cafeterias. Special types of interpersonal violence can break out too, taking the form of assaults (including brutality against fraternity pledges during hazing), drunken brawls after sports events, hate crimes (gay bashings and racial attacks), gang rapes (at parties), and date rapes.

The Controversy Surrounding Acquaintance Rape on College Campuses A bitter maximalist versus minimalist controversy surrounds the incidence of acquaintance rape, especially on college campuses. The sharp disagreement reached a peak right after Congress passed the Federal Campus Sexual Assault Victims' Bill of Rights in 1992, which imposed basic procedures on how college administrations must handle rape complaints. But the dispute continues right up to the present (see Warshaw, 1988; Schreiber, 1990; Bohmer and Parrot, 1993; Faludi, 1993; Leone and de Koster, 1995; Sampson, 2004; MacDonald, 2008a, 2008b; and Koss, 2008).

Anti-rape activists took a maximalist stance based on their belief that they had uncovered statistical evidence that sexual assault was a widespread but severely underreported problem. It was well-known from the annual findings of the *NCVS* that young women in their late teens and early twenties faced the gravest risks of being sexually assaulted. It was clear that attacks by complete strangers in deserted areas of campuses (such as unlit parking lots or isolated offices) were unusual. But it was a shock to find out that unexpected acts of sexual aggression by dates and even mere acquaintances were so common. Maximalists pointed out that the term "date rape" framed the issue too narrowly because surveys indicated that these assailants often were classmates, friends, and other acquaintances and not strictly boyfriends or ex-boyfriends, and that the forced sex took place on occasions other than formal dates (such as after study sessions). Maximalists pictured rapes as the most serious aspect of a much larger set of troubling male-female conflicts, which included incidents of violence during courtship, stalking, indecent exposure (typically in libraries and stairwells), voyeurism (spying by "peeping toms"), obscene phone calls, unwanted sexual touches, sexual harassment, and intense peer pressures to engage in sexual activities. The aftershocks of acquaintance rape paralleled the suffering inflicted by sexual assaults by strangers. The symptoms these young women may experience include outrage, anxiety, depression, guilt, loss of self-esteem, retreat into substance abuse, distrust of others, social isolation, suicidal thoughts, fear of contracting a venereal disease, and sexual dysfunction. Their grades are likely to plunge and they may drop out of school if their concerns escalate about encountering their assailant on campus. Because acquaintance rapes were rarely reported to either parents or college officials, assailants usually went unpunished, the young women's needs for assistance and support were not met, and administrators were misled into thinking that their very limited outreach efforts were sufficient (see Sampson, 2004).

As a result, maximalists launched public education campaigns to alert students, college administrators, and parents to what they perceived to be an epidemic of sexual assaults in dorms, fraternity houses, and off-campus apartments. The extremely low reporting rate, estimated at around 5 percent, was the reason most people were unaware that a "rape pandemic" was raging. The crisis remained under the radar screen because young women were reluctant to bring their troubles to the attention of the campus security force or to the local police for a long list of reasons: they may fear unwanted publicity and exposure; they may feel embarrassed and humiliated; and they may blame themselves for getting drunk or for going to a secluded spot.. Also they may anticipate that they won't be believed by detectives or prosecutors or juries; they may not want their former friends or dates to be severely stigmatized and punished as "rapists"; they may have little faith in the on-campus judicial system; and they could worry about reprisals from the assailant and social ostracism by his friends. Additionally, they may be concerned that their family will find out and may dread that they will be harshly judged, condemned, and slandered for allegedly "precipitating" the young man's out-of-control outpouring of "lust" (see Sampson, 2004).

But minimalist critics wondered whether the problem was really as serious as maximalists pictured it to be. Minimalists pointed out that despite many rape awareness activities, campus rape crisis centers were never overwhelmed by a flood of cases. FBI statistics monitoring crime on college campuses revealed that very few coeds filed complaints. Minimalists concluded that because most college women did not regard themselves as victims of sexual assaults, maximalists were overestimating the threat of forcible rape by dates and acquaintances. If such attacks were rare and isolated, maintaining a rape crisis center was an unnecessary expense and engendered needless anxiety and tension (see Eigenberg, 1990; Gilbert, 1991; Podhoretz, 1991; Crichton, 1993; Hellman, 1993; Roiphe, 1993; MacDonald, 2008a, 2008b).

The only way to estimate the dimensions of the problem accurately is by administering anonymous questionnaires that assure confidentiality for respondents, so they will be willing to disclose intimate details about upsetting experiences. One widely cited survey of more than 3,000 female students at 32 colleges presented the young women with scenarios that described what recently reformed state statutes would legally designate as sexual assaults. Respondents could identify elements of the crime that resembled their own experiences, such as being plied with liquor until their judgment was so impaired that "consent" was meaningless, or being physically held down, or being forced to submit after painful arm-twisting. Based on the survey's findings, the researcher estimated that about 166 out of every 1,000 female students (a shocking 17 percent) suffered one or more attempted or completed acquaintance rapes per year. Fewer than 5 percent reported the assault to police, about 5 percent sought solace at rape crisis centers, and almost half told no one what happened. In 84 percent of the cases, the victim knew the offender; in 57 percent of these nonstranger assaults he was a date. Projecting a yearly incidence estimate into a lifetime prevalence estimate, perhaps as many as one in four college-aged young women might have experienced an attempted rape or a completed rape since she was 14 years old (Koss, Gidyez, and Wisniewski, 1987; Koss and Harvey, 1991; Koss and Cook, 1998; and Koss, 2008).

Similar findings emerged from a telephone survey of a national sample of nearly 4,500 women attending two- and four-year colleges during 1996. The researchers discovered that almost 3 percent of coeds suffered a completed or attempted rape during the nine-month academic year. Projecting that number on to an enrollment of 10,000 female students, nearly 300 will be harmed over two semesters. Over the course of an entire calendar year, as many as 5 percent of young women will experience a completed or attempted sexual assault. Because students often take an average of five years to complete their degrees, between 20 and 25 percent of young women may be raped during their college years. In the overwhelming majority of these attacks, the women knew the assailants. About 90 percent were boyfriends, ex-boyfriends, classmates, co-workers, friends, and casual acquaintances. Faculty members were not identified as perpetrators of any rapes or sexual assaults, but were cited in a small percent of incidents as imposing unwelcome sexual contacts. Most incidents took place off-campus. Furthermore, the study confirmed the results of earlier research projects—that hardly any (5 percent) of the sexual assaults were brought to the attention of local law enforcement agencies or even the campus police. Many women did not report the offenses because they feared embarrassment and blame upon exposure, did not understand exactly how the law defined rape and other forms of sexual assaults, and/or did not want to stigmatize the young man as a rapist. These victims also did not seek medical care or professional counseling services (Fisher, Cullen, and Turner, 2000; and Karjane, Fisher, and Cullen, 2005).

Survey findings also shed light on when and how the attacks took place. The first few weeks of the freshman and sophomore years seem to be a period of greatest vulnerability; the first few days of the freshman term in particular are fraught with danger. Most incidents took place off campus after 6 P.M., and especially after midnight. In only about 20 percent of the assaults did the young women suffer physical injuries, such as bruises, cuts, swellings, black eyes, and chipped teeth. Slightly more than half of these targets of male aggression fought back physically. Most tried at least one resistance strategy, including using force, yelling "Stop!", screaming, begging, and running away (Sampson, 2004).

Skeptics charged that alarmists in the campus anti-rape movement have morphed into an "industry" that is concerned about the limited use by female students of rape crisis centers, sexual assault disciplinary committees, and emergency hotlines. Alarmists were disseminating inflated risk estimates by loosely applying the very serious term, rape, to ambiguous sexual encounters that involved coercion or deceit without threats of bodily harm or actual violence. Minimalists argued that the maximalist definition was too broad, vague, and inclusive. Consequently, cases were being mistakenly counted in which a young woman felt pressured into agreeing to engage in sex, or had lost good judgment because of excessive drinking or drug taking, or had wanted to say "No!" but was not assertive enough to stop the young man's advances.

If the young woman was supplied with alcohol or drugs by the man before intercourse, that does not mean she was "intentionally incapacitated," as the law requires to prosecute and convict a man of the crime of sexual imposition. Verbal coercion, manipulation, deception (about being in love), false promises (of a long-term relationship or marriage), and betrayal of trust—all nonviolent tactics in the male arsenal of seduction—were erroneously equated with "being forced to give in."

But these tactics are not as serious as surrendering due to physical assault, intimidation with a weapon, or a credible threat of bodily harm. What maximalists counted as "date rapes" actually fell into a gray area between sexual assault and consensual sex and should have been excluded from the statistics, minimalists contended. Most of these women deemed "victims" by maximalist researchers did not consider themselves to have been raped, and explained to interviewers that they did not file complaints because their experiences were not "serious enough" to report—a judgment that seems inconceivable from a person who suffered a "real" rape. In fact, more than 40 percent of the women dated their supposed assailants again and engaged in intercourse with them again, surveys revealed.

The *NCVS* statistic indicating that roughly one female in a thousand each year is raped or fends off a would-be rapist is much closer to the truth and puts the problem in its proper perspective, minimalists contended. By overestimating the date rape problem, maximalists were manufacturing a crisis to further their social agenda of unfairly portraying male–female relationships as inherently antagonistic and fraught with danger. Promoting such a negative image of sexuality stigmatized normal heterosexual intercourse as bordering on criminal conduct unless explicit, unambiguous consent had been secured from the female partner before each escalation in intimacy. The presumed adversarial model of bold male initiatives and token female resistance denies the reality of female desires and portrays women as naive, helpless, vulnerable, and more in need of strictly enforced protective codes of appropriate sexual behavior than of equal rights, minimalists insisted. Overestimates unnecessarily alarmed young women, overshadowed those "real" rapes that are genuinely brutal, and undermined the credibility of "real" complainants. The underlying politics of the anti-date-rape movement actually sets back the cause of women's equality, adherents of the minimalist position insisted (see Eigenberg, 1990; Gilbert, 1991; Podhoretz, 1991; Crichton, 1993; Hellman, 1993; Roiphe, 1993; and MacDonald, 2008a, 2008b).

Maximalists point out that whether or not female students realize that their "unwanted sex," "regrettable experiences," or "promiscuous escapades" fit the legal definitions of rape, surveys reveal that they do suffer emotional distress (Koss, 2008). Minimalists scoff that if it truly were the case that large numbers of "campus rape victims" graduated from college each year burdened by serious emotional scars inflicted by male students, their parents would have demanded action and alternative academic institutions would have sprung up to guarantee young women a safer environment in which to live and learn. These skeptics offer a solution that is direct and blunt: the simplest and surest way to prevent these alleged sexual assaults is for college women to reject the "booze-fueled hookup subculture of casual couplings and one-night stands" by exercising more prudence, modesty, and restraint in their interactions with testosterone-charged young men. This sound advice is fully consistent with the theme of female empowerment and recognizes that young women are able to control their fates and take the lead in solving the problem of rape on campus, minimalists insist (see MacDonald, 2008a, 2008b; and Stepp, 2008).

Maximalists assert that because a woman is inebriated is no justification for violating her against her will. Men are supposed to know that it is against the law to impose sex acts on a person who is unconscious or otherwise unable to grant consent due to intoxication (Koss, 2008). Furthermore, a thorough solution requires much more than a victim-blaming "Just Say No! to Casual Sex" approach or an offender-blaming emphasis on punitive solutions. If acquaintance rape on campus truly has reached epidemic proportions of one-in-five or even one-in-four, its roots can be traced to a hyper-masculine subculture. It emanates from some fraternities and some college athletic teams, whose members are encouraged to devalue and degrade women as objects to be toyed with, sexually exploited, and then discarded. Young men have to organize against their socialization into the prevailing campus "rape culture" and in the process redefine what genuine masculinity really entails (see Schwartz and DeKeseredy, 1997; Benedict, 1998; Benedict and Klein, 1998; Martin and Hummer, 1998; Sampson, 2004; and Sanday, 2007).

Regardless of the actual dimensions of the threat, tactics employed to discourage date rapes (such as sensitizing college men to the issue of explicit consent) must be different from those implemented to prevent stranger rapes (for example, guarding campus buildings against intruders). To reduce the threat of assault from male students, college administrations need to sponsor workshops about dating and intimacy during freshman orientation week, complete with re-enactments of dangerous situations and role-playing exercises to encourage bystander intervention. The target audience must include college men, especially those in fraternities, sports teams, and ROTC units. Student governments ought to issue reader-friendly, easily accessible, and widely distributed guidelines and handbooks that clarify and define completely consensual sexual conduct. Administrations should issue no-contact orders to protect victims from harassment, and warn that sexual misconduct and acts of retaliation against women who press charges are punishable by expulsion from the community by a campus judicial committee. Campus rape crisis centers should encourage young women to seek help by devising confidential, third-party, and even anonymous ways of reporting incidents, and by listing the properly trained people to turn to for counseling, medical care, legal advocacy, protection, and other forms of assistance on campus and in the surrounding community. As for actually implementing these measures and complying with federal laws addressing the problem of sexual assaults on campus, four-year colleges and historically black institutions were doing a better job than other schools, according to a survey of about 1,000 institutions carried out in 2000 (Crichton, 1993;

Bohmer and Parrot, 1993; and Karjane, Fisher, and Cullen, 2005).

Because these disturbing and confusing sexual experiences fall into a gray area, they are sometimes called "gray rapes." An outgrowth of flirting, partying, binge drinking, and mutual desires, gray rapes blur the boundaries between the clear alternatives of enthusiastic consent and vehement objection (Stepp, 2007). If a female student decides to lodge a gray rape accusation against a male student with a judicial board or turns to the local criminal justice system for redress, the strength or weakness of her "no weapon and no physical injuries, he said/she said case" will hinge on a number of factors, some of them in contradiction with the others. In terms of consent, she will have to convince those who sit in judgment that she said no and meant it, or clearly did not give permission. The man's defense will be more credible if he did not hear that "No!" or had reason to believe it was part of a game or traditional script. If she initially agreed but then changed her mind, the verdict could depend on the jurisdiction. Court rulings in eight states grant women the right to decide to say no at any time, even in the middle of intercourse. If witnesses testify that they saw and heard her resist his advances, that supports her case. If witnesses observed her acting provocatively and seductively, that undermines her version of events leading up to the alleged assault. As for her immediate reactions, if she quickly got up and left the premises, called the police, or at least disclosed her distress to someone else, her charges seem more credible. But if she stayed the night, had breakfast with him, and continued to date him, that undermines her later reassessment that what took place that evening violated her wishes. If she engaged in heavy drinking, the accuracy of her memory of events might be challenged on cross-examination. But her accusation that she was taken against her will could be believable if there is evidence that she was plied with liquor and was too drunk to actually give consent (Banfield, 2007).

Drug-Facilitated Acquaintance Rape As the debate raged over the true dimensions of the acquaintance rape problem, an ever more explosive charge

arose during the 1990s. Drug researchers and staff members at rape crisis centers began to receive anecdotal reports of women becoming victims of drug-facilitated acquaintance rapes. The charge was that certain predatory men were escalating their acts of aggression, and going beyond weakening their prey with alcohol to loosen inhibitions. They were secretly spiking the drinks of the young women they were targeting with chemical substances that were far more effective than beer, wine, or liquor.

To overcome female resistance, the unscrupulous males would surreptitiously administer certain club drugs that were popular among partygoers: primarily Rohypnol (roofies), and GHB (liquid ecstasy), but also MDMA (ecstasy) and Ketamine (special K). Large doses of these controlled substances rapidly induce sedation and temporary amnesia, and alcohol magnifies those effects. Odorless and colorless, the drugs can be dropped into a drink, and the unsuspecting quarry loses consciousness and the ability to recall events. The fact that they were mentally and physically incapacitated for several hours might not be detected by the females when they wake up, unless they find themselves in compromising circumstances or bruised and sore from rough sexual violations (Ottens and Hotelling, 2001; Pope and Shouldice, 2001).

According to maximalists, sexual predators quickly learned to use these "liquid poisons" to subdue their prey as soon as the drugs became widely available and popular among partygoers during the early 1990s. Law enforcement officials lament that GHB-fueled rapes are a "perfect" crime because females who were "roofied" usually can't prove it. If they don't notify the authorities immediately, and if hospital and laboratory personnel don't perform chemical tests quickly, the traces of the drugs disappear from the target's blood and urine within hours or days of ingestion (depending on the specific substance). Without toxicological evidence indicating foul play, the accused male merely can insist that the woman had not been comatose but had consented to the sex acts that took place. Even if traces of club drugs are found in lab results, the defendant still can claim that she willingly took the drugs to achieve a pleasurable high. Females incapacitated by the drugs will have difficulty recalling specific details of the assault and will tend to be less effective as complainants in police stations and as prosecution witnesses in court (Ottens and Hotelling, 2001; Pope and Shouldice, 2001; and Smalley and Mnookin, 2003).

Maximalists define a date-rape drug to include any substance that renders the user incapable of saying "no" or of asserting herself. Not only club drugs but also alcohol, marijuana, narcotics, prescription medicines (tranquilizers, sleeping pills), and designer drugs can lead to passivity, impaired judgment, and hazy memories of what took place. Maximalist concerns about the possible spread of this insidious line of attack have brought about a number of responses by government, colleges, and even drinking establishments. Congress passed the Drug-Induced Rape Prevention Act of 1996, which imposed stiff penalties for selling or even possessing some of these controlled substances. In 2000, Congress increased the punishments for dealers and users of GHB, which had been banned by the FDA in 1990. The Department of Justice's Office for Victims of Crime has provided training and technical assistance to improve medical examinations seeking evidence of traces of drugs in the aftermath of sexual assaults. A Los Angeles County task force has pioneered a forensic evidence kit to be used specifically in cases when drug-induced paralysis and amnesia is suspected. The U.S. Drug Enforcement Agency has collaborated with anti-rape organizations to sponsor campaigns that alert women about this presumably growing threat, and has dedicated increased resources to investigations of predatory-drug rings. College administrations have undertaken "Watch That Drink" campus awareness events. Students are urged to pay close attention to risk factors that heighten their vulnerability: never leave their beverages unattended; only accept drinks directly from waiters and bartenders; never drink from a punch bowl, keg, or bottle that is being passed around; and, of course, never accept drinks from people they don't completely trust (see Abramovitz, 2001; Drug Enforcement Agency, 2003; Office of National Drug Control Policy, 2003; Bergfeld, 2005; and Fitzgerald and Riley, 2005).

As of 2003, at least 40 universities and thousands of bars also distributed chemically impregnated cardboard coasters that turn colors when doused with a few drops of a beverage laced with club drugs like GHB. The manufacturer of this drug detection device planned to market it to more than 1,000 college campuses nationwide, although critics warned it was far from follproof (Mason, 2002; Ellin, 2003; Smalley and Mnookin, 2003; Maddalenna, 2005).

Despite the attention paid to drug-facilitated sexual assault in recent years, the true scope of the problem remains unknown because of the absence of reliable estimates of incidence and prevalence rates. The number of reports to police departments of suspected drug-facilitated assaults is extremely low, and stories in the press about prosecutions are hard to find. The presumed spread of drug-induced rapes is largely based on anecdotal evidence from rape crisis centers and hotlines, and sporadic newspaper coverage of court cases. The apparent increase in the availability and use of these drugs is based on inferences drawn from ethnographers' observations about the voluntary drug-taking that goes on at dance clubs and parties, and from hospital records about club drug overdoses requiring emergency room intervention or resulting in deaths. Police investigations involving complainants who suspect they were surreptitiously drugged usually turn out to be inconclusive because the window of opportunity for testing their bodily fluids has passed, or local law enforcement agencies do not have the forensic laboratory expertise to collect and preserve this evidence, which does not show up in routine screening procedures (Fitzgerald and Riley, 2005; Jordan, 2005).

A minimalist view that questioned soaring concerns about this "terrifying scourge" first emerged when a British tabloid published the results of a controversial study. It challenged the message, of a "Watch Your Drink" campaign emanating from an "anti-drink-spiking" organization, that innocent and vulnerable young women out with friends and just seeking to have a good time were being preyed upon by dates, casual acquaintances, or even complete strangers who slipped them a dose of an "anesthesia" drug. A forensic science analysis of samples collected in the United Kingdom from more than 1,000 women who alleged drug-facilitated rape did not find traces of Rohypnol in a single specimen. The lab tests did find that a large proportion of the young women had been binge drinking or using recreational drugs, or had taken heavy doses of both (Platell, 2005). A similar investigation by British doctors of evidence collected from 75 women seeking medical treatment because of fears of drink-spiking also concluded that not one tested positive (Hope, 2007.) Skeptics concluded that the imagery of insidious predators on the prowl promoted by alarmists was misleading. Minimalists charged that many of these women simply were "playing the victim" and were not taking responsibility for drinking themselves into a stupor. However, these skeptics conceded that blaming the female for making herself so vulnerable doesn't excuse the man who imposed himself on a semi-comatose woman incapable of granting consent. Even if these girls and women drugged themselves, the male exploiters of weakness were still breaking the law (see Platell, 2005; Weathers, 2005; and Hope, 2007).

Maximalists countered that the threat of drink-spiking is not an urban legend, and that it is an unfair diversion to shift attention back to a young woman's allegedly irresponsible drinking habits and partying lifestyle. A stubbornly pervasive culture of skepticism still causes a complainant to find herself under a cloud of suspicion when she lodges a charge of drug-facilitated acquaintance rape. The rapid disappearance of traces of these drugs from bodily fluids is to blame for the lack of forensic proof to back up her beliefs that she was surreptitiously slipped an incapacitating substance.

A search of newspaper articles from the past three years with the keywords "date rape drug" turned up many warnings in articles and on blogs about the potential dangers to women posed by predatory men who might use powerful chemical substances to immobilize their prey. The news items centered on men arrested for possession of date-rape drugs; individuals who suffered from self-induced overdoses; some criminal cases handled

in other countries; and accounts of young women who suspected that they had been drugged. But only a few actual cases could be found of men arrested for drug-facilitated sexual assaults within the United States, and even fewer news stories told of successful prosecutions such as this one:

> A 17-year-old girl meets a man in bar and then goes to his apartment. She complains of a headache so he gives her a white pill. She wakes up periodically over the next six hours but is unable to move a muscle as he repeatedly takes sexual advantage of her. A week later she goes to the police but can provide no medical or toxicological evidence to corroborate her complaint. But when four other women make strikingly similar charges against the same man over the next two years, a prosecutor of a special victims unit convinces a judge to consolidate the cases. The man is convicted of sexually assaulting four of the five women and is sentenced to a minimum of 30 years in prison. (Warkentin, 2006)

Threats On and Off Campus   America's nearly 8 million part-time and full-time college students face a special problem. Most undergraduates are between the ages of 18 and 24—precisely at the stage of life when the dangers of engaging in violence and theft reach their peak. Simultaneously, people in that same age range face the gravest risks of being harmed by physical attacks and stealing. Demographically speaking, college campuses contain a volatile mix of potential offenders and victims. Drug taking and drinking raise the odds of trouble breaking out. But what is the reality?

It should come as no surprise that college students turn out to be less likely to experience violence than their non-student counterparts. For example, a large proportion of killings that take place on the meanest streets of the nation's toughest neighborhoods involve young men between the ages of 18 and 24 as a perpetrator, a victim, or both. But rarely is either party enrolled at an institution of higher learning. Similarly, young men who are not students are robbed much more often (about 12 per 1,000 per year) than undergrads (just 7 per 1,000), according to an analysis of *NCVS* findings from 1995 to 2002. Non-students 18 to 24 years old also are subjected to aggravated assaults and simple assaults more often than their college counterparts. The most striking difference is that non-student young women suffer acts of violence far more often than college women (71 incidents versus 43 incidents per 1,000, respectively). The dangers of being raped or sexually assaulted are higher for female non-students than for female students (8 compared to 6 per 1,000). Most attackers of college students are strangers (58 percent) rather than acquaintances. Most of these assailants (66 percent) do not use a weapon, and only a small proportion (9 percent) pull out a gun. Surprisingly, college students are less inclined to report their violent victimizations to the police than non-students (35 percent filed complaints compared to 47 percent). Not surprisingly, the overwhelming majority of attacks are carried out off-campus (93 percent), and after dark (72 percent) (Baum, 2005).

Despite the relative safety of college campuses, serious crimes, even murders, can and do take place on the grounds of institutions of higher learning on rare occasion.

Early one morning, a student with a history of drug and alcohol abuse wanders through a campus dormitory, passing through a series of three propped-open doors that should have been locked. He invades the room of a young woman and proceeds to torture, sodomize, rape, and ultimately kill her. He is caught, convicted, and sentenced to die. But her parents discover that crime on campus is "one of the best-kept secrets in the country." The callousness, stonewalling, and cover-up by the college's administration intent on protecting the institution's public image causes the grieving parents to launch a lawsuit charging negligence and failure to warn of foreseeable dangers. The college offers a settlement and the parents use the money

to set up the first national not-for-profit organization dedicated to preventing campus violence and assisting victims. The parents also lead a movement to force colleges to reveal to current and prospective students information about incidents taking place on campus. After nine states pass laws requiring disclosure of crime data within just a few years, Congress passes the Crime Awareness and Campus Security Act of 1990. (Clery and Clery, 2001)

A handful of highly publicized shootings and rapes, as well as a spate of negligence lawsuits filed by distraught parents, have compelled administrators, faculties, and student governments to address threats to personal safety on college and university campuses. Image-conscious administrators initially devised ways to downplay the risks that their students actually faced for fear that such revelations would damage their schools' reputations, scare away potential candidates from applying for admission, and hurt fundraising campaigns seeking donations from alumni. Despite continued opposition by administrators, Congress extended the themes of its 1990 student right-to-know legislation by passing the Higher Education Act in 1992. It mandated that colleges establish sexual assault prevention programs and grant procedural rights to rape survivors.

Congress imposed even tougher right-to-know regulations in 1998 with the enactment of the Jeanne Cleary Disclosure of Campus Security Policy and Campus Crime Statistics Act. It required institutions receiving federal aid to maintain detailed crime logs and issue comprehensive annual crime reports. Now colleges must compile and disclose the nature, date, time, and location of incidents brought to the attention of campus security officers as well as the local police. Crimes committed in residential housing, off-campus buildings, parking areas, and adjacent streets must be included. The log must be made available to the public—especially students, parents, employees, and journalists—during normal business hours. These statistics can be posted on the Internet as well. Timely warnings must be issued to alert the campus community about ongoing threats

TABLE 11.1   Crimes Committed on College Campuses, 2001–2006

Type of Crime	Number of Incidents Per Year					
	2001	2002	2003	2004	2005	2006
Murders	18	23	10	16	11	8
Forcible sex offenses	2,200	2,350	2,580	2,680	2,700	2,700
Robberies	2,140	2,190	2,090	1,980	2,030	1,970
Aggravated assaults	3,180	3,070	3,050	2,910	2,870	3,070
Burglaries	28,140	29,300	29,130	30,740	30,820	32,050
Motor vehicle thefts	6,580	6,610	6,600	6,340	5,890	5,590

NOTE: Numbers of reported incidents, except for murders, are rounded to the nearest 10.
SOURCE: U.S. Department of Education, Campus Crime Statistics Online, 2008.

to personal safety. Administrations face a fine of $25,000 for each willful violation of the reporting requirements (Carter, 2000; Sampson, 2004).

Each year, reports of property crimes on college campuses are much more numerous than violent crimes (see Table 11.1). Larcenies top the list, but some of these thefts are of school property from offices or labs or items from the bookstore rather than students' possessions (and therefore do not appear in Table 11.1). Burglaries (again, not solely of student lockers or dorm rooms) take place more frequently than vehicle thefts. As for violent offenses, aggravated assaults outnumber robberies and rapes. Unlike the streets of poor neighborhoods, where thousands of 18- to 24-year-olds lose their lives every year, murders on campuses are rare, according to the extensive database maintained by the U.S. Department of Education. No across-the-board trends are evident in the data for the first six years of the twenty-first century displayed in Table 11.1. Burglaries and forcible sex crimes seem to have increased over the period, while motor vehicle thefts dropped.

As for killings on campus, the figures presented in the first row of Table 11.1 reveal that a downward drift seemed to materialize by 2006. But in 2007, a deranged undergraduate slaughtered 33 people, and another shooting rampage by a graduate student took place in 2008, snuffing out five lives, reversing this short-lived improvement in campus security (see Hauser and O'Connor, 2007; and Nizza, 2008).

Most of these slayings involved firearms and could be characterized as student-on-student, but some casualties included administrators, professors, and staff. (However, college teaching remains one of the safest occupations.) Some of the bloodiest high-profile shootings by undergraduates and graduate students that broke out on campuses both large and small, in urban and rural settings, and claimed many innocent lives, are listed in Box 11.1.

Parents and students are understandably concerned about campus security. It is tempting to try to calculate the victimization rates per 1,000 students for various campuses to identify the 10 safest and 10 most dangerous in the nation. But comparisons of relative safety can be misleading. The composition of the student body—undergrads versus grad students, men versus women, dorm residents versus commuters—varies dramatically. Also, campus student bodies change in size from day sessions to evening classes to nighttime residence hall populations. Furthermore, some colleges are situated in idyllic rural settings; others are located in densely populated urban neighborhoods or have several scattered satellite centers, branches, or affiliated teaching hospitals. It may even be downright unfair to compare security measures at minimally funded community colleges to those at well-endowed Ivy League universities, and to rank safety levels at large public urban institutions against small, sheltered, private or religious colleges.

B O X 11.1 A Timeline of Some of the Worst Campus Shootings

Year	Campus	What Happened and Who Died
1966	University of Texas	A student climbs a tower and opens fire, killing 16 and wounding 31.
1968	South Carolina State College	State police officers kill three students and wound 27 others during a protest against desegregation.
1970	Jackson State College	Highway Patrol officers kill two students and wound nine others by shooting into a crowd.
1971	Kent State University	National Guard troops open fire on anti-war demonstrators, killing four students and wounding nine.
1991	University of Iowa	A grad student kills three professors, an administrator, a student, and then himself.
1996	San Diego State	A grad student slays three professors during his thesis defense.
2002	Appalachian School of Law	A grad student who failed out of school kills a dean, a professor, a student, and wounds three others.
2002	University of Arizona	A failing student kills three instructors and then himself.
2007	Virginia Polytechnic Institute	An undergrad kills 30 students and two professors, and wounds 24 others, in a rampage that begins in a dorm and ends in a classroom, before taking his own life.
2008	Northern Illinois University	A grad student opens fire in a lecture hall, killing five students and injuring 18 before committing suicide.

SOURCE: Wicker, 1970; Associated Press, 2008b.

Usually, incidents that take place in the immediate vicinity of the campus that would boost the dangerousness ratings are caused by conditions that are beyond the college administration's ability to clean up or control. Non-reporting to the campus security force or the local police may be a larger problem on certain campuses than others, so calculations of victimization rates can be inaccurate and misleading for this reason as well. Finally, published figures may be inaccurate and misleading for institutions whose administrations manipulate the numbers to make their campuses appear safer than they really are to attract security-minded applicants. An example of this would be downgrading burglaries—crimes involving intruders that should be reported to the U.S. Department of Education's National Center for Educational Statistics recording system—to larcenies not resulting from trespassing, which aren't counted by the NCES and don't have

to be publicized to the college community, but are disclosed in the FBI's *UCR* (see Seward, 2006).

Even though the streets around urban universities, and campus buildings and grounds are much safer than they were at the start of the 1990s, self-defense classes for students are growing in popularity. Some colleges offer credit for these courses; some are coed and others are designed to empower women. The syllabus not only centers on physical skills but also teaches about responsible decision making and the dangers of drinking to excess, as well as everyday risk avoidance tactics (Schwab, 2008).

In 2005, Congress designated September as National Campus Safety Awareness Month (Feingold, 2005). To prevent incidents, most campuses now have gates and checkpoints, ID systems, electronic card-key entry systems to buildings, better locking devices, message boards, professional security forces, stepped-up patrols, extensive monitoring via video surveillance cameras, better lighting, indoor and outdoor emergency phones, evening shuttle buses, student escorts, crisis counseling centers, crime blotter columns in campus newspapers, and workshops on date rape and crime prevention as part of first-year orientations. Colleges are now rated in terms of the number and kinds of security measures they have implemented to protect their campus communities. By 2005, most public colleges had sworn officers with firearms and full arrest powers, but many private institutions of higher learning still had only unarmed security guards, according to a federal survey (Purdum, 1988; Smith, 1988; Graham, 1993; Mathews, 1993; Lederman, 1994; Whitaker and Pollard, 1993; Molotsky, 1997; Ottens and Hotelling, 2001; and Reaves, 2008).

After the two bloody rampages of 2007 and 2008, classes were cancelled; students built shrines, posted messages of consolation on the Internet, and organized memorial services. Administrators set up scholarship funds in the names of the victims and offered crisis and grief counseling to distraught members of campus communities. But the reactions go far beyond those immediate responses. Many administrations are enhancing the mental health services offered at counseling centers especially to recognize red flags and identify potentially explosive members of the campus community. Simultaneously, they are arming their security forces, devising lockdown procedures to seal off buildings, and signing up students and faculty to receive emergency notification alerts via e-mail and text messages about incidents as soon as they take place. In the wake of the mass shootings, some parents and students are calling for stricter gun control legislation. However, some took an opposite stance and argued that the problem was not too many guns on campus, but too few—campuses are often designated as gun-free zones. Guns-for-self-defense enthusiasts have convinced legislatures in 15 states to consider measures allowing professors and students (with permits to carry concealed handguns) to bring their weapons to class (Archibold, 2008). In the meantime, hundreds of colleges have paid for a training program that encourages students to dispel feelings that they are defenseless, and to take advantage of their superior numbers and to fight back with

improvised weapons, from backpacks to laptops, to subdue a deranged gunman (Zagier, 2008). Unfortunately, the relaxed and open atmosphere of academia, which was based on freedom of movement and free expression of ideas, is being sacrificed in the name of enhanced campus security (see Fox, 2008; and Mathias, 2008).

Despite the shocking and tragic outbreaks of violence at universities listed in Box 11.1, the special solution—and the best overall risk reduction advice—for the 18 million college students (as of 2008) seeking to avoid trouble, whether they are commuters or live in dormitories, would be to spend as much time as possible on campus because the buildings and grounds of the nation's nearly 3,700 institutions of higher learning still are among the safest locales in the country.

Threats Facing Middle School and High School Students

Teenage students face a special problem. Compulsory education laws compel them to attend their local high school, unless their parents can afford private or parochial school or are able to home-school them. By entering into the mainstream of high school activities, they are forced to interact with potential victimizers. The resulting experiences may be aggravating but can be terrifying, even deadly. On rare occasions, preyed upon students turn the tables on their tormenters, unleash retaliatory violence, and in the process become assailants themselves. Unfortunately, in the absence of an environment free of threats of attacks, counterattacks, and other serious disruptions, teachers will find it difficult to stick to lesson plans, and fearful and distracted targets and their classmates will have trouble learning what they need to know.

To measure the relative safety of various schools and school systems, several government agencies monitor reports of incidents of violence and theft: the FBI, Bureau of Justice Statistics, National Center for Education Statistics (NCES), and the federal government's Centers for Disease Control and Prevention (CDC). These reporting

T A B L E 11.2   Incidents on School Property, Safety Concerns, and Security Measures, United States, 2005

Nature of the Problem	Percentage of Students or Rate per 1,000
Thefts of pupils' possessions	33 students for every 1,000 aged 12 to 18
Victims of serious violence	5 students for every 1,000 aged 12 to 18
Involved in a fight	18 percent of males in grades 9 to 12; 9 percent of females in grades 9 to 12
Threatened with or injured by a weapon on school grounds	8 percent of students in grades 9 to 12
Carried a concealed weapon on school grounds	7 percent of students in grades 9 to 12
Endured hate-related slurs	11 percent of students aged 12 to 18
Experienced bullying	28 percent of students aged 12 to 18
Fearful of being attacked	6 percent of students aged 12 to 18
Skipped school or avoided certain locations because of fear	6 percent of students aged 12 to 18
Protected by security guards or officers	68 percent of students aged 12 to 18
Protected by metal detectors	11 percent of students aged 12 to 18

SOURCE: NCES, 2008.

systems cover about 54 million youngsters from pre-kindergarten to grade 12 who attend about 125,000 schools across the country.

Statistics from the BJS's annual *NCVS* reveal how many adolescents between the ages of 12 and 18 suffer thefts and acts of violence that they are willing to disclose to interviewers, whether or not these negative experiences were reported to the school authorities or the police. One reassuring finding from the *NCVS* over recent years is that the victimization rate for students in middle/junior high schools, and high schools dropped from 1992 to 2002, a trend that mirrored a general decline in crime rates burdening all Americans. The *NCVS* findings for these years also indicated that fewer violent incidents occurred on school grounds than in the communities in which students lived.

However, more thefts took place in schools (33 per 1,000 students) than in the surrounding neighborhoods (23 per 1,000 students) for youngsters between the ages of 12 and 18 during 2005. In general, males were more likely to suffer attacks than females, and urban youth more often than

other students. Similarly, for their teachers, thefts outnumbered physical attacks. Teachers who worked at elementary schools were less likely to suffer acts of violence or theft than those who taught at middle/junior high schools and high schools. Not surprisingly, teachers in urban schools experienced more incidents than their suburban and rural counterparts, which closely reflected the geographic distribution of crimes committed off school grounds (DeVoe et al., 2004, 2005; NCES, 2008). Table 11.2 presents a summary of school incidents, safety concerns, and security measures reported by students to interviewers for the school year ending in June 2005.

As always, murders are the most accurately counted of crime statistics; underreporting is not a problem. Fortunately, there are not many to count—murders of students on school property are quite rare. The graph in Figure 11.1 shows data on slayings of youths between the ages of 5 and 19 since the early 1990s, when school-based data collection and reporting systems were first established.

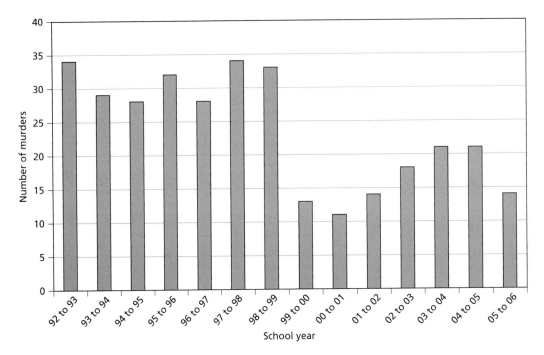

FIGURE 11.1 Trends in Murders of Students at Middle Schools and High Schools in the United States, School Years 1992 to 2006

SOURCES: DeVoe et al., 2005; National Center for Educational Statistics, 2008.

Often a single outrageous outbreak of mass murder accounts for most of the deaths of students in a given year. The annual proportion of youngsters slain on school grounds is a little more than 1 percent of all youth killings. In other words, nearly 99 percent of children who are murdered are killed in settings other than school. For example, during the 2004–2005 academic year, 21 youngsters between age 5 and 19 of a total population of more than 50 million were slain on school grounds, while roughly 1,500 were murdered at other locations. Therefore, statistically speaking, even turbulent high schools remain relatively safe compared to nearby streets, parks, and homes. Put another way, students are 50 times more likely to be murdered away from school than on school grounds (NCES, 2008).

The trend line in Figure 11.1 shows that school security has improved. The number of rare yet tragic murders remained relatively constant and disturbingly high during most of the 1990s, even though killings beyond school grounds declined during this time. At the end of the 1990s, a substantial drop in slayings on school grounds took place, and this reduced level of lethal violence lasted well into the first decade of the twenty-first century. However, the body count of school-related violent deaths rises substantially each year (from 14 to 26 during the academic year of 2005–2006) if a reporting system also counts suicides; the murders of teachers, parents, staff members, and intruders; legal interventions by police officers, accidental fatal firearms discharges; and the slayings of other outsiders at sporting events, dances, and other school functions (NCES, 2008).

Violence among adolescents has declined sharply since the early 1990s. Unfortunately, a spate of school shootings has overshadowed that positive trend in public discourse. Although they are highly unusual, sudden and senseless outbursts of gunfire directed at fellow students, teachers, and administrators by distraught and often suicidal assailants have permanently changed the environment of the nation's middle schools and high schools. To curb violence and theft on school grounds, many superintendents and principals now take security considerations much more seriously. Reports about threats issued by disgruntled students usually are checked out. Many schools have beefed up security by hiring school safety officers, carrying out searches of backpacks, installing metal detectors at their front doors, devising lockdown procedures, and instituting conflict resolution and anti-bullying programs.

However, as with victimization data, the accuracy of school crime statistics must be examined objectively. Manipulating data to make a college or university appear safer was mentioned earlier in the chapter. Occasionally articles in the news claim that middle and high school safety officers (sometimes called school resource officers), principals, and even top school system administrators may seek to suppress initial reporting or the eventual official recording of particular incidents to make schools seem safer than they really are. Principals may be acting in good faith, and certain disruptive behaviors surely fall into a gray area where discretion legitimately can be exercised. But intentional statistical manipulation and underreporting of victimizations violates federal No Child Left Behind legislation. It also does a disservice to students, parents, and members of the staff because if a school does not get the attention and resources that it deserves, everyone inside it will be at greater risk (Gootman, 2007).

INDIVIDUALS MENACED BY STALKERS

Stalking: A New Word for an Old Problem

Terrorists, political assassins, hit men hired by mobsters, and kidnappers always have trailed and hunted their prey before finding an opportune moment to strike. But it was not until the end of the 1980s that the term **stalking** was coined and entered into everyday language. The media began to use it in the aftermath of a widely publicized tragedy in 1989 when an actress was killed by an obsessed fan.

Today the definition includes certain intimidating, harassing, and threatening behaviors that would make a reasonable person fearful. Before an appropriate expression was devised to capture the essence of these intolerable intrusions into another's daily life, individuals who were stalked faced a special problem: being shadowed and hounded was not taken seriously by the authorities unless and until physical injuries were inflicted. Threats of this type are hard to prove and difficult to stop, but in 1990, California's legislature was the first to criminalize these threatening situations. Soon afterward, the Los Angeles Police Department established a Threat Management Unit, the first squad specifically set up to investigate calls for help by people sensing that they were in grave danger.

Two types of victim–offender relationships account for most complaints. In celebrity stalking, the first category, a well-known person (often a pop star, media personality, professional athlete, or political figure) experiences continual, unwanted interference from either a "secret admirer" or an enemy. These cases are relatively few but are highly publicized. In the second, more common, type, the target knows and is repeatedly contacted by the aggressor in a frightening and unwelcome way. This kind of prior-relationship stalking can begin with contacts that are perfectly legal, including phone calls, unannounced visits, faxes, e-mails, cards, gifts, and photographs. But soon the attention becomes a distressing reminder of someone's persisting hostility. Stalkers shadow their targets as they engage in routine activities, and linger in front of their homes, schools, or workplaces. They also might vandalize their target's property, harm their pets, approach their children, steal their mail, and seek to get them in trouble with the law, friends, kin, landlords, and employers.

Like spouse abuse and forcible rape, stalking seems to be an offense that is usually motivated by desires for domination and subjugation. Frequently the terrorized party is a woman followed around by a jealous, possessive, violence-prone ex-boyfriend or ex-husband who refuses to accept her decision that their romantic relationship is over. However, many variations on the themes of "fatal attraction," "murderous obsession," or "erotomania delusions" are possible: a young man's new girlfriend can be trailed and threatened by his old girlfriend; a therapist can be besieged by a former patient who feels abandoned and betrayed after an affair; or a boss might be chased after by a disgruntled worker who was subjected to intense sexual harassment, then exploited, and fired afterward. Most stalkers, according to clinical studies, are primarily motivated by vengeance and hatred of the victim, as opposed to genuine affection or romantic inclinations. They desire to exert power or to regain control over their targets, whom they blame for the falling out (Meloy, 1998).

Victims can suffer in a number of ways. If they are hunted and haunted, they may experience anxiety, panic attacks, depression, sleep disturbances, nightmares, memory lapses, and weight loss, among other emotional and physical symptoms. Financially, the harassment may inflict costs because of damaged possessions, lost earnings, and moving expenses (Brewster, 1998; and OJP, 2008b).

The Scope of the Problem   Each year in the United States, an estimated 1.4 million people (about 1 million of whom are females) consider themselves to be victims of stalking, according to the 1998 National Violence Against Women Survey. That yields a prevalence rate estimate that about 1 in every 12 women (about 8 percent) and 1 in every 45 men (about 2 percent) will be stalked at some point in their lives. Most of the targets were females (78 percent), and most of them (74 percent) were between the ages of 18 and 39. Almost all the stalkers of females were males (94 percent), and most of those who harassed men were other men (60 percent). The typical situation (77 percent of the cases) involved women who knew their male stalkers; the majority of these women (59 percent) were formerly involved in a romantic relationship with these men (ex-spouses, ex-boyfriends, sometimes casual dates), and the stalking often began as soon as their intimate involvement ended. Most of the male victims (64 percent) were hounded by someone they knew, and some of these aggressors (30 percent) were former intimate partners (Tjaden and Thoennes, 1998). Stalking by intimate partners (who often were

younger than their victims) typically was preceded by battering and lasted between one and two years (Brewster, 1998; Tjaden and Thoennes, 1998).

A study of college women yielded a higher victimization rate because it used a broader definition of stalking. Its screening question was posed as follows: "Since the school year began, has anyone from a stranger to an ex-boyfriend repeatedly followed you; watched you; or phoned, written, or e-mailed you in ways that seemed obsessive and made you afraid or concerned about your safety?" About 13 percent of the college women in the sample answered "yes." However, the percent answering "yes" dropped to only about 2 percent when the question was rephrased to ask whether the person who was the source of the unwanted attention actually threatened harm, which is the definition used in many state statutes. Almost one-third of college women disclosed that they suffered emotionally because of a campus stalking incident (Fisher, Cullen, and Turner, 2000).

Although most stalkers do not become physically abusive, their traumatized targets worry that the unwanted intrusions might escalate into a beating, a kidnapping, a sexual assault, or even a murder. Women who previously had been romantically involved with their stalkers face heightened risks of serious violence. Targets of nonsexual obsessions are more likely to be harassed by mentally ill but less dangerous offenders (Farnham, James, and Cantrell, 2000).

An FBI study discovered that 30 percent of slain women had been stalked by their former boyfriends or husbands before the former intimates murdered them (Office of Justice Programs, 1998). A study that focused solely on females killed by their intimate partners revealed that most (76 percent) had been stalked by these murderous men before the fatal encounter (McFarlane et al., 1999).

However, the most common stalking behaviors were harassing the targets by spying on them, following them, and waiting outside their homes, workplaces, or schools. Individuals also complained about unwanted phone calls, letters, and gifts. Less than half of people who considered themselves to be victims of stalking reported that they had been directly threatened.

Turning to the Criminal Justice System for Relief Spurred on by victims' rights groups, all 50 states had, by 1994, criminalized the practice of willfully, purposefully, maliciously, and repeatedly pursuing and harassing someone. Congress passed a comparable Interstate Stalking Act in 1996, making it a felony to travel across state lines with the intent to kill, injure, harass, or intimidate someone who, as a result of these actions, reasonably fears death or serious bodily injury. Anti-stalking laws fill a void in the patchwork of statutes forbidding menacing, trespassing, and threatening behavior, and allow the authorities to take action before the object of the unwanted attention is seriously hurt.

To permit the police to arrest a stalker before an attack is actually carried out, many state laws focus on the victim's state of mind as well as the offender's intentions. These laws take context into account and require that the targeted individual has a reasonable fear of death or grave bodily injury that arises from a credible threat of violence made by the aggressor. In some jurisdictions, stalking is a misdemeanor, while in others it is a felony. Most states have laws that distinguish misdemeanor from felony stalking depending on how ominous the threat is. First offenses usually are prosecuted as misdemeanors. Stiffer punishments can be imposed if the offender actually inflicts bodily harm or confines or restrains the person being pursued, or if there are aggravating factors (such as brandishing a weapon; harassing someone under 16 years of age; disregarding an order of protection; or violating the restrictive conditions of probation or parole) (Beck et al., 1992; Hunzeker, 1992; Kolarik, 1992; Wright et al., 1996; and Stalking Resource Center, 2008).

Only about half of all victims call on the police for help. Less than a quarter of these reported incidents lead to prosecution. Only about half of the prosecutions result in convictions, usually not for stalking per se, but for other minor crimes such as disorderly conduct, harassment, menacing, intimidation, trespassing, vandalism, simple assault (and in the more serious instances, breaking and entering or robbery). Many stalkers violated orders of protection that their intended prey had obtained in court (Tjaden and Thoennes, 1998; Dunn, 2002; and Jordan et al., 2003).

More than one-quarter of female and one-tenth of male victims obtain a restraining order. But most of these court orders of protection reportedly were violated by stalkers (Tjaden and Thoennes, 1998).

Individuals who just want to be left alone will have a tough time convincing the authorities to take action if the police officers are not adequately trained to recognize the various forms that the outlawed behavior might take. Most state laws define stalking so narrowly that planting any high-tech methods of tracking people's movements are excluded. Furthermore, targets often find it unreasonably difficult to document that they are being subjected to meaningful threats. The burden of proof is so high that very few stalkers are found guilty, and most of these misdemeanants are jailed for just a few weeks. For these reasons, victim advocates proposed an updated model stalking code for state legislatures to consider which closes loopholes in existing laws. It would make the following additional behaviors punishable: engaging in obsessive and controlling actions; targeting third parties (family members, children, friends) in order to instill fear; harassing a person when exercising visitation or custody rights; misusing the court system to file motions and suits ("litigation abuse"); applying surveillance technology to monitor movements; impersonating a target to ruin credit or interfere with employment; and posting and disseminating inaccurate and embarrassing information or humiliating photographs (NCVC, 2007).

Whereas victim advocates consider existing laws to be so limited as to be ineffective, civil libertarians consider the wording to be so vague and overly broad as to be unconstitutional. Some admittedly improper acts that victim advocates want to outlaw as constituting stalking behaviors are outgrowths of ordinary interpersonal conflicts that should not be handled as violations of the law. Alleged stalkers may believe that their repeated activities are allowed under First Amendment free-speech protections. These persistent people don't realize that they could find themselves as defendants in criminal and civil courts. Also, some hastily crafted statutes may grant too much discretion to law enforcement agencies, opening the door to arbitrary enforcement (see Endo, 1999; Reno, 1999).

Reducing Risks   Not surprisingly, stalking victims often find themselves blamed for facilitating (through carelessness), precipitating (through rash conduct) or even provoking (through irresponsible incitements) a stalker's preoccupation with initiating or reviving a relationship. Female targets in particular are told that they are imagining that harmless messages foreshadow impending doom, or that they should be flattered by the attention, or that they are somehow encouraging the unwanted contacts through bad judgment. Victim-blaming insists that their behavior is at the root of the problem and that they should examine their own responses and change their reactions (see Meloy, 1998).

To head off serious trouble, victim advocates make the following suggestions: break off contact with the stalker; keep a log or journal documenting acts of harassment and intimidation; formulate plans that will enhance safety at home, when traveling, and while at work; and fully exercise the options for protection and prosecution within the criminal and civil justice systems (Spence-Diehl, 1999).

Stalking victims can take many self-protective measures. In addition to reporting the crime and preserving corroborating evidence, they can go to court for a restraining order, sign up for an unlisted phone number (and a trap to tape incoming calls), change locks, vary their daily routines, practice self-defense techniques, seek the company of trustworthy protectors, and pack an emergency suitcase for a temporary escape to a more secure place. In extreme cases, terrorized people can move away to an undisclosed location and even change their identities to enhance their safety and the well-being of their families.

Unfortunately, stalkers are discovering new high-tech ways to track the movements of their victims, such as by secretly placing a tracking device on a target's car, or by surreptitiously installing spyware to reveal e-mails written and websites visited by the people they are hounding ("When technology gets diabolical ..." 2005).

Cyberstalking: A New Word for a New Problem

A young woman goes to court and gets a no-contact restraining order against a 28-year-old man who is harassing her. In retaliation, during the course of more than a year, the man posts her name and address on popular Internet websites including MySpace, Facebook, and Craig's List, inviting men to visit her home for "sexual gratification." At the same time, he e-mails death threats to her, according to the indictment in federal court that charges him with cyberstalking. (Wood, 2008).

Before the Internet, the prospect of being chased through cyberspace and getting bombarded with unwanted e-mail messages didn't exist. When the potential for abuse was first recognized—that obsessive assailants and sexual predators had a new way to pursue their targets—there wasn't an adequate phrase to characterize this disturbing situation. At first, the problem was referred to as online abuse, online harassment, or even cyberharassment. Those who became alarmed about inappropriate and worrisome communications they were receiving via instant messaging, in their e-mail accounts, in chat rooms, and on widely accessed social networking websites faced a special problem. The authorities to whom they turned for help in moments of despair merely advised them to shut off their computers. Often they were told that the vile suggestions and ominous threats awaiting them when they logged on, or posted about them on others' webpages, did not rise to the level of criminal activity.

The first anguished complainants got the runaround from law enforcement officials because it was unclear which agency, if any, had jurisdiction—local police, state police, local prosecutor, state attorney general's office, or a branch of the federal government. Geographically, the jurisdiction question was whether the crime took place within the sender's area or within the recipient's area. Internet service providers generally were not cooperative with investigators because of concerns about respecting the privacy of their subscribers (Hitchcock, 2002).

By the turn of the century, the term **cyberstalking** was used to describe this potentially dangerous conduct. Within a few years, most states added provisions to their stalking and harassment statutes to outlaw the misuse of computers and electronic communications to pass along threats. The criminal justice system is becoming more responsive as police departments set up units to investigate computer crimes (as the NYPD did in 1995), and county prosecutors establish stalking and threat assessment bureaus (as in Los Angeles) or use the staffs of existing sex crimes divisions.

However, many law enforcement agencies do not have enough adequately trained officers and prosecutors and sufficient state-of-the-art technology to successfully pursue these kinds of cases. Furthermore, the threats might not be taken seriously if the authorities judge the likelihood of an actual physical confrontation to be remote, especially if the harasser lives far away in another region or a different country. Self-help and support groups have sprung up on the Internet to assist and advise those who feel distressed, frustrated, and powerless to stop the unwanted communications. Voluntary online surveys filled out at these websites indicate that of the majority of victims of cyberstalking are female, especially teenage girls and young women, and that most of the perpetrators are male. (These are biased samples of respondents seeking assistance for situations that might not meet the legal threshold of aggravated harassment.) Many offenders seem to be complete strangers, which can be particularly unnerving because their appearances and whereabouts, as well as their credibility, are unknown (Hitchcock, 2002; Riveira, 2002; and D'Ovidio and Doyle, 2003).

Apparently, stalking in cyberspace is not as common as traditional methods—taunting, menacing, intimidating, and threatening someone over the phone, through the mail, via faxes, or face to face. Nationally, during 2001 only 16 percent of prosecutors' offices (77 percent of those serving large cities), handled an e-mail cyberstalking case (DeFrances, 2002). By 2005, corresponding figures

were 36 percent of prosecutors' offices nationwide with 82 percent of those serving more than 1 million residents (Perry, 2006).

TARGETS OF HATE CRIMES

Rediscovering a Very Old Problem

During the 1980s, a long-standing problem finally began to receive the attention it deserved: violence and vandalism motivated by the offender's hatred of the victim's "kind" in terms of race, ethnicity, religion, or sexual preference. Throughout world history, assailants from one group have attacked such "enemies" and suffered counterattacks as reprisals. An examination of U.S. history will reveal that a significant proportion of murders, assaults, and acts of vandalism and desecration were fueled by bigotry. Inter-group tensions break out periodically in mob actions, race riots, lynchings, looting, intentionally set fires, street battles, and even vicious schoolyard fights. Some bias-driven attacks have been spontaneous and isolated while others were planned by organized hate groups as part of a campaign of political intimidation.

Usually, aggressors went after members of groups that lacked social and political influence. In the past, the suffering of these individuals and the fears others who identified with them shared did not often arouse public sympathy or attract media attention. Law enforcement officials did not assign a high priority to investigating these breakdowns in intergroup relations, catching the culprits, and preventing further shockwaves. Many victims felt reluctant to turn to the authorities for help, and many police departments failed to keep accurate records of the incidents that were brought to their attention. Without a standard definition and an appropriate label for this type of crime, no government agency could issue official estimates of the scope of the violence and destruction of property that fell into this category. Therefore, no one knew for sure which groups were being singled out for attack most often and whether this rediscovered problem was growing or subsiding.

That situation changed during the 1980s. Organizations representing constituencies that perceived that they were being targeted (such as racial and religious minorities) began to compile their own statistics and to issue reports. These political activists asserted that the problems of victims of hate-fueled crimes merited special solutions. They advanced the following argument: Recognizing **bias crime** or **hate crime** as a distinct category implies that its impact on the victim and on the community at large goes far beyond the specific harm inflicted. In other words, burning a cross in a predominantly white neighborhood on the lawn of a home that was just purchased by a black family is more than mere criminal mischief; spray painting a swastika on the wall of a Jewish synagogue is more than a minor act of vandalism; and an unprovoked gang attack on a gay couple symbolizes more than simply a random assault by complete strangers.

Hate crimes are assumed to have more profound and enduring consequences than comparable "ordinary" offenses. Hate crimes can be interpreted as symbolic affronts to members of the victim's racial, ethnic, religious, or sexual preference group. People who share the same characteristics as the targets of bias crimes might sense that they are vulnerable too, and even may feel directly harmed themselves. Thus, they tend to identify with and rally around the victim. If other people side with the aggressor, then the community, or even the entire society, becomes polarized. At that point, inter-group relations, which are delicately balanced in a pluralistic society in the best of times, quickly become strained. The resulting rifts could trigger a cycle of aggressive initiatives and violent responses, and perhaps a dangerous escalation in the level of force used in retaliatory attacks. The original act also can inspire copycat crimes by members of the offender's group, which, in turn, could touch off acts of vengeance by members of the victim's group. Therefore, when bias is recognized as a motivation behind an offense, the police and prosecutors must assign a high priority to resolving the case before the situation spirals out of control. Members of the victim's group and of the community at large could misinterpret the authorities' apparent indifference, skepticism, or tendency to blame the victim as tacit official approval of the offender's spiteful actions. The opposite response—taking the crimes very seriously—indicates the government's resolve to provide what the Constitution pledges: equal protection under the law (Wexler and Marx, 1986; Anti-Defamation League, 1999).

Pressures from below finally compelled those at the helm of the criminal justice system to confront this challenge by taking a series of steps: initiating efforts to monitor and measure the frequency and intensity of incidents motivated by raw bigotry; improving the response of police and prosecutors to the victims' plights; and developing community level solutions to these divisive events.

How Much Hate?

A 15-year-old boy comes out and tells classmates that he is a homosexual. When he begins to wear make-up and jewelry, he has to endure teasing and bullying from some of the boys at the junior high school. During a computer lab, in front of 24 other eighth graders, a 14-year-old pulls out a gun and shoots the boy in the head. The prosecutor charges the teenage assailant as an adult who is responsible for a premeditated hate-fueled murder that carries a penalty of 52 years to life in prison. (Cathcart, 2008)

***

After drinking in a park, seven high school students go hunting for a "Mexican" to attack. After harassing and chasing several young men, they close in on a recent immigrant from Ecuador and stab him to death. The hate crime so shocks the conscience of the community that a leading elected official known for his campaigns against illegal immigration declares "that this brutal killing of an innocent, hard-working man for no other reason than he was Hispanic … can be the spark for all of us—yours truly included—to admit our faults, to work more closely with one another, to pay more attention to what our children are doing, and to pay more attention to what we say," (Applebome, 2008).

Bias crimes are motivated in whole or in part by the perpetrator's hatred of the victim's entire group. Those on the receiving end of bigots' wrath usually are members of negatively stereotyped outgroups, in terms of race, ethnicity and national origin, religion, or sexual orientation. Aggressors generally belong to what they consider in-groups. Targets of outbursts of group hatred may be individuals and their personal possessions, commercial property such as stores, or institutional property such as houses of worship, religious schools, and cemeteries. The offenses range from beatings to murders and from criminal mischief to arson and bombings. The perpetrators may be isolated individuals, spontaneously formed mobs, groups of teenagers, loosely structured gangs, or organized hate groups immersed in a subculture built around intense and explicit antagonism directed at their "enemies." Hate crimes often stand out from ordinary acts of interpersonal violence in several ways: The level of brutality can be extreme or excessive; the target is frequently a stranger singled out at random for being "one of them"; and offenders often prowl around and lash out in a group rather than as isolated bigots (Levin and McDevitt, 2003).

In 1990, the rediscovery process was propelled forward when Congress enacted the Hate Crime Statistics Act to generate data that might dispel misperceptions about patterns and trends. The federal legislation authorized the U.S. Attorney General to preside over the collection of the data. The Attorney General delegated that responsibility to the FBI. Its Uniform Crime Reporting Program has issued annual reports on hate crimes reported to the police since 1992. Because hate crimes are not different from ordinary street crimes except for the perpetrator's motive, yearly compilations monitor the same set of offenses as the *UCR*: murder and manslaughter, forcible rape, aggravated and simple assault, robbery, burglary, theft, motor vehicle theft, and arson.

The reporting system also closely tracks crimes of intimidation (threats that place the recipient in reasonable fear of physical injury) and vandalism (damage to and destruction of property, including defacing surfaces with graffiti). **Bias incidents** that involve constitutionally protected speech, such as handing out hate-filled leaflets, no matter how offensive and insulting, don't qualify as criminal activity and are not reported or counted. In 1994, Congress instructed law enforcement agencies to not only keep track of ordinary crimes that were fueled by the offender's bigotry against the victim's race, ethnicity, religion, national origin, or sexual orientation but also to monitor attacks on individuals because of perceived mental and physical disabilities (Harlow, 2005).

Before the government took on this responsibility, civil rights organizations and human relations commissions solicited reports from victims, collected information from police sources, and scanned news media accounts for new cases. When Congress first debated the issue of compiling a national data bank of hate-fueled incidents in 1985, the FBI initially resisted the assignment mainly because of the additional expenses it would impose. Local police departments also wanted to opt out because of unreimbursed start-up costs and administrative overhead ("Lukewarm Reception," 1988). The FBI began to issue reports in 1997. By 2006, about 12,600 law enforcement agencies were participating in the program out of the roughly 17,000 police and sheriff's departments that take part in the compilation of the standard Uniform Crime Report every year (only about 75 percent of potential reporting units). These agencies were responsible for serving and protecting about 85 percent of the nation's population (FBI, 2008b).

Data about people who have been subjected to bias crimes can indicate the intensity of racist, anti-Semitic, homophobic, and other bigoted sentiments at various times and places. Rough estimates about bias crimes can serve as an early warning system for pinpointing areas where relations are strained and trouble is brewing, as well as criteria for evaluating the effectiveness of outreach efforts to defuse potentially explosive inter-group conflicts. But measuring victimization rates reliably and calculating differential risks for experiencing bias crimes is difficult for several reasons. First, many victims still do not report such incidents to the authorities. Second, not all police departments are as yet committed to keeping records of the numbers and types of bias crimes reported to them. Entire states still do not report hate crimes to the FBI. Third, some attacks inspired by bigotry might not be recognized as such by detectives who do not thoroughly investigate suspected cases to discern the offenders' motives (Southern Poverty Law Center, 2001).

The general reluctance of injured parties to report offenses to the police might be magnified when it comes to hate crimes because of the widespread perception that officials will respond with indifference or hostility. People singled out for attack because of their true or assumed sexual preference (victims of "gay bashing") might be especially reticent to press charges and thereby publicize the incident (Maghan and Sagarin, 1983). Sometimes victims who are unwilling to disclose such incidents to the police will provide the information to civil rights groups defending their interests.

Establishing motivation (for purposes of investigation, classification, and record keeping, and later as the basis for harsher sentences after successful prosecutions) can be quite difficult. People who have been targeted for bias crimes might not know why their assailants singled them out. Mere differences in skin color, ethnicity, religion, or sexual preference between offender and victim are not necessarily indications of bigotry, of course. The police and the prosecution, with the assistance of the injured party, must discover the underlying basis for the offender's actions. The clearest evidence would be explicit utterances during the attack or the scrawling of graffiti containing slurs against the victim's group by the offender before the assault, or the perpetrators' use of well-known symbols of hate such as a burning cross, a swastika, or the initials KKK.

Another clue to the offender's motivation might be that the target was a prominent figure in promoting or defending the interests of his or her group, or the offender was active in an organized hate group. Perhaps the incident occurred on a day of special significance to the victim's or the offender's group, such as an anniversary or holiday. The incident might have broken out at a symbolic location, such as a gay bar, a house of worship, or a park frequented by members of a certain group. The target might be one member of a small group vastly outnumbered by members of the offender's group in the immediate area of the crime scene. The person singled out for negative treatment might have received warnings or endured prior acts of harassment or intimidation. Otherwise, the investigators must concentrate on issues such as ongoing neighborhood tensions, patterns of previous incidents, ways the victim stands out from other potential targets, statements made about the offender's behavior by witnesses, or an absence of any other logical motivation such as economic gain (Wessler and Moss, 2001; Turner, 2002; Nolan, McDevitt, and Cronin, 2004).

The difficulty in establishing the offender's motive and whether a reported incident is a hate crime was dramatized when an independent group, the National Coalition of Anti-Violence Programs (NCAVP) issued annual reports for 2003 and 2004, covering incidents reported to its chapters in certain metropolitan areas (where a little more than 25 percent of the population of the United States resided). The NCAVP, which closely monitors attacks against people who are gay, lesbian, bisexual, and transgendered, considered 18 murders in 2003 to embody anti-homosexual bias, whereas the FBI's annual hate crimes report cited 6. For 2004, the discrepancy was greater: the NCAVP deemed 20 killings to be anti-gay. But the FBI reported that five murders across the entire country were considered by detectives at local police departments to be fueled by any kind of bias—race, religion, national origin, mental or physical disability, or presumed sexual preference (Patton, 2005).

According to the FBI's annual report on hate crimes for 2006, agencies sent in information on about 9,650 targets (persons, businesses, religious institutions, even society at large). More than half (57 percent) of the offenses were directed at people, with the remainder aimed at property. Of reported offenses that harmed individuals, nearly half (46 percent) of these incidents were acts of intimidation, and about one-third (32 percent) were simple assaults. Almost one-quarter of the hate crimes directed at people were aggravated assault (22 percent). Only 3 murders out of about 17,000 in that year were attributed to the offender's hatred of the victim's "kind," as were 6 forcible rapes. Of incidents directed at property, the majority (81 percent) involved only vandalism that resulted in damage or destruction, and were not more serious offenses like burglary, motor vehicle theft, or arson (FBI, 2008b).

About 52 percent of these offenses were motivated by racial animosity and an additional 14 percent were driven by hatred for a particular ethnic group or nationality. Roughly 18 percent were fueled by religious intolerance, and 15 percent reflected disapproval of the victim's apparent sexual orientation. Just 1 percent of the incidents seemed to be reflections of the perpetrator's disdain for the victim's physical or mental disabilities (FBI, 2008b). This overall breakdown of targets was virtually the same as in 2004.

Over the years, racial animosity consistently has been the leading motivation, followed by religious intolerance, with hatred of the victim's sexual orientation coming in third. Nearly all the cases embodying the offender's bias against the victim's perceived sexual orientation were attacks by heterosexuals on homosexuals, mostly directed at gay males rather than at lesbians.

In 2006, of nearly 5,000 people harmed by offenses motivated by racial bias, about 66 percent were Americans of African descent. Anti-white bias against whites fueled about 20 percent of the cases, anti-Asian prejudices fueled about 5 percent, and hatred of Native American Indians accounted for less than 2 percent of the incidents (the remainder were hard-to-categorize incidents). As for national and ethnic backgrounds, Hispanics were the main targets (63 percent) of other people's wrath. Of the victims of crimes driven by religious intolerance, the majority (65 percent) were Jewish Americans (suffering more than 1,000 crimes of violence and intimidation). About 12 percent of targeted individuals were followers of Islam, 5 percent were

Catholics, and 4 percent were Protestants. The remainder of the cases reflected hatred for adherents of various other religions and atheists (FBI, 2008b).

In 2001 a disturbing increase was registered in the number of attacks directed against Arabs and other Muslims living in America, mostly during the remaining months of that year after the terrorist hijackings of September 11. In 2000 only about 30 crimes against Americans practicing Islam were reported, while in 2001 that figure shot up to nearly 550, but then subsided. Since 2001, the number of Islamic victims of violence and intimidation has risen and fallen without a clear trend (about 175 in 2002; 155 in 2003; nearly 200 in 2004; almost 150 in 2005; and close to 200 in 2006) as the wars in Iraq and Afghanistan wore on. Fortunately, each year, most of the reported offenses were acts of intimidation and not physically attacks like beatings or shootings.

Besides the FBI's *UCR*, the BJS's *NCVS* (since 2000) also can be used to gauge the extent and seriousness of certain hate-driven activities. The survey asks victims if their attackers uttered derogatory slurs or if thieves and vandals left behind symbolic evidence of their hatred (for example, graffiti). Using these criteria, *NCVS* data indicate that about 3 percent of violent crimes and about 0.2 percent (1 in every 500) of property crimes were fueled by hatred. According to the perceptions of those on the receiving end, the offender's intent was to express racial animosity, followed by antagonism for the target's ethnicity, sexual orientation, religion, or disability, in that order. Less than half (45 percent) of these incidents were reported to the police by either the victim, a family member, a security guard, or a school authority. Then some additional filtering took place: Only about 20 percent of the reported incidents were officially designated as hate crimes after investigations by the police during the first few years of the twenty-first century (Harlow, 2005).

A survey of 450 college campuses in 1998 discovered that hate crimes were committed relatively infrequently. Many institutions had nothing to report, and the remainder only experienced about one illegal incident per year. However, the survey confirmed that underreporting by victims to campus security forces, college administrators, and local police departments continued to be a stubbornly persistent problem. The Department of Justice has prosecuted student offenders for criminal violations of their victims' civil rights at a range of institutions, from small liberal arts colleges to large state universities. The report noted that when hate crimes erupt on campuses, the educational mission of encouraging open discussion and debate is undermined, and young men and women are deprived of an atmosphere free of fear and intimidation (Wessler and Moss, 2001).

Criminal Justice System Reforms

Bias-crime victims and their supporters have been able to improve the response of the criminal justice system in many ways: securing the passage of new laws penalizing hate-motivated acts more severely; spurring police departments to take special steps to investigate and solve these kinds of crimes; and encouraging district attorneys to prosecute hate crimes vigorously.

Starting in the 1980s, a number of state legislatures enacted statutes that applied stiffer penalties to hate crimes to discourage attacks against people considered by bigots to be of the "wrong" race, ethnic group, religion, or sexual orientation.

However, some inconsistencies persist: not all state statutes protect homosexuals.. Many state legislators and congressional representatives have opposed the inclusion of "sexual preference" as a protected category, fearing that specifically prohibiting assaults against homosexuals could be viewed as an endorsement of that lifestyle. In 1984, California became the first state to amend an existing hate crime statute to include attacks against gays and lesbians—as well as people singled out for their age or disability (Gutis, 1989).

Most recent state laws have civil lawsuit provisions that make it easier for plaintiffs to sue bigots who interfere with the exercise of their constitutional rights. Victims can recover out-of-pocket expenses, can collect punitive damages and reimbursement for attorney's fees, and can secure injunctive relief: court orders of protection.

Because many offenders are teenagers who are processed by the juvenile justice system, most states have passed laws that enable injured parties to hold the wrongdoer's parents liable for up to several thousand dollars in damages (ADL, 1999).

The police department in New York City established the country's first specialized unit to investigate possible bias crimes in 1980. Police forces in Baltimore, Boston, San Francisco, and Nassau and Suffolk counties in New York also set up hate crime squads during the 1980s. By 1990, 34 percent of police departments in large cities had established full-time units. However, by 2000, that percentage dropped to 26 percent, although 71 percent of local law enforcement agencies had some officers assigned to investigate bias crimes on a part-time basis (Reaves and Hickman, 2002). When neighborhood tensions soar, these squads can maintain surveillance and monitor people and places judged to be likely targets. They can send police officers as decoys to pose as vulnerable victims to entice would-be offenders to attack—and then be arrested immediately by backup teams lying in wait (Scott and Williams, 1985; Wexler and Marx, 1986).

When bias-crime victims come forward and request help, the police can serve them in many ways. They can respond promptly; be sensitive when questioning them (and not dismissing the incident as a prank, betraying skepticism about whether the event occurred, or implying it was somehow provoked); and make arrests quickly. Detectives can keep victims informed about progress in their cases; can "read them their rights" about opportunities for restitution, compensation, and civil lawsuits; and can try to discourage the news media from revealing names and addresses of complainants. If victims are in continuing danger, the department can provide extra security from reprisals or temporarily relocate them to safer surroundings. Officers also can refer bias-crime victims to community organizations offering hot lines, crisis intervention services, and support groups (Scott and Williams, 1985).

Supporters of a get-tough stance against hate-motivated crimes concede that harmony and mutual respect among people of different races, ethnic groups, religions, and sexual preferences cannot be brought about through legislation. But they believe that the threat of thorough investigations, vigorous prosecutions, and extra-severe sanctions might deter conscious attempts to provoke inter-group strife. Critics of these measures question whether an aggressor's alleged motive—to express his animosity toward an entire group—can ever be established beyond a reasonable doubt in court. Those critics suggest that the harm inflicted rather than the attacker's personal reasons should be the basis for determining the degree of punishment (Klurfeld, 1988; see also Jacobs and Potter, 1998).

The rediscovery of hate crime victims and the emerging consensus that these offenses must be taken very seriously can be seen as a positive development because highly publicized incidents have the potential to sabotage the ongoing experiment of fostering an acceptance of multiculturalism in the United States—at a time when participation in a global economy demands tolerance of diversity.

VICTIMS OF WORKPLACE VIOLENCE

Fearing that he is about to be fired, a part-time letter carrier barges into the back room of his local post office and starts shooting wildly. He guns down 14 people and then kills himself. (Rugala, 2004)

***

A mentally disturbed middle-aged woman, known for muttering to herself and arguing with imaginary opponents, seeks a business license to start a racist publication but is rejected. She confronts a former neighbor and then kills her. She then goes on a rampage at a mail processing and distribution center where she had been employed, shooting to death six former co-workers, including several who were black, Hispanic, and Filipino. Then she kills herself. (Archibold, 2006)

Shocking massacres like these serve as vivid reminders that workers can become injured or murdered while doing their jobs under conditions determined by their employers. Disgruntled or emotionally disturbed employees have attacked bosses or co-workers for many years, but the problem was not monitored or analyzed until its rediscovery in 1989, when the term "workplace violence" was coined. In the wake of a spate of mass murders during the 1980s and 1990s similar to the cases described above, the phrase "going postal" entered everyday conversations (see Ames, 2005). However, a U.S. Postal Commission study concluded in 2000 that the derogatory expression was misleading and unfair because post office employees actually were less likely to be assaulted or killed on the job than other workers (see Rugala, 2004).

On-the-job injuries and deaths certainly are not new: recall images of pirates killing sailors when boarding ships on the high seas, and robbers shooting stagecoach drivers and crews on steam locomotives in the Old West. Now that monitoring systems are in place, it is possible for criminologists and victimologists to determine whether an upsurge in attacks and multiple slayings truly is taking place at job sites or whether more attention is being paid to scattered tragedies. The evidence-based answer is that the shootings that attract sensational media coverage are relatively rare events. The most common on-the-job threats that cause business owners, administrators, and supervisors concern about their employees' ability to focus on the tasks at hand are crimes that are quite mundane—robberies, assaults, stalkings, and acts of intimidation, plus potentially disruptive non-criminal matters such as abusive bullying relationships and sexual harassment (Rugala, 2004).

During the decades since the rediscovery of workplace violence, a cottage industry of security consulting firms offering threat assessment and risk management services has emerged, offering ways to reduce the chances of violence erupting at factories, offices, and other job sites—both to enhance worker safety as well as to fend off lawsuits charging employer negligence. Four kinds of threats must be addressed by high-tech equipment, preventive measures, training sessions, company regulations, and emergency procedures. The first is to prevent an intruder from slipping or barging into the workplace to rob or rape someone. The second is to prevent personal disputes from escalating within the workplace (as when a man invades an office to confront his former girlfriend). The third is to protect employees who must deal with irate customers, angry clients, unruly students, disturbed patients, or dangerous inmates. The fourth is to safeguard workers, bosses, and owners from disgruntled current or former employees (Rugala, 2004).

During the 1990s, the rates of workplace violence declined just as they did both before and after work across the country; incidents at work on average made up about 18 percent of the violent crimes committed each year from 1993 to 1999, according to the *NCVS*. The survey confirmed the existence of differential risks. It discovered that non-fatal violence harmed males more often than females, and younger workers (20 to 34 years old) more often than older workers—patterns that were the same as for similar crimes outside of work. But whites suffered a higher rate of assault than blacks (13 compared to 10 victims per 1,000 workers per year), which was the opposite of the pattern for non-workplace violence. People employed by the government were harmed at about the same rate as employees in the private sector (Duhart, 2001).

Slayings at Work

Certain jobs are far more dangerous than others. Risk factors include working at establishments when few people are around (for example, at night), where escape routes are handy (near highway entrances), and where cash transactions take place (bars and grocery stores). Consequently, injuries and deaths arising from robberies are a real possibility for cashiers in convenience stores, gas station attendants, and taxi drivers. Taxi drivers and chauffeurs of limousines and car services suffer the highest rate of workplace homicides of any occupational group: 18 murders for every 100,000 workers per year. These drivers make up only 0.2 percent of the workforce, but their deaths comprise 7 percent of on-the-job killings. The actual danger of being murdered during

a robbery is even higher for cabbies who collect cash fares from passengers who are strangers than for chauffeurs for limousine services handling credit card transactions. Besides intentional slayings, taxi drivers face additional risks of injury and death from automobile accidents. Police officers and detectives who arrest suspects face high risks of assault and suffer the second highest on-the-job murder rate, more than 4 fatalities for every 100,000 law enforcement agents per year. They too face additional risks from car crashes. Private security guards carry out assignments that are almost as dangerous, and nearly 4 per 100,000 die each year as a result (Sygnatur and Toscano, 2000).

In general, employees engaged in law enforcement (including corrections officers in jails and prisons) faced the highest risks of attack while carrying out their duties, followed by workers in the mental health field. People employed in transportation, medicine, retail sales, and teaching faced much lower risks. Police officers experienced the highest rate of physical assaults (about 260 per 1,000 officers per year), while college teachers enjoyed the safest job of all (just 2 attacks per 1,000 professors per year) (Duhart, 2001). In terms of differential risks, a disproportionate share of work-related deaths were suffered by men, immigrants, and minorities (African Americans, Hispanics, and Asians) (Sygnatur and Toscano, 2000).

As for trends in the odds of being murdered at work—a positive development took place during the 1990s, as Figure 11.2 shows. On-the-job homicides declined across the country, just as they did before and after work. By 2004, deadly assaults at workplaces had declined so substantially that violence was less likely to claim lives than motor vehicle accidents, falls, or being struck by a heavy object. By 2006, the number of killings at work sites had dropped to the lowest level since the early 1990s. Unfortunately, the death toll rebounded in 2007, but it still was almost 45 percent lower than in 1992. Job-related homicides mostly result from gunfire, according to the BLS's Census of Fatal Occupational Injuries (Department of Labor, 2008).

Impressions derived from media coverage about the nature of workplace violence can be

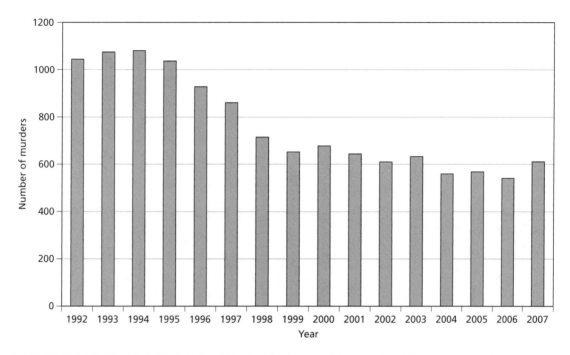

FIGURE 11.2 Trends in Work-Related Murders in the United States, 1992–2007

SOURCES: Census of Fatal Occupational Industries 2004; Bureau of Labor Statistics, 2008.

misleading. More than 67 percent of on-the-job slayings stemmed from robberies, not outbursts of fury by co-workers (13 percent); by customers or clients (7 percent); or by intimates and relatives (9 percent), according to an analysis of the murders at workplaces between 1992 and 1998 in which a victim-offender relationship could be established. Also, except for the killings of taxi drivers and store cashiers, most murders do not take place late at night: midnight to 8 am is the time period with the fewest slayings (Sygnatur and Toscano, 2000).

Of course, murder is just one cause of workplace deaths. Three other leading causes, each of which claimed more lives in 2004 than homicides, were car crashes, falls, and being struck by an object. Taking these risks of deadly accidents into account, the 10 most dangerous jobs (in order of highest death rates per 100,000) are loggers, aircraft pilots of small planes, commercial fishermen, iron and steel workers, refuse collectors, farmers and ranchers, roofers, electric power line repair workers,

truck drivers, and taxi drivers, according to BLS records (Christie, 2005).

LAW ENFORCEMENT OFFICERS INJURED AND KILLED IN THE LINE OF DUTY

Officers who work for law enforcement, probation, parole, or corrections agencies at local, state, and federal levels face special challenges. They must interact with criminals on a daily basis—just the opposite of what risk-reduction strategies would recommend. The police have more dangerous tasks: when people scatter at the sound of gunfire, officers race toward the disturbance to subdue troublemakers known to be armed and dangerous. They patrol the meanest streets of the toughest neighborhoods, break up crimes in progress, search suspicious people, track down fugitives, and guard prisoners. Because badges and uniforms are symbols

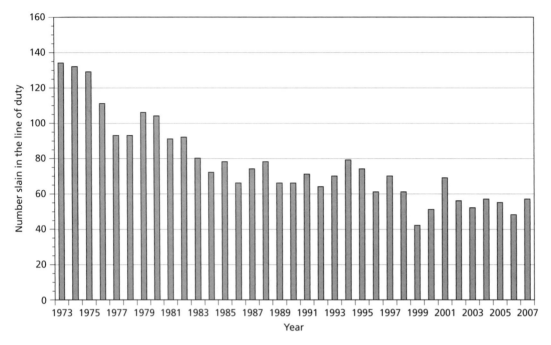

FIGURE 11.3 Trends in the Murders of Law-Enforcement Officers in the United States, 1973–2007

NOTE: The 72 deaths resulting from the September 11, 2001 terrorist attacks are excluded.

SOURCE: Law Enforcement Officers Killed and Assaulted, 2006 (FBI, 2008).

of governmental authority, officers face the risk of ambush by those who oppose what agents of officialdom represent. As the first line of defense for a social order, law enforcement agents serve as lightning rods, attracting and absorbing the bolts of discontent from alienated individuals and hostile groups within society.

Killing a police officer is one of the most heinous of crimes. In most states, it is punishable by death. The National Law Enforcement Officers Memorial Fund keeps track of those who made the ultimate sacrifice to protect the public, as does the FBI's Uniform Crime Reporting Division in its annual analysis, Law Enforcement Officers Killed and Assaulted. Fortunately, deadly attacks on officers are declining, according to records kept by these two sources. The number of line-of-duty murders peaked in 1973, dropped during the early 1980s, and since then has been fairly stable, even though many more people now are engaged in law enforcement duties. The smallest number

of deadly assaults took place during 1999. Over the decades, policing has become a safer occupation, as the graph of trends in Figure 11.3 shows (with the exception of 2001 because of officers killed in New York and the Pentagon on September 11). The leading reasons for this improvement include regulations requiring officers to wear bulletproof vests, better training, improved weaponry, restrictions on the private ownership of assault weapons, and a diminishing amount of interpersonal violence across the country (Butterfield, 1999).

Who, Where, What, When, How, and Why?

The FBI monitors line-of-duty deaths to determine the profile of a typical officer who was feloniously assaulted, how, when, and where the attacks took place, and what the most dangerous situations were during their daily routines, in order to develop insights that can improve training and tactics that will reduce casualties. Figure 11.4 illustrates the similarities as well as the differences between the assignments that led to nearly 580,000 injuries and the missions that resulted in nearly 600 officer slayings during the ten-year period from 1997 to 2006.

The FBI periodically provides a statistical analysis for 10-year periods. As for what the officers were doing at the time they were murdered, the most perilous assignments were making arrests, responding to disturbances (mostly family quarrels and bar fights), and carrying out traffic stops and pursuits, followed by investigating suspicious people and situations. The least likely assignments to result in loss of life were handling prisoners and emotionally disturbed persons. No officers were killed during civil disturbances and riots. Almost 20 percent of slayings were ambushes. Over one-third of officers fired or attempted to use their weapons before dying.

As for where and when officers were slain, almost half were working in the South, while fewer than one-tenth were slain in the Northeast. The most dangerous time to be on duty was between 4 pm and midnight. Thursdays and Fridays were the most dangerous days, and Sundays were the least dangerous. August was the month with the most line-of-duty deaths, and November had the least. About 40 percent were working alone when they died. Nearly 10 percent were off-duty when they were murdered. Practically all (93 percent) were killed with firearms (mostly handguns); being run over intentionally by a driver was the second most frequent cause of death, and being stabbed was a distant third.

A profile of the fallen officers shows that 95 percent were males; 84 percent were whites, and 13 percent were blacks; and 75 percent were between 25 and 45 years old (37 was the average age). During the confrontations, 76 percent were in uniform, and 58 percent were wearing body armor. The fallen officers had been on the job for an average of 10 years. As for the cop killers, 98 percent were males, 56 percent were whites, and 41 percent were blacks; 80 percent had a criminal record (prior arrest); 25 percent were under judicial supervision (on probation and parole, or escapees); and their average age was 29, according to an analysis of the 562 officers murdered by 633 assailants between 1997 and 2006 (FBI, 2007a).

In a study of slayings committed from 1983 to 1992, FBI analysts discovered that a deadly mix was a common element: An easy-going, good-natured officer who was less inclined to use force than his colleagues entered into a fatal encounter with a suspect afflicted with a personality disorder and armed with a handgun. A kind of procedural miscue (such as improperly approaching a vehicle pulled over for a traffic infraction) often played a role in these tragic homicides. The typical law enforcement casualty was a white southern male, 36 years old, married, with a high school education and an average of nine years on the force. The typical assailant was a 29-year-old white man, with a record of previous arrests (FBI, 1993). Between 1980 and 1999, 136 officers of 1,462 (9 percent) were slain by juveniles (Mencken, Nolan, and Berhanu, 2004).

Being assaulted is much more common than being killed, of course. Whereas about 560 officers were slain between 1997 and 2006, more than 1,000 times as many law enforcement agents—nearly 580,000—were assaulted on the job during that 10-year period. A little more than one-quarter of these officers were injured by their assailants. That equals an assault rate of about 12 officers out of every 100 sworn personnel per year, and an injury rate of 3 per 100 in 2006 (FBI, 2007a).

Despite the statistical evidence documenting these disturbing deaths and injuries, media images of gun fights as a typical aspect of police work are misleading. The average officer goes through a 20-year career without ever firing a shot except for target practice. However, undercover officers face much greater chances than their uniformed colleagues of shooting at suspects and of being shot. African American officers in undercover and plainclothes assignments run an additional risk of being hit by "friendly fire"—officers who mistake them for armed criminals (Geller, 1992). (Friendly fire in all kinds of situations—mistaken identity, training exercises, and accidental discharges—during more than a century of policing from 1893 through 2006 has claimed the lives of nearly 200 officers [O'Connor and Pacifici, 2007]). Contrary

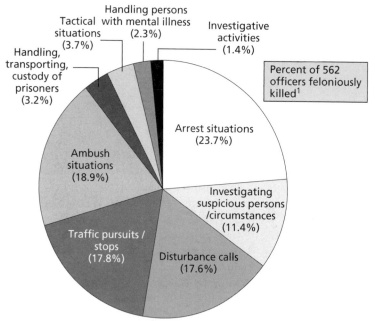

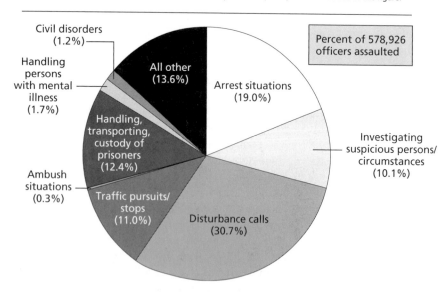

FIGURE 11.4 Why Officers Were Murdered or Assaulted, 1997–2006
SOURCE: Law Enforcement Officers Killed and Assaulted, 2006 (FBI, 2008), Figure 4.

to widespread impressions, federal law enforcement officers who faced the greatest risks of injuries and death from assaults worked for the U.S. National Park Service, and not the FBI, Drug Enforcement Agency, or Bureau of Alcohol, Tobacco, and Firearms (BATF). Agents for the Internal Revenue

Service faced the lowest risks of being attacked on the job (Reaves and Hart, 2001).

Tragically, officers die by suicide more often than at the hands of assailants (Cowan, 2008). Unfortunately, accidents also claim more lives than felonious assaults. For example, during 2007, 83 law enforcement officers died from on-the-job accidents (such as car crashes), and 57 were murdered by criminals (FBI, 2008b). Statistically speaking, policing is not the most dangerous job in terms of intentional plus accidental injuries and deaths—taxi driving is.

Other peace officers endure grave risks of bodily harm. To reduce probation and parole officers' vulnerability to assault, robbery, and car theft when carrying out supervisory tasks and home visits, a growing number of agencies are providing them with firearms, bulletproof vests, alarms, armed escorts, and training in self-defense tactics and crisis management techniques (Lindner and Koehler, 1992; Del Castillo and Lindner, 1994).

Showing Solidarity

As long ago as 1894, an association was established in New York City to take care of the widows and orphans of fallen officers. But over the next 100 years, families of law enforcement agents mistakenly were assumed to be stronger emotionally and better prepared than civilians to cope with losses and grief because they are part of a tightly knit community that "takes care of its own." The inadequate responses of many police departments brought about the establishment of counseling units, death notification training, and peer support groups for injured and disabled officers (see Sawyer, 1987; Stillman, 1987; Martin, 1989; "Does Your Agency Measure Up?" 1999). A national self-help group with many local chapters that is dedicated to addressing the concerns of survivors, mostly young widows and their children, offers many forms of concrete aid and emotional support (for example, advice about sleep problems while grieving, and ways of coping with major holidays). The scope of their services ranges from monitoring the trials of accused cop killers and opposing their eventual parole; sponsoring memorials for those who gave their lives to protect the public; holding peer-support retreats for spouses; and raising money for scholarships and special events (such as summer camps) for their children (see Gibson, 2005). These activities demonstrate how an entire caring community—in this case, police families—can work together to ease the suffering of those who have lost a loved one.

Law enforcement agents demonstrate another kind of solidarity when one of their own is murdered. They are relentless in their pursuit of the killer. In 2007, the assailant was either captured or was killed in an attempt to escape or resist arrest, or committed suicide, in all but one of 51 incidents. Therefore, nearly all the cop killings were solved. Yet not even two-thirds (61 percent) of civilian murders were solved that year (FBI, 2008c).

CASUALTIES OF TERRORISM

Terrorism predates organized warfare. Lone individuals and small bands surreptitiously attacked their enemies long before armies of men were thrown into battle. Terrorism took the form of killing leaders or potential challengers to a throne, and of spreading panic by carrying out barbaric acts.

Although the means and the goals have evolved over the centuries, terrorism still involves the unlawful use of force against persons or property in order to intimidate a government, frighten a civilian population, or coerce a segment of the public to surrender to political or social demands. Unlike common criminals, terrorists do not commit violent offenses to line their pockets. They intend to advance their political cause and seek publicity for their dramatic deeds to score propaganda victories. They attack certain targets to gain the attention of a third party—the audience they are desperately trying to influence. By relying upon stealth and deception, terrorists can disrupt and demoralize more powerful adversaries who would easily defeat them in conventional warfare. Terrorist violence includes bombings, suicide missions, assassinations, airplane hijackings, kidnappings for ransom, and hostage-taking to arrange prisoner exchanges or to negotiate from a position of strength. But modern forms can also can encompass new tactics such as cyberattacks to sabotage and disrupt computer operations (FBI, 2001).

Focused terrorism is aimed at specific targets and symbols such as corporate headquarters and government officials. Indiscriminate acts of violence inflict casualties on innocent, randomly selected targets of opportunity who just happen to be at the wrong place at the wrong time. Usually, the victims have no special connection to, substantial influence over, or particular responsibility for the political and social conflicts that motivated the terrorist attack. The injured parties were pawns or bargaining chips in high-stakes power struggles and fear campaigns designed to spread panic and undermine confidence in governmental bodies.

The public can be affected indirectly in several ways. People may become cynical and pessimistic either about the enemy or about their own side's widely proclaimed lofty ideals, and may lose faith in the ability of their government and its criminal justice system to protect them. Indirect victims are not personally involved in an incident but suffer the adverse consequences of it (for example, their livelihoods are linked to the fortunes of the tourism industry, which experiences business losses in the aftermath of an attack). Besides fearing the terrorists, sectors of the public may also become frightened of their own law enforcement agencies if onerous national security restrictions are imposed and cherished civil liberties are sacrificed in the quest to root out hidden terrorist cells and disrupt clandestine networks conspiring to strike again (Kratcoski, Edelbacher, and Das, 2001).

Assessing the Threat of Terrorism

To determine the number of people harmed by terrorist attacks, and to discern whether or not the threat is growing or subsiding, criminologists and victimologists need a definition for "terrorism" that clearly spells out which incidents should be counted and which belong in other categories (like hate crimes or ordinary street crimes).

Several measurement issues confound efforts by criminologists and victimologists to gauge the threat of terrorist attacks accurately. First, terrorist groups don't always claim responsibility for their violent deeds. Unless arrests are made, the unsolved incidents are recorded as **suspected**, as opposed to **confirmed terrorist attacks**. Some definitional problems add to the confusion. The FBI (2004b) follows the "Code of Federal Regulations" that categorizes terrorism as "the unlawful use of force and violence against persons or property to intimidate or coerce a government, the civilian population, or any segment thereof, in furtherance of political or social objectives. The FBI distinguishes terrorism as either **domestic** or **international**, depending upon the group's origins, base of operations, and objectives. Domestic terrorism encompasses activities that involve acts dangerous to human life such as assassination, kidnapping, or unleashing weapons of mass destruction within the United States and Puerto Rico, in violation of state or federal law, by groups or individuals with no foreign ties. But applying these criteria to real-life situations often raises complications. For example, the many letter bombs mailed by the "Unabomber" from 1978 until his capture in 1995 killed 3 people and maimed 22, including college professors he had never met. But his repeated depredations were not counted as acts of terrorism by the FBI because this federal prison inmate's motivation remains unknown and unclear, and may have reflected either random selection or a peculiar personal vendetta against his unsuspecting targets.

Another complication is that some politically motivated attacks overlap a gray area between terrorism and bias-driven hate crimes. The acts must be counted as either one or the other—not both. For instance, in 1999 when a member of a white supremacist group went on a rampage, shooting at 32 complete strangers (some of them Jewish worshippers leaving a synagogue), killing 2 (one was African American, the other Asian American) and wounding 8, the FBI categorized the incident as an act of domestic terrorism and not a hate crime. Similarly, when a distraught gunman with no known ties to any group opened fire at a ticket counter in an airport, killing a representative of an Israeli airline and one bystander, and wounding another before being shot to death by security officers in 2002, the FBI initially considered the murders to be a hate crime. But later, it classified the incident as international terrorism because the killer was an immigrant from the Middle East. Yet the FBI categorizes assaults and slayings of doctors who perform abortions by extremists in the anti-abortion movement as hate crimes, not as acts of domestic terrorism. Furthermore, some lawbreaking that damages property is not severe enough to be designated as an act of terrorism. These incidents wind up categorized as acts of vandalism, even though the attack might have been carried out by political activists on behalf of a cause.

To further complicate the issue of threat assessment, attempted acts are counted. But what about planned attacks that are foiled? The FBI tabulates these separately as **preventions**, in which law enforcement agencies thwart a terrorist plot (it is "successfully interdicted through investigative activity") before anyone is hurt or any damage is done (FBI, 2001: 15–27; 2007b: iv–v).

The FBI formally began monitoring terrorist attacks in the United States in the mid-1970s (see Figure 11.5). First of all, note that nobody in the United States was hurt or killed during a number of years (1984, 1987–1992, 2000, and 2003–2005). Based on its database, the FBI attributed 327 incidents within U.S. borders from 1980 to 1999 to the work of terrorists. Of these suspected and confirmed acts, 239 (73 percent) were carried out by domestic terrorists; the rest were inflicted by groups with international ties. Even before September 11, 2001, two trends had emerged: the number of specific attacks was decreasing, but the average seriousness of the strikes (in casualties and property destroyed) was increasing. During the 1980s, 267 incidents that took place on U.S. soil claimed 23 lives and injured 105 people. During the 1990s, 182 people were murdered and 1,932 were wounded in just 60 attacks. Overall, the FBI attributed 205 deaths and at least 2,037 injuries to terrorist attacks between 1980 and 1999. Also, during these two decades law enforcement agencies claimed credit for preventing or aborting 130 terrorist plots, of which 47 (36 percent) were planned by foreigners (FBI, 2001: 15–27).

Starting in the late 1960s, extremists in the anti-war movement and the Puerto Rican independence movement engaged in bombings, and militants in the black power movement carried out assassinations of police officers. By the mid-1980s, these outbreaks of left-wing terrorism had faded into insignificance, but terrorism from right-wing extremists emerged as the more serious threat. White racists, neo-Nazis, anti-tax protesters, anti-abortion fringe groups, and extremists in survivalist groups and the militia movement were behind a series of random shootings, targeted assassinations, bank robberies to raise money, and abortion clinic bombings. Right-wing terrorist attacks peaked in 1995 with the blast in Oklahoma City that toppled a federal building and claimed the lives of 168 people, including 19 children in a day care center, and injured 642 others. The homemade car bomb was set off on the second anniversary of the fiery massacre that ended the stand-off between the FBI and a besieged, heavily armed religious cult in Texas. The two perpetrators were hostile to the FBI and BATF, and had indirect ties to the militia movement. Right-wing terrorism diminished after that explosion, but what the FBI terms special-interest terrorism—especially by extremists in the animal rights and environmental movements—became noticeable in the latter part of the 1990s. The only major attack carried out by international terrorists—before September 11, 2001—was the 1993 truck bombing by a small cell of Middle Eastern religious extremists at downtown Manhattan's World Trade Center. The blast failed to topple the twin towers, but the explosion resulted in six deaths and more than a 1,000 injuries.

Looking back over the 1980s and 1990s, about half of the targets of domestic terrorists were civilian or commercial. The remainder were directed at government buildings, or the embassies and other properties of foreign governments (especially of Cuba and of the former Soviet Union) or military sites (FBI, 2001: 15–27).

During 2000, the FBI investigated eight terrorist incidents perpetrated by extremists within the animal rights and environmentalist movements; no deaths or serious injuries resulted. The FBI also prevented one attack on a federal building by a

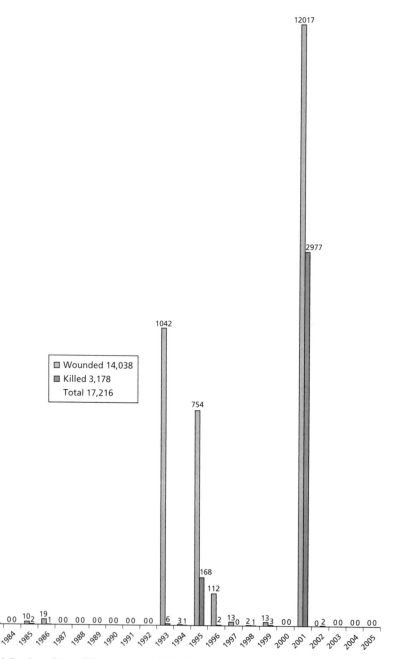

FIGURE 11.5 Casualties of Terrorism, 1980–2005

NOTES: The FBI uses 12,017 as an estimate for the number of those injured as a result of the September 11 attack; the exact number is unknown. Seventeen persons were infected by and recovered from exposure to the anthrax mailings during September-November 2001.

SOURCE: FBI's *Terrorism in the United States*, 2005 (FBI, 2007b), p. 31.

right-wing extremist. During 2001, 13 incidents took place, mostly minor fires and raids by animal rights and environmental extremists; two bank robberies were carried out by an anti-abortion extremist (FBI, 2004). But the relative quiet on the domestic front was shattered on September 11, 2001.

The worst suffering due to terrorism in U.S. history unfolded when 19 hijackers from the Middle East with links to Al Qaeda crashed two airplanes into Manhattan's World Trade Center towers, causing their collapse. The inferno killed 2,838: people inside the aircraft and the skyscrapers, as well as police officers and firefighters working as rescuers. The hijackers smashed another plane into the Pentagon, killing 189 people working for the Department of Defense. A fourth hijacked plane hit the ground and exploded in Pennsylvania, claiming 44 lives, after some of its passengers and crew fought back against the men who had commandeered it (see Arias and Smith, 2003). The FBI estimates that about 12,000 people were injured that day, although hospital emergency rooms in New York City treated very few wounded survivors. (Stories that circulated about orphans who needed to be adopted after the attacks killed their parents turned out to be urban myths [Bernstein, 2001]).

In the aftermath of the September 11 slaughter, what appears to be the first major bioterrorist attack in American history was launched. A spate of letters contaminated with anthrax killed five people, sickened 22 others, disrupted mail deliveries, forced the evacuation of government buildings, and led to numerous "white powder" scares. The suicide in 2008 of a U.S. Army scientist suspected to be behind these murders means that the perpetrator's true motive can never be established (Shane, 2008). Ironically, after the anthrax letters, domestic terrorism during 2002–2005 (also, unofficially, in 2006 and 2007) reverted back to the pattern that prevailed before September 11. Most of the incidents inflicted minor damage on commercial and government property and nearly all were attributed to the efforts of extremists in the animal rights and environmental movements. Except for the airport slaying of two people in 2002 by a distraught individual acting alone (which was originally considered a hate crime), not one person on U.S. soil has been killed or wounded in a terrorist attack since 2001 (FBI, 2007b; MIPT Terrorism Knowledge Base, 2008). That excellent safety record makes it very difficult to assess the true dimensions of the terrorist threat to people and property within the United States, although terrorism surely is on the rise in the rest of the world.

Assistance and Recovery

After a traumatic disaster such as a terrorist bombing, victims are likely to be overwhelmed by intense emotions of shock, anxiety, confusion, sorrow, and grief. Some are immediately beset by outrage and revenge fantasies, or even guilt for surviving, while others undergo delayed reactions. As the unfocused anger dissipates, depression and loneliness may set in. Sleep disorders, panic attacks, sudden weight gains or losses, and abuse of alcohol and prescription drugs are common symptoms of inner turmoil. Sensing that no one understands what they have endured, some might even contemplate suicide. Professional counseling, spiritual support, and membership in a self-help group might stave off the most serious consequences of experiencing this ordeal (Office of Victims of Crime, 2001). However, the "debriefings" during counseling sessions frequently offered to traumatized survivors of disasters such as the September 11 attacks may be ineffective at best or even counterproductive, according to two recent studies. Researchers turned up scant evidence that the recipients of trauma counseling fare better, in terms of their long-term mental health, than victims who get no professional care, or those who just talk to friends and family members (Van Emmerik et al., 2002).

To help victims recover from the financial losses and the side effects of politically driven attacks overseas, the Department of Justice's Office for Victims of Crime established an International Terrorism Victims Compensation Program. The Justice Department also operates a Terrorism and International Victims Unit, and the FBI set up an Office for Victim Assistance in 2002 (Office of Victims of Crime, 2002).

The federal 9/11 Victim Compensation Fund distributed about $7 billion to the several thousand families of those killed and wounded in the attacks. Its formula focused on calculations of lost income, so the families of victims who were making high salaries received the largest payments. For example, more than $6 million was awarded on average to each of the four families who lost a breadwinner making $4 million or more a year. About $1 million was awarded on average to each of the roughly 160 families who lost a member who was earning less than $25,000 a year. As for the injured, 40 survivors who were badly burned received awards averaging about $2 million each (Chen, 2004).

Congress's hasty appropriation of a relatively generous amount of money for a 9/11 Victim Compensation Fund set off a firestorm of debate and soul-searching concerning the weighty moral and philosophical issues surrounding the proper societal response to victimization due to terrorism. Confusing precedents were set, and conflicting principles remain unresolved. Should murders inflicted by terrorists be taken more seriously than slayings committed by robbers or deaths caused by drunk drivers? Should compensation amounts be higher for the survivors of heroic rescuers such as police officers and firefighters who died in the line of duty than for the next-of-kin of average civilians caught up in a disaster? Conversely, is it fair to repay families based on the victim's lifetime earnings potential, which means that wealthy families who lost highly paid executives would receive much more than the families of workers? How much compensation ought to be awarded to the families of immigrant workers who had entered the country illegally, the relatives of single people without dependents, and to the children and domestic partners of victims who were not officially married? Would standard flat amounts for everyone, regardless of status, be fair? Why were the several thousand families of the victims of the attacks on the World Trade Center in 2001 repaid from a special federal fund, whereas the six families who lost loved ones in the 1993 terrorist bombing of the same buildings for roughly the same motives were not? Why were the families of the over 3,000 9/11 victims of foreign religious extremists given more financial compensation than the families of the 168 victims of domestic right-wing extremists in Oklahoma City? Should attacks that take place within the United States evoke more generous outpourings of economic assistance than attacks on Americans on foreign soil? Most importantly, can money really serve as an adequate surrogate or metaphor for other significant public and governmental responses and expressions of collective emotions, such as compassion, support, respect, honor, regret, sorrow, obligation, and appreciation, that are intended to help victims and their loved ones cope with the special problems terrorism imposes? And finally, will such special arrangements for payouts be implemented every time terrorists inflict casualties in the future (Belkin, 2002)? (Until 9/11, people injured by terrorist attacks and the next of kin of those who died in the attacks applied for financial assistance from their state victim compensation funds, which have very limited resources set aside to reimburse individuals who get wounded in ordinary street crimes. See Chapter for a full discussion of the legislation establishing government-run compensation funds.)

Civil lawsuits for damages are another avenue for financial recovery that can be pursued by people injured by terrorists, and for the families of those who perish from their wounds. The obvious target for these lawsuits is the evil-doer himself. But terrorists rarely have assets that can be confiscated. An alternative strategy is to sue some other party that can reasonably be proven to be partly responsible for the injuries and losses. (See Chapter 12 for a detailed discussion of these third-party lawsuits.)

Concerns about the need to enhance security at potential targets predated the 1993 bombing of the World Trade Center. Shortly after that attack, more than 400 plaintiffs (injured office workers and the families of the six who were fatally wounded, plus some owners of businesses in the building), sued the Port Authority, the governmental body that built and operated the Twin Towers, for negligence for failing to safeguard a likely target. Twelve years later, a six-person civil jury unanimously ruled in the plaintiffs' favor. In an historic decision, the jurors accepted the victims' argument that the agency should have realized that the commercial center symbolized American capitalism and consequently ought to have foreseen the likelihood of a terrorist attack, and should have taken steps to prevent it. Specifically, the management did not heed the warning of a 1985 security study its own anti-terrorism unit had commissioned in the wake of a spate of bombings in Europe and the Middle East. The security consultants concluded that the underground garage was highly vulnerable to an explosion from a time-bomb-laden vehicle—which was exactly what happened eight years later. Because the office building's management disregarded the recommendation to shut down the garage—since it would inconvenience thousands of occupants and cost millions in lost revenue from parking fees—the jury considered the Port Authority to be 68 percent at fault for the bombing, and the blameworthiness of the terrorists as 32 percent. That symbolic parceling of responsibility made the government agency fully liable for damages for pain and suffering that the injured plaintiffs might be awarded in their individual lawsuits, along with reimbursement for lost wages (Hartocollis, 2005).

A pending lawsuit that consolidates the claims of 9/11 victims' families, businesses, and the leaseholder of the World Trade Center asks for roughly $23 billion in damages from the airlines and the airport security companies for failing to prevent the hijackings of the four planes. To avoid bankrupting the airlines, the federal government has capped their liability as the maximum amount of insurance coverage they had at the time (Hartocollis, 2008).

The survivors of the September 11 attacks and the families of those who perished also have used third-party lawsuits as a means of empowerment and redress. Because there were so many victims drawn from such diverse backgrounds, more than 20 groups have sprung up to represent them (Voboril, 2005). In their search for the truth about the events leading up to the attacks, they have pursued a wide range of targets in civil court, from terrorist groups and foreign governments that may have harbored them to businesses and charities that may have served as fronts for terrorist fundraising (CNN, 2002). Some survivor organizations also have supported whistleblowers who publicly reveal government blunders and weaknesses in national security strategies (American Civil Liberties Union, 2005).

The worldwide death toll due to countless acts of domestic and international terrorism by disaffected groups in each country is unknown. That body count surely is rising rapidly as many nations take part in the stepped-up war against global terrorism. The specter of terrorists unleashing weapons of mass destruction (biological and chemical agents and radioactive dirty bombs that sicken, injure, and kill huge numbers of people) conjures up scenarios of incalculable victimization, which underscores how the potential threat posed by terrorism is of a far greater magnitude than ordinary street crime.

People concerned about becoming victims of terrorism can take out insurance backed by the federal government. When Congress passed the Terrorism Risk Insurance Act of 2002, it authorized the Secretary of the Treasury, in concurrence with the Secretary of State and the U.S. Attorney General, to determine whether any act inflicting casualties and losses on American soil, or to U.S. airplanes or ships, was committed on behalf of any foreign person or interest. If they decide the injuries and damage was due to terrorism, then the U.S. Treasury will pay 90 percent of the covered losses beyond what the insurance companies must reimburse to their policyholders. Ways of repaying victims of any and all crimes is the subject of the next chapter.

SUMMARY

Groups of victims who face special problems that require special solutions have received a lot more attention in recent years. A spate of school shootings have focused attention on the dangers that students face while at school, but school grounds still are much safer than the streets of surrounding communities. The myth of college campuses as crime-free sanctuaries also has been shattered, but campuses remain among the very safest places for 18- to 24-year-olds to spend their high-risk years. Victims of stalking, until recently, had a difficult time convincing the authorities to take seriously their concerns about being in danger. New legislation, improved law enforcement responses, support groups, and self-protection tactics now help to ease their plight. Meanwhile, the problem of cyberstalking is growing. Fortunately, the number of officers slain in the line of duty is declining thanks to improved training and better equipment. Victims of bias-motivated hate crimes need social support from well-meaning people who are trying to make the ongoing experiment in multiculturalism in America

succeed. Worker safety, including protection from violence, requires greater attention on the part of employers. Police offers face unusual dangers because of their special mission: They interact with criminals daily—just the opposite of what risk-reduction strategies would recommend. To enhance their on-the-job safety, they need better training and improved equipment, but new initiatives also must target suicide and accidents, which claim more lives. In the aftermath of the September 11 attacks, difficult questions arose that still have not been resolved about the proper principles to follow to financially support the casualties of terrorism.

KEY TERMS

stalking, 311

cyberstalking, 315

bias crime, 316

hate crime, 316

bias incidents, 317

suspected terrorist attacks, 328

confirmed terrorist attacks, 328

domestic terrorism, 328

international terrorism, 328

preventions, 329

QUESTIONS FOR DISCUSSION AND DEBATE

1. Outline the maximalist and minimalist positions on the issue of acquaintance rape on campus, including drug-facilitated rapes.

2. Describe the particular problems faced by victims of hate crimes.

3. How serious is the problem of cyberstalking, in your opinion?

CRITICAL THINKING QUESTIONS

1. What might be the most effective strategies to safeguard the lives of police officers?

2. Devise some scenarios in which an individual might feel threatened and falsely accuse someone of stalking, but no real harm was intended by the alleged stalker.

3. Develop your own answers to the difficult questions that arose when the victims of the September 11, 2001, terrorist attacks received more financial compensation than the victims of the 1993 World Trade Center bombing and the 1995 Oklahoma City federal building bombing.

SUGGESTED RESEARCH PROJECTS

1. Find out how many police officers have been killed in the line of duty in recent decades in your home town or state. Try to ascertain the circumstances under which they were fatally assaulted, and what happened to their murderers.

2. Access the Census of Fatal Occupational Injuries report issued each year by the Bureau of Labor Statistics. Look up careers that interest you, and see how often people holding these jobs were murdered while at work and how frequently they died from accidents.

3. Obtain summaries about criminal incidents reported on your campus similar to the data presented in Table 11.1. Compare these figures to reported crimes accessed via the Internet on other college campuses of interest to you.

4. Find out more details about the campus shootings listed in Box 11.1.

5. Draw up a checklist of the possible security measures and risk-reduction strategies that could be implemented either at your workplace or on your college campus. Determine how many have been implemented, and suggest additional measures to make these sites even safer.

12

Repaying Victims

THE COSTS OF CRIME

The social costs of crime-related expenditures are staggering, according to economists' estimates. Victims sustain economic losses whenever offenders take cash or valuables; steal, vandalize, or destroy property; and inflict injuries that require medical attention and recuperation that interferes with work. Theft and fraud bring about the direct transfer of wealth from victims to criminals. Murders terminate lives prematurely, resulting in lost earnings for devastated family members. Non-fatal wounds trigger huge expenses for medical care—bills from doctors, emergency rooms, hospitals, pharmacies, nursing services, occupational therapists, and dentists. The old saying, "it's only money" might underestimate how even modest losses from a robbery or theft can impose serious hardships for individuals living from paycheck to paycheck:

> A knife-wielding robber steals the purse and jewelry of a retired woman scraping by on disability payments. The ID cards and a social security check in her stolen wallet require at least six weeks to replace. In the meantime, she has no cash, no bus pass, and no way to pay for her many prescription drugs, or even dog food for her pet. None of the social service agencies on the list provided by the big city police department offers emergency financial assistance. Finally she discovers a faith-based charity that is willing to pay her rent and electric bill, and give her food vouchers and $50 in cash. "If not for them, I could not have gotten my heart medication, and I'd be going to bed hungry" she tells a reporter. (Kelley, 2008)

Serious injuries may also inflict emotional suffering that requires psychological care for intense feelings of fear, grief, anger, confusion, guilt, and shame. Possible long term consequences include mental illness and suicide, as well as alcohol and drug abuse. Some may get their lives back in order rather quickly, but others could be haunted by disturbing memories and burdened by phobias and by posttraumatic stress disorder (PTSD) for long periods of time. Overall, the lifetime risk of developing PTSD for violent crime victims is much higher than for the general public. Rates of experiencing episodes of major depression and generalized anxiety are also greater. Furthermore, the effects of the victims' emotional turmoil are likely to spill over on to family members, close friends, even neighbors. An

outbreak of crime can have a negative impact on an entire community, fostering a fear of strangers, undermining involvement in activities outside the home, eroding a sense of cohesiveness, and driving out some of the most productive residents (Herman and Waul, 2004).

Huge social expenses arise from the crime-induced production of goods and services that would not be necessary if illegal activities were not such a grave problem. For example, the time, money, and resources spent on manufacturing protective devices (locks, surveillance cameras, and alarm systems); on pursuing the war on drugs, and on running court and prison systems can be considered a net loss of productive resources to society. If the risks to life and health from criminal activity were not so great, these corporate, governmental, taxpayer, and personal expenditures otherwise could have been used to meet basic needs and improve living standards (Anderson, 1999).

Costs imposed by crime cannot be measured solely in monetary terms. Mental anguish and physical suffering cannot easily be translated into dollars and cents. Nevertheless, repairing the damage to a victim's financial standing is an achievable goal and a necessary step toward recovery.

Out-of-pocket expenses can be regained in many ways. Making the offender pay is everyone's first choice, as it embodies the most elemental notion of justice. In criminal court, judges can order convicts to make restitution, generally as a condition of either probation or parole. Insurance coverage also can be a source of repayment. In some cases, financial aid can be forthcoming from a government-run state compensation fund set up to cover certain crime-related expenses. Note that restitution and compensation are alternative methods of repaying losses. Restitution is the responsibility of blameworthy offenders. Compensation comes from blameless third parties, either government-run funds or private insurance companies. In civil court, judges and juries can compel wrongdoers to pay monetary damages. Another possible source of reparations might come in the form of a civil court judgment against a grossly negligent third party, such as a commercial enterprise or a governmental agency that is considered to bear some responsibility for the criminal incident. Finally, in rare instances, victims might be able to deprive offenders of any profits gained from selling a sensationalized "inside story" of their shocking exploits.

This chapter explores all of these means of economic recovery: court-ordered restitution, lawsuits for damages, third-party civil suits, private insurance policies, government compensation plans, and legislation prohibiting criminals from cashing in on their notoriety.

GAINING RESTITUTION FROM OFFENDERS

Back to Basics

A renewed interest in restitution developed during the 1970s. Restitution takes place whenever injured parties are repaid by the individuals who are directly responsible for their losses. Offenders return stolen goods to their rightful owners, hand over equivalent amounts of money to cover out-of-pocket expenses, or perform direct personal services to those they have harmed. **Community service** is a type of restitution designed to make amends to society as a whole. Usually it entails offenders working to "right some wrongs," repairing the damage they are responsible for, cleaning up the mess they made, or laboring in order to benefit some worthy cause or group. **Symbolic restitution** to substitute victims seems appropriate when the immediate casualties can't be identified or located, or when the injured parties don't want to accept the wrongdoers' aid (Harris, 1979). **Creative restitution**, an ideal solution, comes about when offenders, on their own initiative, go beyond what the law asks of them or their sentences require, exceed other people's expectations, and leave their victims better off than they were before the crimes took place (Eglash, 1977).

As a legal philosophy, assigning a high priority to restitution means the financial health of victims will no longer be routinely overlooked, neglected, or sacrificed by a system ostensibly set up to deliver "justice for all." Criminal acts are more than symbolic assaults against abstractions like the social order or public safety." Offenders shouldn't be prosecuted solely on behalf of the state or the people. They don't only owe a debt to society. They also have incurred a debt to the flesh-and-blood individuals who suffer economic hardships because of illegal activity. Fairness demands that individuals who have been harmed be made whole again by being restored to the financial condition they were in before the crime occurred (see Abel and Marsh, 1984).

Usually, wrongs can be righted in a straightforward manner. Adolescent graffiti artists scrub off their spray-painted signatures. Burglars repay cash for the goods they have carted away. Embezzlers return stolen funds to the business they looted. Occasionally, client-specific punishments are imposed, tailored to fit the crime, the criminal, and unmet community needs. For example, a drunk driver responsible for a hit-and-run collision performs several months of unpaid labor in a hospital emergency room to see firsthand the consequences of his kind of recklessness. A teenage purse snatcher who preys on the elderly spends his weekends doing volunteer work at a nursing home. A lawyer caught defrauding his clients avoids disbarment by spending time giving legal advice to indigents unable to pay for it. Such sentences anger those who are convinced that imprisonment is the answer and fervently believe, "If you do the crime, you must do the time." But imaginative dispositions that substitute restitution and community service for confinement are favored by reformers who want to reduce jail and prison overcrowding, cut the tax burden of incarceration, and shield first-time and minor offenders from the corrupting influences of the inmate subculture ("Fitting Justice?" 1978; "When Judges Make the Punishment Fit the Crime," 1978; Seligmann and Maor, 1980).

The Rise, Fall, and Rediscovery of Restitution

The practice of making criminals repay their victims is an ancient one. Spontaneous acts of revenge were typical responses by injured parties and their kin before restitution was invented. Prior to the rise of governments, the writing of laws, and the creation of criminal justice systems, the gut reaction of people who had been harmed was to seek to "get even" with wrongdoers by injuring them physically in counterattacks and by taking back things of value. But as wealth accumulated and primitive societies established rules of conduct, the tradition of retaliatory violence gave way to negotiation and reparation. For the sake of community harmony and stability, compulsory restitution was institutionalized in ancient societies. Reimbursement practices went beyond the simplistic formula of "an eye for an eye and a tooth for a tooth." Restitution was intended to satisfy a thirst for vengeance as well as to repay losses. These transactions involving goods and money were designed to encourage lasting settlements (**composition**) between the parties that would head off further strife (Schafer, 1970).

In Biblical times, Mosaic law demanded that an assailant repay the person he injured for losses due to a serious wound, and required that a captured thief give back five oxen for every one stolen. The Code of Hammurabi granted a victim as much as 30 times the value of any possessions stolen or damaged. Under Roman law, a thief had to pay the victim double the value of what he stole if he was caught in the act. If he escaped and was caught later, he owed the victim three times as much as he took. And if he used force to carry out the theft, the captured robber had to repay the injured party four times as much as he stole. Under King Alfred of England in the ninth-century, each tooth knocked out of a person's mouth by an aggressor required a different payment, depending upon its location (Peak, 1986).

In colonial America before the Revolution, criminal acts were handled as private conflicts between individuals. Police departments and public prosecutors did not exist yet. A victim in a city could call upon night watchmen for help, but they might not be on duty, or the offender might flee beyond their jurisdiction. If the injured party sought the aid of a sheriff, he had to pay a fee. If the sheriff located the alleged perpetrator, he would charge extra to serve a warrant against the defendant. When the suspect was taken into custody, the complainant had to hire a lawyer to draw up an indictment. Then the complainant either prosecuted the case personally or hired an attorney for an additional fee to handle the private prosecution. If the accused was found guilty, the person he harmed could gain substantial benefits. Convicted thieves were required to repay their victims three times as much as they had stolen. Thieves who could not hand over such large amounts were compelled to be servants until their debts were paid off. If the victims wished, they could sell these indentured servants for a hefty price, and they had one month in which to find a buyer. After that, victims were responsible for the costs of maintaining the offenders behind bars. If they didn't pay the fees, the convicts were released (Geis, 1977; Jacob, 1977; McDonald, 1977; Hillenbrand, 1990).

In the years following the American Revolution, the procedures that the British had set up in the colonies were substantially reorganized. Reformers were concerned about the built-in injustices afflicting a system in which only wealthy victims could afford to purchase "justice" by posting rewards and hiring sheriffs, private detectives, bounty hunters, and prosecuting attorneys. Crimes were redefined as acts against the state. Settling individual grievances was no longer regarded as the primary function of court proceedings. To promote equal handling and consistency, local governments hired public prosecutors. State agencies built prison systems to house offenders. A distinction developed within the law between crimes and torts. Crimes were offenses against the public and were prosecuted by the state on behalf of "the people." **Torts** were the corresponding wrongful acts that harmed specific persons. Criminals were forced to "pay their debt to society" through fines and periods of confinement. But injured parties who wanted offenders to repay them were shunted away from criminal court and directed to civil court, a separate arena where interpersonal conflicts were resolved through lawsuits (McDonald, 1977).

The modern rediscovery of restitution in the United States began in 1967, when the President's Commission on Law Enforcement and the Administration of Justice recommended the revival of this old practice that had fallen into disuse. Since the 1970s, opinion polls have indicated widespread public support for its restoration. A greater reliance on restitution also was endorsed by the American Law Institute, the American Bar Association, the American Correctional Association, the National Advisory Commission on Criminal Justice Standards and Goals, the Supreme Court, the National Association of Attorneys General, the Office for Victims of Crime of the Justice Department, as well as reformist groups such as the National Moratorium on Prison Construction. The Federal Victim/Witness Protection Act of 1982 removed restrictions that had limited restitution to simply a possible condition of probation within the federal judicial system.

Also in 1982, the President's Task Force on Victims of Crime noted that it was unfair that people suffering serious injuries had to liquidate their assets, mortgage their homes, make do without adequate health care, or cut back on tuition expenses while criminals escaped financial responsibility for the hardships they inflicted. The task force recommended that judges routinely impose restitution or else clearly explain their specific reasons for not doing so. The Violent Crime Control and Law Enforcement Act passed by Congress in 1994 made restitution mandatory in federal cases of sexual assault or domestic violence. The enactment of the Mandatory Victim Restitution Act of 1996 imposed repayment obligations on all violent offenders in the federal system. The Federal Bureau of Prisons created a payment collection program in the late 1980s that many state correctional authorities have copied. The growing use of alternative, creative, or constructive sentences reflects the rediscovery of restitution by judges (McDonald, 1988; Leepson, 1982; Harland, 1983; Herrington, 1986; Galaway, 1992; National Victim Center, 1991b; Office of Justice Programs, 1997).

In the juvenile justice system, restitution has been ordered more often and for a longer period of time. The oldest existing repayment program for people who have been harmed by delinquents was initiated in Florida in 1945. The earliest community service program was set up in South Dakota in 1965. A Minnesota program established in 1972 was the first to allow youthful offenders to perform direct services for victims instead of paying them in cash. It also pioneered the use of mediation sessions between the two parties to foster a spirit of reconciliation. Hundreds of juvenile restitution projects were set up during the 1970s and 1980s (Warner and Burke, 1987; Klein, 1997; Roberts, 1998; Bradshaw and Umbreit, 1998).

Divergent Goals, Clashing Philosophies

Even though support for restoring restitution to its rightful place in the criminal justice process is growing, its advocates do not agree on priorities and purposes. Some advocates have been promoting this ancient practice as an additional form of punishment, while others tout it as a better method of rehabilitation. Still other champions of restitution emphasize its beneficial impact on the financial well-being of victims and its potential for resolving interpersonal conflicts. As a result, groups with divergent aims and philosophies are all pushing restitution, but are pulling at established programs from different directions (see Galaway, 1977; Klein, 1997; Outlaw and Ruback, 1999).

Restitution as a Means of Repaying Victims

Those who advance the idea that restitution is primarily a way of helping victims (see Barnett, 1977; McDonald, 1978) argue that the punitively oriented criminal justice system offers victims few incentives to get involved. Those who report crimes and cooperate with the police and prosecutors incur additional losses of time and money for their trouble (for example, from missing work while appearing in court). They also run the risk of suffering reprisals from offenders. In return they get nothing tangible, only the sense that they have discharged their civic duty by assisting in the apprehension, prosecution, and conviction of a dangerous person—a social obligation that goes largely unappreciated. The only satisfaction the system provides is revenge. But when restitution is incorporated into the criminal justice process, cooperation really pays off.

If the primary goal of restitution is to ensure that victims are repaid, then they should be able to directly negotiate arrangements for the amount of money and a payment schedule. Reimbursement should be as comprehensive as possible. The criminal ought to pay back all stolen cash plus the current replacement value of lost or damaged possessions, outstanding medical bills from crime-related injuries (including psychological wounds attended to by therapists), wages that were not earned because of absence from work (including sick days or vacation time used during recuperation or while cooperating with the investigation and prosecution), plus crime-related miscellaneous expenses (such as the cost of renting a car to replace one that was stolen or the cost of child care when a parent is testifying in court). Repayment on the installment plan should begin as promptly as possible because victims must foot the entire bill in the interim.

Restitution as a Means of Rehabilitating Offenders

Advocates of restitution as a means of rehabilitation (see Prison Research, 1976; Keve, 1978) argue that instead of being punished, wrongdoers must be sensitized to the disruption and distress that their illegal actions have caused. By learning about their victims' plights, they come to realize the injurious consequences of their deeds. By expending effort, sacrificing time and convenience, and performing meaningful tasks, they begin to understand their personal responsibilities and social obligations. By making fiscal atonement or doing community service, they can feel cleared of guilt, morally redeemed, and reaccepted into the fold. Through their hard work to defray their victims' losses, offenders can develop a sense of accomplishment and self-respect from their legitimate achievements. They may also gain marketable skills, good work habits (such as punctuality), self-discipline, and valuable on-the-job experience as they earn their way back into the community.

If restitution is to be therapeutic, offenders must perceive their obligations as logical, relevant, just, and fair. They must be convinced to voluntarily shoulder the burden of reimbursement because it is in their own best interest as well as being "the right thing to do." However, offenders probably will define their best interests as minimizing any penalties for their lawbreaking. This includes minimizing payments to injured parties, even if restitution is offered as a substitute for serving time behind bars. Offenders most likely will underestimate the suffering they have inflicted, while those on the receiving end may tend to overestimate their losses and want to extract as much as they can (see McKnight, 1981). The sensibilities of wrongdoers must be taken into account, because their willingness to make amends is the key to the success of this "treatment."

Restitution as a Means of Reconciling Offenders and Their Victims

Some advocates of restitution view the process primarily as a vehicle for reconciliation. After offenders have fully repaid the individuals they hurt, hard feelings can dissipate. Also, reconciliation between two parties who share responsibility for breaking the law can be achieved after face-to-face negotiations. In situations without a clearly designated wrongdoer, restitution might be mutual, with each of the disputants reimbursing the other for damages inflicted during their period of hostility. Both parties have to consider the restitution agreement to be fair and constructive if a lasting, peaceful settlement is to emerge. (The philosophy and operating principles of restorative justice, which relies heavily on restitution, are discussed in Chapter 13.)

Restitution as a Means of Punishing Offenders

Those who view restitution primarily as an additional penalty (see Schafer, 1977; and Tittle, 1978) argue that for too long offenders have been able to shirk this financial obligation to their victims. First, convicts should suffer incarceration to pay their debt to society. Next, they should undertake strenuous efforts to repay the specific individuals they harmed. Only then can their entanglement with the criminal justice system come to an end.

Reformers who promote restitution as a means of repaying victims, as a way of rehabilitating offenders, or as the basis for bringing about mutual reconciliation can come into conflict with crime control advocates who view restitution as an additional means of punishment and deterrence. The problem with imposing restitution as an extra penalty following incarceration is that it delays repayment for many years. Because few convicts can earn decent wages while behind prison walls, the slow process of reimbursement cannot begin until their period of confinement is over, either when the sentence expires or upon the granting of parole. When punishment takes priority over reimbursement, the victims' financial needs, the offenders' therapeutic needs, and the community's need for harmony are subordinated to the punitive interests of the state. As long as prison labor remains poorly paid, restitution and incarceration will be incompatible.

The major argument against the centrality of victim reimbursement is that the operations of the criminal justice system are intended to benefit society as a whole, and not just the injured party. Other considerations should come first: punishing criminals harshly to teach them a lesson and to deter would-be lawbreakers from following their example; treating offenders in residential programs so that they can be released back as rehabilitated and productive members of the community; or incapacitating dangerous persons by confining them for long periods of time. Subordinating these other sentencing objectives to restitution would reduce the legal system to a mere debt collection agency catering to victims, according to a 1986 Supreme Court decision (Triebwasser, 1986).

Opportunities to Make Restitution

Restitution is an extremely flexible sanction that is not being used to its full potential. It can be applied at each stage in the criminal justice process, from the immediate aftermath of the crime up until the final moments of parole supervision following a period of imprisonment. Figure 12.1 illustrates how restitution can be an option at every decision-making juncture.

As soon as a suspect is apprehended, an informal restitution arrangement can settle the matter. For example, a storekeeper might order a shoplifter to put the stolen item back on the shelf and never return to the premises, or parents might offer to pay for their son's spray painting on a neighbor's fence. In most states, however, serious offenses cannot be resolved informally. It is a felony for a victim to demand or accept any payment as "hush money" to cover up a major violation of the law, in return for not pressing charges, or as a motive for discontinuing cooperation with the authorities in an investigation or prosecution. A criminal act is an offense against the state in addition to a particular person and cannot be settled privately (Laster, 1970).

After a suspect is arrested, a restitution agreement can be worked out as an alternative to prosecution (diversion). If a defendant is indicted, the district attorney's office can make restitution a condition for dismissing formal criminal charges. Once prosecution is initiated, restitution can be part of a plea bargain struck by the defense lawyer and the district attorney, wherein the accused concedes guilt in return for lesser penalties. Restitution is particularly appropriate as a condition of probation or of a suspended sentence. If incarcerated, an inmate can try to begin to repay the injured party from the meager wages he earns from labor in prison, but he will be more capable of putting money aside if he gets a real job while he is on work release or when he resides at a halfway house. After serving time, restitution can be included as a condition of parole. Restitution contracts can be administered and supervised by various parties concerned about the crime problem: community groups, private and nonprofit charitable and religious organizations, juvenile courts, adult criminal courts, probation departments, corrections departments, and parole boards.

Yet as promising as restitution seems to be, it is not the answer for most victims. Only a small percentage will ever collect anything. The problem is directly parallel to the quest for emotional satisfaction from retribution. Just as most criminals escape punishment, most also evade restitution. The phenomenon of case attrition has been labeled **funneling**, or **shrinkage**, and has been likened to a "leaky net." At the outset, many cases seem

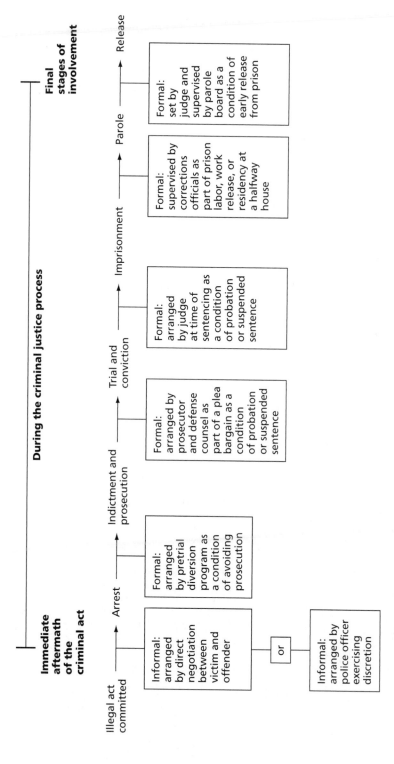

FIGURE 12.1 Opportunities for Offenders to Make Restitution

appropriate for restitution. But at the end of the criminal justice process, only a relative handful of injured parties receive even partial restitution. All the other cases (and offenders) have slipped through holes in the net. Figure 12.2 explains how and why so many "escape" their financial obligations.

First of all, a large number of offenders will never have to make amends because their victims do not report the incidents to the police (see Table 6.1). Next, the majority of offenders get away with their crimes because the police cannot figure out who the perpetrators are (clearance rates are especially low for the most numerous property crimes: burglaries, car thefts, and other forms of stealing; see Table 6.3). Hence, right away most of the people who have suffered harm already have been eliminated from any chance of receiving reimbursement. For example, only about one-half of all robberies are reported, and

only one-quarter are solved, so only one out of eight robbery cases enters the system.

Of the relatively small number of crimes that are solved by an arrest, additional problems can arise during the adjudication process. The overwhelming majority of cases (upwards of 90 percent in many jurisdictions) are resolved through plea negotiations that involve dropping charges or counts. Many complainants are eliminated from consideration if offenders do not admit to hurting them. Some cases that go to trial result in acquittals, and some convictions are reversed on appeal. Of those who are convicted or who plead guilty, many are unwilling or unable to shoulder financial obligations. Judges may not order convicts to repay the people they harmed. Inmates usually cannot earn substantial amounts of money. Prisoners granted parole have trouble finding any work, let alone a job that pays

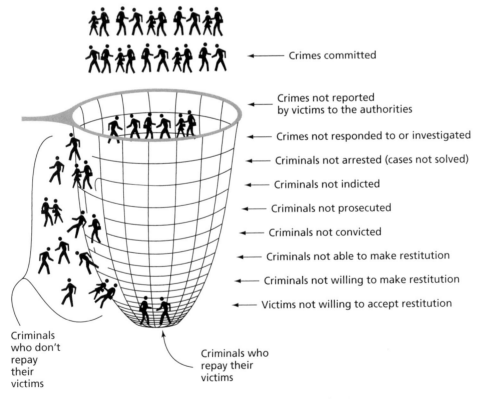

Crimes committed

Crimes not reported by victims to the authorities

Crimes not responded to or investigated

Criminals not arrested (cases not solved)

Criminals not indicted

Criminals not prosecuted

Criminals not convicted

Criminals not able to make restitution

Criminals not willing to make restitution

Victims not willing to accept restitution

Criminals who don't repay their victims

Criminals who repay their victims

F I G U R E 12.2 Case Attrition, Funneling or Shrinkage: The Leaky Net enough to allow them to set aside meaningful amounts after all their other deductions.

Finally, many jurisdictions lack both a tradition of ordering restitution and a mechanism for monitoring and enforcing such arrangements. Actually collecting the funds in a timely manner remains a major challenge for victims (Harland, 1983; McGillis, 1986; Davis and Bannister, 1995).

Obstacles Undermining Restitution

Economic realities limit the ability of many convicts to meet their restitution obligations. Because the street crime problem is in large part an outgrowth of poverty and the desperation it breeds, restitution obligations collide with competing claims for the same earnings. Ex-offenders have more pressing expenses and other debts. Furthermore, restitution is predicated on work that pays a living wage. Offenders must have, must be helped to find, or must be given reasonably well-paying jobs. These jobs need to pay far more than the minimum wage to permit installments for victims to be deducted from total after-tax earnings. But the U.S. economy cannot provide decent jobs for all who want to earn a living, even during the best of times.

Many dilemmas arise when restitution obligations are considered within the context of intense competition for the limited number of well-paying jobs convicts are capable of doing. If a position is found or created for an ex-offender, then the prospects for the successful completion of the restitution obligation are increased. Otherwise, the victims of down-and-out street criminals are denied a real chance to get repaid. If the job pays low wages, then the repayment process cannot be completed within a reasonable amount of time. If nearly all of the ex-offender's earnings are confiscated and handed over to the victim, that would jeopardize the wrongdoer's commitment to the job and to repaying the debt. If the job is demeaning, then its therapeutic value as a first step in the direction of a new lifestyle built on productive employment is lost. If the job is temporary and only lasts for the duration of the restitution obligation, then the risk of returning to a career of crime is heightened.

But if a job found or created for an ex-offender is permanent and pays well, then some observers might object that criminals are being rewarded, not punished, for their misdeeds. Law-abiding people desperately seeking decent jobs will resent any policy that seems to put offenders at the front of the line. Trade union members rightfully will fear that convict labor could replace civilian labor over the long run. But if inmates are put to work in large-scale prison industries, then business interests and labor unions justifiably will complain about unfair competition. If adolescents owing restitution are too young to receive working papers, then a job in private industry would violate child labor laws. Only unpaid community service would be permissible—but then victims get nothing.

When the injured parties are hard-pressed to make ends meet, restitution seems appropriate and fair. But if indigent offenders must hand over money to affluent victims, then restitution smacks of exploitation—taking from the poor and giving to the rich. Conversely, if prosperous offenders (such as white-collar criminals) are allowed to pay off their obligations from their bank accounts and not with hard work, it will appear that they are buying their way out of trouble. If poor people are kept behind bars and denied the opportunity to make restitution as a condition of probation or parole because they lack marketable job skills, such discrimination against an entire class of people seems to be a violation of the equal protection clause of the Fourteenth Amendment.

Yet in jurisdictions where the criterion for release from confinement was a perceived ability to repay, a typical participant in a restitution program turned out to be a white, middle-class, first-time property offender, and the most common recipient of reimbursement was a business, studies showed (see Galaway and Hudson, 1975; Edelhertz, 1977; Hudson and Chesney, 1978; Gottesman and Mountz, 1979; Harland, 1979, 1981a; Outlaw and Ruback, 1999).

Restitution in Action

Courts in every state now have the authority to order restitution. Victims are promised a right to restitution in some states that have adopted pro-victim constitutional amendments. In many states, judges are supposed to impose restitution obligations on convicts whenever possible and if appropriate, unless there are compelling or extraordinary circumstances (which must be entered into the record in writing). Restitution should routinely be part of the sentence after either negotiated pleas or trials. Often, judges are specifically directed to order reimbursement in cases of child abuse, elder abuse, domestic violence, sexual assault, identity theft, drunk driving, and hate crimes. The repayment can cover outlays for medical expenses, counseling bills, replacing property that was damaged or destroyed, lost wages, other direct costs, and even funeral expenses (National Center for Victims of Crime, 2002d).

Statistics compiled by the federal government shed light on the actual rate of ordering convicts to make restitution in state courts around the country. The national data compiled in Table 12.1 reveals that, in general, judges have not been imposing restitution obligations on most offenders. Judges ordered felons to repay their victims in addition to another sentence (usually a term of incarceration, but sometimes a fine or compulsory treatment) in only a small fraction of all convictions for either violent crimes or property crimes. Restitution was part of the sentence in a larger percentage of felony convictions for burglary, larceny, motor vehicle theft, and fraud than it was for murder, rape and other sexual assaults, robbery, and aggravated assault. People who commit fraud are the most likely to have to pay back their victims (who might be businesses rather than individuals). Murderers are the least likely of all felons to be forced to take financial responsibility for the losses they inflicted (presumably to the families of the people they killed).

As for changes over time, the imposition of restitution by judges may have been creeping upward during the late 1990s but slipped backward during 2002. However, by 2004, the ordering of repayment in state courts rebounded and reached new highs that surely were still disappointingly low to those who firmly believe in restitution as an important component of criminal justice. The trends in Table 12.1 were derived from a court monitoring system operated by the Department of Justice that tracks dispositions in nearly one million cases every two years in the nation's 75 largest jurisdictions (see Langan and Graziadei, 1995; Durose, 2004; and BJS, 2008c).

Another set of figures from this federal database is worth examining for national trends (see Table 12.2). In theory, repaying victims is more likely if a convict is on probation rather than behind bars. In practice, restitution doesn't materialize most of the time. Of felons who were fortunate enough to be sentenced to probation for violent acts, only about one in seven was ordered by a judge in state court to try to reimburse those they harmed as one of the conditions

TABLE 12.1   Percentages of convicted felons sentenced to restitution as an additional penalty in the 75 largest jurisdictions nationwide, selected years, 1996–2004

	1996	1998	2000	2002	2004
Convicted for:					
Murder	9	10	11	7	14
Rape and sexual assault	9	11	11	10	16
Robbery	11	13	13	10	16
Aggravated assault	14	14	13	11	15
Burglary	21	23	24	20	24
Larceny	22	21	25	19	26
Vehicle theft	22	21	27	19	37
Fraud	32	29	31	24	30

SOURCE: BJS, 2008c.

TABLE 12.2   Percentage of convicted felons placed on probation who have restitution obligations in the 75 largest jurisdictions nationwide, selected years, 1994–2004

	1994	1996	2000	2002	2004
On Probation for:					
Violent crimes	15	15	14	15	15
Property crimes	34	40	33	32	26

SOURCES: Reaves, 1998; Hart and Reaves, 1999; Rainville and Reaves, 2003; Cohen and Reaves, 2006; Kycklehahn and Cohen, 2008.

they must obey. Felons on probation for property crimes make restitution at a higher rate. But the direction of drift seems downward, from two-fifths of all probationers working off their debt in 1996 down to only roughly one-fourth in 2004. This backward trend toward disuse in property crimes (seemingly the easiest and most appropriate cases), rather than forward toward greater use, is another disappointment to people who believe in the necessity of restitution.

The three most frequently cited reasons for judges failing to impose restitution all fault victims: they didn't request reimbursement, they failed to document their losses, or they were unable to calculate their exact expenses. Often, judges felt that restitution obligations would be inappropriate if convicts also had to "repay society" by serving time behind bars or if they had a very limited potential to earn a living wage.

Despite these obstacles, limitations, conflicting priorities, dilemmas, and ironies, restitution is under way in many jurisdictions. Probation departments run most supervision and collection programs (75 percent) (Office of Juvenile Justice and Delinquency Prevention, 1998b).

When criminologists and victimologists evaluate the effectiveness of these programs, the challenge is to identify the specific goals and to devise appropriate criteria to measure degrees of success and failure. Victim-oriented goals involve making the injured parties whole again by enabling them to collect full reimbursement and to regain peace of mind (recovery from emotional stress and trauma). Offender-oriented goals are achieving rehabilitation and avoiding recidivism. System-oriented goals include reducing case processing costs, relieving taxpayers of the financial burden of compensating people who have been harmed, alleviating jail and prison overcrowding through alternative sentences, and improving citizen cooperation by providing material incentives to injured parties for participating in the criminal justice process. So many different aims and touted benefits coexist that no sweeping conclusions can be drawn about the effectiveness of the programs now in operation (for example, see McGillis, 1986; Butts and Snyder, 1992; Jacobs and Moore, 1994; and Davis, Smith, and Hillenbrand, 1992).

To improve the chances that convicts will make at least partial restitution, notification laws could be strengthened to ensure that victims are advised of their rights. Prosecutors could bear the routine responsibility of requesting restitution, or restitution could be considered mandatory unless the judge specifically excuses the offender from this obligation. Pre-sentence investigation reports and victim impact statements could be used as a standard form to document claims for repayment (NCVC, 2002c). To better enforce restitution orders, judges could routinely investigate the assets of convicts before crafting a workable payment plan. To decrease the likelihood of default, prosecutors could obtain injunctions to prevent defendants from hiding or quickly spending their assets (cash, savings, investments, homes, vehicles, valuable possessions), and probation and parole departments could more closely monitor these court-ordered payments, and either revoke or extend periods of probation and parole if the convict willfully refuses to make timely payments. The money to be handed over can be deducted from inmates' wages from prison labor, state and federal income tax refunds, lottery winnings, inheritances, trust accounts, and collateral used for bail. If convicts default, private collection agencies can be called, and unpaid balances can be converted into civil judgments enforced by seizures of property by sheriffs' departments (NCVC, 2002b).

However, for those who become impatient and dissatisfied with criminal-court-ordered restitution, another avenue for reimbursement can be pursued: lawsuits in civil court.

WINNING JUDGMENTS IN CIVIL COURT

The Revival of Interest in Civil Lawsuits

A young black man is accosted by members of the Ku Klux Klan, kidnapped at gunpoint, beaten, and hanged from a tree. Two Klansmen are convicted of the racially motivated lynching. The victim's mother hires a lawyer experienced in civil rights cases to sue the Klan, not for money or even for revenge, but to shut it down by taking away its resources. A civil jury awards her $7 million, entitling her to ownership of the Klan chapter's headquarters building. (Kornbluth, 1987)

***

A famous retired football player is put on trial for the murder of his ex-wife and her friend, but he is acquitted by a jury that is not convinced by the prosecution's extensive and complicated forensic evidence. The outraged families of the murder victims sue him in civil court. A jury finds him liable for the wrongful deaths and awards the two families more than $33 million in compensatory and punitive damages. (Ayres, 1997)

***

A jury finds an elderly, well-known actor not guilty of murdering his wife. But then her four grown children sue him in civil court, contending that either he killed her himself or hired someone to do it.

Although he did not testify at his murder trial, he is compelled to take the stand and answer questions in the lawsuit. Ten of the twelve jurors conclude that he was behind the killing, and the judge orders him to pay $30 million to his dead wife's four children. He declares bankruptcy. (Associated Press, 2005)

A growing number of victims are no longer content to just let prosecutors handle their cases in criminal court, especially if convictions are not secured. They have discovered that they can go after their alleged wrongdoers and pursue their best interests in a different arena: via a lawsuit in civil court.

Criminal proceedings are intended to redress public wrongs that threaten society as a whole. As a result, the economic interests of injured parties seeking restitution from convicts routinely are subordinated to the government's priorities, whether probation, incarceration, or execution. Injured parties seeking financial redress are directed to civil court. There they can launch lawsuits designed to remedy torts—private wrongs—arising from violations of criminal law. Under tort law, **plaintiffs** (victims) can sue **defendants** and win **judgments** for **punitive damages** (money extracted to punish wrongdoers and deter others) as well as **compensatory damages** (to repay expenses).

Activists in the victims' movement like to call attention to these often-overlooked legal rights and opportunities. Guilty verdicts in criminal courts cost offenders their freedom; successful judgments in civil courts cost offenders their money. Lawsuits can be successful even if charges are not pressed or if the alleged perpetrator is found not guilty after a trial in criminal court. Centers for legal advocacy and technical assistance have sprung up in many cities to make lawsuits an occupational hazard and a deterrent for habitual criminals (Barbash, 1979; Carrington, 1986; Carson, 1986; National Victim Center, 1993).

The Litigation Process

Civil suits can involve claims for punitive damages as well as compensatory and **pecuniary damages**. Awards for compensatory damages (repayment of expenses) and pecuniary damages (to cover lost income) are supposed to restore victims to their former financial condition (make them "whole" again). They can receive the monetary equivalent of stolen or vandalized property, wages from missed work, projected future earnings that won't materialize because of injuries inflicted by the offender, and outlays for medical and psychiatric care (hospital bills, counseling expenses) plus recompense for physical pain and mental suffering (resulting from loss of enjoyment, fright, nervousness, grief, humiliation, and disfigurement). Punitive damages might be levied by the court to make negative examples of lawbreakers who deliberately act maliciously, oppressively, and recklessly (Stark and Goldstein, 1985; Brien, 1992).

In civil courts, victims and their kin can sue offenders for certain intentional torts. **Wrongful death** suits enable survivors to collect compensation for the loss of a loved one without justification or legitimate excuse and for assault, which covers acts sufficiently threatening to cause fear of immediate bodily harm. Suits for **battery** involve intentional, harmful, physical contact that is painful, injurious, or offensive. Suits charging **trespass** center upon the intentional invasion of another person's land. **Conversion of chattel** suits accuse defendants of knowingly stealing or destroying the plaintiffs' possessions or property through theft or embezzlement. Suits alleging **false imprisonment** contend that the offender held the plaintiff against his or her will, even for a brief period of time, such as during a hostage-taking or rape. Charges of fraud can arise from white collar crimes if intentional misrepresentation and deception can be established. Finally, suits can allege that the defendant intentionally or recklessly inflicted emotional distress through extreme or outrageous conduct, such as by stalking the plaintiff (Stark and Goldstein, 1985; Brien, 1992; and National Crime Victims Bar Association, 2007).

Civil actions commence when the plaintiff (also called the **second party**) formally files a complaint (also referred to as a **pleading**). This document includes a brief statement of the legal jurisdictional issues, a summary of the relevant facts of the case (the **causes of action** that show how the harm to the victim was a "direct and proximate result" of the alleged wrongdoer's behavior), and a request for relief for the injuries and damages sustained (monetary compensation). The victim's attorney brings the complaint to civil court and pays a fee. A deputy sheriff (or a privately retained **process server**) must physically hand this written document to the defendant (also called the **first party**), along with a summons requiring a response to the allegations within a stated period of time (usually one month). The accused wrongdoer submits an answer either admitting to the charges or, more likely, contesting them and issuing a defense (or perhaps even launching a countersuit).

In preparing for a trial to resolve the competing claims, both parties engage in a process called **discovery**, in which they exchange written replies to questions, documents, and sworn statements of eyewitnesses (including police officers). Just as in criminal proceedings, the typical outcome is a negotiated compromise agreement. But if an out-of-court settlement cannot be reached, the accused exercises his Seventh Amendment right to a trial, and the injured party has to prove the allegations in court. After considerable delays because of congested court calendars, the trial is held before twelve (or, in some states, six) jurors or perhaps only in front of a judge (Stark and Goldstein, 1985).

In civil proceedings, the defendant in third-party lawsuits is likely to allege contributory negligence (the injured party was partly responsible for what happened). In battery cases, the rebuttal might be victim provocation (leading to responses necessary for self-protection). In other lawsuits, the defense might argue that the plaintiff knowingly and voluntarily "assumed the risk;" for example, a woman alleging rape was drinking heavily and agreed to go to the man's apartment (Stark and Goldstein, 1985; and National Crime Victims Bar Association, 2007).

Following opening statements presented by attorneys for each side, witnesses testify and are cross-examined, and physical evidence is introduced. **Interrogatories** (lists of questions for the other side to answer), **depositions** (answers to the op-posing lawyer's questions) and requests for docu-ments may generate important evidence. Then each party's attorney sums up, and the jury retires to deliberate. The jury votes and then renders its verdict on which of the two versions of events seems more truthful. The jury awards compensa-tory and perhaps punitive damages if it finds for the plaintiff and rejects the defendant's arguments. The losing party is likely to appeal the decision, and a higher court can overturn the trial court's verdict if errors in procedural law are discovered or if the jury acted contrary to the evidence. Appeals may take many years to be resolved (Stark and Goldstein, 1985).

Litigation in civil court usually follows rather than precedes adjudication in criminal court. People who have been badly hurt usually wait to proceed with litigation because the evidence that is introduced during the criminal proceedings can be used again in the lawsuit and generally is sufficient to establish that a tort occurred. Furthermore, if the civil action is filed too early, the defense attorney will use this fact to try to undermine the complai-nant's credibility as a witness for the prosecution, claiming that the testimony is motivated by poten-tial financial gain. But if the civil action is not filed for years, the **statute of limitations** might run out, and it will be too late to sue the defendant. For example, in most states lawsuits alleging assault must be filed within two years, before complai-nants' and defendants' memories fade and material evidence is lost or destroyed (Brien, 1992).

Possibilities and Pitfalls

Injured parties that are considering civil litigation must weigh the advantages and disadvantages of this course of action. One reason civil lawsuits are relatively uncommon is that most victims conclude that the benefits are not worth the costs. In addi-tion, many people are unfamiliar with this option.

Civil lawsuits have several attractions. First and foremost, victims can seize the initiative, haul their assailants into court, bring them to the bar of jus-tice, and sue them for all they can get. In criminal cases, prosecutors exercise considerable discretion and make all the important decisions, even in jur-isdictions where victims have the right to be in-formed and consulted. In civil cases, victims can regain a sense of control and feel empowered. They are principal figures entitled to their day in court, are aware of all the facts surrounding the case, and can't be excluded from the courtroom. It is up to them to decide whether to sue and whether to accept a defendant's offer of an out-of-court settlement. (In small-claims courts, plain-tiffs don't even need an attorney. They can present their own cases using simplified procedures de-signed to expedite trials, because not much money is at stake).

Plaintiffs seeking large awards must hire attor-neys of their own choosing and can participate in developing a strategy and preparing the case in an-ticipation of the trial. Victims can achieve full reim-bursement, perhaps even more money than they lost, through lawsuits. They can collect punitive damages far in excess of actual out-of-pocket ex-penses, and can receive compensation for the men-tal pain and emotional suffering they endured. Defendants' assets, including homes, cars, savings accounts, investments, and inheritances, can be **attached** (confiscated), and their wages can be gar-nisheed. Most attorneys practicing civil law accept cases on a contingency basis and don't charge a fee unless they win. Suits can be brought by the victims' family (parents, children, spouse, or sib-lings) if an injured party is too young, mentally incapacitated, or dies (Stark and Goldstein, 1985; Brien, 1992; and National Crime Victims Bar Association, 2007).

Winning a judgment in civil court is easier than securing a conviction in criminal court—the standard of proof is lower and less demanding. In lawsuits, conflicting claims are decided by a **pre-ponderance of the evidence** (the winning side is the one that presents the more convincing argu-ments, translated as "more likely than not" or "51 percent"), not by guilt beyond a reasonable doubt (proving the charges to a moral certainty). Therefore, a civil suit following a conviction in criminal court is likely to succeed because the same evidence and testimony can be used again in front of a second jury that does not have to reach a unanimous agreement and does not have to be convinced beyond a reasonable doubt. An acquittal in criminal court does not rule out civil action, because a jury still might decide in favor of a plaintiff who presents a more persuasive case than the defendant. Even if the prosecutor drops the criminal charges that were initially lodged by the police, a plaintiff might win if the evidence that came to light during the police investigation is presented in civil court. If plaintiffs win awards but defendants are unwilling to pay up voluntarily, sheriffs and marshals can be enlisted to enforce the courts' judgments by seizing contested assets or property, which can be sold at public auctions to raise cash.

Because defendants in civil court do not face imprisonment or execution, constitutional protections are less stringent than in criminal court. Defendants cannot ignore lawsuits for more than 30 days, or else they automatically lose (a **default judgment**). Nor can the accused plead the Fifth Amendment and refuse to testify on the grounds of self-incrimination. Defendants must reply to the questions put to them or risk a quick defeat. Rules of evidence are more flexible and, for example, allow the plaintiff to reveal the defendant's prior convictions for similar acts, a disclosure that usually wouldn't be permissible in criminal court (Stark and Goldstein, 1985; Brien, 1992).

Successful suits can make victims feel vindicated: The judges and jurors sided with them, accepted their version of events, and rejected the defendants' denials, excuses, or justifications. Victims teach perpetrators the lessons that crime does not pay and that wrongdoers ultimately will be held liable for their misdeeds. Reimbursement is soothing, and revenge is sweet. Civil suits are the only means of redress when the entire injury and loss is intangible and subsumed under the heading of **pain and suffering**.

Despite the prospect of financial reimbursement, several drawbacks deter most victims from pursuing civil actions. Civil proceedings are independent of criminal proceedings. The entire case must be fought all over again in the courtroom,

this time at the victim's expense without the backing of the government and its enormous resources. A statute of limitations may have run out—the time limits for filing a lawsuit vary by crime and by state; those with recovered memories of abuse during childhood may be entitled to extra amounts of time. Victims have to put their lives on hold for years while the litigation process slowly drags on. Cases involve motions, hearings, conferences, negotiations, trials, and appeals. In the meantime, plaintiffs (and defendants as well) undergo a long, drawn-out ordeal punctuated by moments of suspense, anxiety, frustration, despair, and humiliation. Despite their opposing interests and simmering mutual hostility, the warring parties must keep in contact (at least through their respective lawyers) for months or even years after criminal proceedings end. If negotiations fail and last-minute out-of-court settlements are beyond reach, victims must take the stand and once again relive the incident in painful detail. After testifying, victims must submit to a withering cross-examination by the defense attorney that could raise questions of shared responsibility, damage the victims' reputation, and expose the most intimate details about lifestyles, injuries, losses, and suffering. The backlogs and delays in civil court are worse than those in criminal court because litigation has become such a popular way to settle disputes. Win or lose, civil suits drag on for years before they are resolved, forestalling closure for victims who want to get on with their lives. Furthermore, the injured parties run the risk of being sued themselves. Countersuits by defendants against plaintiffs fit into a strategy of harassment and intimidation intended to force victims to drop certain charges, or to withdraw their suits entirely, or to accept unfavorable out-of-court settlements (see Stark and Goldstein, 1985; Brien, 1992; and National Crime Victims Bar Association, 2007).

In the adversary system of civil proceedings, top-notch lawyers are said to be as important a factor as the facts of the case. Unfortunately, they probably won't be interested unless great sums of money are at stake. Their **contingency fees** can range as high as one-third to one-half of the money awarded to plaintiffs, if they are victorious. Even victims who win may have to pay for most litigation expenses other than their attorney's fees, such as filing fees, deposition costs, and expert witness fees.

Most discouraging of all is the problem of collecting the debt. Even in victory there can be defeat. If the offenders have spent or hidden the spoils of their crimes, it will be difficult for the plaintiffs' attorneys to recover any money without incurring great expenses. Most street criminals don't have what lawyers call **deep pockets** (assets like homes, cars, jewelry, bank accounts, investments in stocks and bonds, or business interests). On the contrary, many are virtually **judgment-proof**—broke and with no prospects of coming into money from work or inheritances (see Stark and Goldstein, 1985; Brien, 1992).

No government agency systematically compiles records about the successes and failures of plaintiffs who have sued defendants in civil courts. The actual dollar amounts of some out-of-court settlements are kept confidential. Nevertheless, advocacy groups urge victims to consider exercising their civil court option, especially if the identity and whereabouts of the offender are known, if restitution is not forthcoming from criminal court proceedings, and if compensation is not available from insurance companies or government-administered funds.

Recognizing that few street criminals who commit acts of violence or theft have substantial assets or incomes, attorneys within the victims' rights movement have developed a strategic alternative: lawsuits against financially sound third parties.

Collecting Damages from Third Parties

Even when the perpetrators of a crime are known to be judgment-proof, victims still have a chance to recover their losses. Instead of suing those who inflicted their injuries directly and intentionally, plaintiffs can go after **third parties**: individuals or entities such as businesses, institutions, or government agencies. The twist in these civil suits is to allege that a third party is partly to blame for the victim's misfortunes.

The legal theory behind third-party suits parallels traditional notions of **negligence**. The plaintiff argues that the defendant (the third party) had a duty or obligation, that there was a breach of this duty, and that this breach proximately caused injury to the plaintiff. The plaintiff tries to prove that the third party's gross negligence put the criminal in a position to single him out for harm (Carrington, 1977). For example, in the aftermath of a spate of massacres on school grounds, families of youngsters who were killed or wounded filed lawsuits against the parents of the students who went berserk, the people who inadvertently were the sources of the weapons, the school district, and the manufacturers of the guns (Lewin, 2001).

There are two types of third-party liability suits. The first is directed against enterprises such as private businesses (for example, firearms dealers that failed to take adequate steps to prevent their handguns from being sold illegally to teenage gang members). The second type is aimed at custodial agencies and officials of the criminal justice system (such as municipal police departments, prison wardens, and directors of mental institutions). Whereas suing offenders is reactive, third-party civil suits can be both reactive and proactive. If for no other motive than their own enlightened self-interest, the private enterprises and governmental bodies that are the targets of these kinds of suits are compelled to take reasonable and necessary precautions to prevent further incidents for which they could be sued again. By discouraging the indifference and negligence that facilitate predatory acts, third-party civil suits contribute to security consciousness and crime prevention (Carrington, 1986). A National Crime Victim Bar Association (2007) encourages injured parties to seek redress through civil actions and provides names of attorneys who specialize in lawsuits.

Suing Private Enterprises Several successful suits during the 1970s have served as landmark cases for many subsequent claims.

> A well-known singer is raped in a motel by an unknown assailant who has entered her room by jiggling the lock on the sliding glass

terrace doors. Badly shaken by the experience and unable to appear on stage, the singer sues the motel chain for loss of earnings. Her attorney argues that the motel has shown gross negligence by failing to maintain secure premises for its guests. A jury renders a verdict in her favor of $2.5 million. The motel chain agrees to a settlement by not appealing the verdict and pays her $1.5 million. (Barbash, 1979; Rottenberg, 1980)

***

A security guard at a drive-in hamburger stand is shot in the head during a robbery. He doesn't sue the offender or his employer (the restaurant). Instead, his attorney argues successfully that the chain store that sold the robber the bullet is guilty of gross negligence. The guns and ammunition department routinely ignored an obscure state law that requires two citizens to vouch for the identity of the purchaser of bullets. (Barbash, 1979; Rottenberg, 1980)

Third-party lawsuits against businesses have established new definitions of corporate responsibility and financial liability. The suits never accuse the defendant (business) of intentionally harming the plaintiff because the executives in charge probably never met either the victim or the offender and were two or three steps removed from the criminal action. What is alleged is that the defendant's gross negligence and breach of responsibility created a climate that made the criminal's task easier and the incident predictable (Carrington, 1977, 1978).

Third-party suits against private enterprises can take several forms. Lawsuits can allege that landlords are responsible for crimes committed against their tenants because of inadequate lighting or locks. Hotels and motels may be liable for assaults and thefts committed against guests because of lax security measures (such as failure to install closed-circuit television monitors, store room keys safely, or hire guards). Banks, stores, shopping malls, and theaters can be held accountable for failure to provide ordinary care to protect customers from robbers and thieves. "Common carriers" (bus, train, or airplane companies) might be liable for failure to furnish customary forms of protection for passengers on vehicles or at stations and platforms. Employers who negligently hire known felons and put them in positions of trust might be partly to blame if the ex-cons break laws during the course of their assigned duties. Even college administrations could be responsible for failing to correct security lapses that a reasonable and prudent individual would realize endanger students in campus buildings and dormitories (Austern, 1987). A successful lawsuit by people wounded in the 1993 World Trade Center bombing established negligence about security measures on the part of the agency that managed the twin towers (Hartocollis, 2005). A parallel $23 billion third party lawsuit by 9/11 victims and their families against the airlines and airport security companies is still pending (Hartocollis, 2008).

Plaintiffs can win if they can prove in civil court that the third party did not take sufficient actions to prevent a reasonably foreseeable crime. To prevail, the attorney must convincingly demonstrate that the defendant chronically disregarded complaints, did not post warnings, chose not to rectify conditions and improve security, and did not offer the degree of protection expected by community standards. Most claims fail to meet this test, but the few that succeed can contribute to the improvement of public safety in places like shopping centers, bus terminals, parking lots, hotels, and apartment complexes (Brien, 1992).

As attorneys are honing their skills at security litigation seminars, landlords and businesses are attempting to make their premises suit-proof even if they cannot be crime-proof (Purdy, 1994). Because many lawsuits against property owners are settled out of court, reliable figures about their rate of occurrence and success are hard to find. One estimate from a sample of court records turned up 186 suits against property owners from 1958 to 1982. A later study established that the rate has increased, locating 267 third-party suits from 1983 to 1992. Almost half of all the suits were launched by women who had been raped (Deutsch, 1994).

In recent years, victims of gun violence have filed dozens of claims against the firearms industry, but most of these third-party lawsuits have been dismissed by the courts. A notable exception took place after a pair of snipers terrorized the Washington, D.C. area in 2002. Eight people who were wounded and the next of kin of those who were murdered won a $2.5 million legal settlement from the manufacturer of the high-powered rifle and from the gun dealer who improperly sold it.

However, in 2005, Congress passed "shield" legislation (similar to the existing laws in 33 states) that specifically protected manufacturers and dealers from suits seeking to hold them liable for negligence when their weapons are used to commit crimes. Victorious backers of the gun lobby's measure said it was needed to keep the American arms industry in business in the face of "frivolous" but costly lawsuits. Disappointed opponents argued its passage will deprive wounded people (as well as entire municipalities, such as New York City, that incur huge expenses from gun violence) of a legitimate avenue for financial recovery (Stolberg, 2005).

Suing Governmental Bodies Successful third-party lawsuits against criminal justice agencies and custodial officials, like the two 1970s landmark cases described below, are less common than suits against private enterprises.

> A 14-year-old girl is abducted from a private school, tied to a tree, molested, and then left to freeze to death. The man who kills her had previously attacked another girl from the same school in the same way. He had been committed for treatment while under confinement at a nearby psychiatric institute. The victim's parents sue the mental hospital, a psychiatrist, and a probation officer for arranging the release of the offender into an outpatient program without first receiving court approval. They win a judgment of $25,000. (Carrington, 1977, 1978)

***

An inmate with a record of 40 felony convictions and 17 escape attempts is permitted to participate in a "take-a-lifer to dinner"

program. After eating at the home of the prison's baker, he breaks loose, commits an armed robbery, and kills a man. The victim's widow sues the warden both personally and in his official capacity, in addition to the state prison system, for gross negligence. Her attorney argues that the warden didn't have legislative authority or administrative permission from his superiors to let the inmate out that night. She wins a judgment of $186,000, which the state does not appeal. (Barbash, 1979; Rottenberg, 1980)

The basic charge in civil actions against the government once again is gross negligence. The plaintiffs allege that public officials severely abused their discretionary authority. The crimes are said to have happened because official inaction or incompetence facilitated the offenders' inclinations to harm innocent parties. In a few states, governmental bodies cannot be sued even when the negligence of officials clearly contributed to the commission of crimes; the agents and agencies are protected by the English common law doctrine of **sovereign immunity**. Most states and the federal government permit citizens to sue but impose limitations (for example, financial caps and exemption from punitive damages) and invoke special procedures (Austern, 1987; Carrington, 1978).

Specific charges in third-party liability lawsuits against governmental agencies and officials fit under a number of headings (Austern, 1987). Claims against the police can allege **nonfeasance**: that officers failed to act to protect individuals to whom they owed a special duty, such as witnesses for the prosecution. Claims can also allege police **malfeasance**: that officers acted carelessly or inattentively as victims were hurt, as in the following case.

> A husband stabs his wife 13 times. Nearly 30 minutes later, the police arrive in response to her earlier call for help. As he wanders around screaming, he kicks her in the head, then drops their son on her unconscious body and kicks her again. Finally, the police restrain him and take him into custody. After eight days in a

coma and several months in a hospital, she sues the city, three police chiefs, and 29 officers. Her lawsuit alleges that because the assailant was her husband, the police failed to provide her with equal protection under the law, as guaranteed by the Fourteenth Amendment, by handling her numerous calls for help over the years differently than cases of assaults by strangers. A jury finds the police department negligent for failing to protect her and awards her $2.3 million. The city appeals, and she settles for $1.9 million out of court. (Gelles and Straus, 1988)

When prisoners are not supervised adequately or are released as a result of an administrative error and then inflict harm, suits can allege **wrongful escape**. When dangerous convicts are released and they injure people whom they had previously publicly threatened, suits can be filed for **failure to warn**. Claims can also allege **wrongful release** when, through gross negligence on the part of officials, a high-risk inmate is granted conditional release (probation, parole, or furlough) from a jail, prison, or mental institution and then commits a foreseeable act of lawlessness. The following case illustrates these problems:

> A mental patient walks out of a minimum-security state psychiatric hospital and wanders into a small town. He buys a hunting knife and then, for no apparent reason, seizes a nine-year-old-girl walking down the street with her family and stabs her more than 30 times. He is found not guilty of murder by reason of insanity. The girl's parents sue the state for failing to protect their daughter from this madman. The state agrees to a $1.5 million out-of-court settlement, compensating the mother for the emotional harm of witnessing her daughter's slaying and pledges to improve security at state mental hospitals. (Hays, 1992)

Suits against custodial officials and agencies raise important issues. The Supreme Court ruled in 1980

(*Martinez* case) that neither the Constitution nor the Civil Rights Act of 1964 gave the survivors of a person who was murdered the right to sue a state parole board (Carrington, 1980). In upholding the doctrine of sovereign immunity from liability, the justices of the Court argued that government has a legitimate interest in seeking to rehabilitate criminals. Every treatment alternative to totally incapacitating convicts through maximum-security confinement involves taking risks with the public's safety. Halfway houses, therapeutic communities, work release, educational release, furloughs, probation, and parole all grant conditional liberty to known offenders who may pose a continuing threat to community safety. Underlying a charge of **abuse of discretionary authority** and gross negligence is the assumption that danger can be predicted—it usually cannot be with any statistical certainty. Some patients and inmates thought to be dangerous turn out to be well-behaved (**false positives**), and some out on probation or parole enjoying conditional liberty who were rated as posing a low risk may suddenly act viciously (**false negatives**).

What is predictable is that successful third-party lawsuits by victims against custodial officials and agencies will have a chilling effect on wardens, psychiatrists, parole boards, and others who make decisions regarding confinement versus release. What might develop in these therapeutic relationships is a type of defensiveness comparable to the defensive medicine practiced by doctors afraid of malpractice suits. Fear of legal and financial repercussions could dominate professional judgments and record keeping. Rehabilitation programs could be severely constrained. Eligible convicts could be barred from such programs because administrators wouldn't want to jeopardize their careers by releasing them from total confinement. Qualified professionals could be deterred from taking jobs as custodial officials because of exposure to personal liability lawsuits, unless states protect such employees under a doctrine of sovereign immunity.

On the other hand, vulnerable members of the general public need lawsuits as a vehicle to exert some leverage over justice officials and unresponsive bureaucracies. And aggrieved parties need a way to hold grossly negligent agency officials accountable, as well as a mechanism to recover losses inflicted by dangerous people who should not have been left unsupervised. Some victims' advocates see third-party lawsuits as an appropriate remedy to establish a proper balance between two conflicting policy objectives: lowering the crime rate in the long run by rehabilitating offenders through the judicious granting of conditional liberty, and maintaining public safety in the short run by incapacitating and incarcerating individuals believed to be dangerous to the community (Carrington, 1980).

COLLECTING INSURANCE REIMBURSEMENTS

Private Crime Insurance

Private insurance companies are innocent third parties that can quickly and routinely provide reimbursement for losses. The positive aspect is that a prudent policyholder can be repaid without too many complications as long as a formal complaint is filed with the police. The drawbacks are that a potential target must have the foresight to purchase protection in advance; that a company must be willing to issue a policy (some people and businesses in high-crime areas have trouble finding an insurer); that premiums for the coverage must be affordable (many people are aware of life's dangers but do not have the disposable income to pay for the "luxury" of insurance); and that exclusions of relatively minor losses (because of **deductible clauses**) impose serious financial hardships on low-income families (Sarnoff, 1996).

Cautious individuals can protect themselves against a variety of hazards (see Miller, Cohen, and Wiersema, 1996). Life insurance policies can pay sizable sums to the survivors of loved ones who were murdered. Some policies (which cost more) contain a **double indemnity clause** that grants survivors twice as much if the policyholder dies unexpectedly from an accident or a criminally inflicted injury. Coverage can also be purchased

to offset lost earnings (income maintenance) and expenses due to medical bills (health insurance). Property can be insured against loss or damage. Car and boat insurance covers expenses imposed by theft, vandalism, and arson. Home insurance protects against losses due to burglary, some larcenies (items left on porches or in yards, for example), vandalism, arson, and robbery if the confrontation occurs within the dwelling. Some companies sell robbery insurance that reimburses policyholders for lost valuables such as jewelry or cameras no matter where the crime occurs. A few companies offer protection to businesses whose executives might be kidnapped and held for ransom.

In order for burglary victims to collect reimbursements under homeowner policies, insurance companies usually require receipts, photos or videos of valuables, and perhaps serial numbers of lost items. Deductibles, exclusions, limits, depreciation of value due to age and wear, plus the willingness to pay for optional riders (for example, to cover the theft of very expensive jewelry) make complete recovery unlikely (Weisberg, 2008). If detectives determine that the intruder committed a theft due to a victim-facilitated "no force entry" (see Chapter 5), the insurance adjuster may completely reject the careless policyholder's claim (Reeves, 2006).

Patterns of Loss, Recovery, and Reimbursement

Statistics derived from the *National Crime Victimization Survey* confirm some commonsense predictions about insurance coverage and recovery. First, some types of coverage are more common than others. More people are insured against medical expenses than against property losses. Medical and dental costs are potentially more devastating than theft or vandalism of tangible goods, and health coverage often is provided by an employer as a fringe benefit of full-time jobs. Second, high-income individuals are more likely to buy crime insurance than low-income people (even though the poor are exposed to greater risks and suffer higher victimization rates). Third, larger losses are more likely than smaller ones to be reimbursed through insurance claims. The households that are most likely to receive cash settlements are those whose cars are stolen. Only a small proportion of families who suffer burglaries and larcenies are reimbursed. An even smaller fraction of people who are robbed or pickpocketed are insured against such losses. Most policies have deductible clauses that stipulate that the victim must absorb the first $500 (or some other sum) of the losses and cannot file a claim unless out-of-pocket expenses exceed this figure. Hence, most crime-imposed losses (which usually are small) cannot be recovered (Harland, 1981a).

Studies concerning actual patterns of burglary loss, coverage, and recovery are rare. One revealed that both the average amount stolen and the percentage of victims who are insured are positively correlated with family income. That means that wealthy families lose more to burglars but also are more likely to be insured than low-income households. In one study during the 1970s, only one family in 10 had purchased burglary insurance in the lowest income category, but about half the families in the higher-income category were covered. (Presumably, the rich were fully insured, but those data were unavailable.) In sum, although a small number of families recover substantial amounts, insurance provides relief for relatively few burglary victims (Skogan, 1978; Harland, 1981a).

As for insurance coverage for medical expenses resulting from violent crime, women were more likely to receive reimbursement (73 percent) than men (57 percent). The lowest income grouping (61 percent) and the highest income grouping (95 percent) were much more likely to get their out-of-pocket costs paid by health insurance (from the government in the case of the poor; from private companies in the case of the affluent) than the working poor (45 percent) who usually earn too much for Medicaid but too little to afford their own policies. All senior citizens received coverage of their bills under Medicare, but less than half (45 percent) of injured individuals between 20 and 24 years of age had health insurance coverage, according to the NCVS for 2006 (BJS, 2008).

Federal Crime Insurance

Insurance companies make profits in two ways: They adjust their rates continuously so that they take in more money in premiums than they pay out in claims, and they invest the money paid by policyholders in order to collect interest, dividends, and rents. To contain costs and limit payouts, companies raise their rates, place caps on reimbursements, impose sizable deductibles, and exclude certain kinds of losses. One irony of the for-profit insurance business is that those who face the greatest risks are sometimes either denied coverage outright or charged exorbitant premiums that they can't afford.

The insufficiency and unfairness of private insurance underwriting practices first received public attention during the late 1960s. The National Advisory Panel on Insurance in Riot-Affected Areas (part of the National Advisory Commission on Civil Disorders) in 1967 examined the plights of inner-city residents and businesses that had suffered losses due to looting and arson during ghetto rebellions. The panel cited a general lack of insurance availability as a factor contributing to urban decay: the closing of businesses, the loss of jobs, the abandonment of buildings, and the exodus of residents from high-crime areas.

In 1968, Congress followed some of the panel's recommendations and granted relief to those who suffered from insurance **redlining** (an illegal, discriminatory practice that results in denial of coverage). The Department of Housing and Urban Development Act set up Fair Access to Insurance Requirements plans to make sure that property owners were not denied fire damage coverage solely because the neighborhood had a high rate of arson cases. In 1970, Congress amended the 1968 act to permit the federal government to offer affordable burglary and robbery insurance directly to urban homeowners, tenants, and businesses in areas where such coverage from private companies was either unavailable or unreasonably expensive. Federal intervention into the insurance market to assist actual and potential crime victims was viewed as a last resort (Bernstein, 1972). The Federal

Emergency Management Agency currently runs the Federal Insurance Administration.

Once the government began to sell insurance coverage, it became reasonable to ask whether public funds could be set up to bail out families that faced economic ruin because they were not willing or able to pay for private insurance policies, or were inadequately protected, especially against huge medical bills and lost earnings. Public insurance plans are called crime victim compensation programs.

RECOVERING LOSSES THROUGH VICTIM COMPENSATION PROGRAMS

Most street crime victims never receive criminal court-ordered restitution, for one obvious reason: The offenders are not caught and convicted. For a parallel reason, most victims never collect court-ordered civil judgments: The perpetrators cannot be identified or located, and then successfully sued. Furthermore, rarely can a third party be held partly responsible for the incident and sued for gross negligence. Given the inadequacy of most private insurance coverage when major disasters strike, the only remaining hope for monetary recovery lies with a different sort of third party: a state compensation fund. Reimbursement from a government fund appears to be the only realistic method for routinely restoring individuals to the financial condition they were in before the crime occurred.

> A middle-aged man is blinded by assailants, who are later caught, convicted, and imprisoned. Upon their release, they are ordered by the court to pay restitution to their victim for the loss of his eyesight. Under the arrangement it will take 442 years for the injured man to collect the full amount due him. (Fry, 1957)

***

> A Good Samaritan comes to the aid of two elderly women who are being harassed by

a drunken youth on a subway train. As his wife and child watch in horror, the well-meaning man is stabbed to death by the drunk. The killer is captured and sentenced to 20 years to life in prison. The widow is forced to send her child to live with her mother while she goes to work to pay bills. (Editors, *New York Times*, 1965)

***

> A construction worker and his girlfriend are watching television in their living room when her ex-suitor breaks in and repeatedly hits the man in the head with a baseball bat. The man survives this aggravated assault but needs 10 operations to repair his skull. He has no health insurance and cannot return to work because of dizzy spells. The state's board grants him $45,000 to cover his hospital bills and lost wages. (Mitchell, 2008)

The first two cases, which took place in England in 1951 and in New York City in 1965, dramatized the need for government programs to furnish assistance to innocent people who suffer devastating losses. The remaining case, describing a settlement from a state-run fund, illustrates the kinds of aid that these government boards now provide. Compensation is the easiest, simplest, and most direct way of speeding a victim's recovery and of institutionalizing the notion of helping someone in desperate need of emergency financial support.

The History of Victim Compensation by Governments

The earliest reference to governmental compensation for crime victims can be found in the ancient Babylonian Code of Hammurabi, which is considered to be the oldest written body of criminal law (about 1775 BC). The code instructed territorial governors to replace lost property of someone who was robbed if the criminal was not captured. In the aftermath of a murder, the governor was to pay the heirs a specific sum in silver from the treasury. In the centuries that followed, restitution by the offender replaced compensation by the state. But during the Middle Ages, restitution also faded away. Victims had no avenue of redress except to try to recover losses by suing offenders in civil court.

Interest in compensation revived during the 1800s, when the prison reform movement in Europe focused attention on the suffering of convicts, and in doing so indirectly called attention to the plight of their victims. Leading theorists in criminology endorsed compensation and restitution at several International Penal Congress meetings held at the turn of the century. But these resolutions did not lead to any concrete actions. Legal historians have uncovered only a few scattered instances of special funds set aside for crime victims: one in Tuscany after 1786, another in Mexico starting in 1871, and one beginning in France in 1934. Switzerland and Cuba also experimented with victim compensation (MacNamara and Sullivan, 1974; Schafer, 1970; Silving, 1959).

An English prison reformer sparked the revival of interest in compensation in the late 1950s. Because of her efforts, a government commission investigated various reparations proposals and set up a fund in 1964 in Great Britain. Several Australian states and Canadian provinces followed suit during the next few years. New Zealand offered the most complete protection in the Western world in 1972, when it abolished the victim compensation program it had pioneered in 1963 and absorbed it within a universal accident insurance system. Everyone in New Zealand was covered for losses arising from any type of misfortune, including criminal acts. The nature of the event, the reason it occurred, and the person responsible for it did not affect compensation decisions (European Committee on Crime Problems, 1978; Meiners, 1978).

The Debate over Compensation in the United States

In the late 1950s, the question of compensation surfaced in American law journals. Initially, distinguished scholars raised many objections to the idea of having the government provide financial assistance to innocent individuals wounded or slain by criminals. But support for the notion of compensation grew when a Supreme Court justice argued that society should assume some responsibility for "making whole again" those whom the law had failed to protect. Soon, well-known political figures of the period came to accept the proposition that special funds should be set up to repay victims. Their enthusiasm was in accord with the liberal political philosophy embodied in President John F. Kennedy's New Frontier and President Lyndon Johnson's Great Society: Government should develop programs to try to ameliorate persistent social problems.

The proposals of elected officials, the suggestions of legal scholars and criminologists, and the pressures of coalitions of interest groups were necessary but not sufficient to trigger legislatures to take action. Widely publicized brutal and tragic incidents supplied the missing ingredient of public support in the first few states to experiment with compensation schemes. In 1965, California initiated a repayment process as part of its public assistance system. In 1966, New York created a special board to allocate reimbursements. In 1967, Massachusetts designated certain courts and the state attorney general's office as granters of financial aid to victims.

Starting in 1965, Congress began to debate the question of federal encouragement of and assistance to state compensation programs. No lobby emerged to pressure elected officials to vote against compensation plans. Even private insurance companies did not feel threatened by the potential loss of business. At the hearings, the idea of compensation was endorsed by the American Bar Association, International Association of Chiefs of Police, National District Attorneys' Association, U.S. Conference of Mayors, National League of Cities, National Conference of State Legislatures, existing state compensation boards, judges' organizations, senior citizens' groups, and the National Council on Crime and Delinquency ("Crime Control Amendments," 1973; Edelhertz and Geis, 1974; "Crime Victims' Aid," 1978; Meiners, 1978). The arguments over the pros and cons of governmental compensation raised many

important political, philosophical, and pragmatic issues (see Childres, 1964; Schultz, 1965; Wolfgang,
1965; Brooks, 1972; Geis, 1976; Meiners, 1978;
Carrow, 1980; U.S. House Committee on the Judiciary, 1980; Gaynes, 1981; Elias, 1983a).

The most compelling rationales advanced by advocates presented compensation as additional social
insurance, or as a way of meeting an overlooked governmental obligation to all citizens, or as a means of
assisting individuals facing financial ruin. Proponents
of the **shared-risk rationale** viewed compensation
as part of the "safety net " of the comprehensive
social insurance system that had been developing in
the United States since the Great Depression. All
public welfare insurance programs are intended to
enable people to cope with the hazards that threaten
stability and security in everyday life. Health expenses are addressed by Medicaid and Medicare,
disability and untimely death by Social Security,
on-the-job accidents by workers' compensation,
and loss of work and earnings by unemployment
compensation. The premiums for these state-run
compulsory insurance plans are derived from taxation. Criminal injury insurance, like the other types
of coverage, provides equal protection against dangers that are reasonably certain to harm some members of society but are unpredictable for any given
individual. All taxpayers contribute to the pool to
spread the costs, and therefore everyone is entitled to
reimbursement.

The **government-liability rationale** argues
that the state is responsible for the safety of its citizens because it monopolizes, or reserves for itself,
the right to use force to suppress crime and to punish offenders. Because individuals are not allowed to
routinely carry deadly weapons around for their
own defense wherever they go, the government
has made it difficult for law-abiding people to protect themselves. Therefore, within the social contract, the state becomes liable for damages when its
criminal justice system fails to fulfill its public safety
obligation to its citizens. By the logic of this argument, innocents who have been harmed ought to
have a right to compensation, regardless of their
economic standing and the type of loss they have
suffered.

Those who take a **social-welfare approach**
believe that the state has a humanitarian responsibility to assist victims, just as it helps other needy
and disadvantaged groups. The aid is given as a
symbolic act of mercy, compassion, and charity—
and not as universal insurance coverage or because
of any legal obligation. According to this theory,
receiving compensation is a privilege, not a right,
so eligibility and payment amounts can be limited.

Besides these three rationales, several additional
arguments were advanced to encourage public acceptance of compensation. Some sociologists and criminologists put forward a **social-justice rationale**.
It contended that the "system" (the institutions, economic and political arrangements, and prevailing
relationships within society) generates crime by
perpetuating intense competition, discrimination,
unemployment, financial insecurity, and poverty,
which in turn breed greed, desperation, stealing,
and violence. Therefore, society owes compensation
through its governmental agencies to people who are
harmed through no fault of their own.

Other advocates contrasted the attention accorded to criminals with the neglect shown toward
their innocent victims. They charged that it was
blatantly unfair to attend to many of the medical,
dental, emotional, educational, vocational, and legal
needs of wrongdoers (albeit minimally and sometimes against their will) at public expense while at
the same time abandoning injured victims to fend
for themselves. Compensation partly corrected this
"imbalance." Finally, some pragmatists anticipated
that the prospect of monetary rewards would induce more victims to cooperate with the authorities
by reporting incidents, pressing charges, and testifying against their assailants.

Skeptics and critics objected to the notion of
government intervention on both philosophical and
practical grounds. The earliest opponents of im-
porting this British Commonwealth practice to
the United States denounced what they considered
to be the spread of "governmental paternalism"
and "creeping socialism." They contended that
taxpayer-funded crime insurance undermined the
virtues of rugged individualism, self-reliance, personal responsibility, independence, saving for

emergencies, and calculated risk taking. They considered an expansion of the "welfare state" and the growth of new, expensive, and remote bureaucracies to be greater evils than the fiscal neglect of victims. They contended that, unlike governmental bodies, private enterprises could write more effective and efficient insurance policies for families that had enough prudence and foresight to purchase protection before tragedy struck. Other opponents worried that criminal-injury insurance—like fire, auto, and theft coverage—was vulnerable to fraud. Deserving applicants would be hard to distinguish from manipulators who staged incidents, inflicted their own wounds, and padded their bills.

Finally, certain critics did not dispute the merits of compensation programs but objected to their establishment and expansion on financial grounds. They argued that it was unfair to compel taxpayers to repay victims' losses, as well as to foot the bill for the costs of the police, courts, and keeping convicts in prisons. To accommodate this objection, state programs have come to rely more heavily on raising money from penalties imposed on lawbreakers of all kinds, including traffic law violators, rather than taxpayers (see Childres, 1964; Schultz, 1965; Wolfgang, 1965; Brooks, 1972; Geis, 1976; Meiners, 1978; Carrow, 1980; U.S. House Committee on the Judiciary, 1980; Gaynes, 1981; Elias, 1983a).

A statistical analysis of congressional votes on bills between 1965 and 1980 revealed that Democrats (particularly liberal Democrats) tended to favor allocating federal aid to reimburse crime victims; Republicans (especially conservative Republicans) tended to oppose spending federal tax dollars on state compensation programs. The usual exceptions to these patterns were conservative Democrats (generally from southern states) who sided with conservative Republicans against compensation plans, and some liberal Republicans (often from northern states) who joined with liberal Democrats in support of these pro-victim legislative initiatives. In other words, ideology proved to be a better predictor of voting behavior than party affiliation (Karmen, 1981b).

In 1984, Congress finally reached a consensus about the appropriate role for the federal government on the question of compensation and passed a Victims of Crime Act (VOCA), ending nearly 20 years of floor debates, lobbying, political posturing, maneuvering, and last-minute compromises. VOCA established a fund within the U.S. Treasury, collected from fines, penalties, and forfeitures. Administered by the attorney general, the money was earmarked to subsidize state compensation funds and victim assistance services, and to aid victims of federal crimes (Peak, 1986). In 1989, VOCA guidelines were revised to encourage state programs to expand coverage and to resemble each other more closely. Providing federal matching funds worked out as intended: Every state had set up a compensation program by 1993 (Maine and South Dakota were the last to participate).

How Programs Operate: Similarities and Differences

In all states plus the District of Columbia, Puerto Rico, Guam, and the U.S. Virgin Islands, the question of whether to compensate victims has been answered for the time being. But the programs vary in many ways, reflecting the diversity in the traditions, populations, crime rates, and resources of the states and the differing rationales on which the programs were based.

Certain requirements are the same in each state (see Parent, Auerbach, and Carlson, 1992). All of the programs grant reimbursements only to "innocent" victims. Compensation board investigators always look for evidence of contributory misconduct. If it is established that the individual was partly to blame for getting hurt, the grant can be reduced in size or disallowed entirely. For example, applicants would not be repaid if they were engaging in an illegal activity when they were wounded (such as being shot while holding up a liquor store, being stabbed while buying drugs, or being beaten after agreeing to perform an act of prostitution). Most boards would rule injured parties in barroom brawls ineligible if they had been drinking, uttered "fighting words" and provoked the fracas in which they were seriously hurt. However, applicants can appeal claims that were denied.

Another common feature is that the programs deal only with the most serious crimes that result in physical injury, psychological trauma, or death: murder, rape, assault, robbery, child sexual abuse, child physical abuse, spouse abuse, other types of domestic violence, and also hit-and-run motor vehicle collisions caused by drunk drivers. Most do not repay people for property that is damaged or lost in thefts, burglaries, or robberies (unless they are elderly or their possessions are essential, such as hearing aids or wheelchairs). Only out-of-pocket expenses are reimbursed: bills not paid by collateral sources such as Medicaid or private insurance such as Blue Cross. Payments can be for medical expenses, mental health services, dental bills, and earnings lost because of missed work. Families of individuals who succumb to their wounds are eligible for assistance with reasonable funeral and burial costs; dependents can qualify for a death benefit or pension to compensate for their loss of financial support. Some states go further and pay for the services of home health aides and housekeepers, child care, transportation costs for medical treatments and court appearances, and even for relocation when necessary (New Jersey Victims of Crime Compensation Agency, 2008). Each program requires that all parts of a claim be fully documented with bills and receipts. Every program prohibits double recoveries. Money collected from insurance policies or other government sources (such as Veteran's Benefits) is **subrogated** (subtracted) from the compensation board's final award. In the statistically unusual cases in which offenders are caught, found guilty, and forced to pay restitution, this money is also deducted from the award. For a claimant to be repaid, the assailant does not have to be caught and convicted. But in every state the applicant must report the crime promptly to the police and cooperate fully with any investigation and prosecution to remain eligible.

Despite sharing these basic features, the fifty state programs differ in many ways: how long victims can wait before telling the police about the crime (from one day to three months, with a mode of three days); how long victims can take before applying for reimbursement (from six months

to three years, with a mode of one year); how much claimants can collect (maximum awards of $1,000 to $50,000 plus limitless medical expenses, with modes at $10,000 and $25,000); whether the program will grant an emergency loan before fully investigating a case; and whether lawyers can be hired to help present cases and collect fees. Eligibility rules differ slightly from state to state. For example, survivors of those who are slain can include parents, siblings, and in-laws in some programs, but most states limit coverage only to children and spouses.

In 1988, amendments to the Victims of Crimes Act mandated that eligibility in all states be extended to innocent family members injured by domestic violence, people hurt by drunk driving crashes, and nonresidents (visitors and commuters). Some states have gone further in expanding the list of covered individuals and offenses. For example, besides victims of violence such as kidnappings and carjackings, New Jersey compensates individuals injured in hit-and-run collisions, people sickened by drug and food tampering, bystanders hurt by criminals trying to elude the police, and people brought in to the state by human traffickers (New Jersey Victims of Crime Compensation Agency, 2008). New York's Victim Compensation Board (2008) will consider claims from individuals who were not physically injured if they were Good Samaritans or suffered from stalking, harassment, menacing, unlawful imprisonment, or even frivolous counter-lawsuits by offenders.

On the other hand, whole groups of people can be automatically ruled ineligible. In each state the list varies. Law enforcement officers and firefighters injured in the line of duty generally are excluded because they are covered by Workers' Compensation. In some jurisdictions, prison inmates, parolees, probationers, ex-convicts, and members of organized crime are automatically eliminated from consideration (National Institute of Justice, 1998). In eight states, all persons with a felony conviction are ineligible for aid, even if their current predicament has nothing to do with their past illegal activities (Mitchell, 2008).

Many trends in compensation regulations are worth noting. One change over time has been to broaden coverage to include the cost of cleaning up a crime scene, and replacing essential personal property such as eyeglasses and false teeth. In just a handful of states, money is available to offset pain and suffering. Some programs extend eligibility to include incest survivors, people who were sexually assaulted but escaped without physical injuries, the elderly whose homes were burglarized, and parents of missing children.

Initially, the money given out by compensation programs came from general revenues, which essentially means from taxpayers. The trend since the 1970s is to rely more heavily on funds derived from **penalty assessments** or abusers' taxes (more than half of the programs get all or part of their money this way). These funds are raised from fines and surcharges levied on persons convicted of traffic violations, misdemeanors, and felonies. Some states impose taxes on the earnings of offenders on work release and from collateral forfeited by defendants who jump bail. Offender-funded compensation programs reflect a larger trend that compels convicts in some jurisdictions to shoulder all kinds of financial obligations, including restitution, charges for room and board, fines, court costs, and supervision fees. By the start of the 21st century, 90 percent of state and federal funding came from money extracted from offenders. Taxpayer dollars supplemented these limited and unpredictable revenues in only 13 states. Although making wrongdoers pay their collective debts has symbolic value as a form of group restitution, albeit indirect and impersonal, this is an insufficient source of money to meet all the critical needs of the eligible and worthy claimants seeking financial aid (Herman and Waul, 2004).

Before the 1980s, in about one-third of the states, only claimants who faced severe financial hardships could pass a **means test** to become eligible for reimbursement. The others were told they could afford to absorb their losses. By the end of the 1980s, only 11 programs still required their applicants to establish a dire fiscal need before receiving an award. Encouraged by VOCA's financial support, some states have raised the upper limits for awards because of substantial hikes in the cost of living over the years. In the other states with frozen

maximum benefits (still usually capped at $25,000, even after years of rising prices), compensation payments are failing to keep up with the rate of inflation. Minimum loss requirements and deductible provisions (usually of $100) designed to eliminate minor claims are being scrapped and persist in less than half the states (NOVA, 1988; Parent et al., 1992; NIJ, 1998; and NACVCB, 2008).

Monitoring and Evaluating Compensation Programs

Many arguments about the rightness of compensation hinge on judgments about the type of financial help victims require and on assumptions about the ability of programs to meet these needs. Because many states have operated programs for several decades, a substantial body of data is available for analysis. The differences between state programs can be considered an asset: each jurisdiction can be regarded as a social laboratory where an experiment is in progress. From this viewpoint, various approaches to achieving the same ends are tested to determine which works best. Evaluation is especially important as a means of improving service delivery during periods when the public clamors for additional government aid but is unwilling to pay higher taxes for it.

Program evaluations reveal how well compensation boards are meeting their goals. But assessing whether they are succeeding or failing in their mission requires a clear statement of goals. In the 1960s, the early advocates of reimbursing victims from government-administered funds had ambitious expectations and made optimistic (and perhaps unrealistic) pronouncements. Their noble, charitable, and humanitarian aims of substantially alleviating the economic suffering of injured parties generally have not been realized. Statistics that either support or refute other contentions can be derived from two assessments: process evaluations and impact evaluations.

Uncovering How Programs Work Process evaluations focus on the programs' internal operations and monitor variables such as productivity, overhead costs, and decision-making patterns. Assessments of the efficiency of administrative practices contribute to efforts to eliminate delays, minimize overhead, and iron out inequities. Process evaluations also develop profiles of the typical claimants and recipients of awards. Analyzing data bearing on these questions allows evaluators to provide useful feedback to administrators and board members about trends and patterns that characterize their efforts.

Two process evaluations of a sample of the 50 state funds in operation at the end of the 1980s (Parent et al., 1992) and the start of the 1990s (Sarnoff, 1996) shed light on aspects of how compensation programs actually work. The programs in the survey's sample granted aid to about two-thirds of the applicants. Most of the funds' revenue was raised from fines and penalty assessments levied on all kinds of law violators (including drivers who committed traffic infractions), with the rest derived from general appropriations (taxes), and from the federal government in grants from the Victims of Crime Act (VOCA). Most claims concerned drunk driving crashes, homicides, rapes, robberies, aggravated assaults, and child abuse cases. Very few claims arose from spouse abuse. The volume of cases handled per year varied dramatically by population size and crime rate. Case-processing time (how long it took to resolve a claim) ranged from one month to two years, with a mean of 18 weeks. To aid victims during the interim, most states granted small emergency awards. Some programs were run more efficiently than others, in terms of administrative costs as a percentage of total expenditures.

As for decision-making patterns, denial rates indicated that some boards were much stricter than others. Denials can be issued for technical reasons, such as failure to supply sufficient documentation of expenses; and for fault, such as the stigmatizing moral judgment that the claimant was guilty of contributory misconduct. Some boards seemed more generous, while others were determined to refute the charges that they "gave money away" and were vulnerable to fraud and abuse.

The average award ranged from a low of nearly $700 to a high of roughly $9,000 (in a state where attorney's fees were covered). The rate of compensation, calculated as a proportion (crimes that were compensated compared to reported crimes committed in that state that year that potentially could have been eligible for compensation) also showed tremendous variation. It ranged from a low of 1 percent to a high of 91 percent and averaged 19 percent. The number of "unserved" victims a year in the late 1980s was estimated to be 55 percent of all potentially eligible persons (innocent, injured, suffering out-of-pocket expenses). In other words, despite outreach efforts (such as public service announcements and posters in police stations and hospital emergency rooms), more than half of all possible beneficiaries did not know their rights and/or did not even file a claim. Some state program administrators estimated that 67 percent, maybe even 95 percent, of eligible victims did not apply for financial aid. Of course, if more eligible people had been aware of their rights and sought reimbursement, their claims would have taken even longer to process. Also, the boards either would have had to cut back on the average size of awards or turn down a greater proportion of applicants, unless the directors could somehow raise more money (Parent et al., 1992; Sarnoff, 1996). Setting up storefront offices to accept claims from people living in high-crime areas might help to achieve the objective of reaching the maximum number of deserving individuals in the most effective and efficient manner possible (McCormack, 1991).

The findings from process evaluations about insufficient funding and inadequate outreach confirm that compensation plans are failing to live up to their humanitarian commitments. Because of their limited budgets, many boards maintain low profiles or even face prohibitions against advertising. Lack of interest on the part of police, prosecutors, and hospital emergency room personnel might also be a continuing problem. Some injured parties might be deterred by complex filing procedures and detailed probes into their personal finances (to prevent fraud). Others are discouraged when they hear about high rejection rates, long waits, and disappointingly small awards. On one hand, even with low rates of applications and awards, under-funded programs can run out of money before the year is over (McGillis and Smith, 1983; Sanderson, 1994). On the other hand, inadequate outreach efforts can result in surpluses if injured parties don't realize that they can be reimbursed for expenses such as crime-scene cleanups, counseling, and rehabilitation services ("New Jersey," 2002).

In 1995, state compensation programs across the country paid nearly $250 million to about 120,000 people harmed by violent crimes. Victims of assault (47 percent) and child abuse (especially sexual abuse) (12 percent) were the most numerous recipients. Almost half of the money went to cover medical expenses, and most of the rest was reimbursement for lost wages, mental health treatment, and funeral expenses. The national average for an award was close to $2,000. About a decade later (fiscal year 2007), even though crime rates were down, the number of recipients was up to about 200,000, and the payout total had climbed to more than $450 million. A little more than half the reimbursements were for medical expenses. About $23 million was spent on covering the costs of forensic examinations for those who had been sexually assaulted. The proportion of financial aid recipients who were abused children rose to nearly 20 percent. Assault victims (especially of domestic violence) continued to be the largest group getting monetary help (NACVCB, 2008).

Measuring the Effects of Programs   Impact evaluations are carried out to compare a program's intentions with its actual accomplishments. The studies reveal the consequences of a program for its clients and the community. To determine whether compensation really eases financial stress, the ratio of award payments to submitted losses can be calculated. To assess a program's impact on the participation of compensated complainants in the criminal justice system, those who did and did not receive aid can be compared, in terms of their attendance rates as witnesses in police lineups and court proceedings. The diversity of structures and procedures in different state programs provides opportunities to test which arrangements work best under what conditions.

The findings of research and evaluation studies can have important consequences for the future of compensation. Determining successes and failures can help to resolve the ongoing debates over the pros and cons of compensating crime victims with public funds and the merits and shortcomings of particular rules and practices (Chappell and Sutton, 1974; Carrow, 1980; NIJ, 1998).

The findings of several impact evaluations do not support the hypothesis that the prospect of reimbursement would increase the public's degree of cooperation with law enforcement. In the 1970s, when reporting rates for violent crimes in states with programs were compared with the rates in states without programs, no appreciable differences were found (Doerner, 1978). Comparing the attitudes of claimants in Florida who were granted awards to those whose requests were denied revealed that being repaid did not significantly improve a victim's ratings of the quality of performance of the police, prosecutors, or judges (Doerner and Lab, 1980).

More information is needed about the impact of board decisions on the psychological and economic well-being of physically injured applicants. Those who were rejected because of what they perceived to be mere "technicalities" (such as waiting too long before filing) might feel cheated. Insensitive treatment, lengthy background investigations, extensive delays, and partial reimbursements can make even successful claimants feel victimized once again (McGillis and Smith, 1983).

One researcher who evaluated the New York and New Jersey programs concluded that claimants ended up more alienated from the criminal justice system than nonclaimants. Instead of reducing public discontent with the police and courts, compensation programs provoked additional frustrations. Applicants' expectations probably rose when they first learned about the chance of reimbursement, but these hopes were consistently frustrated when most claimants, for a variety of reasons, were turned down or awarded insufficient funds to cover their documented expenses. Three-quarters indicated that they would not apply for compensation again if they were victimized a second time, largely because of their displeasure over delays, eligibility requirements, incidental expenses, inconveniences, their treatment by program administrators, and, ultimately, the inadequacy of their reimbursements (Elias, 1983a).

The enactment of compensation programs might have been merely an exercise in "symbolic politics." This judgment accuses certain manipulative politicians of voting for programs that look impressive on paper because they want to appear to be "doing something for victims," but these elected officials fail to allocate the necessary resources to make the promise a reality. Nevertheless, the public is favorably impressed by the foresight and concern shown by policymakers and legislators toward victims. Unaware that the majority of claimants are turned down and that the remainder is largely dissatisfied, voters are led to believe that an effective safety net has been set up to cushion the blows of violent crime (Elias, 1983b, 1986).

In sum, four longstanding problems undermine the effectiveness of these programs. First, outreach is inadequate: Too many injured parties are unaware that they are eligible for reimbursement. Only 4 percent of violent crime victims nationwide applied for compensation from state programs in 2002. Second, eligibility is too restrictive: Too many claimants are turned down because of overly strict requirements. Third, the awards that successful applicants receive too often are not enough to bail them out of their financial predicaments. And fourth, money derived from penalizing and fining lawbreakers never is sufficient to meet critical needs (Herman and Waul, 2004).

And yet, the swift action by Congress to establish the September 11th Victim Compensation Fund demonstrates that governmental organizations are capable of taking creative, resourceful, sustained, compassionate, and generous steps to help people rebuild their lives. Could those same unprecedented efforts that aided the more than 4,400 individuals directly injured by the terrorist attack and the nearly 3,000 survivor families be mobilized on a routine basis to assist the 23 million people harmed annually by "ordinary" crimes, advocates ask?

Inspired by the September 11 fund, victim advocates called for many reforms. All innocent parties should be eligible for compensation, not only people injured by violence. All crime-related losses should be reimbursed, and time limits shouldn't be imposed on ongoing problems (such as PTSD). Everyone who files a complaint with the police should be informed about and helped to fill out a claim. The process of granting aid should be fair, respectful, efficient, and easy to understand. Income tax relief should be granted to offset victims' losses (currently most do not lose enough money to qualify for tax deductions). Tax revenue should supplement the inadequate funding raised from offender penalties. Legislatures should determine the best practices already implemented in the various states, as well as in compensation programs in other countries, advocates suggest (Herman and Waul, 2004).

CONFISCATING PROFITS FROM NOTORIOUS CRIMINALS

A lone gunman terrorizes New Yorkers, carrying out ambushes that leave six people dead and many others wounded. Dubbed the "Son of Sam" as well as the "44-Caliber Killer" by the media, he is eventually caught, convicted, and sentenced to a lifetime behind bars. From his cell, he grants interviews to writers and accumulates about $90,000 in royalties from publishers. The individuals he shot and the families of the people he killed sue him to prevent him from benefiting from his notoriety. Eight years later, his attorneys arrive at a settlement: All the money he gained will be divided among those he harmed, and they will share any additional earnings he might receive. (Associated Press, 1984a)

***

A man attempts to rob a bank but bungles the job and winds up taking four employees hostage when his escape route is blocked by the police. After a lengthy siege the four are released, and he is captured, convicted, and imprisoned. Hollywood producers pay him $100,000 for the rights to depict his exploits in the movie "Dog Day Afternoon." The money is seized by the New York State Crime Victims Board and apportioned out to his kidnap victims, his lawyers (to whom he owed fees), and his former wife (for alimony and child support payments). (Roberts, 1987)

One additional option for recovering losses remains open to just a handful of victims or their survivors: going after the profits made by offenders who sell their firsthand accounts of how and why they committed their high-profile crimes. Cases such as the two landmark suits cited above dramatize how victims can fight back when offenders seize opportunities to cash in on the sensationalism surrounding their well-publicized exploits. The practical issue that arises is when and how victims can take these "fruits of crime" away from convicts.

Writing and Rewriting the Law

In 1977, the New York State legislature passed a forfeiture of assets bill to prevent a vicious serial killer (cited in the first example above) from being showered with lucrative offers for book contracts, movie rights, and paid appearances to tell his inside story. In the years that followed, nearly all states and the federal government enacted similar "Son of Sam" laws to head off any financial exploitation of the retelling of criminal acts by their perpetrators and media corporations, and spare victims renewed anguish from the ensuing publicity. Public opinion backed this legislative trend. In one poll, 86 percent of the respondents favored a law that would take away profits gained by notorious criminals and distribute this money to their victims (National Victim Center, 1991a).

These statutes went after financial windfalls: fees, advances, and royalties from re-enactments of the heinous deeds in movies, memoirs, books, magazine articles, tape recordings, records, radio programs, television shows, or other forms of entertainment. If offenders (whether accused or convicted) were

paid for expressing their thoughts, opinions, or feelings about their depredations, or for giving graphic descriptions about these acts, their income could be seized by the government and placed in an escrow account before they could spend it.

For up to five years, individuals who had incurred direct physical or mental injuries or financial losses could argue in civil court that they were entitled to a portion of that money. In some states leftover funds not awarded in damage lawsuits could revert back to the offenders. But in other jurisdictions any remaining money could be used to cover unpaid attorneys' fees plus the court costs arising from the prosecution or to replenish the state's victim compensation fund (Stark and Goldstein, 1985; NOVA, 1988). However, whenever a notorious offender was found guilty of a political crime, or a white-collar swindle, or a vice offense such as running a lucrative prostitution ring or trafficking in drugs, the legal issue of exactly which individuals were entitled to carve up these ill-gotten gains became very complicated.

Notoriety-for-profit laws were primarily symbolic gestures intended to drive home the message that crime doesn't pay. They also were designed to facilitate handing over money to injured parties— but from the outset, these laws were controversial. Critics argued that the confiscation of payments by government had a chilling effect on the First Amendment's guarantee of freedom of expression. In 1991, the justices of the Supreme Court agreed and by a vote of 9 to 0 struck down New York's law and all the others like it in various states. In its unanimous opinion (*Simon and Schuster v. New York State Crime Victims Board*), the Court recognized that states had an undisputed compelling interest to deprive offenders of profits derived from illegal activities, and were pursuing a worthwhile goal in trying to transfer the proceeds from criminals to their victims. However, the justices argued that enacting these overly broad state laws unfairly singled out a convict's "speech-derived income" for a special tax burden and thereby established an inhibiting financial disincentive to create or publish works with a particular content. Publishers, filmmakers, and civil libertarians hailed the Court's landmark ruling as a victory for authors and their audiences. The critics noted that a substantial body of worthwhile literature and redeeming commentary by notable prisoners might never had been written if those laws were in force years ago.

But victims' advocates denounced the Court's decision as a blow to victims' rights. They undertook the task of redrafting provisions about lawsuits, statutes of limitation, fines, forfeitures, and escrow accounts so that they would meet constitutional standards. Soon, state legislatures passed revised "Son of Sam" laws that do not single out royalties from books or movies but target any and all assets these convicts accrue (Fein, 1991; Alexander, 1992). Several states have gone even further, and prohibit law enforcement officials (such as detectives, prosecutors, defense attorneys, judges, and witnesses) from making money by telling about their roles in high profile cases from the time of indictment until the completion of appeals (NCVC, 2008).

However, victims and survivors still face an uphill battle to collect what they believe is due them, as the following account illustrates.

A prisoner writes a book about the nightmare of growing up behind bars in juvenile institutions and state prisons. The inmate's insightful life story sells so well that it becomes the basis for a play, and well-known writers help him to get parole. But just six weeks after he is released, he becomes embroiled in an argument with a waiter over the use of the restaurant's restroom, and stabs him to death. After he is sentenced to prison for manslaughter, the waiter's young widow sues him in civil court. The inmate, representing himself, asserts that the waiter's life "was not worth a dime," but the jury awards her more than $7.5 million. Over the next decade or so, the inmate earns about $115,000 in royalties from his several books and plays, yet the widow collects less than $50,000. In the meantime, he launches two counter-lawsuits against her. Exercising her right to appear before the parole board, she argues against his early release. When he is turned down, the infamous convict-author hangs himself in his cell. "After what he put us through," the widow asserts, "it's more than a relief, it's fresh air. What goes around comes around." (Halbfinger, 2002)

SUMMARY

Victims can try to recover their financial losses in several ways. Restitution payments directly from the offender's earnings seem to be a fair and appropriate method of reimbursement and may provide a solid foundation for redemption and eventual reconciliation. Restitution may be viewed as an additional penalty, but also as a way to sensitize and rehabilitate lawbreakers. Unfortunately, many victims never receive any money because their offenders are not caught, convicted, and sentenced to restitution, or are unable or unwilling to earn adequate amounts of money to pay meaningful installments.

Victims can attempt to sue their offenders in civil court for compensatory and punitive damages. As plaintiffs they have a better chance of winning against defendants than in criminal court because the standard of proof—a preponderance of the evidence—is easier to meet than guilt beyond a reasonable doubt. However, only offenders who are identified and who have substantial exposed assets can be sued successfully. If criminals are not caught or have no tangible assets, victims might be able to launch lawsuits against third parties such as businesses or criminal justice agencies that acted with such gross negligence that innocent parties were harmed in predictable ways by dangerous individuals.

Private insurance coverage can repay losses from assaults, car thefts, burglaries, robberies, and slayings. But many victims could not afford the premiums, did not have the foresight to take out a policy, or could not find a company that would sell them coverage at reasonable rates.

Victim compensation funds have been set up in most states since the 1960s, although they initially met considerable political resistance. Injured parties may receive reimbursement even if the perpetrators are not caught and convicted. However, only innocent victims of violent crimes, not people who have suffered losses from property crimes, currently are eligible for financial aid that covers lost earnings and out-of-pocket medical expenses. Many state funds do not have enough money from penalty assessments and the general treasury to quickly and adequately reimburse all eligible applicants. A small number of individuals might be able to launch lawsuits to claim a portion of the money that certain convicts who viciously harmed them made by cashing in on their notoriety.

KEY TERMS

community service, 338

symbolic restitution, 338

creative restitution, 338

composition, 339

torts, 339

funneling or shrinkage, 342

plaintiffs, 348

defendants, 348

judgments, 348

punitive damages, 348

compensatory damages, 348

pecuniary damages, 348

wrongful death, 349

battery, 349

trespass, 349

conversion of chattel, 349

false imprisonment, 349

second party, 349

pleading, 349

causes of action, 349

process server, 349

first party, 349

discovery, 349

interrogatories, 349

depositions, 350

statute of limitations, 350

attached, 350

garnisheed, 350

contingency fees, 351

preponderance of the evidence, 350

default judgment, 351

pain and suffering, 351

contingency fees, 351

deep pockets, 352

judgment-proof, 352

third parties, 352

negligence, 352

sovereign immunity, 354

nonfeasance, 354

malfeasance, 354

wrongful escape, 355

failure to warn, 355

wrongful release, 355

abuse of discretionary authority, 355

false positives, 355

false negatives, 355

deductible clauses, 356

double indemnity clause, 356

redlining, 357

shared-risk rationale, 360

government-liability rationale, 360

social-welfare approach, 360

social-justice rationale, 360

subrogated, 362

penalty assessments, 363

means test, 363

QUESTIONS FOR DISCUSSION AND DEBATE

1. Explain how restitution can serve many distinct purposes.

2. Review the advantages and disadvantages victims face when they sue offenders in civil court.

3. Why are third-party lawsuits potentially lucrative to victims but also highly controversial?

4. Summarize the arguments that favor the establishment of victim compensation funds by

state governments using tax revenue. Then present arguments that state governments should not provide financial reimbursement to victims.

5. Why is there so much controversy surrounding laws that compel criminals to repay their victims from any profits they gain from their notoriety?

CRITICAL THINKING QUESTIONS

1. Devise a restitution program that would place burglars and robbers in jobs that pay a living wage so that they could repay their victims in installments in a reasonable amount of time. Then anticipate the objections that might be raised against this program.

2. Even though many possible sources of reimbursement exist—court-ordered restitution, private insurance coverage, state compensation funds, civil lawsuits, and "notoriety-for-profit" laws—why do so many victims still fail to receive any repayment of their losses and expenses?

SUGGESTED RESEARCH PROJECTS

1. Locate and interview lawyers who have handled civil lawsuits on behalf of victims. Ask them about their victories and defeats. Were any of the suits against third parties? Find out the details.

2. Locate and interview insurance agents in your area who have handled claims by crime victims. What kinds of losses did these policyholders incur, and what kinds of injuries did they sustain? Were these customers fully reimbursed for out-of-pocket expenses? If not, why not?

3. Look up information on the Internet about the state compensation fund in your hometown or in the jurisdiction of your college. See if the fund issues an annual report. What are the eligibility requirements? What are the caps that limit payments, and what proportion of applicants received awards? What was the average amount of compensation that successful applicants were granted, and for what kinds of expenses were they reimbursed? How long did the process take, on average?

13

Victims in the Twenty-First Century: Alternative Directions

How will victims fare during the rest of the twenty-first century? The answer to that question depends on how several of today's contradictory tendencies work themselves out. On the one hand, the victims' movement is waging a successful campaign to gain additional formal legal rights within the criminal justice system. Activists and advocacy groups want to empower victims so they can be treated with fundamental fairness and exercise greater influence over how their cases are resolved.

B O X 13.1   Dramatic Examples of Victim Activism

Mobilizing against drunk drivers
A mother whose teenage daughter was run over by an intoxicated driver starts a group that successfully changes public attitudes about mixing drinking with driving and persuades criminal justice officials that people injured in drunk driving collisions are victims of crimes—not accidents.

Assisting law enforcement agencies to track down fugitives
A father whose son is kidnapped and decapitated by a killer who is never caught hosts a television program that broadcasts cases from police departments' "most wanted" lists so viewers can phone in tips to capture these suspects.

Covering trials of the rich and famous from a pro-victim angle
A novelist and journalist whose actress daughter is murdered by her lover writes a book about attending her killer's trial and hosts a television program that

focuses on powerful and privileged people who get in trouble with the law.

Assisting the search for missing children
A father whose 12-year-old daughter was abducted and murdered establishes a foundation that helps to locate missing children.

Setting up one of the first victims' rights organizations
A wealthy woman may have been poisoned by her husband (his original conviction for attempted murder was overturned and he was acquitted after a second trial; she remained in a coma for 28 years before dying in 2008). Her son and daughter, convinced that their mother's coma resulted from a crime, use a portion of her fortune to found one of the first organizations that helps all kinds of victims.

Compelling college administrations to publicize information about crimes on campus
The parents of a daughter whose murder in a dormitory was initially played down by college

---

On the other hand, some individuals and groups are moving away from the arena of formal legal rights to explore informal alternatives. Within this tendency toward informal handling are two opposite currents. One leads participants on a quest to settle differences between people embroiled in conflicts in ways that are not as adversarial and legalistic. In this new paradigm of restorative justice, victim-offender reconciliation is the goal, restitution arranged through mediation is the method, and a neighborhood justice center or community-based program is the setting. This search for another forum to resolve disputes is spurred on by a belief that it is unrealistic to attempt to compel a criminal justice system controlled by powerful interests to become more responsive and accountable to the ostensible "clients" or "consumers" of its services. But an opposite current within informal handling rejects this peacemaking approach and reverts to earlier, more violent methods of settling conflicts. These solutions include the legitimate use of force

in self-defense but can drift beyond the limits of the law into acts of vigilantism, in which victims and their allies retaliate against their alleged offenders to make sure they are punished. The situation of victims in the years ahead will be shaped by the interaction of these three tendencies.

TOWARD GREATER FORMAL LEGAL RIGHTS WITHIN THE CRIMINAL JUSTICE SYSTEM

The struggle to gain legal guarantees has been a powerful motivation throughout history. Legal rights serve as a remedy for injustice and abuse as well as a basis for independent and autonomous action. A number of movements seeking liberation, empowerment, equality, and social justice have sought greater rights for their constituencies; the most authorities set up a watchdog group that convinces Congress to impose crime reporting requirements on image-conscious university administrations.

Campaigning for restrictions on gun availability
A White House press secretary, who was shot in the head by an assassin aiming to kill the president, becomes a leading figure along with his wife in legislative efforts to make it more difficult for emotionally volatile and mentally disturbed people to buy handguns.

A nurse, whose husband is shot dead and whose son is severely injured by a man who goes berserk on a commuter train and shoots passengers at random, testifies so dramatically for stricter controls over handguns and assault weapons before Congress that she is later elected to the House of Representatives.

Mobilizing for community notification laws
The parents of a seven-year-old girl, who was raped and murdered by a recently released pedophile living across the street, help to gather support for state and federal legislation that authorizes criminal justice officials to alert the public whenever a convicted sex offender moves into their neighborhood.

Establishing a support group for parents of murdered children
A mother and father whose daughter was slain by her boyfriend set up a self-help group for grieving families that not only serves their emotional needs during their bereavement but also promotes violence prevention activities and lobbies for greater rights for the next of kin within the legal process.

Organizing a national coalition of victim activists
A murdered young woman's parents establish a network of survivors and activists that pledges to be "of the victims, by the victims, and for the victims" in its support and crime prevention actions.

SOURCE: Wikipedia; Rondeau and Rondeau, 2006; National Coalition of Victims in Action (2008).

well-known and influential include the civil rights, women's rights, workers' rights, consumers' rights, students' rights, children's rights, gay rights, patients' rights, and prisoners' rights movements. The **victims' rights** movement that arose during the 1970s falls within this reformist tradition. Many of its most effective activists suffered terrible losses themselves or are close family members of people who perished. These exemplary and resilient crusaders, chosen by fate to become organizers and leaders, channeled their grief and anger into constructive outlets that advanced the cause along many different fronts (see Box 13.1).

The legal rights of journalists, political activists, criminal defendants, and convicts have been derived from the safeguards and guarantees specified in the first 10 amendments to the Constitution, which taken together are referred to as the Bill of Rights. But the framers of the Constitution did not enumerate any rights for crime victims. The pledges, entitlements, privileges, benefits, options, practices, and opportunities for redress commonly known as victims' rights flow from several different sources.

A few rights originated as idiosyncratic policies adopted by certain caring and innovative officials, such as police chiefs, district attorneys, trial judges, and probation officers. Other rights were derived from case law based on court decisions. The remainder was established by laws passed by city and county governments, statutes enacted by state legislatures, acts approved by Congress, and referenda placed on the ballot by advocacy groups and endorsed by voters. As a result, an inconsistent assortment of rights has developed that varies markedly from state to state, jurisdiction (county or municipality) to jurisdiction, and even courthouse to courthouse. However, one trend is certain: Since the 1960s, victims' rights have been proliferating in the legislative arena and expanding geographically. A self-reinforcing cycle is operating: As more victims become aware of their rights and begin to exercise them, these rights become accepted and honored within the criminal justice system. These victories encourage victims and their allies to raise new demands for further rights (Stark and Goldstein, 1985; Viano, 1987).

The Sixth Amendment contains provisions that specify how defendants are to be handled in court. Activists and advocacy groups first raised the possibility of adding pro-victim language to the Sixth Amendment after a presidential task force recommended rewording it in 1982. But in 1986, reformers decided to postpone this plan in favor of concentrating on a "state's first" strategy of securing amendments to state constitutions. By 2007, this approach had succeeded in thirty states (Cassell, 2007). Also, since 1980, almost every state legislature has passed packages of statutes called a Victim's Bill of Rights. The common threads running through these amendments and Bill of Rights packages were these promises to victims: to be handled with fairness, respect, and dignity; to be notified in a timely manner about, to be present at, and to be heard at important judicial proceedings; to promptly get back stolen property that was recovered and held as evidence; to be protected from intimidation and harassment; and to receive restitution or compensation (NVC, 1991a; NCVC, 1996; News Wire Services, 2000).

The National Victim Constitutional Amendment Network's campaign to insert additional phrases into the Sixth Amendment reignited during 1996, when a large number of Republicans and Democrats in both the House and the Senate co-sponsored a bill that received support from many elected officials, including President Bill Clinton. But opponents threatened a filibuster, so the backers of the victims' rights amendment pulled the measure from the Senate floor in 2000. They reintroduced a revised version in 2002 and again in 2003, which received the endorsement of President George Bush and his attorney general. The amendment was introduced again in the House of Representatives at the end of 2007. Both parties incorporated pledges to respect the rights of crime victims in their platforms during the 2008 presidential campaign (NVCAP, 2008).

Proponents of this movement to update the Bill of Rights argued that these federally backed-promises would rectify a Constitutional imbalance—its enumeration of many rights for suspects, defendants, convicts, and inmates versus its silence on victims' issues. A reworded Sixth Amendment could serve as an equalizer that could end institutionalized second-class treatment. However, the degree of opposition is substantial, even from pro-victim quarters. Some critics noted that restricting participatory rights to individuals harmed by violent acts but not by property crimes was an unprincipled cost-saving compromise that would officially disenfranchise the overwhelming majority of victims because theft is so much more common than violence. Furthermore, the language of the proposed amendment eliminated any chances for meaningful redress for injured parties whose rights were violated by criminal justice officials. Lawsuits could not be filed for damages against the United States, a state, a political subdivision, or a public official. Nor were injured parties given any grounds to halt or reopen any proceedings or rulings. The rights pledged in the proposed amendment would be virtually unenforceable, merely symbolic, and practically meaningless advocates insisted (see Gahr, 1997; Pilon, 1998; NCVC, 1999; NOVA, 2002).

Civil liberties groups voiced a different set of concerns. They stated that empowering victims actually strengthens the coercive authority of the government (police and prosecution) to detain, punish, imprison and even execute its citizens. Adding pro-victim measures to the Sixth Amendment could undermine the presumption of innocence before the defendant's guilt has been determined by a jury. Unpleasant as it may be, victimhood must be established in court. The credibility of people claiming to have been harmed and pointing the finger of guilt at defendants must be tested by subjecting them to cross-examination, which is essential to the search for truth. Therefore, victims who testify at bail hearings (presumably to argue that the judge should impose very high bail) must be placed under oath and must be questioned by the defense attorney right at the outset to make sure that their statements entered into the record are accurate and relevant. Also, those complainants who will be called as witnesses must be handled in the same manner as all other witnesses. They should not be permitted to sit in the courtroom to hear what the other witnesses have to say because this information may influence or taint what they testify about later. Furthermore, observing pledges to avoid delays in resolving cases might create a rush to judgment and interfere with the defendant's right to adequate assistance of counsel when the charges are very complicated. Additionally, victims who feel their rights were not respected should not be allowed to reopen and relitigate bail hearings, plea agreements, and sentencing hearings. Finally, changes in the Sixth Amendment could open the door to further federal involvement in hearings and trials in state courts, and this would impose heavy expenses on local criminal justice systems. Victims already can exercise an important right under the Seventh Amendment: They can sue offenders in civil court for reimbursement of losses (Senate Committee, 2003).

In 2004, advocates in Congress of a constitutional amendment adopted a compromise strategy and passed the Crime Victim's Rights Act (CVRA) by a vote of 96 to 1. Also known as the "Justice For All" Act, the CVRA was anticipated to be a "formula for success" and a "model for the states." It resembled the proposed amendment but applied only to the federal criminal code. The Act stated that victims of federal offenses have the right to be treated with fairness and with respect for their dignity, privacy, and safety. It pledged that victims would have the right to confer with prosecutors, to be notified about proceedings, and to be heard on issues involving release, negotiated pleas, and sentences. Victims also would have the right to full and timely restitution. Employees of the Department of Justice and other federal agencies as well as federal judges must undertake their "best efforts" to ensure that these enumerated rights are made known and implemented. The CVRA has the potential to bring about fundamental changes in the Federal Rules of Criminal Procedure that would thoroughly integrate victims into all stages of the justice system's decision-making process, if it is vigorously enforced. If the CVRA proves to be ineffective in the years ahead, then the campaign to amend the

sixth amendment to the Constitution would resume, its backers vowed (Senate Committee, 2003; Morgenstern and Fisher, 2005; Cassell, 2007; and Wood, 2008).

Because many people suffering from acts of violence or theft were harmed by youngsters, the provisions granting them rights in federal and state courts don't apply. Some states have passed an additional bill of rights for victims of crimes committed by minors since acts of delinquency are resolved in a juvenile or family court system, which operates under rules that are different from the adult system's. These unfortunate individuals are promised that they will be entitled to information about developments in their cases and to have a limited amount of input into the proceedings held by judges behind closed doors in juvenile court (Carr, Lord, and Maier, 2003).

The rights that crime victims have fought for and secured are so numerous and varied that they must be grouped for comparison and analysis. One way to categorize these newly achieved rights is to note which groups of victims directly need, want, and benefit from a specific right. For example, in 1984, Wisconsin was the first state to adopt a Child Victims' Bill of Rights. Among other provisions, it stipulated that all legal proceedings must be carefully explained to the young complainant in language he or she can understand.

Another way to keep track of rights is to note at which stage of the criminal justice process these options can be exercised. For example, the right to be present at all court proceedings (with the presiding judge's approval) begins at arraignment when bail is considered. At the other end of the spectrum, the right to address the parole board arises years after the convict has been imprisoned. Still another way to classify victims' rights is to note at whose expense they were gained. Conflicts among individuals, groups, and classes permeate society. Rights gained by one group or class enhance its position with respect to its competitors or adversaries. If this group conflict **zero-sum game model** is accepted, then three categories of victims' rights can be discerned: those gained at the direct expense of criminals (more precisely: arrestees, defendants, convicts, inmates, probationers, and parolees); those gained at the expense of the criminal justice system (agency budgets and the privileges and convenience of law enforcement, judicial, and corrections officials); and those gained at the expense of either offenders or officials, depending on how victims exercise their newly authorized influence.

Rights Gained at the Expense of Offenders

Some advocates argue that victims' rights ought to be gained at the expense of offenders' rights. Too much concern has been shown for the rights of criminals, they say, and not enough for the plights of the innocent people they harm. In the unending battle between lawbreakers and law-abiding citizens, the "bad guys" have gained certain advantages within the legal system over the "good guys." To restore some semblance of evenhandedness to the scales of justice that have been tipped or tilted in favor of the wrong side, victims need rights that can match, counter, or even trump the rights of offenders. In this context, reform means reversing certain court decisions and legal trends and shifting the balance of power away from wrongdoers and toward the parties they injured (see Hook, 1972; Carrington, 1975; the President's Task Force, 1982).

Collisions between the rights of victims versus those of suspects, defendants, convicts, probationers, parolees, and prisoners can arise over many issues. For example, at trials, many victims and their families want to be present in the courtroom; to hear the arguments raised by attorneys for both sides in the adversary process; and to watch the reactions of the accused, the judge, and jurors. In most states, they were routinely barred until new amendments were added to state constitutions or victims' bills of rights were passed that pledged that victims are entitled to attend court proceedings, including trials.

However, restrictions on this promise can be imposed if the defense objects that the injured party's presence interferes with the rights of the accused or violates the rules of evidence. To ensure a fair trial, all witnesses are sequestered during a trial except when they testify, so they won't be influenced by the testimony of others or the arguments put forward by the lawyers. If victims are going to testify on behalf of the prosecution, or even if the defense lists them as potential witnesses, then they can be excluded from the courtroom. However, some recent state statutes and court rulings now allow victims to return to the courtroom after they have finished testifying, and to be scheduled as early on as possible to maximize their attendance. However, even if victims are permitted to attend the trial, they are rarely allowed to sit up front at the same table with the prosecutor and opposite the defendant and defense attorney because their highly visible presence could be deemed too prejudicial to the presumption of innocence (NCVC, 2002a).

To cite another example of victims' rights pitted against defendants' rights, consider the difficulties for sexual assault victims who demand compulsory testing of rapists. These injured parties understandably fear the prospect of contracting HIV/AIDS, so they need to know whether they were exposed to this disease by an infected assailant. Specifically, rape survivors seeking peace of mind want to be able to obtain an immediate court order that would compel suspects (right after arrest but before indictment) to undergo testing. But HIV-positive defendants who insist they are innocent don't want their health status to become known because of the likelihood of social discrimination. In most states, legislators predictably have sided with distraught victims who want to find out: Judges can force convicted offenders (and in some jurisdictions, even defendants before they go to trial) to submit to blood tests, even if that undermines their privacy rights and violates confidentiality laws. Unfortunately, negative test results might lead to a false sense of security. A suspect whose test results are HIV-negative may still be in the "window" period when infection by the virus does not show up. The same could be true for the victim's test results. A safer course of action would be for the victim to undergo a pro-active post-exposure prophylaxis, a 28-day regimen of anti-retroviral medications (Hakim, 2007; and Hofmann, 2007).

Conversely, individuals who endured a sexual assault want their privacy rights to prevail over any demands by defendants through defense attorneys that the records from counseling sessions maintained by rape crisis centers be turned over during the discovery phase of pretrial proceedings. Lawyers for defendants hope to find useful statements in the files summarizing frank conversations about intimate subjects that might indicate confusion about the key legal issue of denying consent, or regarding fears about making a misidentification. In many jurisdictions, judges will order the release of these records but only if the defense attorney can argue persuasively that these notes probably contain relevant information. Counselors who choose to uphold victims' privacy rights rather than accede to defendants' rights to seek exculpatory evidence, and who therefore refuse to hand over their case materials, occasionally have been found in contempt of court and jailed. In response, several state legislatures have enacted victim-counselor privilege laws that shield these communications from disclosure, just like confidential discussions between a husband and wife, doctor and patient, psychotherapist and patient, attorney and client, and minister and parishioner (NCVC, 2002e).

In capital cases, the rights of defendants facing the death penalty are directly pitted against the rights of survivors seeking retribution and closure in the form of either execution or imprisonment for life without any chance of parole. During the penalty phase that follows conviction in bifurcated capital punishment trials, the issue of life behind bars with or without the prospect of parole vs. execution must be decided. The murder victim's next of kin are entitled to present evidence to the jury of the devastating consequences of the killing, in accord with a 1991 Supreme Court decision. Some survivors put together or pay professionals to create a techologically and artistically sophisticated "victim impact video" that dramatically depicts the highlights of the victim's life from cradle to grave via gripping images with musical soundtracks. Apparently showing jurors these videos is permissible, since the Supreme Court during its 2008 term declined to review two cases brought by defense attorneys that challenged these emotional portrayals as highly prejudicial (Markon, 2008).

Those who emphasize punishing offenders in behalf of the individuals they harmed assume that the interests of victims and government officials largely coincide: apprehension, prosecution, conviction, and imprisonment. Victims' rights gained at the expense of offenders' rights would include provisions that facilitate conviction of the accused without unreasonable delays, close legal loopholes that enable the defendants to escape their "just deserts," increase the likelihood of incarceration, and eliminate unwarranted acts of leniency toward these prisoners, such as early release from confinement. The President's Task Force on Victims of Crime (1982) proposed many recommendations of this nature, and some were enacted in California in 1982 when voters passed Proposition 8, which its sponsors called a Victim's Bill of Rights. Additional rights were gained at the expense of offenders in 2008 when California voters approved of a highly controversial ballot initiative called Proposition 9. For example, it established that any threat to the safety of the victim be taken into account when a judge considers setting bail and when a parole board decides whether to grant early release. It also made restitution mandatory without exception for every convict whose criminal actions imposed a loss; increased the number of people who could testify on behalf of the victim at parole board meetings; and limited the number of subsequent hearings inmates are entitled to when they are turned down (NVCAP, 2008). Other gains that victims might secure at the expense of convicts would be the right to preview and perhaps object to the terms of a proposed plea agreement, and to the recommendations in a pre-sentence report (Cassell, 2007).

Some provisions that have been characterized as pro-victim reforms and fit within this punitive/retributory framework are listed in Table 13.1.

Critics of this approach of enhancing victims' rights at the expense of suspects, defendants, convicts, inmates, probationers, and parolees raise a number of objections. First, making convicts suffer more does not mean that the people they hurt suffer less. Second, many of these measures do not really empower victims but simply strengthen the government's ability to control its citizens. Civil libertarians who fear the

T A B L E 13.1   Victims' Rights Gained at the Expense of Suspects, Defendants, and Prisoners

Subject	Right of Victims
Denial of bail	To be protected from suspects whose pretrial release on bail might endanger them
Protection from further harm	To be reasonably protected during the pretrial release period from the accused through orders of protection and by increased penalties for acts of harassment and intimidation
Defenses	To be assured that defendants cannot avoid imprisonment by pleading not guilty by reason of insanity, through the substitution of guilty and mentally ill, which requires treatment in a mental institution followed by incarceration in prison
Privacy	To be assured that medical records and statements divulged to counselors remain confidential even if requested by the defense during the discovery phase of court proceedings
Evidence	To be assured that defendants cannot benefit from the exclusion of illegally gathered evidence by having all evidence obtained by the police in good faith declared admissible in trials
Offender's age	To be assured that juvenile offenders do not escape full responsibility for serious crimes by having such cases transferred from juvenile court to adult criminal court
Restitution	To receive mandatory repayments from convicts who are put on probation or parole unless a judge explains in writing the reasons for not imposing this obligation
Appeals	To appeal sentences that seem too lenient
Notoriety for profit	To have any royalties and fees paid to notorious criminals confiscated and used to repay victims or to fund victim services
Abuser's tax	To have penalty assessments collected from felons, misdemeanants, and traffic law violators to pay for victim services, compensation, and assistance programs

SOURCES: BJS, 1988; MADD, 1988; NOVA, 1988; NVCAP, 2008.

development of a repressive police state warn that the implementation of anti-defendant, pro-police, and pro-prosecutor measures undermines cherished principles: the presumption of innocence and the state's burden of proof. These due process safeguards are subverted when defendants are denied pretrial release, when improperly obtained evidence is used against them, and when the victims' desires for revenge (for example, as expressed in impact statements) are manipulated by the government to enhance its punitive powers (see Henderson, 1985; Fattah, 1986; Hellerstein, 1989; Hall, 1991; Abramovsky, 1992; Simonson, 1994; Dubber, 2002). Finally, these opportunities to press for ritualized revenge benefit only a small proportion of complainants—those whose reported cases were solved by an arrest and then prosecuted vigorously and successfully.

Some measures that directly protect victims from offenders do not strengthen the hand of the state and do not undermine civil liberties. For example, since the turn of the century, many states have passed measures to keep victims' home addresses confidential in cases involving domestic violence, sexual assault, and stalking. Another protective provision requires sheriff's departments to notify a victim of violence that the convicted offender has applied for a permit to obtain a gun (Brown, 2003).

Rights Gained at the Expense of the System

Some rights that victims gain should come at the expense of justice system officials and agencies that have neglected the needs and wants of their ostensible clients for far too long, advocates say. "Society," or more precisely the social system is partly at fault for the crime problems that plague communities. The state, therefore, is obligated to minimize suffering and to help injured parties recover and become whole again through government intervention, even if offenders cannot be caught or convicted. A preoccupation with punishing lawbreakers must not overshadow the need to assist and support the people they harmed. New laws must guarantee that standards of fair treatment be met that respect the dignity and privacy of injured people. Because extra effort, time, and money must be expended to provide services that were not formerly available on a routine basis, these rights can be considered to have been gained by victims at the expense of the prerogatives of officials (including detectives, assistant district attorneys, and probation officers) and the budgets of agencies (such as court systems and parole boards). For example, in many states, sexual assault victims no longer are charged for the costs of medical examinations to collect

evidence ("rape kits"); the police department or the district attorney's office now pays that bill.

Rights gained at the expense of officials and agencies first were enacted in 1980, when Wisconsin's state legislature passed a comprehensive bill of rights for victims and witnesses. The President's Task Force (1982) endorsed similar proposals that were incorporated into federal statutes when Congress approved the Victim/Witness Protection Act. Many states have proclaimed similar assurances, either through specific laws or via more comprehensive legislative packages (see Table 13.2).

TABLE 13.2   Victims' Rights Gained at the Expense of Criminal Justice Agencies and Officials

Subject	Rights of Victims
General rights	To be read their rights as soon as a crime is reported, or to be provided with written information about all obligations, services, and opportunities for protection and reimbursement
Case status	To be kept posted on progress in their cases; to be advised when arrest warrants are issued or suspects are taken into custody
Court appearances	To be notified in advance of all court proceedings and of changes in required court appearances
Secure waiting areas	To be provided with courthouse waiting rooms separate from those used by defendants, defense witnesses, and spectators
Employer intercession	To have the prosecutor explain to the complaining witness's employer that the victim should not be penalized for missing work because of court appearances
Creditor intercession	To have the prosecutor explain to creditors such as banks and landlords that crime-inflicted financial losses require delays in paying bills
Suspect out on bail	To be notified that a suspect arrested for the crime has been released on bail
Negotiated plea	To be notified that both sides have agreed to a plea of guilty in return for some consideration
Sentence and final disposition	To be notified of the verdict and sentence after a trial and of the final disposition after appeals
Work release	To be notified if the convict will be permitted to leave the prison to perform a job during specified hours
Parole hearings	To be notified when a prisoner will be appearing before a parole board to seek early release
Pardon	To be notified if the governor is considering pardoning the convict
Release of a felon	To be notified when a prisoner is to be released on parole or because the sentence has expired
Prison escape	To be notified if the convict has escaped from confinement
Return of stolen property	To have stolen property that has been recovered and held as evidence returned expeditiously by the police or prosecution
Restitution	To repay victims first from any funds collected by the court from the convict before any other legal obligations or fines are paid off
Compensation	To be reimbursed for out-of-pocket expenses for medical bills and lost wages arising from injuries inflicted during a violent crime

SOURCES: BJS, 1988; MADD, 1988; NOVA, 1988; NVCAP, 2008.

Requirements about notification, protection (such as separate waiting areas in courthouses), and intercession (with employers and creditors) increase the justice system's workloads and costs, which could interfere with its public safety priorities. A nationwide survey of prosecutors' offices at the end of the century discovered that most district attorneys reported that new victims' rights laws had imposed significant unfunded burdens on their limited budgets in the form of additional staff and more mailings and phone contacts (Davis, Henderson, and Rabbitt, 2002).

In addition to gaining rights at the expense of the criminal justice system, victims have also achieved some protection from the whims of employers in the private as well as the public sectors. Since the start of the new century, a number of states have passed statutes prohibiting employers from threatening, penalizing, or firing victims of sexual assault, domestic violence, and stalking who must take time off from their jobs ("work leave") to attend to legal or therapeutic matters (Brown, 2003; Bulletin Board, 2004).

Rights Gained at the Expense of Offenders, the System, or Both

The boldest demands raised by advocacy groups within the victims' rights movement concern power. Some victims want to influence the outcome of the criminal justice process at key stages from bail hearings to jury selection to sentencing. Instead of being relegated to the role of passive observers, they want to be active participants in the events that shape the outcomes of "their cases.". This point of view leads to the provision that the injured parties should be present and heard whenever suspects, defendants, and convicts are present and heard.

Participatory rights that victims gain may come at the expense of offenders, agency officials, or both, depending on how this leverage actually is applied. Victims can be seen as allies of the government and as junior partners on the same side as the police and the prosecution in the adversarial system. Therefore, empowering them means strengthening the coalition of forces seeking to arrest, detain, convict, and punish persons accused of wrongdoing. Enhancing the powers of a potentially repressive state apparatus alarms civil libertarians concerned about safeguarding constitutional rights and maintaining checks and balances. But if victims are visualized as independent actors, then they may not agree with the courses of action taken by their ostensible governmental allies. Calls to empower them might provoke resistance from criminal justice professionals who fear that their agency's mission will be compromised and its budget strained, and that their personal privileges and discretionary authority will be jeopardized (see Karmen, 1992; Marquis, 2005).

The critical junctures for victim input are bail-setting arraignments, plea negotiations, sentencing hearings, and parole board appearances. At arraignments, victims concerned about their personal safety can argue that "no contact" be a condition of bail. Opportunities for victims to influence the outcome of sentencing decisions take two forms. The injured party is allowed to submit a written statement. Victim impact statements are objective assessments of the crime's economic, medical, and emotional consequences. They are prepared by probation officers and presented to judges as part of the pre-sentencing investigation report in all states. Victim statements of opinion—written recommendations regarding appropriate sentences—also can be submitted to judges in most states. **Allocution** is the second and more active alternative. This opportunity to speak out before the judge sentences the offender is now permitted in most states. Similarly, victims can make their views known to parole boards in three ways: by submitting an impact statement, through allocution during the hearing, or by sending a videotaped message (NOVA, 1988; NCVC, 1996; Curran, 1999). It is often asserted or assumed that victims' highest priority is retribution and that they are likely to seize every opportunity to press for harsher handling of offenders. Vengeful victims might insist that defendants not be offered low bail or generous concessions in return for guilty pleas, that sentences imposed on convicts be as severe as the law allows, and that parole boards reject prisoners' petitions for early release.

In contrast, victims might have different priorities and find themselves at odds with the authorities over how to handle particular cases. For instance, a battered woman's greatest concern might be securing treatment for a violence-prone lover. If so, she might favor diversion of the case from the criminal justice system to allow the wrongdoer to enter a rehabilitation program. Burglary victims focused on receiving full and prompt reimbursement of their financial losses might favor an alternative to incarceration, such as restitution as a condition of probation.

Thus, involving the victim in the decision-making process constrains the free exercise of discretion formerly enjoyed by prosecutors' offices, judges, probation departments, and parole boards. What victims seek when they exercise participatory rights—for example, when they file victim impact statements or address the court at sentencing hearings—depends to some extent on the viciousness of the crime, but also on their particular notions of the meaning of justice, as the following three cases indicate:

> A gang of teenagers rob and kill a commuter as he walks home from the train station. At the ringleader's sentencing, the widow urges the judge to hand down the maximum punishment by describing the murder's impact on her five-year-old daughter: "She wants to build a time machine to go back in time to be with her dad. She asked to run all her birthdays together so she can go to heaven soon to see her dad." (Givens, 2005)

*****

> A talk show host who routinely denounces a major mob figure on his radio program is shot at point-blank range by a hired hit man. At the gunman's sentencing, the radio personality tells the judge that anything less than the maximum of 20 years in prison would be a horrible travesty of justice. "He meant to kill me. ... The attack was unprovoked and I was

defenseless ... yet [he] showed me no mercy." He is reminded of the shooting every day because the two hollow-point bullets caused permanent damage to his digestive tract and make him double over in pain every time he goes to the bathroom. The shooting helped to wreck his marriage, inflicted emotional turmoil on his parents, and nearly derailed his career. The judge imposes the maximum sentence. (Cornell, 2006)

*****

> A carload of teenagers gleefully hurl a frozen turkey out the window and speed off unconcerned as it bashes the windshield of the vehicle behind them. The heavy object breaks every bone in the driver's face, shatters her eye socket, and knocks her unconscious. After many operations and months of reconstructive surgery, she submits a victim impact statement. It urges the district attorney and the judge to sentence the apologetic and remorseful 19-year-old ringleader to the minimum punishment, six months in the county jail and five years probation, and not the maximum possible sentence of 25 years in prison. She concludes, "God gave me a second chance at life, and I passed it on." After she recovers, she spends much of her time speaking to teenagers about how a thoughtless decision can wreck their lives. (Finn, 2005; and Chang, 2006)

Pledges about the chance to participate in crucial decisions raise several contentious philosophical and policy questions. Should such formal rights also be extended to someone who does not fit the profile of an innocent, law-abiding, mature victim of a serious crime? For example, should assault victims from unsavory backgrounds—who have arrest records as street gang members, drug dealers, mobsters, and prostitutes, or are currently serving time behind bars—be permitted a say in plea negotiations and sentencing? If so, should their requests carry less weight? Should victimized children have input? Should people who represent the victim (in their capacity as survivor of a killing, executor of the estate of the deceased, the legal guardian of a minor, lawyer for the family, or volunteer advocate) be granted consultation rights during plea negotiations, and allocution rights before sentencing and parole decisions? Should participatory rights be restricted to victims of serious crimes such as felonies or, even more narrowly, only to persons physically injured by violence? And what happens when these participatory rights are violated? What remedies should victims have when criminal justice agencies fail to involve them in the decision-making process or don't live up to the standards for fair treatment?

Consider the options for giving victims input into plea negotiations, which are the way more than 90 percent of all misdemeanor and felony convictions curently are secured. Unless complainants are allowed to play a role in this process, they will be effectively shut out of any meaningful participation in the resolution of their cases. They have two chances to affect outcomes: either by conferring with the assistant district attorneys handling their cases during the negotiating sessions, or by addressing the court in oral or written statements before the plea is entered and accepted. However, no state legislation empowers complainants to dictate the terms or to nullify a proposed deal. The terms "to confer" or "to consult" are interpreted as merely to notify, inform, or advise. Victims have a right only to make their opinions known and to offer comments, and prosecutors merely have an obligation to "consider" their views and bring them to the attention of the judge. The terms of the settlement and the sentencing recommendations ultimately are still matters of prosecutorial professional discretion. Most state laws flatly declare that there are no consequences for noncompliance with these rights, and that failure to observe the pledges about opportunities for input shall not be grounds for changing the sentence. Hence, victims only have a voice, not a veto, and even then still are frequently completely excluded from the negotiation process (NCVC, 2002d). Prosecutors generally do not approve of efforts by victims to act as independent parties, for example by challenging an assistant district attorney's sentencing recommendation to a judge (Rothfeld, 2008).

The lack of enforcement mechanisms highlights another related problem: the absence of clear lines of responsibility for implementation. Which officials or agencies can be held accountable for keeping victims informed of their rights? For example, does the duty of notifying the victim about the right to allocution before sentencing fall to the police officer or civilian employee who records the initial complaint; to the assistant district attorney who prosecutes the case; to the probation officer who prepares the pre-sentence investigation report; or to the clerk in the office of court administration who schedules the post-conviction hearing? And how many times must the responsible official attempt to contact a victim before giving up and declaring that a good-faith effort was made?

Providing all complainants with advocates from the outset would be one way to make sure that injured parties find out about all their rights and options and exercise them as best they can. Rape crisis centers and shelters for battered women were the first to empower their clients by furnishing them with the services of dedicated and knowledgeable consultants who understood how the criminal justice process worked and how to make the system responsive to their clients' needs. These pioneers in advocacy usually were former victims who knew firsthand what injured parties were going through. Shortly afterward, prosecutors' victim–witness assistance programs (VWAPs) and family courts (responsible for assigning *guardians ad litem* to abused children) hired professionally trained advocates. But as yet, no jurisdiction has institutionalized and universalized the practice by assigning an advisor to every complainant who wants one, in the same way that lawyers are routinely provided to all suspects, defendants, and convicts.

Furthermore, if victims were read their rights the same way officers read suspects their Miranda warning prior to interrogation, complainants would learn that they have a right to remain vocal about how they are treated and about what they believe should happen at bail hearings, plea negotiations, sentencing hearings, and parole board meetings (see Karmen, 1995). Complainants would also learn, from advocates, that they have a right to consult with a lawyer and to refuse to answer questions or disclose any personal information that was not directly relevant to the investigation (and usually protected by privacy privileges) about subjects such as sexual history, sexual orientation, medical or mental health records; or disclose information in conversations with doctors, therapists, spouses, attorneys, or religious counselors. At the outset, victims would be warned that any disclosures about personal matters would come to the attention of not only the prosecutor but also the defense counsel, the defendant, expert witnesses, and the judge, in addition to the media and the public, during court proceedings (see Murphy, 1999; Cassell, 2007; and Wood, 2008).

Another measure that would substantially empower complainants would be to permit **private prosecution**—allowing them to hire their own lawyers to act as prosecutors—to initiate charges, handle plea negotiations, and present cases at trials. This option is allowed in other countries, and was a standard procedure in colonial America. By the end of the 1990s, only a few jurisdictions still authorized a victim's attorney to directly ask a judge or grand jury to initiate proceedings against a defendant (see Beloof, 1999). However, if this reform were implemented, only the prosperous would be able to afford such "personalized" justice.

Assessing the Effects of Victims' Rights Social scientists have just begun to evaluate the effectiveness of informational and participatory rights that have been granted in recent decades. Criminologists and victimologists are sure to discover evidence of **differential handling** or **differential access to justice**: that certain groups of people are more likely than others to be informed of their rights, to exercise them, and to use them effectively to influence the decision-making process (see Karmen, 1990).

Even with all the new options, does institutionalized indifference toward victims' plights still pervade the justice system? The answer seems to be a qualified yes, according to some preliminary findings gathered from evaluation studies. Only 3 percent of victims who reported offenses to the police in 1991 told *NCVS* interviewers that they had contact with or received advice or help from any office, agency, or program set up to serve them (Dawson et al., 1993).

Several studies carried out shortly after the new rights were enacted discovered that many victims were not informed of their right to be kept posted about progress in their cases and about court dates (Webster, 1988); about filing impact statements that might influence sentences (Wells, 1990); about parole board decisions (NVC, 1991b); and about releases of felons they helped to send to prison (Cuomo, 1992; Dawson et al., 1993). In Texas, only about 20 percent of eligible people filed victim impact statements (Schmidt, 2006).

Similarly, most failed to appear and speak out at sentencing hearings (Forer, 1980). Those who did exercise their in-person allocution rights exerted very little influence, especially when convicts faced determinate (fixed) sentences (Villmoare and Neto, 1987; Walsh, 1992). A survey of New Yorkers turned up no evidence that those who filed victim impact statements experienced a greater sense of involvement or were more satisfied with the city's justice system and the disposition in their cases (Davis and Smith, 1994).

However, when victims submitted impact statements to Pennsylvania parole boards, inmates were less likely to be granted early release (Parsonage, Bernat, and Helfgott, 1994). And when California prosecutors introduced victim impact statements during the penalty phase in capital murder trials, the additional evidence raised the likelihood that the jury would impose execution rather than sentence the killer to life in prison without the possibility of parole (Aguirre et al., 1999). According to a federally sponsored survey of departments of corrections in various states, 98 percent reported that they were notifying victims of parole dates and release dates (Gagliardi, 2005).

Even though many legislatures have added victims' rights amendments to their state constitutions or have passed a victims' bill of rights, much educational work needs to be done, a study conducted by the National Center for Victims of Crime (NCVC, 1999) concluded. It surveyed victims in two states considered to have strong pro-victim protections and in two states where their rights on paper were limited. Overall, those whose cases were processed by the justice systems of states with strong protection fared better, but even they were not afforded all the opportunities they were supposed to get. In the two states that theoretically guaranteed many rights, more than 60 percent of victims interviewed were not notified when the defendant was released on bail; more than 40 percent were not told the date of the sentencing hearing; and nearly 40 percent were not informed that they were entitled to file an impact statement at the convict's parole hearing.

Of those who found out in time, most (72 percent) attended the sentencing hearing and submitted an impact statement, but relatively few went to bail or parole hearings. Only about 40 percent of the local officials surveyed in the two strong protection states knew about the new laws enumerating victims' rights (Brienza, 1999; NCVC, 1999). Overall, a survey of cases handled by prosecutors across the country at the twentieth century's end failed to find evidence of substantial changes in outcomes resulting from the passage of victims' rights legislation (Davis, Henderson, and Rabbitt, 2002).

One explanation for the resistance that thwarts the implementation of victims' rights is that the courtroom work group of "insiders"—prosecutors, defense attorneys, and judges—tends to frustrate attempts by "outsiders" (victims, their advocates, and lawmakers) to influence their rapid, assembly-line processing of cases. These key courtroom figures usually have developed a firm consensus about the appropriate "going rate" (sentence) for various crimes at particular times and places (see Walker, 2005). To the extent that the courtroom insiders are able to resist the interference by outsiders to alter their mutual understandings, victims will find the use of their participatory rights an exercise in futility (see Ranish and Shichor, 1985).

As a consequence of these constraints and obstacles, some activists within the victims' rights movement remain pessimistic, even cynical about the much-heralded reforms that supposedly have empowered victims. Mere pledges of fair treatment

do not go far enough. Being notified about the results of a bail hearing, plea negotiation session, sentencing hearing, or parole board meeting falls far short of actually pursuing one's perceived best interests. Attending and speaking out is no guarantee of being taken seriously and truly having an impact. Victims still have no constitutional standing, which means that they cannot go to civil court and sue for monetary damages if their rights are ignored or violated, and they cannot veto decisions about bail, sentences, and parole that are made in their absence without their knowledge and consent (Gewurz and Mercurio, 1992). Lofty pronouncements that the rights of victims to fair treatment will be carefully respected by officials might prove to be lip service, paper promises, and cosmetic changes without much substance (Gegan and Rodriguez, 1992; Elias, 1993). However, because recent federal legislation grants victims the right to appeal rulings that appear to violate their rights, advocates have convinced the Department of Justice to sponsor victim law clinics to work to boost the degree of compliance by uninformed criminal justice officials (Schwartz, 2007; and Davis and Mulford, 2008).

What is the ultimate goal of victims' rights advocates? What some seek might be called a system of parallel justice; its guiding principles are that the public must be mobilized to support a comprehensive approach to making victims whole again that supplements the efforts of government agencies with additional forms of support from private and nonprofit groups such as community organizations. Local resources must be marshaled to provide a menu of services that can meet both the immediate and long-term needs of individuals harmed by illegal activities that go on in each jurisdiction.

One primary concern must always be to enhance the safety of those who report crimes and serve as witnesses—but victims also need practical assistance and financial compensation for their losses and expenses. The governmental response should include a nonadversarial conference in which victims explain what happened to them, the unwanted event's impact, and what they need to get their lives back on track. The conference should result in an official validation that they have been wronged. Case managers should determine how best to enable them to rebuild their lives with the help of an array of services such as day care, job training, housing, or counseling. Offenders can play a role in constructing a parallel justice system for victims by making restitution and performing community service (Herman, 2000; and NCVC, 2008).

But frustration with inaction and gridlock is causing some activists to abandon their efforts at reforming the bureaucratic process and to redirect their energies into developing an informal venue where injured parties can be central figures who play hands-on roles and take charge of the way their cases are resolved. These activists urge victims to arrange to meet their offenders face to face in the presence of mediators, demand an explanation, and insist that the wrongdoers take responsibility and make amends for the damage and hardships they have inflicted. This informal alternative is called **restorative justice**, and its goals include initiating a dialogue that could lead to reconciliation.

But there is a second kind of **informal justice** that opposes peacemaking. It is an entirely different mode of conflict resolution that relies on the use of force, even deadly force, not negotiation and compromise. Retaliatory justice has a long and bloody history, and its goal is not reconciliation but revenge.

TOWARD RETALIATORY JUSTICE

A man looks out his apartment window when an alarm goes off and spots a thief inside his car. He runs outside, and when the unarmed thief advances in a threatening way, he opens fire, emptying his .22 caliber rifle. He is convicted of manslaughter and sentenced to up to four years in prison for killing a career criminal who had been arrested more than 50 times. A sympathetic judge grants him bail so he can go free while appealing his conviction. (Coleman, 2002)

***

A teenager waiting for a train is robbed of his gold jewelry by six young men. The next night the adolescent spots the gang of robbers at the same station. He comes up to them and says cryptically, "Remember me?" They don't recognize him and look puzzled, until he pulls out a revolver and starts shooting. He wounds three and then flees. When the injured youths tell the police the full story about why they were shot, they are arrested for confessing to the robbery that apparently provoked the victim's wrath. He is never found. (Marriott, 1989)

***

A police officer's wife approaches a 22-year-old man as he watches a basketball game. Believing that the young man had groped her 13-year-old daughter two weeks earlier, she pulls out a gun and shoots him in the chest, yelling, "That's what you get for messing with my children!" The mother is arrested and charged with murder and criminal possession of a weapon. (Celona, 2008)

***

A 26-year-old man forces his way into an unlocked apartment where a 22-year-old mother is playing with five children. Brandishing a knife, he sexually assaults her while some of the children flee. Later, as he gets dressed, the victim escapes and runs to her boyfriend. The boyfriend, in front of a gathering crowd, confronts the accused rapist in the apartment building and a fight begins. The melee spills over into the parking lot. Someone in the mob beats the alleged rapist with a bat and another vigilante shoots him in the head. "He got what he deserved," a neighbor says. "That was just a community watch." (AP, 2008d)

As the above examples show, infuriated victims might seek a very different informal method to settle disputes, involving action, not talk. Their "do-it-yourself" vengeance can be labeled **retaliatory justice**. This outlawed alternative to formal case processing within the criminal justice system in common parlance is dubbed back-alley justice, curbstone justice, street justice, or frontier justice. To government officials, criminologists, and victimologists, it is the modern-day expression of an old-fashioned impulse called **vigilantism**. Clear-cut examples usually attract extensive media coverage and become well-known. Most reported incidents fit into one of four categories (see Shotland, 1976): victims unleashing more force than the law permits under the doctrine of self-defense (Example 1, above); victims avenging an earlier incident (Example 2); and retaliatory actions carried out on behalf of victims by family members or close friends (Example 3). Spontaneous mob actions in which a crowd responds to a victim's plea for help and gets carried away, beating or killing suspects, represents vigilantism by bystanders (Example 4).

Vigilantism's Frontier Origins

Vigilantism has a long and ugly history, especially in the Old West and the Deep South. It began in colonial times as a reaction to marauding bands of desperadoes along the frontier. In Virginia in the late 1700s, a vigilance committee led by Colonel William Lynch developed a reputation for the public whippings it staged. Its escalating violence against lawbreakers gave rise to the terms lynch law and **lynchings**. From 1882 until as recently as 1951, lynch mobs killed 4,730 people. Many targets of these murderous crowds seeking vengeance on behalf of victims, particularly in Southern rural areas, were black men accused of harming white women (Hofstadter and Wallace, 1970).

Over the course of American history, vigilantism, just like lynching, often has arisen as a response to victimization. Vigilantes called for action whenever "honest, upright citizens" became terrified and enraged about what they considered to be an upsurge of criminality and a breakdown of law and order. Pointing to the plights of victims, vigilantes feared that they would be next if they didn't take drastic measures. Hence, "red-blooded, able-bodied, law-abiding" men banded together and pursued outlaws who threatened their families,

property, and way of life. Vigilance committees led by individuals from the local power elite (with a solid middle-class membership) tended to go after people at the bottom of the hierarchy and the margins of society. They lashed out at alleged cutthroats, bushwhackers, road agents (robbers), cattle rustlers, horse thieves, and desperadoes of all kinds. They also crusaded against people they branded as parasites, drifters, idlers, sinners, loose women, uppity members of subjugated groups, outside agitators, and subversives with anarchist and communist leanings. The targets of their wrath were blacklisted, banished (run out of town), flogged, tarred and feathered, mutilated, and in some instances slaughtered (Burrows, 1976). From 1767 to 1909, 326 short-lived vigilante movements peppered American history (mostly as western frontier phenomena), claiming 729 lives (Brown, 1975).

Vigilantes portrayed themselves as true patriots and dedicated upholders of moral codes and sacred traditions. The manifestos of vigilance committees were crowned with references to "the right to revolution," "popular sovereignty," and personal survival as "the first law of nature." Just as they held criminals fully accountable for their transgressions, these rugged individualists held themselves personally responsible for their own security. If duly constituted authority could not be relied on for protection, they would shoulder the burden of law enforcement and the obligation to punish offenders.

The vigilante credo boiled down to a variation on "the end justifies the means": to preserve the rule of law, it is necessary to break the law. Most vigilantes defended their violence in terms of avenging victims and punishing common criminals. Very few of these self-appointed guardians of virtue ever got into legal trouble for their lawless deeds. Teaching lawbreakers a lesson and making an example out of them to deter other would-be offenders was the goal the men in the mob attacks cited to rationalize their own criminality. Surely, vigilantes had ulterior motives as well and, in retrospect, other reasons may have been paramount: to quash rebellions; to reassert control over rival racial, ethnic, religious, or political groups; to intimidate subordinates back into submission; and to impose the dominant group's moral standards on outsiders, newcomers, and defiant members of the community (Brown, 1975).

Currently, vigilantism is argued about much more than it is carried out. The label "vigilante"— a term formerly accepted with pride but now hurled as an epithet—crops up occasionally in news accounts and political debates. Usually, the word is used for shock value by journalists and public officials. When "survivalists" fortify their homes and stockpile weapons, that is not vigilantism—although some of these extremists warn that they will resort to violence if a crisis develops and the government becomes paralyzed or collapses. When neighbors organize citizen patrols and serve as additional eyes and ears for the police, that's not vigilantism, either. (The first such crime-watch patrol in 1964 in a Brooklyn community was dubbed a vigilante group by the authorities, but this overreaction quickly subsided. Ever since, federal money has sponsored local efforts to supplement law enforcement, and police departments have provided training and equipment to civilian anti-crime patrols.) Tenant and subway patrols such as the "Guardian Angels" also have been mischaracterized as vigilante groups. They do not fall into this category as long as they confine their activities to reporting incidents, attending to injured victims, and making citizen's arrests of suspects, and do not cross the line to dish out back-alley justice (Marx and Archer, 1976).

Vigilantism versus Legitimate Use of Force in Self-Defense

A sixth-grader is going door to door, selling chocolates for a school fundraiser. A man sitting on his porch agrees to buy some candy and invites the girl inside while he gets some money. But he whips out a knife and threatens to kill the 11-year-old if she doesn't undress. As he throws her on a couch, she snatches the knife away from him, slashes him on the hand, kicks him in the stomach, and bolts out the front door. Within minutes, the man, who had

served time for raping a 10-year-old relative, is placed under arrest for attempted aggravated sexual assault, kidnapping, and assault with a deadly weapon. (Smith, 1994)

***

An emergency room nurse returning home from work opens her door and is confronted by an intruder armed with a hammer. They clash and she strangles him with her bare hands. Detectives determine that she acted with reasonable force to protect herself in her dwelling, as permitted by state law, so the prosecutor does not bring this homicide, of a convicted felon with an extensive criminal record, before a grand jury. (AP, 2006)

The ultimate right of an individual facing immediate danger is to resist victimization. People under attack are entitled by law to use proportional force to protect themselves. Self-preservation should not be confused with vigilantism.

Statutes governing fighting in self-defense are not worded the same in each state because they have been shaped by four distinct rationales. According to a **punitive rationale**, using force against an attacker is permissible because any injuries the aggressor suffers are deserved. Under the **rationale of necessity**, the use of violence is excused when a victim fearing great harm has no choice but to resort to force as a means of self-protection. According to the **individualist rationale**, a citizen does not have to yield or concede any territory to those who would encroach on his or her autonomy. Under the **social rationale** for self-defense, resistance to attack is justified as a way of preserving law and order (Fletcher, 1988a).

By definition, the **right to self-defense** is the permissible use of appropriate force to protect one's life or that of an innocent third party from an adversary whom one reasonably believes is threatening harm. If a person who meant no harm is hurt or killed, the individual who made the mistake can be held responsible for assault or murder.

Five qualifications within the law are intended to restrain victims in order to discourage needless escalations of hostilities that can increase danger or imperil bystanders, and to prevent tragic misunderstandings that can cause innocent people to be mistaken for dangerous offenders. First, the threat posed by an aggressor must be imminent. A frightened individual may not use force if the would-be aggressor issues a conditional threat ("If I ever catch you, I'll...") or a future threat ("The next time I catch you I'll ..."). Second, if the assailant retreats, removing a victim from imminent danger, force may no longer be used. In some states, the intended target must try to evade a confrontation or attempt to escape before resorting to deadly force. Third, the target's belief that harm is imminent must be reasonable. A reasonable person takes into account the size of the adversary, the time of day, the setting, the presence or absence of a weapon, and similar factors. Fourth, the degree of force the target uses to repel the attack must be in proportion to the threat of injury or death posed by the aggressor. And fifth, the timing of the target's action must be appropriate. A pre-emptive strike initiated before the presumed attacker makes his or her intentions known (too soon) is illegal. A retaliatory strike made after the clash is over (too late) also exceeds the limits of self-defense (see Austern, 1987; Fletcher, 1988).

In every state, the law permits law-abiding people to use deadly force to protect themselves from serious bodily harm, and it spells out the circumstances under which victims of particular crimes can try to wound or kill their adversaries. For example, whether or not citizens are entitled by law to unleash deadly force to protect their homes and property varies substantially from state to state. In most jurisdictions, intruders guilty of forcible entries into dwellings can be shot. In some states, however, residents must be threatened or actually attacked before they can use lethal force against criminals who invade their homes. Trespassers generally are not considered to pose a grave peril and therefore cannot be shot on sight. Only a few states authorize private citizens to use some degree of physical force to safeguard their property from thieves (BJS, 1988).

In fact, *NCVS* findings reveal that people under attack took measures to protect themselves in roughly 60 percent of all robberies, assaults, and rapes. However, not all of their self-defense tactics involved the use of physical force. Their reactions included screaming for help, running away, and reasoning with or threatening the offender, as well as resisting and trying to capture the assailant, and counterattacking with or without a weapon. Willingness to take self-protective measures did not vary dramatically by race, sex, or prior relationship (stranger or nonstranger) but was slightly dependent upon age (older victims were less likely to put up a struggle). Males were more inclined to fight back to resist and capture an assailant, while females were more prone to call for help or threaten the attacker verbally. Most respondents reported that their self-protective measures helped the situation (by enabling them to avoid injury altogether or at least to prevent further wounds, to escape, or to scare off the offender) rather than hurt it (by making the aggressor more violent). Less than 2 percent of victims of violent crimes claimed that they counterattacked by drawing their own weapon (not necessarily a firearm), according to the 2006 *NCVS* (BJS, 2008d).

Would Victims Be Better Off if They Were Armed?

In response to the threat posed by offenders, many people have armed themselves in self-defense, believing that they are improving their odds of surviving a felonious assault. According to gun enthusiasts, the number of privately owned guns and the number of gun owners have reached all-time highs (NRA, 2008b). Surveys during the 1970s and 1980s revealed that almost half of American households possessed at least one gun. However, during the 1990s, the percent of respondents who told interviewers they owned a gun dropped, leveling off at 34 percent in 2002 (Roper, 2004).

At the start of the twenty-first century, about 75 million Americans owned an estimated 200 million to 250 million guns, of which about 70 million were handguns (Riczo, 2001; Kohn,

2005). This arsenal in private homes is much larger than the number of firearms in nonpolice/nonmilitary hands was in 1970, when federal gun control laws first became a major political issue. Nearly half the gun owners cited self-protection as a main reason for acquiring firearms (Morganthau and Shenitz, 1994; Witkin, 1994; Cook and Ludwig, 1997; Riczo, 2001). Gun ownership was higher among men than women, whites than blacks, older people than people under 50, higher-income than lower-income families, Southerners than inhabitants of other regions, residents of rural rather than urban areas, and among Republicans than Democrats (Roper, 2004).

Public opinion is sharply divided over the issue of armed self-defense. The debate centers around whether intended victims would be better off or worse off if they were in a position to draw a gun when threatened or under attack. The gun-enthusiast side sees these weapons as **equalizers** that can save innocent lives and works for policies that provide ready access to firearms for responsible, law-abiding adults. The disarmament side seeks to further restrict gun availability because firearms are seen as **facilitators** that cause minor conflicts to escalate into deadly confrontations. These weapons are considered more dangerous to those who wield them than they are to their opponents. Both sides in the debate admit there is a trade-off between appropriate self-defense uses and improper uses (accidental shootings, shootings of the wrong person by mistake, using firearms to commit suicide, and misusing guns for criminal purposes). But the two opposing camps differ sharply on whether the costs outweigh the benefits (see Kleck, 1997).

Arguments in Favor of Arming for Self-Protection Advocates of armed self-defense tend to cite examples like the following that indicate how lawfully owned guns can be wielded to protect life and property successfully:

Late one night a motorist stops his car at a red light. A robber walks up, shoves a knife through the open window and demands that the driver get out. Instead, the driver, who is a concealed-carry permit holder, pulls out his handgun. Seeing that his intended victim is better armed than he is, the would-be carjacker runs away. ("The Armed Citizen," 2008a)

***

A 22-year-old woman returns home and finds a burglar in her living room. She runs into the bedroom, locks the door behind her, and grabs her husband's gun and ammunition. She then retreats to the bathroom. The intruder breaks down the bedroom door and begins pounding on the bathroom door. She fires a single shot through the door, and the intruder flees in panic. ("The Armed Citizen," 2008b)

***

Three men enter a grocery store. Two of them pull out guns and one points his handgun at the owner behind the counter. The owner grabs the gun he keeps for protection, and they fire a single shot at each other. One robber dies and the other two bolt out into the night. (WTVD, 2008)

Gun-ownership enthusiasts consider keeping a firearm at home or work as well as carrying around a legally registered handgun to be a rational and reasonable antidote to the constant yet unpredictable threat of violent crime. Besides citing the Second Amendment to the Constitution, they offer several arguments in favor of arming for self-protection. First, the likelihood that intended targets would be prepared for battle might dissuade some potential predators from trying to start trouble. Second, the mere sight of a firearm in the hands of the target might intimidate a would-be offender into aborting his plans. Third, when a crime is in progress, recourse to a firearm may enable a victim to fend off an attacker and thwart his criminal intentions. Fourth, an armed, law-abiding citizen could capture and hold an assailant at bay until the police arrive. Finally, in a life-or-death struggle, a gun can improve the victim's odds of surviving a confrontation with a dangerous, more physically powerful foe.

Advocates of gun ownership want to encourage a culture of self-reliance. They believe that heavily armed communities won't be viewed by burglars and robbers as attractive places to operate, and that a well-armed populace can serve as an effective backup for local law enforcement (Reynolds, 2007). They assert that firearms are used by intended victims for self-defense more often than they are used by predators to commit crimes. They suspect that the number of lives saved by guns might exceed the number of lives lost to bullet wounds annually. The crime-inhibiting effect of gun ownership by potential targets counterbalances the lawbreaking of gun-toting criminally inclined persons (see Kleck, 1991, 1997; Will, 1993; and Witkin, 1994).

One measure of how frequently Americans resort to deadly force to protect themselves is the annual body count resulting from justifiable homicides, which are not classified by the FBI as murders or manslaughters because they are legally excusable. Since 1988, the FBI's *UCR* has been keeping track of two types of justifiable homicides: killings of criminals committing felonies by private citizens acting in self-defense, and law enforcement officers slaying dangerous suspects. The yearly data show a pattern in which officers slay more criminals than civilians do. Officers and civilians combined put an end to the lives of more than 800 attackers in 1993, and again in 1994, as Table 13.3 shows. Compared to the number of Americans who were murdered during those years, justifiable homicides accounted for about 4 percent of all violent deaths nationwide. Most of these nonpunishable deaths of felons resulted from gunfire (99 percent of those killed by officers, 78 percent of assailants slain by civilians, in 2007) (FBI, 2008).

As for trends, when the level of lethal violence increased throughout the United States from the late 1980s into the early 1990s, the number of justifiable homicides climbed as well. When the murder rate dropped as the century came to a close, the body count from the defensive use of deadly force unleashed by victims and by law enforcement officers subsided too. Justifiable homicides by police officers peaked in 1994 but tumbled to its lowest

T A B L E   13.3   Justifiable Homicides by Crime Victims and Police Officers, 1988–2007

Year	Number of Killings in Self-Defense	
	By Crime Victims	**By Police Officers**
1988	238	343
1989	273	363
1990	328	385
1991	331	367
1992	351	418
1993	356	455
1994	353	462
1995	268	389
1996	261	358
1997	280	366
1998	196	369
1999	192	308
2000	164	309
2001	222	378
2002	233	341
2003	247	373
2004	222	367
2005	196	347
2006	238	386
2007	254	391

SOURCE: FBI *UCRs*, 1989–2007.

level just five or six years later. Killings in self-defense by civilians showed virtually the same trend, with the death toll topping out in 1993 but then subsiding to its lowest level in 2000. However, during the first decade of the twenty-first century, this correlation came to an end. The number of murders across America basically leveled off, but justifiable homicides by victims and especially by police officers went up considerably (see Table 13.3).

How often victims draw guns to defend themselves in confrontations is a matter of great controversy. Defensive uses (brandishing a gun does not necessarily lead to pulling the trigger) number about 100,000 in a year, according to *NCVS* findings. But gun-ownership advocates dismiss this official estimate as misleadingly low and suspect that many respondents are reluctant to tell interviewers working for the government the full story of how they repelled an attacker.

A 1994 telephone survey yielded a projected nationwide figure of as many as 2.5 million brandishings of a gun with a successful outcome, an entirely different order of magnitude. So the actual number of attempted assaults, robberies, thefts, and break-ins warded off by armed victims is a subject for conjecture. But even if the larger figure is accepted, more is not necessarily better. Some who drew their weapons against perceived threats actually may not have been innocent, unprovoked victims. Also, the threat posed by armed citizens may touch off another round in an escalating arms race, motivating predatory street criminals to get even more powerful guns and to shoot first during the next confrontation (see Kleck and Gertz, 1995; and Cook and Ludwig, 1997).

Gun proponents hail the spread of right-to-carry laws ("shall carry" or "shall issue" legislation) that enable citizens to bring concealed handguns wherever they go. In 40 states, permits are easily obtainable, provided that the applicant is "of good character" and doesn't have a record of arrests and convictions or a documented history of mental illness. In the other states, citizens have to prove that they have a compelling need to be armed, and local police chiefs, sheriffs, and judges decide who gets the limited number of permits (Verhovek, 1995; Ratnesar, 1998; and La Pierre, 2008). Gun proponents claim the growing presence of armed citizens helped to deter crime during the second half of the 1990s (see Lott, 1998); but a blue ribbon commission found no conclusive evidence that the adoption of "shall carry" laws had any impact on local crime rates in the states that had adopted this approach (Vines, 2004).

Some advocates of armed self-defense as well as self-reliance go as far as to argue that intended targets have a "moral responsibility" to fight back if their property, lives, families, and communities are in danger. To do this effectively, law-abiding citizens need to be trained and to be equipped with guns as equalizers. The existence of police departments does not relieve individuals of their obligations to protect themselves, and officers cannot be depended upon to serve as personal bodyguards. Readiness to resist an assault on one's dignity is a prerequisite for self-respect, as well as a deterrent to crime (see Snyder, 1993; Will, 1993).

Proponents of this approach seek to pass "stand your ground" state laws that authorize people to use deadly force—without first trying to back off from a confrontation—against those who threaten them at home, at work, or in public spaces. "Stand your ground" laws (passed in 22 states as of 2008) put forward a "castle doctrine" (NRA, 2007; and Perrusquia, 2008). For example, in Texas, the castle doctrine presumes that the apparent target who feels threatened is acting reasonably if he or she unleashes deadly force against someone who, illegally and with force but without provocation, is entering an occupied home, car, or workplace. The apparent target of an imminent attack no longer has a "duty to retreat" if he or she has a right to be there and is no longer liable to a civil lawsuit by the person who is shot, even if by mistake (Thompson, 2008). Gun control advocates warn that this kind of aggressive "meet force with force" legislation could lead to needless bloodshed (see Goodnough, 2005; and Perrusquia, 2008).

Arguments Against Arming for Self-Protection
Critics of this domestic arms race believe that allowing more people to go about their lives packing guns is a recipe for disaster, and that true public safety rests upon civility (Editors, *New York Times*, 2007). Although many people conjure up fantasies about how drawing a gun will save them, the reality is that gunfire is more likely to claim an innocent life or their own. Advocates of gun control bring up horror stories like the following incidents to illustrate how individuals who mistakenly perceive themselves to be in grave danger might fire their guns in error, causing avoidable tragedies:

> Two teenage boys play hooky from high school. When the father of one of the boys returns home unexpectedly in the early afternoon, they quickly hide in a closet. The father hears muffled noises, mistakes the boys for burglars, grabs his gun, and fires through the closet door. After the 15-year-old friend dies from his wounds, the father is arrested and

charged with assault, reckless endangerment, and criminal possession of a weapon, even though the victim's parents did not want to press charges. (Friefeld, 2000)

***

A 12-year-old boy is showing off his father's loaded handgun, which he discovered in an unlocked box. He pulls the trigger and fatally shoots his fifth-grade classmate. Splattered with blood, he utters a bone-chilling scream and runs outside to a neighbor, shouting, "It was an accident." (Fagen, 2006)

Gun control advocates argue that more guns lead to more crime. Unrestrained access to firearms facilitates accidental shootings or impulsive suicides, homicides and nonfatal aggravated assaults. Restricting gun ownership prevents arguments from escalating into shootouts (see Fox and McDowall, 2008). Owning a firearm for self-defense actually heightens risks and leads to a false sense of security. They point to studies that seem to show that keeping a gun at home, instead of safeguarding the lives of members of a household, increases the likelihood that someone will be killed there in a moment of rage.

According to an analysis of 420 homicides committed in the homes of victims who had access to guns, the majority (77 percent) were slain by a spouse, other family member, or someone else they knew. Only a small proportion (4 percent) was murdered by complete strangers. The remaining cases (19 percent) were not solved. The highest risks of being shot to death at home are faced by people who keep one or more guns handy, reside in a rental unit, and either live alone or with someone who was previously arrested, uses illicit drugs, assaults others, or was hurt in a family fight (see Leary, 1993).

Similar studies have concluded that loaded guns are more likely to be used to slay family members than intruders. The availability of handguns causes ordinary fights between family members, former friends, and neighbors to evolve into deadly showdowns. More people die in a year from handgun accidents than are killed over several years by robbers and home-invading burglars. In shootouts with armed offenders, victims lose more often than they win. In some confrontations, attackers may wrest the gun away and shoot victims with their own weapons—this even happens to well-trained, physically fit police officers. Critics of the guns-for-protection point of view conclude that the gravest threats to members of a household come from within, not from outside; and therefore, on balance, the risks that arise from gun availability substantially outweigh the benefits (see Wright, Rossi, and Daly, 1983; Kates, 1986; Green, 1987; Witkin, 1994; and Butterfield, 1999). The rate of fatal shootings of children under 15 years of age, another important indicator of misuse and misjudged risks, is more than 10 times higher in the United States than in 25 other industrialized countries combined (Children's Defense Fund, 2004).

Victimologists can conduct research to help resolve the heated debate over whether arming for self-defense makes people safer or puts them at more risk for serious injuries or death. Researchers need to assemble an accurate and comprehensive database about all kinds of shootings, whether accidental or intentional, that includes the characteristics of the assailants and their intended targets, the settings, and the circumstances that precipitated the gunfire. This kind of information currently is scattered in the files of police detectives, prosecutors, medical examiners' and coroners' offices, health department death certificate records, and forensic lab reports (Barber et al., 2000). Researchers must also study cases in which a firearm was visibly brandished by a victim but not discharged to see how many confrontations had successful versus tragic endings.

The Dangers of a Drift Back Toward Retaliatory Violence

Once in a while, a case that appears in the news serves as a reminder that victims and their allies can go too far and unleash violence in retaliation for past wrongs—and still garner public support for their misdeeds:

Two robbers barge into a family's apartment in a drug-ridden, high-crime area. One hits the husband on the head, and they flee with some jewelry. The husband recovers and runs outside after them while his wife screams to alert neighbors. Ten men join the chase. The husband catches up with one of the robbers and tackles him. As they wrestle on the ground, the robber pulls out a knife and slashes the husband. Infuriated, the crowd of men close in, kicking, punching, and stabbing the robber to death. Then the mob of neighbors melts away into the darkness. When patrol officers and detectives arrive, they learn nothing from silent and uncooperative eyewitnesses. Local residents tell reporters that they have lost faith in the justice system and that this killing of a "bad guy" might actually be a good thing for the neighborhood's reputation. (Lorch, 1990)

***

A man in court is accused of molesting several young boys. Detecting a smirk on his face as he walks forward to take the witness stand, the mother of one of the boys pulls out a gun and shoots him in the back of the head five times. When she is put on trial for murder, some people rally to her side. Picturing her as a heroic figure who rose up in righteous indignation in defense of her child, they send telegrams offering support and raise money for her defense. But others are skeptical of her portrayal as an anguished parent pushed to the breaking point by an arrogant offender who was about to be coddled by an ineffectual judicial system. When they learn that she waited two years for the chance to shoot the alleged molester, was high on methamphetamine that day, and had a past conviction for auto theft, they view her more as a drug-addled ex-con with a score to settle. Convicted of voluntary manslaughter, she is sentenced to 10 years in prison by a judge who categorizes her courtroom gunplay as an execution that was an intentional and intolerable assault on the justice system. The sentence is hailed by the prosecutor who interprets it as affirming the message that victims must not dish out street justice. But her supporters urge clemency so she can be freed to lead a crusade to toughen the way child molesters are handled by the legal system. (Kincaid, 1993; Associated Press, 1994c)

***

A 48-year-old auto body repairman harasses and bullies his neighbors for years with taunts like, "I know where you live." One day, he warns a retired Navy commander, "You and your family are as good as dead." Those are the last words he ever utters, because the man he threatens pulls out a revolver, starts shooting, reloads, and fires 13 rounds, killing the widely feared but unarmed, methamphetamine-taking loudmouth. Although about eight of ten callers to a talk radio show support his actions, saying, "He should get a medal," and "Put me on that jury, and he'd get off," the retired commander is convicted of second-degree murder. But the judge, declaring that the deceased was a jerk and a ne'er-do-well who got what was coming to him, overturns the verdict, reduces the conviction to manslaughter, and cuts the shooter's sentence in half. (Goldberg, 1996; Associated Press, 1997)

Self-defense involves the use of force to prevent a crime from being completed or to rescue an intended victim from harm. Retaliatory "justice" employs force that is out of proportion to the initial threat and unleashes unjustifiable violence to punish an offender after a crime has been completed. Once the immediate threat has passed, the victim may not use violence to exact revenge. But such distinctions are more easily drawn in classrooms and textbooks than in real-life confrontations. In actual cases, difficult questions must be resolved: Was the victim still in imminent danger? Did the victim still reasonably fear serious bodily harm or even death? Was the response proportionate to the perceived threat, or did the victim overreact?

Police officers grapple with these questions first when they decide whether to make an arrest. Prosecutors confront these issues when they determine what charges, if any, to lodge against an intended target who emerged victorious from a battle with an aggressor. If the case goes to trial, jurors, acting as the conscience of the community, must arrive at a verdict by answering such hypothetical questions as: What would I have done under similar circumstances? Does the abuse the victim endured excuse his or her excessive reaction? Did the assailant get what was coming to him? What message does the verdict send to the public? Juries retain the right to nullify legal principles, disregard the limits imposed by the law, and render a collective decision based on their own interpretations of what is reasonable and appropriate under particular circumstances (Dershowitz, 1988).

When individuals accused of retaliatory violence are not arrested, not vigorously prosecuted, or acquitted by a jury after a trial, commentators try to decipher the meaning or symbolism: Was the person who allegedly dispensed street justice vindicated by public opinion as doing the right thing? Was the prosecution, representing the criminal justice system and the government, repudiated? Were the laws restraining the use of force rejected? Various interpretations are possible when those charged with retaliatory violence are not held accountable for their questionable deeds (see Bahr, 1985; and Dershowitz, 1988).

Retaliation seems to appeal to many people on a gut level. A steady stream of extremely popular movies have capitalized on the theme of personal vendettas and getting even. Even though the plots are transparent and the thirst for revenge is quenched by the end of the story, audiences stand up and cheer for the victims who strike back and make vicious thugs pay in blood for their cruel misdeeds.

No statistics purporting to measure the prevalence of retaliatory violence are available—no government agency or private research group keeps track of such outbreaks. The FBI's *UCR* does not have a category for revenge killings in its Supplementary Homicide Reports. Cases of vigilante violence seem to be relatively infrequent. But if vigilantism is defined broadly as "taking the law into one's own hands" by physically punishing suspected transgressors, then it may be more common than initially realized. Many, if not most, instances of vigilantism are never detected, recorded, investigated, or prosecuted because victims and their allies (relatives, accomplices, or members of a crowd) don't want the authorities to find out their real motives. Bystanders who spontaneously intervene to break up a crime in progress, to rescue a person in trouble, and to catch an assailant might get swept away by a mob mentality or crowd psychology and feel compelled to "get in a few good licks" to punish the offender right then and there. When innocent victims gain the upper hand during confrontations, they, too, may overreact and use more force than the law allows, not only to subdue their attackers but also to make them pay on the spot for their attempted crimes. Additionally, many schoolyard fistfights and barroom brawls probably are touched off by a victim's desire to settle a score with some bully or aggressor. Surely, some incidents of domestic violence are fueled by a yearning for personal vengeance. Some battered wives who fight back or even kill their tormentors go beyond the legal limits of self-defense by launching pre-emptive strikes to forestall another beating or by unleashing retaliatory violence to get him back for a previous assault. A few cases even have come to light in which physically and sexually abused children grow up and slay their parents. Perhaps some incidents in which officers use excessive force to take resisting or unruly suspects into custody (commonly referred to as police brutality) might really be outbreaks of police vigilantism (Kotecha and Walker, 1976).

Criminals act as vigilantes all the time: They routinely resort to brute force to settle their disputes precisely because they cannot bring their personal problems and business quarrels to the police, prosecutors, and courts without incriminating themselves. Vigilantism breaks out whenever street gangs engage in drive-by shootings to retaliate for an ambushing of one of their members, when mobsters hire hit men to "whack" some rival or "rat," or when drug dealers eliminate someone who cheated or stole from them.

Vigilantism also has an overtly political side. It has been part of the ideology of right-wing extremist groups—such as the Ku Klux Klan, neo-Nazis, racist skinheads, and certain militia groups— that openly proclaim their intention to revive the "night rider" tradition to "rid society of undesirable elements," " "troublemakers," and "traitors" (see Madison, 1973; Burrows, 1976; Lasch, 1982; King, 1989; Dees and Corcoran, 1997).

The emotional attraction of the vigilante solution to street crime rests on the notion that retaliation-in-kind is what justice is all about. Offender rehabilitation, restitution, and reconciliation are out of the question. Because the legal system cannot impose far-ranging punishments that directly match the suffering inflicted by offenders, it consistently fails to deliver payment in blood. As the gulf widens between the harsh punishments some people call for and the incarceration penalties the system metes out, street justice gains appeal in some circles as being more appropriate than the sentences imposed by judges.

The impulse toward vigilantism is held in check by two counter-ideologies. Law enforcement officials and responsible figures in government, embracing the tenets of professionalism, reject vigilantism from the conviction that experts, not ordinary citizens, ought to control the criminal justice process. They urge citizens to allow the proper authorities and courts to handle cases and to reject any do-it-yourself impulses.

Civil libertarians marshal even stronger arguments. They insist that due process safeguards and constitutional guarantees must be adhered to faithfully to make sure that innocent individuals are not falsely accused and then subjected to the passions of mob rule. "On-the-spot justice" has been criticized as too swift, too sure, and too informal. Victims and their accomplices dispense with all the rules of the criminal justice game. They assume the roles normally played by the police, prosecutor, judge, jury, and ultimately, executioner. The delicate balance between the rights of victims and of accused persons, hammered out through centuries of competition and compromise, is overturned, and suspects are presumed guilty, no matter how much they assert their

innocence. The history of vigilantism is filled with cases of mistaken identity, when the wrong person was made to pay for someone else's misdeeds, as the following worst-case scenarios show:

> A furious father corners a 17-year-old boy whom his 14-year-old daughter claims raped her on the roof of their apartment building. The father shoots the teenager and then bashes his head with a hammer. But later the girl admits she lied about key parts of her unfounded rape charge. The father is convicted of first-degree manslaughter and is sentenced to 7 to 14 years in prison for his terrible mistake. (Barrett, 1998)

***

> A crowd of 50 teenagers masses in response to a rumor (which later proves false) that a girl from their suburban high school has been raped. Intent on retaliating, they pile into cars and cruise an adjoining neighborhood, spoiling for a fight. Several fistfights break out, and some youths are injured by rocks and bottles. Then the teenagers, armed with baseball bats, corner about 15 boys from a parochial high school and beat one to death. Six students from the mob, who don't know each other and have not been in serious trouble before, are arrested, charged with murder, and tried as adults. All six are convicted of conspiracy to commit murder, and three are found guilty of third-degree murder. (Janofsky, 1994; "Mixed Verdict," 1996)

On-the-spot street justice has been denounced as far too harsh. Physical punishments, including death, are imposed in the heat of the moment for offenses that merit lesser penalties under the law. The vigilante's intent is to settle matters in a manner that mirrors the original act—forcefully— but with the roles reversed.

The widely used phrase "taking the law into one's own hands" does not capture the essence of this reaction to crime. Vigilantes don't *take* the law; they break the law. They don't use force in self-defense, which is legal; they unleash retaliatory violence in order to inflict physical punishment, which is illegal. Their disdain for the technicalities of due process mocks the entire criminal justice process. Unleashed in the name of restoring law and order, vigilantism undermines the legal system and sends shock waves through the social order by trampling the Bill of Rights. In trying to vindicate victims, vigilantes create new ones.

From an academic standpoint, the study of revenge killings and retaliatory justice leads victimology full circle, back to its ancestral origins in criminology. Through vigilantism's role reversals, victims become lawbreakers, physically harming individuals whom they believe made them suffer. Offenders, formerly enjoying the advantage within the oppressive relationship, are compelled to experience firsthand what it is liketo be on the receiving end of criminal violence. But trading places—transforming victims into offenders and offenders into victims—is no solution to the crime problem. In an ironic twist, by striking out against the wrong person or by unleashing excessive force, vengeful victims open themselves up to the risk of being prosecuted in criminal court and sued in civil court. There are too many aggressors out there already. Encouraging do-it-yourself retaliatory "justice" would just add to their ranks.

TOWARD RESTORATIVE
JUSTICE

A 16-year-old girl has an affair with a married 38-year-old man who owns an auto repair shop. The lovestruck teenager shoots the man's wife in the face. The young assailant is quickly captured, pleads guilty to first-degree assault, and is sentenced to a 5-to-15-year prison term. The wife survives, but the bullet remains lodged in her brain, interfering with her eating and drinking and causing her constant pain and suffering. The husband pleads guilty to statutory rape and serves six months in jail before becoming a talk show host. Nearly seven years later, the shooter comes up for parole. She tells the woman she tried to kill, "It was my fault,

and I'm sorry." The wife recommends to the parole board that they release her, and they do. (Associated Press, 1999a)

***

An 11-year-old boy selling candy door to door to raise money for his school is lured into the home of a 15-year-old boy, who sexually assaults and then strangles him. The teenager is convicted of first-degree murder and is sentenced to 70 years in prison. The victim's father, a lawyer, becomes an advocate for victims' rights and a candidate for the state assembly. The killer's parents reach the brink of bankruptcy after financing their son's unsuccessful legal defense, and then are named as defendants in a civil lawsuit along with the psychiatric institutions that ineffectively and negligently treated the disturbed teen. After their minister intercedes, both sets of parents end two years of icy stares and recriminations. The two fathers hug each other and "cry like babies." "The anger has to stop," the victim's father declares. "It's a miracle. It's such a burden lifted," the prisoner's father adds. (Mansnerus, 1999)

***

A 19-year-old shoots a 21-year-old police officer, permanently damaging his right arm. The assailant is released on bail but flees to Canada and lives a conventional life, becoming a husband, father, and librarian. Thirty-five years later the authorities arrest him and extradite him. Facing up to 23 years in prison, his attorney negotiates an unusual plea with the victim's approval. He is sentenced to 30 days in jail, two years on probation, and to make restitution payments that will add up to $250,000 to a foundation that assists families of injured police officers. The wounded officer declares, "Something good had to come of this. The easy way out would have been to have a trial, and cost this county hundreds of thousands of dollars ... and cost the prison system hundreds of thousand of dollars." (Einhorn, 2008)

Even in these cynical times, when calls for rehabilitating criminals are greeted with skepticism and demands for severe punishment receive enthusiastic support, a new approach that assumes the best about people is gaining ground. It is attracting a growing proportion of victims who don't want to use their leverage within the legal system to make their offenders suffer. They are taking advantage of the chance to actively participate in a process whose goals are offender sensitization, victim recovery, a cessation of mutual hostilities, and a sense of closure, in which both parties put the incident behind them and rebuild their lives.

These are the aims of restorative justice, a rapidly evolving way of reconceptualizing and contextualizing the crime problem that many enthusiastic adherents find promising. It draws upon nonpunitive methods of peacemaking, mediation, negotiation, dispute resolution, conflict management, and constructive engagement. These strategies bring about mutual understanding, offender empathy for the victim's plight, victim sensitivity about the causes of the offender's problems, and lasting settlements that reconcile tensions between the two parties as well as within their community.

The Peacemaking Process

Restorative justice embraces themes important to the victims' rights movement, especially empowerment, notification, direct involvement, offender accountability, and receiving restitution. This emerging challenge to the prevailing punitive paradigm incorporates some traditions that helped repair crime's negative repercussions centuries ago, before the state asserted its authority to dominate the justice process. In the distant past, legal systems were victim-focused and restitution-oriented. Detailed lists specified how much a wrongdoer had to pay an injured party for each kind of wound or loss.

But priorities shifted dramatically in most societies when the upper class discovered that the legal apparatus could be used to control the populace. The government symbolically displaced the wounded person as the injured party, and the courts were transformed from a forum to settle disputes between specific individuals into an arena for ritualized combat between representatives of the state and of the accused. If the prosecution succeeded, the state inflicted pain upon its vanquished opponents in order to teach them not to break the law again (specific deterrence) and to make negative examples of them to serve as a warning to others (general deterrence). Later, prisons were invented to serve these purposes, as well as to take troublemakers out of circulation to protect the public (incapacitation), and to force maladjusted people to undergo compulsory treatment (rehabilitation).

In addition to the suffering caused by the deprivation of liberty and the imposition of harsh conditions (retribution), the government often extracted a fine or seized property from convicts, but it never shared the spoils with victims. The overriding concern of the authorities was to impose the appropriate punishment, not to restore the victim's emotional and economic well-being. This paradigm shift to **retributive justice** resulted in a process that was state-centered, offender-focused, and punishment-oriented, rather than injury-centered, victim-focused, and reparation-oriented (see Sullivan and Tifft, 2001).

Centuries later, reformers are promoting another paradigm shift by working to revive the ancient insight that achieving genuine justice requires that something be done *for* the victim and not simply *to* the offender. They point out that street crimes are best viewed as conflicts between individuals rather than as affronts to abstractions such as society's norms or the state's authority. Restorative justice projects are experimenting with two traditional ways of bringing estranged parties together: peacemaking circles and family group conferencing. The use of overlapping **peacemaking circles**, composed of the victim and his support system, the offender and his family, and community members, is derived from Native American tribal culture in the United States and Canada. After frank discussions about what led up to the violation of a law, the groups merge into a disposition circle that develops a consensus on how to restore harmony to the afflicted individuals, their relatives, and their neighbors. A follow-up circle monitors the wrongdoer's progress in making amends (OJJDP, 1998b; Zehr, 1998; Pranis, 1999).

Family group conferencing is another means of conflict resolution that is gaining adherents. Originally, it was developed by the Maori, the indigenous people of New Zealand. It has been adapted to resolve juvenile delinquency cases there and in Australia. Run by a trained facilitator, the conference begins with the wrongdoer undergoing reintegrative shaming by describing the incident to an assembly of relatives, friends, and neighbors. Then the victim explains how this event caused distress, injuries, and losses. Other members of the community fill in details about the impact on their lives. The offender begins to realize how his or her actions caused hardships and how he or she ought to repair the damage. After the victim suggests desired outcomes, the entire group discusses ways to solve the problem. By the end of the conference, a written settlement sets forth the community's expectations about the constructive actions the wrongdoer is obliged to undertake to undo the harm he or she inflicted on others (Bradshaw and Umbreit, 1998; Zehr, 1998).

The development of methods of **alternative dispute resolution (ADR)** around the globe has stimulated interest in reconciliation programs. **Mediation** lies at the center of a continuum bounded by conciliation and arbitration. It requires direct negotiations between disputants with a neutral person, a mediator, who helps the feuding parties arrive at a mutually acceptable compromise by promoting discussion, soliciting viewpoints, and discovering areas of common interest. **Conciliation** simply requires a go-between to facilitate the flow of information from one disputant to another. In **arbitration** a neutral individual is called in to break a deadlock. The arbitrator plays an active role as fact finder and then, after hearing presentations from both sides, imposes a fair, final, and legally binding decision.

A Brief History of Restorative Justice

Starting in the 1970s, innovative activists began to promote dispute resolution as a way to resolve conflicts that involved shared responsibility. They argued that calling the police, pressing charges, prosecuting in court, and seeking vindication through conviction was inappropriate for handling minor violations of the law, especially if they stemmed from ongoing relationships in which each party did something to antagonize, provoke, and harm the other.

In addition, proponents of dispute resolution argued that the adversary system underlying both criminal and civil proceedings is essentially a zero-sum game. At each stage one party gains points at the expense of the other. Strict rules of evidence may prevent the disputants and witnesses from telling the whole story. Both sides are preoccupied with issues of blame, guilt, and liability. At the end of the contest, there must always be a winner and a loser. The victorious side is pleased with the outcome, while the defeated side is angry and disappointed. The two parties may leave court just as they arrived, locked in conflict and seething with hostility, and sometimes even more alienated, bitter, and polarized than at the outset (Wright, 1989; Cooper, 2000). Using ADR was viewed as preferable to adjudication because it could lead to a compromise settlement that might satisfy both sides and resolve their dispute with some degree of finality.

These alternative ways of settling conflicts were made available at places called **multidoor courthouses** or **neighborhood justice centers**. Disputants took their cases to an intake/diagnosis/referral unit, where a screening specialist decided on the most appropriate method of resolving the matter: conciliation, mediation, arbitration, or adjudication within the criminal justice system.

At neighborhood justice centers practicing ADR techniques, hearings were scheduled at the convenience of the participants, not the staff. The use of private attorneys was discouraged. The rules governing the introduction of evidence were minimized. Witnesses were not sworn in. Mediators did not wear robes or sit above and apart from the others. Nontechnical language was used, and only limited records of the proceedings were kept. This moot model of informal justice avoided the constraints of a guilty/innocent, wrong/right, pin-the-blame/deny-responsibility framework. With the mediator acting as a referee, the disputants educated each other by presenting their own versions of their conflict. The intent was to look to the future rather than to dwell on the past. The ultimate goals were to reconcile the estranged parties and repair rifts within their community (Prison Research, 1976; Roehl and Ray, 1986; and Wright, 1991).

Neighborhood justice centers were not sought by activists when the victims' rights movement first emerged during the 1970s. Originally, the idea of relying on informal negotiations to settle criminal matters conjured up the unfavorable image of an unwilling, trembling victim being forced to shake hands with a smirking, unrepentant offender. The impetus for developing this additional forum came from other constituencies.

Attempting to streamline the judicial process, court administrators sought ways to remove the minor criminal cases that clogged their calendars. Judges, including the justices of the Supreme Court, encouraged experiments in conflict resolution so that settling disputes in criminal and civil court at great public expense would become a last resort. Police and prosecutors endorsed weeding out what they considered "junk" cases from their workloads. From their viewpoints, too many people wasted the time of public agencies trying to resolve private matters. They argued that the complex machinery of criminal justice should be reserved for "real" crimes involving large financial losses and serious injuries inflicted by strangers. The limited resources of the court system should not be used to attempt to settle petty squabbles between people with prior relationships. Prosecutors complained that a great many complainants decided to drop charges or failed to appear in court to testify when the defendants were family members, lovers, former friends, classmates, fellow workers, or neighbors. Anticipating that these complainants would change their minds shortly

after an arrest, prosecutors disposed of their "garbage" cases quickly, either by dropping the charges completely or by plea bargaining them down (Silberman, 1978; Ray, 1984; Umbreit, 1987).

The first experiments with ADR techniques for resolving civil and criminal conflicts were launched at the start of the 1970s in Philadelphia and in Columbus, Ohio. The Law Enforcement Assistance Administration provided seed money to cover the start-up costs of other programs. Most experiments were sponsored by and attached to a criminal justice agency such as a court or prosecutor's office; others were run by private nonprofit organizations (such as the American Arbitration Association or the Institute for Mediation and Conflict Resolution), a community group (such as the local bar association), or a county or municipal governmental body. The kind of sponsorship behind a center shaped the way it conducted its business and the types of cases it accepted (Alper and Nichols, 1981; Freedman and Ray, 1982; McGillis, 1982; Goldberg, Green, and Sander, 1985; Harrington, 1985).

In 1980, Congress passed the Dispute Resolution Act, authorizing the creation of a national clearinghouse to conduct research and disseminate information about "storefront" justice. In 1981, New York became the first state to fund new and existing programs. The entire branch of social science known as **conflict resolution** received much-needed recognition, legitimation, and support in 1984 when Congress earmarked money within the military budget to establish the United States Institute of Peace. Courses on the techniques, strategies, and philosophies of conflict resolution and peacemaking are now offered routinely in schools and colleges, and in training programs for lawyers, police officers, and other criminal justice personnel (Cooper, 2000; and Volpe, 2000).

Pilot programs to test whether mediated restitution arrangements could lay the groundwork for reconciliation were pioneered in Canada in the mid-1970s and in Elkhart, Indiana, in 1978. Members of the Mennonite religious sect were among the first enthusiastic supporters of this healing process. Their experimental project became a model for others to replicate and modify, just as the penitentiary (invented by the Quakers in the early 1800s as a nonviolent alternative to corporal and capital punishment) was copied by governments worldwide.

At the start of the 1990s, more than 125 Victim–Offender Reconciliation Programs were operating in 20 states, handling about 16,000 cases a year. By the close of the 1990s, in nearly all states, about 300 programs brought victims and offenders together (Coates, 1990; Umbreit and Coates, 1993; Umbreit, 1994, 1995; Umbreit and Greenwood, 1998). By the early years of the new century, statutes authorizing victim–offender mediation were on the books in 29 states. In some states, the possibility of mediating a conflict was simply listed as one of many sentencing alternatives, but in other states, detailed provisions addressed liability issues, expenditures, the confidentiality of proceedings, training requirements for mediators, and methods for evaluating these programs (Lightfoot and Umbreit, 2004).

In 2002, the United Nations urged member countries to consider setting up experimental programs in restorative justice. Thousands of programs currently operate in more than 50 nations (Butler, 2004a).

How Reconciliation Programs Work

Making restitution, in monetary payments from earnings or by performing direct personal services, is a symbolic gesture that is a prerequisite for reconciliation and reacceptance into the community. Reparations not only help victims recover from the aftershocks of predatory incidents but also provide the basis for forgiveness. The government—through its criminal justice agencies—can strive to maintain order and protect lives and property, but only the community—through its local institutions and traditions—can encourage reintegration. A neutral third party can facilitate and oversee the process of restoring harmonious relations better than an agent of the state—such as a prosecutor, judge, or probation officer who coerces both parties to agree to certain terms (Umbreit, 1989, 1990; Van Ness, 1990; Wright, 1991). The differences between retributive justice and restorative justice are highlighted in Table 13.4.

The kinds of cases considered appropriate for mediation and conflict resolution have grown steadily since the first projects were initiated. Originally, guidelines restricted the types of matters that were referred to neighborhood justice centers to noncriminal quarrels between people with ongoing relationships. Then the scope of eligible cases

TABLE 13.4   **Comparing and Contrasting Retributive Justice and Restorative Justice**

Issue	Retributive Justice	Restorative Justice
Nature of crime	A violation of the state's rules	An act that harms specific individuals
Jurisdiction	Handled by the criminal justice system's agencies and officials	Resolved by community members
Goals	Conviction and punishment for the purpose of retribution, deterrence, and incapacitation	Recovery of victim, rehabilitation of offender, restoration of harmony
Methods	Adversary system, establish guilt according to strict rules of evidence	Mediation, negotiation, frank discussion, consensus, restitution
Victim's role	Limited to complainant and witness for the prosecution	Central figure, direct participant
Offender's role	Must accept blame, suffer consequences	Must accept responsibility, make amends
Orientation	Past wrongful acts, prevention via fear of consequences	Past harm and future recovery, rehabilitation

SOURCES: Adapted from OJP, 1997; Crowe, 1998; and Zehr, 1998.

was broadened to include such misdemeanors as harassment, simple assault, petty larceny, and vandalism, in which the disputants had committed retaliatory acts against each other as part of a simmering feud. Such cases of shared responsibility were not suitable for criminal justice processing because the adversary framework imposed a winner-take-all format that resulted in an undeserved victory for one party and an unjust defeat for the other.

Over the years, the nature of the relationship between the injured party and the offender rather than the nature of the offense became the single most important criterion for diverting cases out of the criminal justice system. Neighborhood justice centers began to handle acts of violence unleashed by offenders who knew their victims. Eventually, even violent incidents perpetrated by complete strangers were considered appropriate cases for face-to-face meetings. Some programs go as far as bringing together for group sessions victims whose cases were never solved and offenders convicted of harming people who don't wish to participate (Umbreit, 1989; Wright, 1989, 1991).

Most programs treat reconciliation as the desired outcome of a process that has four distinct phases: case selection, preparation, mediation and negotiation, and monitoring during the follow-up period. The healing process begins when a case manager selects cases that seem suitable. Next, a trained mediator (either a staff member or a volunteer) contacts the complainant and then the accused to explain the mechanics of the program, discuss the nature of the charges, and test their willingness to participate in a face-to-face encounter. If they both agree, the mediator meets with each side separately, and then brings the two disputants together—at the victim's home, at the jail where the defendant is being detained, or at the program's office. At their conference or dialogue, both parties vent their emotions and share their reactions to the crime and the way it was handled by the criminal justice system. After that they focus on the damage that was done. They attempt to hammer out a mutually acceptable arrangement in which the offender pledges restitution to cover the injured person's expenses. After the meeting, the mediator remains in contact with both

parties, supervising and verifying that the written contract is being completely fulfilled. The agreement usually requires that the wrongdoer make payments from earnings, perform useful and needed personal services, or undertake community service work to benefit a charity (Galaway, 1987; Coates, 1990; Umbreit, 1990, 1994; OJJDP, 1998b).

The heart of the process is the encounter between the person who was hurt and the person who harmed him; it takes place in a structured and secure setting—often at the program's headquarters, a community center, library, or house of worship but occasionally in a courtroom or the victim's home. Usually, each side has met individually with the mediator. The mediator, typically an uncertified volunteer with at least 30 hours of training and experience, tries to make both parties feel comfortable, facilitates their dialogue, and assists them to find common ground.

At the outset the injured party describes how the illegal act inflicted emotional, physical, and financial harm, and asks questions like, "Why me? What did I ever do to you?" and "How could I have avoided this?" The wrongdoer then tells his side of the story, often in the presence of his parents. By the end of the exchange, the wrongdoer comes to appreciate the error of his ways, accepts responsibility, expresses genuine remorse, apologizes, and agrees to try to restore the person who was harmed to the condition he was in before the crime occurred. The mediator, the program's staff, or a probation officer supervises the repayment process during the follow-up period. In cases where compliance lags, continued contacts and renegotiation of the settlement may become necessary. After restitution obligations have been fulfilled, reconciliation becomes a real possibility (see Umbreit and Greenwood, 1998; Price, 2002).

The majority of victim–offender reconciliation programs are run by private nonprofit organizations rather than criminal justice agencies, according to a survey carried out during the mid-1990s. Programs administered by private, community-based groups made up the largest single category (more than 40 percent). Nearly 25 percent were overseen by religious organizations. Criminal justice agencies ran the remainder: probation departments (about 15 percent), corrections departments (nearly 10 percent), and police forces and prosecutor's offices (a few percent each). Almost half of all programs dealt with both juvenile and adult offenders; about 45 percent handled only delinquency cases; and nearly 10 percent only supervised adult lawbreakers.

Local and state governments were the most frequent primary sources of funding. The federal government, faith-based organizations, foundations, private charities, and individual contributors also helped to pay for operating expenses. A typical program had a relatively small budget of just over $50,000, employed two full-time staff members, and relied on 35 or more volunteers to carry out its mission. On average, a program handled about 135 cases concerning juvenile offenders and supervised around 75 involving adults. Roughly 33 percent of the offenses were felonies, and the remaining 67 percent arose from misdemeanors. The most common crimes were vandalism, minor assaults, thefts, and burglaries. But around 33 percent of the programs reported that they occasionally handled more serious offenses, such as attacks leading to physical injuries and assaults with a deadly weapon. Some programs even dealt with sexual assaults by strangers, attempted murders, negligent homicides, and manslaughter. Probation officers, judges, and prosecutors referred all kinds of cases to mediation (Umbreit and Greenwood, 1998).

In every program, victims participated voluntarily, and they could quit at any time. In about 20 percent of the programs offenders had to take part if the people they harmed wanted them to, and they had to admit their guilt before proceeding in 65 percent of theprograms. About 33 percent of all wrongdoers were participating as a condition of diversion before adjudication. A little more than 25 percent had been found guilty in court but had not been sentenced yet, and an equal percentage was attending as part of their sentence.Of the cases in which victims and offenders met in the presence of a mediator, nearly 90 percent were settled by a written agreement, and the overwhelming majority of offenders completed their obligations successfully. However, program directors reported

that a variety of problems plagued their operations. Securing adequate funding from private and public sources presented a continuing challenge. Receiving a steady flow of appropriate referrals from criminal justice agencies required maintaining good working relationships. Cultivating support within the community demanded an ongoing dialogue with the advocates of retributive justice. Similarly, convincing angry victims to give restorative justice a chance required patience to overcome their initial resistance (see Umbreit and Greenwood, 1998).

Evaluating Efforts at Reconciliation

In theory, victim–offender reconciliation offers advantages both to parties and to their crime-plagued communities. A number of criteria for success can serve as the focus of evaluation research. Victims ought to have opportunities to release pent-up feelings and get answers to troubling questions. In addition to emotional catharsis, victims should be able to leave the negotiations with a satisfactory restitution agreement in hand. For offenders, the encounter offers an occasion to accept responsibility, express remorse, and ask for forgiveness. Probably more important to most perpetrators is the chance to substitute restitution obligations for time behind bars. For the community, the pragmatic benefit is that negotiated settlements relieve court backlogs as well as jail and prison overcrowding, and eliminate the need to build more cells to confine greater numbers of convicts at the taxpayers' expense. A less tangible but significant spiritual dividend is the fostering of an atmosphere of tolerance, understanding, and redemption within the community (Coates, 1990; Umbreit, 1990; Viano, 1990b; Sullivan and Tifft, 2001).

Evaluations of different programs highlight many important issues. Offender recidivism rates may not be any lower for adult participants in restorative justice experiments (see Niemeyer and Shichor, 1996; Hansen, 1997), but juveniles may benefit from making restitution. Youthful offenders who passed through mediation committed fewer and less serious offenses than a control group of their peers during the one-year follow-up period (Umbreit, 1994). As for the willingness of people who suffered harm to meet with juveniles placed on probation for property crimes, the percentages ranged from 54 percent to 90 percent. Reportedly, nearly 95 percent of the meetings led to a mutually acceptable agreement. The average amount of money the adolescents pledged to pay their victims ranged from about $175 to $250. The proportion of the contracts that were carried out to the victims' satisfaction ranged from a low of 52 percent in one program to a high of 91 percent in another. In general, research findings show that many victims volunteer to participate in face-to-face confrontations, very few mediation sessions become emotionally explosive, and most victims are not vindictive and do not make unreasonable demands (Galaway, 1987).

Another evaluation of four mediation projects attached to juvenile courts uncovered high levels of client satisfaction, approaching 80 percent of the victims and nearly 90 percent of the offenders. Roughly 85 percent of the participants felt that the process of mediation was fair to both parties. Before meeting their offenders in person, nearly 25 percent of the victims confided that they were afraid of being preyed upon again by the same individual; after the mediation session ended, only 10 percent still harbored that fear. More than 80 percent of the delinquents successfully completed their negotiated restitution arrangements, compared to less than 60 percent of similar offenders ordered to make restitution by juvenile court judges who didn't directly involve victims or use mediation (Umbreit, 1994). Victim dissatisfaction surfaced in those programs that failed to follow up to see to it that restitution pledges were fulfilled (Coates and Gehm, 1989).

Mediators received higher ratings for fairness than judges, according to several evaluations that compared cases handled at selected ADR programs to similar cases adjudicated in court. Most disputants reported that they left the neighborhood justice centers believing that their differences had been settled. The compromise solutions worked out at centers were adhered to more faithfully than dispositions

imposed by criminal or civil court judges (Cook, Roehl, and Sheppard, 1980; Davis, Tichane, and Grayson, 1980; Garofalo and Connelly, 1980). Similarly, meetings between victims and juvenile delinquents and their parents that were facilitated by trained police officers received high satisfaction ratings from all parties (McCold, 2003).

Proponents of mediation in pursuit of reconciliation interpret these findings as evidence of a solid, positive track record. They conclude that the experimental stage can be judged a success and that the time has come for a substantial reallocation of resources that would enable these programs to handle many more cases. They point to polls that demonstrate that considerable public support favors restitution as an alternative to imprisonment, at least for cases involving property crimes and minor assaults (Galaway, 1987, 1989).

Pros and Cons from the Victim's Point of View

For victims of minor offenses who are embroiled in ongoing conflicts for which they admittedly bear some responsibility, alternative dispute resolution offers several advantages over adjudication in criminal or civil court. If the injured parties don't want an arrest to be made or charges to be pressed, they now have the additional option of bringing their problems to a neighborhood justice center. Incidents that otherwise would be too trivial to interest the police or prosecutors can be addressed (see Cooper, 2000).

In more serious cases, victims can tell offenders in their own words exactly how they suffered physically, financially, and emotionally. They can ask troubling questions that only the offender can answer (such as "How did you get in?" or "Were you following me?"), which might finally lead to peace of mind and closure. If they dread the public spectacle of testifying and of being cross-examined in open court, they will be relieved to take part in a low-key proceeding behind closed doors. Informal justice has proven to be speedier, cheaper, and more accessible than formal hearings and trials. Cases are handled sooner, are heard at times and places convenient to the participants, and cost less in terms of time, money, and stress. People who have been harmed can feel a sense of empowerment by representing themselves rather than accepting the services of a prosecutor who primarily looks after the state's interests or, in civil court, a private attorney who is after a share of the judgment awarded to the plaintiff. The settlement can be seen as a vindication if the other party apologizes in writing and undertakes restitution as an admission of responsibility. Such agreements can provide a sound basis for reconciliation for people who want to—or have to learn to—get along with each other in the future within their community. Smoldering tensions that might flare up again and result in violence and retaliation can be smothered (see Price, 2002).

Civil libertarians have some reservations about the way restorative justice is carried out. They are concerned that the emphasis on healing and redemption undermines the presumption of innocence and other legal practices in adversarial proceedings (such as remaining silent) that protect the accused from the power of the state. Suspects and defendants are being pressured to give up their due process rights and readily admit guilt in order to negotiate restitution arrangements and get out of the grip of the punitive system. Offenders from more privileged backgrounds may be more able to buy their way out of trouble or work off their debts than disadvantaged wrongdoers with few marketable skills. Sentence disparity grows because the consequences for committing the same crime vary substantially, depending entirely upon the input from the particular victim and whatever community members take part in the unstructured conferencing process. Whereas court proceedings are generally open to the public to ensure that rules are properly followed, conferencing usually takes place behind closed doors. Also, the willingness of programs to deal with even the most minor infractions stimulates the criminal justice system's appetite for **widening the net**—intervening more intrusively into private matters that previously would have been off-limits to outsiders (see Butler, 2004b).

But from the victims' viewpoints, other drawbacks persist. As with criminal court-ordered restitution, the opportunity for a mediated settlement arises only in cases where a suspect has been apprehended but not necessarily formally convicted. Statistically, that prerequisite excludes most property crime victims. As for violent crimes, the harm inflicted in a moment can last a lifetime. Injuries and losses might be so great that they add up to expenses that far exceed what the offender is able to repay and what a small community can afford to reimburse. The limited capacity of the offender and the community to provide resources might serve as a cap that prevents a seriously wounded person from fully recovering all expenses (Herman, 1998).

Furthermore, a completely innocent victim might find informal justice unsatisfactory. If the process consciously abandons the presumptions of guilt and innocence that underlie the labels *offender* and *victim* and terms both parties *disputants*, then the complainant's conduct is open to scrutiny, especially in the absence of rules governing evidence and cross-examination. The notion of shared responsibility is frequently invoked by mediators, who view disputes as outgrowths of misunderstandings and the pursuit of narrow self-interest by both parties. To reach a compromise, complainants might be pressured to concede more responsibility, fault, or involvement than they feel they should. The entire notion of a compromise solution as a means of achieving reconciliation rests on the practice of both parties giving in, to varying degrees, from their original demands. Complainants who insist that they are absolutely blameless can feel cheated. When their case was diverted from the criminal justice system, that reassignment symbolized a withdrawal of governmental support (prosecutorial backing) from their side. They may feel that they were coerced to give in to a preordained outcome—reconciliation—even if their legitimate feelings of anger and hostility have not dissipated.

For victims intent on revenge, the greatest drawbacks of mediation and restitution are that these processes are not punishment-oriented. Neighborhood justice centers and victim–offender reconciliation programs are not authorized to convict offenders, publicly humiliate them with the stigma of the label of *criminal*, impose stiff fines, or confine them in a penal institution (Garofalo and Connelly, 1980; Butler, 2004b).

The Future of Restorative Justice

In the near future, the number of cases directed to neighborhood justice centers and victim–offender reconciliation programs will grow because there is a movement toward informality throughout the criminal justice system. In practice, informality is marked by a preference for unwritten, flexible, commonsense, discretionary procedures tailored to fit particular cases. As an ideology, informality is characterized by an antipathy toward rigid hierarchy, bureaucratic impersonality, and professional domination.

The growing interest in informal justice is fostered by several beliefs. One is that centralized governmental coercion has failed as an instrument of social change. Consequently, people must solve their own problems in decentralized, community-controlled settings. Another belief is that nonstranger conflicts ought to be diverted from the formal adjudication process whenever possible. The third contention is that both punishment and rehabilitation efforts behind bars have failed to "cure" offenders, largely because criminal justice officials and agencies primarily serve the state's interests (or their own), to the detriment of both offenders and victims. Enthusiasm for informal alternatives is fed by perceptions that the criminal courts are paralyzed by huge caseloads, civil courts are swamped with frivolous lawsuits, and prisons and jails are dangerously overcrowded. As a pragmatic response to such economic and political realities, informality beckons as a solution to the government's fiscal crisis. Neighborhood justice centers and victim–offender reconciliation programs can relieve the overburdened criminal justice system at a time when calls for more services are clashing with demands for less taxation (Able, 1982; Van Ness and Strong, 1997).

Several potential problems could plague the extra-judicial approaches of family group conferencing, alternative dispute resolution, and victim–offender reconciliation programs. If caseloads grow too large, mediators might be inclined to adopt an assembly-line approach to speed up the process and avoid backlogs. Worse yet, overworked staff members might be tempted to eliminate the face-to-face mediation session entirely to dispose of a large caseload more quickly.

Originally, the cases considered suitable for mediation, restitution, and reconciliation involved petty, nonviolent offenses against property. Program staff members acceded to this limitation to perfect their techniques, avoid controversy, and maintain funding and referral sources. But now legislators and judges seem increasingly willing to send conflicts marred by violence between strangers to mediation. Some of these more serious cases don't fit the mediation format, and the harm cannot be repaired through restitution. And other tough cases will require more time to resolve, professional mediators, a greater commitment of resources, and more support from social service and criminal justice agencies (Coates, 1990; Umbreit, 1990; Johnstone, 2001; Wemmers, 2002). The risks of revictimization must be weighed against the prospects for reconciliation when, for example, mediators facilitate victim–offender dialog in father-daughter incest cases (Wilson, 2008).

Signs of conflict already have emerged within the restorative justice movement between practitioners and advocates over the accusation that some programs have strayed too far from the original victim-centered focus of repairing the harm done to individuals by making wrongdoers accept responsibility for their misdeeds. Offenders must show genuine remorse, exhibit empathy, and sincerely apologize in order to elicit the forgiveness response that they seek. Overly enthusiastic staff members and mediators can pressure reluctant victims of serious violence to participate in a dialogue, then insensitively impose simplistic, moralistic, or religious formulas on them: "Forgive and forget; learn to move on; reconciliation brings healing" (see Umbreit et al., 2004; Wilson, 2005; and Armour and Umbreit, 2006).

Furthermore, restorative justice can be oversold as a nonpunitive, redemption-oriented cure-all that can handle most criminal matters. It appears to be the humane and politically progressive alternative to mean-spirited retributive justice. Its popularity arises in part from the imposition of "compulsory compassion" on both good-natured victims and "sinners" seeking redemption (Acorn, 2004). Enthusiasm for other sweeping reforms in the past quickly led to disillusionment when they failed to live up to their potentials. Unfounded optimism greeted the substitution of supposedly rehabilitative reformatories in place of harsh corporal and capital punishment, and of ostensibly treatment-oriented juvenile institutions to supplant a punitive adult court and prison system. A number of other highly touted innovations ultimately disappointed their advocates: the replacement of fixed terms of incarceration with indeterminate sentences that provided incentives for self-improvement; the use of scared-straight visits to prisons to shock delinquents into changing their ways; and the proliferation of boot camps as places to break youthful offenders of bad habits and build self-disciplined, law-abiding young men. Restorative justice programs may fall short too, but promising experimental programs that divert first-time, teenage, and nonviolent offenders into mediation conferences certainly merit an expanded role in the justice system of crime-ridden metropolitan areas.

SUMMARY

During the twenty-first century, victims will pursue three very different courses of action. Most will seek to exercise their recently granted rights within the formal criminal justice process. Some will explore the possibilities that are opening up in a new approach called restorative justice. A few will turn to retaliatory violence to try to get even with the offenders who harmed them.

The victims' movement has secured important new rights that pledge information, protection, and opportunities to participate in decision making. As the movement seeks to make further inroads at the expense of suspects, defendants, convicts, and prisoners, it will encounter resistance from civil libertarians who fear that the government will use victims to enhance its power over individuals. As victims seek more rights from justice system agencies, officials will try to defend their privileges and fend off outside interference and imposed costs. Victim advocacy may become institutionalized and professionalized as the options and obligations become more extensive, complicated, and contested.

Another course of action that some distraught victims will pursue can best be described as vigilantism. This do-it-yourself approach has a long and bloody history. It arises from a preoccupation with exacting revenge and a frustration with the cumbersome criminal justice process. As opposed to legitimate self-defense, retaliatory violence visited upon suspected predators causes a role reversal: victims become offenders, and offenders become victims.

Some victims will direct their energies toward developing more restorative justice programs, which at the start of the twenty-first century handled only a small, but growing, fraction of cases. Restorative justice rejects retributive justice's emphasis on conviction and punishment, and instead substitutes mediation, restitution, and reconciliation. Its goal is to enable the two parties to work out a lasting settlement that restores harmonious relations within a community.

KEY TERMS

victims' rights, 373

zero-sum game model, 375

allocution, 380

guardian *ad litem*, 382

private prosecution, 383

differential handling, 383

QUESTIONS FOR DISCUSSION AND DEBATE

1. Explain how certain rights might be considered to be gained at the expense of either criminals or criminal justice officials, depending on the way victims exercise them.

2. What is the difference between using deadly force in self-defense and unleashing retaliatory violence? Make up some scenarios that illustrate the distinction.

3. Argue both sides of the debate over whether victims would be better off if they were armed.

4. Compare and contrast the principles of retributive justice and restorative justice.

5. From a victim's point of view, what are the potential benefits and drawbacks of participating in a victim–offender reconciliation program?

CRITICAL THINKING QUESTIONS

1. Does a victim "own his case" and therefore have a valid justification to try to control its outcome? If victim input leads to great inconsistency in the way similar cases of robbery or burglary are resolved, is that a problem?

2. Is reconciliation always a worthy goal? Make up some scenarios that would be inappropriate for a mediated dialogue, in your opinion.

3. Should victims be permitted to seek retaliatory justice? Why or why not?

SUGGESTED RESEARCH PROJECTS

1. Why hasn't a victims' rights amendment been added to the Constitution? Look through speeches given by Presidents Clinton and Bush and delivered by members of Congress, and then find out the objections of opponents who defeated this campaign to recast the Sixth Amendment.

2. Look through a database of newspaper and magazine articles and assemble some accounts in which a victim pulled a gun and got out of serious trouble as a result. Then find articles that describe how armed victims suffered serious injuries or were murdered.

3. Look through the accounts of victim–offender mediation programs and assemble some cases in which clever and creative solutions were worked out to settle severe conflicts.

4. Look through the list of real-life activists assembled in Box 13.1. Figure out their names and find out more about their personal tragedies and the activities they have undertaken to further the cause of victim rights, mutual support, and assistance. Discover the names and achievements of a few more of the many other exemplary individuals whose inspiring accomplishments could not be mentioned in Box 13.1.

Glossary

abuse To maltreat, exploit, take advantage of, harm physically, hurt emotionally.

abuse of discretionary authority When a person, acting in an official capacity, takes unfair advantage of an ability to make choices and thereby violates the rights of victims or offenders.

advocates People who represent the best interests of victims and speak, write, or plead on their behalf.

agency The ability of a victim to make choices, seize opportunities, and regain control of his or her future; also, a government bureau.

allocution The chance to speak out and advocate for oneself in court, now available to victims as well as defendants.

alternative dispute resolution (ADR) An option available to victims who are willing to settle conflicts through the use of conciliation, mediation, and arbitration instead of criminal proceedings.

Amber Alert A notification system that uses mass communication to inform and mobilize the public to help search for a kidnapped child.

arbitration A process in which, when two parties are deadlocked, a neutral person engages in fact-finding and then imposes a legally binding, fair settlement of a dispute.

assault In criminal law, an attack intended to inflict bodily harm.

assistant district attorney A lawyer working for the prosecution who handles cases in court representing the

interests of the victim, but also the government and society at large.

attach To seize earnings and hand them over to victims as part of a restitution obligation.

attractiveness How appealing a potential target is to a criminally inclined person.

avoidance strategies Precautions that crime-conscious individuals can follow to reduce their risks of being accosted by criminally inclined persons.

battered-child syndrome Physical and emotional suffering caused by deliberate repeated attacks; also, a defense against criminal charges in which the perpetrator argues that the illegal behavior arose as a result of serious abuse by parents or caretakers that was suffered during childhood.

battered-woman syndrome Physical and emotional suffering caused by deliberate, repeated attacks; also, a defense against criminal charges in which the perpetrator argues that her retaliatory violence arose as a result of repeated physical abuse by a partner.

battery The unlawful use of force during an assault.

bedsheeting A harsh practice of charging a defendant with every possible crime that may have been committed during a single incident.

best practices A collection of recommended procedures that have been proven effective.

bias crime An act of violence or an attack on property that is motivated by the offender's hatred of the victim's kind of person.

bias incident An act that is not illegal but is an expression of the aggressor's hatred of the victim's kind of person.

bifurcated capital trials A two-stage proceeding in which, after the conviction and during the penalty phase, the murder victim's next of kin can testify and recommend a sentence.

blame-the-offender approach A perspective that holds the wrongdoer solely responsible for committing the illegal act.

blame-the-system approach A perspective that holds certain social conditions and institutions partly responsible for causing the illegal act.

blame-the-victim approach A perspective that holds the injured party partly responsible for causing the illegal act.

blind justice An ideal situation in which the victim's characteristics as well as the offender's characteristics do not influence legal proceedings.

blue-book value A standard dollar amount indicating what a vehicle of a particular make, model, and year is worth if it is traded in, totally destroyed, or stolen.

boost explanation A theory holding that repeat victimization occurs because the offender gains important knowledge about the target during the initial crime.

Brady Bill A federal statute, named after James Brady, the White House press secretary, who was shot during an assassination attempt on President Reagan, that imposes a background check and a waiting period on purchasers of firearms.

burnout Physical and emotional exhaustion caused by stress.

carelessly facilitating victims Negligent people who make a thief's tasks easier.

carjacking A robbery in which the offender threatens or attacks a motorist and then drives away in the vehicle.

carnal knowledge An old-fashioned legal term for imposed sexual intercourse by a male in violation of the law.

causes of action In civil lawsuits, the allegation that the harm suffered by the plaintiff (victim) was a direct and proximate result of the defendant's behavior.

character contest A situation in which a slur or insult leads to a confrontation that escalates into a fight because each party wants to save face by not backing down.

child lures Deceitful tactics used by molesters to attract and isolate their victims.

children's rights movement A coalition that advances reforms to prevent the exploitation, oppression, and abuse of youngsters, including those who are juvenile delinquents as well as young victims of crimes.

chop shops Illegal operations that dismantle stolen vehicles in order to sell their parts on the black market.

citizen's arrest A warrantless arrest carried out by a private citizen such as the victim or a bystander in the immediate aftermath of a crime.

civil court An arena in which lawsuits surrounding torts (private wrongs) are settled by a preponderance of the evidence in accordance with civil law.

civil liberties movement A coalition that advances reforms that preserve constitutional rights and due process guarantees placing limits on what a government can do to its citizens, especially those accused of committing crimes.

civil rights movement A coalition that advances reforms intended to prevent acts of hatred and discrimination on the basis of race, ethnicity, religion, sex, or sexual preference, including prejudicial decisions made by criminal justice officials.

claims-making Estimates of the seriousness of the problem, demands for credit, and explanations that appear to be self-serving.

classical school A philosophy developed by Beccaria and Bentham that emphasizes the rational choices facing individuals and the consequences they must accept for making mistakes.

client-specific Outcomes tailored to the needs and wants of victims and criminals in particular offenses.

clinical fallacy Making the mistaken assumption that people who come in for treatment are very similar to those who do not seek help.

Code Adam An emergency procedure to lockdown a facility to prevent a kidnapper from escaping.

cold case squad A special unit of detectives whose assignment is to reopen, re-examine, and resolve unsolved cases.

community policing An approach that emphasizes the importance of maintaining a close working relationship or partnership with neighborhood residents.

comparative rates Weighing the relative risks of experiencing different kinds of misfortunes, such as crimes, accidents, and diseases.

compensatory damages A judgment won in civil court in which a plaintiff (victim) is to be repaid by a defendant for the injuries and losses sustained during a crime.

composition An ancient practice in which the payment of money or goods to a victim by an offender's family was intended to permanently settle a dispute.

conciliation A procedure in which disputants negotiate by communicating through a neutral third party.

confirmed terrorist attacks Incidents in which law enforcement agencies have identified the group responsible and its political motive.

conflict approach An orientation that focuses on laws and policies that reflect opposing interests and clashing goals due to struggles for resources and power.

conflict resolution A informal method that seeks compromise settlements through negotiations and avoids notions of guilt and innocence.

conscientiously resisting victims Individuals who took extra precautions and bear no responsibility for their misfortunes.

consideration Concessions offered by the prosecution during plea negotiations to induce defendants to admit guilt and forgo their constitutional right to a trial by a jury of their peers.

constructionist approach A perspective that notes how powerful groups try to impose their definitions on reality.

contingency basis A financial arrangement in which the attorney representing the plaintiff (victim) in a civil lawsuit is paid a share of the winnings (judgment).

conventionally cautious victims People who did not take extra precautions and therefore can be considered slightly responsible for their misfortunes.

conversion of chattel In civil law, the tort of knowingly stealing or destroying a victim's possessions.

co-orientation A stage during a robbery in which the offender orders the victim to surrender and comply with instructions or else suffer severe consequences.

cop a plea Slang meaning to admit guilt during negotiations in return for "consideration" (concessions) by the prosecution that might disappoint a punitively oriented victim.

co-presence A stage during a robbery where the offender moves within striking distance without arousing either a flight or fight reaction from the target.

correlation An indication that there is some degree of association, connection, and perhaps a statistical relationship between two variables.

cost-benefit analysis A process that weighs the advantages versus the disadvantages (pros and cons) of adopting a certain policy.

courtroom work group Insiders, especially prosecutors, defense attorneys, and judges, who share a common interest in resolving cases routinely and quickly.

creative restitution A situation in which the offender pays the victim back more than was required or expected.

Crime Clock A device used by the FBI in its *Uniform Crime Report* to illustrate how frequently a particular crime is committed within the entire United States.

crime conscious A person who is aware of the risks and ways of becoming a victim.

crime control An outlook that emphasizes the need for a firm and efficient criminal justice system as a means of protecting the law-abiding majority.

crime crash An expression that describes an unanticipated, dramatic drop in the crime rate; the opposite of a crime wave or spike.

crime prevention A social strategy intended to eradicate the social conditions that are thought to be the roots of criminal behavior.

crime prevention through environmental design (CPTED) A specific set of architectural precautions that are intended to make it more difficult for offenders to carry out their tasks.

crime wave A sudden, sharp rise in the crime rate; the opposite of a crime crash.

criminology The scientific study of crimes, offenders, victims, criminal laws, the operations of the criminal justice system, and the social reaction to illegal behavior.

cruelty to children An old-fashioned expression that was parallel to cruelty to animals and that gave rise to the recognition of child abuse.

cumulative risks The chances of becoming a victim over the course of a lifetime.

cyberstalking The use of e-mail, postings on websites, and other methods involving the Internet to threaten and harass someone.

deductible clause An agreement in an insurance policy that the company will not reimburse victims for relatively minor losses and expenses.

deep pockets An expression used in civil court to refer to persons and entities that have substantial assets that could be taken away if a plaintiff's (victim's) lawsuit succeeds.

default judgment A victory that is won in civil court because the other party fails to present a case.

defendants In criminal and civil court, individuals accused of being victimizers and violating laws.

defounding A process in which, after an investigation, the police downgrade the complainant's original accusations into less serious charges.

deviant place factor An explanation for a geographic concentration of incidents that focuses on areas that attract criminally inclined people.

differential access to justice The accusation that criminal justice officials are not yet blind to the wealth, power, and prestige of specific victims and offenders, and consequently handle cases differently.

differential handling The accusation that some people receive better treatment in the criminal justice system than others because of sex, race, or class.

differential rates Substantially different risks of being harmed are faced by individuals who fall into various groupings.

direct or primary victims Individuals who suffer physical, economic, or emotional harm firsthand.

direct transfer Economic harm suffered when thieves steal someone's possessions.

discovery A pre-trial process in which facts are established through depositions.

disposed of Resolved in court; by implication, quickly and efficiently.

district attorney Chief of the government's prosecution unit within a jurisdiction; usually elected, and ostensibly representing victims as well as the organization and the public interest.

doer-sufferer relationship A term that implies shared responsibility within a victim-offender interaction.

domestic chastisement A privilege formerly accorded to husbands to discipline their wives by using reasonable force.

domestic terrorism Attacks to advance a political cause launched by groups within a country.

domestic tranquility A widely held illusion that women were safe when at home.

double indemnity clause A provision in a life insurance policy that pledges a payment of twice the normal amount if the covered individual dies accidentally or is murdered.

dual verbal defense A strategy of victims under attack that involves calling for help while simultaneously reasoning with, pleading with, or threatening the assailant.

duet frame of reference A term that implies shared responsibility within a victim-offender relationship.

elder abuse Harming older people physically, stealing from them, exploiting them financially, or neglecting them emotionally.

English common law The original source of most laws enacted in colonial America; a system of laws not formally written down but supposedly applicable to everyone.

equal protection under the law A pledge derived from the Fourteenth Amendment to the Constitution that promises that criminal justice decision makers will disregard a victim's or a defendant's social class, race, national origin, gender, age, or religion.

equalizers A view that firearms would protect victims under attack from assailants who have initial advantages such as greater size and the element of surprise.

equivalent group An outlook that emphasizes that victims often share many characteristics with their assailants.

exposure A risk factor that emphasizes how individuals and their possessions may be left unguarded and vulnerable to attack.

fabricating simulators People who commit fraud by pretending to be victims to receive insurance reimbursement.

facilitation Careless behavior that makes a criminal's tasks easier.

facilitators A view that firearms would make it more likely that minor quarrels would escalate into shootings.

failure to warn An accusation in a civil lawsuit that a third party was grossly negligent by not notifying a person that he or she was in grave danger.

false imprisonment The unlawful detention or incarceration of an innocent person based on a false arrest, possibly due to a mistaken identification by a complainant.

false memory syndrome A condition that causes some individuals to believe they can recall abusive events that never took place.

false negatives People who are predicted to pose a low risk of criminal behavior but end up acting illegally.

false positives People who are predicted to pose a high risk of criminal behavior but apparently behave legally.

family group conferencing A practice of restorative justice that involves the entire community in negotiations concerning the resolution of a conflict and the repairing of harm.

first party The defendant in a lawsuit who is accused of harming the plaintiff (victim).

flag explanation A theory that repeat victimization occurs because a target has permanent characteristics that attract criminals, such as being at a vulnerable location.

forward telescoping A tendency to believe that an offense occurred more recently than it did; a memory problem that is a source of inaccuracy on the *NCVS*.

funnel model Best pictured as a leaky net: many crimes take place but few offenders end up behind bars.

funneling or shrinkage The reduction in the volume of cases—and perhaps the escape of guilty people—for a number of reasons during the adjudication process.

garnish To seize a portion of a guilty party's earnings and give it to the victim as restitution.

"going postal" Slang for losing control at a workplace and shooting recklessly, derived from incidents of workers going berserk at postal facilities.

going rate A shared notion among members of the courtroom workgroup about the appropriate punishment for conviction of a specific offense at a particular time and place.

government-liability rationale A belief that the state is obligated to pay compensation to violent crime victims because it prohibits law-abiding citizens from going around armed.

gross negligence A basis for a lawsuit that charges a third party with failing to provide adequate protection to a person who was harmed by a criminal in a foreseeable manner.

guardian *ad litem* **(GAL)** A court-appointed advocate who is responsible for pursuing the best interests of a child.

heiress stealing An old-fashioned practice of raping a young woman in order to force her and her parents to agree to a marriage.

hierarchy rule An instruction from the FBI's Uniform Crime Reporting Division to local police departments to classify each incident in which several laws were broken solely in terms of the most serious offense that was committed.

hot spots Locations where crimes repeatedly take place and police are frequently summoned.

House of Refuge movement A coalition in the early 1800s that tried to salvage the lives of abused children by sending them to institutions that housed delinquents.

ideal types A sociological term meaning the clearest cases and best examples for comparison purposes.

implied consent An assumption on the part of a male that a female's behavior indicated that she agreed to engage in sexual intercourse.

incidence rate A research-based estimate of the number of individuals who suffer a particular type of victimization in a year.

index crimes The eight crimes (seven if arson is excluded) in Part 1 of the *UCR* that are closely tracked and are added together to calculate the total crime index for the year.

indirect or secondary victims Individuals who were not directly attacked but also suffer financially and emotionally, such as members of the injured party's family.

individualist rationale A view of self-defense that argues that a person under attack does not have to retreat from an aggressor.

informal justice An alternative approach to resolving cases that does not rely upon arrest, prosecution, and the exercise of formal rights by victims; includes both retaliatory violence and restorative justice.

institution blaming An approach that argues that deep-seated problems in a society's basic structures and fundamental relationships are partly to blame for criminal activity and victimization.

intentional torts Personal wrongs inflicted on purpose.

international comparisons Compilations of statistics showing victimization rates in various countries.

international terrorism Politically motivated attacks carried out by groups based in or originating from foreign countries.

interrogatories A set of written questions that must be answered as part of a lawsuit.

intimate partners People who are or were lovers.

inveiglement Enticement, persuasion to do wrong.

judgment-proof Someone who has no assets and cannot be compelled to make payments after losing a civil lawsuit.

judgment A victorious outcome as a result of a jury verdict in a civil lawsuit.

just deserts A philosophy that argues that offenders have "earned" punishments that are in proportion to the seriousness of the harm they have inflicted on others.

just world outlook A victim-blaming belief that bad things happen to bad people.

justifiable homicide A legal ruling that a killing does not merit punishment, usually because it was the result of an act of self-defense.

law-and-order movement A coalition of victims, officials, and organizations that argued for harsher punishments and an end to unwarranted leniency ("permissiveness").

lifestyle How a person spends his or her leisure time and disposable income.

lifetime likelihood A research-based projection of the proportion of a population that will probably experience a particular type of victimization during the course of their lives.

likelihood or probability A statistical term assessing the odds or chances of something happening.

lynching A violent mob action against a suspect or defendant accused of committing a serious crime, often instigated by vigilantes. The individual is brutally murdered, usually by being hanged by the neck.

macroscopic A view that looks at the larger picture.

malfeasance Carrying out required tasks ineptly.

maximalist An alarmist perspective that assumes the worst and calls for drastic measures to address a crisis.

means test A qualification in compensation programs that eliminates from reimbursement those who are considered able to absorb the loss without financial assistance.

mediation A method of resolving conflicts that counts on the effective intervention of a neutral third party who works with the disputants.

Megan's Law A statute named after a girl murdered by a child molester that requires registration of sex offenders and community notification.

memory decay A problem of forgetfulness that undermines the accuracy of the *NCVS*.

microscopic A view that looks closely at details.

minimalist A skeptical point of view that assumes many statistics are inflated and exaggerate the true scope and seriousness of the crime problem.

misprision of a felony A deliberate and illegal attempt to cover up the fact that a serious crime was committed.

missing children A catch-all phrase popularized by the media to refer to children whose whereabouts are unknown to their caretakers.

moderate correction The permissible use of reasonable force on occasion by a husband who felt compelled to discipline his wife.

moot model The type of informal justice carried out at multidoor courthouses or neighborhood justice centers.

muggability ratings An assessment by robbers of the attractiveness and vulnerability of targets.

muggings Unarmed robberies.

multidoor courthouse A neighborhood justice center that offers conciliation, mediation, and arbitration as ways of settling disputes that might otherwise be sent to civil or criminal court.

National Crime Victimization Survey (NCVS) An annual undertaking that attempts to determine how frequently certain crimes take place, who suffers, and what proportion of victims report the incidents to the police.

needs assessment A research-based report that outlines the kinds of help victims require in order to repair the financial, physical, and financial damage they suffered.

negligence Grounds for a lawsuit; doing something without the care required by circumstances as foreseen by a prudent person, or not taking any action, resulting in harm to an innocent person.

neighborhood justice center A place offering a variety of alternatives to settle minor conflicts that otherwise would be resolved in civil or criminal court.

no-drop prosecution policy A practice adopted by some district attorneys to press assault charges in domestic violence cases even if the battered woman decides to discontinue her cooperation.

nonfeasance Grounds for a lawsuit; not taking action or not doing what is required.

objectivity A stance of neutrality, evenhandedness, and open-mindedness that is desirable in victimology to avoid either pro-victim or anti-victim biases.

offender blaming An approach that holds a wrongdoer solely responsible for harming a victim.

official statistics Measurements and data disseminated from government agencies.

order of protection A restraining order issued by a judge that forbids a specific person from having contact with a particular victim.

outlet-attractor perspective An explanation that accounts for an outbreak of crimes near certain bars and clubs.

overcharging An abusive practice in which prosecutors lodge charges that are not well-supported by the available evidence.

pain and suffering A basis for civil lawsuits, involving an attempt to translate into monetary terms the harm caused to a plaintiff.

patriarchy A system in which men rule over women because of beliefs about male supremacy.

patterns Regularities and predictable relationships that emerge during the analysis of victimization data.

peacemaking circles An approach within restorative justice that attempts to draw interested parties into the process of settling a conflict.

pecuniary damages A basis for civil lawsuits that focuses on financial harm.

penal couple A situation in which both parties bear some responsibility for the development of a victim-offender relationship.

plaintiff A person who is considered a victim and files a lawsuit in civil court against a defendant or a negligent third party.

plea negotiation A longstanding practice in which the prosecution offers some concessions to the defense to convince the accused to admit guilt and settle the case without going to trial.

pleadings Formal arguments about claims and defenses put forward by both parties in a civil suit.

posttraumatic stress disorder (PTSD) A persistent, recurring, intense emotional reaction that is triggered by a highly unusual crisis such as a violent crime.

precipitation A situation in which a victim is partly at fault for arousing the offender's interest or triggering an attack.

precipitative initiators Victims who actually want to be harmed for an ulterior purpose such as insurance reimbursement.

preponderance of the evidence The burden of proof in civil proceedings in which the side that presents the slightly more impressive or convincing case wins.

prevalence rate A research-based estimate of the proportion of the population that has ever experienced a particular type of victimization during their lifetimes.

primary prevention programs Training potential victimizers and victims to avoid resorting to force to settle disputes by refuting myths, challenging stereotypes, and changing their attitudes.

private prosecution An unusual arrangement in a few jurisdictions in which a victim is entitled to hire a lawyer and press charges.

pro-arrest directive A departmental policy that instructs officers to arrest the person who appears to be the aggressor in domestic disturbances.

process server A person hired to inform a defendant that a plaintiff has filed suit in civil court.

profiles Statistically based portraits of the characteristics most offenders or victims share in common.

provocation An act that triggers, instigates, or incites someone to commit an unlawful attack.

provocative conspirators People who pretend to be victims but are in league with criminals for an ulterior purpose, such as insurance reimbursement.

proximity Being within striking distance of an offender.

pseudomemories Recollections of events that never happened.

public prosecutors Lawyers working for the government who represent the interests of their organization, victims, and society at large.

punitive damages A part of a lawsuit that requests additional money beyond expenses for the plaintiff as a way of punishing a defendant for committing a crime.

punitive rationale An argument justifying the use of force in self-defense that rests on the necessity of punishing wrongdoing.

range or confidence interval A statistical notion that predicts that the true but unknown answer is very likely to fall somewhere between the minimum and maximum value.

rape crisis syndrome An intense emotional reaction to being violated that burdens a victim repeatedly in the aftermath of a sexual assault.

rates A way of expressing risks or odds by comparing the number of victims out of every 1,000 individuals, or per 100,000 people or households, in one year.

rational choice theory An explanation for behavior that focuses on how would-be lawbreakers (or potential victims) might weigh the costs and benefits of their voluntary actions.

rationale of necessity A justification for using force in self-defense to prevent serious injury.

raw numbers The actual number of victims, such as a body count or death toll in murders, as opposed to the rate per 100,000 per year.

reasonableness standard An argument that rests on the assumption that most rational people would arrive at the same conclusion.

red carpet or VIP treatment A situation in which victims receive preferential handling by criminal justice officials that is clearly superior to what others experience.

redlining An illegal practice in banking and insurance that involves discrimination against disadvantaged people and troubled neighborhoods.

reform A change for the better in the opinion of supporters, although people holding opposing views would disagree.

restorative justice An approach to resolving criminal cases that rejects punishment in favor of seeking restitution and victim-offender reconciliation.

restraining order An order of protection issued by a judge that forbids a specific person from having contact with a particular victim.

retagging An illegal technique of using false papers to sell stolen vehicles as if they were used cars.

retaliatory justice An approach that emphasizes that the offender must suffer as least as much as the victim suffered.

right to self-defense The philosophy that victims under attack are justified to use as much force as necessary to protect themselves and their property from harm.

risk-benefit analysis An approach that weighs the pros and cons, or potential losses and gains, of a possible course of action.

risk-management tactics Ways to protect oneself against the dangers of being victimized while carrying out unavoidable activities.

risk-reduction activities Ways to limit exposure to dangers and of hardening targets that are likely to be attacked.

road rage An outburst of violence triggered by an incident while driving.

routine activities Everyday responsibilities and behaviors.

rule of thumb Centuries ago, a restriction that limited husbands to using sticks no thicker than their thumbs when beating their wives.

SAID syndrome An accusation, during a child custody battle following a divorce, that one party (usually the wife) will charge the other party with sexually abusing their child.

second party The plaintiff (victim) who pursues a lawsuit against the first party (the defendant).

second wound Additional emotional suffering inflicted on a victim by insensitive caregivers and family members.

secondary prevention programs Training high-risk couples to use negotiation and anger management techniques to settle disputes without resorting to force.

second-class treatment Recognized as part of differential handling; inferior treatment of certain victims by government officials.

security litigation seminars Workshops for employers and landlords that aim to fend off lawsuits.

selective-disinhibition perspective An explanation for misbehavior due to intoxication.

self-help movement A coalition of individuals and organizations composed of people who know from direct experience how a victim is suffering.

self-report survey A research tool that depends upon respondents revealing their experiences as victims or as offenders.

sensationalism A tendency to exaggerate or distort aspects of a crime to attract (usually media) attention for commercial gain.

sentence disparity Sharp differences in punishments imposed on people who committed the same crime.

series victimizations Repeated incidents suffered by the same person.

sexual assault Rape or other unwanted sexual contacts and physical impositions.

shared responsibility The perspective that the offender does not bear total responsibility for the criminal act.

shared-risk rationale The belief that funds set aside for compensating victims should be accumulated in a similar way to the collection of insurance premiums.

shelters Safe houses where battered women and their young children can flee to take refuge during a crisis.

social construction A view that influential people determine which specific individuals are defined as legitimate victims deserving of support.

social rationale A justification for using force in self-defense as a way of preserving law and order in the community.

social-justice rationale A justification for compensating victims of violence because of society's inability to eradicate the social roots of crime.

social-welfare approach A justification for compensating victims of violence because the government has a humanitarian obligation to help needy and disadvantaged persons.

sovereign immunity The protection of certain officials from lawsuits challenging the exercise of their discretion.

speakouts Events at which victims reveal the details of their plight.

spin A way of looking at a situation that can be challenged or questioned.

statutory rape Consensual sex involving a minor considered too young and immature to make such a choice.

stigma contests Struggles to shape public opinion involving attempts to discredit versus attempts to gain respectability and sympathy.

Stockholm Syndrome Behavior by a hostage that appears to be supportive of the situation of the kidnapper.

strong-arm robberies Unarmed robberies in which no weapon is used.

subculture of violence The way of life of a group that appears to condone or even approve of the use of force to settle disputes.

subintentional death Provocative behavior that can cause the victim to get killed.

subjective approach In contrast to the objective approach, reactions to victimizations that are based on emotions and allegiances.

Supplementary Homicide Report (SHR) An information-collection form police fill out and send to the FBI's Uniform Crime Reporting Division.

survivors The next of kin of murder victims; also a positive term for victims who are recovering from an ordeal or trauma.

symbolic restitution Made by offenders, partial repayments or repayments delivered to individuals or organizations that substitute for actual victims.

third parties Parties that are neither victims nor offenders but are accused of gross negligence and are sued in civil court.

throwaways Children expelled from their homes by their parents or guardians.

tort law Civil law governing the redress of private wrongs through lawsuits.

torts Ways individuals can suffer harm that can be redressed in civil court through monetary judgments.

trends Changes in a variable over time.

typification A process of identifying some example that clearly represents or symbolizes a certain concept or situation.

typology A classification system that attempts to sort each case into some category.

unfounded report A complaint that the police reject as untrue or unsupported by sufficient evidence.

Uniform Crime Report (UCR) An annual, national compilation based on a total number of crimes known to local police departments.

unnatural severity An old-fashioned term for child abuse; overly strict parenting.

valve theory of crime shifts The belief that protecting one type of target deflects criminally inclined people toward a comparable but vulnerable type of target.

victim A person who suffers physical, emotional, and financial harm because of illegal activity.

victim blaming An approach that holds an injured party partly responsible for what happened.

victim defending An approach that denies that an injured party should be held partly responsible for what happened.

victimism An outlook that traces deleterious consequences of past injustices right up to the present.

victimization An asymmetrical relationship that is abusive, painful, destructive, parasitical, and unfair.

victimization prevention specific precautions intended to increase the safety of particular persons, in contrast to crime prevention, which is societal in scope.

victimization rates The chances of becoming harmed by a particular crime, usually expressed as "for every 1,000 people per year."

victimology The scientific study of the victim's plight, the criminal justice system's responses, and the public's reactions; a branch of criminology.

victims' rights Pledges as well as guarantees concerning how an injured party will be handled by officials and agencies during the criminal justice process.

video portraits Projections of how a missing child might look as time passes.

vigilantism Retaliatory violence by victims and their supporters against individuals suspected of being offenders.

vulnerability A prediction about the susceptibility of a target to attack.

widening the net A tendency within criminal justice to intervene in situations that in the past had been overlooked or left alone.

women's movement A coalition guided by the ideology of feminism that seeks empowerment, equal rights, and reforms to improve the status of girls and women,

including victims of beatings, sexual assaults, incest, and stalking.

working definition A decision by a researcher about what to include and what to exclude when making measurements.

wrongful death The basis of a civil lawsuit by the family of a murder victim.

wrongful escape The basis of a civil lawsuit by a plaintiff (victim) that alleges gross negligence on the part of a third party in a department of corrections considered responsible for the harm caused by an escaped inmate.

wrongful release The basis of a civil lawsuit by a plaintiff (victim) against a third party in a department of corrections considered grossly negligent for improperly allowing a dangerous inmate to leave confinement.

yokings Unarmed robberies; muggings.

zero-sum game model An approach that assumes that the gains made by one party come at the expense of losses experienced by the other party.

References

ABA. *See* American Bar Association.

Abbey, A. (2005, January). Lessons learned and unanswered questions about sexual assault perpetration. *Journal of Interpersonal Violence, 20,* 39–42.

Abbey, A., Zawacki, T., Buck, P., Clinton, M., & McAuslan, P. (2004, May–June). Sexual assault and alcohol consumption. *Aggression and Violent Behavior, 9,* 271–303.

Able, R. (1982). *The Politics of Informal Justice: Vol. 1. The American Experience.* New York: Academic Press.

Abel, C., & Marsh, F. (1984). *Punishment and restitution: A restitutionary approach to crime and the criminal.* Westport, CT: Greenwood Press.

Abramovitz, M. (2001, March). The knockout punch of date rape drugs. *Current Health, 27,* 18–22.

Abramovsky, A. (1992, Fall). Victim impact statements: Adversely impacting upon judicial fairness. *St. John's Journal of Legal Commentary, 8,* 21–35.

Abrams, A. (1987, December 21). Sharing sorrow: Shelter helps turn victims into survivors. *New York Newsday,* pp. 2, 40.

Abramson, L. (1994, July 25). Unequal justice. *Newsweek,* 25.

Achimovic, L. (2003). *Parent alienation syndrome revisited.* Canberra, Australia: Australian Institute of Criminology.

ACF. *See* Administration for Children and Families.

ACLU. *See* American Civil Liberties Union.

Acorn, A. (2004). Compulsory compassion: A critique of restorative justice. Vancouver, Canada: UBC Press.

ADL. *See* Anti-Defamation League.

Adler, J. (1994, January 10). Kids growing up scared. *Newsweek,* 43–50.

Administration for Children and Families (ACF), U.S. Department of Health and Human Services (2008). Child maltreatment 2006. Retrieved August 9, 2008, from www.acf.hhs.gov/programs/cb.

Aguirre, A., Davin, R., Baker, D., & Konrad, L. (1999). Sentencing outcomes, race, and victim impact evidence in California. *The Justice Professional, 11*(3): 297–310.

Ahrens, J., Stein, J., & Young, M. (1980). *Law enforcement and victim services.* Washington, DC: Aurora Associates.

Ai, A., & Park, C. (2005, February). Possibilities of the positive following violence and trauma. *Journal of Interpersonal Violence, 20,* 242–250.

AIUSA. *See* Amnesty International, USA.

Akiyama, Y. (1981, March). Murder victimization: A statistical analysis. *FBI Law Enforcement Bulletin,* 8–11.

Alexander, R. (1992). Victims' rights and the Son of Sam law: Implications for free speech and research on offenders. *Criminal Justice Policy Review, 6,* 275–290.

Allbritten, R., & Allbritten, W. (1985). The hidden victims: Courtship violence among college students. *Journal of College Student Personnel, 26,* 201–204.

Allen, N. (1980). *Homicide: Perspectives on prevention.* New York: Human Sciences Press.

Allen, H., Friday, P., Roebuck, J., & Sagarin, E. (1981). *Crime and punishment: An introduction to criminology.* New York: Free Press.

Allison, J., & Wrightsman, L. (1993). *Rape: The misunderstood crime.* Newbury Park, CA: Sage.

Allredge, E. (1942). Why the South leads the nation in murder and manslaughter. *Quarterly Review, 2,* 123–134.

Alper, B., & Nichols, L. (1981). *Beyond the courtroom.* Lexington, MA: Lexington Books.

American Bar Association (ABA) Committee on Victims. (1979). *Reducing victim/witness intimidation: A package.* Washington, DC: ABA.

American Civil Liberties Union (ACLU). (2005). 9/11 victims' families and national security whistle-blowers demand an end to government silencing of employees who expose security risks. Press release, January 26. Retrieved November 2, 2005, from www.aclu.org. (2008).

———. (2008). Prisoner's rights—ACLU position paper. Retrieved May 2, 2008, from www.aclu.org.

Ames, M. (2005). *Going Postal: Rage, Murder, and Rebellion: From Reagan's Workplaces to Clinton's Columbine and Beyond.* New York: Soft Skull Press.

Amir, M. (1967). Victim precipitated forcible rape. *Journal of Criminal Law, Criminology, and Police Science, 58,* 493–502.

———. (1971). *Patterns in forcible rape.* Chicago: University of Chicago Press.

Amir, D., & Amir, M. (1979). Rape crisis centers: An arena for ideological conflicts. *Victimology, 4*(2), 247–257.

Amnesty International, USA (AIUSA). (1999). *United States of America: Race, rights, and police brutality.* New York: Amnesty International.

Anderson, B. (2008, April 18). Dead zone of the human spirit. *City Journal.* Retrieved October 13, 2008, from www.city-journal.org.

Anderson, D. (1999, October). The aggregate burden of crime. *Journal of Law and Economics,* 611–642.

Anderson, E. (1999). *The code of the streets.* New York: W.W. Norton.

Anderson, M., & Renzetti, C. (1980, July). Rape crisis counseling and the culture of individualism. *Contemporary Crises, 4,* 323–341.

Andrews, L. (1986, December). Are we raising a terrified generation? *Parents,* 139–142, 228–230.

Anti-Defamation League (ADL). *Hate crimes laws.* Retrieved July 17, 2003, from www.adl.org/99hatecrime.

AP. *See* Associated Press.

Applebome, P. (2008, November 19). Immigrant's death overshadows a debate. *New York Times,* p. A36.

Archambault, J. (2005, January). How many rape reports are false? *The Crime Victims Report, 8,* 83–84.

Archibold, R. (2008, March 5). Arizona weighs bill to allow guns on campus. *New York Times,* p. A14.

Arias, E., & Smith, B. (2003, March 14). Deaths: Preliminary data for 2001. *National Vital Statistics Report* (CDC NVSS), *51,* 1–5.

The armed citizen. (2008a). From the archives of *American Rifleman,* January 1, 2008, issue. Retrieved September 28, 2008, from www.nra.org.

———. (2008b). From the archives of *American Rifleman,* November 1, 2007 issue. Retrieved September 28, 2008, from www.nra.org.

Armour, M., & Umbreit, M. (2006). Victim forgiveness in restorative justice dialogue. *Victims and Offenders, 1*(2), 123–140.

Arriaga, X., & Capezza, N. (2005, January). Targets of partner violence: The importance of understanding coping trajectories. *Journal of Interpersonal Violence, 20,* 85–99.

Ash, M. (1972, December). On witnesses: A radical critique of criminal court procedures. *Notre Dame Lawyer, 48,* 386–425.

Ashman, C., & Trescott, P. (1987). *Diplomatic crimes.* Washington, DC: Acropolis Books.

Associated Press (AP). (1984a, September 20). Victims to get "Son of Sam" cash. *New York Times,* p. B3.

———. (1993a, October 7). A disabled child is seen more likely to be abused. *New York Times,* p. A21.

———. (1993b, October 3). High murder rate for women on job. *New York Times,* p. A29.

———. (1994a, January 1). As cities reach record numbers of killings, youths play grim role. *New York Times,* p. A7.

———. (1994b, April 26). Courts in New Jersey adopt "truth in sentencing" rule. *New York Times*, p. B7.

———. (1994c, January 8). Mother gets 10 years for slaying molester suspect. *New York Times*, p. A7.

———. (1994d, June 12). Notifying the next of kin: The worst job is often poorly done. *New York Times*, p. A35.

———. (1994e, August 7). Witness intimidation is called a growing problem. *New York Times*, p. A30.

———. (1996a, July 3). Menendez brothers sentenced to life in prison. *New York Times*, p. A15.

———. (1996b, July 3). Found memory murder case won't be retried. *Long Island Newsday*, p. A44.

———. (1996c, October 5). 7-year-old Oregon girl escapes as sharpshooter kills kidnapper. *New York Times*, p. A8.

———. (1997, April 18). Judge reduces term for man who killed bully. *New York Times*, p. A8.

———. (1999a, May 7). Amy Fisher wins parole after 6 years in prison for shooting. *New York Times*, p. B12.

———. (1999b, October 15). Some park visitors stroll safely, then claim robbery. *New York Times*, p. B4.

———. (2005a, February 28). Journalist recalls chilling letter from BTK killer. Retrieved October 8, 2008, from www.ap.org.

———. (2005b, November 19). Actor is ordered to pay $30 million in killing. *New York Times*, p. A17.

———. (2006, August 9). Oregon nurse returning home discovers intruder, strangles him with bare hands. Retrieved October 3, 2008, from www.ap.org.

———. (2007a, January 20). Newspaper: 10 months after disappearance, Missouri boy met police to report bike stolen. Retrieved August 8, 2008, from www.ap.org.

———. (2007b, June 14). Data shed light on child sexual abuse by Protestant clergy. *New York Times*, p. A12.

———. (2008a, February 15). List of recent deadly campus shootings. Retrieved September 8, 2008, from www.ap.org.

———. (2008b, March 31). Two freeway shootings, 1 fatal, extend a string in California. Retrieved April 28, 2008, from www.nytimes.com.

———. (2008c, February 10). Man beaten with baseball bat, shot after accused rape. Retrieved September 28, 2008, from www.ap.org.

Aunapu, G., Epperson, S., Kramer, S., Lafferty, E., & Martin, K. (1993, December 27). Robbing the innocents. *Time*, 31.

Austern, D. (1987). *The crime victim's handbook*. New York: Penguin.

Auto theft alert. (1994, Fall). *CAR* (Citizens for Auto-Theft Responsibility) *Newsletter*, 7.

Ayres, B. (1994, May 22). Big gains are seen in battle to stem drunk driving. *New York Times*, pp. A1, A24.

———. (1997, February 5). Civil jury finds Simpson liable in pair of killings. *New York Times*, pp. A1, A16.

Bachman, R. (1994a). *Violence against women: A National Crime Victimization Survey report*. Bureau of Justice Statistics. Washington, DC: U.S. Department of Justice.

———. (1994b). *Violence and theft in the workplace. BJS Crime Data Brief*. Washington, DC: U.S. Department of Justice.

———. (1998). The factors related to rape reporting behavior and arrest: New evidence from the National Crime Victimization Survey. *Criminal Justice and Behavior, 25*(1), 8–29.

Bachman, R., & Paternoster, R. (1993). A contemporary look at the effects of rape law reform: How far have we really come? *Journal of Criminal Law and Criminology 84*(3), 554–574.

Bahr, R. (1985, May). The threat of vigilantism. *Kiwanis*, 20–24.

Baird, S., & Jenkins, S. (2003, February). Vicarious traumatization, secondary traumatic stress, and burnout in sexual assault and domestic violence agency staff. *Violence and Victims, 18*, 71–84.

Baker, Al. (2007, October 25). Road rage passenger offers an account. *New York Times*, pp. B1, B5.

———. (2008, April 26). In man's tale of fatal robbery, police see a contract murder. *New York Times*, pp. A1, B6.

Baldus, D. (2003). Racial discrimination in the administration of the death penalty. *Criminal Law Bulletin (March-April), 39*. 2 (194–220).

Baldwin, J. (1988, May 8). Car thefts (33 a day) becoming an ugly fact of life. *New York Times*, Sec. 12, p. 2.

Balkan, S., Berger, R., & Schmidt, J. (1980). *Crime and deviance in America: A critical approach*. Belmont, CA: Wadsworth.

Banfield, A. (2007). His case vs. her case. *Cosmopolitan Magazine*, September: 204.

Bannister, S. (1992). Battered women who kill their abusers: Their courtroom battles. In R. Muraskin & T. Alleman (Eds.), *It's a crime: Women and justice* (pp. 316–333). Englewood Cliffs, NJ: Regents/ Prentice Hall.

Barbash, F. (1979, December 17). Victim's rights: New legal weapon. *Washington Post*, p. 1.

Barber, C., Hemenway, D., Hargarten, S., Kellerman, A., Azrael, D., & Wilt, S. (2000). "A call to arms" for a national reporting system of firearms injuries. *American Journal of Public Health, 90*(8), 1191–1194.

Barclay, G., & Taveras, C. (2003). International comparisons of criminal justice statistics. London: British Home Office. Retrieved July 30, 2005, from www. homeoffice.gov.uk.

Barden, J. (1987, May 13). Marital rape: Drive for tougher laws is pressed. *New York Times*, p. A16.

Barnett, O., & LaViolette, A. (1993). *It could happen to anyone: Why battered women stay*. Newbury Park, CA: Sage.

Barnett, R. (1977). Restitution: A new paradigm of criminal justice. In R. Barnett & J. Hagel (Eds.), *Assessing the criminal: Restitution, retribution, and the criminal process* (pp. 1–35). Cambridge, MA: Ballinger.

Barrett, D. (1998, July 28). Vigilante dad sentenced in mistaken rapist slay. *New York Post*, p. 6.

Barnett, O., Miller-Perrin, C., & Perrin, R. (2005). *Family violence across the lifespan* (2nd ed.) Thousand Oaks, CA: Sage.

Barnett-Ryan, C. (2007). Introduction to the Uniform Crime Reporting Program. In J. Lynch & L. Addington (Eds.), Understanding Crime Statistics, pp. 55–92. New York: Cambridge University Press.

Barringer, F. (1989, May 30). Children as sexual prey, and predators. *New York Times*, pp. A1, A16.

Bass, E., & Davis, L. (1992). *The courage to heal: A guide for women survivors of child sexual abuse* (3rd ed.). New York: Harper Collins.

Bastian, L. (1993). *Criminal victimization 1992. BJS Bulletin*. Washington, DC: U.S. Department of Justice.

Bastian, L., & Taylor, B. (1991). *School crime: A National Crime Victimization Survey report*. Washington, DC: U.S. Department of Justice.

Baum, K. (2007). *National Crime Victimization Survey: Identity Theft, 2005. BJS Special Report*. Washington, DC: U.S. Department of Justice.

———, & Klaus, P. (2005). *Violent victimization of college students, 1995–2002. BJS Special Report*. Washington, DC: U.S. Department of Justice.

Beall, G. (1980, October). Negotiating the disposition of criminal charges. *Trial*, 10–13.

Beck, A., & Mumola, C. (1999). *BJS Bulletin: Prisoners in 1998*. Washington, DC: U.S. Department of Justice.

Beck, M., Rosenberg, D., Chideya, F., Miller, S., Foote, D., Manly, H., & Katel, P. (1992, July 13). Murderous obsession. *Newsweek*, 60–62.

———, & Hughes, T. (2005). *Sexual violence reported by correctional authorities, 2004*. Washington, DC: U.S. Department of Justice, Bureau of Justice Assistance.

Beckett, K. (1996). Culture and the politics of signification: The case of child sexual abuse. *Social Problems, 43*(1), 57–76.

Behar, R. (1993, August 16). Car thief at large. *Time*, 47–48.

Beirne, P., & Messerschmidt, J. (1991). *Criminology*. San Diego, CA: Harcourt Brace Jovanovich.

———. (2000). *Criminology* (3rd ed.). Boulder, CO: Westview.

Belkin, L. (2002, December 8). Just money. *New York Times Magazine*, 92–97, 148, 150.

Belknap, J., & Melton, H. (2005, March). Are heterosexual men also victims of partner abuse? National Resource Center on Violence Against Women. Retrieved August 20, 2008, from www. vawnet.org.

Bellamy, P. (2005). The murder of JonBenet Ramsey. *Court TV's Crime Library*. Retrieved October 4, 2005, from www.courttv.com.

Beloof, D. (1999). *Victims in criminal procedure*. Raleigh, NC: Carolina Academic Press.

Benedict, H. (1992). *Virgin or vamp: How the press covers sex crimes*. New York: Oxford University Press.

Benedict, J. (1998). *Athletes and acquaintance rape*. Thousand Oaks, CA: Sage.

Benedict, J., & Klein, A. (1998). Arrests and conviction rates for athletes accused of sexual assaults. In R. Bergen (Ed.), *Issues in intimate violence* (pp. 169–179). Thousand Oaks, CA: Sage.

Bensing, R., & Schroeder, O. (1960). *Homicide in an urban community*. Springfield, IL: Charles C. Thomas.

Bent-Goodley, T. (2005, February). Culture and domestic violence. *Journal of Interpersonal Violence, 20*, 195–203.

Bergen, R. (Ed.) (1998). *Issues in intimate violence*. Thousand Oaks, CA: Sage.

Bergfeld, D. (2005, July 22). Students teach others dangers of date rape drugs at Texas Tech. *Texas Tech University Daily*, p. 8.

Berk, R., Campbell, A., Klap, R., & Western, B. (1992, October). The deterrent effect of arrest in incidents of domestic violence: A Bayesian analysis of four field experiments. *American Sociological Review, 57*, 698–708.

Berke, R. (1989, March 28). Capital offers unlimited turf to drug dealers. *New York Times*, pp. A1, A16.

Berliner, L. (1987, March). Commentary: Editor's introduction. *Journal of Interpersonal Violence*, 107–108.

Bernat, F. (1992, March). Book review: "Representing … battered women who kill" by Johann and Osanka. *Justice Quarterly, 9*(1), 169–172.

Berns, W. (1994, April). Getting away with murder. *Commentary, 97*, 25–29.

Bernstein, G. (1972). Statement. In *U.S. Senate, Report on the federal crime insurance program*. Committee on the Judiciary, Subcommittee on Criminal Laws and Procedures, 1st session (pp. 521–529). Washington, DC: U.S. Government Printing Office.

Bernstein, N. (2001, October 26). Thousands of orphans? An urban myth. *New York Times*, pp. B1, B10.

Bernstein, N., & Kaufman, L. (2004, October 2). Women likelier to be slain by a partner than a stranger. *New York Times*, p. B3.

Besharov, D. (1987, November). Federal action urged to protect rights of parents accused of child abuse. *Crime Victims Digest*, 5–6.

———. (1990). *Recognizing child abuse: A guide for the concerned*. New York: Free Press.

Best, J. (1988, Summer). Missing children, misleading statistics. *Public Interest*, 84–92.

———. (1989a). Dark figures and child victims: Statistical claims about missing children. In J. Best (Ed.), *Images of issues: Imagining contemporary social problems* (pp. 21–37). New York: Aldine de Gruyter.

———. (Ed.). (1989b). *Images of issues: Imagining contemporary social problems*. New York: Aldine de Gruyter.

———. (1997, May–June). Victimization and the victim industry. *Society*, 8–10.

Best, J., & Luckenbill, D. (1982). *Organizing deviance*. Englewood Cliffs, NJ: Prentice-Hall.

Biblarz, A., Barnowe, J., & Biblarz, D. (1984). To tell or not to tell: Differences between victims who report crimes and victims who do not. *Victimology 9*(1), 153–158.

Bienen, L. (1983). Rape reform legislation in the United States: A look at some practical effects. *Victimology, 8*(1), 139–151.

Birkbeck, C. (1983). 'Victimology is what victimologists do.' But what should they do? *Victimology, 8*(3–4), 270–275.

Biskupic, J. (2000, May 16). Justices reject lawsuits for rapes. *Washington Post*, p. A1.

BJS. *See* Bureau of Justice Statistics.

Black, D. (1968). Police encounters and social organization. Unpublished doctoral dissertation, University of Michigan, Ann Arbor, MI.

Blau, R. (2006, November 10). Call NYPD crime stats true-blue: Skeptics question findings. *The Chief: The Civil Employees Weekly*, p. 1.

Block, C. (2003, November). How can practitioners help an abused woman lower her risk of death? *NIJ Journal, 250*: 4–7.

Block, R. (1981). Victim-offender dynamics in violent crime. *Journal of Criminal Law and Criminology, 72*, 743–761.

Block, R., Felson, M., & Block, C. (1985). Crime victimization rates for incumbents of 246 occupations. *Sociology and Social Research, 69*(3), 442–449.

Block, R., & Skogan, W. (1986, Winter). Resistance and nonfatal outcomes in stranger-to-stranger predatory crime. *Violence and Victims 1*(4), 241–254.

Blumstein, A. (1995, August). Violence by young people: Why the deadly nexus? *National Institute of Justice Journal, 229,* 2–9.

Blumstein, A., & Rosenfeld, R. (1998, Summer). Explaining recent trends in U.S. homicide rates. *Journal of Criminal Law and Criminology, 88*(4), 1175–1216.

Bochnak, E. (Ed.). (1981). *Women's self-defense cases: Theory and practice.* Charlottesville, VA: Michie Co. Law Publishers.

Bode, J. (1978). *Fighting back.* New York: Macmillan.

Bode, N. (2007, September 5). Rapists' kin taunt, curse victim. *New York Daily News,* p. 16.

Bohmer, C., & Parrot, A. (1993). *Sexual assault on campus: The problem and the solution.* New York: Lexington Books.

Boland, B., Mahanna, P., & Sones, R. (1992). *The prosecution of felony arrests, 1988. BJS Report.* Washington, DC: U.S. Department of Justice.

Boland, B., & Sones, R. (1986). *Prosecution of felony arrests, 1981. BJS Special Report.* Washington, DC: U.S. Department of Justice.

Bonczar, T., & Glaze, L. (1999). *BJS Bulletin: Probation and parole in the United States, 1998.* Washington, DC: U.S. Department of Justice.

Bondurant, B., 2001. University women's acknowledgement of rape: Individual, situational, and social factors. *Violence Against Women, 7*(3), 294–314.

Boston, G. (1977). *Crimes against the elderly: A selected bibliography.* Washington, DC: National Criminal Justice Reference Service.

Bouza, A. (1991). Responding to domestic violence. In M. Steinman (Ed.), *Woman battering: Policy responses* (pp. 191–203). Cincinnati, OH: Anderson.

Bowker, L. (1983, June). Marital rape: A distinct syndrome? *Social Casework,* 340–350.

Bowman, C. (1992). The arrest experiments: A feminist critique. *The Journal of Criminal Law and Criminology, 83*(1), 201–208.

Boyer, D., & James, J. (1983). Prostitutes as victims. In D. MacNamara & A. Karmen (Eds.), *Deviants: Victims or victimizers?* (pp. 109–146). Newbury Park, CA: Sage.

Boyle, C. (2007, April 13). Rape just 1st ordeal. *New York Daily News,* p. 12.

Boyle, P. (1994, April). Travel industry launches drive to protect tourists. *New York AAA Motorist, 1,* 18.

Bradshaw, W., & Umbreit, M. (1998). Crime victims meet juvenile offenders: Contributing factors to victim satisfaction with mediated dialogue. *Juvenile and Family Court Journal, 49*(3), 17–25.

Brandl, S., & Horvath, F. (1991). Crime victim evaluation of police investigative performance. *Journal of Criminal Justice, 19,* 109–121.

Breckman, R., & Adelman, R. (1988). *Strategies for helping victims of elder mistreatment.* Newbury Park, CA: Sage.

Breitman, G. (1966). *Malcolm X Speaks.* New York: Grove.

Breitman, N., Shackelford, T., & Block, C. (2004, June). Couple age discrepancy and risk of intimate partner homicide. *Violence and Victims, 19,* 321–333.

Brents, B., & Hausbeck, K. (2005, March). Violence and legalized brothel prostitution in Nevada. *Journal of Interpersonal Violence, 20,* 270–295.

Brewster, M. (1998) Exploration of the experiences and needs of former intimate stalking victims. Final report submitted to the National Institute of Justice.

Brien, V. (1992). *Civil legal remedies for crime victims.* (Office for Victims of Crime bulletin). Washington, DC: U.S. Department of Justice.

Brienza, J. (1999, May). Crime victims laws sometimes ignored. *Trial, 35,* 103–105.

Briere, J. (1992). *Child abuse trauma: Theory and treatment of the lasting effects.* Newbury Park, CA: Sage.

Briscoe, D. (2005, February 7). Mail order misery. *Newsweek, 54.*

Broder, J., & Madigan, N. (2005, June 14). Jackson cleared after 14-week child molesting trial. *New York Times,* pp. A1, A19.

Brody, J. (2003, January 28). Empowering children to thwart abductors. *New York Times,* p. F6.

Bromley, D. (1991, May–June). The satanic cult scare. *Society,* 55–66.

Brooks, D. (2006a, April 9). Virtues and victims. *New York Times,* p. E 12.

———. (2006b, September 21). Lessons from U.N. week. *New York Times,* p. A31.

Brooks, J. (1972). Criminal injury compensation programs: An analysis of their development and administration. Unpublished doctoral dissertation. Ann Arbor, MI: University Microfilms.

Brown, R. (1975). *Strains of violence: Historical studies of American violence and vigilantism.* New York: Oxford University Press.

Brown, S. (2003, April). Victims' rights legislation in the twenty-first century. *NCSL State Legislative Report, 28*(7), 1–12.

Brown, J., & Langan, P. (1998). *BJS Report: State court sentencing of convicted felons, 1994.* Washington, DC: U.S. Department of Justice.

Brown, J., Langan, P., & Levin, D. (1999). *BJS Bulletin: Felony sentences in state courts, 1996.* Washington, DC: U.S. Department of Justice.

Browne, A. (1987). *When battered women kill.* New York: Free Press.

Brownmiller, S. (1975). *Against our will: Men, women, and rape.* New York: Simon & Schuster.

Brownstein, H. (1996). *The rise and fall of a violent crime wave.* Guilderland, NY: Harrow and Heston.

Bruni, F. (1989, April 3). Maureen Reagan reveals husband beat her. *New York Post,* p. 9.

Buchwald, A. (1969, February 4). Victim precipitation. *Washington Post,* p. 23.

Buchwald, E., Fletcher, P., & Roth, M. (1993). *Transforming a rape culture.* Minneapolis, MN: Milkwood Editions.

Buckler, K., & Travis, L. (2005). Assessing the newsworthiness of homicide events. *Journal of Criminal Justice and Popular Culture, 12*(1), 1–25.

Buckley, C. (2007, January 13). Safe haven laws fail to end discarding of babies. *New York Times,* pp. B1, B5.

Buckley, W. (1994, December 21). Excelsior the counterculture. On the Right (syndicated column). Islamorada (Florida) Free Press, p. 30A.

Bulletin Board (2004, August). Victims get work leave in Hawaii. *The Crime Victims Report, 8*(3), 48.

Bunch, J. (2005, June 28). Justices deny mom's right to sue police; Court: Castle Rock cops couldn't have known dad would kill kids. *Denver Post,* p. A1.

Bureau of Justice Statistics (BJS). (1974–2003). *Criminal victimization in the United States* (Annual Reports). Washington, DC: U.S. Department of Justice.

———. (1988). *Report to the nation on crime and justice* (2nd ed.). Washington, DC: U.S. Department of Justice.

———. (1994a). *Criminal victimization in the United States, 1992.* Washington, DC: U.S. Department of Justice.

———. (1994b). Violence and theft in the workplace. *BJS Crime Data Brief.* Washington, DC: U.S. Department of Justice.

———. (1994c). *Elderly crime victims.* Washington, DC: U.S. Department of Justice.

———. (2005). *Themes for 2005: Deaths in police custody reporting.* Washington, DC: U.S. Department of Justice.

———. (2008a). Intimate partner violence in the U.S. Retrieved August 20, 2008, from www.ojp.usdoj.gov/bjs/intimate/circumstances.htm.

———. (2008b). Homicide trends in the U.S.: intimate partners. Retrieved August 20, 2008, from www.ojp.usdoj.gov/bjs/homicide/intimates.htm.

———. (2008c). State court sentencing of convicted felons – statistical tables. Retrieved September 29, 2008, from www.ojp.gov/bjs/pub/pdf/sc0001st.pdf.

———. (2008d). National Crime Victimization Survey – statistical tables. Retrieved September 30, 2008, from www.ojp.gov/bjs/pub/cvus.

Bureau of Labor Statistics. (BLS) (2008). *Census of fatal occupational injuries, 2007.* Washington, DC: U.S. Department of Labor.

Burgess, A., & Holmstrom, L. (1974). Rape trauma syndrome. *American Journal of Nursing, 131,* 981–986.

Burke, T. (1998). Male-to-male gay domestic violence: The dark closet. In N. Jackson & G. Oates (Eds.), *Violence in intimate relationships: Examining sociological and psychological issues* (pp. 161–180). Woburn, MA: Butterworth-Heinemann.

Burrows, W. (1976). *Vigilante!* New York: Harcourt Brace Jovanovich.

Burt, M. (1980). Cultural myths and support for rape. *Journal of Personality and Social Psychology* 38: 217–230.

——— (1983). A conceptual framework for victimological research. *Victimology, 8* (3–4), 261–268.

Burt, M., & Katz, R. (1987, March). Dimensions of recovery from rape. *Journal of Interpersonal Violence, 2*(1), 57–81.

Burying crime in Chicago. (1983, May 16). *Newsweek*, 63.

Busch-White, L. (2002). *Identity theft victim: Help and support after the crime*. Bloomington, IL: 1st Books Library.

Butler, D. (2004a, September 11). Justice for all. *The Ottawa Citizen*, p. B1.

———. (2004b, September 17). Objection your honor. *The Ottawa Citizen*, p. B1.

Butterfield, F. (1999, October 17). Guns used more for suicide than homicide. *New York Times*, p. A16.

Butts, J., & Snyder, H. (1992). *Restitution and juvenile recidivism: OJJDP Update on Research*. Office of Juvenile Justice and Delinquency Prevention. Washington, DC: U.S. Department of Justice.

Buzawa, E., & Buzawa, C. (1990). *Domestic violence: The criminal justice response*. Newbury Park, CA: Sage.

———. (1996). *Do arrests and restraining orders work?* Thousand Oaks, CA: Sage.

Cable News Network (CNN). (2002, August 16). $116 trillion lawsuit filed by 9/11 families. Retrieved November 2, 2005, from www.cnn.com.

———. (2003, March 13). Police defend Smart probe. Retrieved October 13, 2005, from www.cnn.com.

———. (2005, July 3). Idaho authorities release missing girl 911 tapes. Retrieved October 13, 2005, from www.cnn.com.

Caffaro, J., & Caffaro, A. (1998). *Sibling abuse trauma*. Binghamton, NY: Haworth Press.

Cahn, N., & Lerman, L. (1991). Prosecuting woman abuse. In M. Steinman (Ed.), *Woman battering: Policy responses* (pp. 95–113). Cincinnati, OH: Anderson.

Campbell, R., & Wasco, S. (2005, January). Understanding rape and sexual assault: Twenty years of progress and future directions. *Journal of Interpersonal Violence*, 20, 127–131.

Campbell, J., et al., (2003, November). Assessing risk factors for intimate partner homicide. *NIJ Journal*, 250: 14–19.

Caplan, G. (1991, February 25). Battered wives, battered justice. *National Review*, 15–20.

Carmody, D., & Washington, L. (2001). Rape myth acceptance among college women. *Journal of Interpersonal Violence*, 16(5), 424–436.

Carr, P., Lord, K., & Maier, S. (2003). Keep me informed: What matters for victims as they navigate the juvenile criminal justice system in Philadelphia. *Internal Review of Victimology*, 10(2), 117–136.

Carrington, F. (1975). *The victims*. New Rochelle, NY: Arlington House.

———. (1977). Victim's rights litigation: A wave of the future? *University of Richmond Law Review*, 11(3), 447–470.

———. (1978, June). Victim's rights: A new tort. *Trial*, 39–41.

———. (1980, February 11). Martinez ruling won't bar suits on negligent custodial releases. *National Law Journal*, 26.

———. (1986, June). Preventing victimization through third-party victims' rights litigation. *Networks* (newsletter of the National Victims Center, Fort Worth, Texas), 1, 7.

Carrow, D. (1980). *Crime victim compensation: Program model*. Washington, DC: U.S. Department of Justice.

Carson, E. (1986, September). Crime victims strike back with civil lawsuits for compensation. *NOVA Newsletter*, 1–2, 4.

Carter, S. (2000, September). Covering crime on college campuses. *Quill Magazine*, 8–10.

Cassell, P. (2007). Treating crime victims fairly: Integrating victims into the federal rules of criminal procedure. Retrieved December 6, 2008 from www.nvcap.org.

Catalano, S. (2004). *Criminal victimization 2003. BJS National Crime Victimization Survey*. Washington, DC: U.S. Department of Justice.

———. (2005). *Criminal victimization 2004. BJS National Crime Victimization Survey*. Washington, DC: U.S. Department of Justice.

Catania, S. (2005, July 1). Breaking the silence. *Mother Jones*, 8–10.

Cathcart, R. (2008, February 23). Boy's killing, labeled a hate crime, stuns a town. *New York Times*, p. A16.

CBS News. (2005, February 20). Army rape accuser speaks out. *60 Minutes*. Retrieved February 25, 2005, from www.cbsnews.com.

CCC Information Systems. (2006). Auto News: 2005 most stolen vehicle list shows preference for Hondas. Retrieved July 5, 2008, from www.motortrend.com.

CCRC. *See* Crimes Against Children Research Center.

CDF. *See* Children's Defense Fund.

Ceci, S., & Bruck, M. (1993). Suggestibility of the child witness: A historical review and synthesis. *Psychological Bulletin, 113*(3), 403–439.

Celona, L. (2005, September 26). 'Lie' detectives. *New York Post*, p. 17.

———. (2008, July 10). Cop's wife charged in murder of "kid groper." *New York Post*, p. 8.

Celona, L., Williams, B., & Greene, L. (2005, November 21). Shot Brooklyn cop acted as every victim should. *New York Post*, p. 5.

Center, L. (1980). Victim assistance for the elderly. *Victimology, 5*(2), 374–390.

Chan, S. (2007, September 18). To avoid return to Iraq, soldier arranged to be shot. *New York Times*, p. B3.

———. (2007, December 5). City Room: Legal help for immigrants, even illegal ones. *New York Times*, p. B1.

Chancer, L. (2005). *High-profile crimes: When legal cases become social causes*. Chicago: University of Chicago Press.

Chang, S. (2006, November 3). Source of inspiration. *Newsday*, p. A17.

Chapman, J., & Smith, B. (1987). *Child sexual abuse: An analysis of case processing*. Washington, DC: American Bar Association.

Chappell, D., & Sutton, P. (1974). Evaluating the effectiveness of programs to compensate victims of crime. In I. Drapkin & E. Viano (Eds.), *Victimology: A new focus* (Vol. 2, pp. 207–220). Lexington, MA: D. C. Heath.

Chappell, D., Geis, R., & Geis, G. (1977). *Forcible rape: The crime, the victim, and the offender*. New York: Columbia University Press.

Charkes, J. (2008, March 22). DNA tests lead to arrest in a 25-year-old killing. *New York Times*, p. B2.

Chavez, J. (1992). Battered men and the California law. *Southwestern University Law Review, 22*, 239–256.

Chen, D. (2004, November 18). Striking details in final report on 9/11 fund. *New York Times*, pp. B1, B8.

Chicago police found to dismiss cases erroneously. (1983, May 2). *New York Times*, p. A20.

Child abuse reports rise 2%. (1988, May 15). *Law Enforcement News*, pp. 1, 12.

Child abuse victims get help through interior decor. (1989, May 15). *Law Enforcement News*, pp. 1, 12.

Children's Defense Fund (CDF). (2005). *A moral outrage: One American child or teen killed by gunfire nearly every three hours*. Retrieved December 20, 2005, from www.childrensdefense.org.

Childres, R. (1964). Compensation for criminally inflicted personal injury. *New York University Law Review, 39*, 455–471.

Childress, S. (2006, September 25). Fighting over the kids. *Newsweek*, p. 35.

Chilton, R. (1987). Twenty years of homicide and robbery in Chicago: The impact of the city's changing racial and age composition. *Journal of Quantitative Criminology 3*(3), 195–206.

———. (2004, February). Regional Variations in Lethal and Nonlethal Assaults. *Homicide Studies, 8*, 40–56.

Chilton, R., Major, V., & Propheter, S. (1998). Victims and offenders: A New UCR Supplement. Paper presented at the 1998 annual meeting of the American Society of Criminology, Washington, DC.

Chira, S. (1993, December 5). Sexual abuse: The coil of truth and memory. *New York Times*, p. E3.

Chornesky, A. (2000). The dynamics of battering revisited. *Journal of Women and Social Work, 15*(4), 480–501.

Christie, N. (1986). The ideal victim. In E. Fattah (Ed.), *From crime policy to victim policy* (pp. 125–134). New York: St. Martin's Press.

Christie, L. (2005, September 23). America's most dangerous jobs. CNN Money.

Chu, L., & Kraus, J. (2004, May). Predicting fatal assault among the elderly using the National Incident-Based Reporting System crime data. *Homicide Studies, 8*, 71–95.

Clancy, S. (2005). *Abducted: How people come to believe they were kidnapped by aliens*. Cambridge, MA: Harvard University Press.

Clark, C., & Block, T. (1992, Fall). Victims' voices and constitutional quandaries: Life after *Payne v. Tennessee*. *St. John's Journal of Legal Commentary, 8*(1), 35–64.

Clark, L., & Lewis, D. (1978). *Rape: The price of coercive sexuality*. Toronto: Women's Press.

Clark, R., & Harris, P. (1992). Auto theft and its prevention. In M. Tonry (Ed.), *Crime and justice: A review of research* (Vol. 16, pp. 1–54). Chicago: University of Chicago Press.

Clery, H., & Clery, C. (2001). What Jeanne didn't know. Retrieved September 21, 2005, from www. securityoncampus.org.

Clinton, W. (1996, June 27). President Clinton's memorandum to Attorney General Janet Reno. White House Press Release.

CNN. *See* Cable News Network.

Coates, R. (1990). Victim-offender reconciliation programs in North America: An assessment. In B. Galaway & J. Hudson (Eds.), *Criminal justice, restitution and reconciliation* (pp. 125–134). Monsey, NY: Willow Tree Press.

Coates, R., & Gehm, J. (1989). An empirical assessment. In M. Wright & B. Galaway (Eds.), *Mediation and criminal justice: Victims, offenders, and community* (pp. 251–263). Newbury Park, CA: Sage.

Code Amber. (2008). *Amber alert statistics, 2006.* Retrieved August 8, 2008, from www. codeamber.org.

Cohen, L., & Felson, M. (1979). Social change and crime rate trends: A routine activity approach. *American Sociological Review, 44,* 588–607.

Cohen, L., Kluegal, J., & Land, K. (1981). Social inequality and criminal victimization. *American Sociological Review, 46,* 505–524.

Cohen, P. (1984). Resistance during sexual assaults: Avoiding rape and injury. *Victimology, 9*(1), 120–129.

Cohen, R. (1991, April 21). Should the media name the accuser when the crime being charged is rape? *New York Times,* p. E4.

Cohen, S. (2008, April 1). Drop dead, gorgeous. *New York Post,* p. A19.

Cohen, T., & Reaves, T. (2006, February). Felony defendants in large urban courts, 2002. Statistical tables. Retrieved September 30, 2008, from www. ojp.gov/bjs/abstract/fdluc02.htm.

Cohn, E., Kidder, L., & Harvey, J. (1978). Crime prevention vs. victimization prevention: The psychology of two different reactions. *Victimology, 3*(3), 285–296.

Coleman, C. (2002, July 31). Bail's likely for man who killed thief. *New York Daily News,* p. 8.

Collins, J., & Hoffman, S. (2004). *Identity theft victims' assistance guide: The process of healing.* New York: Looseleaf Law Publishers.

Collins, J., McCalla, M., Powers, L., & Stutts, E. (1983). *OJJDP update on research: The police and missing children – Findings from a national survey.* Washington, DC: U.S. Department of Justice.

Combined News Services. (1993, September 27). NYC man slain on Florida highway. *New York Newsday,* p. 17.

Conklin, J. (1975). *The impact of crime.* New York: Macmillan.

Consumer's Union (2008). *Notice of security breach state laws.* Retrieved July 18, 2008, from www.consumersunion.org/campaigns/Breach_laws.

Cook, P. (1985). Is robbery becoming more violent? An analysis of robbery murder trends since 1968. *Journal of Criminal Law and Criminology, 76*(2), 480–490.

———. (1987). Robbery violence. *Journal of Criminal Law and Criminology, 78*(2), 357–377.

Cook, P., & Ludwig, J. (1997). *NIJ Research in Brief: Guns in America—National survey on private ownership and use of firearms.* Washington, DC: U.S. Department of Justice.

Cook, R., Roehl, J., & Sheppard, D. (1980). *Neighborhood justice centers field test.* Washington, DC: U.S. Department of Justice.

Cooper, C. (2000). Police mediators: Rethinking the role of law enforcement in the new millennium. *Dispute Resolution Magazine, 7*(1), 17.

Cooper, M. (2005, April 7). Racial disproportion seen in applying 'Kendra's Law.' *New York Times,* p. B4.

Corbett, S. (2007, March 18). The women's war. *New York Times Magazine,* pp. 41–57.

———. (2008, July 27). Children of God. *New York Times Magazine,* pp. 36–44.

Corbin, W., Bernat, J., & Calhoun, K. (2001). The role of alcohol expectancies and alcohol consumption among sexually victimized and nonvictimized college women. *Journal of Interpersonal Violence, 16*(4), 297–311.

Cornell, K. (2006, November 11). Avenging angel: Make my torturer suffer too: Sliwa. *New York Post,* p. 29.

Cose, E. (1994, August 8). Truths about spouse abuse. *Newsweek,* 49.

Coston, C. (Ed.) (2004). *Victimizing vulnerable groups.* New York: Praeger.

Council on Foreign Relations (CFR). (2004). *Terrorism: questions and answers: the anthrax letters.* Retrieved October 4, 2005, from www.cfr.org.

Cowan, G., (2000). Women's hostility toward women and rape and sexual harassment myths. *Violence Against Women,* 6(3), 238–246.

Cowan, A. (2008, April 8). Police face a threat deadlier than any criminal's gun. *New York Times,* pp. B1, B6.

Cox, M. (1998, August 4). Kendra's law ready to pass. *Long Island Newsday,* p. A5.

Crecente, B. (2008, March 24). Digg bitch slaps kid for 360 ransom. Retrieved October 1, 2008, from www.kotaku.com.

Crew, R., Fridell, L., & Pursell, K. (1995). Probabilities and odds in hot pursuit: A benefit–cost analysis. *Journal of Criminal Justice,* 23(5), 417–424.

Crichton, S. (1993, October 25). Sexual correctness: Has it gone too far? *Newsweek,* 52–56.

Crime control amendments. (1973). *Congressional Quarterly Almanac,* 29, 370–372.

Crime control needs citizens to do their part in helping. (1985, August). *Crime Victims Digest,* 1–2.

Crime victims' aid. (1978). *Congressional Quarterly Almanac,* 34, 196–198.

Crime Victims Research and Treatment Center. (1992). *The national women's study.* Charleston, SC: Medical University of South Carolina.

Crimes Against Children Research Center (CCRC). (2005). *Fact sheet—Child sexual abuse.* Retrieved October 14, 2005 from www.unh.edu/ccrc.

Crowe, A. (1998). Restorative justice and offender rehabilitation: A meeting of the minds. *Perspectives,* the *Journal of the American Probation and Parole Association,* (Summer): 28–40.

Crowley, K. (2007, October 24). Tiny chop-keeper kicks gunman's ax. *New York Post,* p. 3.

Cruz, J., & Firestone, J. (1998, Summer). Exploring violence and abuse in gay male relationships. *Violence and Victims,* 13(2), 159–174.

Crystal, S. (1988, Summer). Elder abuse: the latest 'crisis.' *Public Interest,* 88, 56–65.

Cuomo, M. (1992, Fall). The crime victim in a system of criminal justice. *St. John's Journal of Legal Commentary,* 8(1), 1–20.

Curran, J. (1999, December 29). Crime victims' families can testify via videotape before parole board. Associated Press.

Curtis, L. (1974). Victim precipitation and violent crime. *Social Problems,* 21, 594–605.

Darnton, N. (1991, October 7). The pain of the last taboo. *Newsweek,* 70–72.

Davey, M., and Einhorn, C. (2007, December 8). Settlement for torture of four men by police. *New York Times,* p. A11.

Davidson, H. (1986, July–August). Missing children: A close look at the issue. *Children Today,* 26–30.

Davies, J., Lyon, E., & Catania, D. (1998). *Safety planning with battered women: Complex lives/Difficult choices.* Thousand Oaks, CA: Sage.

Davis, R. (1983). Victim/witness noncooperation: A second look at a persistent phenomenon. *Journal of Criminal Justice,* 11, 287–299.

———, & Bannister, P. (1995). Improving the collection of court-ordered restitution. *Judicature,* 79(1), 30–33.

———, & Medina-Ariza, J. (2001). *Results from an elder abuse prevention experiment in New York City.* NIJ Research in Brief. Washington, DC: U.S. Department of Justice.

———, & Mulford, C. (2008). Victim rights and new remedies. *Journal of Contemporary Criminal Justice,* 24(2), 198–208.

———, & Murray, D. (1995). *Immigrant populations as victims: Toward a multicultural criminal justice system.* New York: Victim Services Agency.

———, & Smith, B. (1994). Victim impact statements and victim satisfaction: An unfulfilled promise? *Journal of Criminal Justice,* 22, 1–12.

———, Erez, E., & Avitabile, N. (2001). Access to justice for immigrants who are victimized. *Criminal Justice Policy Review,* 12(3), 183–196.

———, Henderson, N., & Rabbitt, C. (2002). *Effects of state victim rights legislation on local criminal justice systems.* New York: Vera Institute of Justice.

———, Kunreuther, F., & Connick, E. (1984). Expanding the victim's role in the criminal court dispositional process: The results of an experiment. *Journal of Criminal Law and Criminology, 75*(2), 491–505.

———, Smith, B., & Hillenbrand, S. (1992). Restitution: The victim's viewpoint. *The Justice System Journal, 15*(3), 746–758.

———, Tichane, M., & Grayson, D. (1980). Mediation and arbitration as alternatives to criminal prosecution in felony arrest cases: An evaluation of the Brooklyn Dispute Resolution Center (first year). New York: Vera Institute of Justice.

Dawson, J., & Langan, P. (1994). *Murder in families: BJS Special Report.* Washington, DC: U.S. Department of Justice.

Dawson, J., Smith, S., & DeFrances, C. (1993). *Prosecutors in state courts, 1992. BJS Bulletin.* Washington, DC: U.S. Department of Justice.

Dawson, R. (1969). *Sentencing. The decision as to type, length, and conditions of sentence.* Boston: Little, Brown.

DEA. *See* Drug Enforcement Administration.

Dean, C., & de Bruyn-Kops, M. (1982). *The crime and the consequences of rape.* Springfield, IL: Charles C. Thomas.

Deane, G. (1987). Cross-national comparison of homicide: Age/sex-adjusted rates using the 1980 U.S. homicide experience as a standard. *Journal of Quantitative Criminology, 3*(3), 215–227.

DeConcini, D. (1989). National child abuse prevention month. *Crime Victims Digest, 6*(2), 4–5.

Dees, M., & Corcoran, J. (1997). *America's militia threat.* New York: Harper Collins.

DeFrances, C. (2002). *Prosecutors in state courts, 2001. BJS Bulletin.* Washington, DC: U.S. Department of Justice.

DeGette, D., Jenson, J., & Colomy, P. (2000). Law and policy surrounding youth violence. *Denver University Law Review, 77*(4), 615–812.

De Koster, K., & Swisher, K. (Eds.). (1994). *Child abuse: Opposing viewpoints.* San Diego: Greenhaven Press.

De Parle, J. (1999, November 28). Early sex abuse hinders many women on welfare. *New York Times,* pp. A1, A28.

Del Castillo, V., & Lindner, C. (1994). Staff safety issues in probation. *The Justice Professional, 8*(2), 37–54.

Demaris, A. (1992). Male versus female initiation of aggression: The case of courtship violence. In E. Viano (Ed.), *Intimate violence: Interdisciplinary perspectives* (pp. 111–120). Washington, DC: Hemisphere Publishing.

Dershowitz, A. (1988). *Taking liberties: A decade of hard cases, bad laws, and bum raps.* Chicago: Contemporary Books.

———. (1994). *The abuse excuse and other cop-outs, sob stories, and evasions of responsibility.* Boston: Little, Brown.

Deutsch, C. (1994, June 3). Victims of violence increasingly hold landlords liable for crimes. *New York Times,* p. B8.

DeVoe, J., Peter, K., Kaufman, P., Miller, A., Noonan, M., Snyder, T., & Baum, K. (2004). *Indicators of school crime and safety, 2004.* U.S. Department of Education. Washington, DC: U.S. Government Printing Office.

DeVoe, J., Peter, K., Noonan, M., Snyder, T., & Baum, K. (2005). *Indicators of school crime and safety, 2005.* U.S. Department of Education. Washington, DC: U.S. Government Printing Office.

Dewan, S. (2005, July 14). Report on court killings is said to lead to firing of deputies. *New York Times,* p. A10.

Dignan, J. (2005). *Understanding victims and restorative justice.* New York: Open University Press/McGraw Hill.

Dobash, R. P., & Dobash, R. E. (1979). *Violence against wives: The case against patriarchy.* New York: Free Press.

———. (1992). *Women, violence, and social change.* New York: Routledge.

Docksai, M. (1979, August). Victim/witness intimidation: What it means. *Trial,* 51–54.

Dodge, R. (1988). *The seasonality of crime. BJS Bulletin.* Washington, DC: U.S. Department of Justice.

Doerner, W. (1978). An examination of the alleged latent effects of victim compensation programs upon crime reporting. *LAE Journal, 41,* 71–80.

Doerner, W., & Lab, S. (1980). Impact of crime compensation on victim attitudes toward the criminal justice system. *Victimology, 5*(2), 61–77.

Does your agency measure up? (1999, November). *Rap Sheet* (newsletter of Concerns of Police Survivors), *6,* 4.

Domestic abusers take it out on pets, too. (1999, February 28). *Law Enforcement News*, p. 6.

D'Ovidio, D., & Doyle, M. (2003, March). A study in cyberstalking: Understanding investigative hurdles. *FBI Law Enforcement Bulletin, 72*, 10–17.

Dowdy, Z. (2003, September 19). U.S. a leader in child abuse deaths. *Long Island Newsday*, p. A16.

Dreher, R. (2001, August 21). Jesse, Sharpton, and Kwesi are problem, not solution. *New York Post*, p. 5.

www.drivers.com Staff. (1997, Summer). The road rage epidemic: Hype or reality? *Driver Education, 7*(3), 15–18.

Drug Enforcement Administration (DEA). (2003). *Ecstasy and predatory drugs*. Washington, DC: U.S. Government Printing Office.

Dubber, M. (2002). *Victims in the war on crime: The use and abuse of victims' rights*. New York: NYU Press.

Dugan, L., Nagin, D., & Rosenfeld, R. (2003). Do domestic violence services save lives? *NIJ Journal, 250*: 20–25.

Duhart, D. (2001). *Violence in the workplace, 1993–99*. BJS Special Report. Washington, DC: U.S. Government Printing Office.

Dunn, J. (2002). *Courting disaster: Intimate stalking, culture, and criminal justice*. New York: Aldine de Gruyter.

Duret, D., & Patrick, R. (2004, October 24). Truck driver is shot along I-44. *St. Louis Post-Dispatch*, p. A1.

Durose, M. (2004). *Felony sentencing in state courts, 2002*. BJS Bulletin. Washington, DC: U.S. Department of Justice.

Dutton-Douglas, M., & Dionne, D. (1991). Counseling and shelter services for battered women. In M. Steinman (Ed.), *Woman battering: Policy responses* (pp. 113–130). Cincinnati, OH: Anderson.

Duwe, G. (2000). Body count journalism: The presentation of mass murder in the news media. *Homicide Studies, 4*, 4 (November): 364–399.

Dwyer, J. (2008, March 29). Kindness for victims when rules don't apply. *New York Times*, pp. B1, B2.

Ebony magazine. (1979, August). Black on black crime (special issue).

Eddy, D. (1990). Supreme Court decides cases involving VOCA, restitution, child witnesses, sobriety checkpoints. *NOVA Newsletter, 14*(3), 6.

Edelhertz, H. (1977). Legal and operational issues in the implementation of restitution in the criminal justice system. In J. Hudson, & B. Galaway (Eds.), *Restitution in criminal justice* (pp. 63–76). Lexington, MA: Lexington Books.

Edelhertz, H., & Geis, G. (1974). *Public compensation to victims of crime*. New York: Praeger.

Editors, *New York Times* (1965, November 20). The Good Samaritans. *New York Times*, p. A34.

———. (2007, April 26). Guns and more guns. *New York Times*, p. A24.

Egger, K., & Egger, S. (2002). Victims of serial killers: the less dead. In J. Sgarzi and J. McDevitt, *Victimology: A study of crime victims and their roles* (pp. 9–32). Upper Saddle River, NJ: Prentice Hall.

Eglash, A. (1977). Beyond restitution: Creative restitution. In J. Hudson & B. Galaway (Eds.), *Restitution in criminal justice* (pp. 91–100). Lexington, MA: Lexington Books.

Eigenberg, H. (1990). The National Crime Survey and rape: The case of the missing question. *Justice Quarterly, 7*, 655–671.

Einhorn, C. (2008, February 23). Four decades after shooting, effort to make punishment fit the crime. *New York Times*, p. A10.

Elderly crime victims. (2003, July 11). *Crime Control Digest, 37*, 7.

Elias, R. (1983a). *Victims of the system: Crime victims and compensation in American politics and criminal justice*. New Brunswick, NJ: Transaction Books.

———. (1983b). The symbolic politics of victim compensation. *Victimology, 8*(1), 210–219.

———. (1986). *The politics of victimization: Victims, victimology and human rights*. New York: Oxford University Press.

———. (1993). *Victims still: The political manipulation of crime victims*. Newbury Park, CA: Sage.

Eligon, J. (2008, August 29). Attack victim charged in death of bystander. *New York Times*, p. A 18.

Ellenberger, H. (1955). Psychological relationships between the criminal and his victim. *Archives of Criminal Psychodynamics, 2*, 257–290.

Ellin, A. (2003, January 12). Here's one way to turn off a date. *New York Times*, Education Life Supplement, *152*, 7.

Ellis, C. (2000, September). Nation's first police shelter for victims of domestic violence. *The Crime Victims Report, 4,* 49–50.

Endo, E. (1999, July 21). Anti-stalking bill stalled by budget. *Long Island Newsday,* p. A45.

Estrich, S. (1986). *Real rape.* Cambridge, MA: Harvard University Press.

———. (1993a, October 25). Balancing act. *Newsweek,* 64.

———. (1993b, October 24). The sympathy defense. *New York Times,* p. E15.

European Committee on Crime Problems. (1978). *Compensation of victims of crime.* Strasbourg, Austria: Author.

Ewing, C. (1997). *Fatal families: The dynamics of intra-familial homicide.* Thousand Oaks, CA: Sage.

Ewing, P. (1987). *Battered women who kill: Psychological self-defense as legal justification.* Lexington, MA: D.C. Heath.

Fagan, J. (1988). Contributions of family violence research to criminal justice policy on wife assault: Paradigms of science and social control. *Violence and Victims, 3*(3), 159–186.

———, Piper, E., & Cheng, Y. (1987). Contributions of victimization to delinquency in inner cities. *Journal of Criminal Law and Criminology, 78*(3), 586–611.

Fagen, C. (2006, June 27). Kid kills playmate in gun-mishap horror. *New York Post,* p. 12.

Fahn, M. (1991, Summer). Allegations of child sexual abuse in custody disputes: Getting to the truth of the matter. *Family Law Quarterly,* 16–21.

Fairstein, L. (1993). *Sexual violence: Our war against rape.* New York: William Morrow.

Falck, R., Wang, J., & Carlson, R. (2001). The epidemiology of physical attack and rape among crack-using women. *Violence and Victims, 16*(1), 79–89.

False accusations of abuse devastating to families. (1989). *Crime Victims Digest, 6*(2), 4–5.

Faludi, S. (1993, October 25). Whose hype? *Newsweek,* 61.

Farmer, A. (2008, January 25). At 101, mugging victim hasher (early) day in court. *New York Times,* p. B5.

Farnham, F., James, D., & Cantrell, P. (2000, January 15). Association between violence, psychosis, and relationship to victim in stalkers. *The Lancet, 355,* 322–323.

Farrell, R., & Swigert, V. (1986, November). Adjudication in homicide: An interpretive analysis of the effects of defendant and victim social characteristics. *Journal of Research in Crime and Delinquency, 23*(4), 349–369.

Fattah, E. (1967). Toward a criminological classification of victims. *International Criminal Police Review, 209,* 162–169.

———. (1976). The use of the victim as an agent of self-legitimation: Toward a dynamic explanation of criminal behavior. In Emilio Viano (Ed.), *Victims and society* (pp. 105–129). Washington, DC: Visage.

———. (1979). Some recent theoretical developments in victimology. *Victimology, 4*(2), 198–213.

———. (1986). *From crime policy to victim policy.* New York: St. Martin's Press.

———. (1990). Victims and victimology: The facts and the rhetoric. *International Review of Victimology, 1*(1), 43–66.

———. (1991). *Understanding criminal victimization: An introduction to theoretical victimology.* Scarborough, Ontario: Prentice-Hall Canada.

———, (Ed.). (1992a). *Towards a critical victimology.* New York: St. Martin's Press.

———. (1992b). The need for a critical victimology. In E. Fattah (Ed.), *Towards a critical victimology* (pp. 3–28). New York: St. Martin's Press.

Faulk, M. (1977). Men who assault their wives. In M. Roy (Ed.), *Battered women: A psycho-sociological study of domestic violence* (pp. 119–126). New York: Van Nostrand.

FBI. *See* Federal Bureau of Investigation.

Federal Bureau of Investigation (FBI). (1954–2008). *Uniform Crime Report: Crime in the United States* (statistics for selected years from 1953 to 2007). Washington, DC: U.S. Government Printing Office.

———. (1993). *Law enforcement officers killed and assaulted, 1992.* Washington, DC: U.S. Department of Justice.

———. (1999). *National incident-based reporting system.* Washington, DC: U.S. Department of Justice.

———. (2001). *Terrorism in the United States, 1999: Terrorism: A retrospective.* Washington, DC: U.S. Department of Justice.

———. (2003a). *Law enforcement officers killed and assaulted, 2001.* Washington, DC: U.S. Department of Justice.

———. (2003b). Press release: *Law enforcement officers killed and assaulted, 2002.* Washington, DC: U.S. Department of Justice. Retrieved May 12, 2004, from www.FBI.gov.

———. (2003c). *Hate Crime Statistics, 2001.* Washington, DC: U.S. Department of Justice.

———. (2004). *Terrorism 2000/2001.* Washington, DC: U.S. Department of Justice.

———. (2007a). *Law enforcement officers killed and assaulted, 2006.* Washington, DC: U.S. Department of Justice.

———. (2007b). *Terrorism 2002/2005.* Washington, DC: U.S. Department of Justice.

———. (2008b) *Hate Crime Statistics, 2006.* Washington, DC: U.S. Department of Justice.

———. (2008c). *Press Release: FBI releases preliminary statistics for law enforcement officers killed during 2007.* Retrieved September 24, 2008, from www.fbi.gov/pressrel/pressrel08/leoka.

Federal rape laws revised: Now apply to male victims. (1986, November). *Crime Victims Digest, 10.*

Federal Trade Commission (FTC). (2002). *ID theft: When bad things happen to your good name.* Washington, DC: U.S. Department of Commerce, FTC.

———. (2005a). *Fight identity theft.* Washington, DC: U.S. Department of Commerce, FTC.

———. (2005b). *Federal Trade Commission Identity Theft Data Clearinghouse, February 2005.* Retrieved October 15, 2005, from www.ftc.gov.

———. (2007). *National and state trends in fraud and identity theft, January–December 2006.* Retrieved July 15, 2008, from www.ftc.gov/idtheft/consumers.

———. (2008). *About Identity Theft – Deter, Detect, Defend, Avoid ID theft.* Retrieved July 15, 2008, from www.ftc.gov/idtheft/consumers.

Feher, T. (1992). The alleged molestation victim, the rules of evidence and the Constitution: Should children really be seen and not heard? In E. Fattah (Ed.), *Towards a critical victimology* (pp. 260–282). Englewood Cliffs, NJ: Prentice-Hall.

Fein, E. (1991, December 11). Decision praised as a victory for free speech rights. *New York Times*, B8.

Feingold, R. (2005). *U.S. Senate recognizes September as first-ever national campus safety awareness month.*

Retrieved December 20, 2005, from www.securityoncampus.org.

Felson, M. (1994). *Crime and everyday life.* Thousand Oaks, CA: Pine Forge Press.

———. (1997). Routine activities and involvement in violence as actor, witness, or target. *Violence and Victims, 12*(5), 209–220.

Fernandez, M. (2007, September 30). Barcelona newspaper casts new doubts on 9/11 account. *New York Times*, p. B30.

Ferraro, K. (1992). Cops, courts, and woman battering. In P. Bart & E. Moran (Eds.), *Violence against women: The bloody footprints* (pp. 165–176). Newbury Park, CA: Sage.

Fine, L. (2001, March 28). Second high school shooting rocks a California school district. *Education Week, 20*(28), 3.

Fingerhut, L., Ingram, D., & Feldman, J. (1992a, June 10). Firearm and non-firearm homicide among persons 15 through 19 years of age. *Journal of the American Medical Association, 267*(22), 3048–3053.

———. (1992b). Firearm homicide among black teenage males in metropolitan counties: Comparison of death rates in two periods, 1983 through 1985 and 1987 through 1989. *Journal of the American Medical Association, 267*, 3054–3058.

Finkelhor, D. (1990, Winter). Is child abuse over-reported? *Public Welfare, 48*(1), 20–30.

———. (1994). Current information on the scope and nature of child sexual abuse. *The Future of Children, 4*(2), 31, 46, 48.

Finkelhor, D., & Asdigian, N. (1996, Spring). Risk factors for youth victimization: Beyond a lifestyle/routine activities theory approach. *Violence and Victims, 11*(1), 3–20.

Finkelhor, D., & Jones, L. (2004). Explanations for the decline in child sexual abuse cases. Washington, DC: U.S. Department of Justice, Office of Juvenile Justice and Delinquency Prevention.

Finkelhor, D., Hammer, H., & Sedlak, A. (2002). *NISMART–2: Nonfamily abducted children: National estimates and characteristics.* Washington, DC: U.S. Department of Justice, Office of Juvenille Justice and Delinquency Prevention.

Finkelhor, D., Hotaling, G., & Sedlak, A. (1990). *Missing, abducted, runaway, and thrownaway children in*

America: First report. Washington, DC: U.S. Department of Justice, Office of Juvenile Justice and Delinquency Prevention.

Finkelhor, D., & Leatherman, J. (1994, March). Victimization of children. *American Psychologist, 49*(3), 173–183.

Finkelhor, D., & Ormrod, R. (2000, June). *Kidnapping of juveniles: Patterns from NIBRS.* OJJDP Juvenile Justice Bulletin, 1–7. Washington, DC: U.S. Department of Justice.

———. (2001). Crimes against children by babysitters. OJJDP Juvenile Justice Bulletin. Washington, DC: U.S. Department of Justice.

Finkelhor, D., & Yllo, K. (1985). *License to rape: Sexual abuse of wives.* New York: Holt, Rinehart & Winston.

Finn, P. (1991). Civil protection orders: A flawed opportunity for intervention. In M. Steinman (Ed.), *Woman battering: Policy responses* (pp. 155–190). Cincinnati, OH: Anderson.

Finn, R. (2005, October 28). Pushing past the trauma of forgiveness. *New York Times,* p. B2.

Fisher, B., Cullen, F., & Turner, M. (2000). *The sexual victimization of college women.* Washington, DC: National Institute of Justice.

———, ———, & Daigle, L. (2005). The discovery of acquaintance rape. *Journal of Interpersonal Violence, 20*(4): 493–500.

Fisher, B., Daigle, L., & Cullen, F. (2008). Rape against women: What can research offer to guide the development of prevention programs and risk reduction interventions. *Journal of Contemporary Criminal Justice, 24*(2): 163–177.

Fitting justice? Judges try 'creative' sentences. (1978, April 24). *Time,* 56.

Fitzgerald, N., & Riley, K. (2005). Club drugs facilitate rape. In K. Balkin (Ed.), *Club Drugs: At Issues Series* (pp. 100–105). Westport, CT: Greenhaven Press.

Fitzpatrick, K., LaGory, M., & Ritchey, F. (1993). Criminal victimization among the homeless. *Justice Quarterly, 10,* 353–368.

Fletcher, G. (1988). *Bernhard Goetz and the law on trial.* New York: Free Press.

———. (1988b). *A crime of self-defense: Bernhard Goetz and the law on trial.* Chicago: University of Chicago Press.

Fleury, R., Sullivan, C., Bybee, D., & Davidson, W. (1998). Why don't they just call the cops? *Violence and Victims, 13*(4), 333–340.

Flynn, E. (1982). Theory development in victimology: An assessment of recent progress and of continuing challenges. In H. Schneider (Ed.), *The victim in international perspective* (pp. 96–104). Berlin: de Gruyter.

Follingstad, D., Rutledge, L., McNeill-Harkins, K., & Polek, D. (1992). Factors related to physical violence in dating relationships. In E. Viano (Ed.), *Intimate violence: Interdisciplinary perspectives* (pp. 121–135). Washington, DC: Hemisphere Publishing.

Fooner, M. (1971, February). Money and economic factors in crime and delinquency. *Criminology 8*(4), 311–320.

Ford, D. (2003). Coercing victim participation in domestic violence prosecutions. *Journal of Interpersonal Violence, 18*(6), 669–680.

Forer, L. (1980). *Criminals and victims: A trial judge reflects on crime and punishment.* New York: Norton.

Forst, G., & Hernon, J. (1984). *NIJ research in brief—The criminal justice response to victim harm.* Washington, DC: U.S. Department of Justice.

Forst, M., & Blomquist, M. (1991). *Missing children: Rhetoric and reality.* New York: Lexington Books.

Fox, J., & McDowall, D. (2008). Brief of professors of criminal justice as *amici curiae, D.C. vs. Heller. U.S. Supreme Court.* Retrieved October 3, 2008, from www.nraila.org/heller.

Fox, J., & Zawitz, M. (2002). *Homicide trends in the United States. BJS Special Report.* Washington, DC: U.S. Department of Justice.

———. (2008, April 16). Topics in university security: Lockdown 101. *New York Times,* p. A25.

Franiuk, R., Seefelt, J., Cepress, S., Vandello, J. (2008, March) Prevalence and effects of rape myths in print journalism: The Kobe Bryant Case. *Violence Against Women, 14,* 3: 287–309.

Franklin, B. (1978). *The victim as criminal and artist: Literature from the American prison.* New York: Oxford University Press.

Franklin, C., & Franklin, A. (1976). Victimology revisited. *Criminology, 14*(1), 125–136.

Freedman, L., & Ray, L. (1982). *State legislation on dispute resolution.* Washington, DC: American Bar Association.

Fried, J. (1982, May 2). Intimidation of witnesses called widespread. *New York Times*, p. S1.

Friedman, L. (1985, November). The crime victim movement at its first decade. *Public Administration Review, 45*, 790–794.

Friedrichs, D. (1983, April). Victimology: A consideration of the radical critique. *Crime and Delinquency, 29*(2), 280–290.

Friefeld, K. (2000, February 11). Man charged in shooting of son's hooky partner. *Long Island Newsday*, p. A35.

Frieze, I., & Browne, A. (1991). Violence in marriage. In L. Ohlin & M. Tonry (Eds.), *Crime and justice: A review of research, Volume 11: Family violence* (pp. 163–218). Chicago: University of Chicago Press.

Frum, D. (1993, January 18). Women who kill. *Forbes*, 20–24.

Fry, M. (1957, November 10). Justice for victims. *London Observer*, p. 8. Reprinted in *Journal of Public Law, 8* (1959), 191–194.

FTC. *See* Federal Trade Commission.

Fulginiti, L. (2008, January). Fatal Footsteps: Murder of Undocumented Border Crossers in Maricopa County, Arizona. *Journal of Forensic Sciences, 53*(1), 41–56.

Fuller, R., & Myers, R. (1941, June). The natural history of a social problem. *American Sociological Review, 6*, 320–328.

Fumento, M. (1998, August). 'Road rage' versus reality. *The Atlantic Monthly*, pp. 18–21.

Furstenberg, F. (1972). Fear of crime and its effect on citizen behavior. In A. Biderman (Ed.), *Crime and justice* (pp. 52–65). New York: Justice Institute.

Fuselier, G. (1999, July). Placing the Stockholm Syndrome in perspective. *FBI Law Enforcement Bulletin, 68*(7), 22–25.

Gado, M. (2005). My baby is missing! *Crime Library*. Retrieved October 13, 2005, from www.courttv.com.

Gagliardi, B. (2005, March/April). Corrections-based services for victims of crime. *The Crime Victims Report, 9*(1), 6.

Gahr, E. (1997, March 10). Advocates raise wide support for victims rights amendment. *Insight on the News*, 42.

Galaway, B. (1977). The uses of restitution. *Crime and Delinquency, 23*(1), 57–67.

———. (1987). Victim-offender mediation as the preferred response to property offenses. In E. Viano (Ed.), *Crime and its victims: International research and public policy issues* (pp. 101–111). New York: Hemisphere.

———. (1989). Prospects. In M. Wright & B. Galaway (Eds.), *Mediation and criminal justice: Victims, offenders and community* (pp. 270–275). Newbury Park, CA: Sage.

———. (1992). Restitution as innovation or unfilled promise? In E. Fattah (Ed.), *Towards a critical victimology* (pp. 347–371). New York: St. Martin's Press.

Galaway, B., & Hudson, J. (1975). Issues in the correctional implementation of restitution to victims of crime. In J. Hudson & B. Galaway (Eds.), *Considering the victim: Readings in restitution and victim compensation* (pp. 351–360). Springfield, IL: Charles C. Thomas.

———, (Eds.) (1981). *Perspectives on crime victims*. St. Louis, MO: C.V. Mosby.

Garbarino, J. (1989). The incidence and prevalence of child maltreatment. In L. Ohlin & M. Tonry (Eds.), *Crime and justice: A review of research, Volume 11: Family violence* (pp. 219–262). Chicago: University of Chicago Press.

Gardiner, S. (2008, May 6). NYPD inaction over a missing woman found dead sparks a historic racial-bias lawsuit. Retrieved October 1, 2008 from www.villagevoice.com.

Gardner, R. (1990). *Sex abuse hysteria: Salem witch trials revisited*. Cresskill, NJ: Creative Therapeutics.

———. (1994). Belated realization of child sex abuse by an adult. In K. de Koster & K. Swisher (Eds.), *Child abuse: Opposing viewpoints* (pp. 217–223). San Diego, CA: Greenhaven Press.

Garfinkle, H. (1949, May). Research note on inter- and intra-racial homicides. *Social Forces, 27*, 370–381.

Garlock, S. (2007, February). Congressional victim's rights caucus offers "a voice of victims" in Washington. *The Crime Victims Report, 10* (6): 85, 89.

Garofalo, J. (1981). Victimization surveys: An overview. In B. Galaway & J. Hudson (Eds.), *Perspectives on crime victims* (pp. 98–103). St. Louis, MO: C.V. Mosby.

———. (1986). Lifestyles and victimization: An update. In E. Fattah (Ed.), *From crime policy to victim policy* (pp. 135–155). New York: St. Martin's Press.

Garofalo, J., & Connelly, K. (1980, September). Dispute resolution centers: Part 1—Major features and processes; Part 2—Outcomes, issues, and future directions. *Criminal Justice Abstracts*, 416–610.

Garrett, D. (2008, June 6). Texas Gov. Rick Perry defends state's seizure of polygamist sect's kids. *Dallas Morning News*. Retrieved August 1, 2008, from www.dallasnews.com.

Gartner, A., & Riessman, F. (1980, February 19). Lots of helping hands. *New York Times*, p. A22.

Gartner, R. (1990, February). The victims of homicide: A temporal and cross-national comparison. *American Sociological Review, 55*(1), 92–106.

Garvey, M., & Winton, R. (2003, June 27). High court's term ends; those who came forward feel betrayed. *Los Angeles Times*, p. 29.

Gately, G. (2005, February 12). Baltimore struggles to battle witness intimidation; prosecutors say violence, threats hinder testimony. *The Boston Globe*, p. A3.

Gaudiosi, J. (2004). *Child maltreatment 2003*. Washington, DC: U.S. Department of Health and Human Services.

Gaynes, M. (1981, November–December). New roads to justice: Compensating the victim. *State Legislatures*, 11–17.

Gegan, S., & Rodriguez, N. (1992, Fall). Victims' roles in the criminal justice system: A fallacy of empowerment. *St. John's Journal of Legal Commentary, 8*(1), 225–250.

Geis, G. (1976). Compensation to victims of violent crime. In R. Gerber (Ed.), *Contemporary issues in criminal justice* (pp. 90–115). Port Washington, NY: Kennikat.

———. (1977). Restitution by criminal offenders: A summary and overview. In J. Hudson & B. Galaway (Eds.), *Restitution in criminal justice* (pp. 147–164). Lexington, MA: Lexington Books.

———. (1983). Victim and witness assistance programs. In *Encyclopedia of Crime and Justice* (pp. 1600–1604). New York: Free Press.

Geller, W. (1992, December 31). Put friendly-fire shooting in perspective. *Law Enforcement News*, p. 9.

Gelles, R. (1987). *The violent home*. Newbury Park, CA: Sage.

Gelles, R., & Cornell, C. (1990). *Intimate violence in families* (2nd ed.). Newbury Park, CA: Sage.

Gelles, R., & Straus, M. (1988). *Intimate violence*. New York: Touchstone Books.

George, M. (2003). Ask the FBI: The white slave trade. *Interactive chat*. Retrieved June 19, 2000, from www.FBI.gov.

Gettleman, E. (2005a, June 28). The Pentagon v. abuse: An interview with Deborah Tucker. *Mother Jones*, 40–45.

———. (2005b, July 1). A new order in the court. *Mother Jones*, 8.

Gewurz, D., & Mercurio, M. (1992, Fall). The victims' bill of rights: Are victims all dressed up with no place to go? *St. John's Journal of Legal Commentary, 8*(1), 251–278.

Giacinti, T. (1973). Forcible rape: The offender and his victim. Unpublished master's thesis. Ann Arbor, MI: University Microfilms.

Giannelli, P. (1997). Rape trauma syndrome. *Criminal Law Bulletin, 33*, 270–279.

Gibbs, N. (1991, June 3). When is it rape? *Time*, 38–40.

———. (1993a, August 16). Hell on wheels. *Time*, 44–46.

———. (1993b, January 18). 'Til death do us part. *Time*, 38–45.

———. (1994, November 14). Death and deceit. *Time*, 43–48.

Gibson, R. (2004). Most-stolen cars? It's debatable. Retrieved September 7, 2005, from www.bankrate.com.

Gibson, S. (2005, Fall). President's message. *COPS Newsletter, 19*(3), 1. Concerns of Police Survivors, Inc., Camdenton, MO.

Gilbert, N. (1991, Spring). The phantom epidemic of sexual assault. *The Public Interest, 103*, 54–65.

Gill, J. (1987, August 14). Let's stop fingerprinting kids. *New York Newsday*, p. 94.

———. (1989, April 11). Missing-kids' groups foster fear rather than facts. *New York Newsday*, p. 65.

Gillespie, C. (1989). *Battered women, self-defense, and the law.* Columbus, OH: Ohio State University Press.

Ginsberg, A. (2005, September 20). Reliving horror at rape trial. *New York Post,* p. 20.

Girdner, L., & Hoff, P. (1994). *Obstacles to the recovery and return of parentally abducted children. Research summary.* Washington, DC: U.S. Department of Justice.

Girelli, S., Resick, P., Dvorak, S., & Hutter, C. (1986). Subjective distress and violence during rape: Their effects on long-term fear. *Victims and Violence, 1*(1), 35–46.

Givens, A. (2005, August 17). 70 years and a rebuke. *Long Island Newsday,* p. A8.

Glaberson, W. (2003, July 6). Justice, safety, and the system: A witness is slain in Brooklyn. *New York Times,* p. A1, B18–19.

Glaze, L., & Palla, S. (2004). *Probation and Parole in the United States, 2003. BJS Bulletin.* Washington, DC: U.S. Department of Justice.

Goldberg, C. (1996, June 18). Support builds for killer who broke cycle of fear. *New York Times,* p. A14.

———. (1998, September 8). Getting to the truth in child abuse cases: New methods. *New York Times,* pp. C1, C5.

———. (1999, November 23). Spouse abuse crackdown, surprisingly, nets many women. *New York Times,* p. A16.

Goldberg, J. (2008, March 19). Yesterday's baggage: Barack in Philly. National Review Online. Retrieved September 27, 2008, from www.nationalreview.com.

Goldberg, S., Green, E., & Sander, F. (1985). *Dispute resolution.* Boston: Little, Brown.

Goldberg-Ambrose, C. (1992). Unfinished business in rape law reform. *Journal of Social Issues, 48*(1), 173–185.

Goldsmith, J., & Goldsmith, S. (1976). *Crime and the elderly: Challenge and response.* Lexington, MA: D.C. Heath.

Goldstein, E. (1993). *Confabulations: Creating false memories, destroying families.* Boca Raton, FL: SIRS Books.

Goldstein, J. (1960, March). Police discretion not to invoke the criminal process. *Yale Law Journal, 69,* 543–594.

Goleman, D. (1993, June 11). Studies reveal suggestibility of very young as witnesses. *New York Times,* pp. A1, A23.

———. (1994, October 31). Proof lacking for ritual abuse by satanists. *New York Times,* p. A13.

Goldstein, K., & Martin, S. (2004, August). Intimate partner physical assault before and during pregnancy. *Violence and Victims, 19*(4), 387–394.

Gondolf, E. (1988). The state of the debate: A review essay on woman battering. *Response, 11*(3), 3–8.

Gootman, E. (2007, September 20) Undercount of violence in schools. *New York Times,* p. B4.

Gonzalez, D. (1992, November 25). Sliwa admits faking crimes for publicity. *New York Times,* pp. B1, B2.

Goode, E. (1999, June 13). Study of child sex abuse provokes a political furor. *New York Times,* p. A33.

Goodell, J. (2001, May 13). Letting go of McVeigh. *New York Times Magazine,* pp. 40–44.

Goodman, B. (2008, January 14). Killing of a young hiker puts North Georgia on edge. *New York Times,* p. A21.

Goodman, R., Mercy, J., Loya, F., Rosenberg, M., Smith, J., Allen, N., Vargas, L., & Kolts, B. (1986). Alcohol use and interpersonal violence: Alcohol detected in homicide victims. *American Journal of Public Health, 76*(2), 144–148.

Goodnough, A. (2003, June 12). City to remove four teachers from classrooms. *New York Times,* p. B2.

———. (2005, April 27). Florida expands right to use deadly force in self-defense. *New York Times,* p. A18.

Gootman, E. (2007, September 20). Undercount of violence in schools. *New York Times,* p. B2.

Gordon, L. (1988). *Heroes of their own lives: The politics and history of family violence, Boston, 1880–1960.* New York: Viking.

Gottesman, R., & Mountz, L. (1979). *Restitution: Legal analysis.* Reno, NV: National Council of Juvenile and Family Court Judges.

Gottfredson, M., & Gottfredson, D. (1988). *Decision making in criminal justice: Toward the rational exercise of discretion* (2nd ed.). New York: Plenum Press.

Grady, D. (2003, March 15). Utah girl may have suffered from Stockholm Syndrome, experts say. *New York Times,* p. A8.

Graham, E. (1993, October 25). Education: Fortress academia sells security. *Wall Street Journal*, p. B1.

Graves, N. (2002, June 3). Schumer rips feds on rape expenses. *New York Post*, p. 19.

Gray, E. (1986). *Child abuse: Prelude to delinquency?* Washington, DC: U.S. Department of Justice.

Gray, J. (1993, July 29). New Jersey court says victims of car chases cannot sue police. *New York Times*, pp. B1, B6.

Grayson, B., & Stein, M. (1981). Attracting assault: Victims' nonverbal cues. *Journal of Communications*, *31*, 65–70.

Green, A. (2008, February 15). Attacks on homeless rise, with youths mostly to blame. *New York Times*, p. A12.

Green, E. (1964, September). Inter- and intra-racial crime relative to sentencing. *Journal of Criminal Law, Criminology, and Police Science*, *55*, 348–358.

Green, G. (1987, February). Citizen gun ownership and crime deterrence: Theory, research, and policy. *Criminology*, *25*(1), 63–82.

Greenberg, M., & Ruback, R. (1984). Elements of crime victim decision making. *Victimology*, *10*(1), pp. 600–616.

Greenberger, S. (2005, July 7). Eyes on Romney as morning-after pill KO'd. *Boston Globe*, p. 8.

Greenfeld, L. (1997). *Sex offenses and offenders. BJS Report*. Washington, DC: U.S. Department of Justice.

Greenfeld, L., Rand, M., & Craven, D. (1998). *Violence by intimates: Analysis of data on crimes by current or former spouses, boyfriends, and girlfriends. BJS Report*. Washington, DC: U.S. Department of Justice.

Greenhouse, L. (1989, June 22). Supreme Court roundup: First Amendment protects paper that named rape victim, justices rule. *New York Times*, p. B9.

———. (1990, June 28). Child abuse trials can shield witness. *New York Times*, pp. A1, B8.

———. (1991, December 11). High court upsets seizing of profits of convict's books. *New York Times*, pp. A1, B8.

———. (1993, June 12). Justices uphold stiffer sentences for hate crimes. *New York Times*, pp. A1, A8.

———. (2008, 27). Justices, ruling 5-4, endorse personal right to own gun. *New York Times*, p. A10.

Griffin, S. (1979). *Rape: The power of consciousness*. New York: Harper & Row.

Gross, J. (1990, September 20). 203 rape cases reopened in Oakland as the police chief admits mistakes. *New York Times*, p. A13.

———. (1992, September 15). Abused women who kill now seek way out of cells. *New York Times*, A16.

———. (1993, December 6). California town mourns abducted girl. *New York Times*, p. A12.

Gutis, P. (1988, April 10). New head of police speaks out. *New York Times* Sec. 12, p. 2.

———. (1989, June 8). Attacks on U.S. homosexuals held alarmingly widespread. *New York Times*, p. A24.

Hackett, G., & Cerio, G. (1988, January 18). When the victim goes on trial. *Newsweek*, p. 31.

Hafemeister, T. (1996, Spring). Protecting child witnesses: Judicial efforts to minimize trauma and reduce evidentiary barriers. *Violence and Victims*, *11*(1), pp. 71–92.

Hakim, D. (2007, May 25). H.I.V. testing bill starts 'war' among assembly democrats. *New York Times*, p. B1, B6.

Halbfinger, D. (2002, February 20). Finding hope as an enemy ties a noose. *New York Times*, p. B1.

Hall, D. (1975). The role of the victim in the prosecution and conviction of a criminal case. *Vanderbilt Law Review*, *28*(5), pp. 932–985.

———. (1991). Victims' voices in criminal court: The need for restraint. *American Criminal Law Review*, *28*, pp. 233–243.

Hall, T. (1990, October 7). Fatal accidents are down as U.S. becomes vigilant. *New York Times*, pp. A1, A32.

Halleck, S. (1980). Vengeance and victimization. *Victimology*, *5*(2), 99–109.

Hampton, R., Oliver, R., & Magarian, L. (2003, May). Domestic violence in the African American community: An analysis of social and structural factors. *Violence Against Women*, *9*(5), pp. 533–558.

Hanley, R. (1994a, September 28). Crime victims call for hard labor. *New York Times*, p. B6.

———. (1994b, January 5). Three lives converge in a killing. *New York Times*, p. B6.

———. (1999, November 11). Killer of New Jersey officer faces at least four more years. *New York Times*, p. B3.

Hansen, M. (1997, September). Repairing the damage: Citizen boards tailor sentences to fit the crimes in Vermont. *ABA Journal, 83*, p. 20.

Harland, A. (1979). Restitution statutes and cases: Some substantive and procedural restraints. In B. Galaway & J. Hudson (Eds.), *Victims, offenders, and restitutive sanctions* (pp. 151–171). Lexington, MA: Lexington Books.

———. (1981a). *Restitution to victims of personal and household crimes.* Washington, DC: U.S. Department of Justice.

———. (1981b). Victim compensation: Programs and issues. In B. Galaway & J. Hudson (Eds.), *Perspectives on crime victims* (pp. 412–417). St. Louis, MO: C.V. Mosby.

———. (1983). One hundred years of restitution: An international review and prospectus for research. *Victimology, 8*(1), pp. 190–202.

Harlow, C. (1985). *Reporting crimes to the police. BJS Special Report.* Washington, DC: U.S. Department of Justice.

———. (1987). *Robbery victims. BJS Special Report.* Washington, DC: U.S. Department of Justice.

———. (1988). *Motor vehicle theft. BJS Special Report.* Washington, DC: U.S. Department of Justice.

———. (1991). *Female victims of violent crime. BJS Special Report.* Washington, DC: U.S. Department of Justice.

———. (1999). *Prior abuse reported by inmates and probationers. BJS Selected Findings.* Washington, DC: U.S. Department of Justice.

———. (2001). *Firearm use by offenders. BJS Special Report.* Washington, DC: U.S. Department of Justice.

———. (2005). *Hate crimes reported by victims and police. BJS Special Report.* Washington, DC: U.S. Department of Justice.

Harrell, E. (2005). *Violence by gang members, 1993–2003. BJS Crime Data Brief.* Washington, DC: U.S. Department of Justice.

———. (2007). *Black victims of violent crimes. BJS Special Report.* Washington, DC: U.S. Department of Justice.

Harrington, C. (1985). *Shadow justice: The ideology and institutionalization of alternatives to court.* Westport, CT: Greenwood Press.

Harris, A., Thomas, S., Fisher, G., & Hirsch, D. (2002, May). Murder and medicine: The lethality of criminal assault, 1960–1999. *Homicide Studies, 6*(2), pp. 128–166.

Harris, M. (1979). *Sentencing to community service.* Washington, DC: American Bar Association.

Harrop, F. (2003, June 1). Editorial: Boys as victims? Oh, please! *Providence* (RI) *Journal-Bulletin*, p. D9.

Harry, J. (2002, July). Focus on victims' rights in Minnesota. *Corrections Today, 64*(4), pp. 12–13.

Harshbarger, S. (1987, March). Prosecution is an appropriate response in child sexual abuse cases. *Journal of Interpersonal Violence*, pp. 108–112.

Hart, T., & Reaves, B. (1999). *Felony defendants in large urban counties, 1996. BJS Bulletin.* Washington, DC: U.S. Department of Justice.

Hart, T., & Rennison, C. (2003). *Reporting crime to the police, 1992–2000. BJS Special Report.* Washington, DC: U.S. Department of Justice.

Hartocollis, A. (2005, October 27). Port Authority found negligent in 1993 bombing. *New York Times* pp. A1, B10.

———. (2008, March 27). Developer sues to win $12.3 billion in 9/11 attack. *New York Times*, p. B5.

Haugrud, L., Gratch, L., & Magruder, B. (1997, Summer). Victimization and perpetration rates of violence in gay and lesbian relationships: Gender issues explored. *Violence and Victims, 12*(2), pp. 173–185.

Hauser, C., & O'Connor, M. (2007, April 16). Virginia Tech shooting leaves 33 dead. *New York Times*, p. A1.

Hawaii return-witness program turns tide against crime. (1982, June 7). *Criminal Justice Newsletter*, p. 1.

Hays, C. (1992, July 29). Family to get $1.5 million in slaying by mental patient. *New York Times*, p. B6.

Healy, K. (1995). *NIJ Research in Action. Victim and witness intimidation: New developments and emerging responses.* Washington, DC: U.S. Department of Justice.

———, & Smith, C. (1998). *NIJ Research in Action. Batterer programs: What criminal justice agencies need to know.* Washington, DC: U.S. Department of Justice.

Healy, P. (2003, June 20). L.I. suspect pleads not guilty in a fatal traffic stabbing. *New York Times*, p. B8.

Heinz, A., & Kerstetter, W. (1979). Pretrial settlement conference: Evaluation of a reform in plea bargaining. *Law and Society Review, 13*(2), pp. 349–366.

Heinz, J. (1982, July 7). On justice to victims. *New York Times*, p. A19.

Heisler, C. (2004, November). Court orders protect victims of stalking and domestic violence. *The Crime Victims Report*, pp. 67–69.

Hellerstein, D. (1989). The victim impact statement: Reform or reprisal? *American Criminal Law Review, 27*, pp. 390–434.

Hellman, P. (1993, March 8). Crying rape: The politics of date rape on campus. *New York Magazine*, pp. 32–37.

Henderson, L. (1985). Victims' rights and wrongs. *Stanford Law Review, 37*, pp. 937–1021.

Hendricks, J. (1992). Domestic violence legislation in the United States: A survey of the states. In E. Viano (Ed.), *Intimate violence: Interdisciplinary perspectives* (pp. 213–228). New York: Hemisphere Publishers.

Henican, E. (1998, July 29). Pretty names don't make these laws effective. *Long Island Newsday*, p. A40.

Hennessy, D. A, & Wiesenthal, D. L. (2002). The relationship between driver aggression, vengeance, and violence. *Violence and Victims* (17) 707–718.

Herbert, B. (2002, April 15). Take the DNA kits off the shelves. *New York Times*, p. A23.

———. (2008, February 19). The wrong target. *New York Times*, p. A21.

Herman, J. (1981). *Father-daughter incest*. Cambridge, MA: Harvard University Press.

———. (1992). *Trauma and recovery*. New York: Basic Books.

Herman, S. (1998). *Viewing restorative justice through victims' eyes*. Arlington, VA: National Center for Victims of Crime.

———. (1999, November 30). Interview: The director of the National Center for Victims of Crime. *Law Enforcement News*, pp. 8–11.

———. (2000). Seeking parallel justice: A new agenda for the victims movement. Retrieved October 3, 2008, from www.ncvc.org.

———, & Waul, M. (2004). *Repairing the harm: a new vision for crime victims compensation in America*. Washington, DC: National Center for Victims of Crime.

Hernandez, R. (2007, April 18). Students panicked and then held off gunman. *New York Times*, p. A21.

Herrington, L. (1982). Statement of the chairman. In the *President's Task Force on Victims of Crime, final report* (pp. vi–vii). Washington, DC: U.S. Government Printing Office.

———. (1986, August). Dollars and sense: The value of victim restitution. *Corrections Today*, pp. 156–160.

Herszenhorn, D. (1999, July 27). Alarm Helps to Fight Domestic Violence. *New York Times*, p. B6.

Hester, T. (1987). *Probation and parole, 1986. BJS Bulletin*. Washington, DC: U.S. Department of Justice.

Hewitt, S. (1998). *Assessing allegations of sexual abuse in preschool children*. Thousand Oaks, CA: Sage.

Hickey, E. (1991). *Serial murderers and their victims*. Pacific Grove, CA: Brooks/Cole.

Higgins, J. (2005). *Don't let identity thieves steal your future!* Retrieved September 23, 2005, from www.ed.gov/about/offices/list/oig/misused/idtheft.html.

Hillenbrand, S. (1990). Restitution and victim rights in the 1980s. In A. Lurigio, W. Skogan, & R. Davis (Eds.), *Victims of crime: Problems, politics, and programs* (pp. 188–204). Thousand Oaks, CA: Sage.

Hills, S. (1981). *Demystifying deviance*. Englewood Cliffs, NJ: Prentice-Hall.

Hilton, N. (1993). *Legal responses to wife assault: Current trends and evaluation*. Newbury Park, CA: Sage.

Hilts, P. (1994, March 3). Six percent of women admit beatings while pregnant. *New York Times*, pp. A1, A23.

Hindelang, M., Gottfredson, M., & Garofalo, J. (1978). *Victims of personal crime: An empirical foundation for a theory of personal victimization*. Cambridge, MA: Ballinger Publishing.

Hines, D., & Malley-Morrison, K. (2005). *Family violence in the United States*. Thousand Oaks, CA: Sage.

Hitchcock, J. (2002, November–December). Cyberstalking and law enforcement: Keeping up with the web. *The Crime Victims Report, 6*(5), pp. 65–66, 73.

Hochstedler, E. (1981). *Crime against the elderly in twenty-six cities*. Washington, DC: U.S. Department of Justice.

Hoffman, B. (2003, September 9). Syracuse sex slaves tell rapist's secrets. *New York Post*, p. 25.

Hoffman, J. (1994, April 22). May it please the public: Lawyers exploit media attention as a defense tactic. *New York Times*, pp. B1, B7.

Hofman, R. (2007, June 28). Help rape survivors quickly. *Newsday*, p. A43.

Hofstadter, R., & Wallace, M. (1970). *American violence: A documentary history*. New York: Knopf.

Holmes, R. (1994). *Murder in America*. Newbury Park, CA: Sage.

Holmes, R., & DeBurger, J. (1988). Serial murder. Newbury Park, CA: Sage.

Hook, S. (1972, April). The rights of the victims: Thoughts on crime and compassion. *Encounter*, pp. 29–35.

Hoover, J. (1994). *Technical background on the redesigned National Crime Victimization Survey*. Washington, DC: U.S. Department of Justice.

Hoover, J.E. (1966, September 22). The car theft problem: How you can help beat it. *Congressional Record: Senate*, 23621.

Hope, J. (2007, February 16). Drug rape myth exposed as study reveals binge drinking is to blame. Retrieved September 24, 2008, from www.dailymail.co.uk.

Horn, M. (1993, November 29). Memories lost and found. *U.S. News & World Report*, pp. 52–63.

Hotaling, G., Finkelhor, D., Kirkpatrick, J., & Straus, M. (1988). *Coping with family violence: Research on policy perspectives*. Newbury Park, CA: Sage.

Houppert, K. (2005, July–August). Base crimes: The military has a domestic violence problem. *Mother Jones*, pp. 8–11.

House Subcommittee on Health and Long-Term Care, Select Committee on Aging. (1992). *Hearings on elder abuse*. Washington, DC: U.S. Department of Justice.

Howell, J. (1989). *Selected state legislation: A guide for effective state laws to protect children* (2nd ed.). Washington, DC: National Center for Missing and Exploited Children.

Hubbard, A. (2006, May/June). Flip-flopping victims. *The Crime Victims Report*, pp. 19, 31.

Hudson, J., & Chesney, S. (1978). Research on restitution: A review and assessment. In B. Galaway & J. Hudson (Eds.), *Offender restitution in theory and action*, pp. 131–148. Lexington, MA: Lexington Books.

Hudson, J., & Galaway, B. (1975). *Considering the victim: Readings in restitution and victim compensation*. Springfield, IL: Charles C. Thomas.

Hunzeker, D. (1992). Stalking laws. *National Conference of State Legislatures' State Legislative Report*, *17*(19), pp. 1–6.

Incident Based Reporting (IBR) Resource Center. (2002). Crime reporting in the age of technology. *CJIS Newsletter*, *4*(1), pp. 1–2, www.jrsa.org.

Identity Theft Resource Center (ITRC). (2003). *About the ITRC*. www.idtheftcenter.org.

Inciardi, J. (1976). The pickpocket and his victim. *Victimology*, *1*(3), pp. 446–453.

Infolink. (1999). *HIV/AIDS legislation*. Arlington, VA: National Center for Victims of Crime.

Ingrassia, M., & Beck, M. (1994, July 4). Patterns of abuse. *Newsweek*, pp. 26–33.

International Criminal Police Organization (Interpol). (1998). *1998 Annual Report*. Paris: Interpol.

Irwin, T. (1980). *To combat and prevent child abuse and neglect*. New York: Public Affairs Committee.

Island, D., & Letellier, P. (1991). *Men who beat the men who love them*. New York: Harrington Park Press.

ITRC. *See* Identity Theft Resource Center.

Jackson, L., Socolar, R., Hunter, W., Runyan, D., & Colindres, R. (2000). Directly questioning children and adolescents about maltreatment: A review of survey measures used. *Journal of Interpersonal Violence*, *15*(7), pp. 725–760.

Jackson, N. (1998). Lesbian battering: The other closet. In N. Jackson & G. Oates (Eds.), *Violence in intimate relationships: Examining sociological and psychological issues* (pp. 181–194). Woburn, MA: Butterworth Heinemann.

Jackson, N. (2007). Encyclopedia of domestic violence. New York: Routledge.

Jacob, B. (1977). The concept of restitution: An historical overview. In J. Hudson & B. Galaway (Eds.), *Restitution in criminal justice* (pp. 45–62). Lexington, MA: Lexington Books.

Jacob, B. (1990, November 28). Bronx jurors fail to indict in slaying. *New York Times*, pp. B1, B3.

Jacobs, A. (2003, April 19). Town loner charged in chilling case of sexual captivity. *New York Times*, pp. D1, D5.

Jacobs, J., & Potter, K. (1998). *Hate crimes: Criminal law and identity politics*. New York: Oxford University Press.

Jacobs, S., & Moore, D. (1994). Successful restitution as a predictor of juvenile recidivism. *Juvenile and Family Court Journal, 45*(1), 3–14.

Jankowski, L. (1991). *Probation and parole, 1990. BJS Bulletin*. Washington, DC: U.S. Department of Justice.

Janofsky, M. (1994, December 5). The "why" of youth's fatal beating in Philadelphia is elusive. *New York Times*, p. A16.

Jasinski, J., & Williams, L. (1998). *Partner violence.* Thousand Oaks, CA: Sage.

Jeffrey, C. (1971). *Crime prevention through environmental design.* Beverly Hills, CA: Sage.

Jennings, K. (1986, August 12). Dispute on abuse survey. *New York Newsday*, p. D3.

Jensen, G., & Brownfield, D. (1986). Gender, lifestyles, and victimization: Beyond routine activity. *Violence and Victims, 1*(2), 85–99.

Jensen, G., & Karpos, M. (1993). Managing rape: Exploratory research on the behavior of rape statistics. *Criminology, 31*, 363–385.

Johann, S., & Osanka, F. (1989). *Representing battered women who kill.* Springfield, IL: Charles C. Thomas.

John Jay College Research Team. (2004). *The nature and scope of sexual abuse of minors by Catholic priests and deacons in the United States, 1950–2002.* Retrieved January 12, 2005, from www.jjay.cuny.edu.

Johnson, G. (1941). The Negro and crime. *Annals of the American Academy of Political and Social Science, 217*, pp. 93–104.

Johnson, J. (1989). Horror stories and the construction of child abuse. In J. Best, *Images of issues: Typifying contemporary social problems* (pp. 5–19). New York: Aldine de Gruyter.

Johnson, K. (2005, March 3). Settlement is reached in Bryant case. *New York Times*, p. A14.

———. (2008, July 10). New DNA technology clears the family of JonBenet Ramsey. *New York Times*, p. A18.

———, and Frosch, D. (2008; April 26). Sect children face another world, but still no TV. *New York Times*, p. A16.

Johnston, J. (2005). Profile: Jennifer Wilbanks: Runaway bride. Retrieved October 1, 2005, from http://marriage.about.com/od/proposingbeingengaged/p/wilbanks.htm.

Johnstone, G. (2001). *Restorative justice: Ideas, values, debates.* Devon, UK: Willan Publishing.

Jones, A. (1980). *Women who kill.* New York: Fawcett Columbine Books.

Jones, M. (2003, May–June). Amber alert system saves children's lives. *The Crime Victims Report, 7*(2), pp. 20, 28.

Jones, R. (2005, September 28). Two plead guilty in child's death in New Jersey. *New York Times*, pp. B1, B5.

———. (2007, February 28). In secret '96 tape, doomed woman tried to bargain with kidnapper. *New York Times*, pp. B1, B5.

———, & Goodnough, A. (2008, April 18). Abuse victims warily consider Pope's words. *New York Times*, p. A18.

Jordan, C., Logan, T., Walker, R., & Nigoff, A. (2003, February). Stalking: An examination of the criminal justice response. *Journal of Interpersonal Violence, 18*(2), pp. 148–165.

Jordan, I. (2005, September 9). Double-shot of fear. *Spokane Spokesman-Review*, p. 12.

Jordan, J. (2004, February). Beyond belief? Police, rape, and women's credibility. *Criminal Justice, 4*(1), pp. 29–59.

Joyce, E. (2004, Winter). Teen dating violence: Facing the epidemic. *Networks*, 1–8. Washington, DC: National Center for Victims of Crime.

Kalish, C. (1988). *International crime rates. BJS Special Report*. Washington, DC: U.S. Department of Justice.

Kalven, H., & Zeisel, H. (1966). *The American jury.* Boston: Little, Brown.

Kanin, E. (1984). Date rape: Unofficial criminals and victims. *Victimology, 9*(1), pp. 95–108.

———. (1994). False rape allegations. *Archives of Sexual Behavior, 23*(1), pp. 81–90.

Kantrowitz, B., Starr, M., & Friday, C. (1991, April 29). Naming names. *Newsweek*, pp. 27–32.

Kaplan, D. (2007, March 7). Gartner: ID theft up 50 percent in three years. *SC Magazine*. Retrieved July 14, 2008, from www.scmagazineus.com.

Kappeler, V., Blumberg, M., & Potter, G. (1993). *The mythology of crime and criminal justice.* Prospect Heights, IL: Waveland.

Karjane, H., Fisher, B. and Cullen, F. (2005, December). Sexual assault on campus: What colleges and universities are doing about it. Washington, DC: Office of Justice Programs.

Karlen, N., Greenberg, N., Gonzalez, D., & Williams, E. (1985, October 7). How many missing kids? *Newsweek*, pp. 32–33.

Karmen, A. (1979). Victim facilitation: The case of auto theft. *Victimology*, *4*(4), pp. 361–370.

———. (1980). Auto theft: Beyond victim blaming. *Victimology*, *5*(2), pp. 161–174.

———. (1981a). Auto theft and corporate irresponsibility. *Contemporary Crises*, *5*, pp. 63–81.

———. (1981b). *Crime victims and Congress*. Paper presented at the meeting of the Academy of Criminal Justice Sciences, Philadelphia, February 15.

———. (1989). Crime victims and the news media: Questions of fairness and ethics. In J. Sullivan & J. Victor (Eds.), *Annual editions: Criminal justice 1988–1989* (pp. 51–57). Guilford, CT: Dushkin Publishing Group.

———. (1990). The implementation of victims' rights: A challenge for criminal justice professionals. In R. Muraskin (Ed.), *Issues in justice: Exploring policy issues in the criminal justice system* (pp. 46–57). Bristol, IN: Wyndham Hall Press.

———. (1992, Fall). Who's against victims' rights? The nature of the opposition to pro-victim initiatives in criminal justice. *St. John's Journal of Legal Commentary*, *8*(1), pp. 157–176.

———. (1995). Towards the institutionalization of a new kind of justice professional: The victim advocate. *The Justice Professional*, *9*(1), pp. 1–16.

———. (2000). *New York murder mystery: The true story behind the crime crash of the 1990s*. New York: New York University Press.

Katel, P. (2005, June). Identity theft: Can Congress give Americans better protection? *Congressional Quarterly Researcher*, *15*(22), 517–540.

Kates, D. (1986). *Firearms and violence: Issues of public policy*. New York: Ballinger.

Katz, L. (1980). *The justice imperative: An introduction to criminal justice*. Cincinnati, OH: Anderson Publishing.

Katz, L., Fletcher, G., & Altman, S. (1993). Blackmail symposium. *University of Pennsylvania Law Review*, *141*(5), 1565–1989.

Keilitz, S., Davis, C., Efkeman, H., Flango, C., & Hannaford, P. (1997, September). Civil protection orders: Victims' views on effectiveness. *NIJ Journal*, 233, 23–24.

Kelleher, J. (2006, January 3). An identity crisis. *Newsday*, p. A8.

Kelly, R. (1983). Addicts and alcoholics as victims. In D. MacNamara & A. Karmen (Eds.), *Deviants: Victims or victimizers?* (pp. 49–76). Newbury Park, CA: Sage.

Kelley, T. (2008, November 15). Bad health and a thief put a woman in crisis. *New York Times*, p. A19.

Kendall-Tackett, K., Williams, L., & Finkelhor, D. (1993, January). Impact of sexual abuse on children: A review and synthesis of recent empirical studies. *Psychological Bulletin*, *113*(1), 164–181.

Kennedy, D. (2004, Spring–Summer). Rethinking law enforcement strategies to prevent domestic violence. *Networks* magazine. National Center for Victims of Crime, 9–15.

Kerner, O. (1968). *Report of the National Advisory Commission on Civil Disorders*. New York: Bantam Books.

Kerr, P. (1992, February 6). Blatant fraud pushing up the cost of car insurance. *New York Times*, pp. A1, D6.

Kesler, J. (1992). *How to keep your car from being stolen*. Houston, TX: Shell Oil Company.

Keve, P. (1978). Therapeutic uses of restitution. In B. Galaway & J. Hudson (Eds.), *Offender restitution in theory and action* (pp. 59–64). Lexington, MA: Lexington Books.

Kidnapping summons city to action. (1993, October 15). *New York Times*, p. A24.

Kilpatrick, D. (1985, February). Survey analyzes responses of female sex assault victims. *Crime Victims Digest*, 9.

———. (1992). *Rape in America*. Fort Worth, TX: National Victim Center.

Kincaid, J. (1993 June 1). Purity, pederasty and a fallen heroine. *New York Times*, p. A17.

Kindermann, C., Lynch, J., & Cantor, D. (1997). *Effects of the redesign on victimization estimates. BJS National Crime Victimization Survey*. Washington, DC: U.S. Department of Justice.

King, P. (1993, October 4). Not so different, after all. *Newsweek*, p. 75.

King, W. (1989, January 1). Violent racism attracts new breed: Skinheads. *New York Times*, p. A35.

Kirkwood, C. (1993). *Leaving abusive partners*. Newbury Park, CA: Sage.

Klaus, P. (1994). *Costs of crime to victims. BJS Crime Data Briefs*. Washington, DC: U.S. Department of Justice.

———. (1999a). *Carjackings in the United States, 1992–1996. BJS Special Report*. Washington, DC: U.S. Department of Justice.

———. (1999b). *Crimes against persons age 65 and older. BJS Report*. Washington, DC: U.S. Department of Justice.

———. (2004). *Carjackings, 1993–2002. BJS Crime Data Brief*. Washington, DC: U.S. Department of Justice.

Klaus, P., DeBerry, M., & Timrots, A. (1985). *The crime of rape. BJS Bulletin*. Washington, DC: U.S. Department of Justice.

Kleck, G. (1991). *Point blank: Guns and violence in America*. New York: Aldine de Gruyter.

———. (1997). *Targeting guns: Firearms and their control*. Hawthorne, NY: Aldine de Gruyter.

Kleck, G., & DeLone, M. (1993). Victim resistance and offender weapon effects in robbery. *Journal of Quantitative Criminology*, *9*(1), 55–81.

Kleck, G., & Gertz, M. (1995, Fall). Armed resistance to crime: The prevalence and nature of self-defense with a gun. *Journal of Criminal Law and Criminology*, *86*(1), 150–187.

Klein, A. (1997). *Alternative sentencing, intermediate sanctions and probation* (2nd ed.). Cincinnati, OH: Anderson.

Klein, E., Campbell, J., Soler, E., & Ghez, M. (1997). *Ending domestic violence*. Thousand Oaks, CA: Sage.

Kleinfield, N. (1995, May 30). Prosecutors paying millions to protect cowed witnesses. *New York Times*, pp. A1, B5.

Klinger, D. (2001, August). Suicidal intent in victim-precipitated homicide. *Homicide Studies*, *5*(3), 206–226.

Klurfeld, J. (1988, June 24). Editorial: Crimes of bigotry deserve harsher punishment. *New York Newsday*, p. 92.

Knudten, M., Knudten, R., & Meade, A. (1978). Will anyone be left to testify? In E. Flynn & J. Conrad (Eds.), *The new and the old criminology* (pp. 207–222). New York: Praeger.

Kohn, A. (2005, May). Straight shooting on gun control. *Reason*, *37*(1), 20–25.

Kolarik, G. (1992, November). Stalking laws proliferate. *ABA Journal*, 35–36.

Koppel, H. (1987). *Lifetime likelihood of victimization: BJS Technical Report*. Washington, DC: U.S. Department of Justice.

Kornbluth, J. (1987, November 1). The woman who beat the Klan. *New York Times Magazine*, pp. 26–39.

Koss, M. (1992). The underdetection of rape: Methodological choices influence incidence estimates. *Journal of Social Issues*, *48*(1), 61–75.

———. (2005, January). Empirically enhanced reflections on 20 years of rape research. *Journal of Interpersonal Violence*, *20*(1), 100–107.

———. (2008). Letter to the editor of the *Los Angeles Times*. Retrieved September 24, 2008, from www.calcasa.org.

Koss, M., & Cook, S. (1998). Facing the facts: Date and acquaintance rape are significant problems for women. In R. Bergen (Ed.), *Issues in intimate violence* (pp. 147–156). Thousand Oaks, CA: Sage.

Koss, M., Gidyez, C., & Wisniewski, N. (1987). The scope of rape: Incidence and prevalence of sexual aggression and victimization in a national sample of higher education students. *Journal of Consulting and Clinical Psychology*, *55*, 162–170.

Koss, M., & Harvey, M. (1991). *The rape victim: Clinical and community interventions*. Newbury Park, CA: Sage.

Kotecha, K., & Walker, J. (1976). Vigilantism and the American police. In J. Rosenbaum & P. Sederberg (Eds.), *Vigilante politics* (pp. 158–174). Philadelphia: University of Pennsylvania Press.

Kramgrow, E., Lentzner, H., Rooks, P., Weeks, J., & Saydah, S. (1999). *Health, United States, 1997, with health and aging chartbook*. Hyattsville, MD: U.S. CDC's National Center for Health Statistics.

Kratcoski, P., Edelbacher, M., & Das, D. (2001). Terrorist victimization: Prevention, control, and recovery. *International Review of Victimology*, *8*, 257–268.

Krauss, C. (1994, January 23). New York car theft draws police priority. *New York Times*, pp. 21, 26.

Kristal, A. (1991). You've come a long way baby: The battered woman's syndrome revisited. *New York Law School Journal of Human Rights*, *9*, 111–116.

Krueger, F. (1985, May). Violated. *Boston*, 138–141.

Kycklehahn, T., & Cohen, T. (2008, April). Felony defendants in large urban counties, 2004 – Statistical tables. Retrieved September 30, 2008, from www.ojp.gov/bjs/abstract/fdluc04.htm.

Kuhl, A. (1986). Implications of justifiable homicide verdicts for battered women. *Response*, 9(2), 6–10.

La Fave, W. (1965). *Arrest: The decision to take a suspect into custody.* Boston: Little, Brown.

LaFontaine, D. (1997). *Speak of the devil: Allegations of satanic abuse in Britain.* New York: Cambridge University Press.

LaFree, G. (1989). *Rape and criminal justice.* Santa Fe, NM: University of New Mexico Press.

Lambert, A., & Raichle, K. (2000). The role of political ideology in mediating judgments of blame in rape victims and their assailants. *Personality and Social Psychology Bulletin*, 26(7), 853–863.

Lamborn, L. (1968). Toward a victim orientation in criminal theory. *Rutgers Law Review*, 22, 733–768.

———. (1985). The impact of victimology on the criminal law in the United States. *Canadian Community Law Journal*, 8, 23–43.

Lamm, R. (2004). Speech: I have a plan to destroy America. Retrieved September 17, 2008, from www.snopes.com.

Land, K., McCall, P., & Cohen, L. (1990, January). Structural covariates of homicidal rates: Are there any invariances across time and social space? *American Journal of Sociology*, 95(4), 922–963.

Lander, E. (1988, May 11). Rough sex defense assailed. *New York Newsday*, p. 26.

Landesman, P. (2004, January 25). The girls next door. *New York Times Magazine*, pp. 28–39.

Laner, M., & Thompson, J. (1982). Abuse and aggression in courting couples. *Deviant Behavior*, 3, 229–244.

Langan, P. (1985). *The risk of violent crime. BJS Special Report.* Washington, DC: U.S. Department of Justice.

Langan, P., & Graziadei, H. (1995). *Felony sentences in state courts, 1992. BJS Bulletin.* Washington, DC: U.S. Department of Justice.

Langan, P., & Harlow, C. (1994). *Child rape victims, 1992. BJS Crime Data Brief.* Washington, DC: U.S. Department of Justice.

Langan, P., & Innes, C. (1986). *Preventing domestic violence against women. BJS Special Report.* Washington, DC: U.S. Department of Justice.

Langan, P., Perkins, C., & Chaiken, J. (1994). *Felony sentences in the United States, 1990. BJS Bulletin.* Washington, DC: U.S. Department of Justice.

Langhinrichsen-Rohling, J. (2005, January). Important findings and future directions for intimate partner violence research. *Journal of Interpersonal Violence*, 20, 108–118.

Langstaff, J., & Sleeper, T. (2001). *The national center on child fatality review. OJJDP fact sheet.* Washington, DC: U.S. Department of Justice.

Lanning, K. (1992). *Child sex rings: A behavioral analysis.* Arlington, VA: National Center for Missing and Exploited Children.

Lanza, J. (2008). *Protecting your identity: Advice from FBI agent Jeff Lanza.* Retrieved July 18, 2008, from www.fbi.gov/page2/aug06/idtheft082106.htm.

LaPierre, W. (2008). Standing guard. Retrieved September 18, 2008, from www.nra.org.

Largen, M. (1981, Autumn). Grassroots centers and national task forces: A herstory of the anti-rape movement. *Aegis*, 32, 46–52.

———. (1987). A decade of change in the rape reform movement. *Response*, 10(2), 4–9.

Lasch, C. (1982, May 17). Why the "survival mentality" is rife in America. *U.S. News & World Report*, 59–60.

Laster, R. (1970). Criminal restitution: A survey of its past history and analysis of its present usefulness. *University of Richmond Law Review*, 5, 71–98.

Lawry, M. (1997, March). Court-appointed special advocates: A voice for abused and neglected children in court. *OJJDP Juvenile Justice Bulletin*, 1.

Leary, W. (1993, October 7). Gun in home? Study finds it a deadly mix. *New York Times*, p. A18.

Lederer, L. (1980). *Take back the night.* New York: Morrow.

Lederman, D. (1994, February 2). Crime on the campuses. *Chronicle of Higher Education*, A31–A42.

LeDuff, C. (2005, March 17). "Baretta" star acquitted of murder in wife's death. *New York Times*, p. A18.

Lee, J. (2005, February 26). Some tourists learn the hard way: Hawaii is not crime free. Retrieved December 9, 2008 from www.ap.org.

Lee, J. (2003a, January 23). Identity theft complaints double in '02, continuing rise. *New York Times*, p. A18.

———. (2003b, May 17). 130 arrested since Jan. 1 in Internet frauds that snared 89,000 victims, Ashcroft says. *New York Times*, p. A18.

Leepson, M. (1982). Helping victims of crime. *Editorial Research Reports*, *1*(17), 331–344.

LeGrande, C. (1973). Rape and rape laws: Sexism in society and law. *California Law Review, 61*, 919–941.

Lehnen, R., & Skogan, W. (1981). *The national crime survey: Working papers: Vol. 1. Current and historical perspectives*. Washington, DC: U.S. Department of Justice.

Leland, J. (2007, February 6). Identity fraud has dropped since 2003, survey shows. *New York Times*, p. A18.

Lengel, A., & Dvorak, P. (2004, May 1). Deepening mystery, enduring pain: Faded from news, Levy case still difficult for investigators, family. *Washington Post*, p. B1.

Lenkowitz, E. (2003, June 21). "Fake cop" busted in teen rape. *New York Post*, p. 8.

———., & Messing, P. (2003, February 26). 12-year-old admits 'rape' all a lie. *New York Post*, p. 5.

Leo, J. (1994, February 14). Watching 'As the jury turns.' *U.S. News & World Report*, 17.

———. (2002, December 23). People who blame people ... *U.S. News & World Report*, *123*(24), 8.

Leonard, E., 2001. Convicted survivors: Comparing and describing California's battered women's inmates. *Prison Journal, 81*(1), 73–86.

Leone, B., & de Koster, K. (1995). *At issue: Rape on campus*. San Diego, CA: Greenhaven Press.

Lerner, M. (1965). Evaluation of performance as a function of performer's reward and attractiveness. *Journal of Personality and Social Psychology, 1*, 355–360.

Letkemann, P. (1973). *Crime as work*. Englewood Cliffs, NJ: Prentice-Hall.

Levin, J., & McDevitt, J. (2003). *Hate crimes revisited: America's war on those who are different*. Boulder, CO: Westview Press.

Levine, J. (1976). The potential for crime overreporting in criminal victimization surveys. *Criminology, 14*(2), 307–331.

Levitt, L. (2004, March 26). Big headache over a box of aspirins. *New York Newsday*, p. 18.

Lewin, T. (1992, April 20). Battered men sounding equal-rights battle cry. *New York Times*, p. A12.

———. (2001, March 7). Legal action after killings at schools often fails. *New York Times*, p. A17.

———. (2002, July 28). Above expectation: A child as witness. *New York Times*, p. E3.

Libai, D. (1969). The protection of the child victim of a sexual offense in the criminal justice system. *Wayne Law Review, 15*, 977–1032.

Libbey, P., & Bybee, R. (1979). The physical abuse of adolescents. *Journal of Social Issues, 35*(2), 101–126.

Lightfoot, E., & Umbreit, M. (2004, December). An analysis of state statutory provisions for victim-offender mediation. *Criminal Justice Policy Review, 15*(4), 418–436.

Lindner, C., & Koehler, R. (1992). Probation officer victimization: An emerging concern. *Journal of Criminal Justice, 20*(1), 53–62.

Lippincott, E. (2006). New kits for sexual assault protective orders. *The Crime Victims Report, 10*, 1 (March/April), p. 3.

Lisefski, E., & Manson, D. (1988). *Tracking offenders, 1984. BJS Bulletin*. Washington, DC: U.S. Department of Justice.

Lisi, C. (2003, June 23). Car-theft lock shock. *New York Post*, p. 23.

Little, K. (2001). *Sexual assault nurse examiner (SANE) programs: Improving the community response to sexual assault victims*. Washington, DC: Office for Victims of Crime.

Livingston, I., & Fagen, C. (2007, September 17). B'klyn mom dead for caring. *New York Post*, p. 11.

Lobdell, W. (2002, March 21). Priests' victims feel vindicated. *Los Angeles Times*, p. A8.

Lockwood, D. (1980). *Prison sexual violence*. New York: Elsevier.

Loftin, C. (1986). The validity of robbery murder classifications in Baltimore. *Violence and Victims 1*(3), 191–202.

Loftus, E., & Ketcham, K. (1994). *The myth of repressed memory: False memories and allegations of sexual abuse*. New York: St. Martin's Press.

Lonsway, K., & Fitzgerald, L. (1994). Rape myths: In review. *Psychology of Women Quarterly, 18*: 133–164.

Lorch, D. (1990, August 24). Robbery suspect dies and a neighborhood is silent. *New York Times*, pp. A1, B3.

Loseke, D. (1989). Violence is 'violence' ... or is it? The social construction of 'wife abuse' and public policy. In J. Best (Ed.), *Images of issues: Typifying contemporary social problems* (pp. 191–206). New York: Aldine de Gruyter.

Loseke, D., Gelles, R., & Cavanaugh, M. (2005). *Current controversies on family violence* (2nd ed.). Thousand Oaks, CA: Sage.

Lott, J. (1998). *More guns, less crime: Understanding crime and gun control laws.* Chicago: University of Chicago Press.

Louden, R. (1998). The development of hostage negotiation by the NYPD. In A. Karmen (Ed.), *Crime and justice in New York City* (pp. 148–158). New York: McGraw Hill Custom Publishing.

Lourie, I. (1977). The phenomenon of the abused adolescent: A clinical study. *Victimology, 2*(2), 268–276.

Lovett, K. (2003, June 12). Peep victim hails deal on vidperv law. *New York Post,* p. 12.

Lubenow, G. (1983, June 27). When kids kill their parents. *Newsweek,* 35–36.

Luckenbill, D. (1977). Criminal homicide as a situated transaction. *Social Problems, 25,* 176–186.

Lueck, T. (2008, March 24). Officials seek benefits for slain auxiliary officers. *New York Times,* p. B2.

Lukewarm reception for new crime-data plan. (1988, May 31). *Law Enforcement News,* pp. 1, 7.

Lundman, R. (1980). *Police and policing: An introduction.* New York: Holt, Rinehart & Winston.

Lundsgaarde, H. (1977). *Murder in space city: A cultural analysis of Houston homicide patterns.* New York: Oxford University Press.

Lurigio, A. (1990). *Victims of crime: Problems, policies and programs.* Newbury Park, CA: Sage.

Lyman, R. (2005, July 7). Missing woman's case spurs discussion of news coverage. *New York Times,* p. A16.

Lynch, C. (2003, October 10). Fighting crime, but diplomatically, at the UN. *Washington Post,* p. A25.

Lynch, J. (2002). *Trends in juvenile offending: An analysis of victim survey data. OJJDP Juvenile Justice Bulletin.* Washington, DC: U.S. Department of Justice.

Lynch, R. (1976). Improving the treatment of victims: Some guides for action. In W. MacDonald (Ed.), *Criminal justice and the victim* (pp. 165–176). Beverly Hills, CA: Sage.

———, & Addington, L. (2007) (Eds..), *Understanding crime statistics.* New York: Cambridge University Press.

Lynn, W. (1981, March 30). What scientists really mean by "acceptable risk." *U.S. News and World Report,* 60.

MacDonald, H. (2007, February 9). Harvard's Faustian bargain. America's oldest university selects a dreadful president. *City Journal.* Retrieved October 13, 2008, from www.city-journal.org.

———. (2008a). The campus rape myth: Bogus statistics, feminist victimology, and university approved sex toys. *City Journal, 18,* 1 (Winter): 15–27.

———. (2008b, March 2). A thought experiment on campus rape. *City Journal.* Retrieved September 25, 2008, from www.city-journal.org.

———. (2008c, September 27). Anti-elitism goes too far: Sarah Palin's defenders shouldn't mock the value of learning. *City Journal.* Retrieved October 11, 2008, from www.city-journal.org.

MacDonald, J. (1971). *Rape: Offenders and victims.* Springfield, IL: Charles C. Thomas.

———, & Michaud, D. (1995). *Rape: Controversial issues—Criminal profiles, date rape, false reports and false memories.* Chicago: Charles C. Thomas.

MacGowan, C. (2007, October 12). Drug-chase killer gets maximum. *Long Island Newsday,* p. A16.

MacNamara, D. (1983). Prisoners as victimizers and victims. In D. MacNamara & A. Karmen (Eds.), *Deviants: Victims or victimizers?* Beverly Hills, CA: Sage.

———, & Sullivan, J. (1974). Making the victim whole: Composition, restitution, and compensation. In T. Thornberry & E. Sagarin (Eds.), *Images of crime: Offenders and victims* (pp. 79–90). New York: Praeger.

MADD. *See* Mothers Against Drunk Driving.

Madison, A. (1973). *Vigilantism in America.* New York: Seabury Press.

Maddalena, D. (2005, September 23). Syracuse officials say new date rape drug test not the answer. *Syracuse Daily Orange,* p. 3.

Maghan, J., & Sagarin, E. (1983). Homosexuals as victimizers and victims. In D. MacNamara & A. Karmen (Eds.), *Deviants: Victims or victimizers?* (pp. 147–162). Newbury Park, CA: Sage.

Maguire, K., & Pastore, A. (1994). *Sourcebook of criminal justice statistics—1993*. Bureau of Justice Statistics. Washington, DC: U.S. Government Printing Office.

Makepeace, J. (1981). Courtship violence among college students. *Family Relations, 30*, 97–102.

Malefyt, M., Littel, K., Walker, A., Tucker, D., & Buel, S. (1998). *Promising practices: Improving the criminal justice system's response to violence against women*. Office of Justice Programs report. Washington, DC: U.S. Department of Justice.

Maltz, W., & Holman, B. (1986). *Incest and sexuality: A guide to understanding and healing*. New York: Free Press.

Mannheim, H. (1965). *Comparative criminology*. Boston: Houghton Mifflin.

Manshel, L. (1990). *Nap time*. New York: Kensington.

Mansnerus, L. (1989, February 19). The rape laws change faster than perceptions. *New York Times* Sec. 5, p. 20.

———. (1999, September 28). Victim's parents reconcile with killer's. *New York Times*, p. B8.

Maple, J. (1999). *The crime fighter: Putting the bad guys out of business*. New York: Doubleday.

Marciniak, L. (1999, Fall). Adolescent attitudes toward victim precipitation of rape. *Violence and Victims, 13*(3), 287–300.

Margolick, D. (1994, January 16). Does Mrs. Bobbitt count as another battered wife? *New York Times*, p. E5.

Mariner, J. (2001). No escape: Male rape in U.S. prisons. New York: Human Rights Watch.

Markon, J. (2008, November 29). Poignant videos of victims valid in court. *Washington Post*, p. A3.

Marquis, J. (2005, June). Prosecutors and victims' rights. *The Crime Victims Report, 9*(2), 17–18.

Marriott, M. (1989, June 12). With a 'Remember me?' man shoots 3 in subway. *New York Times*, p. B2.

———. (1991, November 16). Rising fraud worrying car insurers ... And thefts bedevil automobile renters. *New York Times*, p. 48.

Martin, D. (1976). *Battered wives*. San Francisco: Glide.

Martin, D.E. (1989, June 7). The line of duty: Special officers help their own. *New York Times*, p. B1.

Martin, P., & Hummer, R. (1998). Fraternities and rape on campus. In R. Bergen (Ed.), *Issues in intimate violence* (157–167). Thousand Oaks, CA: Sage.

Martinson, R. (1974, Spring). What works—questions and answers about prison reform. *Public Interest, 35*, 22–54.

Martz, L., Miller, M., Hutchinson, S., Emerson, T., & Washington, F. (1989, January 16). A tide of drug killing. *Newsweek*, 44–45.

Martz, L., Starr, M., & Barrett, T. (1990, January 22). A murderous hoax. *Newsweek*, 16–21.

Marx, B. (2005, February). Lessons learned from the last twenty years of sexual violence research. *Journal of Interpersonal Violence, 20*(2), 225–230.

Marx, G., & Archer, D. (1976). Community police patrols and vigilantism. In J. Rosenbaum & P. Sederberg (Eds.), *Vigilante politics* (pp. 129–157). Philadelphia: University of Pennsylvania Press.

Mash, E., & Wolfe, D. (1991, March). Methodological issues in research on physical child abuse. *Criminal Justice and Behavior, 18*(1), 8–29.

Mason, M. (2002, October 10). Drug coasters that can detect "date rape drugs" may backfire. Associated Press Worldstream.

Mathews, A. (1993, March 7). The campus crime wave. *New York Times Magazine*, pp. 38–47.

Mathias, A. (2008, April 16). Fear and learning on campus. *New York Times*, p. A25.

Mauer, M. (1999). *Race to incarcerate*. New York: New Press.

Mawby, R., & Walklate, S. (1993). *Critical victimology: International perspectives*. Newbury Park, CA: Sage.

Max, W., Rice, D., Finkelstein, E., Bardwell, R. & Leadbetter, S. (2004, June). The economic toll of intimate partner violence against women in the United States. *Violence and Victims, 19*(3), 259–271.

Maxfield, M. (1987). Household composition, routine activity, and victimization: A comparative analysis. *Journal of Quantitative Criminology, 3*, 301–320.

Maxwell, C., Garner, J., & Fagan, J. (2001). *The effects of arrest on intimate partner violence*. NIJ Research in Brief. Washington, DC: U.S. Department of Justice.

May, G. (2002, Spring). Stop thief ! *Journal of Texas Consumer Law, 5*(3), 72–80.

May, J. (2001). *The guide to identity theft prevention*. Bloomington, IL: 1st Books Library.

Mayhew, P., & Hough, M. (1988). The British crime survey: Origins and impact. In M. Maguire &

J. Pointing (Eds.), *Victims of crime: A new deal?* (pp. 156–163). Philadelphia: Open University Press.

McCaghy, C. (1980). *Crime in American society*. New York: Macmillan.

———., Giordano, P., & Henson, T. (1977, November). Auto theft: Offenders and offense characteristics. *Criminology, 15*, 367–385.

McCahill, T., Williams, L., & Fischman, A. (1979). *The aftermath of rape*. Lexington, MA: Lexington Books.

McClennen, J. (2005, February). Domestic violence between same-gender partners. *Journal of Interpersonal Violence, 20*, 149–154.

McCold, P. (2003). An experiment in police-based restorative justice: The Bethlehem (Pennsylvania) Project. *Police Practice and Research, 4*(4), 379–390.

McCormack, R. (1991). Compensating victims of violent crime. *Justice Quarterly, 8*(3), 329–346.

McCurdy, K., & Daro, D. (1994). Child maltreatment: A national study of reports and fatalities. *Journal of Interpersonal Violence, 9*, 75–94.

McDermott, J. (1979). *Rape victimization in 26 American cities*. Washington, DC: U.S. Government Printing Office.

McDonald, D. (1988). *NIJ crime file study guide: Restitution and community service*. Washington, DC: U.S. Department of Justice.

McDonald, W. (1976). Criminal justice and the victim. In W. McDonald (Ed.), *Criminal justice and the victim* (pp. 17–56). Beverly Hills, CA: Sage.

———. (1977). The role of the victim in America. In R. Barnett & J. Hagel, III (Eds.), *Assessing the criminal: Restitution, retribution, and the legal process* (pp. 295–307). Cambridge, MA: Ballinger.

———. (1978). Expanding the victim's role in the disposition decision: Reform in search of rationale. In B. Galaway & J. Hudson (Eds.), *Offender restitution in theory and action* (pp. 101–110). Lexington, MA: Lexington Books.

———. (1979). The prosecutor's domain. In W. McDonald (Ed.), *The prosecutor* (pp. 15–52). Beverly Hills, CA: Sage.

———. (2004). *Trends in child maltreatment statistics*. Administration for Children and Families, U.S. Department of Health and Human Services.

McFadden, R. (1993, May 14). A stranger is stabbed saving a life. *New York Times*, p. B3.

———. (2003, May 20). DNA clears rape convict after 12 years. *New York Times*, pp. B1, B6.

McFarlane, J., et al., (1999). Stalking and intimate partner femicide. *Homicide Studies, 3*, 4 (November): 300–316.

McGillis, D. (1982). Minor dispute processing: A review of recent developments. In R. Tomasic & M. Feeley (Eds.), *Neighborhood justice: Assessment of an emerging idea* (pp. 60–76). New York: Longman.

———. (1986). *NIJ issues and practices: Crime victim restitution: An analysis of approaches*. Washington, DC: U.S. Department of Justice.

McGillis, D., & Smith, P. (1983). *Compensating victims of crime: An analysis of American programs*. Washington, DC: U.S. Department of Justice.

McGrath, K., & Osborne, M. (1989). Redressing violence against elders. *NOVA Newsletter, 13*(2), 1, 4, 5.

McIntyre, D. (1968, December). A study of judicial dominance of the charging decision. *Journal of Criminal Law, Criminology, and Police Science, 59*, 463–490.

McKinley, J. (2006, June 3). The distinction Modesto didn't need: National car-theft capital. *New York Times*, p. A8.

McKnight, D. (1981). The victim-offender reconciliation project. In B. Galaway & J. Hudson (Eds.), *Perspectives on crime victims* (pp. 292–298). St. Louis, MO: C.V. Mosby.

McMillion, R. (2003, February). ABA joins in call for Congress to address elder abuse issues. *ABA Journal, 89*, 62.

McPhee, M. (1999, December 20). Agonizing wait for mom. *New York Daily News*, p. 4.

Mead, J. (2006, May 28). A slow war on human trafficking. *New York Times*, p. B1.

Meadows, S., Johnson, D., & Downey, S. (2003, May 19). Girl fight: Savagery in the Chicago suburbs. *Newsweek*, 37.

Mears, D., & Visher, C. (2005). Trends in understanding and addressing domestic violence. *Journal of Interpersonal Violence, 20*, 2 (February), 204–211.

Mechanic, M., & Uhlmansiek, M. (2000). The impact of severe stalking experienced by acutely battered women. *Violence and Victims, 15*(4), 443–458.

Meiners, R. (1978). *Victim compensation: Economic, political and legal aspects*. Lexington, MA: D.C. Heath.

Meloy, J. (1998). *The psychology of stalking: Clinical and forensic perspectives*. San Diego, CA: Academic Press.

Memmott, M. (2005, July 16). Spotlight skips cases of missing minorities. *USA Today*, p. 6A.

Mencken, F., Nolan, J., & Berhanu, S. (2004, November). Juveniles, illicit drug activity, and homicides against law enforcement officers. *Homicide Studies, 8*(4), 327–349.

Mendelsohn, B. (1940). Rape in criminology. Translated and cited in S. Schafer (1968), *The victim and his criminal*. New York: Random House.

———. (1956, July). The victimology. *Etudes Internationales de Psycho-Sociologie Criminelle*, 23–26.

Menninger, K. (1968). *The crime of punishment*. New York: Viking Press.

Merrill, L. (1994, April 7). A defense that won't go away. *New York Daily News*, p. 6.

Messner, S., & Golden, R. (1992). Racial inequality and racially disaggregated homicide rates: An assessment of alternative theoretical explanations. *Criminology, 30*(3), 421–447.

Messner, S., & Tardiff, K. (1985). The social ecology of urban homicide: An application of the 'routine activities' approach. *Criminology, 23*, 241–267.

Miers, D. (1989). Positivist victimology: A critique. *International Review of Victimology, 1*, 3–22.

Miethe, T., Stafford, M., & Sloane, D. (1990). Lifestyle changes and risks of criminal victimization. *Journal of Quantitative Criminology, 6*(4), 357–375.

Mignon, S. (1998). Husband battering: A review of the debate over a controversial social phenomenon. In N. Jackson & G. Oates (Eds.), *Violence in intimate relationships: Examining sociological and psychological issues* (pp. 137–160). Woburn, MA: Butterworth-Heinemann.

Miller, F. (1970). *Prosecution: The decision to charge a suspect with a crime*. Boston: Little, Brown.

Miller, J. (2005, September 23). Ex-pharmaceutical executive sentenced to 8 years in the beating death of his wife. *New York Times*, p. B4.

Miller, S. (1992). Arrest policies for domestic violence and their implications for battered women. In R. Muraskin & T. Alleman (Eds.), *It's a crime: Women and justice* (pp. 334–359). Englewood Cliffs, NJ: Regents/Prentice Hall.

———. (2005). Victims as offenders: The paradox of women's violence in relationships. New Brunswick, N.J.: Rutgers University Press.

Miller, T., Cohen, M., & Wiersema, B. (1996). *Victim costs and consequences: A new look*. Washington, DC: U.S. Department of Justice.

Miller, W. (1973). Ideology and criminal justice policy: some current issues. *Journal of Criminal Law and Criminology, 64*, 2, 34–59.

Milner, J. (1991, March). Introduction: Current perspectives on physical child abuse. *Criminal Justice and Behavior, 18*(1), 4–7.

MIPT (2008). *Terrorism knowledge base*. Retrieved September 16, 2008, from www.terrorisminfo.mipt.org.

Mitchell, A. (1992, October 23). Strange school ties: A near fatal student-teacher pact. *New York Times*, p. B3.

Mitchell, J. (2008, March 16). Victims fund assists felons. Retrieved September 10, 2008, from www.baltimoresun.com/news/local.

Mithers, C. (1990, October 21). Incest and the law. *New York Times Magazine*, pp. 44–63.

Mixed verdict for six youths in fatal beating. (1996, February 6). *New York Times*, p. A9.

Molotsky, I. (1997, February 26). Two years later, Congress gets report on crime at colleges. *New York Times*, p. A23.

Mones, P. (1991). *When a child kills: Abused children who kill their parents*. New York: Simon & Schuster.

Moore, L. (1985, March). Your home: Make it safe. *Security Management*, 115–116.

Moore, E., & Mills, M. (1990). The neglected victims and unexamined costs of white-collar crime. *Crime and Delinquency, 36*(3), 408–418.

Morganthau, T., & Shenitz, B. (1994, August 15). Too many guns? Or too few? *Newsweek*, 44–45.

Morgenstern, P., & Fisher, E. (2005, July 20). Outside counsel: New clout for victims in criminal proceedings. *New York Law Journal, 234*, 4.

Moss, M. (2003, June 20). Air Force Academy did act on complaints, panel finds. *New York Times*, p. A14.

Mothers Against Drunk Driving (MADD). (1988, Spring). Victim rights: How far have we come? *Maddvocate, 13*.

Muehlenhard, C., Powch, I., Phelps, J., & Giusti, L. (1992). Definitions of rape: Scientific and political implications. *Journal of Social Issues, 48*(1), 23–44.

Mumola, C. (2005, August). *Suicides and homicides in state prisons and local jails.* Washington, DC: Bureau of Justice Statistics, U.S. Department of Justice.

_____. (2007, January). *Medical Causes of Death in State Prisons, 2001–2004.* Washington, DC: Bureau of Justice Statistics, U.S. Department of Justice.

Munson, D. (1989). *The child victim as a witness: OJJDP update on research.* Washington, DC: U.S. Department of Justice.

Murphy, C. (2006, July 22). Little Rock tourism growing, but so is the rate of violent crime. *Arkansas Democrat-Gazette,* p.1.

Murphy, W. (1999, September). Massachusetts initiates victim 'Miranda' law. *The Crime Victims Report, 3*(4), 49, 50, 55.

Mustaine, E., & Tewksbury, R. (1998a, November). Predicting risks of larceny theft victimization: A routine activity analysis using refined lifestyle measures. *Criminology, 36*(4), 829–857.

Mustaine, E., & Tewksbury, R. (1998b, Fall). Victimization risks at leisure: A gender-specific analysis. *Violence and Victims, 13*(3), 232–249.

Mydans, S. (1994, January 29). The other Menendez trial, too, ends with the jury deadlocked. *New York Times,* pp. A1, A8.

Myers, J. (1998). *Legal issues in child abuse and neglect.* Thousand Oaks, CA: Sage.

Myers, M. (1977). The effects of victim characteristics on the prosecution, conviction, and sentencing of criminal defendants. Unpublished doctoral dissertation. Ann Arbor, MI: University Microfilms.

Myers, M., & Hagan, J. (1979). Private and public trouble: Prosecutors and the allocation of court resources. *Social Problems, 26*(4), 439–451.

Myers, R., and Jacobo, J. (2006). Criminal transmission of HIV, Part IV. *The Crime Victims Report, 9*(6): 83–84.

Myrdal, G. (1944). *An American dilemma: The Negro problem and modern democracy.* New York: Harper Row.

NACVCB. *See* National Association of Crime Victims Compensation Boards.

Naim, M. (2005). *Illicit: How smugglers, traffickers, and copycats are hijacking the global economy.* New York: Doubleday.

Nathan, D., & Snedeker, M. (1995). *Satan's silence: Ritual abuse and the making of a modern American witchhunt.* New York: Basic Books.

National Advisory Commission on Criminal Justice Standards and Goals. (1973). *The courts.* Washington, DC: U.S. Government Printing Office.

National Association of Crime Victims Compensation Boards (2008). Crime victim compensation helps victims. Retrieved September 29, 2008, from www.nacvcb.org.

National Center for Child Abuse and Neglect (NCCAN). (1978). *Child sexual abuse: Incest, assault and sexual exploitation.* Washington, DC: U.S. Department of Health, Education, and Welfare.

National Center for Educational Statistics (NCES). (2008). *Indicators of school crime and safety, 2006.* Washington, DC: U.S. Department of Justice.

National Center for Health Statistics (NCHS). (2005, February 28). Deaths and death rates for the 10 leading causes of death. *National Vital Statistics Reports, 53*(15), 27.

National Center for Missing Adults (NCMA) (2008). About our organization. Retrieved September 25, 2008, from www.theyaremissed.org.

National Center for Missing and Exploited Children (NCMEC). (1986). *State legislation to protect children: An update on the nation's progress to implement effective laws preventing child victimization.* Washington, DC: Author.

_____. (1987). *Accomplishing great things.* Washington, DC: Author.

_____. (2005). *Amber Alert – America's missing: Broadcast emergency response.* Retrieved December 20, 2005, from www.ncmec.org.

National Center for Victims of Crime (NCVC). (1996). *The 1996 victim rights sourcebook.* Arlington, VA: NCVC.

_____. (1999). *The NCVC does not support the current language of the proposed crime victims' rights constitutional amendment.* Arlington, VA: NCVC.

———. (2002a). *The crime victim's right to be present.* Legal Series Bulletin 3. Washington, DC: U.S. Department of Justice.

———. (2002b). *Restitution: Making it work.* Legal Series Bulletin 5. Washington, DC: U.S. Department of Justice.

———. (2002c). *Ordering restitution to the crime victim.* Legal Series Bulletin 6. Washington, DC: U.S. Department of Justice.

———. (2002d). *Victim input into plea agreements.* Legal Series Bulletin 7. Washington, DC: U.S. Department of Justice.

———. (2002e). *Privacy of victims' counseling communications.* Legal Series Bulletin 8. Washington, DC: U.S. Department of Justice.

———. (2003, March 9). *Vote of no confidence major factor in low crime reporting rates.* Press release. Washington, DC: NCVC.

———. (2007). *The model stalking code revisited.* Washington, DC: NCVC.

———. (2008). *Parallel justice guiding principles.* Retrieved October 3, 2008, from www.ncvc.org.

National Clearinghouse on Child Abuse and Neglect Information. (1997). *What is child maltreatment?* Washington, DC: NCCANI.

———. (2003). *Child maltreatment 2001: Summary of key findings.* Washington, DC: NCCANI.

National Coalition of Victims in Action (2008). Board of Directors. Retrieved October 4, 2008, from www.rorpf.org/NCVIA Board of Directors.htm.

National Commission on the Causes and Prevention of Violence (NCCPV). (1969a). *Crimes of violence.* Washington, DC: U.S. Government Printing Office.

———. (1969b). *The offender and his victim.* (Staff report by D. Mulvihill, L. Curtis, & M. Tumin). Washington, DC: U.S. Government Printing Office.

National Committee for Prevention of Child Abuse (NCPCA). (1993). *Current trends in child abuse reporting and fatalities.* Chicago: National Committee.

National Criminal Justice Reference Center (NCJRS). (2005). In the spotlight: Identity theft. Retrieved September 21, 2005, from www.ncjrs. org/spotlight/identitytheft.html.

National Crime Prevention Institute (NCPI). (1978). *Understanding crime prevention.* Louisville, KY: Author.

National Crime Victim Bar Association (2007). Civil justice for victims of crime: A handbook. Retrieved September 30, 2008, from www.victimbar.org/vb.

National Highway Transportation Safety Administration (NHTSA). (2008 March 12). Final theft data. *Federal Register, 73* (49), pp. 13150–13155.

National Institute of Justice (NIJ). (1984). *Vehicle theft prevention strategies.* Washington, DC: U.S. Government Printing Office.

———. (1998). *New directions from the field: Victims' rights and services for the twenty-first century.* Washington, DC: U.S. Department of Justice.

National Insurance Crime Bureau (NICB) (1993, Winter). The public speaks out on fraud and theft. *Spotlight on Insurance Crime, 2*(3), 1–2.

———. (1995, Winter). Eye on insurance crime. *Spotlight on Insurance Crime, 3*(3), 8–9.

———. (2004, Summer). Motorcycle theft and fraud. *Upclose Newsletter,* 1–2.

———. (2008). Hot spots, 2007. Retrieved July 6, 2008, from www.nicb.org.

National Opinion Research Center (NORC) (2004). General social survey. Retrieved July 10, 2008, from www.norc.org.

National Organization for Victim Assistance (NOVA). (1988). *Victim rights and services: A legislative directory – 1987.* Washington, DC: Author.

———. (1989). Bipartisan victim rights bill introduced in U.S. Congress. *NOVA Newsletter, 13*(3), 1, 5.

———. (1995). Basic rights revisited. *NOVA Newsletter, 17*(4), 1–2.

———. (2002). Revised victim rights amendment introduced. *NOVA Newsletter, 12,* 15.

National Sheriffs' Association. (1999). *First response to victims of crime.* Washington, DC: Office for Victims of Crime, U.S. Department of Justice.

National Rifle Association (NRA). (2008a). Institute for Legislative Action: Criticism of "Castle Doctrine" bill way off target. Retrieved October 3, 2008, from www.nraila.org/news.

———. (2008b). Institute for Legislative Action: Guns, gun ownership, and RTC at all-time highs. Retrieved October 3, 2008, from www.nraila.org/news.

National Victim Center (NVC). (1990). *Crime victims and corrections.* Fort Worth, TX: NVC.

———. (1991a). *America speaks out: Citizens' attitudes about victims' rights and violence.* Fort Worth, TX: NVC.

———. (1991b). *National victim services survey of adult and juvenile corrections and parole agencies.* Final report. Fort Worth, TX: NVC.

———. (1993). *Civil justice for crime victims.* Fort Worth, TX: NVC.

National Victim Constitutional Amendment Passage (NVCAP), (2008). Marsy's law, California's new VRA, passes. Retrieved December 4, 2008 from www.nvcap.org.

NCCAN. *See* National Center for Child Abuse and Neglect.

NCCANI. *See* National Clearinghouse on Child Abuse and Neglect Information.

NCCPV. *See* National Commission on the Causes and Prevention of Violence.

NCES. *See* National Center for Educational Statistics.

NCHS. *See* National Center for Health Statistics.

NCJRS. *See* National Criminal Justice Reference Center.

NCMEC. *See* National Center for Missing and Exploited Children.

NCPCA. *See* National Committee for Prevention of Child Abuse.

NCVC. *See* National Center for Victims of Crime.

Neidig, P. (1984). Women's shelters, men's collectives and other issues in the field of spouse abuse. *Victimology, 9*(3–4), 464–476.

Neubauer, D. (1974). *Criminal justice in middle America.* Morristown, NJ: General Learning Press.

New Jersey: Crime victims request only 10% of funding. (2002, September 16). *Juvenile Justice Digest, 30*(1), 7.

New Jersey Victims of Crime Compensation Agency. (2008). Benefits in a nutshell. Retrieved September 30, 2008, from www.state.nj.us/victims.

New York Police Department (NYPD). (1992). *Auto theft: A growing business.* NYPD Auto Crime Division.

New York State Crime Victims Board. (2008). *Annual report, fiscal year 2007.* Retrieved September 28, 2008, from www.cvb.state.ny.us/home.

New York State Law Enforcement Council. (1994). *Legislative proposals, 1994.* New York: Author.

New York Times editors. (1987, July 7). Paying victims, freeing prisoners. *New York Times,* p. A26.

———. (1991a, April 17). Growing old under siege of social workers: More funds needed. *New York Times,* p. A24.

———. (1991b, June 25). Warned not to testify, theft victim is shot. *New York Times,* p. B5.

———. (2005a, April 15). Identity thieves' secret weapon. *New York Times,* p. A18.

———. (2005b, June 30). Help for victims of sexual assault. *New York Times,* p. A14.

New study details dangers of holding youth in adult jails. (2008, March). *Juvenile Justice Update, 14*(1): 11.

Newberger, E. (1987, March). Prosecution: A problematic approach to child abuse. *Journal of Interpersonal Violence,* pp. 112–117.

Newman, D. (1966). *Conviction: The determination of guilt or innocence without trial.* Boston: Little, Brown.

Newman, O. (1972). *Defensible space: People and design in the violent city.* London: Architectural Press.

News Wire Services. (2000, February 6). GOP senator advocates push for victims rights. *Bergen (NJ) Record,* p. A21.

NHTSA. *See* National Highway Transportation Safety Administration.

NICB. *See* National Insurance Crime Bureau.

"NICB study shows vehicle theft trends." (1993, August 3). *Corporate Security Digest,* pp. 1–2.

Nicholson, E. (Ed.). (1988). *Sexual abuse allegations in custody and visitation cases.* Washington, DC: American Bar Association.

Niemeyer, M., & Shichor, D. (1996, September). A preliminary study of a large victim/offender reconciliation program. *Federal Probation, 60*(3), 30–34.

Nieves, E. (1994, December 3). Prosecutors drop charges in abuse case from mid-80s. *New York Times,* pp. A25, A29.

NIJ. *See* National Institute of Justice.

Nizza, M. (2007, October 6). Students sue prosecutor and city in Duke case. *New York Times,* p. A24.

———. (2008, February 15). Gunman was once "revered" on campus. *New York Times,* p. A20.

Noe, D. (2005). The killing of Polly Klaas. *Crime Library*. Retrieved October 13, 2005, from www.courttv.com.

Nolan, J., McDevitt, J., & Cronin, S. (2004). Learning to see hate crime: A framework for understanding and clarifying ambiguities in bias crime classification. *Criminal Justice Studies*, 17(1), 91–105.

National Opinion Research Center (NORC) (2004). *General social survey, 2002.* Storrs, CT: Roper Center for Public Opinion Research.

Niesse, M. (2008, January 30). Judge denies request for blackmail emails. Retrieved November 18, 2008, from www.ap.org.

Normandeau, A. (1968, November). Patterns in robbery. *Criminologica*, 2–15.

Nossiter, A. (1994, September 16). Judge awards damages in Japanese youth's death. *New York Times*, p. A12.

———. (1996, April 28). Putative damages: The non-cash value of $43 million. *New York Times* Sec. 4, p. 5.

NOVA. *See* National Organization for Victim Assistance.

National Public Radio (NPR) (2008, March 28). Morning Edition Storycorps Recording America: A victim treats his mugger right. Retrieved October 23, 2008, from www.npr.org.

National Prison Rape Elimination Commission (NPREC) (2008). Sexual Victimization in State and Federal Prisons Reported by Inmates, 2007. Retrieved October 23, 2008, from www.nprec.us/resources.htm.

NRA. *See* National Rifle Association.

Nuwar, K. (2008, July 28). News release: Choicepoint Adam program marks milestone with 100th child recovery. Retrieved August 9, 2008, from www.ncmec.org.

NVC. *See* National Victim Center.

NYPD Detectives. (2008). Victimology. Retrieved April 20 from www.homicidesquad.com.

O'Brien, R. (1985). *Crime and victimization data.* Beverly Hills, CA: Sage.

———. (2000). Crime facts: Victim and offender data. In J. Sheley (Ed.), *Criminology* (3rd ed., pp. 59–83). Belmont, CA: Wadsworth.

Ochberg, F. (1978). The victim of terrorism: Psychiatric considerations. *Terrorism: An International Journal, 1* (2), 147–167.

O'Connell, P., & Straub, F. (1999, Spring). Why the jails didn't explode. *City Journal, 9*(2), 28–37.

O'Connor, A., & Pacifici, S. (2007, April 28). A fatal wound from a colleague's weapon is rare, but always a risk. *New York Times*, p. B3.

Office of the Coordinator for Counterterrorism (OCC). *Patterns of global terrorism, 1999.* Washington, DC: U.S. Department of State.

Office of the Inspector General, Department of Defense. (2003). *United States Air Force Academy: Initial sexual assault survey findings.* Washington, DC: U.S. Department of Defense.

Office of Inspector General, Department of Education. (2005). *Don't let identity thieves steal your future!* Retrieved September 23, 2005, from www.ed.gov/about/offices/list/oig/misused/idtheft.html.

Office of Justice Programs (OJP). (1997). *Implementing the national incident-based reporting system: A project status report.* Washington, DC: U.S. Department of Justice.

———. (1997). *National Victim Assistance Academy (NVAA) handbook.* Washington, DC: U.S. Department of Justice.

———. (1998). *Stalking and domestic violence: The third annual report to Congress under the Violence Against Women Act.* Washington, DC: U.S. Department of Justice.

———. (2008a). Amber Alert, 2006 statistics. Retrieved August 9, 2008, from www.amberalert.gov/statistics.

———. (2008b). Information on stalking victims. Retrieved August 29, 2008, from www.ojp.usdoj.gov/nij/topics/crime/stalking/victims.htm.

Office of Juvenile Justice and Delinquency Prevention (OJJDP). (1998a). *When your child is missing: A family survival guide.* Washington, DC: U.S. Department of Justice.

———. (1998b). *Guide for implementing the balanced and restorative justice model.* Washington, DC: U.S. Department of Justice.

———. (1998c). *National directory of restitution and community service programs.* Washington, DC: U.S. Department of Justice.

———. (2008). The Front Line newsletter, Winter, 2007. Retrieved August 9, 2008, from www.missingkids.org.

Office of National Drug Control Policy. (2003). Rohypnol. Drug Policy Information Clearinghouse Fact Sheet. Retrieved December 20, 2005, from www.whitehousedrugpolicy.gov.

Office of Victims of Crime (OVC). (1997). *Restorative justice fact sheet*. Washington, DC: U.S. Department of Justice.

———. (2001). *Handbook for coping after terrorism: A guide to healing and recovery*. Washington, DC: U.S. Department of Justice.

———. (2002). *Terrorism and international victims unit. OVC fact sheet*. Washington, DC: U.S. Department of Justice.

———. (2003). *First response to victims of crime who have a disability*. Washington, DC: U.S. Department of Justice.

Ofshe, R., & Watters, E. (1993). *Making monsters: False memories, psychotherapy, and sexual hysteria*. New York: Scribners.

Ogawa, B. (1999). *Color of justice: Culturally sensitive treatment of minority crime victims* (2nd ed.). Boston: Allyn and Bacon.

Ohlin, L., & Tonry, M. (1989). Family violence in perspective. In L. Ohlin & M. Tonry (Eds.), *Crime and justice: A review of research, Volume 11: Family violence* (pp. 1–18). Chicago: University of Chicago Press.

OJJDP. *See* Office of Juvenile Justice and Delinquency Prevention.

OJP. *See* Office of Justice Programs.

O'Keefe, M., & Trester, L. Victims of dating violence among high school students. *Violence Against Women, 4*(2), 195–223.

O'Neill, T. (1984). The good, the bad, and the Burger court: Victims' rights and a new model of criminal review. *Journal of Criminal Law and Criminology, 75*(2), 363–387.

Onishi, N. (1994, May 26). Stray gunfire kills man in Bronx. *New York Times*, p. B3.

Orcutt, J., & Faison, R. (1988). Sex-role attitude change and reporting of rape victimization, 1973–1985. *Sociological Quarterly, 29,* 589–604.

Orth, U., & Maercker, A. (2004). Do trials of perpetrators retraumatize crime victims? *Journal of Interpersonal Violence, 19*(2), 212–227.

O'Shaughnessy, P. (2008, February 25). Ex-cop terrorized her. *New York Daily News*, p. 16.

Ostling, R. (2003, June 21). Clergy abuse victims group opens meeting. *Associated Press newswire*.

O'Sullivan, C., Davis, R., Farole, D., & Rempel, M. (2007, September). A comparison of two prosecution policies in cases of intimate partner violence: executive summary by Safe Horizon, NY. National Institute of Justice.

Ottens, A., & Hotelling, K. (Eds.). (2001). *Sexual violence on campus: Policies, programs, and perspectives*. New York: Springer.

Outlaw, M., & Ruback, B. (1999). Predictors and outcomes of victim restitution orders. *Justice Quarterly, 16*(4), 847–869.

OVC. *See* Office of Victims of Crime.

Owsley, S. (2005, June 25). Don't become a victim this vacation season. *Eureka-Times Standard*, p. 4.

Pacepa, I. (2005, June 16). Bolton's bravery. *National Review Online*.

Pagelow, M. (1984a). *Family violence*. New York: Praeger.

———. (1984b). *Women battering: Victims and their experiences*. Beverly Hills, CA: Sage.

———. (1989). The incidence and prevalence of criminal abuse of other family members. In L. Ohlin & M. Tonry (Eds.), *Crime and justice: A review of research, Volume 11: Family violence* (pp. 263–313). Chicago: University of Chicago Press.

Paglia, C. (1993, August 1). Interview on CBS's *60 Minutes*.

———. (1994). *Vamps and tramps*. New York: Vintage.

Parent, D., Auerbach, B., & Carlson, K. (1992). *Compensating crime victims: A summary of policies and practices*. Washington, DC: U.S. Department of Justice.

Parker, K. (1999, November 22). Moral pendulum swings back. *The Denver Post*, p. B10.

Parker, R. (1995). Bringing 'booze' back in: The relationship between alcohol and homicide. *Journal of Research in Crime and Delinquency, 32*(1), 3–38.

Parker, R., & Rebhun, L. (1995). *Alcohol and homicide: A deadly combination of two American traditions.* Albany: SUNY Press.

Parsell, T. (2005) Personal accounts from survivors of prison sexual assaults. Retrieved August 19, 2008, from www.nprec.us/docs/sf_tjparsell_statement.pdf.

Parsonage, W. (Ed.). (1979). *Perspectives on victimology.* Beverly Hills, CA: Sage.

————, Bernat, F., & Helfgott, J. (1994). Victim impact testimony and Pennsylvania's parole decision-making process: A pilot study. *Criminal Justice Policy Review, 6*, 187–206.

Paternoster, R. (1984). Prosecutorial discretion in requesting the death penalty: A case of victim-based racial discrimination. *Law and Society Review, 18*, 437–478.

Patrick, R. (2006, November 5). Blackmail letter brings charges FBI built a case after St. Louis County school employee reported letter. *St. Louis Post-Dispatch*, p. C1.

Patton, C. (2005). *Anti-lesbian, gay, bisexual and transgender violence in 2004: A report of the National Coalition of Anti-Violence Programs.* New York: NCAVP.

Payne, B., & Gainey, R. (2005). *Family violence and criminal justice: A life-course approach* (2nd ed.). Florence, KY: Anderson.

Payne, L. (1989, April 27). Her boyfriend says: Tawana made it up. *New York Newsday*, pp. 1, 3.

Peacock, P. (1998). Marital rape. In R. Bergen (Ed.), *Issues in intimate violence* (pp. 223–235). Thousand Oaks, CA: Sage.

Peak, K. (1986, September). Crime victim reparation: Legislative revival of the offended ones. *Federal Probation*, 36–41.

Pear, R. (2002, March 3). Unreported abuse found at nursing homes. *New York Times*, p. A8.

Pendergrast, M. (1994). *Victims of memory: Incest accusations and shattered lives.* San Francisco: Upper Access.

Pepinsky, H. (1991). Peacemaking in criminology and criminal justice. In H. Pepinsky & R. Quinney (Eds.), *Criminology as peacemaking* (pp. 299–327). Bloomington, IN: Indiana University Press.

Perillo, A., Mercado, C., & Terry, K. (2008). Repeat offending, victim gender, and extent of victim relationship in Catholic Church sexual abusers. *Criminal Justice and Behavior, 35*, 5, pp. 600–614.

Perrusquia, M. (2008, December 1). Standing their ground: More citizens enforcing the law themselves. *Memphis Commercial Appeal*, p. 4.

Perry, S. (2006). *Prosecutors in state courts, 2005. BJS Bulletin.* Washington, DC: U.S. Department of Justice.

Peters, D., Wyatt, G., & Finkelhor, D. (1986). Prevalence. In D. Finkelhor (Ed.), *A sourcebook on child sexual abuse* (pp. 50–60). Beverly Hills, CA: Sage.

Petherick, W. and Turvey, B. (2008). Forensic victimology. New York: Academic Press.

Pfeiffer, S. (2002, November 9). Sex-abuse monitor favors police tipoffs. *Boston Globe*, p. 8.

Pfohl, S. (1984). The discovery of child abuse. In D. Kelly (Ed.), *Deviant behavior* (pp. 45–65). New York: St. Martin's Press.

Pilon, R. (1998, August 31). Victims would be better served by looking to the states, where most laws are enforced. *Insight on the News*, 25.

Plate, T. (1975). *Crime pays.* New York: Simon & Schuster.

Platell, A. (2005, August). The Date Rape 'Myth.' *London Daily Mail*, Sec. 2, p. 12.

Platt, A. (1968). *The child savers.* Chicago: University of Chicago Press.

Pleck, E. (1989). Criminal approaches to family violence, 1640–1980. In L. Ohlin & M. Tonry (Eds.), *Crime and justice: An annual review of research, Vol. 11: Family violence.* (pp. 19–57). Chicago: University of Chicago Press.

Pleck, E., Pleck, J., Grossman, M., & Bart, P. (1978). The battered data syndrome: A comment on Steinmetz' article. *Victimology, 2*(4), 680–684.

Podhoretz, N. (1991, October). Rape in feminist eyes. *Commentary*, 30–36.

Police chief and others do not fit victim stereotypes. (1993, September). *Crime Victims Digest*, 6–7.

Police Department, Cary, NC. (2007, December 14). Cary police advise citizens and business owners to watch for holiday bandits. US States News, Lexis Nexis Academic Universe.

Pollitt, K. (1989, June 18). Violence in a man's world. *New York Times Magazine*, pp. 16, 20.

————. (1991, June 24). Naming and blaming: The media goes wild in Palm Beach. *The Nation*, 833, 847–852.

Pope, E., & Shouldice, M. (2001, January). Drugs and sexual assault: A review. *Trauma, Violence, and Abuse*, 2(1), 51–55.

Porter, E. (1986). *Treating the young male victim of sexual assault: Issues and intervention strategies*. Syracuse, NY: Safer Society Press.

PR Newswire (2005, July 20). Intelius launches ID watch to protect, prevent, and insure against identity theft. Retrieved August 20, 2005, from www. intelius.com.

Pranis, K. (1999, September). Victims in the peacemaking circle process. *The Crime Victims Report*, 3(4), 51.

President's Task Force on Identity Theft (2007). Combating identity theft: A strategic plan. Washington, DC: U.S. Government Printing Office.

President's Task Force on Victims of Crime. (1982). *Final report*. Washington, DC: U.S. Government Printing Office.

Press, A., Copeland, J., Contreras, J., Camper, D., Agrest, S., Newhall, E., Monroe, S., Young, J., & Mattland, T. (1981, March 23). The plague of violent crime. *Newsweek*, 46–54.

Prestia, K. (1993). *Chocolates for the pillows—Nightmares for the guests*. Silver Spring, MD: Bartleby Press.

Preston, J. (2005, September 27). Judge sets Gotti's bail at $7 million. *New York Times*, pp. B1, B6.

Price, B., & Sokoloff, N. (2004). *The criminal justice system and women* (3rd ed.). New York: McGraw Hill.

Price, M. (2002). The benefits of victim-offender mediation. Retrieved November 28, 2005, from www. vorp.com.

Prison Research and Action Project. (1976). *Instead of prisons*. Genesee, NY: Author.

Privacy Rights Clearinghouse (2008). *A chronology of data breaches; updated July 16*. Retrieved July 20, 2008, from www.privacyrights.org.

Prosecutorial discretion in the initiation of criminal complaints. (1969, Spring). *Southern California Law Review*, 42, 519–545.

Puckett, J., & Lundman, R. (2003, May). "Factors affecting homicide clearances: Multivariate analysis of a complete conceptual framework." *Journal of Research in Crime and Delinquency*, 40, 2: 171–193.

Purdum, T. (1988, April 10). The reality of crime on campus. *New York Times Education Supplement*, Sec. 12, pp. 47–51.

Purdy, M. (1994, February 14). Workplace murders provoke lawsuits and better security. *New York Times*, pp. A1, B5.

Purnick, J. (1986, January 22). Manes retracts story and says he cut himself. *New York Times*, p. 1.

Quinn, M., & Tomita, S. (1986). *Elder abuse and neglect: Causes, diagnosis, and intervention strategies*. New York: Springer.

Rainville, G., & Reeves, B. (2003). *State court processing statistics: Felony defendants in large urban counties, 2000*. Washington, DC: Bureau of Justice Statistics, U.S. Department of Justice.

Ramsey, J., & Ramsey, P. (2000). *The death of innocence: The untold story of JonBenet's murder and how its exploitation compromised the pursuit of truth*. Waterville, ME: Thorndike Press.

Rand, M. (1993). *Crime and the nation's households, 1992. BJS Bulletin*. Washington, DC: U.S. Department of Justice.

————. (1994a). *Carjacking: BJS Crime Data Brief*. Washington, DC: U.S. Department of Justice.

————. (1994b). *Guns and crime: BJS Crime Data Brief*. Washington, DC: U.S. Department of Justice.

Rand, M. & Catalano, S. (2007). *Criminal victimization 2007. National Crime Victims Survey*. Washington, DC: Bureau of Justice Statistics, U.S. Department of Justice.

Rand, M., & Rennison, C. (2002). True crime stories? Accounting for differences in our national crime indicators. *Chance Magazine*, 15(1), 8–12.

Ranish, D., & Shichor, D. (1985, March). The victim's role in the penal process: Recent developments in California. *Federal Probation*, 50–56.

Rashbaum, W. (2005, September 23). Arrest in killings of two who dared to rob the mob. *New York Times*, pp. A1, B6.

Rathbone, G., & Huckabee, J. (1999). *Controlling road rage: A literature review and pilot study*. Washington, DC: AAA Foundation for Traffic Safety.

Ratnesar, R. (1998, July 6). Should you carry a gun? *Time*, 48.

Rauber, M. (1991, May 21). Rape victims get a legal break. *New York Post*, p. 22.

Ray, L. (1984, May). Dispute resolution: "A muffled explosion." *NIJ Reports, 185*, 9.

Ready, J., Weisburd, D., & Farrell, G. (2002). The role of crime victims in American policing. *International Review of Victimology, 9*, 175–195.

Reaves, B. (1993). *National incident-based reporting system: Using NIBRS data to analyze violent crime. BJS Technical Report.* Washington, DC: U.S. Department of Justice.

———. (1998). *Felony defendants in large urban counties, 1994. BJS State Court Processing Statistics.* Washington, DC: U.S. Department of Justice.

———. (2008, February). *Campus law enforcement, 2004–05. BJS Special Report.* Washington, DC: U.S. Department of Justice.

———, & Hart, T. (2001). *Federal law enforcement officers, 2000. BJS Bulletin.* Washington, DC: U.S. Department of Justice.

———, & Hickman, M. (2002). *Police departments in large cities, 1990–2000. BJS Special Report.* Washington, DC: U.S. Department of Justice.

Reckless, W. (1967). *The crime problem.* New York: Appleton-Century-Crofts.

Reeves, H. (2006, June 18). What's that word for taking stuff? *New York Times*, section 11, p. 12.

Reeves, C., & O'Leary-Kelly, A. (2007, March). The effects and costs of intimate partner violence for work organizations. *Journal of Interpersonal Violence, 22*, 3: 327–344.

Regehr, C., & Bober, T. (2005). *In the line of fire: Trauma in the emergency services.* New York: Oxford University Press.

Reiff, R. (1979). *The invisible victim.* New York: Basic Books.

Reilly, J. (1981, October). Victim/witness services in prosecutors' offices. *The Prosecutor*, 8–11.

Reiman, J. (1990). *The rich get richer and the poor get prison: Ideology, class, and criminal justice* (3rd ed.). New York: Wiley.

———. (2005). *The rich get richer and the poor get prison: Ideology, class, and criminal justice* (7th ed.). Boston: Allyn and Bacon.

Reiss, A. (1971). *The police and the public.* New Haven, CT: Yale University Press.

———. (1981). Toward a revitalization of theory and research on victimization by crime. *Journal of Criminal Law and Criminology, 72*(2), 704–713.

———. (1986). Official and survey statistics. In E. Fattah (Ed.), *From crime policy to victim policy* (pp. 53–79). New York: St. Martin's Press.

Rennison, C. (1999). *Criminal victimization 1998: Changes 1997–1998 with trends 1993–1998. BJS National Crime Victimization Survey.* Washington, DC: U.S. Department of Justice.

———. (2002a). *Criminal victimization 2001. BJS National Crime Victimization Survey.* Washington, DC: U.S. Department of Justice.

———. (2002b). *Rape and sexual assault: Reporting to police and medical attention, 1992–2000. BJS Selected Findings.* Washington, DC: U.S. Department of Justice.

———. (2003). *Intimate partner violence, 1993–2001. BJS Crime Data Brief.* Washington, DC: U.S. Department of Justice.

———, & and Rand M. (2007). Introduction to the *National Crime Victimization Survey.* In J. Lynch and L. Addington (Eds..), *Understanding crime statistics,* pp. 17–54. New York: Cambridge University Press.

Reno, J. (1999). *Cyberstalking: A new challenge for law enforcement and industry. A report from the attorney general to the vice president.* Washington, DC: U.S. Department of Justice.

Renzetti, C. (1992). *Violent betrayal: Partner abuse in lesbian relationships.* Newbury Park, CA: Sage.

Report exposes lie detector tests that await some Ohio rape victims. (2003, April 15). *Law Enforcement News*, pp. 1, 10.

Resick, P., & Nishith, P. (1997). Sexual assault. In R. Davis, A. Lurigio, & W. Skogan (Eds.), *Victims of crime* (2nd ed.) (pp. 27–52). Thousand Oaks, CA: Sage.

Reuters News Service. (1996, February 18). Loss of evidence impeded inquiry into boy's death. *New York Times*, p. A30.

Reynolds, G. (2007, January 16). A rifle in every pot. *New York Times*, p. A21.

Rhatigan, D., Moore, T., & Street, A. (2005). Reflections on partner violence: Twenty years of research and beyond. *Journal of Interpersonal Violence, 20*(1), 82–88.

Rhode, D. (1989). *Justice and gender: Sex discrimination and the law*. Cambridge, MA: Harvard University Press.

Rhodes, N. (1992). The assessment of spousal abuse: An alternative to the conflict tactics scale. In E. Viano (Ed.), *Intimate violence: Interdisciplinary perspectives* (pp. 27–36). Washington, DC: Hemisphere Publishing.

Rhodes, W. (1978). *Plea bargaining: Who gains? Who loses?* PROMIS Research Project No. 14. Washington, DC: Institute for Law and Social Research.

Richardson, J., Best, J., & Bromley, D. (Eds.) (1991). *The satanism scare*. New York: Aldine de Gruyter.

Richie, B. (1996). *Compelled to crime: The gender entrapment of battered black women*. New York: Routledge.

Riczo, S. (2001). America, guns and the twenty-first century. *USA Today Magazine, 129*(2670), 16–19.

Riedel, M. (1987). Stranger violence: Perspectives, issues, and problems. *Journal of Criminal Law, 78*(2), 223–259.

Riedel, M., & Mock, L. (1985). *NIJ report: The nature and patterns of American homicide*. Washington, DC: U.S. Government Printing Office.

Riley, J. (2005, March 17). Motive, but little proof. *Long Island Newsday*, p. 8.

Rittenmeyer, S. (1981). Of battered wives, self-defense and double standards of justice. *Journal of Criminal Justice, 9*(5), 389–396.

Riveira, D. (2002, November–December). Internet crimes against women. *The Crime Victims Report, 6*(5), 67–68, 75.

Roberts, A. (1990). *Helping crime victims*. Newbury Park, CA: Sage.

———. (Ed.). (1998). Juvenile justice: Policies, programs, and services. (2nd ed.). Thousand Oaks, CA: Sage.

———. (2002). *Handbook of domestic violence intervention strategies*. New York: Oxford University Press.

———. (2005). *Crisis intervention handbook* (3rd ed.). New York: Oxford University Press.

———, & Roberts, B. (2005). *Ending intimate abuse*. New York: Oxford University Press.

Roberts, S. (1987, March 22). Criminals, authors, and criminal authors. *New York Times Book Review*, pp. 1, 34–35.

———. (1989, March 7). When crimes become symbols. *New York Times*, Sec. 4, pp. 1, 28.

Robin, G. (1977, April). Forcible rape: Institutionalized sexism in the criminal justice system. *Crime and Delinquency*, 136–152.

Robin, M. (1991). The social construction of child abuse and 'false allegations.' *Child and Youth Services, 15*, 1–34.

Roehl, J., & Ray, L. (1986, July). Toward the multi-door courthouse: Dispute resolution intake and referral. *NIJ Reports, 198*, 2–7.

Rohter, L. (1993a, September 9). Tourist is killed in Florida despite taking precautions. *New York Times*, p. A16.

———. (1993b, September 16). Fearful of tourism decline, Florida offers assurances on safety. *New York Times*, p. A14.

Roiphe, K. (1993). *The morning after: Sex, fear, and feminism on campus*. Boston: Little, Brown.

Rondeau, G., & Rondeau, E. (2006, February). National coalition of victims in action. *The Crime Victims Report*, pp. 87, 90–91.

Rootsaert, D. (1987). *A prosecutor's guide to victim/witness assistance*. Alexandria, VA: National District Attorneys Association.

Roper Center for Public Opinion Research. (2004). Respondents reporting a firearm in their home. *Sourcebook of Criminal Justice Statistics, 2003* (p. 150). Albany, NY: State University of New York.

Rose, V. (1977, October). Rape as a social problem: A by-product of the feminist movement. *Social Problems, 25*, 75–89.

Rosenthal, E. (1990, June 27). U.S. is by far the homicide capital of the industrialized nations. *New York Times*, p. A10.

Ross, R., & Staines, G. (1972, Summer). The politics of analyzing social problems. *Social Problems, 20*, 18–40.

Rothfeld, M. (2008, October 22). Proposition 9 would give crime victims a stronger voice, but critics say it could violate inmates rights. *Los Angeles Times*, p. A8.

Rothstein, E. (2008, July 5). Good guys, bad guys, and spies, all wrapped in "edutainment." *New York Times*, p. B1, B12.

Rottenberg, D. (1980, March 16). Crime victims fight back. *Parade*, pp. 21–23.

Rubin, J. (2008, March 18). Report urges LAPD to change SWAT unit. *Los Angeles Times*, p. 1.

Rugala, E. (2004). Workplace violence: Issues and responses. Quantico, VA: Federal Bureau of Investigation Academy.

Russell, D. (1975). *The politics of rape: The victim's perspective*. New York: Stein & Day.

———. (1982). *Rape in marriage*. New York: Macmillan.

———. (1984). *Sexual exploitation: Rape, child molestation, and workplace harassment*. Newbury Park, CA: Sage.

———. (1986). *The secret trauma: Incest in the lives of girls and women*. New York: Basic Books.

———. (1990). *Sexual exploitation*. Beverly Hills, CA: Sage.

Ryan, W. (1971). *Blaming the victim*. New York: Vintage.

Sabo, D. (1992). Understanding men in prison: The relevance of gender studies. *Men's Studies Review, 9* (1), 4–9.

Sachs, A. (1994, January 31). Now for the movie. *Time*, 99.

Sagarin, E. (1975, May–June). Forcible rape and the problem of the rights of the accused. *Intellect*, 515–520.

Sakheim, D., & Devine, S. (Eds.). (1992). *Out of darkness: Exploring satanism and ritual abuse*. New York: Macmillan.

Salfati, C, James, A., & Ferguson, L. (2008). Prostitute homicides: A descriptive study. *Journal of Interpersonal Violence, 23*(4), 505–543.

Salmivalli, C., & Nieminen, E. (2002). Proactive and reactive aggression among school bullies, victims, and bully-victims. *Aggressive Behavior, 28*, 30–44.

Salzinger, S., Feldman, R., & Hammer, M. (1991, March). Risk for physical child abuse and the personal consequences for its victims. *Criminal Justice and Behavior, 18*(1), 64–81.

Sampson, R. (2004). *Acquaintance rape of college students*. Washington, DC: Office of Community Oriented Policing Services, U.S. Department of Justice.

San Mateo Section (2006, November 24). It's time to treat innocent bystanders fairly. *Inside Bay Area, California*, p. 2.

Sanday, P. (2007). Fraternity gang rape: sex, brotherhood and privilege on campus, second edition. New York: NYU Press.

Sanderson, B. (1994, November 30). Victim fund slashes its payouts. *Bergen (NJ) Record*, pp. A1, A12.

Sargeant, G. (1991, April). Battered woman syndrome gaining legal recognition. *Trial, 27*(4), 17–20.

Sarnoff, S. (1996). *Paying for crime: The policies and possibilities of crime victim reimbursement*. Westport, CT: Praeger.

Saunders, D. (1986). When battered women use violence: Husband-abuse or self-defense? *Victims and Violence, 1*(1), 47–59.

Saunders, P. (2005). Traffic violations: Determining the meaning of violence in sexual trafficking versus sex work. *Journal of Interpersonal Violence, 20*(3), 343–360.

Savage, D. (2003, January). Getting back your name. *American Bar Association Journal, 88*, 24–25.

Savitz, L. (1982). Official statistics. In L. Savitz & N. Johnston (Eds.), *Contemporary criminology* (pp. 3–15). New York: Wiley.

———. (1986). Obscene phone calls. In T. Hartnagel & R. Silverman (Eds.), *Critique and explanation: Essays in honor of Gwynne Nettles* (pp. 149–158). New Brunswick, NJ: Transaction Books.

Sawyer, S. (1987, November). Law enforcement officers and their families face special difficulties when victimized. *NOVA Newsletter, 11*(11), 1–2.

Scafidi, F. (2006a, July 24). California tops nation in motorcycle thefts. Press release. *National Insurance Crime Bureau*. Retrieved July 5, 2008, from www.nicb.org.

———. (2006b, November 1). Hot wheels: Do you know where your car is? Press release. *National Insurance Crime Bureau*. Retrieved July 5, 2008, from www.nicb.org.

———. (2008a, April 22). Modesto, California regains the nation's top spot for vehicle thefts. Press release. *National Insurance Crime Bureau*. Retrieved July 5, 2008, from www.nicb.org.

———. (2008b, July 9). Hot wheels: vehicle theft continuing to decline. Press release,. *National Insurance Crime Bureau*. Retrieved July 15, 2008, from www.nicb.org.

Schafer, S. (1968). *The victim and his criminal*. New York: Random House.

———. (1970). *Compensation and restitution to victims of crime* (2nd ed.). Montclair, NJ: Patterson Smith.

———. (1977). *Victimology: The victim and his criminal*. Reston, VA: Reston Publishers.

Schanberg, S. (1984, March 27). The rape trial. *New York Times*, p. A31.

———. (1989, April 28) We should be outraged at all rapes. *New York Newsday*, pp. 94–95.

Schaye, K. (1998, July 27). Judgment called the end of the Tawana Brawley story. *New York Daily News*, p. 8.

Schechter, S. (1982). *Women and male violence*. Boston: South End Press.

Schemo, D. (2002, December 18). Harvard advertises for people abducted by aliens, but the truth is out there a little farther. *New York Times*, p. B13.

———. (2003, September 23). Air Force ignored sex abuse at academy, inquiry reports. *New York Times*, p. A16.

Scherer, J. (1982). An overview of victimology. In J. Scherer & G. Shepherd (Eds.), *Victimization of the weak: Contemporary social reactions* (pp. 8–30). Springfield, IL: Charles C. Thomas.

Schmidt, J. (2006, October). Victim impact statements in El Paso. *Crime Victims Report*, 10 (4), 49–50.

Schmitt, E. (1994, May 23). Military struggling to stem an increase in family violence. *New York Times*, pp. A1, A12.

Schneider, A. (1981). Methodological problems in victim surveys and their implications for research in victimology. *Journal of Criminal Law and Criminology*, 72(2), 818–830.

———. & Schneider, P. (1978). *Private and public-minded citizen responses to a neighborhood crime prevention strategy*. Eugene, OR: Institute of Policy Analysis.

———. (1981). Victim assistance programs. In B. Galaway & J. Hudson (Eds.), *Perspectives on crime victims* (pp. 364–373). St. Louis, MO: C.V. Mosby.

Schneider, E. (1980). Equal rights to trial for women: Sex bias in the law on self-defense. *Harvard Civil Rights and Civil Liberties Review*, 15, 623–647.

———. (1991). The violence of privacy. *The Connecticut Law Review*, 23, 973–999.

———. (2000). *Battered women and feminist lawmaking*. New Haven, CT: Yale University Press.

Schneider, H. (Ed.). (1982). *The victim in international perspective*. New York: Walter De Gruyter.

———. (1996). Violence in the institution. *International Journal of Offender Therapy and Comparative Criminology*, 40, 5–18.

Schneider, P. (1987, February). Lost innocents: The myth of missing children. *Harper's Magazine*, pp. 47–53.

Schreiber, L. (1990, September). Campus rape. *Glamour*, 23–26.

Schultz, L. (1965). The violated: A proposal to compensate victims of violent crime. *St. Louis University Law Journal*, 10, 238–250.

———. (1968). The victim-offender relationship. *Crime and Delinquency*, 14, 135–141.

Schur, E. (1984). *Labeling women deviant: Gender, stigma, and social control*. New York: Random House.

Schwab, N. (2008, August 21). Self-defense techniques help you to survive on campus. Retrieved September 25, 2008, from www.usnews.com/articles/education/best-colleges/2008/08/21/self-defense-techniques-help-you-survive-on-campus.html.

Schwartz, M. (2005). The past and the future of violence against women. *Journal of Interpersonal Violence*, 20(1), 7–11.

———, & DeKeseredy, W. (1997). *Sexual assault on the college campus: The role of male peer support*. Thousand Oaks, CA: Sage.

Schwartz, E. (2007, December 13). Giving crime victims more of their say. *U.S. News and World Report*, p. 32.

Schwendinger, H., & Schwendinger, J. (1967). Delinquent stereotypes of probable victims. In M. Klein (Ed.), *Juvenile gangs in context*, pp. 92–105. Englewood Cliffs, NJ: Prentice-Hall.

———. (1974). Rape myths in legal, theoretical, and everyday practice. *Crime and Social Justice*, 1, 18–26.

Sclafani, T. (2005, April 11). Fighting fire with wire. *New York Daily News*, pp. 4–5.

Scott, E., & Williams, A. (1985). *Racial and religious violence: A model law enforcement response*. Landover, MD: National Organization of Black Law Enforcement Executives (NOBLE).

Screening (2006, May 30). Women often hide domestic abuse from doctors. *New York Times*, p. C4.

Sedlak, A., Finkelhor, D., Hammer, H., & Schultz, D. (2002). *NISMART National estimates of missing children: An overview*. Washington, DC: Office of Juvenile Justice and Delinquency Prevention, U.S. Department of Justice.

Seebach, L. (1999, March 28). How to give the campus left a taste of its own medicine. *Denver Rocky Mountain News*, p. 2B.

Seligmann, J., & Maor, Y. (1980, August 4). Punishments that fit the crime. *Newsweek, 60.*

Senate Committee considers proposed victims' rights amendments to Constitution. (2003, April 16). *Criminal Law Reporter, 73*(3), 74–76.

Senate Committee on the Judiciary. (2003). *Report: The Violence Against Women Act of 1993.* Washington, DC: U.S. Senate.

Senate Judiciary Committee (Majority Staff). (1993). *The response to rape: Detours on the road to equal justice.* Washington, DC: U.S. Senate.

Serbin, R. (2002, May). When clergy fail their flocks. *Trial, 38*(5), 34–41.

Seward, Z. (2006, October 23). FBI stats show many colleges understate campus crime. *The Wall Street Journal*, pp. B1, B12.

Sexton, J. (1994, December 3). Brooklyn drivers fear reckless young guns. *New York Times*, pp. A1, A26.

Shane, S. and Lichtblau, E. (2008, June 28). Scientist is paid millions by U.S. in anthrax suit. *New York Times*, p. A10.

———. (2008, September 17). Senator, target of anthrax letter, challenges FBI finding. *New York Times*, p. A14.

Shanahan, E. (2006, June). ID thieves' new tricks. *Readers Digest*, 82–87.

Shapiro, L., Rosenberg, D., Lauerman, J., & Sparkman, R. (1993, April 19). Rush to judgment. *Newsweek*, 54–60.

Shelden, R. (1982). *Criminal justice in America: A sociological approach.* Boston: Little, Brown.

Sheley, J. (1979). *Understanding crime: Concepts, issues, decisions.* Belmont, CA: Wadsworth.

Sheridan, R. (1994). The false child molestation outbreak of the 1980s: An explanation of the cases arising in the divorce context. In K. de Koster & K. Swisher (Eds.), *Child abuse: Opposing viewpoints* (pp. 48–55). San Diego, CA: Greenhaven Press.

Sherman, L. (1986). *NIJ crime file: Domestic violence.* Washington, DC: U.S. Department of Justice.

Sherman, W. (2005, May 15). How they'll steal your I.D. *New York Daily News*, p. 8.

Sherman, L., & Berk, R. (1984, April). The specific deterrent effects of arrest for domestic assault. *American Sociological Review, 49,* 261–272.

Sherman, L., Berk, R., & Smith, D. (1992, October). Crime, punishment, and stake in conformity: Legal and informal control of domestic violence. *American Sociological Review 57,* 680–690. Washington, DC: Police Foundation.

Sherman, L., Gartin, P., & Buerger, M. (1989, February). Hot spots of predatory crime: Routine activities and the criminology of place. *Criminology, 27*(1), 27–40.

Sherman, L., Steele, L., Laufersweiler, D., Hoffer, N., & Julian, S. (1989). Stray bullets and "mushrooms": Random shootings of bystanders in four cities, 1977–1988. *Journal of Quantitative Criminology, 5,* 297–316.

Shichor, D., Sechrest, D., & Doocy, J. (2000). Victims of investment fraud. In H. Pontell & D. Shichor (Eds.), *Contemporary issues in crime and criminal justice* (pp. 81–96). Upper Saddle River, NJ: Prentice Hall.

Shifrel, S. (2007a, July 19). Rape victim hummed to soothe drug-crazed beast, she testifies. *New York Daily News*, p. 26.

———. (2007b, July 25b). Raped ma wins fight for DNA justice. *New York Daily News*, p. 8.

Shipp, E. (1987, April 21). Defense lawyers' tactics: Unfair or just aggressive? *New York Times*, pp. B1, B4.

Shotland, L. (1976). Spontaneous vigilantism: A bystander response to criminal behavior. In J. Rosenbaum & P. Sederberg (Eds.), *Vigilante politics* (pp. 30–44). Philadelphia: University of Pennsylvania Press.

Siegel, J., Sorenson, S., Golding, J., Burnham, M., & Stein, J. (1987). The prevalence of childhood sexual assault. *American Journal of Epidemiology, 126,* 1141–1153.

Siegel, L. (1998). *Criminology* (6th ed.). Belmont, CA: West/Wadsworth.

Sieh, E. (1990). Diplomatic immunity: A reconsideration of an ancient concept. *International Journal of Comparative and Applied Criminal Justice, 14*(1, 2), 269–280.

Silberman, C. (1978). *Criminal violence, criminal justice.* New York: Random House.

Silberman, M. (1995). *A world of violence: Corrections in America.* Belmont, CA: Wadsworth.

Silverman, J. (2005, May 4). The rush is on to increase penalties on drunk drivers who kill. *AM New York*, p. 1.

Silverman, R. (1974). Victim precipitation: An examination of the concept. In I. Drapkin & E. Viano (Eds.), *Victimology: A new focus* (pp. 99–110). Lexington, MA: D.C. Heath.

Silving, H. (1959). Compensation for victims of criminal violence – A roundtable. *Journal of Public Law, 8,* 236–253.

Simon, D. (1991). *Homicide: A year on the killing streets.* New York: Fawcett Columbine.

Simonelli, C., Mullis, T., Elliott, A., & Pierce, T. (2002). Abuse by siblings and subsequent experiences of violence within the dating relationship. *Journal of Interpersonal Violence, 17*(2), 103–122.

Simonson, L. (1994). The victims' rights movement: A critical view from a practicing sociologist. *Sociological Imagination, 31,* 181–196.

Sinason, V. (1994). *Treating survivors of satanist abuse.* New York: Routledge.

Singer, S. (1981). Homogeneous victim–offender populations: A review and some research implications. *Journal of Criminal Law and Criminology, 72*(2), 779–788.

———. (1986). Victims of serious violence and their criminal behavior: Subcultural theory and beyond. *Violence and Victims, 1*(1), 61–70.

Sivers, H., Schooler, J., & Freyd, J. (2002). *Recovered memories.* New York: Elsevier Science.

Skogan, W. (1978). *Victimization surveys and criminal justice planning.* Washington, DC: U.S. Government Printing Office.

———. (1981a). Assessing the behavioral context of victimization. *Journal of Criminal Law and Criminology, 72*(2), 727–742.

———. (1981b). *Issues in the measurement of victimization.* Washington, DC: U.S. Department of Justice.

———. (1986). Methodological issues in the study of victimization. In E. Fattah (Ed.), *From crime policy to victim policy* (pp. 80–116). New York: St. Martin's Press.

Skogan, W., & Maxfield, M. (1981). *Coping with crime: Individual and neighborhood reactions.* Beverly Hills, CA: Sage.

Skuse, D., et al. (2003, February). Development of sexually abusive behavior in sexually victimized males: A longitudinal study. *The Lancet, 361,* 471–476.

Sloane, L. (1991, November 16). Rising fraud worrying car insurers … *New York Times,* p. 48.

Slosarik, K. (2002). Identify theft: An overview of the problem. *The Justice Professional, 15*(4), 329–343.

Smalley, S. (2005, February 3). 'The Perfect Crime.' *Newsweek,* 52.

———, & Mnookin, S. (2003, May 5). A house of horrors. *Newsweek,* 49.

Smith, B. (1985). Trends in the victims' rights movement and implications for future research. *Victimology, 10*(1–4), 34–43.

———, Sloan, J., & Ward, R. (1990). Public support for the victims' rights movement: Results of a statewide survey. *Crime and Delinquency, 36*(4), 488–502.

Smith, K. (1994, September 19). Outrage over new attack by freed N.J. kid molester. *New York Post,* p. 6.

Smith, M. (1988). *Coping with crime on campus.* New York: American Council on Education (ACE).

Smith, P., & Welchans, S. (2000). Peer education: Does focusing on male responsibility change sexual assault attitudes? *Violence Against Women, 6*(11), 1255–1268.

Smith, S. (1994, July). Have screwdriver, will steal. *Car and Driver,* 157–167.

Smith, S., & Freinkel, S. (1988). *Adjusting the balance: Federal policy and victim services.* New York: Greenwood Press.

Smith, S., Steadman, G., Todd, M., & Townsend, M. (1999). *Criminal victimization and perceptions of community safety in 12 cities, 1998. BJS Report.* Washington, DC: U.S. Department of Justice.

Smothers, R. (2003, September 27). New Jersey creates independent child advocate office. *New York Times,* p. B6.

Snell, J., Rosenwald, R., & Robey, A. (1964, August). The wifebeater's wife: A study of family interaction. *Archives of General Psychiatry, 11,* 107–112.

Snyder, J. (1993, Fall). A nation of cowards. *The Public Interest 113,* 40–56.

Snyder, H., & Sickmund, M. (1995). *Juvenile offenders and victims: A focus on violence.* OJJDP Statistical Summary. Washington, DC: U.S. Department of Justice.

Sokoloff, N., & Pratt, C. (2005). *Domestic violence at the margins: Readings on race, class, gender and culture.* New Brunswick, NJ: Rutgers University Press.

Sokoloff, N., & Price, B. (2003). *The criminal justice system and women* (3rd ed.). Englewood Cliffs, NJ: Prentice Hall.

Sontag, S. (2002, November 17). Fierce entanglement. *New York Times Magazine*, pp. 52–62.

Sorenson, S., & White, J. (1992). Adult sexual assault: Overview of research. *Journal of Social Issues, 48*(1), 1–8.

Southern Poverty Law Center (SPLC). (2001, Winter). Discounting hate. *Intelligence Report*. Atlanta: SPLC.

Southern Regional Council. (1969). *Race makes the difference: An analysis of sentence disparity among black and white offenders in southern prisons*. Atlanta, GA: Author.

Sparkman, E. (2003). SUVs, pickups, minivans favorites on thieves' shopping lists. Retrieved September 10, 2005, from www.nicb.com.

Sparks, R. (1981). Multiple victimization: Evidence, theory and future research. *Journal of Criminal Law and Criminology, 72*(2), 762–778.

Spears, J., & Spohn, C. (1997). The effects of evidence factors and victim characteristics on prosecutors' charging decisions in sexual assault cases. *American Journal of Criminal Justice, 20*, 183–205.

Spector, M., & Kitsuse, J. (1987). *Constructing social problems*. New York: Aldine de Gruyter.

Spelman, W., & Brown, D. (1984). *NIJ report: Calling the police: Citizen reporting of serious crime*. Washington, DC: U.S. Department of Justice.

Spence-Diehl, E. (1999). *Stalking: A handbook for victims*. Holmes Beach, Fla.: Learning Publications.

Spitzer, N. (1986, June). The children's crusade. *Atlantic*, 18–22.

Spohn, C., & Horney, J. (1992). *Rape law reform: A grassroots revolution and its impact*. New York: Plenum Press.

Spunt, B., Goldstein, P., Brownstein, H., Fendrich, M., & Langley, S. (1994). Alcohol and homicide: Interviews with prison inmates. *Journal of Drug Issues, 24*(1): 143–163.

Spunt, B., Tarshish, C., Fendich, M., Goldstein, P., & Brownstein, H. (1993, Spring). Research note: The utility of correctional data for understanding the drugs–homicide connection. *Criminal Justice Review, 18*(1), 46–60.

Stalking Resource Center (2008). Federal interstate stalking law. Retrieved September 13, 2008, from www.ncvc.org.

Stammer, L. (2003, February 23). National advocacy group helps victims break their silence. *Los Angeles Times*, p. A8.

Stark, J., & Goldstein, H. (1985). *The rights of crime victims: An American Civil Liberties Union handbook*. New York: Bantam Books.

Steinman, M. (1991). The public policy process and woman battering: Problems and pitfalls. In M. Steinman (Ed.), *Woman battering: Policy responses* (pp. 1–18). Cincinnati, OH: Anderson.

Steinmetz, S. (1978a). The battered husband syndrome. *Victimology, 2*(4), 499–509.

———. (1978b). Battered parents. *Society, 15*(5), 54–55.

———. (1988). *Duty bound: Elder abuse and family care*. Newbury Park, CA: Sage.

Stephens, M. (1988). *A history of the news*. New York: Penguin.

Stepp, L. (2007, September). A new kind of date rape. *Cosmopolitan*, 199–203.

———. (2008). Unhooked: How young women pursue sex, delay love, and lose at both. New York: Penguin, Riverhead Trade.

Stets, J., & Pirog-Good, M. (1987). Violence in dating relationships. *Social Psychology Quarterly, 50*, 237–246.

Stevens, D. (1999). Interviews with women convicted of murder: Battered women's syndrome revisited. *International Review of Victimology, 6*(2), 117–135.

Stewart, E., Schreck, C., & Brunson, R. (2008). Lessons of the street code. *Journal of Contemporary Criminal Justice, 24*, 2: 137–147.

Stillman, F. (1987). *NIJ Research in brief. Line-of-duty deaths: Survivor and departmental responses*. Washington, DC: U.S. Department of Justice.

Stolberg, S. (2005, October 21). Congress passes new legal shield for gun industry. *New York Times*, pp. A1, A21.

Stone, L. (1984). Shelters for battered women: A temporary escape from danger or the first step toward divorce? *Victimology, 9*(1), 284–289.

Straus, M. (1978). Wife beating: How common and why? *Victimology, 2*(4), 443–458.

———. (1991). Conceptualization and measurement of battering: Implications for public policy. In M. Steinman (Ed.), *Woman battering: Policy responses* (pp. 19–42). Cincinnati, OH: Anderson.

———. (1999). The controversy over domestic violence by women. In X. Arriaga & S. Oskamp (Eds.), *Violence in intimate relationships* (pp. 109–119). Thousand Oaks, CA: Sage.

Straus, M., & Gelles, R. (1986). Societal change and change in family violence from 1975 to 1985. *Journal of Marriage and the Family, 48,* 20–30.

———. (1990). *Physical violence in American families.* New Brunswick, NJ: Transaction.

Straus, M., Gelles, R., & Steinmetz, S. (1980). *Behind closed doors: Violence in the American family.* New York: Doubleday.

Struckman-Johnson, C., & Struckman-Johnson, D. (2002). Sexual coercion reported by women in three midwestern prisons. *Journal of Sex Research, 39*(3), 22–28.

Study points to reasons behind mammoth nationwide DNA backlog. (2005, September 15). *Law Enforcement News,* pp. 1, 17.

Study puts facts behind some child kidnapping assumptions. (1997, August 15). *Law Enforcement News,* p. 9.

Study shows intimidation of witnesses affects verdicts. (1990, October 3). *New York Amsterdam News,* p. 18.

Sugarman, D., & McCoy, S. (1997, Summer). Impact of expert testimony on the believability of repressed memories. *Violence and Victims, 12*(2), 115–126.

Sullivan, A. (1993, February 9). Gay values, truly conservative. *New York Times,* p. A21.

Sullivan, C. (2005, June 20). End sought to "outdated" rape statute. *New York Post,* p. 14.

Sullivan, D., & Tifft, L. (2001). *Restorative justice: Healing the foundations of our everyday lives.* Monsey, NY: Willow Tree Press.

Sygnatur, E., & Toscano, G. (2000, Spring). Work-related homicides: The facts. *Compensation and Working Conditions,* 1–8.

Sykes, C. (1992). *A nation of victims: The decay of the American character.* New York: St. Martin's Press.

Sykes, G., & Matza, D. (1957). Techniques of neutralization: A theory of delinquency. *American Sociological Review, 22,* 664–670.

Symonds, M. (1975). Victims of violence: Psychological effects and after-effects. *American Journal of Psychoanalysis, 35*(1), 19–26.

———. (1980a). Acute responses of victims to terror. *Evaluation and Change* (special issue), 39–42.

———. (1980b). The 'second injury' to victims. *Evaluation and Change, 7*(1), 36–38.

Synovate. (2003). *Federal Trade Commission – Identity theft survey report.* McLean, VA: Synovate, Inc.

———. (2007). *Federal Trade Commission – 2006 Identity theft survey report.* McLean, VA: Synovate, Inc.

Taibbi, M., & Sims-Phillips, A. (1989). *Unholy alliances.* San Diego, CA: Harcourt Brace.

Tardiff, K., Gross, E., & Messner, S. (1986). A study of homicides in Manhattan, 1981. *American Journal of Public Health, 76*(2), 139–145.

Task Force on Assessment. (1967). The victims of crime. In The President's Commission on Law Enforcement and Administration of Justice, *Task force report: Crime and its impact – an assessment* (pp. 80–84). Washington, DC: U.S. Government Printing Office.

Tatara, T. (1993). Understanding the nature and scope of elder abuse with the use of state aggregate data. *Journal of Elder Abuse and Neglect, 5*(4), 35–57.

Taveras, C., and Thomas, T. (2008). Crime and criminal justice: Homicide, European Union countries. Retrieved September 19, 2008, from http://epp.eurostat.ec.europa.eu/pls/portal/docs.

Tavris, C. (1993, January 3). Beware the incest survivor machine. *New York Times Book Review,* pp. 1, 16–17.

Taylor, B. (1989). *Redesign of the national crime survey.* Washington, DC: U.S. Department of Justice.

Teaching children how to escape from abduction. (1999, February 14). *New York Times,* p. 32.

Teevan, J. (1979). Crime victimization as a neglected social problem. *Sociological Symposium, 25,* 6–22.

Terr, L. (1994). *Unchained memories: True stories of traumatic memories, lost and found.* New York: Basic.

Thomason, T., & Babbilli, A. (1987). *Crime victims and the news media.* Fort Worth, TX: Texas Christian University Department of Journalism.

Thompson, M. (1984). MADD curbs drunk drivers. *Victimology, 9*(1), 191–192.

Thompson, S. (2008, March 16). Prosecutors fear castle law's presumption will allow real murderers to go free. *Dallas Morning News*. Retrieved September 15, 2008, from www.dallasnews.com.

Thyfault, R. (1984). Self-defense: Battered woman syndrome on trial. *California Western Law Review, 20*, 485–510.

Timrots, A., & Rand, M. (1987). *Violent crime by strangers and non-strangers. BJS Special Report*. Washington, DC: U.S. Department of Justice.

Timrots, A., & Snyder, E. (1994). *Drugs and crime facts, 1993. BJS drugs and crime data center and clearinghouse*. Washington, DC: U.S. Department of Justice.

Titterington, V., & Abbott, B. (2004, February). Space city revisited: Patterns of legal outcomes in Houston homicide. *Violence and Victims, 19*(1), 83–95.

Tittle, C. (1978). Restitution and deterrence: An evaluation of compatibility. In B. Galaway & J. Hudson (Eds.), *Offender restitution in theory and action* (pp. 33–158). Lexington, MA: Lexington Books.

Titus, R., Heinzelmann, F., & Boyle, J. (1995). Victimization of persons by fraud. *Crime and Delinquency, 41*(1), 54–72.

Tjaden, P., & Thoennes, N. (1998). *Stalking in America: Findings from the National Violence Against Women Survey*. Washington, DC: National Institute of Justice.

———. (2000). *Extent, nature, and consequences of intimate partner violence: Findings from the National Violence Against Women Survey*. Washington, DC: National Institute of Justice.

Toby, J. (1983). Violence in school. In M. Tonry & N. Morris (Eds.), *Crime and justice: An annual review of research* (Vol. 4, pp. 1–47). Chicago: University of Chicago Press.

Tomz, J., & McGillis, D. (1997). *Serving crime victims and witnesses* (2nd ed.). Washington, DC: U.S. Department of Justice.

Toobin, J. (2003, September 1). The consent defense, Kobe Bryant, and the changing law of rape. *The New Yorker*, pp. 40–47.

Topping, R. (2005, February 24). Drama in an unmarked car. *Newsday*, A3.

Treanor, W. (1986, August 25). The Missing Children's Act has been misused, abused. *Juvenile Justice Digest*, 7–10.

Triebwasser, J. (1986, June 28). Court says you can't run from restitution. *Law Enforcement News*, 6, 8.

———. (1987a, June 9). Court leaves death penalty alive and well. *Law Enforcement News*, p. 5.

———. (1987b, September 29). Victims' non-impact on sentence. *Law Enforcement News*, p. 5.

Troup-Leasure, K., & Snyder, H. (2005, August). Statutory rape known to law enforcement. *Juvenile Justice Bulletin*. Washington, DC: Office of Juvenile Justice and Delinquency Prevention.

Trump, K. (2005). School deaths, school shootings, and high-profile incidents of school violence. National School Safety and Security Services. Retrieved November 16, 2005, from www.schoolsecurity.org.

Turman, K. (1999). *Breaking the cycle of violence: Recommendations to improve the criminal justice response to child victims and witnesses*. Washington, DC: Office for Victims of Crime, U.S. Department of Justice.

Turner, J. (1990). Preparing individuals at risk for victimization as hostages. In E. Viano (Ed.), *The victimology handbook: Research findings, treatment, and public policy* (pp. 217–226). New York: Garland.

Turner, N. (2002). *Responding to hate crimes: A police officer's guide to investigation and prevention*. Alexandria, VA: International Association of Chiefs of Police (IACP).

Tyler, K., Whitbeck, L., Hoyt, D., & Cauce, A. (2005, May). Risk factors for sexual victimization among male and female homeless and runaway youth. *Journal of Interpersonal Violence, 19*(5), 503–520.

Tyre, P. (2001, June 18). Betrayed by a badge. *Newsweek*, 38–39.

Ullman, S. (2007). Comparing gang and individual rapes in a community sample of urban women. *Violence and Victims*, 22,1, pp. 43–51.

Umbreit, M. (1987, March). Mediation may not be as bad as you think; some victims do benefit. *NOVA Newsletter*, 1–2, 6.

———. (1989). Violent offenders and their victims. In M. Wright & B. Galaway (Eds.), *Mediation and criminal justice: Victims, offenders and community* (pp. 99–112). Newbury Park, CA: Sage.

———. (1990). Victim–offender mediation with violent offenders: Implications for modifications of the VORP model. In E. Viano (Ed.), *The victimology handbook: Research findings, treatment, and public policy* (pp. 337–352). New York: Garland.

———. (1994, Summer). Victim empowerment through mediation: The impact of victim offender mediation in four cities. *Perspectives*, special issue. American Probation and Parole Association. 25–28.

———. (1995, March). Restorative justice: Implications for organizational change. *Federal Probation*, *59*(1), 47–54.

———, & Coates, P. (1993). Cross-site analysis of victim–offender mediation in four states. *Crime and Delinquency*, *39*, 565–585.

———, & Greenwood, D. (1998). *National survey of victim–offender mediation programs in the United States.* Washington, DC: Office of Victims of Crime, U.S. Department of Justice.

———, Vos, B., Coates, R., & Brown, K. (2004, April). Victim–offender dialogue in violent cases: The Texas and Ohio experience. *The Crime Victims Report*, *8*, 1–2.

United Nations, Department for Economic and Social Information. (1998). *Demographic yearbook, 1996.* New York: United Nations.

Unnever, J., & Cornell, D. (2003, February). Bullying, self-control, and ADHD. *Journal of Interpersonal Violence*, *18*(2), 129–147.

U.S. Attorney General's Advisory Board on Missing Children. (1986). *America's missing and exploited children: Their safety and their future.* Washington, DC: U.S. Department of Justice.

U.S. Center for Disease Control and Prevention (CDC), National Center for Health Statistics. (1999, October). *National Vital Statistics Report*, *47*(25), 27–28.

U.S. Conference of Catholic Bishops (USCCB). (2002, September 19). Sex abuse committee releases preliminary survey results. *Communications*.

U.S. Department of Labor (2008). Census of Fatal Occupational Injuries, 2007. Retrieved September 24, 2008, from www.bls.gov.

U.S. Department of Health and Human Services (DHHS). (1999). *Child fatalities fact sheet.* Washington, DC: National Clearinghouse on Child Abuse and Neglect Information.

U.S. Department of Justice, Fraud Division (2008). *Identity theft.* Retrieved July 18, 2008, from www.usdoj.gov/criminal/fraud/websites/idtheft.html.

U.S. General Accounting Office (GAO). (2002). *Identity Theft: Prevalence and cost appear to be growing.* Washington, DC: U.S. Government Printing Office.

U.S. House Committee on the Judiciary. (1980, February 13). *Victims of Crime Act of 1979: Report together with dissenting and separate views.* 96th Cong., 2nd session. Washington, DC: U.S. Government Printing Office.

U.S. Supreme Court holds: No constitutional duty to protect. (1989). *NOVA Newsletter 13*(2), 6.

Vacca, J. (2002). *Identity theft.* Upper Saddle River, NJ: Prentice Hall.

Vachss, A. (1993). *Sex crimes.* New York: Random House.

Vansickle, A. (2005, September 10). Detective defends questioning of Couey. *St. Petersburg Times*, p. 8.

Van Emmerik, A., Kamphuis, J., Holsbosch, A., & Emmelkamp, P. (2002). Single session debriefing after psychological trauma. *The Lancet*, *360*, 766–771.

Van Ness, D. (1990). Restorative justice. In B. Galaway & J. Hudson (Eds.), *Criminal justice, restitution and reconciliation* (pp. 7–14). Monsey, NY: Willow Tree Press.

Van Ness, D., & Strong, K. (1997). *Restoring justice.* Cincinnati: Anderson.

Vazquez, S., Stohr, M., & Purkiss, M. (2005, March). Intimate partner violence incidence and characteristics: Idaho *NIBRS* 1995 to 2001 data. *Criminal Justice Policy Review*, *16*(1), 99–114.

Verhovek, S. (1994, October 7). Gang intimidation takes rising toll of court cases. *New York Times*, pp. A1, B8.

———. (1995, March 6). States seek to let citizens carry concealed weapons. *New York Times*, pp. A1, B8.

———. (2001, November 7). 'Code Adam' soon finds lost children in big stores. *New York Times*, p. A33.

Viano, E. (1976). *Victims and society.* Washington, DC: Visage.

———. (1983). Victimology: The development of a new perspective. *Victimology*, *8*(1–2), 17–30.

———. (1987). Victims' rights and the constitution: Reflections on a bicentennial. *Crime and Delinquency*, *33*, 438–451.

———. (1989). Victimology today: Major issues in research and public policy. In E. Viano (Ed.), *Crime and its victims: International research and public policy issues* (pp. 3–16). New York: Hemisphere Publishing.

———. (1990a). Introduction: Victimology: A new focus of research and practice. In E. Viano (Ed.), *The victimology handbook: Research findings, treatment, and public policy* (pp. xi–xii). New York: Garland.

———. (1990b). The recognition and implementation of victims' rights in the United States: Developments and achievements. In E. Viano (Ed.), *The victimology handbook: Research findings, treatment, and public policy* (pp. 319–336). New York: Garland.

———. (1992). Violence among intimates: Major issues and approaches. In E. Viano (Ed.), *Intimate violence: Interdisciplinary perspectives* (pp. 3–12). New York: Hemisphere.

Villmoare, E., & Neto, V. (1987). *NIJ research in brief: Victim appearances at sentencing under California's victims' bill of rights.* Washington, DC: U.S. Department of Justice.

Vines, V. (2004, November 28). Press release: Data on firearms and violence too weak to settle policy debates; comprehensive research effort needed. *The National Academies.*

Vitello, P. (2008, November 13). Sexual abuse complaints subpoenaed. *New York Times*, p. A33.

Voboril, M. (2005, September 6). 9/11 groups: Dedicated to the memory. *Newsday*, p. 8.

Vollmer, A., & Parker, A. (1936). The police and modern society. San Francisco: University of California Press.

Volpe, M. (2000). ADR in the criminal justice system: Promises and challenges. *Dispute Resolution Magazine*, 7(1), 4–7.

Von Hentig, H. (1941, March–April). Remarks on the interaction of perpetrator and victim. *Journal of Criminal Law, Criminology, and Police Science, 31*, 303–309.

———. (1948). *The criminal and his victim: Studies in the sociobiology of crime.* New Haven, CT: Yale University Press.

Voss, H., & Hepburn, J. (1968). Patterns in criminal homicide in Chicago. *Journal of Criminal Law, Criminology, and Police Science, 59*, 499–508.

Wakin, D. (2003, April 15). Two sexual abuse lawsuits filed against L.I. diocese. *New York Times*, p. B8.

Walker, L. (1984). *The battered woman syndrome.* New York: Springer.

Walker, S. (1982, October). What have civil liberties ever done for crime victims? Plenty! *ACJS Today*, 4–5. Academy of Criminal Justice Sciences.

———. (2005). *Sense and nonsense about crime and drugs: A policy guide* (6th ed.). Belmont, CA: Wadsworth.

Walklate, S. (1991). Researching victims of crime: Critical victimology. *Social Justice* 17(3), 25–42.

Waller, I., & Okihiro, N. (1978). *Burglary: The victim and the public.* Toronto: University of Toronto Press.

Walsh, A. (1992). Placebo justice: Victim recommendations and offender sentences in sexual assault cases. In E. Fattah (Ed.), *Towards a critical victimology* (pp. 295–311). New York: St. Martin's Press.

Walsh, M., & Schram, D. (1980). The victim of white-collar crime: Accuser or accused. In G. Geis & E. Stotland (Eds.), *White-collar crime* (pp. 32–51). Beverly Hills, CA: Sage.

Warchol, G. (1998). *Workplace violence, 1992–1996. BJS Special Report.* Washington, DC: U.S. Department of Justice.

Warkentin, G. (2006, June). Special victims unit. *Crime Victims Report*, 10, 2, pp. 17, 28.

Warner, J., & Burke, V. (1987). *National directory of juvenile restitution programs.* Washington, DC: U.S. Department of Justice.

Warrior, B. (1977, February). Transition house shelters battered women. *Sister Courage* (Boston), 12.

Warshaw, R. (1988). *I never called it rape.* New York: Harper & Row.

Washington Crime News Service. (2003, June 27). $200 million in grants to prevent child abuse. *Crime Control Digest, 37*(25), p. 2.

Weathers, H. (2005, August 8). Drug rape: The disturbing facts. *London Daily Mail*, p. 26.

Websdale, N., & Johnson, B. 1997. Structural approaches to reducing women-battering. *Social Justice, 24*, 54–81.

———. (2003, November). Reviewing domestic violence deaths. *NIJ Journal, 250*: 26–31.

Webster, B. (1988). *Victim assistance programs report increased workloads.* National Institute of Justice, Research in Action. Washington, DC: U.S. Department of Justice.

Weed, F. (1995). *Certainty of justice: Reform in the crime victim movement.* Hawthorne, NY: Aldine de Gruyter.

Weigend, T. (1983). Problems of victim/witness assistance programs. *Victimology, 8*(3), 91–101.

Weinberg, S. (1955). *Incest behavior.* New York: Citadel Press.

Weinraub, B. (1994, January 26). Michael Jackson settles suit for sum said to be in millions. *New York Times,* pp. A1, A18.

Weis, K., & Borges, S. (1973). Victimology and rape: The case of the legitimate victim. *Issues in Criminology, 8*(2), 71–115.

Weisberg, L. (2008, July 13). Home burglary: Even with insurance and good police work, odds are against a full recovery. *San Diego Union-Tribune,* p. H1.

Weisel, D. (2005). *Analyzing repeat victimization. Problem-oriented guides for police series, Number 4.* Office of Community Oriented Policing Services (COPS). Washington, DC: U.S. Department of Justice.

Wellford, C., & Cronin, J. (2000, April). Cleaning up homicide clearance rates. *National Institute of Justice Journal,* 2–8.

Wells, R. (1990, September). Considering victim impact: The role of probation. *Federal Probation,* 26–29.

Wemmers, J. (2002). A victim-oriented approach to restorative justice. *International Review of Victimology, 9,* 43–59.

Wertham, F. (1949). *The show of violence.* New York: Doubleday.

Wessler, S., & Moss, M. (2001). *Hate crimes on campus: The problem and efforts to confront it. Office of Justice Programs,* Washington, DC: Office of Justice Programs, U.S. Department of Justice.

Wexler, C., & Marx, G. (1986, April). When law and order works: Boston's innovative approach to the problem of racial violence. *Crime and Delinquency, 32*(2), 205–223.

Wexler, R. (1990). *Wounded innocents: The real victims of the war against child abuse.* Buffalo, NY: Prometheus Books.

"What a way to dye." (2008, May 6). Retrieved August 8, 2008, from www.snopes.com.

What sheriffs need to know about the Prison Rape Reduction Act of 2003. (2004, March–April). *Sheriff, 56*(2), 58–59.

When judges make the punishment fit the crime. (1978, December 11). *U.S. News & World Report,* 44–46.

When technology gets diabolical: Florida trains its sights on digital stalkers. (2005, May 15). *Law Enforcement News,* p. 11.

Where's the car? (1992, March 30). *U.S. News & World Report,* 51.

Whitaker, C. (1989). *The redesigned National Crime Survey: Selected new data. BJS Special Report.* Washington, DC: U.S. Department of Justice.

Whitaker, L., & Pollard, J. (Eds.) (1993). *Campus violence: Kinds, causes, and cures.* Binghamton, NY: Haworth Press.

Whitcomb, D. (1986). *NIJ research in action: Prosecuting child sexual abuse: New approaches.* Washington, DC: U.S. Department of Justice.

———. (1988). *Evaluation of programs for the effective prosecution of child physical and sexual abuse.* Washington, DC: Institute for Social Analysis.

———. (1992). *When the victim is a child* (2nd ed.). Washington, DC: Office of Justice Programs.

White, J., & Wesley, J. (1987, April). Male rape survivors: Guidelines for crisis counselors. *Crime Victims Digest,* 3–6.

Whitman, H. (1951). *Terror in the streets.* New York: Dial Press.

Wicker, T. (1970, October 4). Jackson State and Orangeburg. *New York Times,* p. A10.

Widom, C. (1995). *Victims of childhood sexual abuse—later criminal consequences.* NIJ Research in Brief. Washington, DC: U.S. Department of Justice.

———. (1989). Child abuse, neglect, and violent criminal behavior. *Criminology, 27*(2), 251–270.

Widom, C., & Maxfield, M. (2001, February). *An update on the "cycle of violence."* NIJ Research in Brief. Washington, DC: U.S. Department of Justice.

Wiehe, V. (1997). *Sibling abuse: Hidden physical, emotional, and sexual trauma* (2nd ed.). Thousand Oaks, CA: Sage.

Wiehe, V., & Richards, A. (1995). *Intimate betrayal: Understanding and responding to the trauma of acquaintance rape.* Thousand Oaks, CA: Sage.

Wikipedia. (2008). *Elizabeth Smart kidnapping.* Retrieved August 8, 2008, from www.wikipedia.com.

Wilgoren, J. (2005, June 28). Kansas suspect pleads guilty in 10 murders. *New York Times,* pp. A1, A20.

Will, G. (1993, November 15). Are we a nation of cowards? *Newsweek*, pp. 93–94.

———. (1998, July 31). President feeds the culture of victimology. *Houston Chronicle*, p. A42.

Williams, B. (2002). *Reparation and victim-focused social work*. Philadelphia: Kingsley Publishers.

Williams, C. (2009: January 2). Rise in Young Killers Worries D.C.; City Recorded 186 Homicides in '08, an Increase of 5; Area Slayings Up Slightly. *Washington Post*, p. B1.

Williams, K. (1976). The effects of victim characteristics on the disposition of violent crimes. In W. McDonald (Ed.), *Criminal justice and the victim* (pp. 172–214). Beverly Hills, CA: Sage.

———. (1978). *The effects of victim characteristics on judicial decisions: PROMIS research project report*. Washington, DC: Institute for Law and Social Research.

———. (2005, February 14). Policing video voyeurs. *Newsweek*, 44.

Williams, L. (1984). The classic rape: When do victims report? *Social Problems, 31*, 459–467.

Williams, T. (1987, February). Post-traumatic stress disorder: Recognizing it, treating it. *NOVA Newsletter*, 1–2, 7.

Willis, C., & Wells, R. (1988). The police and child abuse: An analysis of police decisions to report illegal behavior. *Criminology, 26*(4), 695–714.

Wilson, D. (2007, June 16). Facing sanction, Duke prosecutor plans to resign. *New York Times*, pp. A1, A11.

Wilson, D. G., Walsh, W., & Kleuber, S. (2006). Trafficking in human beings: Training and services among U.S. law enforcement agencies. *Police Practice & Research: An International Journal, 7*(2) 149–160.

Wilson, J. (2005, October). Victim-centered restorative justice: An essential distinction. *The Crime Victims Report, 9*(4), 49–50.

———. (2008, June). Victim-centered victim–offender dialogue in father-daughter incest cases. *The Crime Victims Report, 12*(2), 17–18.

Winton, T. (2005, August 11). FBI to probe child's death. *Los Angeles Times*, p. 1.

Witkin, G. (1994, August 15). The great debate: Should you own a gun? *U.S. News & World Report*, 24–31.

Wolf, R., & Pillemer, K. (1989). *Helping elderly victims: The reality of elder abuse*. New York: Columbia University Press.

Wolff, C. (1993, February 7). Hostages mean hard lessons for police. *New York Times*, p. A37.

Wolfgang, M. (1958). *Patterns in criminal homicide*. Philadelphia: University of Pennsylvania Press.

———. (1959). Suicide by means of victim-precipitated homicide. *Journal of Clinical and Experimental Psychopathology and Quarterly Review of Psychiatry and Neurology, 20*, 335–349.

———. (1965). Victim compensation in crimes of personal violence. *Minnesota Law Review, 50*, 229–241.

Wolfgang, M., & Ferracuti, F. (1967). *The subculture of violence: Towards an integrated theory in criminology*. London: Tavistock.

Wolfgang, M., & Riedel, M. (1973, May). Race, judicial discretion, and the death penalty. *Annals of the Academy of Political and Social Science, 407*, 119–133.

Wong, P. (2003). Elizabeth Smart and the Stockholm syndrome. International Network on Personal Meaning. Retrieved October 13, 2005, from www.meaning.ca.

Wood, J. (2008). The Crime Victims Rights Act of 2004 and the Federal Courts: Federal Judicial Center. Retrieved December 5, 2008 from www.uscourts.gov/rules/cvra0806.pdf.

Wood, J. A. (2008). Press release: United States Attorney's Office, Western Missouri. Retrieved September 20, 2008, from http://kansascity.fbi.gov/dojpressrel/pressrel08/cyberstalking050908.htm.

Wood, N. (1990). Black homicide—a public health crisis: Introduction and overview. *Journal of Interpersonal Violence, 5*, 147–150.

Wooden, K. (1984). *Child lures: A guide to prevent abduction*. St. Louis, MO: Ralston Purina.

Wright, E. (1973). *The politics of punishment*. New York: Harper & Row.

Wright, J. (1995). Guns, crime, and violence. In J. Sheley (Ed.), *Criminology: A contemporary handbook* (2nd ed., pp. 495–514). Belmont, CA: Wadsworth.

Wright, L. (1994). *Remembering Satan*. New York: Knopf.

Wright, M. (1985). The impact of victim–offender mediation on the victim. *Victimology, 10*(1), 630–646.

Wright, M. (1989). Introduction. In M. Wright & B. Galaway (Eds.), *Mediation and criminal justice: Victims, offenders and community* (pp. 1–13). Newbury Park, CA: Sage.

———. (1991). *Justice for victims and offenders.* Philadelphia: Open University Press.

Wright, J., Burgess, A., Burgess, B., & Laszio, A. (1996). A typology of interpersonal stalking. *Journal of Interpersonal Violence, 11*(4), 487–502.

Wright, J., Rossi, P., & Daly, K. (1983). *Under the gun: Weapons, crime, and violence in America.* New York: Aldine de Gruyter.

WTVD (2008, October 3). Robbery suspect shot, killed. Retrieved October 4, 2008, from www.abclocal.go.com/wtvd.

Wyatt, E. (2005, February 24). A Mormon daughter's book stirs a storm. *New York Times,* pp. E1, E7.

Wyatt, G. (1985). The sexual abuse of Afro-American and white American women in childhood. *Child Abuse and Neglect, 9,* 507–519.

———., & Powell, G. (1988). *Lasting effects of child sexual abuse.* Newbury Park, CA: Sage.

Yapko, M. (1994). *Suggestions of abuse: True and false memories of childhood sexual trauma.* New York: Simon & Schuster.

Yardley, J. (1999, December 26). A flurry of baby abandonment leaves Houston wondering why. *New York Times,* p. A14.

Yllo, K., & Bograd, M. (1988). *Feminist perspectives on wife abuse.* Newbury Park, CA: Sage.

Young, C. (1999, November 26). Feminists play the victim game. *New York Times,* p. A43.

Young, M. (1991). NOVA protests NBC's 'Naming Names.' *NOVA Newsletter, 15*(4), 1.

Young, M. (2008, April 11). North Carolina deputy paralyzed by shooting sets new life in motion. *The Charlotte Observer.* Retrieved September 28, 2008, from charlotteobserver.com.

Zagier, A. (2008, August 26). Campus training program. Retrieved September 8, 2008, from www.ap.org.

Zawitz, M. (1994). *Domestic violence: Violence between intimates. BJS Selected Findings.* Washington, DC: U.S. Department of Justice.

Zehr, H. (1998). Justice as restoration, justice as respect. *The Justice Professional, 11*(1), 71–87.

Zernike, K. (2003, August 3). What privacy? Everything else but the name. *New York Times,* p. D4.

Ziegenhagen, E. (1977). *Victims, crime, and social control.* New York: Praeger.

———., & Brosnan, D. (1985). Victim responses to robbery and crime control policy. *Criminology, 23*(4), 675–695.

Zgoba, K. (2004). Spin doctors and moral crusaders: The moral panic behind child safety legislation. *Criminal Justice Studies, 17*(4), 385–404.

Zimring, F., & Hawkins, G. (1997). *Crime is not the problem: Lethal violence in America.* New York: Oxford University Press.

———., & Zuehl, J. (1986, January). Victim injury and death in urban robbery: A Chicago study. *Journal of Legal Studies, 15*(1), 1–40.

Name Index

Subject Index